LEGACY OF A LIFETIME

The Governor, wearing the informal type of clothing he preferred, is standing in front of the Katahdin Stream boulder bearing the plaque that reads:

Man is born to die. His works are short lived. Buildings crumble, monuments decay, wealth vanishes but Katahdin in all its glory forever shall remain the mountain of the people of Maine.

P.P.B.

# LEGACY OF A LIFETIME

*The Story of Baxter State Park*

*Dr. John W. Hakola*

1981.

**TBW** *Books*

Woolrich, Maine

© 1981 by the Baxter State Park Authority
All rights reserved.
Except for purposes of review, no part of this book may be reproduced in any fashion
whatsoever without the consent of the Authority and publisher.
Library of Congress Catalog Card Number: 80–54368
Published by Thea Wheelwright, TBW Books
Box 58, Day's Ferry Road, Woolwich, Maine 04579
ISBN 0–931474–18–3
Composition by Yankee Typesetters, Biddeford, Maine
Manufactured in the U.S.A. by Halliday Lithograph Corporation, Quincy, Mass.

### Illustrations Reproduced Courtesy of the Following

Avery Collection, Maine State Library, Augusta, Maine: pp. 25, top 32, 40, 65, 80, 81, 90, 100, top 110, 139, 140, top 244

Baxter State Park Authority, Millinocket, Maine: frontis., pp. 192, bottom 244, 287

Dr. A. E. Brower, Augusta, Maine: flowers, p. 4 of insert

Maurice (Jake) Day, Damariscotta, Maine: pp. xx, 2, 4–5, 18, 24, 31, bottom 32, 35, 64, 72, 77, bottom 110, 124, 134, 136, 174, 182, 228, 257, 260, 266, chipmunk, p. 4 of insert

Harold J. Dyer, Albany, New York: p. 160

Dr. John W. Hakola, Orono, Maine: pp. 54, 292

Frank Knaut, Minnesota: jacket photo

Paul Knaut, Jr., Dover-Foxcroft, Maine: bottom p. 112, pages 1–3 of insert

Information & Education Section, Maine Department of Conservation, Augusta, Maine: fire photos, pp. 302–03

Inland Fish and Wildlife Department, Augusta, Maine: p. 206

Lawrence Mansur, Bedford, Massachusetts: maps, pp. 75, 270

Laurence M. Sturtevant, North Belgrade, Maine: p. 196

Austin H. Wilkins, Augusta, Maine: pp. 45, top 112, 296, 307

### DISCLAIMER

The contents of this book were prepared for the Baxter State Park Authority by Dr. John W. Hakola, but were not independently verified and therefore are not officially endorsed by the Authority.

# FOREWORD

Percival Proctor Baxter, "Uncle Percy," as he was always thought of and addressed by me, my sisters, and his other nieces and nephews, was twenty years older than I. Actually it was nineteen and a half years, and actually he was a half-uncle; for he was the middle child of my grandfather and his second wife. He and his brothers referred to each other as "of the first litter" and "of the second litter." And he was much closer to some of those "first litter" brothers than some of them were to each other. The youngest of those brothers, Uncle Rupert, was only five years older than he; and was his best friend. My father, Hartley, twenty years older, came next, especially because they both were fond of the ocean. Although his brothers knew he had largely written their father's will, which left almost all of his large fortune to him, they did not seem to hold that against him; rather their attitude seemed to be that he had earned it for devoting so much of his life to taking care of his father and his father's property.

Turning from a glimpse of his background, I shall try to give you a few comments, odds and ends, about him as he seemed to me over the forty-seven years during which we became increasingly close in our relationship.

He was a fine-looking man, tall, blond, erect. He considerably resembled General George C. Marshall, and was sometimes mistaken for him. He was a man of many contradictions, friendly but generally rather remote; his brother Rupert was his only real close friend. He was fond of women, but never married. He was very generous in his way to charities. In small ways he was "close," to put it mildly. When he and his dear brother Rupert went fishing and such together, Rupert was always stuck with somewhat more than half the expenses; small items, gasoline, tolls, tips, that sort of thing. He and I would often walk over together from his office to the Cumberland Club for lunch. After lunch he always paid for his in cash, without even a gesture to pay for mine, which I would sign for.

On the other hand, during his later years he would send five of us, two nephews and three nieces (half ones, that is!) a generous check for Christmas. Just the check, without a card or comment. The other three, who seldom saw him, got nothing.

Once after he gave Macworth Island, a very valuable piece of property, to the state, I asked him what he did about federal income tax deductions   vii in such cases. He said, "Oh, John, I don't take any deductions for what I give away. I wouldn't want people to think that the purpose of my gifts was to avoid taxes." I was tempted to point out that the saving in taxes would give him additional money to give away. But, although we often disagreed, we usually avoided discussing subjects about which we differed; and I said no more.

On his seventieth birthday he mailed me the following poem:

**AFTER SEVENTY**

*From P.P.B.—on his 70th birthday to J.L.B.*

Pamper the body
Prod the Soul
Accept Limitations
But play a role.

Withdraw from the front
But stay in the fight.
Avoid isolation
Keep in sight.

Beware of reminiscing
Except to a child.
To forgetting proper names
Be reconciled.

Refrain from loquacity,
Be crisp and concise
And regard self-pity
As a cardinal vice.

*Olive H. Prouty*

I've carried the original copy in my wallet; and now, thirty-three years later, it is rather the worse for wear. He adhered to the poem's advice for the next ten years. Then he became shy, and would have me represent him on occasions when he felt a response was required.

I could go on and on about "the Uncle," but as the poem warns old people to "refrain from loquacity," I will add only one more anecdote about him. Before he was governor, and for several years afterward, he was looked upon by the "vested interests" as a "red-eyed radical," "a socialist," "a traitor to his class." In 1926 it was those "vested interests" who ran Gould against him in the special primary election and beat him, though considerably through his own default. Not more than ten years later, the Republicans had no strong candidate for governor and a move was afoot to urge him to run. "The young Republicans," then a fairly active group, opposed him publicly as being "too conservative." He had no intention of running, he told me, but was amused to be called "too conservative," commenting, "Once I was called a socialist, now I am called too conservative, but I haven't changed. It is the times that have."

As for John Hakola's history of Baxter State Park, it is a monumental book, the result of a tremendous amount of skillful research. It is a sort of biography of my Uncle Percy's "child" whom he loved so deeply, a fitting final tribute to the decades he devoted to creating it. Although it would not have been written during his lifetime, I regret that he never had the opportunity to admire and enjoy reading this fine book.

JOHN L. BAXTER, SR.

# ACKNOWLEDGMENTS

Bringing this book from the initial basic research through to the final product which you are now reading has been a labor of love for many individuals. The commitment of these people reflects not only the uniqueness of Governor Baxter's gift to the people of Maine, but also their respect for him as a man.

Beginning in 1970, the Baxter State Park Authority recognized the need to document the process by which Percival Proctor Baxter acquired and donated the land, as well as those events which affected the acquisition.

Dr. John W. Hakola, University of Maine Historian and outdoors person, agreed to conduct the research under contract to the Authority.

Until the completion of the manuscript, the final form the project would take was unclear. However, when the value of information documented became evident in 1980, the Authority determined to proceed with publication in order to make it as widely available as possible. A contract was consummated with TBW Books to edit and publish the manuscript.

Many others have participated in or assisted with this project.

Photographs were furnished by Paul Knaut of Dover-Foxcroft, whose son Frank Knaut did the jacket photo; Gerald Merry of Stacyville; and Dr. A. E. Brower of Augusta; and a great number are from the collection of Maurice (Jake) Day of Damariscotta. Several were also obtained from the Myron Avery collection at the Maine State Library; and the caribou and fire and blowdown photos are from the Maine Inland Fisheries and Wildlife Department and from the Maine Department of Conservation.

A special note of appreciation is due former Park Supervisors Helon Taylor and Harold L. Dyer for their recollections and reminiscences with the author. Also, retired Forest Commissioner and former Authority Chairman Albert D. Nutting provided many insights in his review of the manuscript. A citizen's committee assisted in the preliminary editing process through review of the draft manuscripts; they were John Baxter, Sarah Redfield, Ethel Dyer, Walter Birt, and Austin Wilkins.

The latter deserves special recognition. As chairman of the Authority when the history project was conceived, Austin Wilkins did not allow interest to flag, even after his retirement from state government. He played a critical role when the process of publication began by chairing the review and editing committee, and he acted as liaison between the Authority, its staff, and the publisher to ensure a quality publication.

Professional artist and outdoors person Maurice "Jake" Day, of Damariscotta, has kindly allowed the use of several of his whimsical cartoons of the denizens of Baxter State Park. The story of Baxter State Park would not be complete without recognition of Jake and his famous "Jake's Rangers," who were long-time visitors and supporters of the Park. During his many visits to the Katahdin area, he became a close friend of LeRoy Dudley, the famed and popular Mt Katahdin philosopher and guide. Listening to Roy's tales of Pamola, Jake sketched the well-known "portrait" of Pamola seated on South Peak and talking with Roy Dudley who is seated on Baxter Peak. In the early 1970's, Jake designed the park medallion found on the back of the jacket of this book.

Members of the Baxter State Park Authority throughout the period provided invaluable support and guidance for the project. These have included Forest Commissioner Austin Wilkins, Directors of the Bureau of Forestry Fred Holt, John Walker, A. Temple Bowen (Acting), and Kenneth Stratton; Commissioners of Inland Fisheries and Wildlife Ronald Speers, George Bucknam, Maynard Marsh, William Peppard (Acting), and Glenn Manuel; and Attorneys General James Erwin, Jon Lund, Joseph Brennan, Richard Cohen and James Tierney.

Finally, it has been the continued interest of citizens, lovers of wilderness, back-country recreationists and history buffs that has given the real impetus for completion of this project. Your patience and enthusiasm is acknowledged. Enjoy!

# PREFACE

In the annals of the state park movement in the United States there are few stories to equal that of Baxter State Park. Currently (1979), the fourth largest state park in the nation, after the Adirondacks and Catskills in New York and the Anza-Borrego Desert of California, it is unique for its size and in the way in which it was put together. While many parks were carved out of federal or state-owned land, or were purchased with funds from these units of government, Baxter State Park is the direct result of the zeal and drive of a single remarkable individual who pieced it together with purchases from private corporations. Percival Proctor Baxter, after nearly a decade and a half of trying to convince his own state government to do the job, finally decided that if it were to be done at all he would have to be the one to do it. He dedicated more than half of his life to an unrelenting quest for the land needed to make his cherished dream a reality. What could be a better legacy to one's state?

The centerpiece of the Park, of course, is Katahdin. It is known under a wide variety of names, but most Maine citizens prefer "Katahdin" to "Ktaadn," which was more common with groups and individuals from outside the state until long into the 20th century. Katahdin is the anglicized derivation of the Indian terms "ket," "k't," or "keette," meaning big or greatest and "adene," meaning mountain, and was officially adopted in 1893 by the U.S. Geographic Board. Because of Indian legends concerning it, because of its relative isolation for so long and because of its striking appearance, particularly when viewed from the south and southeast, where it rises so dramatically from relatively flat country, the mountain fascinates many individuals. The literature concerning it is as extensive and as interesting as for any other mountain in the nation.

Commissioned by the Baxter State Park Authority, this study will trace the history of Katahdin and the Park created by Percival P. Baxter. The year 1969 has been selected as the terminal point, since, with the death of Baxter in that year and the availability shortly after of his magnificent endowment for maintaining the Park, its operation and management were considerably modified.

I am indebted to the Baxter State Park Authority and its staff for providing unrestricted access to all available materials in its possession and for xiii additional information when it was requested. I am also indebted to the Authority for its patience—more than I had the right to expect—with my delays in completing the work.

The staffs of the Maine State Library, Bangor Public Library, Maine Historical Society, National Archives, and particularly the Special Collections Division of the Fogler Library at the University of Maine at Orono were most helpful in finding and providing needed research materials. I am also indebted to several work-study students at the University of Maine who performed a good deal of newspaper research for me. Finally, I owe an enormous debt to my wife, Judith, who kept encouraging and prodding when progress was slow.

# CONTENTS

# ILLUSTRATIONS

## TABLES

## MAPS

xviii

FROM THE WEST WALL LOOKING EAST AT PAMOLA PEAK
When one looks at this grim, overpowering structure, it is easy to understand the
Indians' fear of spirits dwelling in the mountain.

No account of its history would be complete without some discussion of the role Katahdin played in the lives of Maine Indians. Long before the arrival of the white man in the area, Katahdin had acquired an important place in the legends of the local Abenaki Indian tribes, though there is little indication that they came near the mountain. Indeed, the very legends themselves would seem to indicate that they did not climb it, since they feared retribution by spirits living there. Since the East and West branches of the Penobscot River lay to the east and south of Katahdin, Indians moving back and forth between the coast and lower river and hunting grounds as far north as Canada traversed the streams flowing from it and saw it in all its moods.

The first mention we have of Indian legends concerning Katahdin comes from John Giles. Giles was captured at Pemaquid by a band of Maliseet Indians in 1689, when he was nine years old, and was not freed until 1698. Several decades later, after he had become commander of a Massachusetts military garrison on the St. George River, he wrote of his captivity and provided the first accounts we have in English of Indian legends of "the Teddon," as he called Katahdin:

> I have heard an Indian say that he lived by the River at the Foot of the Teddon, and in his Wigwam, seeing the top of it thro' the Hole left in the top of the Wigwam for the passing of Smoke, he was tempted to travel to it; accordingly he set out early on a Summer's Morning, and laboured hard in ascending the Hill all Day, and the Top seem'd as distant from the Place where he lodged at Night, as from the Wigwam whence he began his Journey; and concluding that Spirits were there, never dare make a second attempt.
>
> I have been credibly inform'd that several others have fail'd in the same Attempt; particularly, that three young Men towr'd the *Teddon* three days and an half, and then began to be strangely disordered & delirious, and when their Imagination was clear, and they could recollect where they were, and been, they found themselves return'd one Days Journey; how they came down so far, they can't guess, unless the Genii of the Place conveyed them. [1]

Giles travelled with his captors along the coast and up the Penobscot

## PAMOLA, THE INDIAN GOD OF KATAHDIN

Maurice "Jake" Day describes how he came to draw this well-known cartoon: "We prevailed upon Roy Dudley, who is now more or less a legend of the mountain, to tell us a few of his Pamola yarns one night at his Chimney Pond cabin. It was around 2 A.M. that I drew a rough sketch of Pamola on South Peak conversing with Roy on Baxter Peak, as described by Roy. I worked in light from two plumber's candles."

River to the Mattawamkeag, which they then followed eastward to the St. Croix and St. John.

Many later visitors and observers left versions of these legends, usually obtained from the Indians. Not all such stories or legends were authentic, but mistakes were usually honest ones and resulted from lack of knowledge by whites of the Indians' language and culture. In one case, the Penobscot Indians willfully misled a priest from Old Town who had interfered in a tribal quarrel. His accounts of the legends were often reprinted and his errors compounded. Maine guides and such individuals as Leroy Dudley, at Chimney Pond, popularized the old legends around evening campfires and developed new ones.

Fannie Hardy Eckstorm (1881–1946) is an excellent source on Katahdin legends. She had a lifelong acquaintance with the Penobscots and a questioning though sympathetic attitude toward these stories. Her views therefore have considerable validity. At least three different concepts, she maintained, were included in the Indian word *bumole*, the white's *Pamola*. *Wuchowsen*, the spirit of the night wind, was one of these. An old Indian woman described *Wuchowsen* as having "no body, only leetle mite here [indicating her chest], all legs, hands." This description provided the basis for many caricatures of *Pamola*. The spirit made the breezes by flapping his wings and was considered harmless.

Another concept was the Storm-bird, a variation of the Passamaquoddy and Maliseet *Culloo*. He was a monstrous creature with an awesome beak and claws and a huge head. Some depictions give him a human head, while a modern illustrator shows a varied agglomeration—birdlike feet, wings, and lower body; a human torso and arms; and the upper portion representing a moose's head and rack. When irritated, as frequently happened, the Storm-bird used his great powers to create violent winds and fierce snowstorms.

The third aspect, or Spirit of Katahdin, was a human figure, with eyebrows and cheeks of stone, who lived inside the mountain with his Indian wife and two children.[2]

Legends of the Storm-bird, often depicted as the Spirit of Pamola, concern his intention of preventing men from climbing the mountain. While they remained below treeline, all humans were safe from his anger. Above treeline he showed no mercy, using blizzards, severe winds, mist and fog to keep away intruders.

John Neptune, the famous Penobscot chief, was the subject of the most famous Storm-bird legend. On one occasion Neptune went hunting and spent the night on the mountain in a hut with a strong door. Pamola was enraged at his effrontery, and swooped down from above to destroy him. Though he blew fiercely and hammered Neptune's door, he could not get in and stormed away, greatly agitated. Neptune reached safe ground at lower elevations the next day.

A MODERN PAMOLA YARN AS TOLD, AND ILLUSTRATED, BY JAKE DAY

"In 1933 I took off with my friend Lester Hall in an old Dodge, which was the first car to cross Avalanche Brook—we built the log bridge to get across—and park at old Depot Camp, also known as Avalanche Field. Close to the 20th of October while we were still there we had very cold weather and snow flurries. It was so cold we made friends with Old Pamola and warmed our hands against his tarbarrel pipe; but we couldn't sit there forever. So Caleb Scribner of Patten, then a warden supervisor, took pity on us and brought us an old iron schoolhouse stove which we set up in our tent. Now don't be surprised if I tell you that Old Pamola helped us in putting the stovepipe through the top of the tent.

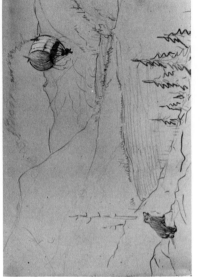

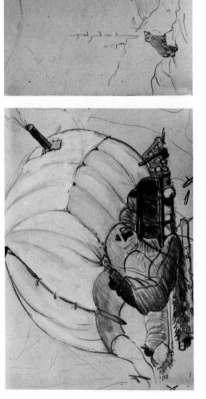

"Now an old-fashioned schoolhouse stove stoked with wood in a small tent can really generate hot air; in fact, so hot that the tent lifted, pulling out the tent stakes. I was left on the ground but Hall hung on. The tent took off down the valley with Hall tangled up in the ropes. He and the tent headed straight toward Katahdin. Fortunately Pamola saw it coming and just reached up and grabbed the ropes as it was about to sail over Pamola Peak and on to heaven knows where. So good Old Pamola (we have always been indebted to him) just flew back up the valley to our campsite and deposited the tent and Hall right over the stove. Needless to say, we kept a very low fire after that."

The Spirit of Katahdin, unlike the more malevolent Pamola, exhibited an amicable attitude toward the Indians. The most frequent tale concerning him involves his taking a bride. A number of versions have been preserved, each unique, but with some features in common: A young Indian maiden was once picking blueberries on the lower reaches of Katahdin. While gazing at the mountain, she hoped that it was a man and would marry her. While thinking about this she lay on the ground and slept. When she woke, the Spirit of Katahdin stood before her. He took her inside the mountain to live with him and she bore him two children. After a time she missed her family, so Katahdin returned her and the children to her relatives. Before they left, Katahdinosis, the little boy, was given the ability to kill whatever he pointed at. The girl was granted the power to make come true whatever she said, but only if she first passed her fingers over her lips. Arriving for the visit, they found the tribe dreadfully affected by a terrible famine. The children provided for the needs of the tribe by using their magical powers to obtain fish and game. Unfortunate accidents, however, usually forced the return to Katahdin of the woman and her children.

In one version, the mother remains and assists her tribe in defeating the Micmac Indians. Each century she reappears to visit her people. In still another variant, Katahdin instructs her to tell her people not to raise questions about the boy's father and to refuse to reply if questions are raised. When the inevitable happens and questions are asked regarding the boy's father, she finally can no longer contain herself and says that the boy is the son of Katahdin and also that the Indians have lost the chance for Katahdin to lead them and make them a great tribe. Thereupon, she and her children return to the mountain and are not seen again.

While the Indians feared and revered the mountain it is unlikely that they often, if ever, climbed it before the arrival of the white man.

The precise date when white men first saw Katahdin is not known. John Giles may have seen the mountain. Undoubtedly French missionaries and soldiers moving between Quebec and the Kennebec used the route on some occasions or saw the mountain from the Kennebec and Moosehead Lake areas, but the accounts in the *Jesuit Relations* make no mention of this.

In 1760 Colonel John Montresor, a British engineering officer, while travelling from Quebec to the Kennebec River after the English seized Quebec, "had the pleasure," along the west side of Moosehead Lake, "of beholding at the same time the Panavansot hill, higher [than Onegla], at the foot of which runs the Penobscot, the most considerable mountain in this part of the world."[3] Whether this was Katahdin or some nearer mountain such as Big Spencer or Whitecap, it is impossible to determine; most likely, however, it was Katahdin.

Four years later came the first definite recorded sighting. After the Treaty of Paris of 1763, the colonial government of Massachusetts and the British government determined to survey a route for a road between Quebec

6

and the Atlantic seaboard. One possibility was along the Penobscot. Governor Bernard of Massachusetts sent Joseph Chadwick, a surveyor, to follow and map the full length of the Penobscot River from Fort Pownal (present Fort Point) to its source and then continue beyond the height of land to Quebec. Captained by John Preble, the party left Fort Pownal in early May, followed the Penobscot to the Piscataquis, then went up that stream, across portages to Moosehead Lake and the West Branch of the Penobscot. At that point Chadwick continued on to Quebec before returning to follow the West Branch downstream for its entire course, while a smaller group immediately turned down the West Branch and mapped tributary streams.

Chadwick and his party left Quebec in late June or early July. During the trip he sighted and possibly climbed part way up Katahdin. His journal entry, which is not entirely clear on this point, reads as follows:

### SATINHUNGEMOSS HILL

Lays in the Latitude of 45° 43″ and from Fort Pownall 184 miles as we travel$^d$ and 116 miles by Computation. Being a remarkable Hill for highteth & fig$^r$ The Indines say that this Hill is the highest in the Country. That they can ascend so high as any Greens Grow & no higher. That one Indine attempted to go higher but he never returned. The hight of Vegetation is as a Horizontal Line about halfe the perpendicular hight of the Hill a & intersects the tops of Sundrey other mountines. The hight of this Hill was very apperent to ous as we had a Sight of it at Sundre places Easterly

Westerly at 60 or 70 Miles Distence—It is Curious to See—Elevated above a rude mass of Rocke large Mountins—So Lofty a Pyramid— One which is another Rarity From a. Decendes a Stream of water.— If the observer places himselfe at such a place that the Rays of Light are Diverging with the falls then the Splay of water as it falls from the hill will appear in as grate a Veriety of Collers as may be View$^d$ in a Prism glass.[4]

According to Fannie Eckstorm, Chadwick was giving his spelling of Nesowadnehunk in naming the mountain. The sketch of the mountain to which the letter *a* refers has been lost. On one of the maps Chadwick prepared, Katahdin is named *Satinhungemoss Hill;* in another map, drawn by an unidentified member of the party, it is called *Mount Todden.* These were the first maps to show the location of Katahdin. From Chadwick's narrative it is impossible to determine just how far up the mountain he climbed, if indeed he climbed it at all. Most writers have assumed that he did, but I believe he could have been referring to falls on one of the streams that seemingly emerged from the mountain. In any event, since Chadwick's journal and maps were not widely known until much later, they appear to have had little immediate impact on the public's awareness of Katahdin's presence.

Four decades elapsed before the next mention and the first actual climb of Katahdin occurred. Undoubtedly English surveyors and travellers and colonial and American sojourners visited the general area. Charles Turner, Jr., in his account of the first complete ascent in 1804 notes that a mountain lying to the N.N.W. of Katahdin was "called by the English Fort Mountain." A citizen of Scituate, Massachusetts, Charles Turner held a variety of positions including postmaster, and after his Katahdin climb, a seat in the U.S. House of Representatives. In 1804 he was employed as a surveyor to locate the so-called Eastern Lands being sold by Massachusetts. On August 13 his party left their canoes at the "head of Boat-waters, in a small clear stream of spring water, which came in different rivulets from the mountain, . . ." and crossed the tableland, as he called the lower elevations above the West Branch. From this tableland they followed a ridge, probably the present Hunt Spur, for two miles, trying to "gain the summit, at the west end, which appeared most easy of access." The party followed this ridge, which, since it had not been burned over in the great fire of 1795, was easier to traverse than the area in the lower elevations to the south and east of Katahdin that had been burned and also "were from their steepness inaccessible." The Abol Slide had not yet come down. They reached the plateau, or current tableland, where the "elevation was so great as sensibly to affect [our] respiration," and followed it to the east end and the highest point of the Natardin or Catardin, as Turner spelled it. He wrote of the difficulty in expressing precisely the Indian pronunciation, saying that "No-tar-dn or Cata-din" were as close as anyone could come. Before leaving the summit, the party "deposited the initials of our names . . . and the date cut upon sheet lead, and a bottle of rum corked and leaded, on the highest part."[5]

When the party returned to Old Town, members had difficulty convincing the Indians that they had been on top of the mountain until the Indians who had accompanied them verified the fact. While Turner's written version of the expedition was not made public for a decade and a half, the participants undoubtedly wrote and spoke of their trip a good deal. Some, perhaps, returned to the mountain region later on and provided information for Moses Greenleaf's 1815 map.

A decade and a half elapsed before the next ascent of Katahdin, in what could be termed the "surveyors' era" on the mountain. The Treaty of Ghent, which ended the War of 1812, provided for the establishment of a Maine Boundary Commission to settle the Maine-New Brunswick boundaries remaining in dispute after the Treaty of 1783. Both the British and Americans hired commissioners and surveyors to make the general survey of northern and eastern Maine. Though working in conjunction, they made separate reports and prepared their own maps. From 1817 to 1820, each side tried to establish the most favorable position for their nation of the lines of mountains mentioned in the Treaty of 1783. In 1817 surveyors determined the precise point, agreed on nearly two decades earlier, at which the St. Croix River arose and the Maine border began to follow a route due north. Here, at the head of a stream subsequently named Monument Brook, a yellow birch tree was rimmed with iron hoops.

The first surveyors to climb Katahdin in 1819 were a British party headed by Colin Campbell, who had been active with British surveying parties during previous years, searching for the height of land mentioned in the Treaty of Paris. Low water had prevented an approach to Katahdin from the north and northeast by way of the Aroostook River and its tributaries connecting to Penobscot East Branch waters. Campbell volunteered to head a small party to climb Katahdin to make needed observations from its summit. He left St. Andrews, New Brunswick, in late September of 1819. At Mill Town, on the St. Croix, he hired a Penobscot Indian to guide his group to the Penobscot River and up the West Branch. The party ascended the St. Croix to Grand Lake and then crossed a portage to Baskahegan Stream and followed it down to the Mattawamkeag River and the Penobscot. That and the West Branch were then followed upstream through the lakes to the mouth of Aboljackomegas (Abol Stream), which was reached on October 13. The party carefully chained the entire distance from Mill Town. On the West Branch they encountered a group of lumbermen from Bangor. At Abol Stream, which "appears to lead toward Cathardin & corresponds with one laid down in Greenleaf's Map (1815)," the party followed a route through "low meadow and burnt Land" for a mile and a half before low water stopped them; they thereupon returned to the river and moved upstream and camped at the mouth of what is now Katahdin Stream "on a hard wood point, where there was an appearance of a number of persons having encamped before probably on their way to Cathardin."[6]

During the next week two vain attempts were made to climb the snow-covered mountain. A third attempt, on October 19, was successful. A route from Katahdin Stream, probably along Abol Stream and up the Abol Slide, was followed. A hut was built on a terrace about a mile above the foot of the slide, which came down in 1816. On the summit, though hindered by high winds, Campbell took many magnetic bearings toward points visible as much as a hundred miles away. His observations concerning heights of lands and the separation of watersheds as seen from Katahdin show that his primary task was to work toward a solution favorable to Britain in the boundary dispute.[7]

In August of the following year, a mixed party of British and American surveyors, one of whom was Campbell, again ascended the mountain by the same route. With three tents and rations, the group "proceeded on the route to Katahdin." Aside from Greenleaf's map of 1815, this is the first use of the now-accepted spelling of the mountain.* As Campbell's group had done the previous year, they erected a base camp on the terrace of Abol

---

* Greenleaf used the name "Katahdin" rather than "Ktaadn," in his *Survey of the State of Maine,* (p. 47n), because he thought it hard to pronounce. Katahdin, he said, "is written therefore in such a manner as will most naturally express in English form the nearest approximation of the Indian name."

Slide. An American surveyor by the name of Loring, using the barometer
of a British member of the party, William F. Odell, estimated the altitude
of Katahdin to be 5,385 feet, though the figures he listed total 5,335 feet.
This was apparently the first attempt to measure accurately the altitude of
Katahdin. After spending several hours on the summit, the party started its
"difficult descent" but not before "one of the gentlemen of the British party
had left our names in a small bottle amidst a pile of stones."[8]

The work of the boundary commission coincided with Maine's drive
toward statehood. One of the provisions of the Act of Separation in 1819
was for an equal division of the remaining public lands of Massachusetts
with the new state. A commission was set up to effect this within ten years.
In 1825, the commission decided that in order to survey lands north of the
settled portion of Maine, a base line would be run westward from the monument in the upper reaches of the St. Croix set up in 1817.[9] From this base
line, or Monument Line as it came to be known, which was to be drawn
westward to the border of Quebec, townships could be laid out to the north
and south. The townships subsequently laid out bear the subscript W.E.L.S.,
meaning West of the East Line of the State.

The commission hired Joseph C. Norris, Sr., and his son to begin running the line from the New Brunswick border. Near the end of the year
1825 they had accomplished the fourth recorded complete ascent of Katahdin, and they were at a point four miles west of the northeast corner of
T3R9, the township on which Katahdin is located. Further progress was
barred by approaching winter and the difficulties involved in trying to
survey the Northwest Basin and the Klondike, which they were probably
the first to see. They crossed the tableland, climbed to the highest point on
November 11, 1825, and then descended by way of the Abol Slide, after
first making a false start south of that point, to their boats on the West
Branch. Their exploit, given the lateness of the season and the ruggedness
of the terrain, was a remarkable one. They were probably the first individuals in the Wassataquoik Valley and undoubtedly the first party to
climb the east flank of Katahdin.

In the next and later years, the survey was resumed west of Chesuncook Lake. It was not until 1833 that Edwin Rose, in the fifth recorded
ascent of the mountain, completed the line. He drew the first detailed map
of Katahdin that year. The offset in the southwest corner of T4R10 shown
on survey maps demonstrates the difficulty Rose experienced in making the
east and west lines finally meet. His party undoubtedly made the first descent
into the Northwest Basin and the Klondike, and its members were the first
to climb the Brothers and Double-Capped (Doubletop). The Northwest
Basin was not entered again until 1886.

In 1828 other surveyors in the area may have ascended Katahdin. Moses
Greenleaf, writing in 1829, while arguing for the American position in the
10 boundary dispute, took issue with claims concerning continuity of mountain

ranges made by Colin Campbell and noted that his (Greenleaf's) description was confirmed by the "observations of surveyors employed in May and June 1828 in exploring the townships in this region for the Commonwealth of Massachusetts; and proves the deception of Mr. Campbell's vision on his reported view from Katahdin . . ."[10] While the surveyors in 1828 were undoubtedly on the mountain or around it, it is not known whether they actually climbed it and reached the summit. Greenleaf estimated the height of Katahdin to be 5,623 feet.

The work of the Monument Line surveyors marks the end of the surveyor period on Katahdin. In subsequent years townships were laid out north and south of the Monument Line and many were soon purchased. Scarcely a decade later, the first lumbering activity occurred on the East and West Penobscot branches and on the Wassataquoik. Though few of the early accounts other than Greenleaf's *Survey* and maps received wide distribution at the time, the fact that Indians accompanied most of the parties and that citizens of the lower Penobscot Valley were on some of them meant that the area became much more widely known.

In the period following, scientific exploration was mixed with recreation in motivating visitors to the mountains. The accounts left by some of the visitors reached a much broader national audience and led to greater interest in the mountain and its environs. By the next recorded ascents from the south or the West Branch route, logging was going on; both accounts of ascents in 1836 mention farming or logging activities.

That year witnessed two climbs of Katahdin—one apparently for sheer recreation, the other motivated primarily by scientific interests. In late July and early August the Reverend Joseph Blake of Bangor, a recent graduate of Bowdoin College, and two of his friends followed the West Branch route, hired the services of two men and a batteau at Grand Falls (present day Millinocket) and then, after moving up the river, made a partial ascent to the tableland in cold, stormy weather. They retreated to the base of the mountain and spent a night at a cabin occupied by two men who were cutting hay in a large clearing in the woods, probably on Sourdnahunk Stream. They later moved up the West Branch and hiked overland to Moosehead Lake and Monson before returning, penniless, to Bangor.[11] Since this account did not appear in print for nearly a century the trip had little immediate impact.

More important was that taken several weeks later by J. W. Bailey, professor of chemistry at the U.S. Military Academy at West Point. While visiting in Waterville he became curious about Katahdin from accounts he read. With two friends, Professors George Keely and Phinehas Barnes of Waterville (Colby) College, he made the trip. The construction of the Military Road to Houlton earlier in the decade made the first part of the journey to Mattawamkeag much easier and faster than it had been for others in the past. After the new bridge over Mattawamkeag Stream, paid for by the federal government, the rest of the route was by trail, without guides, along the north bank of the Penobscot. At the Indian settlement of Nickatow at the junction of the East and West branches, Bailey found an abundance of *Swertia deflexa,* a member of the gentian family, then considered a rarity in New England. On reaching the settlement at Grand Falls, his party hired two members of the MacAstlin (McCauslin?) family to take them by boat the rest of the way.

They left the boats at the mouth of what Bailey called Hoyt's Stream, probably either Abol or Katahdin Stream, and struck out overland toward the Abol Slide. Since they did not find the paths established by earlier climbers they had an exceedingly difficult hike over burnt lands into the drainage of Abol Stream. The first night was spent on the slide, probably at the terrace used by earlier parties. The next day, August 13, was marked by drizzle and rain. To save their strength, Bailey and Keely turned back before reaching the summit, while Barnes and the two guides continued on. Since the party had been unable to procure a mountain barometer in Waterville or Bangor, the men could not measure the altitude of Katahdin, but concluded that it was considerably lower than most previous estimates, since Barnes found vegetation on the top and the party did not notice any rarification of the air or significant changes in temperature. As a scientist, Bailey made numerous observations about the geology of the area and the plants and trees he found. Also important historically, is the fact that at Debsconeag Lake, on the approach, he drew a sketch of Katahdin and the surrounding mountains that showed the Abol Slide and the Avalanche, or East Slide, as well as Doubletop Mountain, which he called Sugar Loaf. This is the first publicized sketch of the mountain. Aside from its thoroughness and readability, Bailey's account is important, since his was the first scientific expedition to the mountain. His paper was published in the *American Journal of Science,* therefore receiving national distribution.

Two years later, in 1838, Charles T. Jackson led an expedition of ten persons to Katahdin. As state geologist for both Maine and Massachusetts, he was charged by those states to do a geological survey of the lands they owned. As his assistant, he named James T. Hodge of Massachusetts. William C. Larrabee, who later wrote a vivid essay about the trip, also joined the party. Larrabee was an educator and was then principal of Maine Weselyan Seminary at Kent's Hill. At Old Town, Jackson hired an Indian guide, Louis Neptune (?). A batteau had been specially built for the expedition and with that, handled by boatmen from Old Town, and a canoe, the party left Old Town on September 13, 1838, and made the entire journey upriver and through the lakes by boat. Larrabee's account is particularly interesting since he described the Indians, the techniques of handling the boats, and the countryside through which the party travelled.

A week after they left Old Town, the party camped on a small island in Pockwockamus Deadwater, about three miles below Abol Stream. From this

12

island "Katahdin, the prince of eastern mountains . . . stood wild, grand,
and solitary before us." Thereafter, the party moved in light skiffs to the
mouth of Abol Stream, where the approach route was picked up. Larrabee
wrote of the difficult trip through the burned-over land from which the
"original forest had disappeared . . . Some careless lumberman had, some
years before, kindled a fire in the dry season, in a pine forest . . . There
had sprung up thickets of white birch, patches of gigantic ferns, and immense fields of blueberry bushes, loaded with the finest fruit." Larrabee was,
of course, talking about the fire of 1795 mentioned earlier.

The expedition met the same fate as the Bailey party had two years
earlier. They camped near the base of the Abol Slide, which they climbed
the next day in the middle of a violent wind and snowstorm. Several of the
party turned back before the summit was reached. The Indian guide "declared that Pamola was angry with us for presuming to measure the height
of the mountain, and revenged himself upon us by this storm," Larrabee
wrote. "An Indian of the Penobscots, who was one of the party, averred that
Pamola, the mythological demon of the mountain, had sent this terrible
storm up on us, in punishment of our impiety in visiting his dominions."
Pamola "is the genious of Katahdin, of Hurculean strength, occupying a
throne of granite, and reigning as sole despot over those lofty peaks and dark
ravines." No mortal had seen him, but Indians often heard his voice, particularly during storms. The Penobscots continually feared him "and it is with
difficulty that you can urge them to approach the mountain." [13]

During the short stay on the top, Charles Jackson continued the scientific and barometric observations and measurements that he had been making
during the entire trip and estimated the altitude of Katahdin to be 5,300 feet.
He concluded that during the last ice age the mountain had been covered by
glaciers.

The descent was a difficult one. Fortunately the Indian guide had made
a number of stone monuments at the top of the slide and along the route to
facilitate the return over the snow-covered tableland; otherwise the party
might have become lost. Larrabee left a particularly vivid description of the
scene from the edge of the tableland during the storm:

> As we were passing down along the brink of one of the ravines,
> which I had not noticed in our ascent, owing to the dense mist sur-
> rounding us, I looked down the dizzy abyss. How wide it was I know
> not, as I could not in the storm see across; but it was at least a thousand
> feet deep, and walled up by perpendicular precipices. The scene was
> intensely sublime. The emotion was indeed overwhelming. On one side
> was the naked mountain peak, drear and desolate, its rocks rived by
> the frosts of six thousand winters; on the other was the deep dark
> chasm, whose recesses, formed by jutting crags and overhanging cliffs,
> no adventurous foot had ever trod; above us, and around us, was the

13

storm, the wintery winds whirling the fast falling snow into many a fantastic drift. The scene made the blood run chill and the teeth chatter.[14]

The storm magnified the normally harsh features of the mountaintop. Larrabee overreacted, as did a number of other writers, by assuming that the sides of the mountain were perpendicular for thousands of feet.

While most of the party waited out the storm at the encampment on the slide, Larrabee and two boatmen decided it would be best to return to the island camp. Along the way Larrabee dislocated his shoulder. The boatmen went to the island camp ahead of him, while he struggled along the shore of the river. He was saved from spending a very uncomfortable, cold and possibly disastrous night on the river bank when some lumbermen camped across the West Branch heard his cries for help and rescued him. After the party was reunited on the 25th of August, they moved downriver, replenished their supplies, and then travelled up the East Branch.

All of the early recorded ascents of Katahdin to this point, except that by Norris in 1825, appear to have been from the south or west. After Jackson's ascent, the situation changed somewhat as approaches to the eastern part of the mountain were opened. At the time the Military Road was opened between Mattawamkeag and Houlton in the early 1830s, the Aroostook or Fish River Road, beginning at Molunkus and eventually leading to Fort Kent, was also begun. By 1832 it had been built through what became Benedicta and then to present-day Sherman. Apparently in that same year William Hunt, who had bought a tract of land on the east side of the Penobscot River, began cutting a road westward from what became Stacyville to his farm. For several decades the Hunt Farm, built in 1835, was the last outpost of civilization on the East Branch. In 1838 Ezekiel Holmes led his party along the East Branch into Matagamon Lake and up Hay Brook to reach Aroostook waters in the course of his exploration and survey of the territory drained by the Aroostook River. Holmes mentions the existence of the Hunt and Dace farms on the East Branch as "the last inhabitants that the traveler finds as he proceeds up the river."[15] In 1841 lumbermen began taking the white pine out of the Wassataquoik drainage and by the middle of the decade a tote road had been built at least as far as the junction of Wassataquoik Stream and its south branch.[16] Several lumbering camps were located on the main stream as well. According to Edward Everett Hale, one of these lumbermen, whom he hired as a guide in 1845, stated that he "had ascended the mountain two or three times himself with sundry of his workmen, . . ." No record remains of these ascents.

The first known party to use this eastern and northern approach to Katahdin was that of Hale and his Harvard classmate, William Francis Channing, in 1845. The two men had served with Charles T. Jackson's Geological Survey of New Hampshire in 1841, and now Channing proposed the

14

hike to Katahdin for pleasure as well as for scientific observations. Whereas most earlier ascents had been from the south, the Boston men deliberately chose the Wassataquoik route. At Mattawamkeag they hired the guide mentioned above and then took a wagon to Molunkus where they stayed at the Molunkus House. From there they had to walk since the road was then unsuitable for wagons. They spent the night with the "hospitable Lowell family"—perhaps the Stacy family was meant—on the road to "Hunt's Inn," where supplies were procured the next day. Hunt Farm was "a large, rambling place, partly built of logs and partly of frame" in a clearing "grass and grain covered sweeping down the hill to the river" a position which "is for picturesque beauty unsurpassable."

From Hunt's they were rowed upstream for half a mile and brought across to the north side of Wassataquoik Stream. They followed the tote road along the north bank of the stream and spent the night at a logger's hut along the way. The next day, at the camp of a logger by the name of Jackins, they first crossed the Wassataquoik by batteau and then its south branch, then called Katahdin Brook. They climbed the northeast side of Russell Mountain, following the stream draining that portion of the mountain, and fought their way through woods and thickly-matted, dense black spruce that mantle Katahdin above timberline on all sides. They spent the night on the southeastern side of the North Peaks. The next day they were disappointed as a driving wind, rain, and hailstorm made it impossible for them to progress to the highest peak. From Hale's description it appears that they did not get beyond the North Peaks or Hamlin Peak. The short visibility in the driving rain did not allow him to describe the landscape with clarity.

Hale had promised the Harvard botanist Asa Gray that he would pick specimens of alpine plants on the mountain to enable Gray to compare them with the growth on Mount Washington. He returned with at least twenty specimens each "of twenty alpine species or varieties." Hale published an account of the trip in his father's newspaper, the *Boston Daily Advertiser*, after his return. Thus, in the year before Thoreau's trip, Katahdin was widely publicized in a well-written letter.[17]

The following year was of major importance for the exploration and history of the mountain. Thoreau's vivid and beautiful account of his partial ascent of Katahdin is so widely known and available that it will not be discussed in any detail here. He was repelled by the mountain, but his story of the approach to Katahdin and the climb itself is one of the finest idylls of wilderness and the forest ever written. His description of the cloud cover on the day he tried to ascend to the summit is particularly fascinating for its imagery and force. Whether he ascended to the tableland or to the ridge between Baxter and South peaks remains a matter of dispute. He did more than most individuals to make known the Penobscot Indian guides, the inhabitants of the small settlements along the river on the approach to Katahdin, and the nature and character of early lumbering operations. His account was first published under the title "Ktaadn and the Maine Woods" in the *Union Magazine of Literature and Art* in 1848. In 1864, after his death, this was combined with the essays on "Chesuncook" and "The Allagash and East Branch" and published as *The Maine Woods*.[18]

Thoreau is important in our context, not for information that he imparted about Katahdin, but because he expressed himself so beautifully and argued for wilderness values. In recent decades he has been a hero of wilderness advocates and environmentalists. The fact that the essay was printed soon after his trip and subsequently published in a book that has been continually reprinted since is also of consequence. A writer and thinker of Thoreau's stature was of immense importance in spreading knowledge of the mountain to Americans and adding to its mystique. Fannie Eckstorm, who felt that his knowledge and ability as a woodsman and scientist had been overrated, summarized his significance in this fashion: "So, though he was neither woodsman nor scientist, Thoreau stood at the gateway of the woods and opened them to all future comers with the key of poetic insight. And after the woods shall have passed away, the vision of them as he saw them will remain . . . Indeed, this whole description of Katahdin is unequaled."[19]

During the same summer that Thoreau approached the mountain from the south, the Reverend Marcus Keep, then at Fort Kent, made a partial ascent from the east, the first of many over a period that extended until 1881. Keep was born in Swanton, Vermont, in 1816 and was educated at Middlebury College, Andover Seminary, and the Bangor Theological Seminary. He began his career as a Home Missionary at Fort Kent during the period 1846–48 and thereafter served at such points as Burlington and Passadumkeag in Penobscot County and later at a variety of places in Aroostook County, ending up at Ashland where he died in 1894.

Keep was an interesting individual. A decade after his death the *Bangor Daily Commercial* published a letter describing him in this way:

> Marcus R. Keep was considered to be a little odd. He would start off and be gone a week without letting anyone know where he was going. One leg was a little shorter than the other, his feet were large, his stride long—born of the impatience of his enthusiasm.[20]

When Reverend Joseph Blake made his second trip to Katahdin in 1856 with a party of which Keep was a member, he described him as:

> Peculiar in more respects than one, somewhat uncultivated in appearance, he had considerable mind and a strong will, and politically and in his social and moral opinions was so conservative that I was about to say that he leaned backwards . . . He was like the Scotch-

man who prayed that the Lord would keep him right because when he once took a wrong way it was so terribly hard to change him. But whatever his peculiarities he was the man of the party; the tallest when he stood erect, the stoutest, the one who could carry the heaviest load and endure the most fatigue, the one who always led the way, not only because he knew it best, but because it was a right belonging to him as the strongest and least disposed to lag. He stopped indeed occasionally, and I suppose sometimes from the need of rest, but more frequently from a regard to his companions.[21]

Whatever his personality, Keep was important to the history of the mountain for over two decades.

In 1846, in company with James H. Haines, Keep made a partial ascent, evidently along the route through Hunt's Farm, the Wassataquoik Stream, then southward to Katahdin Lake, and finally along a route he selected to Avalanche Brook and the slide on the south side of what is now Keep Ridge, which had apparently occurred about the same time as the Abol Slide. Little is known of this trip except references in later communications.

Keep was more active in 1847. In mid-September he led a group of seven men, primarily ministers from Brewer, Bangor, Lincoln and Patten, on a climb, following the route from the Aroostook Road to the Hunt Farm and then up the Wassataquoik to a camp on the north side of the stream slightly upstream from the mouth of Katahdin Brook. Reverend Keep had been chosen captain and guide since, he wrote, "I was the only one at hand who knew any thing of the route . . ." The next day they crossed Wassataquoik Stream on a raft of their own making at what became known as Lower Katahdin Crossing and "left the river and all traces of human footsteps" to follow a course to Katahdin Pond, as he called it. That night they camped in a swamp west of Katahdin Lake. There he predicted "the time is not far distant when 'The Katahdin Mountain House' will stand near the outlet." The next day the party moved across Roaring Brook and travelled to Avalanche Brook, which they followed upstream to the foot of the slide (East Slide or Avalanche Slide) on present-day Keep Ridge. In separate sections on the following day, the group climbed the slide, ascended the ridge and reached Pamola, and then crossed the Knife Edge to the monument on the highest peak. Keep described the topography and shape of the mountain in some detail. The party then descended by the route they had followed to the summit.[22]

Within a month Keep returned to explore the Great Basin. "So far as I can learn I was the first human visitor to this fabled residence of the Indians' 'Pamolah' and was not surprised about the Indian traditions concerning the mountain," he wrote. He descended to Katahdin Lake, apparently "spotting" a line to Roaring Brook, and returned to Hunt's Farm. On his descent below Katahdin Lake he noted that a logging road had been con-

**THE GREAT BASIN IN MT. KATAHDIN**
The "fabled residence of the Indians' 'Pamolah'," as Reverend Marcus Keep called
it, when claiming himself to be the first human visitor there, on his journey in 1847.

structed to a height-of-land near Katahdin Brook and to within two miles of Katahdin Lake. It was to be completed to the lake the next year, and from the lake it was only five miles to the foot of the East or Avalanche Slide or into the Great Basin. "When this is done any one may 'go to Katahdin' that wishes."[23]

In June 1848, Reverend Keep, with the assistance of John Stacy, marked a route over the intervening distance between the end of the tote road and Katahdin Lake—and the Keep Path was completed. Soon the road was extended to Katahdin Lake.

In the years following, Keep led parties to Katahdin once a year or more. Soon after his marriage in 1849, he led an expedition that was to include the first women to climb to the highest peaks of the mountain. But just before this party approached the mountain, James H. Haines, who had accompanied Keep in 1846, had guided Mrs. Elizabeth Oakes Smith of Portland along the Keep Path, apparently as far as Pamola. Mrs. Smith was the wife of Seba Smith, a former Portland journalist famous as "Major Jack Downing." She left a letter in a bottle on Pamola for the Reverend Keep. This was done to taunt Keep, who had earlier boasted that his wife would be the first woman to reach the top of Katahdin.

In 1861, Keep led the Hitchcock geological survey party in its ascent of the mountain. Finally, after a twenty-year hiatus, he accompanied Charles E. Hamlin on his ascent in 1881. For his work in opening up what is known as the Keep Path, the Maine Legislature in 1859 accepted Keep's petition that he be granted two hundred acres at the outlet of Katahdin Lake, where he had cleared several acres and built a crude camp, and granted him title to the land in 1860. The Keep Path remained a favored route to Katahdin until the 1870s when lumbering activities in the area forced changes in trail location.[24]

In 1847, several weeks before Keep's trip to Katahdin, the mountain was visited by another scientific expedition. The legislature in that year appropriated six hundred dollars for a botanical survey of the state and Dr. Aaron Young, an accomplished botanist from Bangor, was appointed state botanist and asked to head the survey. Young decided that Katahdin, which had never been explored by a "practical Botanist," should be the first area to be visited. He recruited six others to make the trip. Most were trained in botany to some degree. The party included Dr. George Thurber of Providence, Rhode Island, and the Reverend Ariel P. Chute of Harrison, Maine, both accomplished botanists and correspondents of Young. Two were Young's students—John Emerson of Glenburn, a deaf mute, and his brother George Emerson of Bangor, a botanist and also noted as a marksman. A Bangor journalist, J. K. Laski, probably sent by the *Bangor Courier*, and James Cowan, a Bangor lumberman who had worked on the Wassataquoik and served as guide, completed the party. Cowan reportedly had previously ascended Katahdin.

19

The expedition travelled by road to Mattawamkeag and Molunkus, and followed the Aroostook road, which could now be travelled by wagon as far as Sherman. The road from there to Hunt's Farm was so bad that the wagon and all but one horse were left behind. The group stayed briefly at the house of John Stacy, at present-day Stacyville, before moving on to Hunt's Farm. Leaving that point on the 23rd of August, they walked up the Wassataquoik tote road, using an old camp en route as a shelter for one night, to the point where the northeast shoulder of Russell Mountain approaches the stream. After another night of camping, on August 25 they ascended through the difficult, dense forest over the top of Russell Mountain and into the valley between that and the North Peaks. As they neared the North Peaks they dropped their packs, assuming they were on the top of Katahdin. Disappointed, they moved over those peaks and Hamlin Peak, which Young called the Camel's Back, descended the Saddle, and reached Monument Peak, or "Old Pamola," as John Laski called it. Along the route above timberline, Young and the other botanists gathered as many arctic plants as possible. Some of the specimens were deposited eventually at the Gray Herbarium at Harvard University. On their return from the mountain's east flanks, they moved farther to the south over the North Peaks and on descending from the mountain struck the South Branch of the Wassataquoik, which they called Katahdin Stream. From that point they descended to the main stream and moved on to the East Branch. Three accounts of the trip found their way into print within a short period of time. It was important, therefore, not only for the botanical information gained, but because it also further publicized the grandeur and beauty of the mountain.[25]

Visits to Katahdin became more frequent after the Keep Path was opened. An ill-founded rumor concerning discovery of gold near the mountain in late 1848 did not increase traffic to the area.[26] In 1852 or just before, the Reverend John Todd from Massachusetts was apparently the leader of a party that followed the Keep Path to Pamola and Baxter peaks. A Penobscot Indian, Nicola, was the guide. Todd's reaction to the first sight of the Knife Edge and Baxter Peak from Pamola was similar to that of many others. It was "nearly as lofty as the highest of the White Mountains; but it stands alone, solitary, naked and awful." On reaching the highest peak he wrote:

> Your first feeling is, you want to be and must be alone. When I reached the summit, my companion and guide were more than half a mile off, and right glad I was. I did not want to see or hear any thing human. I did not want any one to ask, What means the tear in your eye? You are communing with nature and with nature's God, and you feel as if you had no right to be there. At every few minutes the wind draws into the chasm, and in an instant the air is condensed into a cloud, and up it rolls towards you, up higher and higher, and all is thick cloud beneath and over you, and about you, and then it floats off, light and gladsome,

and the chasm is there,—the cloud-former!—clear and deep and awful, just as it was before. Perhaps we saw clouds created a dozen times in that hopper.

Several more times, in describing the beauties of the scenes, he used the term *awful*. "Nature is here unfashioned by man, stern savage, awful, but beautiful."[27]

Also in the summer of 1852, the governor of Maine toured the Moose-head Lake area. Governor John Hubbard's party descended the West Branch "to Katahdin Mountain," but it is not known whether the members actually ascended to the summit.[28]

A young man from Minot Center made the trip in 1853 with some un-named companions. William L. Jones left Bangor in mid-April and, using the Keep Path when he and his friends could find it, must have experienced a great deal of water and snow in reaching Avalanche Brook and the slide. They first ascended Pamola and then came down again, and, perhaps skirt-ing the southern side of the mountain, the next day they "went up the avalanche brook to the top of the highest peak." There they found a rock monument about five feet high and a bottle filled with pieces of birch bark and paper with the names of persons who had visited the top along with the date of the climb. "They were all of a later date than the time when Uncle M. went up." From the main peak, as they termed it, they followed a "sort of 'horseback' over rough rock about a quarter of a mile to another peak on the north."[29] Obviously the rock monument and bottle were at what is now called South Peak, which many early visitors thought higher than Baxter Peak. As Professor Lucius H. Merrill noted, decades later, "by a curious optical delusion, the point on which the observer stands always seems the lower."[30]

Thomas Wentworth Higginson, in 1855 a Unitarian Minister in Worces-ter, Massachusetts, and later an officer in the Civil War, a noted author, and president of the Appalachian Mountain Club, led a party from Massa-chusetts and Bangor that included five women. This was the third party to include women to hike on the mountain. After planning the trip for the better part of a year, the group finally gathered in Bangor and moved up-river by stage to Mattawamkeag and on to Molunkus and the hotel there. They were able to obtain the services of "Alick McClane" as a guide. After leaving Molunkus they could not reach the Hunt Farm as planned on the next day and therefore stayed at the Stacy house west of Sherman. They were as pleased and surprised with the Stacy household as Edward Everett Hale had been ten years earlier. There they felt fortunate in being able to hire John Stacy, "the fine looking youth in a red shirt," who had helped spot Keep's Path and was "the best woodsman in that region." The party had a copy of Hale's account and were also familiar with the trip made by Mrs. Smith in 1849. At Hunt's the group heard that the painter Frederic Church 21 had been the last visitor during the course of a trip along the East Branch.

From Wassataquoik Stream the Keep Path was followed to Pamola, the highest point reached by the party. From this vantage point, Higginson wrote: "The top of the mountain can be depicted at a single stroke, to any well instructed woman. Merely fancy the rim of a teacup, five miles round, with a piece broken out of one side. Beside this, the whole is jagged and uneven; nibbled, in truth, by a thousand or two of hungry winters." To mystify his companions and make them believe that one of the five women present on the trip had written the account, published in *Putnam's Monthly Magazine*, Higginson used a style that seemed to indicate that it had been written by a woman. Before his death, he admitted that he was the author.[31]

Several significant ascents were made in 1856. The Reverend Joseph Blake, who had been on the mountain two decades earlier, climbed Katahdin again in 1856. By now an accomplished botanist, he made the trip with a Reverend Whittlesey of Bath who was later a professor of rhetoric and oratory at Bowdoin College. Marcus Keep served as guide along the route he had pioneered. On the approach they stayed with the Stacy family, whom they regarded as highly as had the Higginson expedition of the previous year. The most remarkable incident on the otherwise commonplace trip was the discovery on July 4 by Blake of a plant previously unknown in Maine. While descending from Chimney Peak to the head of the Chimney, he found a number of specimens of *Saxifraga Stellaris* var. *comosa*, a small arctic plant not previously found south of Labrador. Blake gathered specimens of this as well as many more arctic plants. These were later given to various herbariums, while his own collection ultimately was given to the University of Maine. The plant was not found again on the mountain until 1873. While Blake's discovery was soon widely known among botanists, his account of the trip was not published for seven decades.[32]

A second trip in 1856 was not widely publicized until very nearly a century had elapsed. In August, Henry Ingersoll Bowditch, a physician from Boston and the son of Nathaniel Bowditch, led a party that included his teen-age son, three young nephews, and a lawyer friend, John W. Browne. Instead of taking the usual Penobscot River route from Bangor, they chose to go to Greenville and Moosehead Lake. There they engaged Z. (Zeb) D. Mitchell and Tim Meservy, an Indian, as guides. They purchased and rented canoes, took boats to Northeast Carry, and travelled across the carry to the West Branch, which they descended. They camped at various points along the river until they reached the mouth of Sourdnahunk Stream, where they again put up their tents. The next day they canoed to Abol Stream and left for the mountain. Neither guide had been on the lower West Branch nor on the mountain. Instead of ascending the slide when they reached the foot of it, they crossed it and moved farther west in order to intersect the Hunt Spur, a route which Mitchell thought would be easier, if longer. They had a difficult ascent through the thickly-matted spruce, but eventually

22

gained their objective. The remainder of the trip was pleasant, if uneventful. Since the river was very high, they were unable to return upstream and had to descend to Bangor. Bowditch's account, written from his diary immediately after the trip ended, remained with the family until 1927 when it was deposited with the Islesford Historical Collection.[33]

The third known ascent in 1856 was probably the most significant historically in terms of its total impact. Theodore Winthrop, author of the delightful account of *Life in the Open Air* and a number of other books, and Frederic E. Church, the famous landscape painter, set out from New York to Lake Champlain, after which they crossed northern Vermont and New Hampshire and entered Maine through the Rangeley Lakes area. From there they canoed to Moosehead Lake and, in Greenville, made preparations to go down the West Branch. They hired a guide whom they named "Cancut" and took the steamboat to the northern end of the lake. Winthrop and later artist groups on Katahdin used pseudonyms (Church was "Iglesias" in Winthrop's account). They both felt the need to be "somewhere near the heart of New England's wildest wilderness. We need to see Ktaadn, the distinctest mountain to be found this side of the continent." Katahdin "was the great object of all our voyage, with its educative preludes,—Ktaadn and a breathless dash down the Penobscot."

Winthrop's account is buoyant and exciting. His expedition camped opposite the mouth of Abol Stream. As with so many groups, on awakening the next morning they found the mountain covered with clouds. Then,

the sky was clear and scintillating; but there was a white-cotton nightcap on the head of Ktaadn. As we inspected him, he drew his nightcap down farther, hinting that he did not wish to see the sun that day. When a mountain is thus in the sulks after a storm, it is well not to disturb him; he will not offer the prize of a view. Experience taught us this; but then experience is only an empiric at the best.

Besides, whether Ktaadn were bare headed or cloud-capped, it would be better to blunder upward than lounge all day in camp, and eat Sybaritic dinners. We longed for the nervy climb. . . .

Of the climb to Abol Slide Winthrop wrote:

Even on this minor mountain the law of diminishing vegetation can be studied. The great trees abandoned us, and stayed indolently down in shelter. Next the little wiry trees ceased to be the comrades of our climb. They were no longer to be seen planted upon jutting crags, and, bold as standard-bearers, inciting us to mount higher. Big spruces, knobby with balls of gum, dwindled away into little ugly dwarf spruces, hostile as dwarfs are said to be always to human comfort. They grew man-high and lodged themselves together in a dense thicket. We could not go under, nor over, nor through. To traverse them at all, we

23

PITCHER PLANTS NEAR MARTINS PONDS, 1938

At one time Jake Day worked for Walt Disney. When "Bambi" was in the planning stage he persuaded Disney to make it the story of a Maine whitetail deer, so Jake was sent to the Katahdin region to photograph the flora and fauna of that area for background use.

PICTURES FROM A 19th-CENTURY JOURNEY
These two photographs were taken by James Stodder when he accompanied the well-known artist Frederic E. Church on a trip to Katahdin in 1874. The serenity of the Ripogenus Chasm, above, is in great contrast to the boulder-strewn confusion of Katerskonegan Carry, which the travellers used.

must recall the period when we were squirrels or cats, in some former state of being.

On reaching the terrace where other Bostonians had camped (the Higginson or Bowditch parties?) they could not stay "and sympathize with the late tenants" since they planned to do the whole hike in one day. Though Ktaadn "meant to wear the veil all day," they continued to the summit. Before reaching the cloud cover on the plateau, Winthrop observed: "Ktaadn's self is finer than what Ktaadn sees. Ktaadn is distinct, and its view is indistinct. It is a vague panorama, a mappy, unmethodic maze of water and woods, very roomy, very vast, very simple,—and these are capital qualities,—but also quite monotonous." Winthrop was obviously less enamored of the view than most visitors. "Besides sky, Ktaadn's view contains only the two primal necessities of wood and water. Nowhere have I seen such breadth of solemn forest, gloomy, were it not for the cheerful interruption of many fair lakes and bright ways of river linking them." After "studying the pleasant solitude and dreamy breath of Ktaadn's panorama for a long time," they decided to continue to the summit. "We made ourselves quite miserable for Naught. We clambered up into Nowhere, into a great, white, ghostly void." When they "reached the height of our folly and made nothing by it," they descended almost immediately. Though perhaps overdone, Winthrop's description ranks with that of Thoreau.[34]

Church had been on a canoe trip on the East Branch the year before. Probably the outstanding painter of the American Landscape School, he had studied under Thomas Cole and travelled widely to find subjects for his canvasses. According to Myron Avery, the 1856 expedition was the fourth Church had made to the Katahdin area. Winthrop noted that "Iglesias" earlier had gone up Katahdin's "eastern land-slide with a squad of lumbermen."[35] He had previously been on both branches of the Penobscot. Later he bought property on Millinocket Lake and spent time there until the water level was raised by construction of a dam.[36]

In 1876 Church made another canoe trip on the West Branch. This time he had with him James C. Stodder, a photographer from Bangor who took at least thirty-five photographs of scenes along the route, including camp scenes, views of the old Ripogenus Dam, and a view of Katahdin from that lake. It is not known if he climbed Katahdin on that trip.

Church and three other noted American landscape painters—S. R. Gifford, H. W. Robbins, and Lockwood de Forest—spent much of the month of September 1877 at Katahdin. They took the European and North American Railroad to Mattawamkeag and then followed the road through Molunkus and Sherman to Hunt's Farm. They were based at the head of Katahdin Lake, but spent considerable time in the Great Basin as well. Much of their time was spent sketching and painting, but they also explored a good part of the area, reaching the summit of Katahdin by means

26

of a slide coming down from the Saddle. The delightful account of the expedition, "perhaps the most famous assemblage of artists to visit a single peak in the United States," contains eleven of the sketches by different members of the group.[37]

Colonel Luther B. Rogers of Patten made his first trip to Katahdin over the Keep Path in the 1850s. He led a party of twenty-two individuals to the Great Basin, probably along the route from Sandy Stream spotted by Keep. John Stacy acted as guide. One of the party, Harriet Scribner, was the first woman to enter the Great Basin.[38] At about the same time, in 1857, a dozen ministers from Bangor, with six boatmen from Old Town, ascended by way of the Abol Slide.[39]

The next recorded ascents were made in 1861 when members of the Scientific Survey of Maine visited Katahdin. Early in that year the legislature had authorized a scientific survey to prepare a geologic map of the state and to investigate the coastlines, check out the iron and slate producing areas and the Penobscot River, and study the settled and unsettled portions of Aroostook County to determine their geology, natural history, agriculture, and physical geography. Ezekiel Holmes, the noted advocate of agriculture, and Charles Hitchcock, a well-known geologist, were asked to lead the survey. As assistants they chose George L. Goodale of Saco, a botanist and chemist; John C. Houghton of Still River, Massachusetts, a mineralogist; A. S. Packard, Jr., of Brunswick, an entomologist, and C. B. Fuller of Portland, a marine zoologist. Beginning on June 1, the party split and performed various portions of their assignments along the Maine coast and in the western part of the state. In early August they met in Bangor to explore the Penobscot region and western Aroostook County. In the course of exploring the Penobscot and the East Branch regions, members of the party hiked in the Traveler region and visited Trout Brook Farm as well.

While investigating the area around Hunt's Farm, the party, by prearrangement, met with Marcus Keep and a Mr. Maxwell of Golden Ridge, an independent hiker. Keep had been asked to guide the group to Katahdin. Hitchcock, Goodale, Packard, and Edmond H. Davis, of Wayne, an assistant brought along to help carry provisions, made up the party. Hitchcock wrote the account of the ascent of the mountain by way of the Keep Path. Along the way he described the geological features. On the Knife Edge, three-quarters of a mile was travelled along a "very narrow ridge, whose top was often only a foot wide, while on both sides of us we could look down for 3,000 feet over precipices too steep to be descended with safety." So awesome was the sight that "some of the party crawled upon their hands and knees over a large part of the distance." They never imagined that in New England "localities could be found so nearly resembling the peaks and ridges of the Andes." Contrary to what Jackson had argued two decades earlier, Hitchcock and his group felt that the continental ice sheet had not moved over Katahdin; he could find no evidence of drift. In noting other

27

mountains from the summit, Hitchcock suggested that the name Mount
Pomola be given to the North Peaks and concluded that in comparison with
the view from Mount Washington, "There is less grandeur and more beauty
in the view from Katahdin." Guided by Keep, the party descended into the
Basin and then moved out by a route "extremely difficult to travel" to Roaring Brook and Katahdin Lake. Along with many other visitors, Hitchcock
noted the potential tourist appeal of the mountain.

> If a good carriage road could be built from the Hunt farm to Chimney
> Pond in the Basin, and a good foot or bridle path from there to the
> summit, an immense number of visitors would be attracted to Mt.
> Katahdin, especially if a Hotel should be built at Chimney Pond, the
> most romantic spot for a dwelling-house in the whole State. As the roads
> are now constructed, it is easier for travellers to ascend from the
> west branch of the Penobscot, because less time is required away from
> the water. With the road thus constructed, travellers would hardly
> know that they were climbing a high mountain. With the Present con-
> veniences, lovers of adventure and recreation will find a trip to Mount
> Katahdin invigorating, and fraught with pleasure.[40]

John C. Houghton and G. L. Vose of the same expedition ascended to the
Southeast Slide and then followed the path to the Hunt Spur spotted by the
Bowditch party several years earlier.[41] Since official publications had a fairly
wide audience in the 19th century, the mountain received additional publicity through the Hitchcock party while at the same time more had been
learned of Katahdin's geology and natural history.

Also in 1861 or the following year, appeared the account of a canoe trip
down the West Branch from Moosehead Lake in which an anonymous writer
made observations about the mountain, though he did not climb it, that were
typical of many in the 19th century. After passing Sourdnahunk Falls the
writer's guide said, "Now I will show you the finest sight in America." On
looking upward as directed from the proper spot, the writer noted:

> Three miles off, like a huge uncut emerald, towered Mt. Katahdin, its
> base swept by the water at our feet, with a front of two miles. Its
> grandeur was oppressive. There it stood, stern, solemn, silent. Silent,
> did I say? Nay, from every tree, nook, and copse, swept toward us the
> hum of nature's voices, as if singing doxologies in adoration of Him
> whose hand upheaved its granite front.

Later the guide told him: "I have seen Katahdin a hundred times from this
very spot and it always seems new to me." After viewing the mountain from
other points along the river and noting its grimness, the writer concluded:
"I could not keep my eyes from it, and I watched it for an hour as we glided
28  slowly down the stream. It fascinated me as nothing else ever did. There is

something about it and its surroundings that rivets the attention, awakening a feeling of reverence and awe, causing a man to shrink within himself and cower before the silent demonstration of the power of Jehovah."[42]

In 1864 Frederic S. Davenport, J. P. Moore, and F. A. Appleton made an excursion to the mountain, an account of which was not publicized for over half a century. All apparently Bangor residents, they left that city in late August and travelled by way of Moosehead Lake and the West Branch, ascending Katahdin by the Abol Stream and Slide route. Later Davenport wrote a long series of articles about the trip, giving much historical detail as well as observations of the route and comparing the situation as it existed in 1864 with that of 1919. On the descent they met a party that included a Mr. Banks of Boston, a Mr. Russell of Lincoln, and Mr. Tomah, an Indian from Lincoln, who were ascending the peak. The guide Tomah had used the footprints left by the Davenport group in leading his party to the Abol Slide. Davenport made four additional trips to the summit of Katahdin by this route in the next dozen years.[43]

The Keep Path was used until the mid-70s, after which it appears to have become overgrown. John DeLaski (formerly J. D. Laski), who had accompanied the Young party, made an ascent of the mountain in 1871 to study glacial action there. In his account of the trip, DeLaski discussed the geologic situation of Katahdin, the highest point of which he called Pomola, at considerable length. He agreed with Charles T. Jackson, though he could find no evidence of glacier polish or scratches, "that the top of Katahdin was overridden by the glacier, and the icecap has everywhere degraded its summit, . . ." At the conclusion of his article, he described the various paths to Katahdin. From the east he said the Keep Path was still the usual one, though he preferred the approach over Russell Mountain farther up Wassataquoik Stream, which he thought was easier since one could camp in the trees near the top of Russell and reach the summit of Katahdin "without that exhausting labor which attends ascents by the other routes."[44]

In 1873 and 1874 a party led by President Merritt C. Fernald of the Maine State College (University of Maine at Orono) and the botanist F. Lamson-Scribner made the trek to Katahdin along the Keep Path to measure more accurately the altitude of Katahdin and to make botanical studies. Fernald found the altitude to be 5,215.5 feet with an error not to exceed 4.2 feet. F. W. Hardy, a well-known photographer of Bangor, accompanied the group on both trips and made some excellent stereoscopic views of the mountain. John C. Stacy was hired as guide. By this time, Hunt's Farm was owned by C. R. Patterson, who provided the same hospitality his predecessors had. Lamson-Scribner collected a large number of plants and reported that the only species peculiar to Katahdin was the *Saxifraga stellaris* var. *comosa*, which he said was found only "under the shade of rocks on the ridge north of the summit of the mountain."[45] This is the same plant found by the Reverend Blake seventeen years earlier on the side of Chimney Peak. 29

By the 1870s substantial developments had taken place in the Katahdin region. The white pine phase of lumbering had ended, except in the more remote areas, and loggers were increasingly turning their attention to spruce and other species. Lumbermen had penetrated far up the East Branch, made the Telos Cut, and were bringing down timber from farther and farther afield. Luther Rogers of Patten was taking white pine out of Trout Brook in 1857. During this period a welter of logging roads and tote roads were constructed in the whole area. Some, such as the one along the route of Trout Brook became the basis for a permanent road, but most of them were abandoned and soon became overgrown once lumbering was completed. This process was repeated several times as areas were recut. Since they were distant from the Katahdin region, most of these roads were little used by hikers or any others not associated with lumbering or the various scientific expeditions.

Lumbering on the upper reaches of the West Branch began during the 1830s, and the first dam at Chesuncook was built around 1834, while that at North Twin came a decade later.[46] Thoreau refers to a crew repairing the dam there in 1846. The Penobscot Log Driving Company was organized in 1846 as a cooperative by landowners in the West Branch to systematize earlier driving practices on the stream. All owners of land who logged them were participants in the concern. The company constructed a number of dams on the Penobscot and its tributaries as lumbering operations extended farther and farther upstream. Little was done in the area immediately south and east of Katahdin during most of this period since it had been burned over in 1795. This delayed the construction of roads in that area for some time and meant that the approaches to that portion of Katahdin would be by water rather than over land.

By the 1870s there was lumbering on the lower reaches of Sourdnahunk Stream and in 1878 the owners of property drained by the stream organized the Sourdnahunk Dam and Improvement Company. In the following year the first toll dam was constructed, as was the first dam at the foot of Sourdnahunk Lake; in 1880 the first slide dam was built. The supplies for the operations at Sourdnahunk in 1880 and for a time thereafter came by a circuitous route. They were moved to Mattawamkeag by rail, freighted to Patten, and then taken on wagons over tote roads by way of Shin Pond, Seboeis Farm, and along a route north of First Grand Lake, to Trout Brook, Dwelley Pond and on to Sourdnahunk Lake, a distance of fifty-two

*Opposite, above:* The remains of an old dam on the East Branch, now replaced by a new bridge. *Below:* Remains of the old Nesowadnehunk (Sourdnahunk) Dam on the road that "goes round the mountain" and over this bridge and dam. Reproduced from a painting by Jake Day.

30

**THE OLD HERSEY DAM ON SANDY STREAM.**
*Above:* Mt. Katahdin, knife edge and basin rims sharp against the sky, rises above remains of the old dam as photographed by Samuel Merrill long ago. *Below:* The Hersey Dam as "reconstructed" in Jake Day's painting.

miles from Patten. The road later was extended along the course of Sourdnahunk Stream to the West Branch. It remained open for travel into the
next century and as late as 1900, buckboards could make the two-day trip
from Patten to the lake. Burton W. Howe of Patten was then operating Trout
Brook Farm.[47]

Obviously this lumbering activity brought many people to the West
Branch region. The accounts of canoeing on the river or of those hiking the
mountains often mentioned the assistance rendered by those engaged in the
work. The history and folklore of the lumbermen and river drivers is enormous and rich and no attempt will be made here to cover the subject. A
good starting point on the literature is Fannie Hardy Eckstorm's *The
Penobscot Man*.[48]

The commencement of lumbering operations on Sandy Stream in 1874
modified some trail approaches to the mountain for a time. Edwin A. Reed,
later of Orono, but then in the shingle making business with his father in
Springfield, Maine, entered the operation to assist his father's brother-in-law,
William R. Hersey, who died before the operation really got underway. A
dam at the outlet of lower Togue Pond and two on Sandy Stream were
built to facilitate the movement of lumber. The uppermost of these dams
was called the Hersey Dam and was later reconstructed slightly farther
downstream by the Great Northern Paper Company. A depot camp was
established about a mile upstream from Hersey Dam and, to supply this,
the road to Katahdin Lake was extended to Sandy Stream in 1874. The Reeds
cut many logs, but when the Hersey Dam went out in 1875 the drive was
hung and considerable money was lost. Edwin Reed was the hero of the
"Sandy Stream Song," one of the famous Maine lumbering ballads.[49]

Lumbering obliterated the Keep Path west of Sandy Stream and in the
fall of 1874 two "young guides" spotted a trail from Hersey Dam into the
Great Basin. The route had been cut earlier by Keep and was used by several parties. In the early seventies two men, Lang and Jones, who ran
stages between Mattawamkeag and Patten, made a trail from a point above
Daicey Dam on the Wassataquoik to Katahdin Lake and then used the road
to Sandy Stream. Later called the Lang and Jones Trail, this route was used
by Frederic Church's party in 1877. The old road from the Lower Katahdin
Crossing to Katahdin Lake that had been cut in 1847 and was Keep's route
to the lake had become overgrown and was rebuilt in 1881 to bring supplies
to the crews rebuilding the dam at the outlet of Katahdin Lake to store
water for impending lumbering operations on the Wassataquoik. Lang and
Jones built the first sporting camp on Katahdin Lake, but apparently never
had much business. By the end of the decade of the 70s the road routes to
and along Sandy Stream from the east were very rough and practically unusable.[50]

Though becoming overgrown, this was probably the route used by the
young Harvard student, Theodore Roosevelt, when he climbed the moun-        33

tain in 1879. Sickly as a youth, Roosevelt embarked on a rigorous program of work and travel to regain his health and build his body. During the 1870s he came to the Maine woods a number of times at all seasons of the year. He developed a lasting friendship with two Maine guides, William Dow and William W. Sewall, and later brought them to his Dakota ranch. He spent a month in northern Maine during August and September of 1879, just before he began his senior year at Harvard. Accompanying him was his cousin, W. Emlen Roosevelt and his tutor, Arthur H. Cutler. They made an eight-day trip up Katahdin but did not indicate the departure point or route. To his surprise Roosevelt found that he "could carry heavier loads and travel faster" than his companions. Though the swarms of black flies didn't bother him much, they did annoy Cutler particularly, whose face gradually came to look "like a roughly executed map of the Rocky Mts." While fording a stream Roosevelt lost a shoe and had to do the rest of the hike using moccasins "which protect the feet just about as effectually as kid gloves would." Though footsore, he was the only one of the group to reach the summit. Immediately afterward he left for an arduous two-week trip to the Munsungun Deadwater on the Aroostook River with William Sewall, "the roughest work I have yet had in the way of camping out; our trip to Katahdin was absolute luxury compared to it."[51]

During the 1880s, with commencement of the Tracey-Love operations on Wassataquoik Stream, a new stage of lumbering on and use of the Wassataquoik was entered.[52] A number of small operators had cut timber on the lower reaches of the stream in earlier decades to clean out the remaining white pine and some spruce. In 1883 Foster J. Tracey and his son-in-law Hugh Love began preparations for lumbering in T4R9 for the owner of the land, T. H. Todd of St. Stephen, New Brunswick. Tracey moved from Milltown, New Brunswick to Stacyville. The year 1883 was spent in cruising the town, building dams on Wassataquoik Stream, and performing other necessary preliminaries to lumbering. For depot camps Tracey and Love constructed Old City Camps at the junction of Pogy Brook and the Wassataquoik. Later they built the Russell Camp (the site of New City Camps) on the middle branch of the Wassataquoik and Bell Camp near the junction of the Wassataquoik and its South Branch. Operations began in mid-October and were commemorated by the inscription carved on a huge boulder in the stream at Mammoth Dam: "Tracey and Love commenced operations on Wassataquoik October 16th 1883." Within a month the plans were modified when a terrific windstorm, locally known as the "Maine Cyclone," uprooted enormous numbers of trees from Daicey Mountain westward. Thus the first year of logging was spent in cleaning up blowdowns. During the next summer two careless fishermen at Norway Falls let a fire they had built to chase away black flies get out of hand. Before it burned itself out, the fire had ravaged 22,000 acres, including Old City Camps and other outlying camps.[53] Tracey and Love rebuilt and continued their operations until 1891.[54]

34

These operations were important since they opened new routes to Katahdin, including the Tracey and Love Trail to the North Peaks, cut in 1885. Starting from their Russell Camp on the middle branch of the Wassataquoik, they first followed the stream and then cut the trail in the valley to the west of Russell Mountain and east of Tip Top. In the same year Madison Tracey, to collect $100 offered by Lang and Jones, who still had their camp on Katahdin Lake, to help defray the cost of the trail, took a horse to the top along this route. Late in that summer a party of fourteen, including Mrs. Luther B. Rogers of Patten, "the only party of tourists which visited Katahdin last year," used buckboard wagons to the end of the road and then proceeded to climb the mountain. In her description, Mrs. Rogers exaggerated the depths below the "Narrows" as she called the Knife Edge.[55] George Witherle also used the route in 1886. Later, when lumbering operations were moved to different areas it began to be overgrown. In 1927, after he opened the camps at Russell Pond, William Tracey, the nephew of

THE KNIFE EDGE

A good head-on photograph of this famous part of the Katahdin ascent. It was taken in 1960 on the occasion of a climb to Mt. Katahdin by Governor Curtis and friends.

Foster J., relocated portions of the trail and cleared it for use. Parts of the original trail remain in use today.[56]

During the same period changes had occurred at the Hunt Farm on the East Branch. Hunt had sold out his operation to C. R. Patterson, who in turn in 1881 sold out to S. B. Gates, a hotel operator from Winn and Mattawamkeag. Patterson moved upstream about two miles to the so-called Dacey Clearing, which Ezekiel Holmes had noted as existing in 1838. Patterson built a road connecting the two clearings and built a house or inn there which he called Lunksoos.[57] During the next decade when Ayer and Rogers were lumbering the Wassataquoik, they leased the Patterson place, then called the East Branch House, and on a portion of it built a large and elaborate sporting camp called Lunksoos Camp.[58] This remained in use long into the 20th century. While Gates made some repairs at the Hunt Farm it never regained its former significance.

The pace of exploration of Katahdin increased during the last decades of the 19th century. Ascents become too numerous to discuss in detail. Botanists and geologists particularly made a large number of trips to the area and ascents of the mountain in this period. For citations to their work and particularly that of Francis L. Harvey of the University of Maine, consult Smith and Avery's *Annotated Bibliography of Katahdin*.

However, the explorations of two men should be discussed in some detail. The first is Charles E. Hamlin, professor of geology at Harvard University. Hamlin made his first trip to the Katahdin area in 1869 when he climbed the Southwest or Hunt Spur. Subsequently he made at least four other trips to the region in 1871, 1879, 1880, and 1881. In the course of his wanderings he covered most sections of the mountain except the northern basins and in 1881 published two important articles concerning the mountain. In the first he discussed extensively the physical characteristics and geologic features of the Katahdin area.[59] He was particularly interested in the extent of the granite formations on and around the mountain. His description of the geology and physical features of Katahdin accompanied by a heliotype of the model of the mountain he had prepared, was the most detailed to that time. His was probably the first model made of the mountain. In the course of his explorations he found a fossil-bearing chunk of sandstone about 600 feet below the West (Baxter) Peak, and while he was certain that the continental glacier had overrun much of the mountain, he made no final conclusions as to whether it had covered it completely.[60]

In "Routes to Ktaadn," the second article, he not only discussed approaches, but summed up much of the previous exploration on the mountain and discussed many of its features.[61] The latter article, as the first, was accompanied by a map drawn by J. W. and J. Sewall of Old Town. The first route listed was by way of Mattawamkeag and the Penobscot River. From Mattawamkeag to Medway one could go by trail or by river. From Medway to "Old Fowler's" on Millinocket Stream a road could be used if one chose.

Beyond Fowler's a road existed over the carry to Quakish Lake and the
upper West Branch. Camps existed at the outlet to Ambejijis (Ambajejus)
Lake—the Boom House or Ambejijis House—and at the north Twin Dam.
They were the only two between Chesuncook and Fowlers. The remainder
of the route is already familiar. On the mountain itself Hamlin took a course
to the southwestern spur, which he thought would make a good alternative
to the slide if the dense spruce were cut.

A second approach, probably not much used, also started from Bangor.
Hamlin apparently took this route to allow study of the granite features
along the way. Those using this route first took the railroad to Old Town
and Milo. Beyond Milo, stage transportation was available to Brownville
and thereafter private conveyances were used on the regular roads for five
more miles. A woods road then led for twenty-one miles more to Middle Joe
Merry (Jo-Mary) Lake. (An alternate route for part of the way included
the use of Schoodic Lake.) From Middle Jo-Mary Lake canoes were used to
navigate Lower Jo-Mary, the Thoroughfare, Pemadumcook Lake, and the
usual West Branch route.[62] The third approach was from Moosehead Lake
and the upper West Branch.

The fourth route, via Sherman, Wassataquoik Stream, and Katahdin
Lake, Hamlin thought the best. The alternative over the North Peaks he
thought was too long, since he believed that the Great Basin was the most
logical center for climbing activities in the Katahdin area. To reach the
Basin by any other route entailed too much exertion. From the Great Basin
there was ready access to the higher peaks. Hamlin thought a good wagon
road should be built to Katahdin Lake, which he felt would make an ideal
site for a summer resort. After talking with guides, resort owners, and
others he estimated that not more than fifty people per year had visited
Katahdin during the previous decade.

Much more extensive were the explorations conducted by George
Witherle of Castine, Maine. During the period 1880 to 1901, Witherle, at
first with his wife and two guides and later alone with the guides or with
his daughter, made eleven major trips to the Katahdin region. For most of
the early trips the guides were Paul R. Peavey and his son Clarence, of
Patten. Witherle visited virtually every major point in present-day Baxter
State Park south of Trout Brook. In addition, he investigated the ranges of
low mountains paralleling the East Branch not within the Park. Over five
decades after the Monument Line surveyors had discovered the Northwest
Basin (to Witherle the West Basin) and the Klondike, he visited and explored them several times. On one of his trips, he walked the length of the
road along Trout Brook to Dwelley Pond. He climbed nearly every mountain of significance in the region and was the first to explore what is now
Witherle Ravine between the Klondike and the Owl. He kept a detailed
record of his travels and published the results of two of the expeditions in
*Appalachia.* Several decades later the diaries of the remaining trips were

37

published by the Maine Appalachian Trail Club.[63] His record of exploration of the region was unsurpassed in the 19th century.

The Appalachian Mountain Club was organized in Boston in 1876 by a small group of people, mainly scientists, who were interested in the mountains. The objectives of the Club were "to explore the mountains of New England and the adjacent regions, both for scientific and artistic purposes; and, in general, to cultivate an interest in geographical studies."[64] Thriving from the first, the Club concentrated its activities primarily in the White Mountains of New Hampshire where to this day it has been a potent force in the conservation movement. Hamlin became a member in early 1877, and Witherle in 1883. The Club's journal, *Appalachia*, has been the outlet for an enormous number of articles on the Katahdin region. Probably influenced by the work of Hamlin and Witherle, the Club gradually became interested in the Katahdin area. Its work was to be inextricably intertwined with Katahdin and later Baxter State Park into the decade of the 1960s.

A group of five club members travelled to Katahdin in 1886 and approached the area from the east, apparently reaching the Great Basin over the North Peaks on the new Tracey-Love Trail. A woman member of the party, Rose Hollingsworth, was a photographer who took over fifty excellent pictures of the region, many of which were later published in *Appalachia* or other publications such as *In the Maine Woods*. No mention is made of the party's guide but it was undoubtedly Clarence Peavey or his father.[65] Either then or during the ensuing year the department of improvements of the Club determined to follow Hamlin's advice and improve the route to Katahdin. It was the Club's first improvement work outside of the White Mountains. The Club also planned an excursion to Katahdin for the following August—this was the first in what became the Club tradition of August Camp.

Clarence Peavey was hired to cut out a trail where necessary since the Lang and Jones trail was nearly impassable. As cut by Peavey, the Appalachian Trail, as the route or portions of it were to be called for fifty years, followed the Wassataquoik Stream to the Upper Katahdin Crossing about nine miles above the East Branch. Peavey then utilized a lumber road leading toward Katahdin Lake through the so-called Green Woods, which had not been burned in the fire of 1884. From the end of that road, he cut a trail to Katahdin Lake. From Katahdin Lake, Peavey went almost due west through an extensive blowdown area below Turner Mountain and north of Sandy Stream Pond until he reached Roaring Brook. After following that for a mile, he crossed and then improved the route Lang and Jones had laid out to the Basin ponds and then on to Chimney Pond (then called Basin Pond by AMC members and others). From the Basin ponds area Peavey cut a route to Pamola and also one to the North Basin from a point just below Chimney Pond. He also erected a fairly large camp at Katahdin Lake and a smaller one at Chimney Pond for the Club.[66]

Between August 15 and September 15, 1887, nineteen club members, including ten women, and five guides as well as twenty-six other individuals, used the new route. The AMC members climbed the various peaks in the area, erected a number of signs at various key points, and improved the trails. To reach the Saddle, in the next two years they opened up and cleared a route up an old slide south of the present Saddle Trail.[67] Lore A. Rogers, son of Luther, used this route in his first ascent of the mountain in 1887.[68] Then, for unknown reasons, club members lost their intense interest in the area and within less than a decade both camps had burned and parts of the trail, particularly in low areas, had become obscured.[69] Some hikers continued to use it, however, until the great fire of 1903 obliterated the lower portions of it.[70]

The Wassataquoik route remained a favored one during the following decade. In 1891 the firm of Ayer and Rogers of Patten, seemingly led by Luther Rogers, took over the lumbering operations on the Wassataquoik. Both men had lumbered on the Penobscot and its tributaries for several decades. As indicated earlier they bought the Patterson place on the East Branch and built Lunksoos Camp as a headquarters and adjunct to the lumbering operations. The firm built a good road up the valley of the South Branch of the Wassataquoik in 1892, and early in that year Lore Rogers made a winter ascent from the Russell Camp. One of the lumbering camps was located where a large stream from the east side of Katahdin joined the South Branch of the Wassataquoik and was named McLeod Camp after the man who was the boss there. What became known as the McLeod Trail was built up the mountain westward to the North Peaks. A small camp was built near timberline. The trail was often used as a means of descending the mountain. Lore Rogers took a party to the McLeod Camp in 1894. Since it was only three miles from the Great Basin, his brother Edwin marked and cut a trail for the party to use to reach Chimney Pond. The Rogers Trail, which connected with the Appalachian Trail at the Basin ponds, was used for a number of ascents, including that of George Witherle in 1898. Though longer, this route offered easier access to the summits of Katahdin than the Appalachian Trail. Moose and caribou hunters also used this route in the '90s. In 1900 Edwin Rogers led George Kennedy and a group of botanists from the New England Botanical Club to Chimney Pond along this trail and built a short-lived camp in the Great Basin.[71] A year later a similar botanical expedition organized by the Horn's Club in Boston followed the same path and used buckboards as far as the McLeod Camp.[72] The fire of 1903, which burned through Pogy Notch and burned the east side of Katahdin and much of the valley of the South Branch of the Wassataquoik, obliterated parts of the Appalachian and Rogers trails, including the McLeod Camp.[73] By then Ayers and Rogers had ceased their lumbering operations.

In the upper Wassataquoik, the trails were kept open for periods of time by continued lumbering operations. The Katahdin Pulp and Paper

Company, very active at the time in the Trout Brook region,[74] succeeded
Ayer and Rogers in 1901 and attempted to cut long logs, but were beaten by
the fire of 1903. In 1910 Edward B. Draper of Bangor, an official of the
company, urged that pulpwood be cut in the upper reaches of Wassataquoik
Stream. As a result, the dams were rebuilt and new ones constructed higher
up the middle branch north of Katahdin. A sluice for bringing pulpwood
from the northern flanks of Katahdin was constructed to the west of the
Tracey and Love Trail. The Draper operations extended up the Wassataquoik as far as the steep slopes of the Brothers. During this period and for
years after, the sluices and roads offered other approaches, sometimes confusing, to the mountain and its neighbors. In addition, Draper constructed
roads on Pogy Mountain and a sluice from there leading into Wassataquoik

UPPER SOUTH BRANCH POND
In the background The Traveler towers to the left; Pogy Notch is in the center; and
Black Cat Mountain is at the right. Photo by E. S. C. Smith.

Lake, thus opening up additional areas. Lumbering operations ceased in 1914 and in the following year a fire swept Pogy Mountain. The Pogy area tote roads had been tied in with roads coming in from the upper reaches of the South Branch of Trout Brook and thus offered a long and little-used route to Katahdin.[75] During the same period, roads were opened up to the Upper South Branch Pond, through Pogy Notch.

After the turn of the century, the approaches to Katahdin from the east were continually modified by lumbering activities and the attendant construction of roads. John Ross, the noted lumberman from Bangor, began cutting operations in the Sandy Stream area in 1902. The dams were rebuilt and new lumbering camps developed. Earlier, a lumbering firm had extended the road utilized in part for the Appalachian Trail all the way to the AMC camp on Katahdin Lake. Madison M. Tracey and John Cushman had opened the second sporting camp on Katahdin Lake about 1896. They utilized the Appalachian Trail and this new road to supply their operation. Tracey sold out to Cushman about 1900, and the latter operated the camp alone for two and a half decades. From this camp after 1896, hunters frequented Katahdin to shoot moose and caribou, the latter of which disappeared from the mountain about 1905.[76]

In the course of the Ross lumbering operations, Edwin Rogers, who held a lease on Lunksoos Camp and was also working for Ross at the time, extended a road from Lunksoos to Sandy Stream Pond. This route, not to be confused with the Rogers Trail described above, for a short time afforded another trail into the Great Basin from the east. In the course of his work for Ross, Rogers built a road along Roaring Brook almost to the Basin ponds. Few records of the use of this route exist, though on occasion in 1902 there were as many as fifty people in the Great Basin at one time.[77] Professor Leroy Harvey, the noted botanist from Chicago, used the Rogers route when in 1902 he was the leader of a distinguished group of scientists who explored the Katahdin region. Their work in the Northwest Basin was of particular importance.[78]

In the second decade of the 20th century the AMC once again became interested in the Katahdin area. Individual members began frequenting the region more often. In 1916 the Club held another August Camp there. Madison Tracey cut a trail for them. Travellers could use the Upper Katahdin Crossing on the Wassataquoik or another route along the line of Katahdin Brook to reach Katahdin Lake. Tracey's trail then followed a lumber road westward from the pond near Sandy Stream and Sandy Stream Pond before ascending to the Basin Ponds.[79] This trail lasted a short time before approaches from the south and the west became more practicable. The Baxter expedition of 1920 used portions of the route.

The Sandbank Trail was opened in 1920, up the stream of the same name, from the East Branch to Katahdin Lake. Developed as Stacyville's move to be the major gateway to the Park, its future was doomed by devel-

opments of the Great Northern Paper Company.[80] However, the Wassataquoik Stream route remained open due to the operations at Russell Pond in
in the decades of the 1920s and '30s. Also, the Maine Forest Service maintained personnel in the area to spot and fight fires.

The end of the century saw a new era in the Katahdin region and the
Penobscot River. The completion of the Bangor and Aroostook Railroad to
Norcross, Millinocket, and Stacyville in 1894 modified travelling arrangements to Katahdin to a considerable degree. More modern means of transportation moved closer to the mountain, so that even more people could
experience the pleasures offered by the trip. By the late '90s a number of
small steamboats brought passengers to the lakes and the river above Millinocket. Sporting camps flourished along both the East and West branches
as they had not done before.[81] Early in the new century the Bangor and
Aroostook Railroad began publication of *In the Maine Woods,* and other
promotional literature. *In the Maine Woods* was an interesting mixture of
articles featuring recreational attractions along the route or near the railroad, written, as often as not, by well-known authors or enthusiastic ama-
teurs. All extolled the great fishing to be found or the beauties of the region
made accessible by the railroad. With these were included advertisements
of ever more numerous sporting camps. Similar in scope and even wider in
coverage were *The Maine Sportsman* and also *Forest and Stream,* a national
periodical published in New York City.

Of the sporting camps two were of particular importance for the history
of Katahdin. During the 1890s Irving O. and Lyman A. Hunt, grandsons of
William Hunt of Hunt's Farm, operated a sporting camp on Indian Pitch on
Sourdnahunk Stream. Here they guided sports in the summer and fall, and
hunted and trapped in the winter. A few years later, probably in 1900, they
established Hunt's Camp on Kidney Pond, which they owned until the
1920s. One authority says the Hunts would have located at Daicey Pond had
Maurice York, who established the Twin Pine Camps on that lake, not
beaten them.[82] In 1900 the Hunts marked and cut the trail from Kidney
Pond up the southwestern spur of Katahdin, which now bears the name.[83]
Their clientele, as that of York, included not only fishermen and hunters, but
also hikers and those who wished to have a wilderness experience. In their
operations trails were opened up, not only to the numerous small ponds and
lakes nearby, but to surrounding mountains as well. Approached from the
river route before 1916, they became more accessible once the Great Northern Paper Company opened roads into the area.

In the late 19th century the inexorable consolidation movement in
American industry resulted in the formation of the International Paper
Company in 1899, combining many small paper plants in Maine and other
states. One of the participants was Garret Schenck, who had opened a
paper mill in Rumford and had earlier taken part in the construction of
42  sulphite mills in Orono and Old Town. Unsatisfied with the new situation,

even before the final organization, Schenck withdrew the same year, and with banking help from New York, chartered the Great Northern Paper Company, to replace the Northern Development Company, a firm organized two years earlier in Millinocket.[84] Schenck had been called upon when it ran into financial difficulties. Working with Franklin W. Cram, president of the Bangor and Aroostook Railroad, Schenck was able to raise the needed capital to organize and expand the operations of Great Northern after 1899. He brought into his service Fred A. Gilbert, a native of Orono, who had long experience in lumbering on the Penobscot and had headed the operations of the Penobscot Log Driving Company on the West Branch in 1900. Until Schenck died in 1928 and Gilbert resigned the following year, their work was to be inextricably mixed in the affairs of lumbering on the West Branch and its tributaries. After 1900 Great Northern purchased properties in the drainage areas of the West and East branches of the Penobscot, as well as in other river areas, whenever it could do so, and soon it became the largest landowner in Maine. By 1903 it was able, after a very difficult legislative battle, to organize and control the West Branch Driving and Reservoir Dam Company. It then controlled the affairs of the Penobscot Log Driving Company, the Sourdnahunk Dam and Improvement Company, and numerous similar concerns on the river and its tributaries. In the future all logs destined to go to the Penobscot Log Driving Company would be delivered at Shad Pond, below Millinocket; all other logs would be controlled by the new concern. After that, only a small part of the annual drive went to Shad Pond. In effect, the new corporation controlled lumbering above the Millinocket area.

The Great Northern Paper Company built dams along the West Branch and its tributaries as needs dictated. During the next three or four decades, it moved pulpwood from a number of areas around Katahdin as well as from the more far-flung portions of its holdings. Lumbering roads were gradually extended into new areas; roads which might be followed for a few years only, until lack of hard use led to decay and made them obscure. Other roads provided the basis for more permanent routes into the area. The Sourdnahunk tote road was pushed through late in the 19th or early in the 20th century; but though it was occasionally used by visitors to the mountain, it was unusable for automobiles until 1933.[85]

During the second decade of the century, the company decided to build the high dam at Ripogenus Gorge. Begun in 1915 and completed several years later, this project merged three lakes—Ripogenus, Chesuncook, and Caribou—into one larger lake. To allow movement of construction materials to the dam site, the company, beginning in 1910, improved an existing tote road from Lily Bay on Moosehead Lake to the Grant Farm and then extended it to Ripogenus Gorge and beyond to Sourdnahunk Field by way of Harrington Lake.[86] After 1916 it was possible for visitors to the Katahdin area to drive automobiles through Greenville, over the new dam, and on to    43

Sourdnahunk Field. From that point existing tote roads were used by the
owners of Kidney Pond Camps and Twin Pine Camps to shuttle their clients
by buckboards. Though the river route remained in use, the new road became the more common approach by visitors to the area.

These Great Northern operations were coupled with developments on
the southeastern side of Katahdin. There, in T3R9, Great Northern had
acquired considerable land along with John and Harry Ross. Under the
leadership of Superintendent Patrick E. Whalen, the company began logging the northern portion of the township in 1920. Old dams were rebuilt or
relocated so as to speed the movement of pulp along Roaring Brook and
Sandy Stream. Camps were built in favorable locations to house personnel
in the area of Basin Ponds, Sandy Stream, Roaring Brook and Turner Mountain. To supply these camps the company rebuilt and extended the old
Sandy Stream tote road until it reached the Basin Ponds. With this change
the new road became a favored approach to Katahdin.[87]

The work of the Maine Forestry District and its impact in the Katahdin
region should also be noted. The District was created by the legislature in
1909 after disastrous fires had swept many portions of Maine's forest lands
in 1903 and 1908. An organizational structure for the District was developed, supervisory personnel was hired, and a network of fire lookout towers
was built. The first in the nation had been built on Squaw Mountain in 1905
by a local lumber company. William Hilton, later vice president of Great
Northern, was the first person to man this tower. By the time the District
was established, several other towers had been built by private landowners.
The new agency, headed by the forest commissioner, was charged with fire
protection of forest lands in unorganized townships, some plantations,
coastal and inland islands, and some towns. The expenses of the District,
with its fire warden force, lookout towers, administrative cost, and the cost
of fighting fires, were paid from the proceeds of a tax levied on the lands
protected. Landowners paid the self-imposed tax in proportion to their
holdings. The District, unique in the nation at the time, lasted until it was
phased out in 1972.[88]

Within the present area of Baxter State Park several towers or lookout
stations were established during the first decade of the District's existence.
In 1913 a cabin was built by Frank Sewall, who also served as the watch-
man, on the south side of Katahdin, at the terrace on Abol Slide where
hikers had often camped en route to the summit. The cabin was often used
by hikers. Because of its location, which allowed a view only in certain directions and was in an area of much fog and clouds, the lookout was abandoned in 1920, though the cabin was used by hikers for several more years
before it collapsed.[89] A tower was erected on Doubletop, also in 1913, and
replaced with a steel tower of newer design in 1918. It remained in use
through the decade of the 1930s. Others were built at Horse Mountain
above First Grand Lake in 1917, and at Burnt Mountain in T5R10 in 1924,

44

FIRE TOWERS
On the left, typical of the very early primitive structures; on the right, one of the
latest models

both of which remained operational for several decades; and at Center
Mountain for a brief period. The opening of these towers and others in the
surrounding region were of some significance in making scenic points in the
area more accessible. To supply them various routes had to be kept open,
routes which were used by visitors to the area as well. Combined with activities of employees of the Inland Fisheries and Game Commission, the
work of the Maine Forestry District added significantly to the public's
knowledge of and ability to visit the area. Representatives of both agencies
assisted the Baxter party in the summer of 1920.

By the early 20th century the Katahdin region had been fairly thoroughly explored. Timber in most of the area had been cut at least once and
much of the land area was under the control or ownership of a small number of individuals or corporations. While the mountain was more readily
accessible than a century earlier, a trip there still involved a good deal of
time and effort. However, more visitors travelled to the mountain for recreational purposes and the wilderness experience, and more citizens of Maine
began to feel that the Katahdin region should be protected and preserved
from future exploitation.

On March 3, 1931, former Governor Percival P. Baxter wrote to Governor
William Tudor Gardiner offering to give the state of Maine his interests in
just under 6,000 acres of land, which included the bulk of Katahdin. The
legislature speedily accepted his offer, and the effort to acquire complete
ownership of the property and officially establish Baxter State Park was
begun. Baxter pointed out that it had long been his ambition to have Maine
own the mountain, which to his mind was "the grandest and most beautiful
of all the natural attractions of our State." He declared that since his many
attempts to have the state establish a park had been unsuccessful, he had
decided to do it himself. Baxter's bequest culminated a long and often terribly involved process, which began long before he became interested in
the area. With dogged persistence he succeeded where others had failed.

The first discussion of the potential recreational values of the area thus
far discovered had come in 1861, when C. H. Hitchcock climbed Katahdin
in the company of the Reverend Marcus Keep and advocated a good car-
riage road from Hunt Farm to Chimney Pond, and a "good foot or bridle
path" to the summit.[1] Two decades later, Charles Hamlin envisioned the
development of a road from Sherman to Katahdin Lake with hotels at the
lake and in the Great Basin.[2] He apparently did not think of the creation
of a park or forest reserve. In the early 1890s Dr. Augustus Hamlin of
Bangor (no relation) envisioned the creation of a game preserve there.[3]

For most of the 19th century, while the people of Maine were engaged
primarily in developing the agricultural and forest potential of the state,
they were not interested in setting aside preserves for use by the public.
As long as the Katahdin area was difficult to reach no greater pressures for
doing so arose. Maine provided a great many alternatives for recreation,
and the mountains and lakes, though usually privately owned, were generally accessible to all. Only as the national park movement developed in
the nation as a whole, as population pressures built up, and the tourist industry began to reach greater proportions did the first conservation movement in the Maine forest emerge. In the 1890s and early 1900s, the gradual
consolidation of landholdings by the rapidly growing paper industry spurred
interest in setting aside natural areas for public use.[4]

A very early proposal to create a state park came in 1895 when *The*    47

*Industrial Journal* of Bangor, the official paper of the Maine Hotel Proprietor's Association, urged the creation of a state park of nine hundred square
miles centering on Katahdin before the region was "devastated by lumbermen, fires and a squatter population." If the state did not have the money
to buy the land at the time it could wait until lumbering had been completed and then purchase it for a "trifling sum per acre. . . . Nature indeed,"
argued the editor, "would seem to have designed it as a public park." He
also argued that the same should be done with the Moosehead and Rangeley Lakes areas, since they were unfit for agriculture. Such actions would
attract many tourists from around the nation and protect areas from despoliation.[5]

A year later, the Maine Sportsmen's Fish and Game Association, a
leader in conservation lobbying in Maine before 1900, urged Maine people
to note the possibilities available in the state "to develop it, by preserving our forests, our fish and our game."[6] Early in the new century, the
*Bangor Daily Commercial,* after noting recent accounts of botanists' trips to
Katahdin, argued editorially that before the region was developed com-
mercially "it should be made the duty of the state to own Katahdin, to be
forever kept for the use of the people as a great public reservation."[7] The
work of the forest commissioners, whose office had been established in 1891,
the publication by the Bangor and Aroostook Railroad of *In the Maine
Woods,* and the efforts of the Maine State Federation of Women's Clubs
helped to spur interest in preserving the forests of Maine. In the late 1890s,
Fish and Game Commissioner Leroy T. Carleton developed a "pet scheme
of a game preserve, to include the caribou grounds on and around Katahdin."[8] Undoubtedly events on the national level, particularly the conservation work carried on during the administration of Theodore Roosevelt,
also helped to publicize the forest resources of Maine and to spur local
action.

Percival Baxter often indicated that he had first become interested in
preserving the forests and other natural resources around Katahdin and in
Maine generally while he served in the legislature in 1905. Two years
earlier, he had first seen the mountain close at hand when he accompanied
his father on a fishing trip to Kidney Pond, which they reached by "railroad
tote team and on foot."[9] A close check of the *Legislative Record* for 1905,
however, indicates that he was not particularly active during the session,
though he did introduce a petition for eight members of the Maine State
Federation of Women's Clubs calling for enactment of laws to preserve the
beauty of the fields and forests of Maine and for planting trees along its
highways.[10] Nothing came of the petition.

The Federation was one of the first groups to seek some protective
status for the Katahdin area. In 1904 Mrs. Joseph A. Thompson of Bangor,
one of its 6,000 members and a member of its forestry committee, had urged
that the Federation adopt as one of its projects the acquisition of the Ka-

48

tahdin area as a state park and forest preserve.[11] The petition of 1905 was undoubtedly an early result of her campaign. In 1908 the group drew up a bill to create a commission to ascertain the costs of purchasing Katahdin as a state park. Perhaps the State Water Storage Commission, created by the legislature in 1909, was the product of this effort, since it was directed to ascertain which lands could be purchased and their cost. Such lands were to be of value as forest reserves for conserving waterpowers of the state and burnt-over lands capable of being reforested. The Commission contacted the owners of the Katahdin area and though some were willing to sell, no agreement on price was reached. The Commission lacked purchase funds and also funds needed to determine the cost of denuded and burned lands.[12]

At a meeting of the Maine State Board of Trade in 1908, its president, Charles E. Hichborn, told the assembly that he knew of no question that could better be brought before the people of Maine than that of conservation of its natural resources. "We believe it is possible to have not only a White Mountain forest preserve but a Katahdin preserve as well."[13] Another delegate, George Otis Smith, writing to Baxter three decades later in support of Baxter's stand against a national park status for Katahdin, said that when asked about the advantages of making Katahdin a national park at the 1908 Board of Trade meeting, his answer had been prompt and unequivocal: that he would be ashamed of his native state if it "conceded that a forested peak up here in northern Maine could be better administered as a public reservation from Washington than from Augusta."[14]

The discussion among Maine conservationists undoubtedly stimulated the thinking and ideas of Congressman Frank E. Guernsey from Dover-Foxcroft who, in 1910, introduced a resolution in the national House of Representatives calling for federal purchase of forest reserves in the Appalachian and White mountains, the Katahdin area, and the headwaters of Maine rivers. The Mt. Katahdin Forest Reserve would serve the same purposes as those envisioned in the White Mountains—conservation of forests and water supply and control of waterpower.[15]

The Weeks Act of March 1, 1911, which authorized the creation of the National Forest Reservation Commission to accept or purchase lands in various parts of the eastern states for forest purposes, and provided for aid to states with private and state fire-protection plans, did not make any specific mention of locations of possible forests.[16] Representative Guernsey soon introduced a bill in Congress providing for the creation of a national park and a national forest reserve around Katahdin. The Maine State Federation of Women's Clubs, the powerful Maine Sportsmen's Fish and Game Association,[17] the Commissioners of Inland Fisheries and Game,[18] and many state newspapers supported the bill. The Maine Legislature in 1913 also passed a resolution asking the federal Congress to pass the measure.[19] Despite the widespread backing the bill did not advance in Congress.

Undaunted, in 1916 Congressman Guernsey again introduced a bill authorizing the Secretary of Agriculture to examine, locate, and report to the National Forest Reservation Commission on such lands in the Katahdin area as he thought might be suitable for a national park and national forests. Though he was supported by the same conservation groups as before, nothing came of it.[20] Continued proposals of a similar nature made during the three years following were equally fruitless.

After 1916 most of the efforts on behalf of the Katahdin area and the creation of some sort of preserve were engineered by Percival P. Baxter. However, he was generally opposed to increasing the powers of the federal government and was not a particularly strong supporter of federal acquisition, preferring state control instead. He was the leading member of a constantly enlarging group that wanted to establish some special status for the mountain. Along the way, that issue became embroiled with the waterpower controversy and with the public lands conflict. Certainly opposition to Baxter's position on waterpower and public lands led to more opposition to his park schemes.

In 1917 he introduced a bill into the legislature to create a Maine Water Power Commission. The bill, which passed in the House but failed in the Senate, authorized the proposed commission to determine what townships or parts of townships could be purchased by the state, their cost, and their value as forest reserves or for conserving waterpower and reforestation. The proposed commission would also be empowered to investigate the extent and value of burned-over or barren lands with a view to possible purchase by the state.[21] Baxter, in discussing the bill, noted that the Water Storage Commission in 1909 and the Public Utilities Commission after 1913 had been empowered to do the same things, but the pressure of other duties had made this impossible. The increasingly powerful representative from Portland was interested in having the state recover land that it once owned, land that could be purchased "for a very small sum per acre" and was taxed for almost nothing. He stressed the value of the forests of Maine, second in importance only to its waterpower and argued that state holdings could be developed by the Water Power Commission or by Land Agent and Forest Commissioner Forrest W. Colby. Finally, he noted the increasing concentration of timberland holdings, especially by such groups as the Coe Estate of Bangor and the Great Northern Paper Company, which together held 1,800,000 acres of the 15,000,000 acres of timberland in the state at the time. He asked whether it was not time "for the State itself to step in and buy back some of our squandered inheritance in order that the foundation of a policy may be laid which will tend to prevent the timberlands of Maine from getting into the hands of a few large owners?"[22]

Some people believed that Baxter was using these various issues as a means of catapulting himself into a strong political position. Garret Schenck of Great Northern was one of these. Early in 1918 in a letter to an associate, he said of Baxter: "If you are acquainted with his record, you will see what

kind of philanthropist he is, and that it is generally believed he is trying to
boost himself into prominence by making an attack on the water power
owners of our State."[23] Whether Schenck was correct or not regarding Baxter's ambitions and motivations cannot be determined. Until his death a
decade later, Schenck remained an implacable foe of Baxter and his natural
resource projects. The fact that Baxter clung to his position for a decade
despite continued defeats indicates his sincerity.

After his reelection to the legislature in 1918, Baxter became even
more deeply concerned with conservation and preservation issues. A survey of 154,000 acres in the Katahdin region made by the United States
Forest Service in the summer of 1918 showed that 53 per cent was burned-
over land, 15 per cent was bare rock and stunted growth, 12 per cent,
virgin growth then being cut, and 5 per cent, timber under one hundred
years old. Half of the area consisted of very steep mountains, with the
grandest scenery in Maine.

Several months previously Baxter had obtained from the federal
government a list of landowners in the area. When the legislature met in
January he introduced a bill calling for the creation of state parks and
forest reserves in the Katahdin region and elsewhere. The bill provided for
an appropriation of $10,000 for each of the years 1919 and 1920 to buy
and obtain by condemnation such lands as were determined by the Governor and Council to meet the purposes of the bill. At a meeting of the
Committee on State Lands and Forest Preservation in late January, Baxter
argued that a small beginning should be made and he pointed to the
progress being made on Mount Desert Island and in the White Mountains.
He mentioned earlier efforts by Representative Guernsey and federal
officials with regard to establishment of a park. A counsel and lobbyist for
Great Northern objected strongly, at the late January hearing on the bill,
to the proposed use of eminent domain and said that the power should
be more specifically outlined. But Commissioner Forrest Colby and Dr.
John M. Briscoe, professor of forestry at the University in Orono, testified
in favor of the measure.[24]

The opposition by the powerful Great Northern Paper Company was
a formidable obstacle and Baxter well understood this. Shortly after the
hearing he wrote to Garret Schenck and asked him to reconsider his position. Garret's reply was icy; he referred Baxter to the company lawyer. In
further correspondence, Baxter reiterated his position, but his battle was
a futile one, despite the support of such outside assistance as Austin Cary,
formerly a forestry leader in Maine and currently an engineer for the United
States Forest Service, who came to Maine in mid-February to support the
bill. In late February and early March, an extended debate on the issue
was held in the House of Representatives. Soon after, although because of
Great Northern's opposition, the eminent domain features had been removed from the measure, the Committee on State Lands and Forest Preser-

vation submitted an ought-not-to-pass report that doomed the bill.[25] Another was introduced in its place, presumably with Baxter's support, that emerged from the same committee under the title of "An Act to provide for the acceptance by the State of gifts of land and for the establishment of a State park and forest within the State of Maine." This bill eventually became law.[26]

Though Baxter had again lost the immediate battle, the law which did finally emerge was a crucial one for it was still in effect a dozen years years later when he made his first grants of land for Baxter State Park. Briefly, the law provided that the forest commissioner, with the advice and consent of the Governor and Council, could accept for the state gifts of land for forest and park purposes. The purpose of acquisition was to be "the preservation of scenic beauty, facility for recreation as nearly unrestricted and general as is practicable by the people of this state and those whom they admit to the privilege, and the production of timber for watershed protection and as a crop." There were additional details regarding control and operation of properties so acquired.

Advocates of public preservation of the Katahdin area had reacted to the defeat in the spring of 1919 by developing a wider basis of support for Baxter's proposals. To what extent Baxter, who decided to run for the State Senate from Cumberland County in 1920, coordinated or led the movement is difficult to determine precisely, but by mid-1920 he was clearly a leader. In his Report for 1919 Forest Commissioner Colby again advocated increased expenditures for the fiscal years 1921 and 1922 to allow him to buy cut-over lands. Though he did not mention the Katahdin area by name, a picture of the mountain was juxtaposed on the same page as his request for funds.[27] In January, William F. Dawson, a member of the AMC and a participant in its 1916 expedition to the mountain, spoke at a meeting of the Maine Sportsmen's Fish and Game Association and strongly urged that the area be made a national park or else set aside as a park by the state. He believed that facilities for travellers in the form of housing at Sandy Stream, a foot trail to Chimney Pond, and a lodge at that point were imperative.[28]

Two months later Baxter succeeded in getting a plank in the Republican state platform of 1920 advocating state purchase of waste, burned-over, denuded, and unproductive forest lands to be used for "reforestation, for the establishment of state parks or forest reserves, for the protection of water sheds, for refuges for wild game, for agricultural purposes, or for the establishment of national parks in connection with the United States."[29] During and after the Republican primary election in June, Baxter adopted a personal platform to save and develop Maine's waterpower for Maine people and provide "State Forest Reserves and Re-forestation of Timberlands."[30]

Later that summer occurred an event of tremendous significance in
the history of the Katahdin area and in the drive to secure a park. In
August, a party of prominent politicians, newspapermen, and state officials
made an expedition to Katahdin. The trip resulted from a discussion among
members of the Maine delegation to the Republican National Convention
in June, 1920, as they were returning from Chicago by train. Burton W.
Howe, a Patten lumberman and one long familiar with the Katahdin area,
extolled its virtues to his friends and challenged them to allow him to
prove his claims by organizing a trip to the area in which he wanted to
develop a park. Many in the group agreed and during the following
months Howe, who Baxter later said "was the man who first brought my
attention to the beauties of Mount Katahdin," organized the expedition.

Described in newspaper releases as a surveying party, the group
gathered at Howe's Patten home on August 5. By this time the plans had
matured sufficiently for members of the group to state that it was designed
to secure firsthand information to be used in the next legislature for the
creation of a "Centennial State Park." The trip was designed to provide as
much publicity and political support as possible for the creation of a park.
In addition to Howe and Baxter, by now an avowed candidate for the
presidency of the State Senate, the party included Charles P. Barnes of
Houlton, candidate for speaker of the Maine House at the next legislative
session; Charles H. Fogg, editor of the *Houlton Times;* Arthur G. Staples,
editor of the influential *Lewiston Evening Journal;* Sam E. Connors, a reporter for the *Journal;* George M. Houghton, an official of the Bangor and
Aroostook Railroad who was in charge of publishing *In the Maine Woods;*
Willis E. Parsons, fish and game commissioner of Maine; Howard Wood,
chief game warden of Maine; John T. Mitchell, district chief fire warden;
Leroy Dudley, the famous Katahdin guide making his thirty-eighth ascent
of the mountain; Nat Howe of Ashland, cousin to Burton; Elroy J. Parker,
a prominent farmer of Patten who provided horses for the expedition; his
son-in-law, Oscar Smith, and other local citizens who served as drivers
and cooks.[31]

The group travelled by buckboard and foot to Lunksoos Camp, then
owned by E. B. Draper, on the East Branch, and followed Wassataquoik
Stream to the turn-off to Katahdin Lake. They followed the old AMC
route of 1916 to Sandy Stream and the Basin and Chimney ponds.

Once in camp at Chimney Pond, the group used different routes to
reach Monument Peak. Baxter, who agreed that "climbing Katahdin is a
rugged job," and "the hardest thing I ever undertook," in company with
Dudley, Houghton, Barnes, Fogg, Smith, and Parker, climbed Pamola by
the Dudley Trail and then crossed the Knife Edge to the summit. There
they met the other party, which used the fresh slide below the Saddle to
reach the tableland and then the summit. While resting and eating lunch, 53

the group animatedly discussed their plans for the creation of a park. With
the return trip to Chimney Pond and the long walk back to Patten they
covered seventy-two miles in five days.[32]

The expedition was of utmost significance in several ways. Most im-
portantly, Pervical Baxter became more committed than ever to the idea
of a park. "While I was there that day," he later wrote, "I said to myself,
'This shall belong to Maine if I live.' I have never lost sight of it."[33] Many
members of the party wrote accounts of the trip or were interviewed by
the press of Maine and New England so that Katahdin received more
publicity than ever before in a short time. All the articles emphasized the
area's value as a park and game preserve. Individuals such as Arthur G.
Staples continued to use their influence and that of their papers in publicizing the group's plans. Staples wrote that "Katahdin got me as noth[ing]
else ever did" and told Burton Howe that they "simply must all get together and do something practical to save this mountain and sufficient part
of its surrounding territory for our children and our children's children,
and save it in its primeval condition." He was sure that a good publicity
campaign to inform the people of Maine what they possessed would encourage them to spend the money to save the area.[34]

While still on the expedition, the members planned some of the details
of their publicity campaign. Shortly after his return from the trip Howe
saw Colonel Frederic H. Parkhurst of Bangor, destined to be the new
governor of Maine, and obtained Parkhurst's assurance that he would help
Baxter in every way possible. Howe advised Baxter to see officials of Great
Northern and others who might oppose the park idea. He also told Baxter
who the owners of land in the Katahdin area were and suggested areas to
purchase first. He thought landowners might oppose the park or "try to
make the State pay high and, while admitting that the State may acquire
the same by 'eminent domain,'" would put "all the 'trigs' possible in causing as much delay as possible." Howe suggested that while he and others
"holler Katahdin," Baxter and his friends see the Stetsons of Bangor and
obtain an option on land which included Katahdin Lake. This would provide a base of operations and might forestall purchase of the land by Great
Northern. Once this land was obtained additional areas could be added
readily.[35]

Baxter apparently followed Howe's advice and wrote to a Bangor lumberman for assistance in obtaining land. Though the lumberman was sympathetic and agreed to assist and suggested other desirable areas,[36] Baxter
did not follow up by obtaining options. Several months later, the park pro-
moters lost ground when Great Northern succeeded in buying a 3/8 undivided interest in T3R9, the township which included Katahdin. In one

ROY DUDLEY
*Opposite,* The famous guide and spinner of Pamola yarns geared for a mountain climb.     55

case a former owner may have been willing to sell land to the park pro-
moters.[37]

Those interested in promoting the park concept acquired the name
"Katahdin Club," though there was never a formal organization. Undoubtedly most members had been on the summer trip to the mountain.[38] Their
efforts were not well-coordinated. One of them, John Mitchell, was asked
to obtain as much information as possible about the operation of the federal
forests and game preserves. His plan was to visit such reserves in the Appalachian chain from New Hampshire southward. To finance this he unsuccessfully solicited funds from Forest Commissioner Colby and Governor
Milliken; then he looked to the National Forest Service, supervisors of
forests, and private individuals for assistance.[39] Though these efforts were
also unsuccessful, he continued to work for the park idea.

During his election campaign to the State Senate, Baxter continued to
hammer on his themes of public power and the creation of a Mount Katahdin park as a centennial memorial. After an easy victory in the September
election, he completed the task of rounding up the necessary votes for election as president of the new Senate and took the lead in preparing the
final version of the new park bill.[40] Though there is no proof available, he
was undoubtedly influential in obtaining passage by the legislature of an
order inviting William F. Dawson of Lynn, Massachusetts, to give an illustrated lecture on Katahdin before the members of the legislature and their
guests on February 2. Before Baxter's bill was actually introduced on
February 25, the legislature directed that Forest Commissioner Colby prepare 200 copies of a map of the proposed park.[41]

The bill to create Mount Katahdin State Park provided for the establishment of a board to take charge of the project. It would consist of the
commissioner of Inland Fisheries, the state land agent and forest commissioner, and three citizens appointed by the governor. The board was empowered to purchase, on behalf of the state, lands it thought suitable for
the creation of the park. It was also empowered to take by eminent domain land for roads, trails, rights of way, and campsites. An appropriation
of $50,000 for each of the two years in the biennium was provided.[42] The
bill was referred to the Committee on State Lands and Forest Preservation.

Proponents of the park were optimistic at the outset since it had a
long list of prominent endorsers. Both parties had supported the idea in
their platforms in 1920, and Governor Parkhurst had urged it in his inaugural address. Both Senate President Baxter and Speaker of the House
Barnes supported the bill. In addition, various groups around the state
urged its passage.[43] Baxter provided additional momentum in a much publicized and reprinted speech to the annual meeting of the Maine Sportsmen's Fish and Game Association in late January. By this time, he was in the
midst of his continued fight over the waterpower issue with the large private
56 landowners and power interests in the state. Much of his impassioned argu-

ment was a discussion of the history of land disposal in Maine, the previous history of the park drive, and a vivid description of the mountain and proposed park. He concluded his address on a note that may have made any compromise impossible when he argued: "This park will prove a blessing to those who follow us, and they will see that we built for them more wisely than our forefathers did for us. Shall any great timberland or paper-making corporation, or group of such corporations, themselves the owners of millions of acres of Maine forests, say to the People of this State, 'You shall not have Mount Katahdin, either as a memorial of your past or as a heritage for your future'?"[44]

The situation changed dramatically scarcely a week later, when Governor Parkhurst became ill and died on February 2. As president of the Senate, Percival P. Baxter automatically succeeded him. In some respects, his loss of leadership in the Senate may have been a costly blow to his dreams of development of waterpower by the state and the establishment of parks for, as governor, in many ways he had a weaker power base from which to operate. After the normal delay with tributes and services for the departed chief executive, Baxter asserted his position in an inaugural address to the legislature on February 10. In the course of the address, in which he generally favored reorganization and retrenchment and a reduction of expenditures, the new governor returned to his former stand on the Katahdin issue. Noting once again that millions of acres had passed into private hands, he pointed out that in the heart of these lands "stands Mt. Katahdin, the greatest monument of nature that exists east of the Mississippi River. This moutain raises its head aloft unafraid of the passing storm and is typical of the rugged character of the people of Maine." Its purchase would be "a fitting memorial to the past century and an inspiration to the new." The cost would be small given the nature of the asset. Finally, he invoked the opinion of the recently deceased Governor in support of his proposal.[45] Baxter's position had been supported in the House chamber several days earlier when William Dawson strongly urged that the Katahdin area be saved, either by state or national efforts. Dawson's speech was part of the larger campaign to establish the park.[46] Dawson's and Baxter's efforts were supported by Speaker of the House Charles P. Barnes, who described in graphic terms the glories of the Katahdin area and pressed his arguments for the park.[47]

The park bill generated so much interest that the Committee on State Lands and Forest Preservation obtained use of the hall of the House of Representatives for a hearing on February 17. Several nights earlier, representatives of lumber companies and landholding interests met with Burton W. Howe of Patten, Willis E. Parsons, commissioner of Inland Fisheries and Game, and other citizens to discuss the bill. The meeting adjourned without action being taken.[48]

Most of the arguments presented at the hearing had been heard many times before. Speaker Barnes led off for the proponents and was followed by Ora Gilpatrick of Houlton, who argued that seventy-five per cent of the people in the hall would favor the park idea if they were to visit Katahdin. They were followed by William Arnold, a timber cruiser and scaler from Houlton, who argued that there was no merchantable timber on the mountain; former Congressman Frank E. Guernsey, who said that while he could not be classed as a proponent of the bill, he had long favored the concept and felt that the bill could be amended and redrafted to remove objectionable provisions; and the president of the Cumberland Audubon Society and Mrs. J. A. Thompson of Bangor, representing the Maine Federation of Women's Clubs, who also argued for the bill.

Strong opposition came from representatives of the landowners. Taber D. Bailey of Bangor, a former president of the Senate, was most vociferous. Speaking as a regular taxpayer, he derided the expenditure of $100,000 as a luxury that Maine could ill afford and argued that the construction of a road to the mountain would be enormously expensive. He emphasized that Maine people currently could go to Katahdin and other wild areas of the state without interference. Louis C. Stearns of Bangor, representing the Lincoln Pulpwood Company, a subsidiary of the Eastern Manufacturing Company, also strongly opposed the measure, principally because of the eminent domain provision and the high costs involved. Charles B. Carter of Auburn, counsel and lobbyist for Great Northern, reiterated earlier arguments and added: "If the State of Maine can afford—if it has the money for this Katahdin park, and that is a question for the people of Maine to say, I will say that if the majority of the people want it, within certain limits and under certain conditions the Great Northern Paper Co. offers to make a free deed of gift to the State of Maine for park purposes of any interests it may have in such lands."[49] Though this latter item gained much publicity at the time, the paper company never followed up on the offer, presumably because no proof was offered that the people of Maine wanted a park. James Q. Gulnac, president of the Maine State Chamber of Commerce and Agricultural League, believed the money could be better spent for a much-needed health program and did not like the idea of laying so much stress upon the state's being a playground rather than a workshop. He considered questionable the effects of guides and tourists upon the people of Maine.[50] Colonel Harry F. Ross of Bangor, owner of much of the land around Katahdin Lake and the mountain itself, concluded the opposition arguments. In his closing remarks, Speaker Barnes criticized the activities of the lobbyists for the landowners.

The merits of the Katahdin proposal were debated in the newspapers of the state. At about the time of the hearing, the *Bangor Commercial* strongly opposed the measure and based most of its argument on the need for economy in government. The *Daily Kennebec Journal*, controlled by Guy P. Gannett, who was allied to land and water interests strongly op-

posed to Baxter, also editorially opposed the measure.[51] The staunchest
supporter among the major papers was A. G. Staples's *Lewiston Evening*
*Journal.* The Portland press was divided.

After the hearing it was obvious that the pressure exerted by landowners was having an impact on legislators, despite continued support by
the Maine Federation of Women's Clubs.[52] Baxter's continuing fight for
state development and control of its waterpowers more deeply divided him
from the managers of land and water concerns and undoubtedly increased
their opposition to the Katahdin bill. Baxter himself increased the likeli-
hood that the bill would get nowhere when in a major speech to the legislature on March 10 he urged the practice of strict economy in all aspects
of government and suggested severe cuts in many appropriations, including that for the University. In effect, he signed the death knell for his Katahdin bill when he recommended changes in it. He felt that since he had
asked others to sacrifice for the sake of economy he should be prepared to
do the same. Though the requested park appropriation would mean a very
small tax increase, and while he defended the concept and the right of the
state to take land by eminent domain, he abandoned his request for the
$100,000 appropriation. In its place he suggested that half of the increased
revenues coming to the state from an appropriation for cruising wild lands
and half of the funds appropriated for the use of the forest commissioner
for the "Purchase of Land and for General Forestry Purposes" be set aside
for the Mount Katahdin State Park. In this way no additional taxes would
have to be levied.

Finally, he attacked the Great Northern Paper Company. He referred
to the vague offer made at the hearing by the company, but again regretted
that a concern "which itself has been given rights of untold value in the
water resources of Maine should oppose this Park." He argued that Great
Northern opposed the park idea, not because it wanted to save the state
money, but to defeat the eminent domain provision. It dominated the legislature in such a way, he said, that the true interests of the people could
not be heard on the issues. It was also somewhat ironic, he noted, that
Great Northern should oppose the state's using its rights to eminent domain since that company, "to its own great profit, has been freely given
this right by the State."[53]

A week later the Committee on State Lands and Forest Preservation
issued its divided report. The majority report recommended ought not to
pass; the minority report, signed by three members, including the governor's brother, Rupert Baxter of Bath, recommended ought to pass in a new
draft. In the proposed draft the $100,000 appropriation was dropped and
the park board authorized to buy lands when it received appropriations or
gifts of money. No assessments for roads or trails could be made against
landowners, but the right of eminent domain could be exercised by the
board if landowners declined to sell. The Senate accepted the majority

committee report on March 23, and the House concurred the next day. With that action the Katahdin bill was lost for the 1921 legislative session. Evidently some legislators confused the park issue with Baxter's proposed waterpower constitutional amendment that he had introduced late in the session.[54]

Baxter's immediate reaction to the defeat of the park bill is not known. Undoubtedly he was disappointed and bitter, since he had also lost in his attempt to get the state into the waterpower business. He could take some solace in knowing that the issue had been more widely publicized than before, and he undoubtedly immediately began planning future moves. Whether he was connected at all with the bill to create a Mount Katahdin national park that was introduced into Congress by Representative Ira G. Hersey shortly after the defeat of the state park bill is impossible to determine, but given his growing opposition to an increase in the power of the federal government it is unlikely.[55]

More important was the creation by Willis E. Parsons, commissioner of Inland Fisheries and Game, of the Katahdin Park Game Preserve. Parsons and his counterpart in the Forest Service had advocated creation of the park, which also would have made the area a game preserve. When twenty-five citizens of Maine led by John Francis Sprague of Bangor and former Congressman Frank E. Guernsey petitioned him for the creation of a game reserve during the early summer of 1921, he used authority granted him under Chapter 219 of the Public Laws of 1917 to create one on August 1, 1921. For four years after that date it would be illegal to hunt, chase, catch, or destroy game or birds in an 85,000-acre tract that encompassed Townships 3 and 4 in the 9th Range, W.E.L.S. and parts of Townships 3 and 4 in the adjoining 10th Range, where the Millinocket-Sourdnahunk tote road marked the general western boundary of the reserve.[56] Within a year the legislature ratified Parsons' actions and slightly revised the boundaries on the west to follow the Sourdnahunk Stream and Lake, thereby increasing the acreage to about 90,000 acres. Great Northern Paper Company officials believed that this measure was a good one. At the same time, the life of the preserve was continued indefinitely; and changes in ensuing years increased its size.[57]

During the period between sessions of the legislature, Governor Baxter continued to promote the park concept. In a major address to the Maine Forestry Association in Augusta in January 1922, he dealt with most aspects of state government and defended his positions. He maintained that the Mount Katahdin Park would prove to be of benefit to the state as a suitable centennial memorial and an attraction to tourists. He referred to the battles of the previous legislative session, but felt that tempers were cooling and saner councils were likely to prevail in the future. The timberland owners had nothing to fear, he argued, since the amount of land concerned was small and they would be paid well for it. He felt that no burdens such as costs of roads and campsite construction should fall to the landowners.[58]

During the rest of the year, while he successfully ran for renomination and then easily defeated his Democratic opponent in September, the Governor continued to argue his case for his water proposals and the Katahdin park.

A bill that he probably drew up was introduced into the legislature by a Republican representative from Parsonsfield and was quite similar to the final version that had failed in 1921. In the new draft the governor, the commissioner of Inland Fisheries and Game, and the forest commissioner would constitute a Mt. Katahdin state park board authorized to purchase lands with appropriated funds or gifts. The right of eminent domain was once again specifically granted. The purposes of establishment of a state park were for "the promotion and preservation of the public health and welfare and for the preservation and propagation of wild game and fish of the state, . . ." The lands to be purchased eventually would total 90,000 acres, including all of T3R9 and T4R9 and parts of T3R10 and T4R11 W.E.L.S., Piscataquis County. These were the same bounds set for the Katahdin Park Game Preserve as redefined by Commissioner Parsons and the legislature in 1923.

As before, the document was referred to the Committee on State Lands and Forest Preservation where it was duly reported out in March with an ought-not-to-pass recommendation. The most significant debate on the bill came in the Senate where Senator Ralph Owen Brewster of Portland, destined to succeed Baxter as governor and to play a major role in the history of Baxter State Park, argued at length for passage of the measure. He stressed the fact that no costs would be incurred by the bill, that the mountain area was unfit for forestry (though the Great Northern Paper Company had been logging in the Basin Ponds area for several years). He compared Katahdin favorably with western mountains and argued that it was coming into its own as a resort and asked whether it should be with or without restrictions. Other members of the Senate opposed the creation of the park, because they felt it would open the door for later expenditures that would burden the state. Some felt the state should not again get into business enterprises, and others stressed the dangers of the eminent domain provision. When the vote was taken only three senators voted for passage.[59]

Baxter continued his interest in the Katahdin area. Very soon after the park proposal was defeated, he enthusiastically endorsed a plan for the introduction of reindeer into the new preserve. The chief proponent of the idea was Almon S. Bisbee of Portland, who interested the Cumberland County Fish and Game Association in the matter of bringing reindeer from Lapland for introduction into the Katahdin area where terrain and climate were similar. Members of that group made plans for a late spring tour of the area, obtained the agreement of Great Northern, and then visited Governor Baxter. He readily assented to the scheme and felt that the game preserve would be a good place to try it. He had become familiar with reindeer herding in earlier trips to Norway and Sweden. Since no state funds were available, he suggested that Fish and Game Associations in the state start a fund drive to which he would gladly contribute. But after the initial enthusiasm ebbed, no party seemed willing to try to raise the needed funds.[60]

Several months later when Senator Charles L. McNary of Oregon, chairman of the United States Senate Reforestation Committee, held a hearing in Bangor, Baxter extended his official welcome. He wrote of his efforts to establish a state forest preserve and argued that development of the Katahdin region would afford the people a playground and the state an opportunity to practice modern forestry and to carry on experiments in reforestation. If Maine continued to neglect the opportunity to acquire the Katahdin district, he wrote, "I hope the Federal Government will make this a National Forest Reserve."[61]

The Katahdin park idea remained an issue into 1924. Though Baxter decided not to seek reelection, he did attend the state Republican Convention and pushed for his favorite waterpower and park planks for the platform.[62] When the Cumberland County Fish and Game Association studied the Katahdin project early in 1924, it formed a Mt. Katahdin association to push the issue. After meeting with its representatives, the Governor turned most of his data over to the new group. However, after an initial burst of activity, the enthusiasm of the group ebbed. Ironically, the additional publicity generated by these proposals encouraged significantly larger numbers of tourists and hikers to visit the Katahdin area.[63]

Late in 1924, Governor Baxter had an extended controversy with the Great Northern Paper Company, which closed its lands during the fire season to hunting without a guide. Baxter was fearful that if other owners followed the lead of Great Northern, a large part of Maine would become a private preserve. He pointed out that the company's actions went counter to its arguments used against the Katahdin park idea: that its woods were open to all and there was no need for a park. If the practice were continued, he argued, the tax structure for the wild lands should be re-examined. He urged the people of the state to fight the Great Northern Paper Company's decision.[64] During the following winter, Great Northern and other landowners made preparations for defense of their right to control access to and use of their lands. Since the fire danger was lower the following season and since Baxter was then out of office, the issue faded.[65]

As Baxter neared the end of his administration, he made certain that a bill for creation of a park would be introduced into the legislature. As he entered his last days in office, he decided to deliver a precedent-setting

62

farewell message to the people of the state. In this address he reiterated his stand on most important public issues and defended his administration. Once again he urged creation of a park at Katahdin and made an offer to the state: if the legislature would create a park and appropriate $10,000 annually for the two years following, he would contribute his salary as governor for the years 1923 and 1924.[66] Few came to his support.

In February a senator from Kennebec County introduced still another bill to create a Mount Katahdin state park. With Baxter out of office and despite the backing of Ralph Brewster, his successor, the measure had little legislative support. In late February it was reported out of comittee with an ought-not-to-pass recommendation, with which the Senate and House concurred on the same day.[67] This represented Baxter's last attempt to obtain passage of a Katahdin park bill through the legislature until he was in a position to provide the land himself. Later that year representative Ira G. Hersey introduced another Katahdin national park bill into Congress, where it met the same fate as previous bills on the subject.[68] Other than brief arguments in occasional speeches, Baxter himself had little more to say about Katahdin until 1930 and 1931.[69]

During his first year in office, Governor Brewster aggressively pushed creation of the park. He suggested at one point that private individuals furnish the money to buy the top of the mountain and that the National Forest Service obtain surrounding lands. He further supported the idea of the creation of a park when he became the first governor of the state to climb Katahdin while in office. The immediate occasion was to inspect the new state camp built in 1924 and 1925 by the Department of Inland Fisheries and Game for the use of the deputy game warden who would be in charge of the Katahdin Park Game Preserve. At that time the famous guide, Leroy Dudley, who had assisted in Baxter's trip in 1920, was the deputy game warden. For years he had had a cabin on Chimney Pond, and several lean-tos had been constructed for the use of campers. Dudley was charged with supervision of the preserve during the summer months. In addition to the Governor and his wife, others in the party were Commissioner Parsons of Inland Fisheries and Game; Dr. George W. Dorr, superintendent of Lafayette National Park; Phil Coolidge, a photographer for Pathe News, who took movies of the expedition; Philip R. Shorey, director of publicity for the State of Maine Associates; Leroy Dudley and several other guides and assistants. In early July the group travelled by auto from Millinocket to a point three miles beyond the new Togue Pond camps and then walked the rest of the way to Chimney Pond. After ascending the mountain by way of the Saddle Trail, the group had lunch at one of the springs on the plateau. Parsons immediately renamed it "Governor's Spring" in Brewster's honor. The party decided to spend the night on the tableland and were rained out early the following day. Though Katahdin thus received a great deal of publicity, the trip seem-

**SCRUB SPRUCE**
"Little ugly dwarf spruces, hostile . . . to human comfort," the prominent 19th-century explorer Winthrop called these trees, found on the Katahdin tableland and photographed by Jake Day for his Disney research project.

**LOG ROLLING**

Closeup of a tense moment in driving the big logs downstream.

65

ingly did little more to enhance the chances for the development of a park.[70]

Later in the year, Brewster talked with Great Northern officials about the possibilities of a park. He apparently misconstrued what he had been told and stated in a speech that the company would not let its lands go into other private hands pending public development. This led one newspaper editor to give fulsome, if misplaced praise, for the company's position.[71]

While the political battles over the future of the Katahdin area raged, it not only became much more widely known and publicized, but more and more accessible. In 1920, when Baxter and his party had made the trip, the approach was long and difficult from almost any direction. By 1927 a Maine newspaper could feature a headline: "Climbing Katahdin Without Hazard or Hardship."[72] A major factor in opening up the area was the lumbering activity of Great Northern. On the eastern side, the company had begun operations in 1921 to take the remaining spruce from the lower reaches of Katahdin and from Turner Mountain. The base camp was on Sandy Stream, with side camps distributed through the area. Most notable and important was No. 3 on the southeast corner of the Basin Ponds. Aside from the facilities for the firm's personnel, the company improved a structure originally erected by the builders of the dam at the outlet to the ponds. There Fred Gilbert, superintendent of the Spruce Wood Department, had established a residence and guesthouse. It served as a haven for many travellers to Katahdin, both summer and winter. Gilbert also had ordered that a 500-foot strip of spruce woods be kept around Chimney Pond during the course of lumbering operations on the east side of Katahdin.[73] In the course of its operations, Great Northern extended the tote roads from Millinocket so that by 1923 it was possible, when conditions were right, for some cars to go to the depot on Sandy Stream, beyond the famous Windey Pitch.[74] Unfortunately, a fire in that year destroyed most of the camp at Basin Ponds, including Gilbert's house, and it was not rebuilt.[75]

To the south and west, the mountain could be approached by Great Northern's road system from Greenville to Sourdnahunk Field. The distance to Kidney Pond camps and to what later became Katahdin Stream campground was only about eight miles.[76] While the older canoe routes were still used at times during the decade, some steamers operated until the late '30s, and the new approaches allowed a much larger number of people to visit the mountain and the new game preserve.

The AMC continued to be an important factor in the opening of the area. Periodically since the formation of the Club in 1876, members such as C. E. Hamlin and George Witherle had explored and written classic accounts of the Katahdin region. In the 20th century the Club spearheaded a major expedition to the mountain in 1916, and in the process opened a variant of the route from Stacyville on the east that was used for several years. In 1923, 1925, 1926, and again in 1927 the Club sponsored other expeditions to the mountain.[77] Club officials also talked with officials of Great Northern and other landowners, seeking permission to cut trails and erect signs on and about Katahdin.[78] The Club published as part of its *White Mountain Guide* its first trail guide to the area around Katahdin in 1917. Improved and expanded in subsequent editions, it was published separately in 1928 as the *AMC Katahdin Guide.* In 1925 the Club published the first contour map of the area.[79] Through these guides and through articles that appeared in almost every issue of *Appalachia,* Katahdin became more widely known. The Club was publishing, beginning in 1922, the series of bibliographies of the area compiled by Edward Smith and Myron Avery.[80] The Club's expeditions and individual members provided a great deal of trail construction and maintenance in the Katahdin region and were instrumental in some of the early planning and tracing of what became the Appalachian Trail.

The United States Geological Survey, using federal appropriations and matching state funds, surveyed the Katahdin region in detail during the summer of 1927 in the course of preparing a topographic map. Survey crews carefully measured the height of Katahdin and arrived at an elevation of 5,268 feet, a figure that still stands.[81]

Probably of greater importance in publicizing the area was the promotional publication of the Bangor and Aroostook Railroad, *In the Maine Woods.* Each of the yearly volumes during the '20s and '30s had at least one article on Katahdin. These articles were written by officials of the railroad, members of the Appalachian Mountain Club and similar groups; faculty members of Maine's colleges; sportsmen, and many others. Though concentrating on the mountain itself, they did not omit discussion of the surrounding area. *The Northern,* published by the Great Northern Paper Company until 1928 as a source of information primarily for its employees, also contained a great many articles. Of Maine's newspapers, many of which began to carry more news of the mountain once the political squabbling began, the best reporting came in the *Lewiston Evening Journal,* and particularly in its celebrated *Magazine Section.* Finally, professional and scientific publications such as the *Maine Naturalist* carried articles that had a wider appeal than merely the scientific. While these made Katahdin much better known, they were not sufficient in the decade of the 1920s to convince the legislature of Maine to provide the funds for a park.

Little is known of Baxter's thinking regarding the establishment of the park between 1925 and 1930. When Arthur Staples again advocated creation of a state park at Katahdin in 1927, he undoubtedly did so after conferring with Baxter on the issue.[82] Baxter had been preoccupied with politics for much of 1926, when he was unsuccessful in his bid for the Republican nomination to fill a vacancy in the United States Senate. Opposition of landowners, waterpower interests and much of the press to his nomination was strong and bitter.[83] That Baxter intended to provide for the creation of a park after his death if he did not do so during his lifetime is indicated by his establishment of a trust for this purpose in July 1927.[84]

When Herbert Hoover became President in 1929, Baxter was mentioned prominently as a possible ambassador to Japan or some other major nation. When this did not materialize, Baxter seemingly made up his mind to turn his attention to the creation of the park.

He obviously had planned, at some point in the late '20s, to attempt to purchase the land himself. Whether he had had any previous discussions with Harry Ross or the leaders of Great Northern is uncertain. Perhaps he sensed that the situation at the latter company had changed sufficiently to allow him to be hopeful. President Schenck had died in January 1928 and within a year Fred Gilbert had been forced to resign. Both had been bitter opponents of Baxter's proposals and had fought them for a decade. The new management, headed by William A. Whitcomb, had not been as deeply immersed in the political battles as had Schenck. Whitcomb, indeed, respected Baxter "for having the courage of his convictions, and for the battle he had put up for what he believed in." General Manager William O. McKay also thought highly of him, for the reasons stated above and also because, as he put it, "He is a gentleman. He treats everyone as an equal, . . ." Thus the atmosphere at Great Northern headquarters "was favorable to his plans."[85]

John McLeod, an official in the Boston office of Great Northern from the 1920s until the office was moved to Bangor three decades later, has written a monumental multi-volume history of the paper company. He was present and played a role until the 1950s in all of Baxter's acquisitions from that company. He too admired Baxter, who called McLeod his "helper" in the Boston office. McLeod states that Baxter came into the office in September or October, 1930, carrying "a well-worn map, on which he had marked in red pencil," a block of land four miles square containing over 10,000 acres. With this, Baxter told President Whitcomb, his dream of establishing a park at Katahdin would become a reality, and "he wanted nothing more." McLeod was sure that Baxter was sincere when he told President Whitcomb that all he wanted was the top of the mountain.[86]

At a meeting on November 12, the company's directors authorized the president to sell Baxter the company's 3/8 undivided interest in the northern 2/3 of T3R9, an area comprising about 5,760 acres and embracing the major part of Katahdin. The legal documents were signed on November 18, 1930 and Baxter paid the agreed-upon price of $25,000. At the same time he agreed to attempt to buy the other 5/8 interest owned by Colonel Harry Ross, a strong critic of Baxter's earlier park schemes. Baxter felt that now he would have more leverage with Ross to obtain the balance of the 10,000 acres he wanted. A condition of the original purchase from the paper company was that if he obtained all of the northern 2/3 of the

68

township, Baxter would turn it over to the state, with the various restrictions noted below; also that he could sell the land back to the company within five years for the price he had paid, and that in the event he
died and his heirs did not grant the land to the state, the company had the
right to buy it back at the same price. Soon after the agreement was made,
lawyers realized that "the company had no right to impose restrictions
unilaterally on undivided property.[87] Two months later, this agreement
was cancelled and a new one was signed, involving only the westerly 2/3
of the northern 2/3 of T3R9: Baxter, in his conveyance to the state, would
impose the following conditions:

> (a) that the land so conveyed shall be forever used for public park
> and recreational purposes, (b) shall be forever left in its natural wild
> state, (c) shall be forever kept as a sanctuary for wild beasts and
> birds, (d) and that no roads or ways for motor vehicles shall hereafter
> ever be constructed therein or thereon.

Baxter also agreed that if he could not get the remainder of the northern
2/3 but conveyed what he had to the state, he would ask that the above
conditions somehow also be effected by the state for the westerly 2/3 of
the northern 2/3 of T3R9.[88]

Baxter was unable to induce Colonel Ross to part with his 5/8 interest
in the area of the original purchase. He had to decide, therefore, whether
or not to deed that which he had purchased to the state. He made drafts of
necessary legal documents and soon contacted Governor Gardiner, Attorney General Robinson, and probably Forest Commissioner Violette to
discuss his intentions. The Attorney General began assisting Baxter in the
technical legal aspects of the deeds, even while he was urging him to delay
making the grant to the state.[89] Robinson warned of the dangers inherent
in a situation in which the state would be receiving a 3/8 interest in a large
area of land where the other portion was held privately. No definite bounds
could be given for the state's holdings until the property was properly
divided. He also feared adverse publicity and embarrassment to all concerned. Baxter replied in a handwritten note, saying: "I know that this is a
generous act, prompted by genuine public spirit. If there be those who
criticize it, I shall not be broken hearted. Let us go through with it and
take the consequences."[90] Baxter and Robinson held another conference
to work out the many details. In memorandums to the Governor, Robinson
noted that Baxter was determined to go ahead despite possible criticism
and despite the fact that he might have to pay much more for the additional land later on. "Criticism of his motives he has experienced before
and survived," Robinson wrote. "The eventual price of the five-eighths
which particularly impressed Mr. Nichols [Baxter's attorney] does not
bother P.P.B. at all."[91] Robinson then completed the necessary arrangements with Baxter.

69

In making his first grant to the state, Baxter developed a procedure which became his standard mode of operation. To impress upon all concerned the depths of his feelings and to protect his grants from encroachment, he made a formal offer to the governor and the Senate and the House of Representatives. He drew up a deed that formally transferred the property to the state and then asked that the rules of the legislature be waived so that the necessary legislation accepting the grant could be speedily enacted. In his first as well as later offers, he moved ahead rapidly before all legal niceties were arranged, because "owing to the uncertainty of life, and being apprehensive lest something might happen to thwart my plans, . . ." he wanted them legalized. In this grant, and particularly in later ones, he and his lawyers drew up the legal documents with minimal advisory assistance from state officials.

On March 3, 1931, Baxter, in order to "show to the people of my native State my appreciation of the honors they conferred upon me in the years gone by," officially offered to donate his undivided 3/8 interest in the western 2/3 of the northern 2/3 of T3R9 W.E.L.S. in Piscataquis County.[92] Baxter also held a 3/8 interest in the eastern 1/3 of the northern 2/3 of the town, but withheld it pending his attempt to buy the remainder. The terms of the gift were as Baxter had provided in his January agreement with Great Northern. On the following day, the legislature speedily accepted Baxter's offer.[93] No name was given to the park at the time, but in the following month the legislature officially changed the name of Monument Peak to Baxter Peak.*

While the citizens and the newspapers of the state were praising the former governor for his generosity,[94] Baxter and state officials set about the unenviable task of acquiring complete ownership of the land in which the state now held a part interest. In mid-March Baxter again talked with Harry F. Ross, who indicated he might ask the courts for a partition of the property. Baxter asked Attorney General Robinson to watch the matter closely; if Ross attempted to obtain a partition, the Attorney General was to see the Governor and begin condemnation proceedings to obtain the property by eminent domain. Baxter was willing to stand behind the state to the extent of $6.00 per acre, the assessed valuation and more than it was worth, he felt. He was thus willing to pay up to $38,400 for the property in question.[95]

Baxter indeed took a chance when he decided to give the state his 3/8

---

* *Laws of Maine, Private and Special, 1931: Chapter 94 (p. 578): Resolved:* That as a token of the appreciation of the People and Legislature of the State of Maine, for the gift by former Governor Percival P. Baxter to his native State, of a tract of land including Mt. Katahdin; and in recognition of the generous and public-spirited desire evinced by said gift that the natural scenic beauties of this noble mountain may forever be preserved for the enjoyment and pleasure of our people; Monument Peak, so-called, on said Mt. Katahdin, shall hereafter be designated and called Baxter Peak.

*Approved April 2, 1931*

undivided interest in the property on Katahdin. When he continued his negotiations with Harry Ross he found that his erstwhile foe in park proposals during the previous decade was as stubborn as ever in refusing to sell. "Baxter was almost sick over it, for days," wrote the Attorney General. Baxter and his attorney, Charles J. Nichols, held meetings in Boston with officials and attorneys for Great Northern, and it was, rather ironically, that company which eventually assisted him in resolving the situation. On June 23, 1931, the directors of Great Northern agreed to allow a court division of the township; to this Harry Ross assented. In September the state courts legally divided the town. The northwestern corner of the township—an area 2.25 miles by 4 miles—with 5,760 acres and a lot along the western edge of the town were given to Great Northern, which gave Ross $10,000 and the remainder of its 3/8 undivided interest in the rest of the town. The 5,760-acre tract containing the summit was immediately deeded to Baxter.[96]

By early October the necessary legal arrangements had been made and in a letter to Governor Gardiner, the Executive Council, and Forest Commissioner Violette, Baxter proudly stated that he was ready to transfer full title to nine square miles of land in the Katahdin area to the state. Neil Violette, under the provisions of Sections fifteen and sixteen of the Revised Statutes of 1930 (actually the law as passed in 1919) accepted the land for the state. The Council and Governor concurred.[97] The next legislature in early 1933 formally accepted Baxter's gift. Almost immediately the legislature approved an act setting aside the area of his grant—approximately 5,960 acres—as Baxter State Park.[98]

A myriad of problems regarding its operations had already arisen and would arise in the immediate future. But Baxter's dream, a firm one since at least 1917, was at last realized.

LOOKING WEST FROM KATAHDIN SUMMIT TO BASIN PONDS BELOW

The story of Baxter's long, tedious acquisition of the more than 200,000 acres that constitute the Baxter State Park cannot be told in complete detail, because many important documents are missing. It is also a difficult story to delineate clearly because of the complexities of the acquisition process itself. Baxter generally granted the land to the state soon after it was purchased, but in some cases, he held off for a number of years until his title was completely clear. Because the townships were often owned jointly by several different parties who had not actually divided the land, all owners had to be satisfied before complete title could be claimed to a section.[1] Fitting the pieces together perhaps most resembles the putting together of a jigsaw puzzle, or, as Baxter put it: "A map showing the different acquisitions both small and large over the years would remind you of your grandmother's patchwork quilt, which finally in some mysterious way came out of the confusion into one large piece."[2] At the end, several small pieces were still missing.

Baxter, in the process, showed amazing diligence and patience. In some cases, he pursued pieces of property for over two decades before reluctant owners would sell to him. Fortunately, the tendency toward longevity in his family favored him and benefited the state, for the last land was acquired in 1962, when he was eighty-seven years old. After the attempt to create a national park in the 1930s, if not before, Baxter made the creation of a large state park in his memory his life's work. He was willing to be patient in acquiring land, willing to pay higher prices than the land would normally have brought in order to obtain it; and sometimes he purchased lands in outlying areas—often considerably better in quality than those he sought—in order to exchange them with owners who were fearful of losing production potential for wood needed in the papermaking process and persuade them to part with their land. He was not above using moderate pressures to coerce reluctant owners to sell, pressures such as the national park threat, with reminders that he had been primarily responsible for stopping its creation; finding common ties in family backgrounds, and similar stratagems. Though he did not like the idea, at times he was willing to make some rather important concessions in his ideals for the Park to obtain property.

TABLE III–1

Parcels of land acquired for the state by Percival Baxter

| Gift # & Township | When Acquired by Baxter | From Whom | Dates Accepted by State |
|---|---|---|---|
| 1. T3R9 | 11/18/30 | Great Northern Paper Company (GNP) | P&S, 1931, ch. 23 3/3/31 10/7/31 & P&S, 1933 ch. 3 2/2/33 |
| 2. T5R9 | 6/15/38 12/1/37 | Piscataquis Land Co. St. John Smith | 11/9/38 Gov. & Exec. Coun. 1/17/39 P&S, 1939, ch. 1 |
| 3. T5R9 | 6/15/38 12/1/37 | Piscataquis Land Co. St. John Smith | 11/9/38 Gov. & Exec. Coun. 1/17/39 P&S, 1939, ch. 1 |
| 4. T3R10 | 1938 & 1939 | GNP | 7/22/40 Baxter's deed P&S, (Spec. Sess.) 1939-40, ch. 122 |
| 5. T4R9 | July-Aug., 1939 | Eastern Mfgr. Co. | P&S, 1941, ch. 1 |
| 6. T4R9 | July-Aug., 1939 | Eastern Mfgr. Co. | P&S, 1942, ch. 95 |
| 7. T5R9 | 6/15/38 12/1/37 | Piscataquis Land Co. St. John Smith | P&S, 1943, ch. 1 |
| 8. T5R9 | 6/15/38 12/1/37 | Piscataquis Land Co. St. John Smith | P&S, 1943, ch. 1 |
| 9. T5R10 | Aug., 1940 | Eastern Corporation | P&S, 1943-44 (Spec. Sess.) ch. 91 |
| 10. T3R9 | 2/15/39 | GNP | P&S, 1945, ch. 1 |
| 11. T3R9 | Jan., 1941 | Harry F. Ross | P&S, 1945, ch. 1 Deed dated 1/2/45 |
| 12. T3R9 | Jan., 1941 | Harry F. Ross | P&S, 1945, ch. 1 Deed dated 1/2/45 |
| 13. T3R10 | 1939-1940 | GNP | P&S, 1945, ch. 1 Deed dated 1/2/45 |
| 14. T3R10 | 1/29/39 8/11/48 | Piscataquis Land Co. Cassidy Estate | P&S, 1945, ch. 1 Deed dated 1/2/45 P&S, 1949, ch. 1 |
| 15. T3R10 | 1/29/39 8/11/48 | Piscataquis Land Co. Cassidy Estate | P&S, 1945, ch. 1 Deed dated 1/2/45 P&S, 1949, ch. 1 |
| 16. T3R10 | 1/29/39 8/11/48 | Piscataquis Land Co. Cassidy Estate | P&S, 1945, ch. 1 Deed dated 1/2/45 P&S, 1949, ch. 1 |
| 17. T4R10 | 2/15/39 | GNP (exchange for land in T2R9) | P&S, 1945, ch. 1 Deed dated 1/2/45 |
| 18. T4R10 | 1944 | GNP | P&S, 1945, ch. 1 Deed dated 1/2/45 |
| 19. T4R10 | Oct., 1946 | GNP (land Exchange) | P&S, 1947, ch. 1 Deed dated 1/8/47 |
| 20. T6R9 | Aug. 20, 1947 | Eastern Corporation | P&S, 1949, ch. 1 Deed dated 1/3/49 |
| 21. T6R9 | Aug. 1947 | Eastern Corporation | P&S, 1949, ch. 1 Deed dated 1/3/49 |
| 22. T6R8 | Dec. 12, 1947 | Garfield Land Co. Pingree Heirs | P&S, 1949, ch. 1 Deed dated 1/3/49 |
| 23. T6R8 | June 14, 1951 June 27, 1951 | Sada Coe Robinson Irving Pulp & Paper, Ltd. | Exec. Council 7/16/53 P&S, 1955, ch. 3 |
| 24. T6R9 | 1/4/54 | Eastern Corporation | Deed dated 1/12/54 Exec. Council 1/20/54 P&S, 1955, ch. 3 |
| 24-1 T6R9 | 9/1/54 | East Branch Improvement Co. | Baxter deed 12/1/54 P&S, 1955, ch. 1 |
| 25. T3R9 | 12/1/53 | GNP | Exec. Council 1/20/54 P&S, 1955, ch. 3 Deed dated 1/12/54 |
| 26. T6R9 | 3/10/55 | Eastern Corp. & GNP. Eastern traded with GNP & sold to Baxter | P&S, 1955, ch. 61 Deed dated 3/17/55 |
| 27. T6R10 | 4/20–21/55 | Eastern Corporation | P&S, 1955, ch. 171 Deed dated 5/2/55 |
| 28. T2R9 | Nov. 18, 1962 | GNP | Baxter Deed 8/6/62 Gov. & Council 9/5/62 P&S, 1963, ch. 1 |

# MAP III-2

## LOCATION OF LAND ACQUISITIONS WITH DATE GRANTED TO STATE

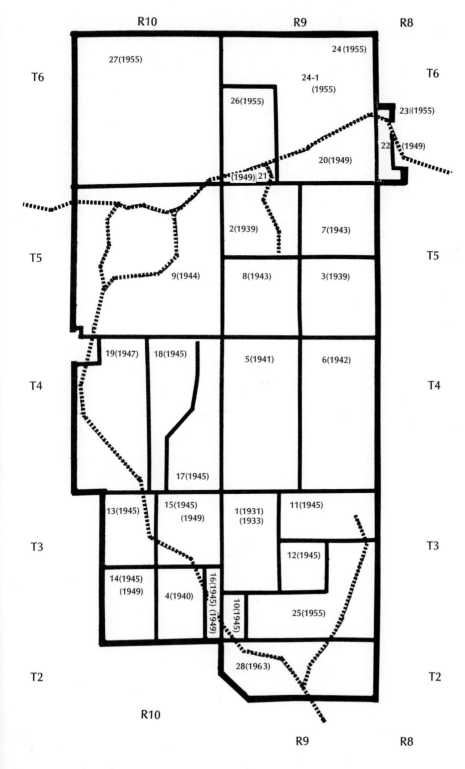

His approach in purchasing property also reflected his personal life-style and his political and economic philosophy. In several instances, completion of sales agreements was delayed or deferred indefinitely while he made his annual cruises. At other times, when Franklin D. Roosevelt or some other political leader with whom he did not agree did something that particularly bothered him, he would withdraw offers to buy land. He had a nagging fear that Roosevelt's policies would drag the United States down economically. From the late thirties on, he was particularly concerned that he might die before lands he purchased could formally be accepted by the legislature, so he generally followed the procedure used in his first bequest, when he and his lawyers drew up the language that became the basis for subsequent formal legislation. The variant wordings of these deeds later caused some difficulty in interpreting Baxter's intentions for the Park.

No attempt will be made here to provide all details involved in the acquisition of lands that eventually went into the Park. Table III-1 and Map III-1 list the gifts to the state in the order in which they were granted. An attempt has been made to determine the date of purchase, the date of cession to the state, the acreage, and the party or parties from whom the land was purchased. (It has been impossible to determine all acreages precisely, since those listed by Baxter at the time and other estimates given then, or made later, vary to some degree.)

During the year after Baxter made his first grant to the state, he started negotiating to purchase part of T4R9, the township immediately to the north. The Eastern Manufacturing Company, after taking care of some legal problems regarding its mortgage, agreed to sell a portion that Baxter wanted. At the last minute he backed out because of financial uncertainties created by difficulties he was having with tenants in his buildings in Portland.[3] By the time the problems were corrected, no further progress could be made. The deepening depression undoubtedly made Baxter's financial situation worse for some time, for there is no evidence that he sought to buy property until later in the decade. Then the threat posed by the possible creation of a national park spurred him into action. Whether he started negotiations before or after Congressman Brewster's bill was introduced is not known, but it is certain that very shortly afterward he obtained an option on a piece of property adjoining T4R9.[4]

Most of Baxter's early efforts were directed toward the two townships immediately north of the original park area. Township T5R9, 23,000 acres embracing The Traveler area, had been sold by Massachusetts and Maine soon after it was surveyed in 1832. David Pingree of Salem, Massachusetts and his heirs obtained a portion of it that by 1934 had been vested in the Piscataquis Land Company, a creation of the Pingree Heirs. The remainder was owned by St. John Smith of Portland.[5] Those in charge of the Pingree Estate were willing to sell their portion at a price lower than they might otherwise have obtained because, they wrote Baxter, they felt a great

**LESTER "SAWDUST" HALL**
Crossing a stream on North Traveler trip via Fowler Ponds and Barrel Ridge in the early 1930s.

sympathy with his "desire to create a state park and keep the land out of the hands of the Federal Government. . . ."[6] Legal complications in obtaining final title clearance to Smith's part of the township made it impossible for Baxter to turn it all over to the state immediately. In November 1938, he gave a deed to the northwest quarter.[7] During the next year he gave a deed for the southeast quarter and had both formally accepted by the legislature.[8] The remaining portions of the township were not formally transferred by Baxter until 1943.

While acquiring The Traveler area, he again began long negotiations to buy the intervening township, T4R9. According to John McLeod, Baxter's ideas about a larger state park "jelled at this time into a plan to create    77 one, of indeterminate size, but big enough to eliminate any excuse for a Federal project of the kind in Maine."[9] Unfortunately, the Eastern Manufacturing Company was in such poor financial condition in 1937 that it was placed under the control of federal Judge John A. Peters for reorganization under Section 77B of the federal bankruptcy statutes. Nothing much could be done until 1939 when Baxter again wrote to the company's president in an attempt to buy T4R9 and T5R10. He said his one object was to make "this park 100,000 acres and when that is accomplished I shall feel that my life's work is done." By then he had acquired 47,603 acres and the inclusion of the two towns would give him 96,241 acres. "I have set my heart on this Katahdin area," he said, "because I want to leave behind something worth while for the People of Maine from whom I ask nothing but their respect."[10] By this time the company was in a position to move since the Boston trust company that held a lien on the property was willing and able to release the land upon payment by Baxter. The deeds were ready by late July and Baxter paid for the property, though final transfer of ownership was delayed until the next year.[11] Baxter apparently visited the new property in September, 1939, when he travelled the sixteen miles in and out on horseback, following an old lumber road, probably the Wassataquoik tote road.[12] The western half of T4R9 was deeded to the state in 1941, the eastern section a year later. In his communication to the legislature in 1941 Baxter noted that in addition to the 35,000 acres already donated, he owned about 64,000 more that would eventually be turned over to the state. His sights on total acreage were already higher, for he said he intended to purchase even more land to straighten out the lines of the Park and fill in the gaps.[13]

Even before the purchase of T4R9 was consummated, Baxter pushed the Eastern Company to sell him T5R10, the township which includes Strickland, Lord, Howe, McCarty and Burnt mountains. So that the company would not lose valuable timber production, he first offered to trade that town for an equal amount of land elsewhere. When that was turned down and a hint made that the company might sell while retaining cutting rights for a period of time, Baxter jumped at the chance. Negotiations continued until the summer of 1940, when ownership was transferred.[14] To get the land Baxter had to grant cutting rights for a period of twenty-five years, until August 7, 1965, but he praised the actions of the Eastern Company and indicated that the land was sold to him "only because it was willing to help me carry out my Park project," and would have sold it to no one else. A 20-acre tract in the township, located on the shores of Nesowadnehunk Lake and owned by Charles A. Daisey, was not included in the transfer. As then, it has remained the site of Camp Phoenix, a private sporting camp opened early in the century. Baxter transferred his land to the state in 1944.[15] This was the first time he had provided for cutting rights in lands he ceded. During the ensuing period the operations of cutters was to cause Baxter and park authorities a good deal of difficulty.

The national park threat forced Baxter into land purchase operations in other areas surrounding Katahdin. To provide adequate access to the initial park area and obtain land for campgrounds and approach trails, additions east, south, and west of Katahdin were desirable. Baxter concentrated on T3R10 and T4R10.

He faced special problems in T3R10. The acquisition of this area was crucial to the creation of a workable park in the long run, since it was traversed by the Hunt and Abol trails and included Doubletop, Barren, O-J-I, and Coe mountains and Sourdnahunk and Katahdin streams. The campground at Katahdin Stream was then the major starting point for trips up the mountain. At the time Great Northern owned various amounts of land in each quarter of the township; the estates of John Cassidy, T. U. Coe, and David Pingree owned other portions of the northeast and southwest quarters and also a strip, the "Polish Corridor" (#16 on the map), 250 rods wide and three miles long along the east side of the southeast quarter. The affairs of these estates were handled by various legal and land management firms in Bangor. In the latter sections the holdings had not been divided but were held in common. Baxter faced a difficult job in acquiring the property, since the terms of the trust establishing the Cassidy Estate prohibited the sale of real estate.

Baxter first tackled Great Northern. He was fortunate in that President Whitcomb disliked the New Deal as much as he did and feared the potential impact of a national park. Thus, after Baxter excitedly told him of his purchase of T5R9 in late 1937, the company was willing to assist him by selling 4,442 acres in the northeast and southeast quarters of T3R10 in September of 1938.[16] He then convinced the company to sell him two more pieces of land totalling 6,400 acres in the north half of T3R10 so that the park would include O-J-I and Doubletop. The company retained a "corridor" of 3,000 acres along Sourdnahunk Stream. By now company officials knew what Baxter was up to in his park planning, "and everybody joked about it, wondering what he would turn up next." When the other landowners in the southern half of T3R10 sold a portion of their holdings to Baxter and cut off the new "corridor," he asked the company to sell it to him since, he said: "If I could just have that, I would have a solid block here"; and it was sold to him, after some good-natured banter.[17] Soon after, Great Northern sold him its share in the Polish Corridor as well; by late 1939 Great Northern had sold him a total of 15,073 acres in the town.[18] The company reserved the right in some portions to cut timber for five years and the right of way for its road in the Sourdnahunk Valley, and retained driving rights on Sourdnahunk Stream.

In January 1939 the Piscataquis Land Company, controlling the Pingree Heirs lands in the town, sold Baxter its interest in the northeast 79

CABLE BRIDGE ACROSS WEST BRANCH OF THE PENOBSCOT

Built by the Patten CCC crew in the 30s, this bridge was swept away in the 1963 hurricane that wrought so much damage in the Katahdin area. The photograph was taken in 1937 by Allan Rinehart.

KATAHDIN STREAM CAMPGROUND
Photo taken in 1937 by Allan Rinehart

81

quarter and in the Polish Corridor.[19] Baxter was able to trade some of the land acquired from the paper company to the Cassidy Estate to acquire complete ownership of some portions of the tract. He also began negotiating in December with George T. Carlisle of Prentiss and Carlisle in Bangor, which managed the lands of the Cassidy Estate. Carlisle tried unsuccessfully to convince the trustees of the Estate to trade their remaining lands in the township for lands in one adjoining to the south that Baxter had bought for trading purposes.[20] At that time, late in the decade, Baxter or the state held all but 6,017 acres in the township.

Once Baxter had obtained some of the lands discussed above he hastened to transfer them to the state. Though by now the chances of creation of a national park in the area were well-nigh nonexistent, the vague possibility of its happening spurred Baxter on and affected the method by which he deeded lands to the state. To insure the legality of his actions and to prevent raids on the trust arrangement in the future, he contacted several legal experts and jurists in Maine. A copy of a typical deed was sent to Judge John A. Peters of Ellsworth. Peters said, "I especially wanted to note any conditions in the deed in connection with the possibility that someone might want to change the title or the use of the property or convert it into a National Park." He added "I do not see how anything could be more clear or definite" than the terms in the trust deed, and he said that it could be enforced later, if necessary, by Baxter or his successors. "So, as I look at it," he concluded, "you have well taken care of the contingency which we both somewhat feared."[21] This type of advice supported and reinforced Baxter in his desire to spell out the conditions of acceptance of lands to a series of governors and legislatures in the expectation that his ideas would be more carefully followed.

With these ideas in mind, during the year 1940 he decided to cede certain portions of T3R10, the crucial area to the west of Katahdin, to the state. The area he donated (#4 on the map) included Katahdin Stream camp and the start of the Abol Trail and much of the western side of the mountain.[22] As Baxter aged and became more concerned about the uncertainties of his life and longevity, he finally decided to cede the remainder of his holdings in the town. In 1945 he deeded his portion of 8,299 acres in the remainder of T3R10 to the state; at the time, however, it was still undivided with the Cassidy Estate.[23]

Baxter waited until some time after the conclusion of World War II to continue his pursuit of the remaining lands in T3R10. Little is known of the origins of the lawsuit leading to a final settlement. By late 1947, he was working in conjunction with the State Attorney General's office, with Raymond Fellows, justice of the Supreme Judicial Court in Equity in Bangor, and with Justice Edward P. Murray, of Bangor, a trustee of the Cassidy Estate, in the planning and preparation of a friendly suit to provide a legal means for the Estate to dispose of the property in T3R10 that

82

it held in common with the state as successor to the Baxter interest. By the time the suit was commenced, Maine held ownership of 114/254 (8,299 acres) of the southwest and northeast quarters of the town, a similar holding in the Polish Corridor, and a fourth (250 acres) of the public lot in the town. Technically, the state, through the attorney general and the Baxter State Park Authority, brought suit against the beneficiaries and trustees of the Cassidy Estate and against Baxter, who personally held land in the town not yet granted to the state, asking for division and sale of the lands in T3R10 owned by the Estate. The state argued that since Baxter had given the land in trust to the state with certain conditions and limitations regarding its uses and improvements that could be made, and since the trustees could not sell their interest in the land, the wild lands could not be divided without depreciation in value and could not be occupied as tenants in common by the state and the trustees. To obtain relief, the state asked for a partition. Baxter, the bill in equity continued, stood ready as trustee for the state, to purchase the land described, for the purpose of making a gift to the state. He was willing to pay whatever price the court fixed.

Justice Fellows held initial hearings in early 1948. Consideration of technical details continued the case through the winter and spring, as time had to be allowed for defendants to file answers to requests made by the court for their thoughts and feelings with regard to division of the property. At the final hearing on July 16, Judge Fellows held that the town should be divided and that Baxter should be allowed to buy the Cassidy interest in trust for the state. George T. Carlisle was named to assess the value of the property.

Before Carlisle had a chance to set a figure, Baxter offered the Cassidy Estate eight dollars per acre for 5,767 acres and whatever price the judge might name for the 250 acres in the public lot. Baxter thought the price "excessive" and "liberal" but he was happy to pay it, "for this will complete my Park project on which I have labored for more than thirty years."[24] The offer was accepted. While acting as trustee for the Superior Court, Baxter granted the final share in the town to the state in 1949.[25]

Of equal long-range importance for the establishment of a workable park area was the acquisition by Baxter of additional lands in T3R9, the township in which the first portion of the Park was located. In one sense, his problem there was a bit simpler than in the township to the west, for in 1931, as a consequence of his first purchase, the courts had divided the remaining land. Harry Ross at that time became the owner of the remainder of the town except for a small lot of 1,920 acres in the southwest corner (#10 on the map), ownership of which was held by Great Northern after the division of the township.

Baxter began negotiating with them for the small segment in 1938. He "gently pointed out" that the land "was not much good" to the company, but it was important to him since the Abol Trail crossed a corner of the lot. But in order to obtain the piece at that time, Baxter would have had to grant Great Northern the right to remove merchantable timber for five years.[26] Undoubtedly this was a major reason why he held off transferring the property until 1945. No cutting rights were mentioned in his deed to the state in that year.[27]

Harry Ross was a different and more difficult person to deal with than the officials of Great Northern. The son of a famed Bangor and Penobscot lumberman and river driver, Ross was the pugnacious owner of the *Bangor Commercial*. A fiercely proud and independent individual, he did not like to be pushed around by anyone and reacted negatively when he felt this was being done to him. After he finished college, he and his father had purchased a half-interest in T3R9 in 1899 from Nathan C. Ayer, who in 1874 had joined Samuel H. Blake in purchasing the property from Francis Reed, the original owner, who had bought the township from the state in 1870. Blake's half of the property was sold by his heirs after his death, one quarter of it (one-eighth of the whole town) to Frank W. Goodwin in 1892. Goodwin subsequently sold it to Minnie Ross Holman, Ross's sister, who willed it to him on her death. The remaining portion of the Blake holdings (3/8 of the total) was sold to Great Northern in 1920; it was that holding that Baxter had originally purchased in 1930.[28]

From their correspondence, it is obvious that at first Ross did not particularly care for Percival Baxter. When Congressman Brewster's park bill was introduced, Baxter promptly contacted Ross as well as other owners of land surrounding the Park. Ownership of the Ross lands by Baxter and the state was crucial to the development of a coherent park since they contained the Roaring Brook Road, the proposed Roaring Brook camping area, Turner Mountain, the Basin Ponds area, and much of the slopes of Pamola. Baxter first tried for the lands immediately east of the original park area (numbers 11, 12, and the northern part of 25 on the map). The first extant correspondence shows that the two had been negotiating earlier, but that Ross was not interested in selling his lands. Baxter renewed his efforts late in 1939, this time limiting his request to a smaller northern portion of Ross's holdings rather than the entire tract. Baxter's initial offers apparently were too low for he then offered to buy land elsewhere that was more productive and not so liable to fire. Ross had often expressed concern that his lands might be destroyed by fires set by the large number of persons travelling through them to reach the east base of Katahdin. Baxter expressed his sentiments about the mountain and park issues and said he was leaving money for maintenance in his will. Ross turned down his latest offer and rather testily added: "If you will permit me to say so, my dear sir, you forget that other people as well as yourself indulge in sentiment." He said he had tried to be courteous to Baxter at all times and added that he knew the value of timberland better than Baxter and

84

that he would sell to Baxter to help him round out his park, but not at the price Baxter offered.[29]

The matter remained closed until late in 1940 when Baxter again reopened negotiations and even made a trip to Rockland to visit Ross. They apparently nearly agreed on the exchange of 7,360 acres (numbers 11 and 12) for $40,000, when Baxter suddenly withdrew his offer because of a misunderstanding regarding ownership of the public lot in the town. He said he did not know who owned the public lot, a strange statement coming from one who had been governor, had been in the midst of a controversy over public lands, and had also purchased other lands that contained rights to cut grass and timber on the public lots. He finally admitted, rather ruefully, that "you will see I know very little about the wild lands of Maine and about the customs that prevail in buying and selling these areas."[30] Thereafter the negotiations were somewhat more amicable, and Ross, after some urging by Great Northern finally parted with the land, though Baxter had to concede cutting rights to a portion of it (#12) until 1946.[31] Ross had already contracted with Abe Chase to cut the area which included the famous and lovely birch grove at the base of Avalanche Slide. It had been used as a camping ground since the 1840s when Marcus Keep first discovered the stand. By 1946 the entire grove was wiped out.[32] Baxter thus secured part of the eastern approaches to the mountain. He deeded the lands to the state in 1945.

Baxter immediately attempted to buy another portion of the township, an area about four and a half square miles to the south and east of his holdings (number 25). The land contained a portion of the Roaring Brook Road and much of the drainage of Rum, Spring and Beaver brooks on the southeastern slope of the mountain. Ross felt that it had "some of the best spruce growing on any land" and refused to sell except at a substantial price. When he set off on another extended trip in 1941, Baxter withdrew his offer.[33]

The matter remained dormant until 1950 when negotiations were reopened. It is not known whether Baxter initiated the attempts or whether Ross and his agent Ralph A. Dyer, Jr., of R. A. Dyer & Sons Real Estate Corporation in Bangor did so. The first evidence is a letter from the state tax assessor to Baxter in reply to an earlier letter of inquiry about who paid the taxes on the land.[34] Dyer apparently visited Baxter in Portland in April 1950 and urged him to make a substantial offer for the land. He noted that a New York buyer was interested in the property and might want to close the Roaring Brook Road. Later in the year, he intimated to Baxter that Ross was not feeling well and was making "very definite arrangements relative to some of his properties," and suggested that Baxter make a liberal offer for the remaining land in T3R9.[35]

Baxter at first increased his offer, but refused to pay more, and then, after receiving a suggestion that he pay an even higher price, bluntly asked

Dyer if he were representing Ross directly. After some hesitation and exchange of telephone calls, Dyer wrote that he was "acting solely on behalf of H. R. Ross" for the remaining lands, though several weeks earlier, in response to an inquiry from Baxter, Ross had stated: "I have never sent anybody to you at any time for anything." Dyer's aggressive behavior was apparently on his own initiative. Baxter again refused to pay Ross's asking price and wrote Dyer that he had dismissed the matter from his mind and "come to the conclusion that it will not be possible for me to make this purchase."[36] Ross thereafter sold the land to Great Northern, which in 1953 conveyed it to Baxter,[37] who deeded it to the state two years later. But to obtain the property Baxter had to grant cutting rights to Great Northern for a twenty-year period, to December 1, 1973. These rights created a major issue near the date of their expiration, but the acquisition rounded out Baxter's and the state's ownership of that key township.

Of as much immediate interest to Baxter was the land in T4R10 to the northwest of Katahdin. Aside from the Sourdnahunk (Nesowadnehunk) campground area, this township includes much of the route of Wassataquoik Stream and North Brother, Center, and Wassataquoik mountains, and the Cross Range. Baxter had acquired an irregular portion (number 17) of the eastern half of the township in 1939.[38] This section included the upper reaches of streams draining into Wassataquoik Stream and Lake and was cut by Great Northern in the late 1930s and early 1940s. When Baxter tried to buy the lands immediately to the west (number 18) to complete the holding in the eastern half of the township, he ran into more serious problems, since the company was still cutting in the area. Woodlands Manager William Hilton thought the company was selling more land than it should and apparently opposed a sale until Baxter agreed to exchange lands he had bought outside of the park limits in T2R9, immediately south of Katahdin in the Togue Ponds area and in T4R8.[39] He also had to concede cutting rights to Great Northern in the most recently acquired area until December 28, 1969.[40]

In his diligent attempts to obtain the sections of land discussed above and to obtain the western half of the town, Baxter evidently made rather frequent trips to Boston and corresponded regularly with officials of Great Northern and other concerned companies. In 1943 Edward Graham, president of the Bangor Hydro-Electric Company, while discussing mutual land dealings wrote Baxter that he had visited Great Northern offices in Boston and had talked with Vice President William O. McKay, since President Whitcomb was not there at the time. "I am sure that you have in Mr. McKay a friend who will be very helpful to you in persuading Whitcomb to recommend the sale of . . . land . . .," he wrote. "I told McKay about my pleasant relations with you and how you deserve every consideration in accomplishing your life's work. I left him with a definite feeling that you have made much progress there in the last two or three years."[41]

However, McKay's "persuasive powers" were not sufficient, and Baxter again argued his case before President Whitcomb. He said that he already had 1,250 acres of unproductive land in T2R9; and that a local broker was attempting to get him to buy shares in the St. Croix Paper Company, but he preferred to stay with Great Northern.[42] In a subsequent letter he again referred to his efforts in defeating the national park proposal and said he believed the company would eventually let him have the land he wanted, adding, "As the well-known advertisement reads, 'eventually, why not now?' "[43]

While company officials by now were more than sympathetic to his plans, such blandishments did not move them. To get the remainder of T4R10 Baxter had to purchase lands elsewhere. For this purpose he worked through George T. Carlisle again. In the late summer of 1945 Baxter closed negotiations to purchase over 11,000 acres from Prentiss & Carlisle, which he intended to trade with Great Northern for the lands he wanted.[44] The company was still reluctant to give up its productive land and particularly wanted to hold the dam lot at the foot of Sourdnahunk Lake. Baxter told one correspondent that it was "hard, very hard" to get the lands but he was proceeding with purchases from Carlisle, "hoping Mr. Whitcomb will soften & exchange with me." If Whitcomb did not, Baxter planned to give the exchange lands to the state even though they were not contiguous to the park area.[45]

Whitcomb softened and was ready to complete the exchange. Just fifteen minutes before Baxter's scheduled appointment with him, he was shot and killed for unknown reasons by a former employee, who later took his own life.[46] The tragedy delayed completion of negotiations until October, though the new president, William McKay, admired Baxter. Great Northern reserved the 880-acre dam lot at the outlet of Sourdnahunk Lake, cutting rights for five years, and a right of way for the road on the tract between Sourdnahunk Lake and Field.[47]

After the flurry of land purchasing during the war years, Baxter had slowed down for some time. The lands in various towns surrounding the Park that remained in private hands were evidently so valuable for timber or other purposes, such as water rights and storage, that he had made little headway in obtaining them. He made some futile attempts in 1946 to obtain land near Katahdin Lake in T3R8.[48] He also continued attempts to buy land in other areas near the Park, lands to be used as part of the Park or, more likely, for exchange purposes.[49] Very soon, however, he concentrated his efforts in T6R8 and T6R9, which included the major portion of Trout Brook and most of Grand Lake Matagamon (the Second Lake and the westerly portion of First Grand Lake). The crucial lands in

T6R8 were owned by the Pingree Heirs, while lands in T6R9 were divided between the Eastern Corporation* and Great Northern.

The situation was complicated by the intricate corporate interrelationships among the various owners of the land in the area. Unravelling these relationships and problems before looking at the actual process of land acquisition is made doubly necessary because of various agreements Baxter had to make before and after acquiring different parcels. Close study of the map and table at the beginning of this chapter is also necessary to understand these relationships.

The Eastern Corporation had sold Baxter T5R10 in 1940, but had retained cutting rights in the town until 1965. Portions of the perimeter road in the southwest corner of the town had not yet been constructed; the old tote road running west from Patten to Sourdnahunk Stream in the late 19th and early 20th centuries was now impassable. The only practical access to the land was by an extension or continuation of the Grand Lake (Shin Pond) road along Trout Brook that, after traversing the central and southern portions of T6R9, crossed a corner of T5R9 (deeded to the state by Baxter in 1939), and then entered T5R10. In 1945 Baxter prohibited further construction of roads in the Park except for maintenance of the Millinocket-Sourdnahunk (or Baxter State Park) road and the roads then being built by the Eastern Corporation in T5R10. These terms were accepted by the legislature in 1945 and reiterated with the state's acceptance of another gift two years later.

Baxter apparently had made these restrictions on the land before he became committed to further expansion of the Park. It should be remembered that his goal was 50,000 acres at first. After that, the objective was increased to 100,000, then 150,000, and finally, as long as he remained in good health, to 200,000 acres. Aside from lands in T2R9, at the southern border, the most obvious areas for expansion were in the towns to the north of the existing Park—T6R8, T6R9 and T6R10. The latter town was owned completely by the Eastern Corporation. It had independent access to the area, but one obvious route was through T6R9. The Corporation also owned the bulk of T6R9, though a portion (number 26) in the southwest was held by Great Northern. The sections of T6R8 west of First Grand Lake and the East Branch of the Penobscot River were held by the Pingree Heirs through the Garfield Land Company. The Eastern Corporation, in postwar years, was busily engaged in cutting in the area of T6R9, north of Trout Brook, with a base of operations at Trout Brook Farm. From that point a lumbering road ran northwestward, south of Second Grand Lake, to Webster Stream and beyond. The concern also maintained a base on First Grand Lake to supply its operations. The Corporation thus had a vital interest in maintaining and keeping open roads that would

* Late in the 1930s the Eastern Manufacturing Company had become a corporation.

give access to the lands it owned and to land on which it held cutting rights. The same applied to Great Northern holdings on T6R9.

To further complicate the situation, water rights on the East Branch of the Penobscot and on Grand Lake Matagamon were involved. The Bangor Hydro-Electric Company, through ownership of the East Branch Improvement Company (successor to the East Branch Dam Company in 1903), owned the water rights on the river and the lake, and owned the dam at the foot of Grand Lake Matagamon. Included in these rights was that of raising the level of the lake by 10 feet to 665 feet, which entailed flooding lands along the lake and streams flowing into it.[50] Since the lake system described bordered lands in T6R8 and comprised a good part of T6R9, in which Baxter was interested, all of the various interests had to be satisfied.

Finally, in their negotiations, Baxter and the various landowners had to consider the feelings of citizens in Patten and other areas of Maine. Some of them were increasingly concerned by the continued extension of the Park, the restrictive provisions demanded by Baxter, and the continued expansion of the Katahdin game refuge, which unduly restricted the areas in which they could hunt. In the process of acquiring additional lands, therefore, Baxter had to steer a course that would satisfy the various needs and demands, while at the same time preserving the essentials of his wilderness concept. He also was convinced that he could do something to educate the people of Maine in methods of scientific forestry. Along the way he had to make a good many compromises, some of which would return to haunt him and park administrators at a later date.

Baxter first tried to deal with the president of the Eastern Corporation, Clyde B. Morgan, on a one-to-one basis. He argued that he and Morgan did not need "all the whys and wherefores that lawyers often work into their documents." This is doubly interesting since Baxter, a lawyer, insisted on legal technicalities in his deeds to the state. Morgan argued for the legal language in the proposed deeds to the land his company was willing to sell, on the basis that there is "a reversion clause which covers the corporation in case some citizen of Maine for some silly reason tries to upset some of the plans you have laid." Baxter wanted the land so badly that he was willing to change the restrictions imposed on roads in the Park and said he would ask the next legislature to effect them. The Eastern Corporation wanted legal reassurance in its deeds. In a polite form of blackmail both sides argued their points. Baxter was willing to make whatever concessions were needed regarding roads; if Eastern did not sell him the land, it would have no access through T5R9 to T5R10. The Corporation was willing to sell the southern section of T6R9, but only with assurances that its larger interests would be protected. Baxter reassured the Corporation that if he was living in 1949 he would obtain from the legislature a change in the terms of his deeds to the state; if Eastern

89

**TROUT BROOK FARM**

An early photograph of the main house at the farm, taken "before the fire." Many early explorers of the Katahdin area stopped at this farm on their way up.

did not sell and the change were not made in the law, or if Baxter died BAXTER STATE PARK
before the legislature met, the company would be forever excluded from   ACQUISITION
access to the land through Baxter Park. Finally Baxter noted that he had
been examined recently by his cousin, Dr. Elliott P. Joslin of Boston,
"probably the best known Doctor in the East," who "pronounced me
sound in every respect both inside and out."[51] Indeed he was to live for
twenty-two more years.

After further discussions, Baxter sufficiently protected the interests of
the Eastern Corporation for it to agree to sell him the land (numbers 20
and 21). Just prior to the conclusion of the sale of number 20 on August
twentieth, Baxter sent his check for $15,000. He was following, he said,
the practice of his aged aunt "who always insisted on paying her bills in
advance and I may have inherited this trait." A recent visit he had made
to the Trout Brook area convinced him that it was in the "public interest
to make this road available for persons who visit the Park as well as for
your Company."[52] Eastern reserved the 136-acre area at Trout Brook
Farm from the sale, since it was an important headquarters for its operations on lands within and to the north of the Park.[53] A year later Baxter
bought the small 536-acre segment south of Trout and Wadleigh brooks
in T6R9 from Great Northern.[54]

At the same time he was negotiating with Eastern, Baxter was
trying to get as much as he could of the western portion of T6R8 (number
22) from the Pingree Heirs through the Garfield Land Company. Baxter's
negotiations for this land were also complicated by road-access problems
as well as the preexisting water rights of the Bangor Hydro-Electric Company and increasingly vociferous objections by sportsmen, and the Eastern
Corporation had to be granted landing rights and transit rights through
the Garfield Company territory as well as on the land it was selling.

Once the sale of Number 20 was completed, the sale of Number 22
followed, on December 12, 1947. In obtaining this land for $7,500
Baxter had to reserve passage rights to the Garfield Land Company as
well as to the Eastern Corporation and also had to continue the East
Branch Improvement Company's rights to flowage on First Grand Lake
and tributary streams.[55] At the time, he could not purchase a minor interest (Number 23) in the undivided property held by two other parties;
this was done in 1951.[56] Also in 1951, during the Korean War, the Pingree
Heirs offered to sell Baxter additional lands in T6R8. Baxter demurred,
"in view of the uncertainty that prevails in our domestic and foreign
affairs."[57] He did not get another chance after the "present confusion"
passed.

While all of the foregoing land deals were being completed, Baxter
busied himself with preparing legislation to uphold the promises he had
made to the various interests concerned. In early 1948 he began drafting
a bill to change the trust provisions regarding roads. By October the   91

wording apparently had been completed. When the Ninety-fourth Legislature met in early January, among its earliest official actions it passed
the various bills Baxter had prepared to convey the purchases in northern
regions as well as lands in T3R10 in the southwest. With regard to roads,
both the legislature and the Governor accepted Baxter's revision, which
changed the trust provisions of 1945 and 1947 by deleting former restrictions and adding the wording that in all areas of Baxter State Park the
state of Maine was empowered to construct and maintain "such roads and
ways as said State as such Trustee shall deem to be in the public interest
and for the proper use and enjoyment of those citizens of said State who
may visit the area known as BAXTER STATE PARK, subject however to
the conditions, limitations and restrictions that said roads and ways be
constructed and maintained in a manner not to interfere with the natural
wild state now existing in said areas."[58]

The act by which the state accepted the latest grants was passed
without difficulty, to take effect on August 6, 1949. Almost immediately
the first real opposition from within the state to further acceptance of
lands from Baxter arose. It originated among sportsmen's groups in Aroostook County, particularly fish and game clubs in Presque Isle and Houlton.
They asked Republican Senator George B. Barnes, whose father had been
an early advocate of the Park and who had climbed Katahdin with Baxter,
to table the act. Accepting the lands, the sporting groups felt, would
"mean taking some of the most valuable hunting territory away from the
public and creating another area where the predatory animals such as the
bear and wildcat can thrive." They also complained that previous landowners had been granted cutting rights and were practically denuding
the land and that in the meantime Baxter would receive significant sums
for the cutting rights; also that the loss of taxes when such lands fell into
the hands of the state was too great.[59] Barnes apparently felt the same
way and during the remainder of the session worked in the interest of the
sportsmen's groups.

Baxter was ill at home when the first attacks were made. As soon as
he recovered, he wrote directly to Barnes and other officials and legislators. To Senator John F. Ward of Millinocket, who had introduced the
legislation accepting the land gifts, he referred to his letter to Barnes and
sent a copy of a newspaper article attacking the gift. He attacked the attitudes of what he believed to be "a small selfish group of hunters." The
law had been passed and the trust created, and, he wrote, "nothing can
be done to break it. . . . Some time in the future if we enlarge the Park
we shall want to have this situation well in hand."

Further trouble arose, however, when legislation drafted by Baxter
and his attorneys was introduced in the normal course of events to enlarge
the boundaries of the "Katahdin Wildlife Sanctuary" in order to incorporate

the newly added lands. Baxter made an attempt at the same time to have
the name changed from "Katahdin Wild Life Sanctuary" to "Baxter State
Park Game Sanctuary." In support of his proposal, he gave Senator Ward
a brief history of the sanctuary and said it seemed unnecessary to have a
separate name. In a later memorandum he asked that the old name be
changed simply to "Baxter State Park."[60] When a bill incorporating the
changes reached the Senate, Senator Barnes had it tabled and then offered
an amendment that would have limited the size of the game preserve.
However, he was pressured into withdrawing his amendment and allowing the bill to be passed. A correction in the description of the boundaries
of the area concerned in the bill had to be passed at the next legislative
session when it was learned that half of the Bangor Hydro-Electric Company's dam lot at the foot of First Grand Lake had been included in the
game preserve.[61]

The attacks on increasing the size of the Park continued during the
following summer, though they did not generate much support. In June,
Senator Robert N. Haskell, chairman of the Legislative Research Committee, suggested that future grants of land for the Park be studied before
being accepted. He gained support from some legislators, particularly
Senator Barnes, who felt that future gifts should go through the normal
legislative process rather than be rushed through in one day; in this way
residents of Maine could express their opinions. While a number of residents in areas surrounding the Park sympathized with the legislators, most
newspapers and citizens defended Baxter, who said that he was "undis-
turbed by the criticism," and was continuing his project, because he believed it was "for the benefit of the present and future generations of
Maine people. I have faith," he went on, "in their sympathy with my aims,
and I have faith, too, that their legislators will never break the Katahdin
trust."[62] Little more was done, but Baxter had learned much from the attacks, and the opposition served to force him to make concessions on the
issue in the future.

After the attacks died down, Baxter continued his efforts to purchase
the remaining lands in the northern end of the Park and to round out his
holdings in the township in which he had made his first purchase. In the
northern section, he moved to obtain the lands north of Trout Brook in
T6R9. As long as the Eastern Corporation was logging its section of the
town (number 24) it was not interested in selling, but it agreed to the
sale of lands north of Trout Brook, which included Trout Brook Farm as
well, by January 1954. Thereafter Baxter prepared a deed for the state,
which he signed on January 12, 1954, and presented to the Governor and
Executive Council for approval.[63]

At once a storm of protest arose. Opposition was centered in Piscataquis, Aroostook, and northern Penobscot counties. Most vociferous were   93

the people of the Patten area. The protesters again were headed by Senator Barnes of Houlton, who presented the Executive Council, at a closed-door meeting on January 20, with a petition bearing names of four hundred individuals in the regions affected. Particularly notable in their opposition were Caleb Scribner of Patten, an old friend of Baxter, camp owner Arthur Augustine of Shin Pond, and State Representative Raymond Potter of Medway.[64] Though present in Augusta, Baxter refused to argue his case personally. He had noted earlier that "almost every great public improvement that is being undertaken in some small way or other interferes with a few individuals." The 10,000 park visitors the previous summer, he pointed out, spent far more money than hunters coming to Maine for a forty-day season.[65] Continued strong support for the park concept far outweighed the complaints, and the Executive Council readily accepted the latest gift by a 6 to 1 vote. The single negative vote came from a council member from Milo, who stated that his constituents opposed the gift because it harmed people, adversely affected hunters, ruined camp trade and cut into the tax base of the county; and also because Baxter stopped hunting and prevented use of outboard motors in the Park.[66]

As in the case of earlier purchases from the Eastern Corporation, Baxter had to agree to certain rights and privileges for that concern, the East Branch Improvement Company, and the Bangor Hydro-Electric Company. After the Executive Council accepted the land in January 1954, Baxter had to make certain changes that were incorporated in the legislative enactments the following year. In the process of conveying the land to Baxter, the Eastern Corporation excepted certain rights which it then conveyed to the East Branch Improvement Company and the Bangor Hydro-Electric Company on the same date. To the East Branch Improvement Company was thus conveyed the right to raise the level of First Grand Lake by 10 to 665 feet above sea level and to flood an estimated 2,000 acres of land in the process. The Bangor Hydro-Electric Company was granted the right to build a dam or dams on Webster Brook, downstream from Webster Lake, for water storage and/or power purposes and was also given the right to flood the necessary land. The Eastern Corporation also reserved the right to store supplies and equipment at Trout Brook Farm for five years and the right of way for roads from Trout Brook Farm north and west along the Diamond Match Road and the "Old Indian Carry" tote road near the upper end of Second Grand Lake. Also reserved was the right to use wood and other materials to maintain a right of way and to construct and maintain needed telephone lines, and the right to operate motorboats in connection with log-driving activities. The East Branch Improvement Company late in 1954 conveyed its lands in the area to Baxter while reserving all the above rights.* The original deed to Baxter

---

* Number 24–1 on the map and table.

of January 4, 1954, was modified on December 1, 1954, to incorporate the changes, and the agreements were signed on that date.[67] Baxter had written Attorney Peabody in September that in order to complete the transaction it was necessary for him to make certain concessions, which he was pleased to do. "It really may mean something to Governor Cross to have this matter settled promptly," he wrote, "and he will make a brief announcement after I hear from you that the matter has been closed."[68] The legislature duly approved the modifications early in its 1955 session when it also, without opposition, accepted various grants of land.[69] Baxter thus stilled some of the more strident criticism of local citizens.

One more minor problem involving the Eastern Corporation's holdings in T6R9 arose during the legislative session in 1955. This involved a small parcel of about 40 acres on First Grand Lake that was part of Baxter's purchase in 1947. The land would be flooded if the level of the lake were raised to 665 feet. When Baxter purchased the flowage rights for the 2,000 acres in 1954 he had endorsed needed legislative changes to guarantee flowage rights to the East Branch Improvement Company, as indicated above, but no provision was made for the 40-acre parcel. The corporation wanted a specific legislative enactment, endorsed by Baxter, to provide for correction. Baxter balked and sought other means. He recognized the problem and said if he had the power to change his deed he would do so, but felt that a letter admitting the East Branch Improvement Company's right to flood the land would be sufficient. Vice President Robert Haskell of the Bangor Hydro-Electric Company urged Baxter, his lawyer John Willey, and the firm's lawyer to get together to try to work out some legislation or some secure legal means of getting around the problem. He thought there was some solution acceptable to Baxter and acceptable to his firm that would remove any "legal doubt hanging over a $400,000 investment and maybe make us the victims of some fisherman's whim, come the 665 elevation." The method worked out at a series of meetings in Augusta, at which Baxter was present, was to have the Baxter State Park Authority issue a permit. Since Baxter was somehow afraid of violating the trust conditions (though he did not hesitate to ask for changes at other times), a permit was more acceptable to him than a conveyance of the land or the right to flood. In any event, he provided the wording for a permit to be issued by the Authority that included the statement: "Governor Baxter is of the opinion that the raising of this lake will be a major public improvement and will greatly add to the appearance of Baxter State Park. It will also give to the people of the State a beautiful lake for fishing and recreation."[70]

Later in the session of the 97th Legislature in 1955, that body passed a bill accepting two other grants of land in the northern part of the Park. The first involved a parcel of 3,567 acres (including a sixth of the public lot that was located on the parcel) owned by Great Northern. Baxter had first tried to purchase this "poor" land, located miles apart from other company lands, in 1951.* While praising Baxter for his efforts on behalf of the Park, the Company said it wanted to keep its remaining lands, since it had sold Baxter so much already.[71] Baxter delayed two years before pushing the matter again and then he once more reminded President McDonald of Great Northern that he had saved his company from the establishment of the Katahdin National Park and that he had been a company stockholder for thirty years. If he bought the land, Baxter wrote, "my life work begun in 1917, will have been completed and my State Park finished. *Never again* shall I ask for more land from the Great Northern." He pointed out that the land was of little value and difficult of access through the Park and over the Eastern Corporation's land and that its acquisition would give him ownership of the entire town.[72] Great Northern was sympathetic but still did not want to sell or lose productive land. Baxter thereupon started looking for other lands in order to effect an exchange. He asked the assistance of Justice Edward P. Murray, still a trustee of the Cassidy Estate, but without avail. Finally, a chance meeting with Robert N. Haskell of the Bangor Hydro-Electric Company and the Eastern Corporation led to a solution. Baxter prevailed upon Eastern to exchange an equivalent acreage of its lands in T5R11 to Great Northern for its holdings in T6R9. These were then sold to Baxter,[73] who deeded them to the state in the next year.

Acquisition of land in the northern section of the Park was completed also in 1955 when Baxter acquired the entire area of T6R10.** Virtually no evidence of his negotiations for the land is available. The Eastern Corporation as owners of the property insisted on the same conditions of sale as for T6R9 to the east. Baxter at first demurred but ultimately agreed.[74]

Finally, with regard to the northern section of the Park, Baxter began negotiating with the Pingree Heirs for the western portions of T6R8 not yet held by the state. Ownership of these would have given control of the remainder of First Grand Lake. The extent to which he had modified his views regarding wilderness status is indicated by the fact that he was willing to allow hunting in the area as well as to give the state power to restore the premises in the event of blowdowns, fire, or insect infestation. In another appeal for the land, Baxter noted that his family had come from Salem, as had the Pingree family.[75] Baxter wanted this land to "complete the Park," and it would, he promised, "be definitely my last acquisition." He offered $50,000 for the acreage, with the right to remove timber for ten years. Family difficulties and problems delayed decisions until October of 1957 when, at the outbreak of the Israeli-Arab War, Baxter

---

* Number 26 on the map.
** Number 27, consisting of 25,025 acres.

96

decided: "In view of the troubled conditions in the World that have developed within the past few days it seems best for me to buy no more
land for the Park." Since the future was not clear he wanted no offers
outstanding.[76] The opportunity did not arise again, so the possible acquisition of land near the northeastern corner of the Park was not consummated.

What remained in Baxter's mind was the acquisition of the northern
portion of T2R9. Baxter had begun to acquire this parcel earlier, since its
ownership would give him and the state better control of access to the center of the Park. Ownership of the town was divided between Great
Northern and several individuals and estates. In 1941 he had bought
1/32 interest;[77] three years later, he added a 1/48 interest.[78] At the same
time he was trying to buy 10,000 acres from Great Northern, working
chiefly through Vice President McKay. But Great Northern had remained
firm in its refusal to part with the property.

The matter had remained quiescent for a dozen years while Baxter
bided his time. By the late fifties, as traffic to the park area increased, members of the Authority and officials in the Park as well as Baxter gradually
became more concerned about controlling access to the area. The Roaring Brook Road and the Sourdnahunk tote road (now Baxter State Park
Road) to the area west of the mountain left the Millinocket-Greenville
road at points several miles apart. Those concerned with the Park wanted
to have a single southern entrance to the area and began developing
plans for a new road west and slightly north of the Togue Ponds and then
on to Abol and Katahdin stream campgrounds. Baxter had seen such a control system work effectively at the Laurentides Park in Quebec. A road
atop an esker or horseback between lakes would provide scenic outlooks
and allow closing a portion of the old Sourdnahunk tote road. By the end
of the decade plans had evolved to develop entrance gatehouses.

With these considerations in mind, Baxter reopened negotiations in
1957, though without immediate effect; the paper company felt that the
Park's boundaries were clear and needed no enlargement.[79] Two years later
Baxter turned down an offer by Great Northern of a right of way through
the coveted land and a lot for the park custodian on the basis that "it
would humiliate me" to go to the state with such an offer.[80] As plans for
the gatehouse system progressed, park officials assisted Baxter in the acquisition process. Commissioner Wilkins wrote to William Hilton of Great
Northern in 1960 and summed up his latest talk with Percival Baxter regarding the 7,764 acres in question, usually referred to in round numbers
as the 8,000-acre tract. Acquisition of it would increase the size of the
Park to over 200,000 acres and would provide effective control of the park
area.[81] Negotiations continued through the next two years. At first Great
Northern insisted on its proposals to give a right of way only and argued
that the debate over the Allagash area and the possibility of losing lands     97

there had determined it not to sell. But as plans for the gatehouse system were firmed up, the company gradually became more receptive to the idea of selling the needed lands.[82]

Baxter made another appeal to President McDonald in the late summer of 1961. He mentioned the gatehouse and road plans and said he had heard that McDonald was about to retire. Maine, he argued, "needs you for ten more years." Then Baxter made his pitch and asked that before McDonald left office he sell the 8,000 acres previously discussed. He was willing to pay $50,000 for the tract. Baxter felt that a proposed new regulation on registration would allow control of the number of people visiting the Park, and he again tied his ideas to policies he had seen in use elsewhere. He noted that he had recently given a considerable sum of money to the state to protect Katahdin and the adjoining land and said he would later on take over or provide funds for the total operation of the Park. Finally, he indicated that he had been asked by the National Park Service to give his views regarding the Allagash wilderness proposal. He had told them, "I am against Federal ownership and control." But he concluded his letter to MacDonald with a mild threat: "The Park Service wants to talk to me about it; our relations have been cordial."[83]

During ensuing months, Helon Taylor and other officials of the Park were brought into the planning for the additional land. Taylor gave alternative proposals for increasing the size. By the summer of 1962, after the retirement of William Hilton, "who had always been reluctant to sell any part of T.2,R.9 . . . ," Baxter and Great Northern agreed on Baxter's purchase of 7,764 acres there.[84] Baxter deeded the land to the state early in August and the legislature formally accepted it early the next year.[85]

In acquiring the tract Baxter again had to make a number of concessions. First, he had to grant Great Northern cutting rights and use of the Roaring Brook Road for entrance and access to T3R9 to December 1, 1973. No express provision was made that the new land be included within the game preserve so the land was thus left open to hunting under the laws of Maine. Finally, the conveyance to the state was made subject to three existing camp leases: 1) on the north shore of Abol Stream at the outlet of Abol Pond, to the Fin and Feather Club of Millinocket; 2) the lease on the shore of Abol Pond, to the Abol Pond Scout Camp Committee; and 3) the lease on Togue Stream, to Ronald Budreau and others: "so long as said lessees use said leased premises for the purposes as now established, each of said lessees may continue its and his occupation under said lease in accordance with the terms thereof." All of these provisions were to cause problems for administrators of the Park at a later date.

In completing this purchase, Baxter finally realized his dream of creating a park area exceeding 200,000 acres in size. In the individual grants and cumulative totals, it is difficult to give an acreage with any degree of real precision. The amounts of land provided by different surveys,

the problems of private lots excluded for the park area, and similar problems led to differing totals. As Table III-2 indicates, in 1962, shortly before the last acquisition of park lands, the actual acreage and the acreage
given in deeds from Baxter differed slightly. Thus, any final determination
of the precise acreage of the Park must await more definitive surveys.
What is known, is that it does exceed 200,000 acres.

### TABLE III–2

Acreages in Baxter State Park by Township as of January 29, 1962

| Township | Actual acreage of town, less any private ownership | Actual acreage in the deeds from Baxter |
|---|---|---|
| 3 R 9  Piscataquis County | 23,040 | 23,040 |
| 4 R 9          ” | 22,881 | 22,881 |
| 5 R 9          ” | 23,017 | 23,017 |
| 6 R 9          ” | 25,372 | 25,493 |
| 3 R 10         ” | 24,277 | 24,443 |
| 4 R 10         ” | 22,360 | 22,360 |
| 5 R 10         ” | 24,702 | 24,702 |
| 6 R 10         ” | 25,025 | 25,025 |
| 6 R 8  Penobscot County | 1,562 | 1,562 |
|  | 192,236 | 192,523 |

Source:  Austin H. Wilkins to John Maines, Great Northern Paper Company, Jan-
uary 29, 1962, BSPA. The figures were obtained from the Bureau of
Taxation, which used cruise figures developed by the James W. Sewall
Company. These did not agree with the figure of 193,254 acres, which
Baxter gave in his last deed of trust in 1955.

When the 7,764 acres accepted by the state in 1963 are added to these
totals, the ultimate acreage of the Park is 200,000 or more.

Even given the lower cost of land in earlier decades, Baxter's ob-
stinacy and courage were the key factors in the gradual enlargement of his
lifetime work. It is fortunate, as he indicated, that he came from a family
that was long-lived; but he continuously feared that he might not live until
the next legislative session met. In his method of deeding lands to the
state he created important precedents, only to flaw them with some of his
later acquisitions and deeds. Why he did so is understandable; the methods
he chose are regrettable. Yet, in their totality, the grants remain a major
milestone and monument to the perseverance, foresight, and determination of a major conservationist.

KATAHDIN LAKE

Many early trails led to this lake, which lies like a jewel in a rugged setting made up of the Great, North, and Little North basins.

When in the winter of 1931 former Governor Baxter made his first donation of land for the creation of Baxter State Park, he made the grant on
condition that the land "shall forever be used for public park and recreational purposes, shall forever be left in the natural wild state, shall forever
be kept as a sanctuary for wild beasts and birds, and that no roads or
ways for motor vehicles shall hereafter ever be constructed thereon or
therein." The state and its people accepted the conditions with alacrity. It
seemed a fitting beginning for a noble objective for which Baxter had
fought for over a decade. At the time it also appeared that there would
be no difficulty attending the conditions of the grant. As matters turned
out, no single issue concerning the Park has created so much controversy
for so long a time as that of an adequate definition of "natural wild state"
or of "wilderness." Had the Park not been increased in size the matter
might not have arisen, but since the land was acquired and deeded to the
state over a period of more than three decades, virtually every aspect of
the problem underwent change. The concept of itself changed; and particularly during the past two decades, the desirability of conserving
wilderness areas was much more widely accepted by American society.

Baxter changed the wording of his deeds of trust over the years; in
the end, he provided for land uses completely counter to his original
wilderness concept. Political pressures brought by Maine citizens living
near Baxter State Park and conditions imposed by landowners who sold
him land for park additions forced changes in his original concept.
Baxter himself, for a variety of complex reasons, changed his mind on or
made exceptions to most of the major aspects of the wilderness concept.
This has made the task of trying to unravel his thinking and wishes for
the future of the Park exceedingly difficult.

Precisely when and how Baxter developed the wilderness concept
he evoked in 1931 is impossible to determine. As a youth he had gone
fishing often with his father, perhaps visiting the Kidney Pond area in
1903, and particularly frequenting the Rangeley Lakes area. Since he
travelled widely he was undoubtedly well aware of conservation practices being carried on by the federal government. Its renewed and expanded activities in 1916, when the National Park Service was created,

IV
Percival P. Baxter
& the Wilderness
Concept

undoubtedly increased his awareness. To what extent he was reading the works of John Muir, Aldo Leopold, and other early wilderness advocates is unknown. In any event, during the second decade of the 20th century he became acutely aware of the extent to which the forest resources and waterpowers of Maine were being abused.

In a widely publicized address to a sportsmen's group shortly before he assumed the governorship, Baxter argued among other things that the state should acquire burned-over timberlands in the Katahdin area "in order to make a beginning toward maintaining and increasing the supply of timber and pulp, and in order to provide a recreation ground in the most picturesque region of the State." If Maine were to "acquire large areas of land which are now practically worthless, but which in the future will yield a harvest that will bring to the State an annual income on the investment," he argued, "it will prove a profitable investment, and a direct income will be derived from it when the crop of timber is harvested, while an indirect income will be obtained from the tourist travel that is bound to come. . . ." On the recreation side, he said that the Park would be a major attraction for state residents and tourists as well. As a game sanctuary the Park would provide protection for wildlife. "Roads, trails, and camps will be built in the most favored locations, and the camps will be rented for nominal sums to those who wish to use them. For those who want hard mountain climbing, trails will be laid out over difficult routes to the top of the mountain, while easier trails will be provided for those who do not desire to make the supreme effort." Katahdin would become a "recreation center for those who seek the woods that are unspoiled by fashionable hotels with liveried attendants, or by costly club houses frequented by the devotees of tennis and golf."[1]

In the drafts of legislative bills to create the "Mt. Katahdin State Park" in 1923 and the "Mt. Katahdin State Park and Forest Reserve" in 1925 that are found in the Baxter Papers, the thrust of expected use is essentially the same. In 1923, while stressing recreation and excluding hunting, the draft bill provided that no live timber would be removed "except for the purpose of improving the forest growth therein; but timber not needed for the purposes of this act or for the preservation of the scenic beauty of said park may be sold therefrom. . . ." The provision in the 1925 draft was essentially the same: "Timber not needed for the purposes of this act or for the preservation of the scenic beauties of said park may be sold therefrom. . . ."[2] In 1924 he wrote to a United States Senator telling of his efforts to establish a state forest preserve and argued that the development of the Katahdin region would afford the people a playground and the state an opportunity to practice modern forestry and to carry on experiments in reforestation.[3]

Baxter's last known statement before his first donation of land for the Park in 1931 came in 1927 when he created his trust. In this trust he

left funds to the state for the "purchase of or other acquisitions of additional lands for said Baxter State Park. . . ." If acquired, these lands
were to be held by the state "in Trust for the benefit of the people of
Maine for development, improvement use, reforestation, scientific forestry,
and the production of timber and sale thereof. . . ." Baxter's intentions
at this point were much the same as they had been earlier in the decade.

Since Baxter's deeds of trust to the state were conveyed over a
period of thirty-one years and various lawyers were involved in preparing
them, the precise wording of each differs to a considerable degree. Baxter
himself, in the trust created on July 6, 1927, viewed the creation of the
Park through these deeds as a "continuing evolving trust."[4]

With regard to the purposes for which the state was to hold and use
the land there are six different wordings that have vastly different significance. Even with the first parcel, which Baxter conveyed to the state in
three separate actions between 1931 and 1933, there are as many different wordings. In March he provided that the land "shall forever be
used for public park and recreational purposes." Later in the year
when the Governor and Council accepted the remaining undivided interest in the first grant, the words used were "said premises shall forever
be used for forest and park purposes"; but in 1933 when the legislature
officially accepted the land, the wording was that it "shall forever be
used for State forest, public park and recreational purposes." Quite obviously, these might be open to variant interpretations. Baxter used the
third version for his next two grants in 1938 and 1939 and then used still
another form—"shall forever be retained and used for state forest, public
park and public recreational purposes"—for the next six grants extending
through 1944. Undoubtedly he added the word "retained" to try to rein-
force the sanctity of the trust arrangement after the proposed creation
of a national park in the area. He reverted to the 1933 version for nine
more parcels granted in 1945, and asked that the legislature apply the
same wording on all areas previously granted. In 1947, he introduced
still another version for land he donated in the west half of T4R10 when
he stipulated that it "forever shall be kept for and as a state forest and
public park for public recreational purposes." Thereafter, until 1954, he
reverted to an earlier form and provided that the land "shall forever be retained and used for state forest, public park and public recreational purposes."

In 1955 he dramatically changed his position to one that he had held
in the twenties. In deeding a large parcel in the northwestern part of
the Park (T6R9), he provided that it "shall forever be held for and as
a State Forest, Public Park and Public Recreational Purposes and for the
practice of Scientific Forestry, reforestation and the production of forestry
wood products. All harvesting of said products shall be done according
to the most improved practices of Scientific Forestry and all revenue de-

rived from the sale of said products shall be used by said State for the care and management and protection of Baxter State Park as now or hereafter defined."[5] Later in the year he deeded an even larger amount of land with the provision that it be "forever held by said State for State Forest, Public Park and Public Recreational Purposes and for the Practice of Scientific Forestry and Reforestation. The trees harvested may be cut and yarded on the premises but no manufacturing operations shall be carried on or within said township. All revenue derived from the sale of timber shall be used by the State IN TRUST for the care, management and protection of Baxter State Park as now or hereafter defined, . . ."[6] In his letter to Governor Edmund S. Muskie on this occasion, Baxter wrote: "I want this township to become a show place for those interested in forestry, a place where a continuing timber crop can be cultivated, harvested and sold; where reforestation and scientific cutting will be employed; an example and an inspiration to others. What is done in our forests today will help or harm the generations who follow us."[7] No matter how laudable the objectives of this portion of Baxter's hopes and desires, to add practices of scientific management to a portion of a wilderness park makes it more difficult to come up with any clear-cut concept of wilderness for the area as a whole. For the other transfers made in 1955 and in the early 1960s, Baxter reverted to the wording "shall forever be retained and used for state forest, public park and public recreational purposes."

With regard to the second restriction Baxter placed in his deed of trust in 1931—"shall forever be left in the natural wild state"—there were no really significant changes in three decades as far as the official transfers of ownership are concerned. The variant readings amount to the same thing. What is important in this regard are Baxter's actions during his lifetime. Until his death he expressed his desires and ideas on numerous particulars of what constituted the "natural wild state." It is probably in the interpretation of this restriction that most controversy will arise in the future, as it has in the past. Baxter's ideas can be used to support very different arguments.

The third restriction he placed in 1931—"shall forever be kept as a sanctuary for wild beasts and birds"—changed relatively little over the years as far as the wording was concerned. Again, what is important here are the exceptions Baxter made to the sanctuary provision as he acquired more land.

A fourth restriction included in his first grant in 1931 was a provision that he retained "the right to determine, and to place whatever markers or inscriptions shall be maintained or erected on or within the area hereby conveyed." He included this provision through the first six grants, or until 1942. Why it was dropped is not known. He did use his rights under this restriction until the late 1960s.

104

A more important restriction involved roads. In 1931 Baxter provided "that no roads or ways for motor vehicles shall hereafter ever be constructed thereon or therein." He retained the restriction when he deeded the remaining undivided interest in the first grant to the state two years later, but thereafter did not include it again until 1945. No explicit reasons for the change have been found, but several can be surmised: In order to obtain some lands, he had to allow the owners to cut timber for varying periods of time; to allow them to exercise this right he had to allow roads. Also, in one of the grants made to the state, other parties held an undivided interest and could not be excluded from access to their properties. Finally, the Civilian Conservation Corps had been doing a good deal of roadbuilding in both the northern and southern sections of what became park land. Baxter wanted to obtain these properties and until he did so he did not oppose roadbuilding.

By the end of World War II, after he had consolidated his holdings in much of the Park, he dramatically reversed himself once more. In making a new grant of land he asked that no roads be built in the new section and that, with stated exceptions, the ban on new road construction be applied to all previous grants. In his letter transmitting his deed of trust, Baxter gave no explicit reason for changing his mind, but in spelling out some of his thoughts with regard to the future of the Park, he appeared to be afraid that too much new road construction would interfere with its wilderness aspects.[8]

Baxter might have been influenced by a letter BSPA member Attorney General Frank I. Cowan wrote him and other Authority members, late in 1944. He and Commissioner of Inland Fisheries and Game George J. Stobie had discussed the merits of widening roads in the Park and clearing places for people to park to see the mountain. He also advocated construction in the postwar years of a paved road, an extension of the CCC road from south of Togue Ponds, across the West Branch of the Penobscot to connect with a Great Northern road south of Ripogenus Dam. It might even be a toll road, he added. Unless something such as this were done, he feared that the Millinocket-Sourdnahunk road would be developed "as a broad turnpike," thereby increasing the fire danger and vitiating Baxter's purpose.[9] In his reply, Baxter praised Cowan for the thought he had given to the situation and said he would speak with Stobie next time he went to Augusta.[10] No record exists of what, if anything, transpired thereafter. The legislature concurred with his wishes and the law accepting the land barred new road construction on it and made the ban retroactive to all earlier deeds. The only exceptions were the Millinocket-Sourdnahunk road in T3R10 and T4R10, the Roaring Brook road from Togue Ponds to Roaring Brook, and a provision that rights of co-owners of land in T3R10 would not be restrained. A lumber road that the Eastern Corporation was building in T5R10 to enable it to exercise its cutting 105 rights was closed and abandoned.[11] At this point Baxter seemed to be most determined to maintain rigidly the wilderness aspects of the Park. The ban on roads was extended to another parcel in T4R10 conveyed to the state in 1947.

By then, shortly after his latest restriction, Baxter began negotiating for land in T6R9, to the north of the Park, which he desperately wanted to help fulfill his goal of 200,000 acres. The Eastern Corporation refused to sell him more until the ban was legally lifted. Baxter agreed that when the legislature met in 1949 he would ask for the change, and meanwhile he provided access to lands in T6R9 that the Eastern Corporation finally sold to him after being satisfied that the ban would actually be lifted so it could construct a road through lands in T5R9 to obtain access to the park area in T5R10 to which it had cutting rights until 1955.[12] By mutual consent in 1949, Baxter and the state lifted the roads ban "subject however to the conditions limitations and restrictions that said roads and ways be constructed and maintained in a manner not to interfere with the natural wild state now existing in said areas."[13] There were no further bans on roads in the deeds of trust.

Another restriction dealing with the wilderness concept that Baxter placed in some of his trust deeds dealt with the use of firearms. As has been noted elsewhere, the Katahdin Park Game Preserve consisting of 90,000 acres had been established by the legislature in 1923 with Baxter's blessing. Later, the "Katahdin Wild Life Sanctuary" was renamed the "Baxter State Park Wild Life Sanctuary."[14] The land that Baxter deeded to the state for the first fifteen years was included in the game preserve and therefore needed no special protection. As the Park grew, however, lands outside of the preserve were acquired, and, given Baxter's strong feelings against hunting and killing game, his next actions were not uncharacteristic. In deeding numerous parcels to the state in 1945 he provided that land then donated and also that which had been given earlier "shall forever be kept in their natural wild state and as a sanctuary for wild beasts and birds and use of firearms, trapping and hunting, not including fishing, shall be forever prohibited within the same and aircraft forbidden to land on the ground or on the waters within the same." This provision was added to succeeding trust deeds into 1954.

The people in surrounding communities, particularly Millinocket, Patten, and towns in southern Aroostook County became increasingly irritated as Baxter bought more land and granted it to the state with these sanctuary provisions. Though the area open to hunting remained enormous, they resented the fact that favorite hunting spots were being closed to them. As has been discussed in Chapter III, major attacks on continued expansion of the park and game sanctuary came in 1949 and continued into 1954, when citizens petitioned the Executive Council not to accept another grant of land. Baxter won all of these battles, but by the end of

1954 he felt sufficiently pressured into maintaining the good will of the people in the area and of legislators to ask the governor and legislature to amend the deeds of trust of 1949 for lands in T6R9, north of Trout Brook, removing restrictions on the use of firearms, hunting, and trapping in the area. The lands were removed from the game sanctuary. This was done, he said, when he "learned that the closing of this area might be detrimental to the citizens in Patten and surrounding territory who operate stores and camps . . ."[15] In his last deeds for land in T6R9, T6R10, and T2R9, he did not impose the restriction. Though the reasons for the change are understandable, the result is unfortunate, since once again, in a crucial area, the concept of wilderness is flawed.

Another restriction concerned the use of aircraft in the Park. No mention was made of this until 1945 when at the same time that Baxter banned further roads and hunting, he stipulated: "Aircraft [are] forbidden to land on the ground or on the waters within the same." Later variants included that "aircraft forever be forbidden to land on the ground or on the waters within the same." In 1948, while he was visiting the Park, Baxter was disturbed to see that the lessors of the Kidney Pond camps, despite warnings, continued to use an airplane on the pond. He expressed disappointment in seeing the plane and speculated: "Apparently I was not expected to come to the Park as late in the season as this." He thought if the situation continued he might make it difficult to renew the lease, or that he might go to the legislature to impose a penalty for the infraction of the trust deed restriction.[16] But he gave no reasons for his actions in late 1954 when he removed the ban on aircraft landing in the Park at the same time he removed the ban on hunting.[17] Then for some inexplicable reason, he reimposed the ban on aircraft in his deed for the portion of T2R9 that he granted to the state in 1962.

A curious final restriction in the deeds appeared in late 1954 when, in ceding additional lands in the northeastern section of the Park to the state, he added a provision that it "shall forever be named Baxter State Park." This reappeared in the next two grants, but was deleted from the final donation. There is no explanation for this change except, perhaps, that a different lawyer handled the transaction.

The deeds of trust are the most important legal basis for determining precisely what Governor Baxter meant by wilderness or "forever wild." It has been shown that he often changed his mind on what he meant or believed. Another way of looking at his view of the concept is to see how he followed it up with public statements, official or unofficial, as to his intentions.

During the decade of the 1930's, few additional statements of his can be found. In his strong fight against the creation of a national park, he began to correspond with national leaders in the wilderness or preservationist movement, such as Robert Sterling Yard, formerly of the National

Park Service and then president of the Wilderness Society, and Robert
Marshall of the office of Indian Affairs. He sent them copies of newspaper
articles in which he attacked the park service for its overdevelopment and
catering to large numbers of people. They replied in terms strongly upholding Baxter for the stand on wilderness that he espoused and supporting his fight against the federal government.[18] His discussions with the
park service officials and former leaders such as Horace Albright undoubtedly sharpened his thinking with regard to the wilderness concept.
Yet, while acquiring and ceding additional areas of land, he was not always
willing to follow his own philosophy. For example, he continued many
leases in park areas for non-wilderness uses, often simply because he did
not want to dislodge current holders. During the 1940s, Supervisor Harold
Dyer in various annual reports suggested that outlying areas in the Park
be managed on a scientific basis for timber production; in one case he
even suggested that spot burning be done to improve the wildlife habitat.
The general thrust of his work and suggestions was in the direction of a
managed, though basically wild, park. Baxter kept very closely in touch
with developments in the Park and it is unlikely that he did not see these
reports; yet none of his reactions regarding them have come to light. Perhaps his actions in the middle of the decade provide the answer, but those
came before Dyer's return from military service after a three-year absence.

Early in the decade, Baxter did use the opportunity afforded by some
of his larger grants to make more widespread and public his views concerning the operation of the Park. In a very widely publicized statement
late in 1941, he eloquently expressed his thinking with regard to the Park
in terms that merit a direct quotation:

> Katahdin always should and must remain the wild stormswept,
> untouched-by-man region it now is; that is its great charm. Only small
> cabins for mountain climbers and those who love the wilderness should
> be allowed there, only trails for those who travel on foot or horse-
> back, a place where nature rules and where the creatures of the forest
> hold undisputed dominion.
>
> As modern civilization with its trailers and gasoline fumes, its
> unsightly billboards, its radio and jazz, encroaches on the Maine wilder-
> ness the time yet may come when only the Katahdin region remains
> undefiled by man. To acquire this Katahdin region for the people of
> Maine has been undertaken by me as my life's work, and I hope as
> the years roll on that this State Park will be enjoyed by an ever-
> increasing number of Maine people and by those who come to us
> from beyond our borders.
>
> Katahdin stands above the surrounding plain unique in grandeur
> and glory. The works of man are short lived. Monuments decay, build-
> ings crumble and wealth vanishes, but Katahdin in its massive gran-
> deur will forever remain the mountain of the people of Maine.

Throughout the ages it will stand as an inspiration to the men and women of this State.[19]

Not long afterward, in deeding another parcel of land, Baxter explained to Governor Sewall why he was deeding land in small portions instead of all at once and asking succeeding legislatures to accept the gifts by regular legislation. Obviously he had been scared by the national park controversy, and after consulting eminent jurists and lawyers, had decided that by having succeeding legislatures accept the land with its wilderness restrictions he could create a series of precedents that would be difficult to break.[20] A year later, he wrote to Governor Sewall at greater length and detailed his rationale and said that before he finished, at least ten legislatures would have officially approved his proposals. In this way, he thought, the trust agreements would be very difficult to break.[21] This emphasis on legislative acceptance, sacredness of the trusts, and the significance of precedents continued throughout his life. Ironically, he was responsible for the most basic changes.

His next major official statement regarding his plans and hopes for the Park came in 1945 when he imposed his ban on roads. In his letter communicating the deeds of trust for additional lands and for the laws needed to accomplish his ends, he again spelled out, in even greater length, his intentions. They are worth quoting in their original form:

In all the deeds from me to the State the phrases "natural wild state" and "as a sanctuary for wild beasts and birds" have been used. By these I do not intend that the Park forever shall be a region unvisited and neglected by man. I seek to provide against commercial exploitation, against hunting, trapping and killing, against lumbering, hotels, advertising, hot-dog stands, motor vehicles, horse-drawn vehicles and other vehicles, air-craft, and the trappings of unpleasant civilization. Nor is the Park to be kept exclusively for professional mountain climbers; it is for everybody.

I want pleasant foot-trails built and attractive camp-sites laid out in the valleys, by the brook and on the shores of the waters. Sites where simple forest lean-tos and small log cabins are available for those who love nature. A suitable shelter also should be erected on the summit of Katahdin to give protection to those who climb the mountain and who may be caught in a storm or compelled to remain overnight.

With the protection of wild life the deer, the moose and the birds no longer will fear man and gradually they will come out of their forest retreats and show themselves. I want hunting with cameras to take the place of hunting with guns. Aircraft frighten wild life and disturb the peace and solitude of the wilderness. Would that the day may come when all of Maine will become a sanctuary for the beasts and

109

*Above:* Deer at South Branch Pond, another in series of Jake Day photos for use in Disney production of "Bambi." *Below:* Located on the Penobscot East Branch, Lunksoos Camp was a famous stopping place for Katahdin area explorers. Photo by Dr. Lore A. Rogers, taken in 1903.

110

birds of the forest and field and when cruelty to the humbler orders of life no longer stalks the land.

Everything in connection with the Park must be left simple and natural and must remain as nearly as possible as it was when only the Indians and the animals roamed at will through these areas. I want it made available to persons of moderate means who with their boys and girls, with their packs of bedding and food, can tramp through the woods, cook a steak and make flapjacks by the lakes and brooks. Every section of this area is beautiful each in its own way. I do not want it locked up and made inaccessible; I want it used to the fullest extent but in the right unspoiled way.[22]

These eloquent sentiments were deeply and sincerely felt. In practice, however, a close analysis of them demonstrates numerous inconsistencies, inconsistencies that would cause problems in future years and force Baxter to change the deeds of trust in significant ways. How, for example, if the Park was to be for all people, including those of moderate means, could they reach many sections of it, far distant from roads? What would happen in terms of excess population and the inevitable death due to starvation of animals if all of Maine became a game sanctuary?

From time to time in the ensuing decade after 1945, Baxter modified his trust provisions, generally in the direction of easing them in the light of social and political pressures as well as the realities of the day. Increased use of the Park forced numerous modifications of his ideas with regard to roads, buildings, and how the Park should be used. In addition, he had to come to grips with the problem of establishing more workable guidelines in dealing with the problems faced by the Baxter State Park Authority. What would happen, for example, if predators threatened to destroy animals or trees in the park area? What should be done in case of natural disasters, such as very strong winds that flattened timber? Should beaver colonies that erected dams that flooded roads be removed? In an increasingly scientific age, should chemical pesticides or other means be used to control vegetation on the narrow roads in the Park?

The question of predatory animals was raised in 1952 when Oliver Cobb, owner of the Katahdin Lake camps east of the Park, evidently wrote a complaint to Baxter, who asked Supervisor Helon Taylor for his reaction. Taylor, after talking with the members of the Baxter State Park Authority, supported Cobb's position and argued that a state-paid vermin hunter should be hired to eradicate troublesome animals.[23] Some time during the summer, Baxter met with members of the Authority and apparently agreed to a proposal that predatory animals should be destroyed. But on returning to Portland, he changed his mind and wrote that while the idea at first appealed to him, the more he thought about it, the more he felt that matters should be left as they were and sanctuary provisions of

SEEN ALONG A KATAHDIN TRAIL

112

the trust deeds should hold. He again stated his fear that unfortunate precedents might be created by hasty action.[24]

Early in 1954, Baxter began to reconsider the treatment of predators and also damages caused by acts of nature. Two years earlier, the issue of what to do with blowdowns had arisen. In June Baxter had visited the Park and apparently had been shown a blowdown area in which Great Northern had some interest. He had talked with William Hilton of that company, who argued that the cost of salvaging the timber was ex-cessive. Baxter wrote Forest Commissioner Nutting that he did not want to "establish a precedent [in salvaging] for it might be used in the future to the disadvantage of the Park." Nutting replied that he would like to discuss the subject further with Baxter, since, he said, "I believe this is a long time problem which I think the Authority and you should carefully consider and review."[25] Though no records exist, discussions were apparently conducted with the result that in the early spring of 1954, while Baxter's latest grants of land were under attack because they excluded hunting in the northeastern section of the Park, he wrote to Nutting regarding some of the restrictive clauses. While he did not want to, or was then not able to, alter the trust deeds he stated he would not regard as a breech of the trust certain interpretations, which he outlined. Should the number of predatory animals in the Park increase sufficiently to threaten the deer and moose population, he was willing, though reluctant, to have the Authority take care of the problem in cooperation with the Fish and Game Department. He was also willing to have damages caused by fire, winds, floods, mountain slides, infestation of insects, and disease "or other-wise by acts of nature or carelessness of man" taken care of by the Author-ity in cooperation with the forestry department at the University of Maine.[26]

Then during the summer Baxter thought the problem over again and decided that it was "best to make no change in the existing trust con-ditions" and asked Nutting to return his earlier memorandum.[27] Early in August Baxter made a trip through the Park with members of the Authority and noted the devastation caused in one area where cutting rights were being exercised. An agreement to leave a 50-foot strip of trees beside the highway was not being followed. Baxter, as a result, felt that the trust deed restrictions should remain.[28] Nutting responded to Baxter's decision by stating that he would do all he could to uphold his wishes. As a pro-fessional forester, he took the opportunity to point out some things that he felt would be valuable to the Park in administration and management of the lands. He believed that Baxter should leave in the the hands of the Authority the handling of natural disasters. Experiences with such disas-ters in other states such as New York, he pointed out, produced many management problems if they were not taken care of promptly. He also declared that his proposals were not opening up any area to commercial timber cutting.[29]

Baxter was apparently convinced by Nutting's arguments. Probably current attacks on the expansion of the Park also helped to force a change of mind. In any event, by the end of August, he wrote to Commissioner Nutting interpreting the trust deeds in such a way as to allow the Authority to deal with predators and natural disasters. In modified, but very nearly identical, form these were put into a revised deed of trust, sent to the legislature early the next year, and enacted into law.[30] After the introductory phrases, the revision reads:

## NATURAL WILD STATE

The State of Maine is authorized to clean, protect and restore areas of forest growth damaged by ACTS OF NATURE such as blow-downs, fire, floods, slides, infestation of insects and disease or other damage caused by ACTS OF NATURE in order that the forest growth of the Park may be protected, encouraged and restored.

The State is authorized to build trails and access roads to camp sites, to use timber from this area for fire control and firewood and to construct shelters and lean-tos for mountain climbers and other lovers of nature in its wild state.

This area is to be maintained primarily as a Wilderness and recreational purposes are to be regarded as of secondary importance and shall not encroach upon the main objective of this area which is to be "Forever Wild."

The existing leases of the land and buildings at Kidney Pond, Daicey Pond and on the shores of Matagamon Lakes may be continued by and in the discretion of the Baxter State Park Authority.

## SANCTUARY FOR WILD BEASTS AND BIRDS

The State is authorized to maintain the proper balance of nature among the different species of wild life; to control predators that may become a menace to other species; to control disease and epidemics of the wild life of the Park. Such control shall be exercised by the Baxter State Park Authority. The destruction of any species of wild life shall be carried on exclusively by the Personnel of said Authority and of the Forest and Fish and Game Departments.

All work carried on by the State in connection with the above shall be in accordance with the best forestry and wild life practices and shall be undertaken having in mind that the sole purpose of the donor in creating this Park is to protect the forests and wild life therein as a great wilderness area unspoiled by Man. Nothing shall be done for the purpose of obtaining income but should there be incidental income it is to be used solely for the care, operation and protection of this Wilderness area.[31]

There is no question that this constituted an enormous relaxation of the deed restrictions Baxter had laid down. Only time would tell how he would actually interpret them in practice. It must be remembered that he kept close contact with the operation of the Park until shortly before his death.

Five years later, in 1960, after the membership of the Authority had changed completely, one member, probably Austin Wilkins, the new forest commissioner and chairman of the Authority, asked Baxter for an interpretation of the restrictions in the several deeds. Baxter complied and wrote to the governor and asked that his reply be incorporated in his records and those of the Executive Council. Before giving his interpretations, Baxter pointed out: "While I am living I fear no encroachments on the Park, but as time passes and new men appear upon the scene there may be a tendency to overlook these restrictions and thus break the spirit of these gifts. I ask that the Park be separately administered free from any connection with the larger State Park Commission." Obviously, he still felt the impact of the national park controversy though nearly two decades had passed. Again, it is important to give the precise wording on Baxter's interpretation of the restrictions in his various deeds:

## NATURAL WILD STATE

This language allows the State to clean, protect and restore areas of forest growth damaged by blow-downs, fires, floods, mountain slides, infestation of insects and disease or other damage caused by acts of nature in order that the forest growth may be encouraged and restored. It permits the cutting down of trees needed for roads, bridges, fire control and fire-wood which are incident to the care, operation and protection of the Park but not otherwise.

Encroachments are often threatened, one being that a Museum for old lumbering tools be placed in the Park and another that prisoners be put to work there. Any such matters would directly conflict with the terms and spirit of the Trust, and nothing should be done that will disturb the peace of mind of our visitors and spoil the free atmosphere of that remarkable region.

The erection of a few lean-tos and tent platforms in suitable locations for campers with walk-in trails are not objectionable. I want this area to be unique and kept as a wild, unspoiled wilderness.

All work in connection with the above should be in accordance with the best FORESTRY and WILD LIFE practices and should be undertaken having in mind that the sole purpose is to protect the public's right and use of the forests under the restrictions of the Trust Deeds. This is not to be done for the purpose of obtaining any income, but should there be incidental income it is to be used solely for the care, improvement and extension of the Park.

## SANCTUARY

The proper balance of nature among the different species of wild life is to be maintained. Predators such as wild-cats, bears and foxes may become a serious menace to other creatures in the Park such as deer and moose, for deer and moose are the chief wild life attraction in Maine. Such a situation may need correction to maintain this proper balance. This should be done only by the Park Authority in cooperation with the Wardens of the Fish and Game Department.

As to roads within the Park this must be left to the discretion of the Park Authority but I request that no additional roads for automobiles be constructed therein and that no additional camps be erected such as those at Katahdin Stream, Abol, Trout Brook, Roaring Brook, Sourdnahunk Stream, Chimney Pond and Russell Pond.[32]

This was the last official interpretation of the deeds of trust by Percival Baxter. The task of trying to sort out his thinking on the various facets of the concept during the last two decades of his life remains. Until near the date of his death, Baxter kept very close contact with the operation of the Park. Any major decisions on the expenditure of funds and construction of roads and buildings were first approved by him. Until the last several years of his life, he made at least one and usually two or three inspection trips to the Park each season. His last trip came in the late summer of 1967. In dealing with the Authority or in newspaper comments during these last decades, he had the opportunity to make a number of comments and decisions which had a bearing on his concept of wilderness.

During one of his visits to the Park in the early fall of 1955, Baxter noted that a woods camp on Matagamon Lake, recently made a part of the Park, was being occupied. On his return he immediately asked Forest Commissioner Nutting to check it out, since occupancy would violate the "Natural Wild State" clause. Nutting investigated and reported that the camp was temporarily occupied by agents of a company that was cutting in a town to the north and had access, by deed from Baxter, across park land. Apparently with the company's approval, Nutting solved the problem by ordering that the camp be burned.[33]

A year later when he read a newspaper article describing mineral searches in the region around Katahdin by airplane, Baxter quickly asked Nutting to investigate. Nutting reassured him that the Park could not possibly be affected since the trust deeds and a state law putting public lots in the park area on the same basis as the trust deeds took care of the matter.[34]

Even earlier, a game warden wrote Commissioner of Inland Fisheries and Game Roland Cobb, asking whether firearms, if kept locked up, could be transported through the Park; the existing law seemed to preclude this. Cobb consulted with Baxter, who replied that he thought it all right for the owners of Daicey Pond and Kidney Pond camps to keep guns locked up at their camps as long as they were registered and open for inspection by game wardens. He also felt that hunters could carry guns through the Park to destinations outside of it, as long as they were locked up.[35] This

116

was a reasonable interpretation of the existing statute, but it somewhat
clouded stricter interpretations of the trust provisions.

In 1957, when reacting strongly in opposition to a development plan
of the State Park Commission in cooperation with the National Park
Service, which proposed spending a million dollars to improve the Park
through construction of more roads, nature trails, information centers, and
other facilities "in keeping with the wilderness character" of the Park,
Baxter reiterated some of his concepts. In the process he attacked the State
Park Commission and upheld the work of the Baxter State Park Authority.

> . . . These state parks are picnic grounds, with all the confusion
> of trailers and soda pop and all that.
> Baxter State Park was created for an entirely different purpose.
> Some day—maybe in your day—there won't be any really wild areas
> left. This park may be the only place where future generations can see
> Maine as it really was.
> I wanted a place just as near what it was when the Indians were
> there.
> The park is for mountain climbers, trail walkers, naturalists and
> campers—people who are willing to put up with certain primitive
> conditions.
> Anybody can go into the park, but its use is restricted. No more
> roads are to be built. We have a road around the park. Then if you
> want to enjoy it you must go in on the trails with a pack on your back,
> carrying food and bedding—you're on your own.[36]

A year later, when Chairman Wilkins on behalf of the Authority sought
his reaction to the hunting of weasels in some portions of the Park and
the cutting of a large Christmas tree, presumably for Rockefeller Center,
Baxter demurred. He agreed that both proposals were small ones, "but if
we yield we shall have created a crack in the armor of our protection of
the Trust provision," he said. If these were allowed others would follow.
"Now is the time for us to take a firm stand against any incursion in our
wilderness." At the same time, Baxter opposed an increase in camping
facilities in the Park and felt that it should be different from other parks
and more of the nature of Laurentide Park in Quebec, which could be
used only on a reservation basis. Baxter Park, he argued, was not for tourist
campers, but "should be kept for hikers, mountain climbers and lovers of
the primitive."[37]

Attorney General Frank E. Hancock raised the Christmas tree issue
once more a year later. This time is was Maine's turn to provide the tree
for the White House lawn in Washington. Baxter again demurred, arguing
that there must be many other fine trees in Maine and New Hampshire
outside the Park. He feared the creation of precedents and countered Hancock's argument that the tree presentation would be good advertising for

117

the Park by saying that it was best *not* to advertise, since it "sufficiently advertises itself by those who visit it." Such advertising would bring more people for whom there were no facilities. Baxter felt that no more facilities should be built since, he said, "the Park is really for a select group who want it left as an untouched wilderness insofar as this is possible and who are willing to put up with minor inconveniences." He added that after he finished his work he hoped there would "be no further buildings constructed in the Park," and that all visitors should register and those staying overnight should be by reservation ahead of time. Hancock expressed his disagreement on the need to advertise the Park and his reluctant agreement that its development should be slow."[38]

Another aspect of the wilderness problem that has been discussed with regard to the trust deeds earlier is that of roads. By 1950, Baxter had agreed to the contruction or improvement of a road from Sourdnahunk Field, at the end of the Millinocket-Sourdnahunk tote road northeastward to connect with the Shin Pond Road, as it was then called, in T6R9. He not only permitted construction of this link, which would allow access to the northern part of the Park from the southern end, through park lands, and also enable the Eastern Corporation to use its logging rights in T5R10, but he paid for half the cost of construction out of his own funds.[39] He was obviously deeply concerned with the entire planning of the road and its construction. It was completed in the way he desired, a narrow road, barely wide enough for two cars. When the job was done, he travelled the route and expressed his complete satisfaction with the way it had been handled.[40]

Later in the decade, another facet of the roads problem emerged, a facet that has caused controversy to the present. This was the question of what to do about the brush and small trees that constantly grew up along the roads in the Park. Since they were so narrow and curved a great deal, the brush, once it reached a certain height, cut into the ability of drivers to check the conditions of the road far ahead. As use of the park roads increased, this slowed travellers and increased the danger of accidents. Once the State Highway Commission started providing maintenance for the roads in the Park, crews from that agency from time to time cleared the edges of some of the roads without comment from Baxter. In the autumn of 1957, on an inspection trip to the Park with Forest Commissioner Nutting, Baxter noticed that state highway crews were cutting brush along the approach road, and he apparently felt that they were making the road too wide. He wrote to the state highway commissioner expressing his opposition to the work. He again invoked the wilderness concept and said that this meant "that the roads should not be boulevards, only they should be reasonably safe. With too many improvements the Wilderness idea will no longer be maintained and I shall be pleased if you will give consideration to this matter." He said that those visiting the Park did not

118

mind the state of the roads or the many turnouts since they "give a little zest to the journey." He reiterated that though he might be considered "somewhat backward and conservative . . . , the whole idea of the Park lives in my mind as a Wilderness and therefore I want primitive conditions to remain insofar as possible." Highway Commissioner Stevens replied that crews cutting brush on the approach roads had been removed and in future maintenance within the Park no cutting of roadside growth would occur.[41]

In 1960 United States Supreme Court Justice William O. Douglas, having just returned from a visit to the Park, wrote to Baxter telling of rumors he had heard of possible construction of a road from Roaring Brook to Russell Pond. Baxter quickly checked into the matter and was assured that no such road was contemplated, though apparently someone in some agency had raised the possibility. He finally answered Douglas and declared: "I want you to feel assured that there will be no additional roads built in the Park at least while I am living."[42]

Even while Baxter was writing in such a manner to Douglas, he was discussing with park officials the possibility of and apparently agreeing to construction of at least one new road. This involved long-term planning for more adequate control of traffic moving into the southern end of the Park. Travellers to the park area at the time approached the southern and western sides on the Millinocket-Sourdnahunk road. Much of this was on Great Northern lands. In T2R9 the road to Roaring Brook left the main tote road, which then reentered the Park to lead to Abol, Katahdin Stream, and Nesourdnahunk campgrounds. To obviate the need to have two control points in the southern end of the Park, a scheme was developed to have Baxter acquire land in T2R9 and then utilize a glacial ridge or esker between several small lakes just north of Togue Pond as the route of a road connecting the park headquarters and the Roaring Brook road with the Millinocket-Sourdnahunk road. This would allow a section of road leading from Great Northern's haul road to Ripogenus Dam to be abandoned. All motor traffic into the Park from the south would then have to come through this one entrance.

Authority members apparently consulted Baxter in the matter. He agreed verbally to the scheme and promised $15,000 to help defray the costs of the road. Supervisor Helon Taylor, commenting favorably on Baxter's recent visit to the Park in May 1959, noted that he had "forgotten all about what he said about giving $15,000 to build the road. When I asked him about it, he said 'What road?' So I said no more about it." Off the record, Taylor noted that Baxter "seemed a little more feeble than last fall but he is still a grand old man and he had a fine time."[43] A year later Baxter was again in favor of the proposal and turned down an offer of a right-of-way for the road over Great Northern lands. He did not want to spend the money on a road and control building unless he held

119

ownership to a twelve square-mile area.[44] Once Baxter got the land and
deeded it to the state in 1962, planning for the new project continued. This became part of a larger plan to establish three control gates to the park
area, with appropriate buildings and roadwork.

By 1964 members of the Authority and the State Highway Commission were completing detailed plans for the three-mile road in the southern
end of the Park. The cost was estimated at $15,000. Baxter had been in on
the discussions, yet, when Authority Chairman Wilkins wrote him concerning payment for the road and suggesting that Helon Taylor's camp at
Togue Pond be moved to the road and used to establish a toll gate at an
additional cost of $10,000, Baxter demurred and said he didn't want to
put that amount of money into the project. He felt that park officials were
doing beautifully, and said, "It is well for us to be content." He saw no
sound reason for such heavy expenditures.[45]

However, as use of the Park continued to increase, Baxter ultimately
came to see the utility and need of the control gate scheme and new
roads. In early 1966, after members of the Authority met with him in Portland, he gave his permission for their construction.[46] He agreed that the
monies needed would come from accrued interest in the Baxter State
Park Trust Fund, and when it was obvious that cost of the road would be
more than the $35,000 estimated in 1966 (inflation had continued from
1964), Baxter, in a Portland meeting with Attorney General James S.
Erwin and Highway Commissioner Stevens, agreed that the added costs
could come from the trust fund.[47]

Baxter similarly changed his views with regard to new buildings in
the Park. A final issue with regard to them arose in January 1967, when
Helon Taylor's house at Togue Pond burned, with great loss of personal
effects. The question of whether to rebuild arose. During the late winter,
Baxter expressed a desire to see it rebuilt in or near the Park, and not
in Millinocket. At the same or later date he gave permission to use interest
from the trust funds for this purpose, only to rescind it in late spring. He
apparently had other plans for reconstructing the supervisor's headquarters.[48] During the next year the Authority continued to consider the
construction of a new headquarters, and when mention of this was made
in Taylor's report, of which Baxter received a copy in May of 1968,
he reacted strongly in a letter to Chairman Wilkins. He said he wanted
more information before anything was done and stated: "I do not want
any buildings started without my consent." He again expressed his fear
that the trust might be broken after he died: "I now want to keep everything as it is with no new buildings. . . . While I am here," he concluded,
"I can prevent any encroachment but once permission is given it will be
hard to call a halt. Please do not allow any mistakes that would make
trouble later on. *NO NEW BUILDINGS*.[49] The members of the Authority
120   assured him that his wishes would be respected, even though the need

for a new headquarters was acute. Wilkins made plans to meet with Baxter to discuss the situation,[50] but apparently no meeting was held, and no more planning was possible until after Baxter's death.

Another major area of controversy concerning wilderness and Baxter's interpretation of it is that involving his "natural wild state" clarification, which the legislature had accepted and enacted in 1955 (see page 114). The first real test of this came after October 1963, when extremely hard winds accompanying a blizzard destroyed 300 acres (3,400 cords) of spruce near the Abol campground. This was the same storm that caused the deaths of Ranger Ralph Heath and Mrs. Margaret Ivusic. (See Appendix.) Chairman Wilkins, after consulting with other members of the Authority and obtaining from the Attorney General an opinion that the group possessed sufficient legal authority to clean up the hurricane blowdown, began laying plans.[51] During the winter, the clearing program was discussed with various pulpwood cutters. Commissioner Wilkins discussed the proposal with Baxter and stressed the extreme fire hazard that would be created if the area were not cleared. He also explained that if it were not done fairly promptly, insect borers would begin getting into the wood and render it valueless for lumber or pulpwood. Baxter at first appeared agreeable to the operation, but then had second thoughts concerning the "forever wild" implications.[52] He wanted to delay a final decision until he could see the area during his regular visit in June, but Wilkins asked for and apparently got permission to begin earlier. With Baxter's knowledge, a contract was drawn up with Gerald Ladd, a pulpwood cutter from Milo, to take out the wood. The Great Northern Paper Company agreed to buy the pulpwood while the Maine Forestry District purchased 100,000 board feet of lumber. When the former governor toured the area in September with Helon Taylor, he viewed the devastation, which "certainly left a bad scar," and asked how much wood was removed and to what account the receipts were credited.[53] Taylor observed that Baxter was "not disturbed with the logging on the east side or the blowdown operation on the west."[54] The cleanup was completed by the end of 1965, and when the accounts were settled they showed a net income of $7,676.06, which was deposited in a special account that also contained income from camp leases.[55]

As a result of the same storm, the bridge at Trout Brook near the South Branch Pond road and the bridge at Little Sourdnahunk were washed out. In addition, much washing occurred on the roads in the Park. The State Highway Commission sought and obtained an additional appropriation of $50,000, over and above its usual $30,000, for repairing the damage done. Baxter was kept aware of this work as well.[56]

In a final area of controversy regarding interpretations of the "forever wild" clauses of the deeds of trust, Baxter's actions remained ambiguous. This involved the use of snowmobiles inside the Park. It has been enormously controversial with regard to Baxter State Park, as it has with many other areas of the nation. Not many citizens are neutral on the topic.

Early versions of the modern snowmobile might have been used earlier in the 20th century in what is now the park area, and undoubtedly private individuals did use the machines in the Park not long after they began to appear in significant numbers in the late 1950s. The first known, official use of one came in late 1961, or early 1962, when Helon Taylor personally purchased one and used it extensively to haul supplies and materials to various distant points in the Park. Perhaps through his monthly reports or otherwise, Baxter heard of his purchase and decided that Taylor should not bear the cost of such an expensive machine himself and promptly sent him a check. The check was processed through state channels, and Taylor was reimbursed so that the machine became state property.[57]

For several years snowmobile use increased enormously in Maine, and more and more people from the surrounding region apparently began making trips to the immediate area of the mountain and probably penetrating farther. Funds for their control were practically nonexistent, and they were not really noticed until 1964 or early 1965, when an article entitled "A Day on the Mountain" appeared in the *Bangor Daily News*, describing some of the popular drives owners of the new machines were making in the area. The article elicited some angry responses, particularly from a citizen of Old Town, who wrote to the newspaper and to Baxter directly, complaining that he had seen a picture of a man with his snowmobile on Baxter Peak.[58] Baxter wrote Helon Taylor, enclosing a clipping of the story and the citizen's letter, and said he would take the problem up with Taylor on his next trip north. Taylor replied immediately, suggesting that Baxter let him and Austin Wilkins handle such petty complaints, since, he said, "We are the ones who are supposed to be running the Park and we wish and strive to run it exactly as you want it run." He denied that a photograph supposedly taken on Baxter Peak was genuine and said it had been taken about a half mile above his camp. He continued:

> As far as I am concerned I can see no harm in people enjoying our Park in winter with their motor toboggans. Maybe in the future we will have to control it but up to now it has caused no trouble. They do not cut our trees, disturb our wild life or harm our Park in any way. Those who come in summer would never know they had been here unless they are told. I have talked with Austin [Wilkins] about this and he and I are agreed that there is no harm in it.[59]

Ironically, on the same day Taylor wrote to Baxter, Baxter wrote again, saying he had thought it over, and suggested:

These skis should be prohibited in the Park except for one for you as Supervisor to use in case of emergencies. I feel strongly about this for they will frighten away the wild animals and we certainly would not see a caribou again. This same reason prompted us to forbid the use of motor boats on our lakes. I can see the damage they would cause.

I would be much pleased if the AUTHORITY would add this to the list of what is forbidden in their regulations. Will you please bring this to the attention of the AUTHORITY members for this is the time to kill it.[60]

In reacting to the exchange, Taylor wrote Wilkins that he should be forewarned and said he did not care whether they allowed motor toboggans in the Park in winter or not, but, he wrote, "It will take more than one Ranger and a broken down old Supervisor to police the area if we do not." He went on to admit that a game warden and park ranger had indeed made it to the top of Katahdin in a snowmobile. It was done at Taylor's order to search for caribou tracks and survival equipment left after caribou had been set down by helicopter on the mountain. He said no one else could find the route used or tell that they had been there.[61] In response Wilkins said he had discussed the use of motor toboggans and Hondas in Baxter Park with Baxter, and the topic would be on the agenda of a forthcoming Authority meeting. Wilkins opposed the use of trail bikes, but was more sympathetic to allowing snowmobiles.[62]

Several years later, when the Authority issued a rule permitting the use of snowmobiles on the perimeter road, the Roaring Brook road, the Chimney Pond trails, and some roads on Rum Mountain, the public outcry was so great that the rule was amended to allow them on the perimeter road only, and on the Roaring Brook road as far as the turnoff to Katahdin Lake. Wilkins stated that when the original regulation was issued, the matter had been thoroughly discussed with former Governor Baxter, and that Baxter had given his approval of the use of snowmobiles in the Park by other than rangers. "I am sure that in his declining years he still understood what was meant by this snowmobile regulation," Wilkins said.[63]

When the need, desirability, or utility of a change was put forcefully enough to him, Baxter modified his stance. But it can be seen that it is impossible to come up with a really workable and tightly-knit formulation of what Baxter meant by his wilderness or "forever wild" concept.

**BAXTER PEAK**
Once called Monument Peak, this massive mountain was renamed in honor of Baxter upon the occasion of his first major gift of park territory to the state of Maine.

The history of Baxter State Park during its first decade was in many ways a dreary one. Administratively, it was loosely handled, and financially the state did little for it; so little, in fact, that this was a major reason for the attempt to create a national park in the area. Baxter was unable to increase the size of the Park until late in the decade. By the time World War II broke out, the lines of administration and operation were being clarified. Ironically, in view of the national park struggle, most constructive work in the Park during the decade was done by the National Park Service in conjunction with the CCC.

Just what had the state received from Percival P. Baxter? The total acreage was unclear. Baxter and many other sources used the figure 5,960 acres after the second grant late in 1931; others used the figure arrived at by computing the number of acres in nine square miles—5,760. The park area included the main bulk of Katahdin with Baxter and South peaks; the Knife Edge; Pamola; most of the tableland; Chimney Pond; the Northwest plateau with Harvey Ridge; Hamlin Peaks; the North Peaks; Rum Mountain and the Great, North, and South basins. It was enclosed by privately owned lands.

If weather and road conditions allowed, two automobile approaches to the Park were possible by 1931.[1] One led from Millinocket by Togue Ponds and on to Windey Pitch; the other approach was from Greenville over the Great Northern road across Ripogenus Dam and on to Sourdnahunk Stream. From the Millinocket end, old roads and trails could be followed to the Great Basin. From Chimney Pond the so-called Appalachian Trail led to the tableland or Saddle, following the route of old slides; the Dudley Trail, opened by Leroy Dudley in 1923, led up Pamola and then across the Knife Edge. From the Togue Pond area the St. John Trail,[2] soon to fall into disuse, followed the Keep Ridge route toward Basin Ponds and then followed a slide up Pamola. From either roadhead, approaches could be made for the trail up the Abol Slide to the tableland and on to Baxter Peak, or from the sporting camps on Daicey and Kidney ponds up the Hunt Trail. The latter route had been selected as the route of the Appalachian Trail. In the first two years after

the Park was created, the final location of the latter trail was determined
and marked.[3]

The only accommodations available in the Park itself were the few
lean-tos and the state camp at Chimney Pond where Leroy Dudley still
resided. Most travellers to the mountain stayed at private sporting camps
in the area. The major ones were Earl York's Twin Pine camps on Daicey
Pond; the Kidney Pond camps of Roy and Laura Bradeen; William Tracy's
camps at Russell Pond; the Togue Pond camps and the camps on Katahdin
Lake. From these locations an estimated twelve hundred hikers reached
the top of Katahdin in 1932.[4]

During the first two years of its existence Baxter State Park was
under the administrative direction of the forest commissioner, who was
charged by law to administer lands granted to the state. The Forestry
Department had had officials in the area for some years, since it organized
and manned the Maine Forestry District.[5] The Katahdin Park Game
Preserve was also continued, and its 90,000 acres encompassed an area
much larger than the Park. The commissioner of Inland Fisheries and
Game, with one camp at Chimney Pond and others located in the general
area, was in charge of maintaining the preserve and upholding game
laws. No separate appropriation was made for the Park in 1931; the
minimal costs of maintenance came from the regular budgets of the offices
named above. In 1932 the forest commissioner noted the continued difficulty of access. The existing roads were in terrible shape so that the Park
was not readily accessible to most people of the state. He recommended
improvement of the road approaches and, when funds were available,
construction of "some sort of hotel or camp . . . at Chimney Pond" and
the hiring of a corps of wardens or forest rangers to serve as guides and
to patrol the trails.[6] But no improvements or long-range planning could
be accomplished.

Quite properly, Baxter was more deeply concerned about the Park's
development than most citizens of Maine, but in view of later events,
some of his actions in connection with his initial gift are hard to explain.
He deliberately omitted any reference to forfeiture or reversion in his
deeds of trust to the state. He felt it sufficient at the time, he said to
Governor Gardiner, to have the solemn promise of the people of Maine
made through their governor and legislature that Katahdin forever would
be held by the state as a sacred trust. "Mt. Katahdin is now safe," he is
reported as saying. "The word of the State of Maine is enough for me.
There are no forfeitures or reversions in my gift."[7]

After the legislature renamed Monument Peak in his honor,* Baxter
sent a copy of the resolve to the United States Geological Survey to make
certain that the United States Geographic Board would change the name

* See page 70.

officially. After this was done he wrote again, suggesting that in order that the records may be complete, the following words be added: "and who [Baxter] in 1931 donated Mt. Katahdin to the State of Maine to be forever held for public park and recreational purposes."[8] Late in 1932 he wrote again to the Geological Survey, asking for copies of special maps of the Katahdin area. He was preparing a small map of "the Mount Katahdin gift which is now called BAXTER STATE PARK."[9]

Baxter's gift to the state was further commemorated in the form of a bronze tablet placed on a rock near the summit of Katahdin. The Executive Council and Governor on March 16, 1932, ordered the forest commission to procure and erect the tablet at a cost not to exceed $350. Baxter was to approve the tablet and its inscription. This was done and in September the tablet was carried to the top of Katahdin by a party that included Baxter, the commissioner of Inland Fisheries and Game, a representative of the forest commissioner, members of the Millinocket Chamber of Commerce, and personnel from Great Northern who helped to install it.[10] The inscription on the tablet gave the date and size of the gift, mountains and landmarks in the area, and the conditions of Baxter's grant to the state.

Within six months after the erection of the tablet, the situation at the Park changed dramatically. Baxter's old friend, President Herbert Hoover, was beaten decisively in his bid for reelection in November. Though Maine remained loyal to Hoover, its citizens elected the Democratic candidate, Louis J. Brann, to the governorship. The administration of Franklin D. Roosevelt was to provide many services for the Park, which Baxter appreciated; but at the same time he opposed bitterly many other facets of the New Deal. His reactions were to affect the Park's history in several ways. On the state level, the newly-elected Governor Brann was to support Baxter's ideas in some cases while threatening his plans and ideals in other ways. Given Baxter's political emphasis on states' rights as opposed to centralization of power at the federal level, he was torn in several directions. Ultimately he repudiated the general thrust of federal programs and officials while having to accept some of their specific programs and assistance. In all of this he was bedevilled to a certain degree by a state legislature that was not willing and, indeed, could do little to assist in the development of his beloved project.

A major change in the administration of the Park came late in 1933. Early that year, when the legislature accepted additional areas of land on the mountain, it had made no specific changes in administration; undoubtedly Baxter had not asked for them. But the coming of the New Deal and the work of the CCC and the National Park Service in the park area during the summer of 1933 forced establishment of a more formal organization to provide continuous supervision as required by federal law.[11] In the absence of a regular state park commission, and undoubtedly at Bax-

ter's behest, an act creating a Baxter State Park Commission was approved
in mid-December.

The five-member Commission was to consist of the governor, the
forest commissioner, the commissioner of Inland Fisheries and Game, and
two public members to be appointed, after the first round, for three-year
terms. At least one of the public members had to be from either Greenville or Millinocket. The Commission was given the responsibility for
operating the Park—to receive gifts and disburse them as well as funds
granted by the legislature; control erection of monuments and structures;
improve trails; and establish rules and regulations for protection and
preservation of the Park. The State Highway Commission, upon order of
the governor, was to make all suitable equipment available for the use
of the Park, free of charge when not otherwise occupied. The law provided for fines for violating the rules established by the Commission and
procedures for trying violators. Finally, the commissioner of Inland
Fisheries and Game and the forest commissioner were protected in the
enforcement of laws relating to their duties.

Little is known about the operations of the Baxter State Park Commission during most of the decade. No records of its meetings are available. The reports of the forest commissioner and the correspondence relating to the work of the CCC and the National Park Service indicate that
the forest commissioner handled most of the detail work of the Commission. There is no evidence that Baxter worked through the Commission
structure when dealing with state officials or federal agencies. No record
of establishment of rules and regulations remains. Until late in the decade
no appropriations were made for the Park. Even the *Maine Register* did
not list the membership of the Commission each year. What costs were incurred for administration seem to have come from the budgets of the
forest commissioner and his counterpart in Inland Fisheries and Game, or
from the federal government. Soon after passage of the act, Governor
Brann appointed Frederick P. Bonney of Rangeley and John F. Ward of
Millinocket as public members of the Commission.[12] Ward, who served as
chairman a good part of the time, was a lawyer in Millinocket, a member
of the local Chamber of Commerce, later a member of the legislature and always a proponent of the development of Baxter Park. Mr.
Ward later told a friend that no regular meetings of the Commission were
scheduled; they were called when problems arose.[13]

The activities of agencies of the federal government over a period of
several years provided most of the monies to construct access roads and
improve and maintain trails. What became in 1937 the Civilian Conservation Corps, or CCC, was born during the very early days of the New Deal.
President Roosevelt was concerned with the preservation of two of the
nation's most vital resources—forests and manpower. Various meetings in
early March 1933 resulted in legislation passed by early April creating

the Emergency Conservation Work Agency, which was charged with coordinating the conservation work. Roosevelt named an old acquaintance,
union leader Robert Fechner, as first coordinator. This agency utilized the
knowledge, administrative skills, and manpower of existing agencies, including the army, agriculture department, labor department, and the
interior department, particularly its National Park Service. Each would
have a role, coordinated by Fechner, in recruiting, organizing, and directing the work of the CCC.[14]

In Maine the officials most directly concerned were Governor Brann,
Forest Commissioner Neil Violette, and James Sewall of the Maine Forest
Service. Sewall had written to Roosevelt during the summer of 1932, suggesting a major federal effort in conservation work. He assisted Violette
in general planning and then came to direct all CCC programs in the
Maine Forestry District. In April 1933, Maine officials began a series of
conferences with federal officials that established a policy for creation of
CCC camps in Maine. State officers emphasized that much work in the
state would have to be on private lands, since over 97 per cent of the
land was owned by private interests.[15] Agreements were worked out by
which the Maine Forest Service would help supervise various camps for
the CCC. By the end of April, plans for the establishment of twelve camps
around the state were nearly complete. Nine of these were managed
through the Department of Agriculture and the U.S. Forest Service. In
addition, plans were made for work to begin to improve the approaches
to and premises of Acadia National Park. By midsummer a number of
CCC companies were scattered throughout the state.[16]

North and west of Millinocket, the CCC established various camps
that had a long-range impact on the Katahdin area and Baxter State
Park. In June 1933, Company 193 was located in Millinocket and Company 159 in Patten. Both were supervised by the Maine Forest Service
in conjunction with federal agencies. Late in the same year and early in
the year following, side camps from these two bases were established
at Togue Pond and Seboeis Lake. Federal policy prohibited payment for
constructing side camps, so these facilities were provided from state funds.
The National Park Service in 1934 and 1935 established side camps near
Baxter State Park: at Foster Field in June 1934, and at Avalanche Brook
a year later.[17] The major purpose of all of these camps was to speed the
construction of roads, as often as not for the benefit of private interests,
but in the long run opening up the Katahdin area for recreational purposes. Along the way, the National Park Service became deeply involved
in plans for the creation of a second national park in Maine.

The men at the Patten camp spent much of their time improving and
rebuilding the Grand Lake road from Patten, across Seboeis Stream and
the East Branch of the Penobscot for three additional miles, to near the
present boundary of Baxter State Park. This shorter route replaced the   129

old route to Trout Brook that led to the north of First Grand Lake. Plans to continue the road up Trout Brook and over the watershed to Sourdnahunk Stream had to be dropped when work was stopped in 1937.[18] Portions of this road were not completed until the 1950s, after Baxter had purchased the area for the Park.

The establishment of the CCC camp at Millinocket was a natural one and seems not to have been promoted initially by ex-Governor Baxter. Once Company 193 arrived in August, however, the new camp, about a mile east of town near the present-day airport, was named Camp Baxter in his honor.[19] Its major task from the outset was the construction and improvement of roads in the Millinocket area. Baxter visited the camp in September, during his trip to install the plaque on the mountain commemorating his gift. He expressed his approval of the work being accomplished.[20]

Of most immediate significance for the Katahdin region was the conversion of the old tote road leading from Millinocket toward the mountain into a truck route. Citizens of Millinocket were arguing for the continuation of State Route 157 from their city along a route south of the mountain to Greenville. Baxter's September trip to the CCC camp and Katahdin seems to have been part of a plan to promote this particular route, which never was completed as a state highway though a road was pushed through.[21] During 1933 the CCC unit rebuilt the section from Millinocket to Millinocket Lake; installed bridges; built a campsite on the lake; cleared the roadsides for fire protection; fought forest fires; and continued improving the old tote road beyond the lake. That road, which had been used in the previous decade, had deteriorated. Baxter's party went by auto to Katahdin Stream. A CCC official reported in the late spring of 1934 that only the first twelve miles from Millinocket could be considered a Class 2 road, and that the remainder of the thirty-two-mile route to Foster's Field

> . . . is a one way truck trail, when two cars meet, it is necessary for one of them to back up until such time as he finds a spot wide enough for two cars to squeeze by. The road is so narrow and the rocks so numerous that it is almost impossible for the trucks with their dual wheels to get through, already four tires have been ruined by the Army trucks alone, through continually hitting against the rocks on the side of the road. The forestry trucks are running with light loads and I advised the taking off of the outside dual wheel.[22]

During 1934 and 1935, until the abandonment of Camp Baxter at the end of the latter year, the contingent continued construction and improvement of the roads, still all over privately-owned lands.[23] The main road forked near Pockwockamus Bridge, with one branch leading right to Togue Pond and the east side of Katahdin, the other leading left to Foster's Field and by the end of 1934 to Sourdnahunk Field. On the branch leading beyond Togue Pond, the road was completed for some distance beyond Windey Pitch when work was discontinued. Plans to do more elaborate work on the Sourdnahunk section were dropped.

Just after Camp Baxter was authorized in the summer of 1933, ex-Governor Baxter made a request that eventually had momentous consequences for himself and his beloved Park. In early July he wrote to Governor Brann apparently asking that the federal government, through the CCC and the National Park Service, establish a work camp in Baxter State Park to provide many improvements. Brann forwarded the letter to Secretary of the Interior Harold Ickes with a request that work be done in the Park by his department. Ickes replied that when the conservation program was first established, appropriate forms were sent to the forest commissioner in Maine, but none had been completed and it was now too late to apply for the first six-month period. After indicating that he was asking the National Park Service to send additional forms for the next period, Ickes added: "I am much interested in the Mount Katahdin region which has been proposed as a national park."[24] Secretary Ickes's last comments probably reflected the new expansionist ideas of the National Park Service, and the eagerness of Governor Brann to interest the New Deal in projects in Maine, particularly in the Moosehead and Katahdin areas. At the time the park service recommended caution, since so much of the area had been cut over and supposedly was not suitable for a national park.[25] Governor Baxter's apparent lack of concern about the ambitions of the National Park Service at this time is notable.

As part of its work in connection with the CCC, the National Park Service coordinated work programs in the national parks and was also authorized to assist the states in the improvement of state parks. In 1933 and 1934 the agency developed an extensive program at Acadia National Park and began working with Maine on the development of several areas that eventually ended in the creation of Camden Hills State Park, Mount Blue State Park, and Rangeley Lakes State Park, among others. The park service apparently had changed its cautious stance of the summer of 1933 and had become eager to take hold in the Katahdin area as well. During the remainder of the decade, it remained the only area in Maine in which the state government really cared to create a national park. The immediate issue was to get the federal government involved in some way.

Federal plans, state needs, and Baxter's desires produced much discussion during the summer of 1933. In late August the newspapers reported that Governor Brann had suggested that the federal government take over Baxter Park and the surrounding area as a national park or a national forest to be improved by the CCC.[26] The federal government was deeply interested and might have established another CCC unit closer to the Park than Millinocket in late 1933, had not Maine officials suggested waiting until 1934 when the needed work could be accomplished more easily.[27] The planning continued, and it probably was this factor that helped to force the creation of a Baxter State Park Commission in order to have an agency legally responsible for the area in which the work was to be accomplished. By the late winter of 1934, the establishment of Camp SP-2 Baxter (State Park-2), in the Katahdin area was assured. The recruitment of personnel to man this side camp was pushed, and the camp itself was finally established at the site of the old lumbering camp at Foster Storehouse (Foster Field) on Sourdnahunk Stream in early June.[28]

The personnel for the new National Park Conservation camp were transferred for the season from another at Alfred, Maine. Upon their arrival in Millinocket, most of the group were detained and assigned to fight forest fires, which were raging south of Katahdin. The men were at first "somewhat inclined to be resentful over the change" from Alfred to the wilds of northern Maine and were further irritated, soon after arrival, upon being subjected to the fury of the scourge of the north woods—black flies.[29] After settling in at the temporary camp at Foster Field and adjusting to the new environment, the men were set to a variety of tasks in and about the park area. Until late in the decade, most of the land on which they made improvements was privately owned, though some of the officials wrote and acted as if it would eventually become part of the Park.

The unit completed a number of valuable projects. First priority was given to further improvement of the Millinocket-Sourdnahunk road from Abol Field to Sourdnahunk Field. Two miles back toward Millinocket from Foster's Field, the present Katahdin Stream campground was developed. The site was an open, gravelly area beside Katahdin Stream that had formerly been the location of a lumbering camp and a campsite for some Katahdin hikers. It was on the route to Katahdin from sporting camps at Daicey and Kidney ponds. Improvements made consisted of a parking area, six tables with shelters and fireplaces, four lean-tos, a log cabin for the ranger, latrines and water supply; and the construction of a dam across Katahdin Stream to provide a pool on the campsite. The campground was maintained by the Maine Forest Service until it was merged into the Park after Baxter acquired the land. The CCC crew also relocated the first mile and a half of the Hunt Trail to follow the stream and pass Katahdin Stream Falls. Farther on, at the 2,450 foot elevation, the crews constructed a log lean-to for emergency purposes. The entire Hunt Trail was cleared, blazed, and marked with white paint and metal markers. The other trails on the tableland and on the east side of the mountain were also signed and marked with blue paint. The CCC crew relocated the Abol Trail, the lower part of which had been relocated a decade earlier by members of the AMC, to a more attractive site to avoid lumber-

132

ing activities of Great Northern Paper. They also repaired the Sewall forest warden's camp at the base of the slide, just within the park boundaries.[30]

When the camp was broken up in the fall and the men moved back to Alfred, the site was left in charge of Fred Pitman, a Maine Forest Service warden who had been a construction foreman during the summer. Pitman, a river man and logger since early in the century, owned "Katahdin View Camps" on the West Branch, about four miles below Abol Stream. As an employee of the Maine Forest Service and later of the Park, Pitman was to play a key role in the management and operation of the Park for the next two decades.

The State Park Division of the National Park Service envisaged several years' work in the development of Baxter State Park through the use of CCC crews. Technicians made plans for protection and care of wildlife in the Park. Late in the 1934 season, for example, a wildlife technician for the National Park Service reported enthusiastically about the wildlife potential of the Katahdin region, though he was less than happy with the protection that wildlife had thus far received. Leroy Dudley, "for many years game protector of this State Game Preserve, and now the sole permanent summer dweller of a hut near the mountain," told the federal expert about wildlife in the preserve and alluded to the widespread poaching of game in the area, which had not had a protector since 1927. The federal expert advocated hiring a naturalist (or a botanist and a zoologist) and three game protectors to assist a forester, landscape architect, and road engineer to help develop and manage "the Mt. Katahdin State Park, or National Park, as the case may be," an area he felt offered "unusual opportunity for wildlife, the most important and the most valuable to posterity in the northeastern United States."[31] In September of 1934 Baxter met at Togue Pond with members of the AMC; James W. Sewall of the Maine Forest Service; a representative of the CCC; and Arthur C. Sylvester, a landscape architect of the National Park Service who had been lent by the Interior Department to direct conservation work in the area. Baxter may not have learned all the details of various individuals' thinking, but the question of possible creation of a national park must have emerged. He appeared to be proud of the work of the CCC and was as yet unafraid of encroachments on his gift to the state.[32]

Before the work was completed at Foster Field in 1934 the National Park Service planned to establish another CCC work project on the east side of the mountain at the old Depot camp of the Great Northern Paper Company on Avalanche Brook. Plans were made for completion of the road to Roaring Brook; improvement of the trail from Roaring Brook to Basin Ponds; and construction of a horse trail from Roaring Brook and Basin Ponds to the top of Katahdin over the North Peaks area. Sites for cabins and a lodge at Basin Ponds were to be cleared and the ground

## LESTER HALL IN THE THIRTIES

*Above:* Busy outside an old Basin Pond bunkhouse. *Below:* Looking down into The Klondike. Lester was one of two honorary members of a group of local business and professional men to whom Jake Day introduced the beauty of the Katahdin area. They called themselves "Jake's Rangers" and had their own insignia designed by the artist.

134

prepared for construction in 1936. Plans were also laid for cabins and lean-to construction at Chimney Pond as well as for an adequate tote road and foot trail connecting Basin and Chimney ponds.[33] In May and June of 1935 personnel from the 192nd Company at Princeton were transferred for the summer to the temporary campsite on Avalanche Brook. National Park Service officials were in charge of what was officially known as Camp SP-3.[34] During the summer the crews worked mainly on improving and extending the road from Windey Pitch toward the planned terminus at Roaring Brook. The route was cleared for the last mile, but the work was not completed. Some work was done on trails, and a suspension bridge for the Appalachian Trail was constructed across the West Branch of the Penobscot River, but the more elaborate plans enunciated above were not carried through.[35]

This was the last major work actually accomplished by the CCC and the National Park Service in the Katahdin area. During the summer of 1936, though somewhat late, another work camp was authorized for the Depot campsite on Avalanche Brook to complete the road to Roaring Brook and to begin development of another campsite, but nothing was done.[36] In ensuing summers short side camps from the Camden Hills Recreational Demonstration Area were detailed to the Katahdin area to do a bit more work on the Roaring Brook road and raze the camps at Foster Field and Avalanche Brook.[37] Any possibilities for additional camps were precluded later in the decade by the controversy over establishment of a national park.[38] By 1940 the personnel of the CCC in Maine had been so reduced that the forest commissioner's request, approved by Baxter, for the establishment of a side camp out of Camden was turned down.[39]

After his initial expressions of approval of the work done by the CCC, it is impossible to determine the precise role played by Baxter or the Baxter State Park Commission in planning, approving, or determining the work of the CCC. Though Baxter was consulted at crucial moments by the National Park Service and by members of the Commission, it appears that no one group had a really strong hold on the Park's operations during the middle years of the decade. Until it burned in 1936, the old Great Northern Camp number 3 at Basin Ponds, though just outside the Park, was maintained by the owners of Togue Pond camps. It was a base for much activity within the Park proper. At Chimney Pond, where the state cabin was transferred from the Department of Inland Fisheries and Game to the forest commissioner during the decade, Leroy Dudley remained in charge of the often large influx of users, related his stories, maintained trails, and generally tried to keep control. Much of the time he was not an employee of the state or federal government, but simply kept charge at Chimney Pond and retained the receipts from the 25¢ per night users' fee. The nearest fire warden was at Togue Pond. On the south side of the

THE DUDLEYS
Roy and his wife Abby, photographed by Jake Day in 1934.

mountain, Fred Pitman alternately seemed to be an employee of the federal government and of the state of Maine at Katahdin Stream and other points on the perimeter. The only camping site actually within the Park until very late in the decade was at Chimney Pond. The Maine Forest Service maintained other campsites in the area at Millinocket Lake, the Narrows on Upper Togue Pond, Rum Brook and Avalanche Brook on the Togue Pond road, Abol Field and Sourdahunk Stream.[40] The Abol Field site was built by the CCC.

Mention should be made of the activities of other groups on the mountain or in the immediate area during the decade. W. F. Tracy, who had opened a sporting camp at Russell Pond in the previous decade and reopened the North Peaks Trail, continued his operations. From the Roaring Brook area, which gradually became more and more accessible as the CCC improved the approach road, he kept open a horse trail to Basin Ponds and also up the valley between Katahdin and the Turners to Russell Pond. Most parties exploring the area north of Katahdin made use of his services.[41]

Also of major significance during the decade was the activity of the AMC on and around Katahdin. As in the twenties, the Club sent annual excursions to Katahdin. Most significant of the members was Ronald L. Gower who, aside from Myron H. Avery, knew more about the region than any other individual. Three decades later, Baxter wrote him: "I regard you as one of the founders of the Katahdin Park. . . .[42] In the late summer of 1934 when Baxter, "by prearrangement," met with one of Gower's expeditions at Togue Pond, he told how he appreciated the Club's sending the excursion and "extended an invitation to the Club to build a hut or cabin of their own." Presumably this would be at Chimney Pond. Though the cabin was never built, the Club retained an interest in the region and probably did more than any other group or institution except the federal government to maintain the area during the next decade. Early in the thirties, the Club reopened the trail from Basin Ponds to Pamola and made extensive repairs on it from Basin Ponds to North Basin. In 1940 the Club checked and cleaned the vast majority of the trails on and around Katahdin.[43]

Perhaps the major achievement of the Club in the thirties was its role in the opening of the Northwest Basin, over half of which lay inside the original park boundaries. Prior to the late twenties, few hikers had been in the area for many decades. The Monument Line surveyors, lumbermen, George Witherle, and botanical parties early in the 20th century had visited the remote glacial cirque, but as access routes changed, it was again nearly forgotten. During the twenties, interest in the Klondike and the Northwest Basin had increased, and the areas were most commonly approached from the Saddle. In 1929 a group of AMC members, including two women, had spent two weeks climbing around the mountain while based at Chimney Pond. In the course of their explorations they descended into the Northwest Basin from the plateau and left the area via Wassataquoik Stream, Russell Pond, and the North Peaks Trail. In 1931, the same group, now including Mr. and Mrs. Leroy Dudley, had descended into the Basin by way of Harvey Ridge and thoroughly explored it. In leaving the Basin the group located and began blazing what is now the Northwest Basin Trail. Roy Dudley and others subsequently brushed out the trail more thoroughly and, with the initial exploratory group, decided to erect a shelter at Davis Pond. This was accomplished during the next two summers, and in 1934 cairns were placed along the tableland to mark the completed route.[44] In this as in many other aspects of the Park's development during its first decades, the Park benefited from the work of agencies, groups, or individuals not directly tied to the state of Maine.

Literally dozens of fateful decisions regarding the Park were made during the 1930s with no solid indication that Baxter worked with or through the Commission. It is obvious that Governor Brann, as a member of the Commission, followed a policy counter to Baxter's much of the time. The roles played by Forest Commissioner Violette until his death in September 1935 (ironically it was Baxter who originally appointed Violette to the position) and Waldo N. Seavey, his successor, must have been equally ambiguous, because their membership in the Baxter State Park Commission often seemingly conflicted with what they had to do in coordinating federal-state programs such as the CCC. An indication of the tenuous relations came in 1938 when Baxter, in the midst of the national park controversy, wrote to a national park official saying that the Baxter State Park Commission was planning to erect a simple log cabin at Chimney Pond and that he had written "them to find out what steps have been taken to do this."[45]

On the strictly personal side, during the decade Baxter twice evoked the proviso in the original trust agreement that he could name or rename park areas during his lifetime. The first time was in 1933 when he asked that the notation "Governor's Spring" on the Geological Survey map be changed to "Thoreau Spring," in "honor of the man who first brought Mount Katahdin to the attention of the people of New England." He declared that the original name had no real or historical significance, though actually it had been named eight years earlier to honor Governor Ralph Brewster, the first Maine governor to climb Katahdin, with whom Baxter fought bitterly later on over the national park issue. The second time was when Baxter asked in 1935 that the North Peaks and the ridge of the Katahdin massif extending north from Hamlin Peak, and only slightly lower in elevation, be renamed the "Howe Peaks," in honor of Burton W. Howe (1874–1922), the Patten lumberman and politician who a decade and a half before had been so instrumental in introducing Baxter to the Katahdin area. Baxter's wishes were gratified in both instances without question.[46]

By 1939 the organization of the Park was changed considerably. The rationale and precise reasons for the change in direction are not entirely clear. Perhaps it was connected, as Myron Avery charged, with the fact that the maintenance and operation of the Park had become difficult or nearly impossible under the existing structure. An administrative arrangement that made it more possible for the forest commissioner to finance park operations out of his budget was needed.[47] More likely the reason for change was Baxter's bitterness over the national park fight and his fear of the Commission as it had been constituted. The citizen members of the Commission from Greenville and Millinocket often had difficulty getting to meetings, and Baxter thought the arrangement had worked poorly.[48] He undoubtedly had a major role in 1939 in the planning and introduction into the legislature of a bill that provided for abandonment of the Baxter State Park Commission and its replacement by a new governing group. The law as passed in late February repealed all the old legislation and placed "full power in the control and management" of Baxter State Park in the hands of the attorney general, the forest commissioner, and the commissioner of Inland Fisheries and Game.[49]

SHELTERS AT CHIMNEY POND
Travelers often spend the night at Chimney Pond before starting up one of the trails to the top of Katahdin.

CHIMNEY POND CABIN

A bustling scene as, their gear packed on burros, hikers get ready for a climb up the mountain.

The controversy in the 1930s concerning the creation of a national park in the Katahdin region deserves separate discussion from other federal and state activities in the area. The struggle typifies much of the federal activity during the decade and illustrates the attitude of many of the citizens of Maine toward an enlarged role for the federal government. It forced the people of the state to look more favorably on Baxter Park, and it was instrumental in speeding enlargement of the initial acreage. Finally, the battle illustrates differing attitudes concerning conservation and wilderness practices and the development of Baxter's own thinking on the same topic.

The attempt to create a national park was not surprising in view of earlier proposals to this end by Maine citizens, including Baxter himself. The impoverishment of the government of Maine during the depression and the suddenly acquired resources of the National Park Service and its aggressive policy of increasing its scope of operations added to the pressures. A Democratic governor interested in tapping the federal treasury and unafraid of federal encroachments upon the state provided further impetus. The work of the CCC, beginning in the summer of 1933 in the Millinocket area and then in the park area itself in the following year, made such proposals well-nigh inevitable.

During the summer and fall of 1933 various proposals to create a national forest or park were aired.[1] Late in the autumn, as New Deal programs were growing in size and scope, Governor Brann, after returning from a planning meeting in Washington, proposed the creation of a Roosevelt National Park consisting of a million acres in the Katahdin region as part of federal efforts to employ more people under the civil works programs. In his message to a special session of the legislature meeting in December, Brann asked for legislation to permit the federal government to purchase land in the Katahdin area for a national forest, and he was instrumental in the introduction of a bill to this end. He announced that the President had earmarked $2,000,000 at his request for purchase of the land. The bill was amended to allow the acquisition by purchase or gift, but not by eminent domain, of lands for national park purposes while holding on to the state's rights in watersheds, dam sites, 141 and water storage facilities. A week before Christmas it was approved by the legislature and the Governor.[2] State officials and congressional representatives urged quick action by the federal government, only to learn in April that the act as written was not satisfactory to federal officials since the rights noted above had been withheld.[3] The Great Northern Paper Company had fought hard but vainly against passage of the measure; but were more successful against later proposals to establish national forests in the Moose River area, Aroostook County, and the Grand Lake region east of the Penobscot River. From the correspondence available it is obvious that the company leaders were terribly worried by federal encroachment.[4]

Baxter's park cause benefited considerably, later in the decade, as a result of this threat. Governor Brann thereafter remained in a somewhat ambiguous position, since he continued to favor a national park while at the same time serving as a member of the Baxter State Park Commission created by the same legislature.

During the next two years, as the State Park Division of the National Park Service planned the work to be done by the CCC in the Katahdin area and sent experts in geology, biology, and other disciplines to make studies and provide recommendations for future work, it was obvious that upper echelon employees, at least, had the ultimate goal of national park status for the region.

At this stage ex-Governor Baxter was cooperating closely with those in charge of the work at Katahdin. Then, in the summer of 1936, Governor Brann officially requested the National Park Service to investigate the feasibility of establishing a national park in the Katahdin region.[5] Whether he worked through the Baxter State Park Commission or discussed the matter with the donor of the land is impossible to determine, though it is unlikely that he talked with Baxter. Brann had decided to run for the United States Senate and was a lame-duck governor. During the month of July, two officials of the park service studied the Katahdin region extensively, even flying over the area. They reported that Katahdin, by itself, was not sufficiently large to warrant park status, but that an area of at least five hundred square miles, including the mountain, would be worthy of setting aside.[6] While in the state they met in the Governor's office with Alfred Mullikin, associate consultant for the Maine State Planning Board, and Colonel Harry Ross of Bangor, owner of much of the land immediately south and east of the Park as it then existed. One outcome of the meeting was the request of Mullikin for assistance from the federal government in purchasing 10,000 acres owned by Ross. Ross did not wish to continue paying taxes on his holdings while the public was making a playground out of the land and exposing it to fire hazards beyond his control. Ross said if the federal or state government did not buy it, he would have to sell it to a paper company.[7]

142

Also in July, Dr. Earle A. Pritchard, associate recreation planner for the National Park Service, investigated the situation around Katahdin, visited state officials, and called on Baxter, who confided his long-range plans for the development of the Park.[8] Whether during the visit or later by letter, Pritchard asked Baxter for his views on possible acquisition by the park service of lands contiguous to Katahdin and about the possibility of the federal agency taking over Baxter State Park for inclusion in a larger national park.

Baxter wrote at length, thanking him for his advice and information on state and national parks. In reply to Pritchard's requests for his thoughts on national status for the Park, he wrote: ". . . I certainly hope the Federal Government will not come into this region and as to the second suggestion that Baxter State Park be merged into a National Park it just cannot be done as I will explain." He related his long struggle to establish the Park; repeated the trust provisions established by Maine law in 1931 and 1933; he referred to the long-range plans he had discussed with him, including what was to be done in case of his decease; and added, "now I ask you and your associates to be patient and to leave this area to me. . . . In due time from these plans of mine a large and suitable State Park will develop in the Katahdin region. . . . All the land outside is just more wild land, such land as can be found in countless places within our State. If your Park Service wants a National Park in Maine there is available much land and many lakes and streams in Washington and other counties, with no State Park to restrict and limit your purchases."

He said he could explain his plans for the Katahdin region to Pritchard's associates, "for I know you will all be discreet." Governor Brann had been told, "and he has given me his word he would not favor the National Government's entry into the Katahdin region. I depend upon his word in this matter." Baxter then referred to his earlier struggles with private landowners of Maine who now were suddenly "park-minded and public-spirited! . . . If I know anything about the undercurrents here in Maine, these recent converts have but one thought and the interest now shown by them is solely for the purpose of selling their property to the government. You have no conception of the political strength of this opposition in our Maine Legislature. From long experience they know just how to handle anything that they consider is likely to trespass on their sacred privileges. They to-day are as strong as ever and their repentance and reform is too recent to be genuine." (Baxter did add that there were some broad-minded and public-spirited landowners in the state whom he respected.) He had accomplished what had been done only after a long fight, "absolutely single-handed and in the face of abuse and bitterness that you would not believe possible where a man merely was trying to do something worthwhile for his Native State." His sole desire, he said, was

143

to serve the state as a private citizen by building a great park and forest reserve for future generations, something big and lasting which would be the state's biggest natural asset. "You and your associates and I speak the same language, so let us continue to do so without interference from those we may not too disrespectfully call outsiders."[9]

Pritchard replied that he only regretted that Baxter had not included a statement of his willingness to see the area turned to the administration of the State Park Commission if and when the resources of that Commission were increased to allow it to take on the work. He hoped that Baxter or the State Park Commission would request the National Park Service to send proper technicians to Katahdin for an evaluation that would show the "adequate size, appropriateness of land and the proper buffer area required for best use in making this an outstanding scenic and wildlife recreation area for Maine." He reiterated the desire of the park service to be of assistance.[10]

Though nothing more of moment occurred during the autumn, the park service continued its planning and sought support for the creation of another national park in Maine. A major proponent emerged publicly in the person of Myron H. Avery of the United States Maritime Commission. Avery had grown up in Lubec, where he still maintained his legal residence. Like Baxter, he was a graduate of Bowdoin and the Harvard Law School, but unlike Baxter, he entered the federal service. From his early youth he had become intimately acquainted with the Katahdin region, had done enormous amounts of research on the area, published a great many articles, and probably knew more about the region than any man then living. He had been an early promoter of the Appalachian Trail and out of his base in Washington, D.C. he had helped develop the trail in Maine and other states. His long tenure as chairman of the Appalachian Trail Conference began in the 1930s. He had become closely associated with leading officials in the National Park Service and in 1938 was named to head a National Park Service advisory committee on hiking. In his role as government official, hiker, one long interested in recreation and public service, and also a resident of Maine, he became probably the strongest private individual promoting the national park concept.[11]

It was Avery who pointed to some of the major problems involved in state ownership and development of the Katahdin area. Baxter had earlier indicated that he was going to Chimney Pond to see the improvements that had been made there. Avery wrote to warn him that instead of improvement, with all that LeRoy Dudley, who had no official authority, was able to do, "conditions at Chimney Pond are short of chaotic." There was abuse of Chimney Pond itself and destruction of the environment in the camping area. Avery and his friends felt most strongly the need for supervision in the area and the development of a long-range plan. He

144

urged Baxter to use his influence with the legislature to obtain an appropriation for supervision. "I do not want to under-emphasize our apprehension," he wrote, "and our feeling that the seeming laissez faire policy is bound to produce—and already has produced—consequences which are close to irreparable." Baxter asked the Governor for "the modest sum of $2,000" for the Baxter State Park Commission, quoting at length from Avery's letter to supplement his suggestion. The money would be used to provide caretakers on both sides of the mountain and a few additional camping shelters for the "several thousand" visitors who ascended the mountain each year.[12]

Soon after, Baxter left on his annual winter cruise, during which time he was out of contact with events in Maine. Only on his return in early April did he learn of momentous developments that had occurred during his absence. The legislature, in an economy move, had eliminated the appropriation proposed for the Park. This may have helped to spur Congressman Brewster to introduce H. R. 5864, "A Bill to provide for the establishment of the Katahdin National Park in the State of Maine, and for other purposes," which had been drafted by the Appalachian Trail Conference leadership, and particularly by Myron Avery after the initial studies of Katahdin in 1936 had provided promising results.

Brewster had carefully considered the measure, "both as to the merits of the area as a national park and on its own merits," before he agreed to introduce it. He said he had tried to contact Baxter and finally decided he could not wait for him to return before introducing it on March 23. The major reasons he gave for his action were that the Park, given the state's financial problems during the decade, was a "white elephant"; that the area was deteriorating rapidly with increased use, and that only the National Park Service had the facilities, money, and expertise to develop a park properly.[13] Brewster had talked with the leaders of the AMC, trying unsuccessfully to obtain their agreement; and he had also huddled with Avery and park service officials.[14] Early in March, Senator Wallace H. White had written to Baxter concerning the intentions of the National Park Service and said that Brewster had spoken with him about it, but they had agreed "that we ought not to enlist ourselves in this cause, without having some idea as to how such a project would be regarded by those having a special familiarity with the region and all other considerations."[15]

A final reason why Brewster may have introduced the measure stems from his relationship with Baxter. The two had been firm political friends and allies and had worked effectively together until the end of Baxter's tenure as governor. Thereafter they fought bitterly; and Baxter's nephew later surmised that Brewster favored the national park idea as much as anything else "to plague Uncle Percy."[16] Baxter felt that Brewster's motives were apparent: "first to injure me and second to get some political advantage by being instrumental in having a National Park in Maine."[17]

The goals of the bill introduced by Brewster in late March were ambitious ones. A month later, on April 22, it was replaced by H. R. 6599, which was identical except for some of the land areas to be included. The area planned for the Park encompassed all or parts of a total of about sixteen townships from the range of towns immediately east of the present eastern boundary of Baxter State Park, westward to the next range of towns to the west, the present northern boundary, and on the south, the West Branch of the Penobscot River, with a southward jut on the southeast to encompass an area south of the current boundary. The total area was about 400,000 acres, or twice the size of Baxter Park as currently established. A crucial provision was that title to the lands would have to be vested in the United States before the national park would be established. The United States was prohibited from purchasing lands with public funds, and lands "shall be secured by the United States only by public or private donations." The Secretary of the Interior was authorized to accept title to the park lands provided that no land could be accepted "until exclusive jurisdiction over the entire park area, in form satisfactory to the Secretary of the Interior, shall have been ceded by the State of Maine to the United States." The third section provided that the administration of the Park would come under the jurisdiction of the National Park Service, provided that no general development of the area was to be undertaken until all of the lands had been accepted by the Secretary of the Interior. One further provision was that the Secretary of the Interior could accept, for administration and protection by the National Park Service, title to the area comprising the existing Baxter State Park, or such other portions of the area described in Section 1, subject to the agreement by the state of Maine that if at least 90 per cent of the lands in Section 1 had not been conveyed within ten years of passage, the establishment of the national park would be abandoned and the lands reconveyed to the state of Maine. This last section was obviously designed to get around the limiting provisions of the second section and allow national control over a lesser area pending receipt of the larger holdings.[18]

Baxter returned to Portland about two weeks after the first bill was introduced. His reactions were predictable and quick. He established his unwavering hostility in a stream of letters and then began planning further action. In letters to the senators from Maine he reiterated his stand that he would never consent to ceding Baxter State Park to the federal government. To Senator Frederick Hale he wrote:

> My one great interest in this State is the Mt. Katahdin area. I shall be glad to tell you of my plans for the future but owing to their personal nature prefer not to put these plans on paper. All I ask is that the Federal Government leave this area alone and in due time the State will have a splendid Park that will be a credit to the State, to be held forever for the use of the people. I want nothing from the

146

people of the State of Maine other than their respect and I am no longer interested to hold any public position whatsoever.

During the past years I have worked with and for you and have made certain enemies by so doing. I shall continue to help you in the future and now I ask you to stand by me in this matter and see to it that this bill dies almost before it is born.

Nothing could be more unfair and unkind than to advocate a bill of this sort after what I have done for Maine. As I said in my letter to Dr. Pritchard, if the Federal Government wants to establish a National Park in Maine they have twenty million acres other than Mt. Katahdin from which to make a selection.

Nothing of a public nature could arise that touches me more intimately than this bill and I shall not rest in peace until I am convinced that it is definitely killed and there will be no further agitation in regard to it.[19]

Baxter also sent a copy of this letter and his letter to Pritchard of August 13, 1936, to Horace M. Albright, former director of the National Park Service, who had written Baxter asking his opinion of the park bill.[20] Albright was an old friend whom Baxter respected very much.

The replies from Maine's congressional delegation were interesting. Senator White stated that he would be reluctant to see the Brewster bill pass in view of Baxter's feelings and plans.[21] Senator Hale was more ambivalent than White. He noted that Brewster was still strong for the bill and said that he (Hale) would try to get Baxter to come to Washington to discuss the matter with the congressional delegation and the National Park Service in order to work something out. Finally, Hale noted that Brewster was working up considerable support in eastern Maine and that unless something were done to improve and take care of the park properly, Brewster "will soon work up strong public sentiment for his bill."[22]

Congressman Brewster wrote Baxter soon after his return and reminded him that his bill called for a ten-year period to determine what was best for the area. He also asked for a meeting in Augusta. When Baxter could not get to Augusta, he wrote a letter to be delivered to Brewster there. He urged him not to press the matter "because everything is going along well at present and the State is under little or no expense." He realized that Brewster was not aware of his plans "and of the establishment of a definite Trust in regard to the Mountain." Brewster's reply expressed concern over management of the park area and noted the advantages that the National Park Service had that no state or individual could match. But he said his mind was "entirely open with only the one objective in view of the greatest good of the greatest number . . ."[23]

Baxter also wrote to Governor Barrows, who had taken office three months earlier, stating the situation and reminding him of the state's

147

promises in the trust agreement. Barrows said the first he had heard of the proposed park was when a copy of the bill arrived, and he concluded: "I know of nothing more."[24] Since the Governor was a member of the Baxter State Park Commission it is difficult to see how he could have known nothing of the situation, unless that group was totally inactive.

At about the same time Baxter also wrote to his nephew John. Copies of much of the previous correspondence were enclosed. Baxter felt that while he was alive and well nothing could be done to break the trust, but that if anything happened to him, Brewster might accomplish his goals. He wanted to explain his plans to his nephew the next time they met "so that if anything should happen to me you can represent me and stand up for the honor of the family. As you are about twenty years younger than I am, perhaps between us we can outlive friend Brewster and thus defeat his plans."[25] Baxter, of course, took care of the matter himself by living for over three decades more.

He continued his attack on the proposed park by writing directly to National Park Service officials. Late in April he wrote to the director reiterating the various views already expressed and enclosing copies of letters sent earlier. He asked that these be read carefully despite their length. He noted that various good friends had suggested that he go to Washington to oppose the bill directly but, for the time, he refused. It seemed to him, he wrote, "that the man who gives to his native State its highest and greatest mountain, its chief natural attraction, in Trust to be forever held by said State, should not be called upon to defend his gift. Both ethically and legally the gift should defend itself against any attack such as that in H. R. 5864."[26]

Baxter, in some ways, was fighting against a federal-state financing situation with which he had disagreed while he was governor. Through the whole arrangement ran the question of where and how the Baxter State Park should be administered. At times, earlier, Baxter had felt that a national forest or park administered by the national government would be satisfactory, though it was obvious he preferred state control. After the creation of the Park, when better administration became imperative, he had pushed for the creation of a separate state commission to do the job. At that time no regular state park commission was in existence so the move was natural enough. His reactions to the creation in 1935 of the State Park Commission at the behest of the federal government are not recorded. He might have approved in theory of the Commission, with its modest appropriations that made possible continued federal expenditures in various proposed state parks, but he did not want that Commission to control his own cherished creation.

The State Park Commission, as created in 1935, consisted of the commissioner of Inland Fisheries and Game, the forest commissioner, and three citizens with staggered terms, of whom no more than two should be from the same political party. Four classes of "park" lands were set up: (1) any area of considerable size but not exceeding 10,000 acres combining either superlative or distinctive scenic characteristics and a reasonably varied or extensive or exceptional opportunity for active recreation; (2) areas not exceeding 1,000 acres, with or without distinctive characteristics, but containing such natural features as afford ample opportunity for development and use as an active recreational area; (3) any area included in the first two, not part of the highway systems, the primary purpose of which was to preserve the natural beauty of lands bordering such roads or to afford temporary stopping points along roads; (4) any strip or strips of land, with or without roads, highways and/or improvements required for ingress and egress to or from any of the areas described above, not exceeding in length the distance required to connect such areas with the nearest arterial or trunk-line highway, railroad line or terminal, or other public transportation facility or way. The term "memorial" was to define land areas for public use primarily because of their historic, archaeological, or scientific interest or value. The Commission was granted various powers and rights to acquire or accept land for parks, to make recreational and park studies and make recommendations to the Governor and Council, and to set aside, with their consent, lands for parks and/or memorials. The Commission also had the right to set rules for areas under its jurisdiction, though certain areas, including Baxter State Park, were specifically exempted. Finally, a major provision allowed the Commission to cooperate and make needed legal arrangements with the federal government.[27]

The Commission was given only $500 for each of the first two years of its existence. The federal government provided that after July 1, 1937, no work would be undertaken on other than federally owned land, unless the state had made adequate provision for maintenance, supervision, and similar responsibilities. By the spring of 1937 Maine had not done this and the Governor asked Robert Fechner, head of the CCC, to provide a statement of what was needed. The State Park Commission, working with National Park Service officials, was developing a plan of organization for the Commission based on an appropriation request of $15,000. In commenting upon the small appropriation request, a park service official pointed out that Maine had never been particularly "state park-minded" in the past and that the Commission was trying to develop the proper attitudes by means of education and instruction, "but without alarming or antagonizing those who have not yet been converted to the proper viewpoint." They therefore decided to keep the budget request small in order not to alarm opponents of park concepts. Among budget figures projected was a $2,500 total for Mt. Katahdin. This was planned under the assumption that the Commission would be able to acquire in the "near future, other land on the side of Mount Katahdin which can be developed into the more usual type of recreational area." Baxter State Park, it was felt, was one in name only since by terms of the gift, "the area is to be considered largely as a game refuge and preserve."[28] The Commission obviously never got the land at Katahdin, but the new federal policy also made it impossible for the Baxter State Park Commission to obtain more government aid. It is also possible that the close cooperation of the State Park Commission and the National Park Service and the announced intentions of buying land at Katahdin did much to alienate Baxter and caused him to oppose thereafter *any* suggestion that the State Park Commission take over administration of Baxter State Park.

The new developments also forced closer cooperation between Baxter and Great Northern. Relations between them had improved considerably. An official of the company wrote Baxter early in May, 1937, asking if the story he had heard that Baxter favored Brewster's bill was true. He realized that the bill allowed only for the acceptance of gifts, but he said Great Northern considered it an opening wedge and felt that once the limits of the proposed park were legally defined, pressures to appropriate funds to purchase it would arise. Since the lands were in the heart of the company's operating territory, the extreme effects would put the company on a liquidating basis instead of continuous operation. The company needed the lands, he said, and did not want them sterilized by "creation of a fancy park idea." On receipt of this letter, Baxter informed Great Northern of his opposition to the bill by telegraph first and in a following letter expressed his strongest opposition. He praised the company as Maine's finest business concern and said that with its opposition, the bill "certainly ought not to make any progress whatsoever."[29]

In his history of Great Northern, John McLeod said Baxter and President Whitcomb often discussed the proposed creation of a national park. Both disliked the New Deal intensely; and it is McLeod's belief that if Baxter "had ideas about a larger State Park, they jelled at this time into a plan to create one . . . big enough to eliminate any excuse for a Federal project of this kind in Maine."[30]

In late April Baxter also wrote to Mr. and Mrs. David Gray, residents of Portland who were related to Mrs. Eleanor Roosevelt, enclosing copies of his letters to Pritchard and Hale and asking them to intercede with the President. Roosevelt forwarded the letter to the Interior Department, requesting a reply. In a memorandum to the President in early July, Director Cammerer provided a brief biographical sketch of Baxter, indicated his attitude toward the national park concept, and briefly summed up the role of the park service in park planning. He said that the Brewster bill was introduced at the request of the people in Maine and not by his agency, though he did note that it was "contemplated that a final report upon the bill will be withheld until we have made further and detailed study of the project, which study will be undertaken this summer."

Roosevelt sent the memorandum on to the Grays and asked them to send it to Baxter and tell him "that I know of the splendid work which he has done for conservation and wild life."[31] The President did not commit himself in any way.

Baxter waited until early May to make his first major public statement concerning Brewster's bill. Then, in an interview, the results of which were widely published in Maine and other parts of the country, he made his views known.[32] The interview became the basis for a broad attack on Brewster's proposal by conservation groups throughout the nation. Baxter opposed Brewster's bill in much the same language he had used privately earlier—the inviolability of the trust provisions, the question of ethics, and the need of Maine to keep its promise to him. A major addition to earlier statements was his attack on a statement by Congressman Brewster, published first in a Millinocket paper, in which Brewster advocated location in the park area "of great log cabin hotels similar to those which have been established in the Yellowstone and Yosemite Parks."

During the remainder of May, Baxter continued his attack. He wrote letters to park service officials and to the Secretary of the Interior reiterating his arguments and adding that the state was financially capable of handling the costs of park maintenance. From Governor Barrows he asked for assistance. He distributed copies of his press release rather widely and did what he could to get groups in Maine to oppose the proposed national park. Most influential in this regard, perhaps, was the adamant opposition of the 5,000-member Federated Garden Clubs of Maine and a resolution of the AMC. Baxter was able to convince the Millinocket Chamber of Commerce to rescind an earlier resolution in support of the national park. These pressures, plus the need of the National Park Service to make a more detailed scientific survey of the proposed park prompted the Department of the Interior to request that the Committee on Public Lands of the House of Representatives take no action on the measure until the study was completed.[33]

During the summer, the intensity of the fight over the national park issue was probably responsible for eliminating some planned CCC work in the area. In April, Myron Avery had written to the park service requesting that a group from the Camden Hills State Park camp of the National Park Service be sent to complete the Roaring Brook road and build some lean-tos at the site of the campground proposed at that road's terminus. He reiterated his request in late May.[34] While the possibilities were being investigated, Avery again wrote, but this time he asked that his request for CCC workers at Roaring Brook be withdrawn. "In view of the Katahdin Park bill situation," he wrote, "it might be more beneficial to the area in the long run to have no CCC activity there this year and leave the completion of the road project until next year."[35] Avery also discussed the matter with Forest Commissioner Raymond Rendall, a

member of the Maine State Park Commission and of the Baxter State Park
Commission (still in existence at the time), who recommended to regional
officials of the park service that additional work by the CCC be put off
until 1938.[36] Avery's reasons were not spelled out, but it does seem apparent that he did not want much more work to be done in the Katahdin
area until the national park was assured; if too much were done the state
would find it easier to maintain the Park.

Conservation groups were split on the issue. The Appalachian Trail
Conference meeting in the Great Smoky Mountain National Park in the
early summer endorsed the national park concept when the delegation
from Maine remained silent on the proposal. At the same conference the
delegation from the AMC took no stand.[37] Robert Marshall, of the
United States Forest Service and a leading conservationist and proponent
of the wilderness concept, wrote to Baxter in early May and strongly
supported his stand. He felt that Baxter's views on what the National
Park Service did to areas it entered were fair and true: Katahdin would
not remain in a wilderness condition if the park service took over. He
understood, "from quite direct sources that some of the Park Service
people are already greatly annoyed that they can not go in there with
their development programs."[38]

More important was the support Baxter received from Robert Sterling
Yard, permanent secretary and president of the newly-formed Wilderness
Society in Washington, D.C. Yard had been a publicist for the park service
in his earlier years, but increasingly became estranged from it and used his
new organization to oppose its expansionist drive.[39] The correspondence
between the two men began in May and continued for several years.
Yard passed on information he gathered to Baxter and kept reiterating
that the park service could not be trusted; that it was attempting to rival
the forest service in size and appropriations. He praised Baxter for his
campaign and said that if the park service could learn of the attitudes in
Maine, it would "kill the alertness that now inspires them. 'Not yet,' I
can hear them say a little grimly."[40]

The team conducting the National Park Service study during the summer of 1937 consisted of five specialists in various disciplines who stayed
in the Katahdin area for eight or ten days. In addition to studying the
terrain and natural geographical and geological features, they prepared
special reports on animal and plant life. When Robert Yard passed this
news to Baxter, he said the report would recommend creation of an enlarged park. He was afraid that the park service would not consider it a
difficult matter to obtain the land from the state or private companies.
Baxter calmed Yard's fears about the attitudes of the landowners and
reiterated his faith that the people of Maine would uphold the Baxter State
Park trust provisions, and maintained that while he was alive the legisla-
152  ture would not violate its trust. "Moreover," he noted, "I come from a long

lived family and may be spared for many years. My father was ninety and had it not been for an accident my mother without doubt would have lived almost to that age."[41]

Although the field work for the report was completed during the summer of 1937, the actual preparation of the final report dragged on through the fall and winter. During the early fall, Baxter indicated his willingness to go to Washington to discuss matters with park service officials. Senator Hale prepared the way, and Baxter went in late October and talked with his adversaries. He found the federal officials fair and reasonable. Acting Director A. E. Demaray indicated it would not be ethical for them to push the national park matter until the report had been completed. He told Baxter, however, that while they felt the Katahdin area was of national park status, they would report to the Committee on Public Lands that they would not wish to recommend passage of the bill on account of the existence of Baxter State Park and Baxter's "unwillingness to transfer the lands."[42] Baxter returned home "much relieved in spirit" and hoped the matter had been settled.

Not long after his return to Maine, he added another dimension to the controversy and went a long way toward providing a solution favorable to himself. By November he succeeded in consummating the purchase of the 18,000-acre tract separated from the original park by an intervening town. He quickly arranged to turn it over to the state so as to buttress his argument against the National Park Service, and prepared a news release to appear in the papers for December 3, 1937. After describing the new acquisition, saying "there is no wilder region in the entire state," he emphasized that quadrupling the size of the Park did not complete his plans, for he had in view "extending the present Baxter State Park to even larger areas by the purchase of additional land." He again attacked Brewster's bill and repeated his view that Maine would never break its trust, and added that park service officials were men of "long range vision, uninfluenced by selfish or political motives and they can be depended upon in every way to do what is fair and right."[43] In the event anything happened to him before official transfer to the state of the land, he made necessary provisions in his will.

The release was widely printed throughout the state and was accompanied by favorable editorials. Baxter busied himself in clipping these and sending copies to Department of Interior officials.[44] Demaray wrote Baxter that as a result of the past summer's field investigations the service was preparing, as part of a report to Congress, a "suggested long range use plan for the area if it were to be administered as part of the national park system. This plan is being drawn along wilderness lines and admits only the minimum development essential to proper protection and public use by other than motorized means." He concluded by reminding Baxter that in his recent visit, he had said he and the park service had about 153 the same ideas, and he asked whether it would not be well for Baxter "to go over our plans in order that you might have the benefit of any ideas of value suggested by them?" Baxter was away on vacation when the letter arrived, so his reply was delayed for nearly two months. He had hoped the new acquisition would end the pressure by the National Park Service, but, he wrote, "I still see that you are interested and confess I am disappointed."[45]

Meantime, the proponents of the Brewster bill were not inactive. Brewster's insertion of Avery's article in the *Congressional Record* in June has already been noted. He played on the theme that the park area was in danger from overuse if adequate means of protecting it were not found. In October, Avery published another and similar article in *Nature Magazine*.[46]

By May of 1938, Baxter had been able to purchase 4,500 more acres for the Park. In his usual fashion, he sent copies of the clippings announcing the fact to his adversaries, with reminders of what he was doing and suggestions to the effect that they stay out of Maine. Director Cammerer praised Baxter's "good citizenship," but added: "I would be derelict in my duty, however, if I did not voice again the hope which has been expressed to you before, that the Katahdin region may sometime become a national park."[47]

The controversy achieved a new level during the late spring and summer of 1938, when several major newspaper articles appeared on different sides of the issue. In late April a Portland paper published a long article by Ronald L. Gower, editor of the AMC's *Katahdin Guide*. The article generally followed the lines Baxter had laid down earlier. Gower stressed that most of the important scenic points in the area were already safe, that a great park was being built without taxpayers' money. The Park was yet a young one; "perhaps certain unimportant mistakes have been made— perhaps others will be." But most important needs were being met and, he noted, the last legislature had made an appropriation for the Park (evidently he meant the $5,000 provided for highway work in the area). "It is better," he argued, "to bear with underdevelopment for a while and build wisely and well for the future." He emphasized the wilderness and trust deed provisions of the original grants and argued that they should be kept inviolate, and quoted prominent citizens of Maine to this effect. He refuted objections made by the proponents of Brewster's bill to increase the size of the Park by noting that the legislature, when creating the State Park Commission in 1935 had placed a 10,000-acre park size, but had specifically exempted Baxter State Park. Percival Baxter, he noted, contrary to some statements, was not a member of the Baxter State Park Commission. On the issue of maintenance, Gower wrote that there had always been two and sometimes three caretakers in the Park. His arguments tried directly to counter those put forward by Avery in the articles

154

cited earlier. Gower then listed the group of outdoor and conservation associations that were opposed or had expressly refused to support the creation of a national park. Aside from those already mentioned, were the Green Mountain Club, Brooklyn Institute of Arts and Sciences, Cosmopolitan Club, Explorers Club, and the Massachusetts Forest and Park Association. Finally, he recapped earlier Baxter warnings about the possible impact of national park stewardship: ". . . it is inevitable that many civilizing influences will of necessity be brought to bear upon Katahdin and the wild lands adjacent to it. Roads, skyline drives, concreted parking places at frequent intervals, and iron pipe balustrades are all right in their proper situation—so are sidewalks and office buildings. All would be equally out of place at Katahdin."[48]

Following his usual practice, Baxter sent reprints or copies of the article to Demaray, Cammerer, Marshall, and others. The article, he argued, represented "the overwhelming sentiment of the people of Maine." He also noted that if Maine broke the trust, the mountain would revert to him.[49] Robert Marshall replied that while he was a strong believer in federal activity, "in the case of Mt. Katahdin I believe your plans for it are best."[50] Baxter expressed his hope to Demaray that they would not get into "a long and perhaps bitter controversy." Demaray replied that he likewise would like to avoid conflict and reassured Baxter that "no unjustified action on our part will be taken," though a report had to be prepared for the congressional committee.[51]

Myron Avery presented a rebuttal to Gower's arguments in two lengthy and tightly-argued articles in the same Portland paper in late July and early August. They have all the aspects of lawyers' briefs, which, in effect, they were. He expressed astonishment at the bitterness of the opposition who, he said, made the proponents "the target of entirely unwarranted and unbecoming personal attacks, . . ." He argued that the proponents of a national park were solely interested in saving the Katahdin area from despoliation. Gower's attack, he felt, was "typical of the would-be rabble-raising, flag-waving demagogic tactics," calling on Maine to maintain her sovereignty and denouncing the "meddlesome outsiders, which we have seen in the past in connection with other conservation projects." In calling Gower an outsider as a resident of Newton, Massachusetts, Avery did not add that his own residence in Lubec was at best quite occasional. He also noted that, except for the Maine Garden Clubs, all organizations cited by Gower as opposing the national park concept were located outside of Maine. He argued that there was no necessary conflict between Baxter State Park and the national park proposal: the national park could be constructed to surround the State Park, which could be kept intact. Indeed, a national park would provide a buffer zone for Baxter Park. There was ample precedent in the west for such an action.

He discussed the "trust" issue, which he believed the state was not necessarily honor-bound to maintain. The 1933 action was "little more than a declaration of legislative policy and it is well-known that one Legislature cannot foreclose the right of a later session to amend earlier action." He argued that the rapid deterioration of conditions at Katahdin, the result of the huge influx of visitors as access was improved during the thirties, was the major reason for introduction of the national park bill. Since he and the Appalachian Trail Conference wanted to protect the northern terminus of the trail, they had drafted the bill to create the park and asked Brewster to introduce it. Whether the proposed bill passed or not, its introduction had stimulated activity in the area: "It has focused attention on the problems."

Avery went on to discuss the "emphasis on the preservation of the area in its primeval or wilderness aspect" that characterized national parks. He had seen the national park plan for Katahdin drawn up after the investigations of 1937, a report that had not yet been made public. He said it was predicated, not on the preservation of the wilderness aspects of the Katahdin area "but on the restoration of wilderness features, which have been dissipated by ill-advised and unfortunate developments." The Chimney Pond area and developments, an area virtually denuded in recent years, would be obliterated and allowed to revert to its original beauty. The Katahdin Stream campsite would be abandoned. Many of the roads recently constructed would be eliminated or terminated at such points as Togue Pond. The Millinocket-Nesowadnehunk road and its branches would be removed. Camping facilities would be constructed at Togue Ponds and at the west side of Nesowadnehunk Lake.

Avery next centered on the costliness to Maine citizens of continued state ownership and operation. As the Park was enlarged, the cost to the state would increase constantly. He questioned how the acquisition of Traveler Town in 1937 legally could be considered part of the Park. He noted the land in between would have to be acquired. He attacked Baxter's motives directly. He repeated an earlier charge that Baxter regarded the Park as a personal memorial, one which he developed after having been beaten in the race for the U.S. Senate in 1926. He questioned the extent to which natural features should give up control of their outstanding scenic asset to Baxter's undisclosed and unknown plans in return for the contributions of land he would make to the state. Then followed a rather unconvincing argument to which Avery would return a good many times. Any further increase in the size of Baxter State Park was illegal, he felt, because the statute creating the Maine State Park Commission had placed a limit of 10,000 acres on state parks. He dismissed the specific exclusion from this law of Baxter State Park by arguing that the provision referred to administration and not to park size, ignoring his own earlier argument that one legislature could not bind another.

156     He next turned to specific conditions at Katahdin. The lack of adequate

funding was reiterated and the fact that the Baxter State Park Commission had not exercised its power in the area during the Park's existence was stressed. The Abol and Sandbank trails (then outside the Park proper) had been obliterated by lumbering, and the magnificent stand of birches on Avalanche Brook was slated for the woodsmen's axes. Roy Dudley had provided the only supervision in the Chimney Pond area, but as a private individual had real difficulties when as many as sixty campers tried to crowd his cabin. Baxter's recent offer of $300 to the Millinocket Chamber of Commerce to build a hut on top of the mountain was to Avery an indication of "a complete failure to appreciate the problems involved." He derided Baxter's lack of concern for the financial situation. The $500 appropriation for each of the years 1937 and 1938 was ludicrously small, considering the $2,000 requested. He also noted Baxter's subsequent comment that "the mere fact that a leaderless Legislature declined to make a small appropriation is of no significance whatsoever." The decision of the Park Commission to build another cabin or bunkhouse at Chimney Pond was denigrated. Avery rather savagely indicated that $116 of the first year's appropriation was used to erect a bronze plaque of dedication similar to that on the summit.

He listed the imperative needs of the Park: the 24-person cabin should be built anywhere but at Chimney Pond; the Chimney Pond development should be obliterated and the area reforested; a custodian armed with adequate authority should replace the private individuals such as those who had functioned at Chimney Pond and elsewhere; reasonable public accommodations in a suitable area should be provided. Trails should regularly be maintained and signed.

Avery next attacked the Appalachian Mountain Club, of which he had been a member longer than Gower. Using Gower's words, he commented on the earlier lack of interest on the part of the AMC in the Katahdin area and noted its "outsider" status. The Club, he said, had refused to take part in measures to help improve the situation in the Park, such as extending its hut system to the area. He therefore questioned its sudden conversion.

Finally he wrote a plea for cooperation. All of those interested in the region could engage in constructive activity. Let Baxter and the AMC, he said, go through with their plans to add to Baxter State Park, but "let them particularly give heed, while they talk of the future, to the present situation at Katahdin and check the impending chaotic conditions which will become intensified with increased travel to the mountain. Let there be no more sanctioning of ill-considered developments."[52]

Avery's long articles were important in various ways. There is no question but that he pinpointed a great many of the difficulties surrounding maintenance and operation of the now rapidly expanding Baxter State Park. The state was obviously unwilling to provide funds for its adequate

157

maintenance. Percival Baxter, intensely proud of what he was doing, had ill-defined but long-range plans for solving these very problems.

What Avery and the National Park Service could not cope with was a seemingly implacable dislike of many Mainers for the New Deal. While Baxter was willing to go along with portions of the New Deal, when his interests were threatened he developed a major campaign to thwart federal encroachment. The people of Maine, now eager to support his ideas (though not financially), went along with him in favor of a state-based program. This situation was to be reenacted three decades later in the Allagash Wilderness Waterway issue.

There is little doubt but that Avery was right in arguing that his group's stance forced the people of Maine to begin to face up to the situation at Katahdin. Improvements were started, though they were never adequately financed. Funds were soon made available to hire a regular ranger for at least one section of the Park. Better arrangements were developed for administration; in 1939 a major change was made in this regard, as we have seen.

Finally, the charges and accusations levelled by Ronald Gower and Myron Avery in their exchange probably started a split or feud between two of the major conservation groups interested in the mountains of Maine. Both men were longtime members of the AMC. But the gradual development of the Appalachian Trail and Avery's position of leadership in the Appalachian Trail Conference (of which the AMC was a member), led to different approaches. Avery's Washington experience brought him close to the National Park Service; Gower's base in New England, where most wild lands were privately owned, led to a different outlook. During ensuing decades both groups made major contributions to the development of Baxter State Park. Had their activities been combined they might have done much more.

The immediate controversy over the proposed creation of a national park at Katahdin cooled quickly after the summer of 1938. When Congress adjourned in late June without having taken any action on the Brewster bill, it died, since the congressional session had been completed and unpassed bills could not be continued into the next congress. There is no indication that it had even emerged from the Committee on Public Lands. By the time the next term approached, Brewster was not willing to introduce the bill again. Brewster and Baxter had a talk, after which Baxter announced: "Brewster tells me that he will not take up the matter again."[53] After that time letters from National Park Service officials, Avery and his associates, and others indicated that a basic decision had been reached not to pursue the matter; however much some may have wanted a federal park, Baxter had stopped them.

Baxter's relations with federal park officials improved thereafter. He faithfully informed them of his latest purchases, probably to help ward off possible future attacks. He was asked to write articles for park service journals and was continually offered the advice and assistance of federal park officials at Acadia and elsewhere for betterment of the Park,[54] but there is little evidence that much actual cooperation took place.

The controversy was undoubtedly a major instrument also in delaying completion of the Appalachian Trail Conference agreement for the part of the Appalachian Trail in Baxter Park. Under this blanket agreement, the Conference had negotiated with landowners to run the trail through certain areas and to provide some protection for the routes. These were gradually adopted after the trail was completed. In 1939 and 1940, the Baxter State Park Commission (Authority) for a time refused to sign the agreement. The reasons were not stated, though in a letter asking for approval, Myron Avery alluded to the fact that it might have been because of "the personal opposition of Mr. Baxter."[55] Ultimately, as tempers cooled, the agreement was approved. By 1950, Baxter even became more well-disposed toward Avery.[56]

The coming of war and the rapid expansion of Baxter State Park finally stilled the national park controversy. In 1952, when Brewster was running for reelection to the United States Senate, Attorney General Ralph W. Farris opposed him in the primary election. Farris recalled Brewster's attitude in the late thirties and wrote to Baxter asking him to look into his records for more detailed information. Farris planned to use Brewster's stand on the national park issues to attack him during the primary campaign. Baxter replied, giving some information on the fight, but said: "In view of his having made complete amends and of his having assured me that he would withdraw the Bill and would never take any further action to interfere with Baxter State Park, it would seem unwise and unfair to bring the matter into the present political campaign." Baxter was trying to keep out of political controversy and feared that if the Park was brought into controversy his name would also become involved because "the Park and myself are inseparable. This being so I hope you will not disturb the present peaceful situation." Farris agreed that he would not disturb the situation, but noted that it was a matter of public record and "can be borne out by the Congressional Record that such a bill was introduced by Mr. Brewster when he was a member of the House and it was aimed against the rights of the people of Maine, and if this matter should be brought into the campaign you may rest assured that I have not had anything to do with it as I will regard your wishes in this matter."[57]

HAROLD J. DYER

Thawing out on the trail in a setting that epitomizes the spirit of mountain woods. Looking at this photograph taken in the 1940s, one can imagine the cushioned silence of a Katahdin trail in winter.

One of the consequences of the national park controversy was a change in the administration of the Park in 1939. The law was a brief one. It simply repealed the 1933 measure creating the Baxter State Park Commission and provided that all the lands in townships 3, 4, and 5 in range 9, and 3 and 4 in range 10, W.E.L.S., that had been given to the state, or which would be given thereafter, would forever bear the name Baxter State Park. The lands will be "under the joint supervision and control of, and shall be administered by the state forest commissioner, the commissioner of inland fisheries and game and the attorney-general and the said commissioners and attorney general shall have full power in the control and management of the same."[1] Two years later, the act was amended to include township 5 range 10 and any lands already given or to be given thereafter by Baxter in Penobscot and Piscataquis counties.[2] This was undoubtedly done to clear up problems that might have arisen over any lands to be acquired and given by Baxter in T5R10 and areas of Penobscot County. Baxter acquired title to T5R10 in 1940 and from time to time was interested in the Katahdin Lake area and in lands in T6R8 in the Grand Lake region.

Neither law specifically named the administering group, though it very quickly assumed the name Baxter State Park Authority.[3] The law said nothing as to the limits of the power of the Authority in administering the Park, enforcing the laws, leasing of lands turned over to it, and numerous other key questions. It was left to the Authority itself to set up its own internal operations and procedures.

Not until 1949 did the legislature spell out some of the Authority's powers. It was then empowered to establish "such rules and regulations as it deems necessary" to protect and preserve the Park, protect the public, and uphold and observe conditions provided in the deeds of trust. Before any rules were promulgated they were to be checked by the attorney general to make certain they were in conformity with the law, and were then to be published once a week for two successive weeks in a newspaper printed or published in either Piscataquis or Penobscot County. Then, after being posted in four places in the Park, they would become effective. Violators of the rules could be punished with fines of no more than $50

and costs, or by imprisonment for not more than thirty days, or both. Anyone convicted of mutilating park property or structures or any posted notice, rule, or regulation was subject to similar punishment.

The law also gave the Authority police supervision over the Park. The agents or representatives designated by the Authority were "authorized and empowered to arrest with or without warrant any person within the state who is committing, or to detain, until a warrant has been obtained, any person within the state who has been seen by said agents or representatives committing any offense against the state laws, or any violation of any rule or regulation" of the Authority. Dwelling houses could not be searched without a warrant and then only in the daytime, and no sealed railroad car could be entered "for purpose of such arrest without such warrant." Trial justices and municipal courts within their counties were given original and concurrent jurisdiction with the superior court in all prosecutions. Violators who were arrested were to be taken "with reasonable diligence" to the municipal court nearest the site of the violation, even if that meant taking the violator to a municipal court in a different county than the site of the violation. However, if a trial justice held court in the county where the offense was committed and if that court was closer to the scene of the violation than any municipal court, violators could be taken to trial justices for warrant and trial. Finally, there was a provision that the Authority would not interfere with members of the Maine State Park Commission, the Department of Inland Fisheries and Game, or the Forestry Department and their duly appointed agents in the legal exercise of their duties.[4]

Under these laws the Authority gradually developed a set of procedures and policies. Not all of the pertinent records are available, so it is difficult to determine how often the Authority met and how it arrived at decisions. Unlike the situation that was to occur after 1950, when the forest commissioner was chairman and handled much of the detailed work, all three members appear to have been involved to a considerable degree in the decision-making process. The attorney general had a good deal of legal work to do in the matter of accepting lands from Baxter as well as in drawing up leases. The fish and game department was involved with enforcing game laws and protecting the sanctuary; while the forest commissioner was involved with forest-fire protection and other work. George J. Stobie, commissioner of Inland Fisheries and Game, was a member of the Authority during the entire period. His office took charge of the bookkeeping and detailed paper work for the Authority during his tenure. Raymond E. Rendall was forest commissioner until January, 1948, when he was succeeded by Albert D. Nutting, who served for a decade. Most changes occurred in the office of the attorney general. Franz U. Burkett served from 1939 to 1941; Frank I. Cowan from 1941 to 1945; and Ralph W. Farris from 1945 to 1951. Because of the limited documentation available, it is difficult to assess the quality of their work for the Park or compare their effectiveness. From what material is extant, Baxter seemed to work most effectively with Stobie.[5]

There appears not to have been an official chairman until 1946; letters to members of the Authority before that date do not indicate who was in charge, though the attorney general signed much of the correspondence. Perhaps the term "joint supervision" in the legislation setting up the Authority was taken to mean just that. In 1946, after a spring meeting, Attorney General Farris wrote to his fellow member Raymond Rendall, commenting on receipt from Rendall of minutes of the last meeting in which he, Farris, was elected chairman. Forest Commissioner Rendall had penned a note on the letter: "You are the official Sec'y. George & I framed you last time in making you Chr. for the meeting only. Otherwise we have no Chr."[6] From that point on, despite Rendall's disclaimer, Farris became the actual chairman and remained so until he left office.

In the Park itself there appears to have been no one individual outside of the Authority who exercised supervisory powers until Harold Dyer, of South Portland, who had graduated from the University of Maine with a degree in Forestry and Wildlife in June 1940, was hired to make a reconnaissance in the Park. By the end of the summer he held the title of ranger and later on was styled chief ranger and finally supervisor, when, after an interruption of four years of service in the United States Army, he returned to the Park and remained until the summer of 1950.

The financial situation for the Park had remained grim for a number of years after 1939. In that year the legislature had failed to provide funds for the use of the new Authority. At the beginning of the year, just as the legislature was about to meet, Baxter sent a telegram asking incoming Governor Barrows to speak positively of Baxter State Park in his inaugural address. Baxter was particularly concerned to have Barrows uphold the trust concept against encroachment by the national park scheme and sent a suggested wording for Barrows • address.[7]

In 1941 the Authority requested an appropriation of $5,000. Attorney General Burkett appeared before the budget committee to justify the request, and after he left office agreed to watch progress of the request through the legislature. This he did not do; the committee cut the item out of the appropriation bill, and by mid-March the Authority wrote: "We did not realize that no appropriation had been provided for in the budget committee's request until just recently."[8] Its restoration in the reduced amount of $4,000 for each year of the biennium was requested and granted.[9] For the following biennium the allocation was $3,500.[10] From this was deducted $1,506, authorized by law in 1943, to be paid the Maine Forestry District for the protection of the Park.[11] For the fiscal year July 1, 1946 to June 30, 1947, the legislature appropriated $3,000 over and above the amounts needed for paying the Maine Forestry District and the estimated $500 that would be received in fees. Of the total $3,500 actually available, $3,066 was for salaries. The clerk for the Authority noted that aside from the $2,400 paid to the supervisor, only $666 was left for hiring seasonal help—this would allow one man for eighteen weeks or two men for nine weeks. Since the Authority had already committed itself to personnel and operating expenses at a considerably higher level, it applied for and received an Executive Council grant of $2,000 from the contingent fund of the state to balance the budget.[12]

By the fiscal year 1949–50 the legislative appropriation had risen to $12,064 (up from $7,500 in 1947–48), of which $4,251.36 went to pay the Forestry District tax. With revenues amounting to $3,864.82, a total of $11,677.46 was available for expenditures. Of this, $896.92 was allowed to lapse back to the general fund at the end of the year. In the same fiscal year the first $12,000 of the $25,000 for capital expenditures at Roaring Brook and in the northern part of the Park were disbursed.[13] Senator Roland H. Cobb, of Denmark, later to be a valuable member of the Authority and commissioner of Inland Fisheries and Game, played a vital role in obtaining passage of appropriations.[14] Fees received during the period had risen from $245 in 1940–41 to $1,599.50 in the fiscal year 1947–48. Though expenditures remained very low for the size of the Park, progress had been made.

By the end of the decade of the thirties there was only one campground actually within Baxter State Park. That was at Chimney Pond. Leroy Dudley was caretaker and kept the fees he collected; he was not a park employee. In 1938 the Baxter State Park Commission had authorized construction of a large camp at the site, and in the following year Baxter requested and received $500 from the Executive Council's contingent fund to assist in its construction.[15] But by the end of that year the camp still was not completed.

Myron Avery continued his attacks on Baxter and the whole concept of state control. The topic, while not on the official agenda of the meeting of the ninth Appalachian Trail Conference held at York's Twin Pine camps at Daicey Pond from August 18 to August 26, 1939,[16] was widely discussed, since one of the trips during the conference was a hike over the Hunt Trail, past Katahdin Stream campground, to Baxter Peak and then down to Chimney Pond. Avery had long singled out Katahdin Stream and Chimney Pond as the most blatant examples of neglect and mismanagement by the state in his arguments for the creation of a national park. In an issue of the *Appalachian Trailway News* in the following year, he took the opportunity to reiterate his argument.[17]

At Avalanche Field and Roaring Brook, the road terminus on the east side of the Park still on private land, camping increased late in the decade. Forest Ranger Jack Grant operated a string of packhorses out of Avalanche

Field. On the other side of the mountain, the campsite at Katahdin Stream
often called Baxter Camp, was further developed in 1939 with the addition of four lean-tos. Also off the Park, it was administered by the Maine Forest Service, as it had been since its development by the CCC earlier in the decade. It was manned in 1939 by Richard Holmes, later an engineer in Presque Isle. Just who paid for Holmes's services is unclear from the records. There are some indications that either the Maine Forest Service or the Department of Inland Fisheries and Game did so. Former Baxter State Park Supervisor Harold Dyer stated in an interview several decades later that Holmes was paid by the Authority and that he was, therefore, the first regular employee of the Park.[18] Since Holmes's successsor was paid by the Forestry Department, it is likely that was the case in 1939.

For all of these areas the problem of use by large numbers of people was intensified during the late summer of 1939 by the incredible adventure of Donn Fendler. After his return to civilization, hundreds of hikers, attracted by the publicity given to the long search, headed for the Katahdin region. According to the Maine Development Commission, "Record-breaking throngs of hardy hikers and outdoor lovers from all parts of the country are flocking to this section. . . ." Chimney Pond, which normally had 25 to 35 hikers a night, saw an increase to 125 to 150 per night; and on one night in mid-August 210 people camped there.[19]

The saga of Donn Fendler is probably the single most widely publicized event in the history of Baxter State Park. On July 17, shortly after noon, the twelve-year-old youth from Rye, New York, set off from Katahdin Stream campsite to climb Katahdin by way of the Hunt Trail. He was accompanied by his father, two brothers, and two friends, Henry Condon and Fred Eaton. Young Fendler and Henry Condon moved ahead of the main party and reached cloud-enshrouded Baxter Peak. Since he became cold because of the clouds and strong wind, Fendler decided to descend from the summit and go back toward Thoreau Spring to meet the rest of the party, although Condon tried to dissuade him and urged him to wait for the arrival of another hiker who was approaching the peak from the Knife Edge. In the driving wind and dense clouds, Fendler soon lost the trail and did not meet his father and brothers.

During the next eight days, until the afternoon of July 25th, when Nelson McMoarn, the proprietor of the Lunksoos Camp on the East Branch of the Penobscot River, heard his weak cries for help and hurriedly crossed the river to bring the emaciated boy back, Fendler made an epic journey of at least thirty miles through incredibly rough country. In the course of the trip he lost his clothes and subsisted for much of the time on berries. Those most knowledgeable about the area believed he had crossed the plateau to a point near the head of the Saddle Slide, continued on an irregular course through the dense brush farther northward, and then either descended into The Klondike, the Northwest Basin, or else followed over the Howe Peaks to the Tracy Trail and then descended to Wassataquoik Stream. He followed the stream or the tote road beside it past New City and Old City clearings and other points, and then diverged from the stream and followed the Robard Pond route and reached the East Branch, which he followed southward along the west bank on the old Telos road to a point opposite Lunksoos Camp.[20]

Fendler was the object of one of the most intensive search efforts in the history of the Maine woods. At the peak, at least six hundred persons—private individuals as well as members of the Maine National Guard, many Maine Guides, and dozens of wardens and patrolmen from the Maine Forest Service and the Department of Inland Fisheries and Game—scoured the area thoroughly. They concentrated their search around the Hunt and Abol trails, as well as in the Great Basin around the Saddle Trail, at the top of which bloodhounds had lost their scent. Little did they realize that Donn had crossed to the northern side of the mountain and each day was farther away from the area in which they were searching.

The boy was fortunate indeed to survive such an ordeal. He had violated several of the cardinal rules of hiking in leaving his party. But he also showed an amazing desire and ability to survive under adverse circumstances. He received a hero's welcome in Millinocket and a medal when he was released from the hospital in Bangor.

The Fendler drama and its publicity led to a rapid increase in the use of the area during the remainder of 1939 and on into 1940, with an estimated ten thousand people visiting the area and Baxter Peak in 1940.[21] The Fendler incident pointed up other problems on the mountain. One was the nearly total lack of supervision and control of the area. Another was the fact that there were virtually no signs on the trails of the mountain. The rapid growth in the size of the Park after 1940 created more problems since decisions had to be made regarding use of the land. By then Baxter had purchased the portion of T4R9 that contained Russell Pond and the private camps on that lake owned by William F. Tracy. In early 1941, the Authority formally ordered him to vacate the premises. He was not offered any money for his improvements, so he appealed to the legislature and was awarded $2,600 in 1943. All but two of the camps on the site were torn down.[22] The land on which the Katahdin Stream campsite was located became part of the Park in 1941, and formal control over the operation of that site was transferred from the Forestry Department to Baxter Park.[23]

In 1940 the Baxter State Park Authority made one last try to have a CCC camp located in the area. Forest Commissioner Rendall wrote to the National Park Service director in early March that Baxter had contacted him to "inquire as to the possibility of constructing trails to and around the mountain and bridal [sic] trails to the summit." He asked whether it would be possible to obtain a CCC camp for the park area if

166

development plans were available from the BSPA. He was told that there would be a camp at Camden until September 1, but that side camps were increasingly difficult to set up; yet he was urged to make an application. This he did in mid-June. On the day before, June 13, Rendall met with two park service officials, one of whom was Conrad L. Wirth, supervisor of recreation and land planning for the park service. As Wirth reported later, he told Rendall:

> . . . we could not put camps in areas which had a limited work program and which had no means of maintaining the improvements when they were put in. I told him as I recalled it the Katahdin area is governed by a board with no appropriation whatsoever, and we had no assurance that if any improvements were put in they would be maintained. I told him that if he was on the spot and had to make a request for a camp that he should write the letter and we would answer, telling him frankly that we could not consider the matter under the present circumstances.

Rejection of Rendall's proposal followed in a letter shortly after.[24]

The situation in the Park had begun to change when, on June 1, 1940, Harold Dyer started service as a park ranger. His friendship with Richard Holmes, Dyer later stated, got him the job. Whether he was paid by the Authority or the Forest Service is unclear, but he was clearly a park employee, hired to develop a management plan for the rapidly growing Park.[25] A "reconnaissance" would best seem to describe his activities, since during much of the first summer he spent his time "going over the country to get a feel of it." His report of what he did during his first month shows an extraordinary pace of activities.

During the two and a half-week period after he actually began working in the Park on June 4, Dyer brushed out the Hunt Trail and cleaned up around Thoreau Spring and Baxter Peak (June 4); checked out the trail to West Branch of the Penobscot (June 5); checked the Abol Trail and met with Leroy Dudley at Chimney Pond and returned to Katahdin Stream (June 7); travelled around the Foss-Knowlton Ponds, Abol Stream and West Branch (June 8); looked over the trail from Roaring Brook to Chimney Pond (June 9); attended his commencement at the University of Maine (June 10); checked Hamlin Ridge Trail, cleaned out Caribou Spring and helped hikers over the Knife Edge to Pamola (June 11); met with Rendall and checked York's camps (June 12); travelled to Roaring Brook, Katahdin Lake and returned to Katahdin Stream through Chimney Pond (June 13); travelled up Sourdnahunk Road to Slide Dam, climbed Mt. Coe and went into the floor of the Klondike and returned (June 14); travelled Abol Trail to Abol Mountain and Rum Mountain (June 16); went down Katahdin Stream to Foss-Knowlton Ponds, across to Lost Pond, to York's, and returned to Katahdin Stream (June 17); to Chimney Pond to help the Bates College Outing Club (June 18–19); after helping the club went through the Northwest Basin to Russell Pond (June 20); from Russell Pond to Chimney Pond to Katahdin Stream in "a hard snow storm" (June 21); to Kidney Pond and nearby ponds to check on fishermen (June 22). Based at Katahdin Stream, he walked (and often brushed) practically every trail on Katahdin and travelled as far north as Russell Pond and as far south as the Penobscot River. In his reports he made running comments on what he saw and did and also included a lengthy list of jobs a CCC side camp might do.[26]

From fragmentary evidence, his pace scarcely slowed during the summer. In July he wrote to Myron Avery and asked for a list of needed trail signs for Katahdin that had been prepared during the Ninth Conference at York's Twin Pine camps the previous summer. The list had been given to Everett F. Greaton of the Maine Development Commission, who had hoped to get help from the CCC or elsewhere in having the signs prepared and installed. In his reply, Avery asked Dyer to repair the roof of the lean-to on the Hunt Trail and also suggested that the downed shelter on Davis Pond in the Northwest Basin not be rebuilt, since the danger from fire was so great.[27]

More important during the summer were Dyer's contacts with the AMC. Just before he left the service of the Park on September 15 to attend graduate school at the University of Maine, Dyer had talked with Ronald Gower, who had led an AMC expedition/trail maintenance group based at Wassataquoik Lake during the first week of September. The Club made the trip with Baxter's blessing and cleaned up all trails on the mountain and in the Russell Pond area, except the Hunt and Abol trails. In the process Gower and his crew painted the four trails leading out of the Great Basin and installed signs at their own expense. Gower promised to prepare and forward additional signs during the fall. This cooperation was to become much closer the following year.[28]

The accomplishments of 1940 and the overall situation with regard to Baxter State Park in that year can be best analyzed by summarizing the lengthy report Dyer submitted as part of his work during the summer.[29] In his analysis of the situation and in his suggestions for change, Dyer demonstrated a keen intelligence and an ability to envision the potential exhibited by a much larger park.

He began his report by stating that the development policy to be set up for the "present and proposed park" depended on several factors. One was whether the state wanted to develop the Park as a whole immediately or develop each new acquisition. It also depended on the availability of CCC manpower. He went on to divide his report into sections on recreational development, forest development, fish and game development, personnel, and equipment. He thought the three eastern townships in range 9 were most susceptible, because of their forest type, to game management,

while the western ones were primarily for timber development. Recreational interests were concentrated in T3R9.

He first dealt with these. At the Katahdin Stream campsite were the
caretaker's cabin; nine lean-tos with tables and fireplaces; six sheltered
picnic tables and fireplaces. There were overnight accommodations for
sixty people in the lean-tos and thirty in tent sites. The caretaker was John
O'Connell, in the pay of the Maine Forest Service, who was allowed to
run his own small store and sell wood. Dyer noted a long list of maintenance problems and abuse of the area by users. On July 22, the land on
which the campground stood was deeded to the state by Baxter and on
August 1, after hiring Bernard Gardner to collect them, fees of 10 cents
per person per night were assured for camping privileges. (A week later
the Authority received its first complaint regarding the fees.)[30] Two highway patrolmen lived at the campground as well. In 1939 the Forest
Service had built a lean-to type camp, which was used by Dyer, Gardner,
and occasional game wardens. Dyer discussed at length the repairs and
construction necessary at Katahdin Stream. Aside from a new dam and
caretaker's building, he suggested that six shelters and two picnic tables
be added. The removal of rubbish and garbage had become a problem,
particularly after the campground was turned over to the Park. Dyer noted
that a half-ton truck was needed for the next season. Finally, he suggested
that a park supervisor's cabin should be located at the main camp entrance.
If CCC labor were available, he suggested that an additional four lean-tos
be constructed.

Foster Field, he felt, should be developed as a tenting and trailer
campsite. In effect, this would be an overflow site for Katahdin Stream.
Tied with it would be redevelopment of the trail to Doubletop Mountain.

At Chimney Pond Dyer thought the problems not as intense as at
Katahdin Stream because of Dudley's effective management. The campground contained eight lean-tos; the caretaker's cabin (built by the state
in 1924); the new and incomplete camp authorized in 1938, and a number
of tent sites. Leroy Dudley was completing nearly fifty years of work
and service at the site as caretaker. Dyer and Gardner did much work
on the new cabin and performed other maintenance work. Dyer suggested
possible uses for the new cabin and for the caretaker's cabin, which needed
much work on the interior. He thought the Authority would have more
control over the caretaker and the campground by placing Dudley on the
state payroll; but since Dudley had indicated his intention of retiring in
two years, Dyer suggested continuing the present system until that time.
With the adverse weather conditions and the dangerous fire situation at
Chimney Pond, Dyer thought the cabin there should be "developed into
a camp similar to the A.M.C. huts of the White Mountains." If land at
Basin Ponds became available to Baxter and the state, he thought the 169

lean-tos should be removed from Chimney Pond and a new campground built at Basin Ponds. Trails from Basin Ponds to Pamola and Hamlin Ridge could then be reopened.

Contrary to most thinking at the time, Dyer believed that the road from Avalanche Brook to Roaring Brook should be closed and a campground developed at Avalanche Brook. Jack Grant was already at the site with his packhorse string. Avalanche Brook could serve as a basis for reopening the Keep Trail, continued maintenance of the three and a half-mile route to Basin Ponds, and as the center for a horse trail system. For the time being, however, Roaring Brook was made an official lunch ground in 1940. Neither Baxter nor the state yet owned the site.

In the newly-acquired Traveler area and Wassataquoik region, Dyer argued that development of facilities should not precede control of the area by park personnel. Finally, he noted the existence of unofficial campsites in the Northwest Basin "with its broken down leanto," Klondike Pond, Saddle Spring, New City, Old City, South Branch ponds, and Slide Dam.

Turning to trails, Dyer had many suggestions. The development of trails in the "back area," he argued, should be from Avalanche Brook, and the approaches from Grand Lake on the northeast and from Stacyville on the east should be eliminated or discouraged. The Hunt Trail he found generally in good shape, though cairns and paint blazes were needed above timberline. He also noted that signs warning about climbing under adverse weather conditions should be posted at Katahdin Stream and at timberline; this was a suggestion destined to be repeated for decades afterward to no avail. Dyer then discussed the work of the AMC and Ronald Gower on the trails from Chimney Pond, and, as so many did before him and were to do after him, complained of the condition of the trail between Roaring Brook and Chimney Pond. The Basin Ponds-Chimney Pond section he said could easily be redone, but from Basin Ponds to Roaring Brook, on land owned by Harry Ross of Bangor, the situation was far worse and reconstruction would be a "sizable task." If done, he thought, it should be developed as a horse trail and a fire break.

The trails on the mountain itself were adequate for the present, and there were ample trails into the back wilderness; "future trail building and improvement should develop along with the campsites and their control." The existing horse-trail system from Avalanche and Roaring brooks to Chimney Pond and into the Wassataquoik Valley could be extended easily to the North Peaks and elsewhere if sufficient demand arose. In this connection, Dyer was critical of Jack Grant in his practice of rerouting existing trails to accommodate his horses. While most of this was being done on lands owned by Harry Ross, Dyer suggested that "a letter would curb his [Grant's] ambitions somewhat."

The need for more signs was also stressed. Aside from those set up by Ronald Gower, Dyer suggested using the Appalachian Trail Conference list sent by Myron Avery to Everett Greaton; but that the ATC mark should be eliminated and "some symbol for the State Park" substituted. The roads, he thought, should be widened to two-car width and straightened out and should include turn-offs.

Dyer next turned to forest management practices. He noted that in large fires in 1867, 1903, and 1915 large parts of the current park area had been burned and that lumbering operations had removed most of the merchantable timber from the upper Wassataquoik and from the Trout Brook and Nesowadnehunk watersheds. The differences between the western portion of what became the park area, which had been burned very early, and the eastern portion, which had been cut over or burned several times in the 20th century were still vivid and dramatic at this time. He noted the sorts of forest that were returning in these areas and the cutting that was going on in various parts of the region. Dyer suggested that as new lands were added to the Park they be surveyed and cruised to learn what timber resources were available. Cutting of wood for campsites and for the sporting camps should be done under the direction of the supervisor with emphasis on "silvicultural stand improvement, particularly along the roads" and restriction of intensive cutting within 100 feet of roads and trails.

He had many recommendations concerning forest protection. Fishermen and hunters built fires without permits or control in all sections of the Park, thus creating hazards. Until W. F. Tracy was evicted from Russell Pond early in 1941, he had some control over the Wassataquoik region; Dyer recommended opening of additional fire towers, the placement of a patrolman at Togue Pond, and changes in the telephone system, which entered the park areas from Millinocket, Stacyville, and Patten, to provide more effective communication.

On fish and game management Dyer said that much poaching was going on in fly-fishing areas. He recommended close studies of the existing fish and game resources, and if CCC labor was available, the development of a fish hatchery below Katahdin Stream campground.

To administer the Park Dyer felt that the position of park supervisor should be created and said that the services of two rangers, in addition to campground caretakers, should be obtained. Each ranger would have a commission as a deputy game warden and should wear a distinctive uniform and badge (also to be worn by the caretakers). For the rangers he set down a list of responsibilities for the period before opening of the campgrounds and after, much like that developed in later years. Until July 1 the rangers' chief job, aside from trail, campsite, and telephone maintenance, would be to help game wardens control fishermen; after that date, their primary duties would be to serve hikers. After Labor Day would come reconstruction work, surveying, trail maintenance and construction, cutting firewood, and similar tasks.

171

In this report Dyer showed that he had developed a fairly deep knowledge of the existing park area and what it might become in the future. He stressed the need for the Authority to gain real control over the areas it acquired and then plan specific developments. He was wrong, as events later demonstrated, in his suggestions regarding Basin Ponds, but otherwise his recommendations for development could be readily defended. All that was lacking was money.

Dyer returned to Orono to begin graduate work in wildlife research and to write a thesis on wildlife management in Baxter State Park. This particular topic was developed as the result of a plan by the University of Maine, the Cooperative Wildlife Research Unit, the United States Bureau of Biological Survey, the Maine Department of Inland Fisheries and Game, the Maine Forestry District, and Baxter State Park to apply for a federal grant from the Fish and Wildlife Service of the Department of the Interior to investigate and survey the status of mammals and game birds in Baxter Park and the larger wildlife sanctuary. The carrying capacity of the sanctuary would be estimated and plans prepared for game management and development. In making the application it had been decided that Dyer would represent Baxter State Park. The grants were made possible by passage of the Federal Aid in Wildlife Restoration Act, or the Pittman-Robertson Act as it is usually known, which passed Congress in 1938. The application was approved in late January 1941, at about the same time that another grant to construct cabins for fish and game personnel work in the wildlife sanctuary was awarded.[31]

The research team, of which Dyer was the co-leader, went to work immediately and, under trying circumstances with the impact of war and the difficulties in obtaining trained personnel, submitted its complete report by the deadline on July 1, 1942.[32] In the interim, leadership was changed six times and sixteen men were hired to maintain a six-man team. During the winter of 1941 the team ran the boundaries and then ran east-west cruises at half-mile intervals through townships 3R10, 4R10, and 5R10. A decision had been made to survey all of these towns even if they were not yet officially in the Park, since it was expected that they eventually would be. Notes were taken regarding forest-type changes, physical features, and signs and observations of wildlife. In the late spring and summer, close surveys were made of deer and moose yards in various parts of the Park and surrounding areas; these were reported on at length. In midsummer part of the eastern boundary of the Park and sanctuary were run. Forty-five miles of park and game preserve boundaries were marked before all work ended on December 15, 1941. During a four-month inactive period beginning in August, the team from the other Pittman-Robertson project (5-D) built new camps at Roaring Brook, Katahdin Stream, Burnt Mountain, and Lower South Branch Pond; and rebuilt one of the buildings at Russell Pond that the Park had taken over

the year before. These buildings were for the use of fish and wildlife personnel in administering the wildlife sanctuary, but were turned over to the
Park fairly quickly. Later reclaimed by fish and game personnel, they became a source of considerable controversy.[33]

During the last part of the winter the research team concentrated on
the three eastern townships. They mapped several areas in detail for the
first time. Except on Turner Mountain, where moose yards were located,
the team found far fewer moose and deer in the eastern townships. In
view of a later experiment in the Park, it is interesting to note that the research team constantly kept in mind the feasibiliy of liberating caribou.
Katahdin had been the last stronghold of the caribou in the eastern United
States. Though the team concluded that further investigation was necessary before making a final decision, the tentative conclusion was that the
area did not seem "too promising as caribou range. . . ."[34]

Due to the war and the shortage of personnel there could be no immediate follow-up on the research program. Dyer went into the service
almost as soon as the program was completed. Much had been learned
about the wildlife present in the Park, however, and a number of valuable
buildings had been constructed, which eased considerably the administration of the area. Baxter's reactions to this construction are not recorded.

While working with the wildlife research project, Dyer had also returned to his duties as park ranger at the Park in the summer of 1941. The
Authority accepted his suggestion regarding park leadership; and after
interviewing several candidates for the position, selected Dyer as supervisor. With apparently a fairly wide degree of freedom in making policy
decisions, he assumed his position in May.

Late in the season he helped escort Governor Sumner Sewall and
Attorney General Frank I. Cowan on a hike up Katahdin. Sewall was the
first Governor since Owen Brewster to climb the mountain while in office.
After his return Cowan wrote a fine description of the trip in a letter to
Myron Avery.[35] Otherwise, Dyer's work in the Park is best described by
discussing his report for 1941.

As in the previous year, Dyer presented a long, well-organized summary of work done during the summer and proposals and recommendations for further action. He divided it into three sections on recreational
development, forest fire control, and forest and wildlife management. In
his introduction he noted passage of the 1941 law on park administration
which he said provided a development policy to include the entire proposed park area. He considered his report of 1940 as a basis for park
management and development and based his 1941 work schedule on that
report. The $4,000 appropriated by the legislature for the fiscal year be-
ginning July 1, 1941, allowed the Authority to buy a pick-up truck, "its
most needed piece of equipment."

Dyer noted a sharp drop in attendance during 1941. This was attribut-  173

GOVERNOR KENNETH CURTIS AT BAXTER PEAK

able to fire bans imposed on three different occasions, totalling nearly three weeks; the horrible condition of the roads; and a gasoline shortage scare that had developed as the nation mobilized for war. Dyer detailed the terrible condition of the roads and said that few vehicles got through to Katahdin Stream or Roaring Brook without dents, scrapes, or broken tires, springs, or crankcases. Unless some maintenance were performed the roads would be impassable by 1942.[36]

A major need, he felt, was to get specific control over the camp-grounds, for this would mark the beginning of active management of the Park. At Katahdin Stream he convinced the caretaker, John O'Connell, to relinquish his position in favor of his son-in-law Fred M. Pitman. Pitman, "a competent and knowledgeable woodsman," had worked on the CCC project in the area during the previous decade and ran a sporting camp nearby until 1935, when he was burned out in a forest fire. Dyer felt that Pitman was much better suited for the job than O'Connell, who stayed on to run his small store at the campground for the season. Pitman was to serve the Park as caretaker, ranger, and occasional temporary supervisor until his retirement in 1954. Dyer had again based his operations at Katahdin Stream and with the assistance of Pitman and two patrolmen, presumably paid by the Forest Service, had begun expanding the campground. Late in the year, when the new camp built with Pittman-Robertson Act funds was finished, the Park took charge of it and Dyer moved in and used it as his headquarters. The fee for lean-to use was increased to 15¢ per night while the cost of tent and trail sites remained a dime.

At Chimney Pond Leroy Dudley was placed on the park payroll at the start of the season and the 25¢ fees he collected were taken by the Authority. With 1,800 camper nights, the use of Chimney Pond was about half that at Katahdin Stream. Dudley and his wife were allowed to rent out blankets, sell wood and various sundries, and retain the receipts. In addition, Mrs. Dudley cooked for some camp groups. At the end of the regular season, the entire park crew moved to Chimney Pond and virtually completed work on the large bunkhouse or "Hotel," as Dyer called it, which was originally authorized in 1938. For the 1942 season Dyer recommended the addition of a kitchen wing and also allowing campers, for a fee of 50¢ or 75¢ per night, to use it, with the Park providing mattress pads and blankets. He did note that the vegetation at Chimney Pond had "shown a remarkable increase in height" and that nearby cut-over areas "are also responding beyond expectations." He again recommended development of a campground at Basin Ponds.

At Roaring Brook Dyer appeared to back away from his recommendations of the previous year. He recommended further improvements of the road and parking lot at the terminus and improvement of the lunch ground by the addition of picnic tables. No lean-tos should be built then, he thought, "though they may be desirable in the near future." No mention was made of developing Avalanche Field.

Important developments regarding trails came in 1941. The Hunt Trail was maintained and also the Appalachian Trail as far as the West Branch of the Penobscot. Dyer recommended that the Park assume responsibility for maintenance of the trail from the summit all the way to the West Branch. Also, he felt, the Park should make certain that the cable bridge across the West Branch, built in 1935 by the CCC with some state funds, be maintained, since it was the only place to cross the West Branch between Ripogenus Dam and the lakes. He expected that the University of Maine Outing Club would assume responsibility for its ongoing maintenance.

Most of the remaining trails in the park area were maintained by a trail crew from the AMC, which visited the Park for two weeks in July.[37] As-     175 serting that he had the authority to act, but also acting with Baxter's knowledge of what was to take place, Dyer had negotiated with Ronald Gower and on June 4 signed an agreement by which the Club adopted as "official club trails" the Dudley, Knife Edge, Saddle, Northwest Basin, Cathedral, Hamlin Ridge, North Basin, and Basin Cut-off trails. The Avalanche Trail would be added as soon as it was cleared of slash. Later in the decade, the Club cleared and assumed maintenance on the North Peaks Trail as well. In addition, the Club agreed that in 1942 it would rebuild and maintain the shelter at Davis Pond in the Northwest Basin. The Park Authority would maintain the Great Basin Trail to Chimney Pond. The AMC agreed to provide signs for the trails named and for other trails if the Authority desired.[38] Gower had prepared 38 signs in 1940 and added 15 more in 1941.

Dyer saw a need to develop wilderness trails in the Russell Pond area and suggested that a forest service patrolman be stationed at Tracy's old camp there. He indicated that the Wassataquoik tote road within the Park would be cleared and also that a tote road was to be built northward from Roaring Brook to meet an existing road in the Wassataquoik Valley. This would be on land still privately owned. There is no indication that Baxter knew anything of this possibility, which fortunately was never carried out.

Development of horse trails was also contemplated for the Park. Dyer noted that a horse trail had been developed from Avalanche Field to the site of an old lumbering camp on the side of South Turner Mountain in 1941 and thought it could easily be extended to the summit. He listed alternative routes to the North Peaks from the north and east, but thought a usable horse trail from there to Baxter Peak "may prove difficult due to boulder fields."

Dyer's recommendations regarding forest and wildlife management are interesting. He noted the terms of the deeds of trust and recommended that definite primitive areas be established which would remain untouched. But he noted that there were many, many acres with no scenic value "that should be managed as a forest crop for future years, and there are now small areas of merchantable timber that can be managed with an expected yield a few years hence." If this were done the remaining stands would be improved. Not to cut such areas, he said, was a "waste of resources." As for game management, he noted that there was no hunting of predators in the Park, as was the case in many game preserves elsewhere; but that "animals doing malicious damage, like the bear and porcupine around camps, are removed." He concluded the report with a discussion of the Pittman-Robertson wildlife management project.

Dyer raised a number of interesting ideas and proposals for the action of the Authority in this report. He presumed that sufficient funds would be made available beginning the next year. If the personnel situation remained unchanged, the proposals were obviously overly ambitious. There THE 1940s is no record of any reaction by the Authority or by Baxter to most of the items in the report, except the sections on roads and the agreement with the AMC. Baxter must have seen copies and it would be fascinating to know his reactions to Dyer's ideas on forest management within the Park, since they coincided closely with one aspect of Baxter's work and interests. In any event, most of the program had to be abandoned with the entry of the United States into the Second World War late in the year.

Two of the issues Dyer discussed were followed up during the ensuing period. The first was the condition of the roads in the immediate area of the Park. Baxter had indicated his concern about them in September 1941 and planned a talk with members of the Authority. After a gasoline company travel editor reiterated Dyer's statements about the lack of maintenance, some action was promised. Undoubtedly under pressure from the Maine Development Commission, the Authority, and Baxter, the chairman of the Maine Highway Commission requested and received $2,200 from the state's contingent funds in the spring of 1942 to repair the Sourdnahunk road.[39] In 1943, the legislature designated the existing road between Millinocket and Greenville by way of Katahdin and Ripogenus Dam as the Baxter State Park road and provided $2,500 per year for its maintenance, particularly in the area of the mountain.[40] Though there was some improvement in the roads during the next year or two, their condition was very bad at the end of the war.

The other issues involved the assumption of responsibility for the maintenance of many miles of park trails by the AMC. Despite wartime conditions, the Club sent a crew to clean up the trails in 1942 and fulfilled its promise to reconstruct the shelter at Davis Pond. A twelve-person, enclosed-type shelter was erected.[41] Thereafter, in most years, especially from 1944 onward, AMC trail crews, usually led by Ronald Gower, spent some time each year performing the promised maintenance work. In 1946, to celebrate the hundredth anniversary of Thoreau's climb of Katahdin, the Club held its annual August Camp at the mouth of Abol Stream.[42] Working with Dyer in mid-decade, the crews rerouted the North Peaks trail and brought it to standard. This work was continued until 1960 when it was converted to cash payments.

Although Harold Dyer included a copy of the agreement he had made with the AMC concerning the shelter at Davis Pond in his report for 1941, the members of the Authority apparently forgot about it. Two years later, when Vice President Ronald Gower of the Club wrote to Baxter on several occasions, he discussed the construction of the shelter. Baxter also had apparently forgotten the agreement and contacted Attorney General Cowan and gave him copies of the letters. Cowan asked Gower by what authority the shelter had been built; Gower, in turn, produced relevant portions of the lengthy correspondence he had had with Dyer 177 and other park officials. In a letter dated May 2, 1941, Dyer had declared: "Under the present setup, I have been given complete charge of the administration of the area; and of course it is essential that all activities such as your trail crew and its work, be approved by me and work under my supervision." Gower had written to Baxter on April 5, 1941, and told him that the Club would rebuild the shelter. Baxter replied a week later and said he would see the Authority and discuss the matter.[43] It is obvious that the administration of the Park was extremely loose at the time. Dyer did not feel that the Authority should clear all major policy decisions. Even when members of the Authority were informed of what was going on, they did not always react.

During the war years the AMC was the most active group in the Park and its aggressiveness and presence ultimately caused a reaction. In 1944 Attorney General Cowan, then the member of the Authority most interested in development of the Park, made two trips to the region to learn more about the situation. He concluded a report to Baxter and Authority members by noting: "Many people [feel] that the Appalachian Mountain Club has charge of the Park area or at least has full authority in regard to trail marking and shelter building on Mount Katahdin." He recognized the fine work done by unselfish volunteers and "would not for an instant suggest that we be other than most friendly with all mountain lovers and especially with the members of the Appalachian Trail Conference." He felt, however, that the Authority should "keep in touch with Mr. Avery and with his successors in the Appalachian Mountain Club to the end that the Authority and the Club may work in perfect harmony."[44] In the last two sentences he confused the Appalachian Trail Conference and the Appalachian Mountain Club, but it was obvious that he felt the Authority should play a firmer role in administering the Park than it had in the past.

In 1942 the impact of American entry into World War II had been felt deeply in the Park. The number of visitors had dropped off sharply. Even more important were changes in personnel. On February 15, Leroy Dudley was crushed beneath the wheels of a pulp truck in which he was riding from Stacyville on his way to check his trap lines, one of his activities in the off season.[45] He had spent five decades in the Katahdin area and was the most widely known and beloved individual connected with Katahdin and the Park. Early in the summer, Harold Dyer, who had been given a healthy raise by the Authority,[46] had entered the Mountain Troops as a second lieutenant, and his services were lost for the duration of the war.[47]

Before his departure, Dyer prepared a report on his activities to date. With Fred M. Pitman in charge once more at Katahdin Stream campground, the usual maintenance work and improvements were being carried out.[48] At Chimney Pond the use was so slight that a caretaker had not been appointed to replace Dudley. Though the lean-tos were being used, the camps were closed for the season. Irwin Maker, the patrolman who had come onto the park payroll during the previous year, was loaned to the Fish and Game Service until July 1; after that he took charge at the Roaring Brook camp in order to control and observe movements in that portion of the Park. Dyer had several conferences with William F. Tracy concerning his working at Chimney Pond or at Russell Pond as a patrolman. He decided that Tracy could be best used at Russell Pond and hired him for that purpose. The weekly wage included the use of Tracy's horses for fire patrol work. Near Russell Pond the immediate large project was construction of a six-man lean-to at New City to shelter hikers in the area. Dyer laid out additional work on trails, camp maintenance, and repair of telephone lines for Tracy and others. Finally, Dyer provided the Authority with information and suggestions regarding communications systems and campground facilities.

The Authority placed Fred M. Pitman in charge of the Park after Dyer's departure. Pitman spent much of the summer carrying out the work plan that had been laid out.[49] He remained in charge, without official title, until the end of the war and Dyer's return.

Some personnel problems arose very soon after Dyer's departure. Dyer had not obtained the approval of the Authority when he hired Tracy for Russell Pond and in early July the Authority instructed Pitman to terminate Tracy's services. Tracy's arguments that he was not interested in the job at Chimney Pond and that he was hired by Dyer to work at Russell Pond as caretaker until October 1 were to no avail when in late August the Authority decided to refuse to pay him after July 11. Tracy had worked nearly a month and a half after his termination notice.[50]

Little is known regarding activities in the Park during the remainder of World War II. In 1943 the U.S. Army Air Force was given permission to use a portion of the Park for training purposes for a one-month period.[51] Pitman remained in charge at Katahdin Stream, and the Maine Forest Service had a man at Roaring Brook camp or other points in 1943 and 1944.[52] No record is available as to the total number of visitors in the Park during these years. The number of people reaching the summit of Katahdin and signing the register there declined from about 2,500 in 1940, to 234 in 1942 and then rose gradually to 276 in 1943 and to about 400 in 1944. In 1946 the total had increased to 1,908.[53] The editor of the *Appalachian Trailway News* noted in 1943 that the drop in the number of visitors would undoubtedly be beneficial, particularly for the Chimney Pond area.[54] But the region was virtually totally open, with no controls on those who could obtain the needed gasoline or who had the time to visit the area.

Baxter visited the Park on several occasions during the war. He was generally accompanied by Chief Game Warden Caleb Scribner of Patten, with whom he was very close. In September 1944 he spent several days at the warden's camp on Lower South Branch Pond, built earlier in the decade with Pittman-Robertson Act funds. During this trip, his first to the area, they used the newly-constructed tote road along Trout Brook from Matagamon Lake to "The Crossing," and then the rough tote road, still usable for horse-drawn wagons, to the pond. While they were in the area, a large party of AMC members came in to camp on Upper South Branch Pond. Baxter and Scribner greeted them and later paid them a visit at their campsite.[55] Later in the decade Baxter began his regular inspection trips when Dyer and members of the Authority would "show him his park."

As noted earlier, Attorney General Frank Cowan visited the area twice in 1944 to study "local problems at first hand." Cowan stressed the need to mark the boundaries and suggested that a strip of land on the boundary be cleared so as to mark it clearly. He modified arguments he had presented earlier regarding severely limiting roads in the area and suggested that the proposed CCC road from Togue Ponds across the West Branch of the Penobscot to a point south of Ripogenus Dam would provide a fine vantage point for those wishing only to view the mountain. He believed this project should be put on the postwar building agenda for the state; otherwise pressure would rise to build a broad turnpike from the Togue Pond locality to the junction of Sourdnahunk Stream. He even toyed with the idea of making this a toll road that would exempt hikers who had climbed Katahdin from payment. He felt that there should be a closer supervision of trails and better maintenance at the various campgrounds. After the war, he argued, Chimney Pond campground should be carefully reconditioned and developed.[56]

The most exciting incident to occur in the Park during World War II was the crash on the night of June 19, 1944, of a C-54 cargo plane on the northeast slope of Fort Mountain, about 300 feet below the summit. Seven crew members and passengers were killed. Rescue workers cut a trail from the tote road near Katahdin Stream campground. After the bodies and essential cargo were removed, the bulk of the plane was left where it crashed and is visible to this day. The approach route used in the rescue was used as a trail by curious hikers for several years but soon became overgrown.[57]

Harold Dyer was discharged from the Army in January 1946 and soon obtained reappointment as supervisor. Almost immediately he made preparations for the summer season. The budget he prepared and considered essential for simple maintenance with little development called for a deficit of over $2,000. He believed that his work plan of 1941 should be completed and detailed his plans for improvements at the campgrounds. He urged that use fees at all campgrounds be set at 25¢ per night for shelters and tent sites and 50¢ for the large cabin at Chimney Pond. He also made numerous recommendations regarding telephone communication,

180

fire control, trail development, and control in the Wassataquoik Valley,
where he argued the Maine Forest Service should maintain a patrolman,
since the Park could not afford one.[58] In general, the Authority approved
Dyer's suggestions. Increased use fees and an allocation from the state contingency fund took care of the expected deficit.[59]

The summer was a busy one. Fred Pitman continued to serve as caretaker at Katahdin Stream campground, which again was the busiest one
in the Park. Dyer hired Ralph Robinson to serve at Chimney Pond, where
there had been no caretaker since 1941. Jack Grant again operated his
string of packhorses out of Avalanche Brook, which was still privately
owned. The use of the Park was about 80 per cent of the totals for 1941,
but with the increased availability of gasoline and automobiles, a more
rapid growth was expected the next year. The park staff and trail crews
from the ATC and the AMC performed their usual maintenance work.

During the postwar years, Dyer and others connected with the Park
continued the long-range planning he had started earlier in the decade.
Late in 1946 Dyer again provided members of the Authority with an extensive report and set of recommendations regarding development of the
Park.[60] He noted that the size of the Park, then 116,228 acres and soon
to be 141,605 acres, created control problems not normally encountered in
smaller park areas. Since its isolation limited travel and use of the area,
fees charged to users at campgrounds would pay only for their maintenance. Funds for general administration and development would have to
come from the legislature.

Dyer recommended a better location for the park headquarters than
at Katahdin Stream, where it had been since 1939. A site near Togue
Ponds would provide more efficient communication and fire-fighting coordination and allow for more effective work in emergencies; and it could
be leased from Great Northern.

Next the supervisor recommended the establishment of three ranger
districts in the Park—in the Sourdnahunk, Wassataquoik, and Trout Brook
watersheds. Developments in the latter area could be delayed for the
present. The northern part of the Park had been made more accessible
during the war when the Eastern Corporation began to exercise its cutting
rights in T5R10. The Grand Lake Fire road was extended to Black Brook
Farm by the summer of 1944, and further extended to McCarty Camp,
only five miles from Sourdnahunk Lake, two years later.[61] The Sourdnahunk and Wassataquoik districts would be controlled out of Roaring Brook
and Katahdin Stream campgrounds respectively. The rangers would handle
campground maintenance at first, but as funds became available the functions would be separated. The ranger districts would also serve the Maine
Forestry District for forest-fire protection. Rangers, he said, should be
employed on a full-time basis.

The wretched condition of the roads was described. Only $2,500 was   181

AT TOP OF CHIMNEY POND TRAIL
The "Chimney" stands out in this fine photograph by Jake Day, and it is easy to see how this trail got its name.

available to provide maintenance for twenty-six miles of road from
Millinocket to Sourdnahunk; in 1946 an extra $1,000 was earmarked for
the Togue Ponds-Roaring Brook road, the last four miles of which had
never been worked on by a road machine. Brush growing beside the narrow roads had not been cut since 1940 and provided a real hazard to
drivers. At least $10,000 annually was needed to maintain the one-car
width gravel roads.

Dyer next discussed recreation development. Though camper use of
the facilities in 1946 was less than in 1941, more money had been realized
since the 25¢ per camper night charge had been established at both campgrounds. Dyer recommended construction of additional facilities at Katahdin Stream and a continuation of the rehabilitation program at Chimney
Pond, though he reiterated his earlier argument that the latter campground be removed entirely since it marred the scenic attractiveness of the
Great Basin. Also adverse weather conditions in the Basin rendered it a
less than ideal camping place. With a major campground at Basin Ponds,
where "the weather is more settled," the old trail to Pamola could be reopened.

Dyer also argued for the development of a large campground at
Roaring Brook. This was necessary to provide adequate control of the
eastern side of the Park. He preferred a location at the Maine Forest
Service campsite at Avalanche Brook, but since that was still in private
hands he settled on Roaring Brook. While operating his packhorse string
at Avalanche Field, Jack Grant also served as a relay in the inadequate
telephone communication system from Chimney Pond to the outside
world and maintained some oversight and control of the movement of
hikers into the Wassataquoik Valley, where forest-fire protection was weak
and needed improvement.

In addition to the major campgrounds, Dyer recommended that
wilderness campsites be maintained at one-day intervals along first-class
foot trails. Currently, the double shelter in the Northwest Basin was the
only such facility available. Plans to build shelters near the crossing on
Wassataquoik Stream and to improve trails in that area had to be abandoned for lack of funds. Dyer felt that campsites should be provided near
the inlet brook of Wassataquoik Lake, McCarty Field, Black Brook Farm,
the outlet of Lower South Branch Pond, and at Pogy Notch.

The continued dependence on outside assistance for maintenance of
trails was noted. In addition to the organized clubs maintaining trails,
private individuals also maintained trails to O-J-I and other mountains.
The rotting of the slash along the Abol Trail had proceeded sufficiently to
allow reopening of that route, which, with the Hunt Trail, would provide a
convenient loop trail to Baxter Peak. A new shelter at the site of the
collapsed Sewall camp on the route was recommended. Trails to Mt.
Coe and South Brother were to be opened to travel and the Double Top

trail would be cleared and signed in 1947. Dyer was also surveying the possibilities of building horse trails on Katahdin.

Finally, he discussed at some length the development of forest and wildlife resources in the Park, which, he said, "go hand in hand." He noted particularly the damage done to much of the white birch in the Park by the bronze birch borer.[62] The most notable loss was the well-known stand of pure white birch trees at the headwaters of Avalanche Brook, on land owned by Harry Ross. Abe Chase had built a sawmill on the approach road above Togue Pond to cut the timber.[63] With the exception of areas being cut over, Dyer wrote, the forests "are approaching a solid block of second growth which is only slightly broken up by natural openings and recent burned-over areas." As the forests approached maturity, he said, there would be a marked change of types and populations of wildlife in the areas; deer, beaver, woodcock, and ruffed grouse would decline in numbers; while moose, marten, fisher, snowshoe hare, red squirrels, spruce grouse, most small mammals, predators, and to some extent bear would increase in population. To insure that certain animals would not be driven out by the extremely dense growth, Dyer urged that small openings, in valleys away from scenic areas, should be created by controlled burning or cutting. He recommended the continued maintenance of a forest and wildlife management program.

Various recommendations made by Dyer were acted on during the years following. In the late spring of 1947 Great Northern leased a plot of land in T2R9 near Togue Pond to the Authority as a site for the proposed headquarters building.[64] Construction began in the fall of 1947 on the double lot. The lumber for the main building was obtained from the camps at Slide Dam previously built by Great Northern. The rest of the camp, "built in bits and pieces" from lumber and materials scrounged from various places, was soon closed in and was used during the 1948 season. Finishing touches and various outbuildings were added later as time and money became available.[65] Dyer's recommendations regarding the establishment of ranger districts and the separation of functions of rangers and campground caretakers had to await larger appropriations. At Roaring Brook controlling the increased number of visitors became more difficult after the 1947 season, when Jack Grant discontinued running his string of packhorses.[66] Before the 1948 season began, Dyer again urged quick construction of the campground at Roaring Brook, or at least the allocation of funds to allow him to maintain a ranger at Roaring Brook to control movement of hikers and campers on the east side of the Park and to develop camping facilities at the site. Nothing could be done until the legislature met the following year.[67]

Dyer's reports undoubtedly helped spur the Authority and Baxter to request legislation further clarifying the power of the Authority. The law passed in 1949 has already been discussed. Dyer and the Authority drafted

184

a set of regulations but they were not put into effect until the summer of 1950. Enforcement of any rules, Dyer felt, required more singular identification of the rangers as employees of the Park. This would take the form of new badges to identify their proper employer rather than badges which carried the designation of Ranger, Maine State Park Commission, or Maine Forest Service. In addition, Dyer thought that he and the three men he would have working for him on a semi-permanent basis after July 1 should have distinctive uniforms. The Authority approved of these suggestions,[68] but uniforms were not purchased for over a decade.

The Authority requested funds from the legislature in 1949 for the construction of campgrounds at Roaring Brook and in the Trout Brook section, which was still largely undeveloped. As indicated earlier, the legislature appropriated $25,000 for this purpose. Construction at Roaring Brook began in August when a bulldozer roughed out the campground area. Before the first snow fell a garage and ranger's quarters were erected; the parking lot was enlarged and the necessary roads and camp sites were cleared and partially graded. The area was sufficiently developed to allow camping the next season when the campground was officially opened.[69]

Work was delayed in the northern end of the Park while all efforts were directed toward completion of the Roaring Brook facility. The ultimate location of the proposed campground remained uncertain. In 1949 and 1950, Dyer and presumably the Authority members were leaning in the direction of building on the shore of Matagamon Lake. An initial reconnaissance was made in 1949 but detailed surveys remained to be done.[70] In the end, the campground was built at Lower South Branch Pond.

The initial development of the campground at Roaring Brook was Harold Dyer's last major accomplishment in Baxter State Park. During the late spring of 1950, he was offered and accepted the position of director of state parks for the Maine State Park Commission. He had been considering the new position for some time and had discussed it with members of the Authority. He made certain that administration of Baxter Park was going smoothly and promised that he would check into the operations with his successor, Robert H. Dyer (no relative), who was coming from Mt. Blue State Park to replace him. Fred Pitman, the veteran ranger at Katahdin Stream, was asked to take care of transitional problems.[71]

Dyer had performed extremely well with the limited funds available to him. In leaving, he provided still another report summing up the developmental work done to that point and making recommendations for the future.[72] He reiterated most of the issues discussed in previous reports. The increased size of the Park, he argued, called for additional campgrounds and greater emphasis on the development of the Trout Brook region. Lack of funds, he admitted, had made impossible adequate maintenance of facilities and trails in much of the Park. The Russell Pond area, for instance, had seen little maintenance work since it was acquired in 1941. The construction of campsites along the Trout Brook road and at McCarty Field was recommended. There was particular need for implementing the ranger district concept and for adopting the rules and regulations that had been discussed. A new campground should be constructed on the shores of Matagamon Lake in the northeastern corner of the Park where more land had recently been acquired; Dyer foresaw rapid growth there.

In the late spring of 1950 five men were employed on a regular basis. Aside from Robert Dyer, Fred Pitman was in charge at Katahdin Stream where he was regularly slated to work eighty-four hours a week. Edward C. Werler at Chimney Pond, Ralph D. Robinson at Roaring Brook, and Ralph G. Dolley at Russell Pond rounded out the crew. Dolley was employed for a sixteen-week season, the others for thirty-two weeks. Though the Park had been divided into ranger districts, as Harold Dyer had recommended earlier, no distinction had yet been made between district rangers and campground operators; the employees performed both functions. Robert Dyer was the only individual employed for the entire year.[73]

Though interrupted by the war and plagued by the serious shortage of funds, much had been done by the Authority and Dyer and his crews during the previous decade. Their job had been made more difficult by the rapid increase in the size of the Park. In contrast to the situation in the 1930s, when no real planning for the future had been done, it was apparent that members of the Authority and Dyer were making and developing long-range plans to provide for more orderly administration. The steady improvement of highways leading northward toward the park area meant that the number of visitors would continue to increase at a rapid rate and that even more facilities would have to be provided for them. Percival Baxter continued to visit the Park several times a year and was deeply involved in all major decisions regarding its operation. Something of his long-range financial plans for maintaining the Park was becoming apparent when he established the trust fund in 1946. At this time, however, he had not developed the close contact with park employees that was to come while Helon Taylor was supervisor.

Much had been accomplished but more remained unfinished. Given the size of the staff and the level of appropriations, one can only marvel at how much had been done. The meager state appropriations were supplemented by federal aid through the Pittman-Robertson program and the personnel of the Maine Forestry Department and the Department of Inland Fisheries and Game, both of which kept wardens in the area. The progress made was a monument not only to Governor Baxter, but also to the extraordinary efforts of the employees who were willing to work extremely long hours for small salaries.

The year 1950 marked the departure of Harold Dyer as supervisor of the Park, and after a short hiatus, the assumption of that role by Helon Taylor, who served until his retirement in 1967. The actions of his immediate successors provided no change in the style of operations, but in 1969 Percival Baxter died and when the funds he left to the state for the operation of the Park became available, the nature of the whole operation changed dramatically. The period was marked also by considerable stability in the make-up and nature of the Baxter State Park Authority.

Following Baxter's wishes, the governance of the Park remained unchanged during the period. Even though he complained about some actions by the Authority late in his life, until the time of his death Baxter continually reiterated his confidence in it and its members and resisted any attempts to reorganize it or place the Park under control of the State Park Commission. In 1945 he wrote a warden in the Maine Forest Service that the park administration "is perhaps the best we can do," but asked for comments on how it might be improved. "I hesitate to turn it over to the State Park Commission," he wrote, "and prefer that it be maintained as a separate unit independent of all other areas."[1] He often discussed the structure of the Authority with Albert Nutting, who later wrote that Baxter's "review of the subject ended with a statement that he knew a dead man couldn't run a park, but a designated group could under outlined principles."[2]

Most suggestions for changing the administration never got beyond the talking stage. When the Maine State Park Commission in 1956 suggested spending a million dollars to develop park facilities, Baxter reacted violently to the idea that the Commission should presume to determine policies for his Park.[3] In the same year a Chicago consulting firm, the Public Administration Service, under contract to the state to recommend changes in governmental organization, bluntly recommended that the Authority should be abolished; the State Park Commission should have jurisdiction over Baxter Park. Upon being told of this recommendation, Baxter asked Austin Wilkins to appear before the legislative committee handling the PAS Report and express Baxter's feelings. "I am quite sure that my wishes will be respected, but if it ever comes to the Governor we

187

would have another chance to prevent the absorption of the Authority into the Park Department."[4] The recommendation was not accepted by the legislature.

In 1967 Representative Leon Crommett of Millinocket, at the behest of the local Fin & Feather Club, introduced a bill in the legislature that provided for adding the representatives from Greenville and Millinocket to the Authority and also provided for a rotating chairmanship. The Fin & Feather Club, which held a lease on park land beside Abol Pond, had long been unhappy with the administration of the area and the restrictions placed on their activities within it. This was an attempt to make the Authority more amenable to local pressures. Baxter reacted strongly; he argued that the Authority had "taken extra good care of the Park," and said the bill was "a personal attack against what I have done in creating Baxter State Park." The present membership of the Authority, he felt, was familiar with the operations. "I want them to carry on without any change being made." Those suggested, he said, "would ruin harmony." Besides, any changes made without his permission would violate the terms of the trust deeds by which the land was given. "I hope the time has not come when the wishes of one who has created the most unique park in the country, would be disregarded," he added. When hearings were held on the bill only members of the Fin & Feather Club supported it; the legislative committee recommended that it not pass.[5] What is important about this last attempt to change the nature of the Authority is that it once again provided Baxter with an opportunity to state unequivocally his position with regard to the administration of the Park. It would make difficult any later attempt to alter it, whatever the merits might be. In a letter to Austin Wilkins late in the same year, Baxter said, "I shall never forget what you and the Commissioners with you have done. I want to keep in close touch with those of you who have charge of this wonderful area. It is difficult for me to express the feeling I have for you and those who have worked with you."[6]

The membership of the Authority varied somewhat over the years, but overall there was a good deal of stability and in no year was more than one member changed. George Stobie, commissioner of Inland Fisheries and Game, was chairman of the Authority when he left office early in 1951. He was succeeded as commissioner by Roland Cobb of Denmark, who as a member of the Senate in 1949 had done a great deal to secure passage of the largest operations and capital expenditures budget for the Park to that point. Cobb served ably for ten years and in turn was succeeded by Ronald T. Speers. The next position in the Authority, that of attorney general, was held by Ralph W. Farris until early 1951. He was followed by Alexander LaFleur until 1957; Frank Harding until 1959; Frank Hancock to 1965; Richard Dubord to 1967, and James S. Erwin until the end

188

of the period. The third member of the Authority, the forest commissioner,
was by far the most important in this period. Albert Nutting served until
1958 when he became director of the School of Forestry at the University
of Maine. He was succeeded by Austin H. Wilkins, who had had a long
career in the Maine Forest Service. Wilkins became chairman immediately
and remained so until his retirement.

Members of the Authority varied widely in their degree of interest in
park matters. Least interested appeared to be the various attorney generals.
It should be remembered that the position was a half-time one. Unless an
incumbent took a personal interest in the Park and its welfare as Erwin
did after 1967, the attorney general's contribution was not likely to be
a major one. The various commissioners of Inland Fisheries and Game
played a more important role, since they were concerned with enforcing
the fish and game laws in the game preserve. They regularly used park
facilities and controlled several cabins in the Park that had been built in
the 1940s. Since none of them became chairman of the Authority during
this period, they were less concerned with the details of operation. Most
important by far were the roles played by Nutting and Wilkins. Both men
worked very effectively with Baxter, and both were devoted to development of the Park. Assuming the functions in 1951 that had previously
been handled by the fish and game department, the forest commissioner's
office provided bookkeeping, ordering, secretarial help, and other essential
administrative services for the Park. This allowed the Authority to function
with a much smaller budget than otherwise would have been the case.

There were no set dates for meetings of the Authority. The members
generally convened in the late winter or early spring to act on plans for
the coming season; and usually they met during the summer months when
they, in company with Baxter, made an inspection of the Park. These
annual inspections were important in planning, and they usually lasted two
days and three nights. Baxter, Authority members, Taylor, and others
generally met in Millinocket the night before the park tour began. The
next two days or portions of them were spent in checking the facilities and
discussing plans. In the late summer or fall, the inspection was often
concluded by a dinner meeting in Millinocket that was attended by park
rangers and their wives. Otherwise the Authority met whenever the
pressure of business warranted. As the Park was expanded and its use increased during the two decades, meetings tended to be held more frequently. The Authority generally dealt with larger policy, such as development of the campgrounds, establishment of rules and regulations, determination of budgets (though most of the detailed work here was done
by the Forest Service), establishing fee schedules for use of park facilities
and similar duties. For a while, however, valuable time was spent deciding
on whether or not to grant refunds on fees paid when facilities were not

used—a practice which continued until a more specific policy was adopted. As the modern ecological movement became stronger in the sixties, more time was devoted to discussions of that issue.

The Authority from time to time developed intermediate plans for construction of facilities, but it never had the funds or the time to develop a really comprehensive plan for the future of the Park. Baxter never seemed particularly interested in detailed long-range planning beyond the setting of a basic philosophy concerning the wilderness character of the Park.[7] Helon Taylor in the mid-sixties made reference to a six-year plan he had developed.[8] The most detailed analysis of alternative schemes for recreational development of the park area was made by a graduate student from the University of Maine.[9] Attempts to include Baxter State Park in master plans for recreational development in the state were stoutly resisted by Baxter. Since all of the members had multitudinous and widely varied duties to perform, comprehensive planning was next to impossible. Nor, until the late sixties did there appear to be great public pressure for it. Any decisions on the future of the Park, or any major decisions on financing had to gain the approval of Baxter, and this often took long periods of time.

Though the Authority by law had complete control of the Park, that control was always subject to the wishes of Baxter. Details of budget requests were generally not discussed with him, unless large capital expenditures or the addition of personnel were involved, but decisions as to whether or not to build campgrounds were cleared. Construction of new roads and the maintenance of existing ones were also subject to his approval.[10] After he made bequests to the Park he tightly controlled their use. He continued to play a major role in defining the wilderness concept and in making decisions as to clearing up blowdowns. He even cleared the printing of some promotional brochures.[11] In some cases he gave final approval to or rejected applications of scientists desiring to work in the Park.[12] When a member of the Authority once suggested using prison labor to perform trail work and forestry duties in the north end of the Park as a means of rehabilitating them, Baxter responded by writing: "No prison labor of any kind ever should be used in my Park. It is for free men only forever."[13] The list could be expanded, but what is important here is that Baxter's activities were one of the factors that made the development of a comprehensive policy or plan very nearly impossible during his lifetime.

Another area in which Baxter remained adamant and consistent in his actions was in the placing of memorials or plaques in the Park. He insisted that any memorials placed would be only with his permission.[14] After the tragic deaths of Mrs. Margaret Ivusic and Ranger Ralph Heath in October, 1963, the AMC Club voted to provide $5,000 from one of its Maine-related endowment funds to erect two bunkhouses at Chimney Pond in Heath's memory. The buildings were erected with Baxter's

190

knowledge, but shortly before the official dedication ceremonies, he abruptly terminated them and sent a check to the Club for the cost of the bunkhouses and mountain rescue equipment for which it had paid. Baxter was deeply concerned that a wooden plaque commemorating the gift and noting the source of it would be placed near the bunkhouses. He wrote the Authority: "Any building or Memorial that is erected in my Park will be paid for by myself after my approval. Once we allow anybody to erect a building or memorial in the Park it will create confusion. Everything that is done there of this nature will be done by myself under the supervision of the AUTHORITY." He regarded the plaque installation, if not the bunkhouses, a breech of the trust deeds and also "contrary to the spirit of my gift." He asked that the memorial be removed immediately and concluded by saying, "This Park is not to be used in Memorial to anybody not even to myself."[15]

Two years later when Baxter State Park was placed on the National Register of Natural Landmarks and the Interior Department wanted to erect a bronze plaque on the site, Baxter rejected the proposal since, as Wilkins wrote after consulting him, he wanted the Park to "remain as a gift from him to the people of Maine with no other identification."[16]

From 1950 until 1966 Baxter visited the Park two or three times during the season. At times Helon Taylor would go to Portland to drive him to and around the Park; on other occasions Baxter would "borrow" a game warden or forest ranger, generally Supervisor Arthur Rogers or David Priest, for the purpose. Occasionally his personal chauffeur drove him. Depending on weather and road conditions and the state of his health, he would attempt to visit most of the campgrounds and other scenic areas in the company of Helon Taylor, and particularly for the late summer visit, the members of the Authority who could be present. In 1953 he introduced Horace M. Albright, former director of the National Park Service and a longtime friend, to the Park. On these trips Baxter often had a meal or stayed at private sporting camps within the Park. He was careful to note the highway and campground maintenance and other management details. On his return to Portland he wrote to those who had taken part, thanking them for their assistance and then discussing any issues that had created concern for him in the inspection.[17]

He developed a high regard for the rangers and particularly for Supervisor Helon Taylor. He had complete faith in the effectiveness of his work and at times authorized him to do things without consulting the Authority directly. By 1963 he took the position that "anything about Baxter Park if approved by Mr. Taylor automatically receives my consent. Helon is a grand man, devoted to his important position in the Katahdin Park area and with him to guide, you will do no harm."[18] Though on a number of occasions thereafter, particularly with regard to construction in the Park, Baxter did not follow Taylor's views, the general thrust of

191

THE BAXTER STATE PARK AUTHORITY POSES
WITH GOVERNOR BAXTER IN 1960
Reading from left to right: Chairman Austin H. Wilkins, Supervisor Helon Taylor,
Governor Percival Baxter, Attorney General Frank Hancock, and Commissioner
Roland H. Cobb.

the quotation is true. As Taylor's retirement neared, Baxter tried to talk him out of it. He wrote: "There must be some way to have you remain in command. Your personality makes the Park and without you I would lose most of my interest and probably I would not visit the Park again." He offered to pay Taylor's salary "either from the Park Trust Fund or from my own pocket rather than have you leave us."[19] Baxter's trip to the Park later that summer was indeed his last.

Once general policies had been determined, the details of their implementation were generally left to the chairman of the Authority and the supervisor. If questions arose regarding interpretation of procedures or policy they would be referred by the forest commissioner as chairman to the entire Authority. Both Nutting and Wilkins were devoted and able public servants. They got along enormously well with Baxter, who relied on them for advice and assistance. Both men were professional foresters, and that aspect of their duties came first. A careful reading of the extant manuscript materials indicates that they had a sincere and dedicated interest in the well-being of the Park and faithfully attempted to comply with Baxter's wishes. He trusted and respected both of them.[20] However, since Baxter's wishes sometimes changed, and since they were at variance with ideas of various and varied pressure groups in the surrounding area and in the state, the chairman of the Authority was increasingly in the center of public controversies.

In 1955 in his request to the legislature for operating funds, Chairman Nutting neatly summarized the administration of the Park:

192

Probably no park is administered with so little overhead as Baxter. The Authority, . . . determines general policy; the bookkeeping details are handled by the Forestry Department. Game control is taken care of by the Fish and Game Department assisted by the Park Rangers, and the Maine Forestry District is responsible for fire control. At present the only administration charge from Park funds is for the Park Superintendent who spends from one-half to three-quarters of his time in actual ranger and construction work.[21]

During the fifties and sixties, personnel in the Forest Service such as Fred Holt, later forest commissioner, William Whitman and William Cross, both business managers for the Maine Forest Service, and a great many others, including patrolmen on the scene, performed an enormous number of services for the Park at no cost to the Authority.[22] Forest service as well as fish and game department buildings and vehicles were often used for park business. The forest commissioner, as chairman of the Authority, coordinated the work of individuals involved, maintained contact with the Authority, worked with Governor Baxter in trying to implement his wishes or convince him of the propriety of various courses of action, and also spent a good deal of time directing the work of the supervisor. Final decisions on expenditure of funds and construction were with the chairman or the Authority as a whole. The Authority, or at least the chairman, generally reviewed the supervisor's personnel decisions, but for the most part did not attempt to interfere with his responsibility. Because of the difficulties of coordinating work between Millinocket and Augusta, the supervisor was left with a good deal of discretionary authority. In practice he kept the chairman and other members of the Authority informed of his actions and generally referred delicate or difficult problems to the chairman for decision. Within the budgetary limitations the situation seemed to work tolerably well until park attendance soared in the 1960s and a multiplicity of new issues arose.

Increasingly during the late sixties the controversial problems in the Park were ecological in nature—such as the use of snowmobiles, roadside spraying, use of pesticides generally, and the exercising of cutting rights. Most of these problems involved the attorney general and his department. It became more difficult for one member, even the chairman, to speak for the Authority. All those concerned were extremely busy with their regular jobs, so the proliferation of problems at Baxter Park at times became trying. The major problem became increasingly one of interpreting Baxter's wishes and communicating them to the public at large. The issue was focused neatly by the owner of Camp Phoenix, the private enclave within the Park on Nesowadnehunk Lake. He had talked with Attorney General Erwin on some issues and later wrote him. He noted the increasing criticism of the Authority by groups, individuals, and newspapers and added that this was due primarily to lack of proper communication    193 between members of the Authority and the public, a situation which "often breeds suspicion, distrust and provides the seeds for false information." The writer went on to recommend the creation of a full-time executive secretary to act as liaison between the Authority and the press and public. Such a person, he argued, should be skilled in public relations and could do many of the time-consuming tasks then done by the Authority.[23] Though in this and some other cases, the individuals concerned harbored personal grudges because of past conflicts over policy, the general thrust of the argument was correct.

Erwin, in responding, agreed that the Authority was aware that the demands on its time were one of its greatest problems. He pointed out that the Authority had discussed the same issues and had created the position of business manager to perform many of the functions mentioned.[24] But while William Cross, formerly of the Maine Forest Service, became the first park business manager and performed well in financial and administrative functions, the public continued to work primarily with the chairman and members of the Authority on controversial policy issues.

Next to the Authority in power, and perhaps more important in the actual administration and operation of the Park, was the supervisor. During most of the history of the Park his specific duties and responsibilities were not spelled out. In the 1940s Harold Dyer operated as supervisor with minimum, though gradually increasing, supervision and direction from the Authority.[25] Once the powers of the Authority were more clearly delineated in 1949, a more rational method of operation gradually emerged. Policies regarding collection and deposit of fees and the keeping of records were gradually developed. Procedures were set up for the orderly purchase of supplies, even though communication problems between Millinocket and Augusta sometimes created snags or delayed needed purchases. After late 1950, the Authority began a practice of having the supervisor provide monthly as well as annual reports of his activities.[26] Copies went to each of the members of the Authority, at least part of the time to Baxter, and occasionally to newspapermen in the state. Though Baxter now and then disregarded the chain of command by dealing directly with Helon Taylor, most matters regarding park policy were funnelled through the chairman. But the supervisor did the actual hiring and firing of personnel, referring to or consulting with the chairman on questionable cases. Much, then, depended on the ability and character of the supervisor.

During 1950–1969, there were four supervisors. Three of them covered such short terms that it is difficult to assess adequately their effectiveness and abilities. Robert Dyer served only from June 19 to August 18, 1950; Helon Taylor served from August 20, 1950, through November 1967; Rodney Sargent became acting supervisor through April 30, 1968, when Irvin Caverly, Jr., was named to replace him. Caverly's tenure was brief. Effective November 1, 1968, Harry Kearney was named to the position.

During Robert Dyer's brief tenure the construction work at Roaring
Brook proceeded very slowly and the quality of maintenance in the Park
deteriorated. During the summer Dyer's relations with his staff became
sufficiently embroiled for him to be dismissed after a hearing in Augusta,
"for the good of the service and the morale of the personnel of the Park
Authority. . ." Fred Pitman was asked to take charge on August 19 to
serve until a successor arrived.[27] His tenure was short-lived indeed, since
on August 21 Helon Taylor assumed responsibility.

For many visitors to the Park during the next two decades, Taylor
was the Park. In his friendly, easy-going manner he worked effectively
with the Authority, with Governor Baxter, with the personnel in the Park,
and with citizens in the surrounding communities and visitors to the Park
generally. In his mid-forties when he took the job, Taylor came from a
position as Chief Forest Warden of the Dead River District. Earlier he had
been a Warden Supervisor for the Department of Inland Fisheries and
Game and, for a time, had managed the Lake Megantic Club. He was an
early member of the Maine Appalachian Trail Club, had served on its
governing board, and had been instrumental in establishing parts of the
Bigelow Range Trail and the Appalachian Trail on Sugarloaf. He was
recommended for the position by Albert D. Nutting and George Stobie,
and his appointment was approved unanimously "because of his practical
experience and background in management of woods areas and fish and
game."[28]

No attempt will be made here to detail his long career as supervisor.
He accomplished an enormous amount at Baxter Park with miniscule
budgets. As supervisor, particularly during the first part of his tenure, he
spent half to two-thirds of his time doing the work other rangers would do.
For several years he was the only year-round employee of the Park. At
times he seemed rather loose in his administrative and managerial practices;[29] but with the very small budgets, a small staff, and the huge land
area with which he had to work, it is no wonder that more was not
done. He had to keep the good will of all concerned to get the job done
at all. Until 1954 he answered all correspondence regarding accommodations
and reservations himself! He served a very important function at a critical
time in the history of the Park.

In ill health periodically, Taylor took a leave of absence in 1967 and
finally resigned late in the year.[30] Rodney Sargent, ranger at Abol Campground, was named acting supervisor until the Authority selected Irvin
Caverly Jr. to the position on a probationary basis, effective May 1, 1968.[31]
He relinquished the position at the request of the Authority on November
1, to Harry Kearney, who served into the following decade.[32]

A LOMBARD STEAM LOG HAULER

One of three old lumber haulers, not made after 1917, that went up in a garage fire in 1928. (Illustration from *Lombards of Maine: Inventors from the Penobscot Frontier*, by Lawrence M. Sturtevant, to be published soon.)

Although funds increased considerably over what they had been in the 1940s, the situation still remained grim in the 1950s, as far as appropriations for operating Baxter State Park were concerned. They were simply never sufficient to provide enough personnel, equipment, and services to administer the Park properly. A good overview may be obtained by consulting Table IX–1. The figures do not include appropriations for maintenance of roads, which were made through the State Highway Commission; nor do they include costs incurred by the Maine Forestry Department, the Attorney General's office, and the Department of Inland Fisheries and Game for administrative work performed for the Park. Despite this, it seems clear that appropriations remained inadequate.

The reasons for this inadequacy are several. Generally low income levels in Maine limited funds available for recreational purposes. In a state such as Maine, where recreational opportunities in the outdoors are readily available for a large part of the population, there appears to be a real reluctance to appropriate large sums for formal park purposes to serve a clientele that consists of many out-of-staters. The policy of various governors was that state parks should pay for themselves as much as possible. The Authority was always modest and conservative in its appropriation requests. In its unwillingness to push for much larger sums, it was undoubtedly following specific requests of Governor Baxter, as he was addressed by many. Commissioner Nutting later wrote that the legislature would not approve a budget that had not been cleared with Baxter.[1] In late 1956, for example, he wrote to Chairman Nutting: "It seems to me that at the present time it would be just as well not to ask for funds to extend our activities. Is it not better to improve what we have rather than to branch out into a new location?" Nutting replied that he would be happy to review the appropriation requests with Baxter and added: "The Authority believes we should provide the legislation [legislature?] with an opportunity to go along with a conservative, continuing program. In any case, the best way for us to review it would be to sit down together."[2] Several years later, when Maine's financial situation was tight, the Authority, at Baxter's request, withdrew a $30,000 capital expenditures request from legislative consideration.[3] A final factor leading to modest appropri-

IX
Administration
1950–1969:
Finances

197

Table IX-1

## BAXTER STATE PARK
Use Fees/Expenditures 1945 to 1973 incl.
FINANCIAL DATA/STATISTICS

| | EXPENDITURES | | | | | | | USE FEES | |
| | General Fund | | TRUST FUND | | | | | | |
| F.Y. | Operations | Special | Maint. & Imp. | "Major" | Spec. Rev. | Appalachian Mt. Club | TOTAL | (NET) | GROSS |
|---|---|---|---|---|---|---|---|---|---|
| 1945 | 3,569.48 | | | | | | 3,569.48 | 122.15* | |
| 1946 | 4,459.72 | | | | | | 4,459.72 | 124.55* | |
| 1947 | 8,392.80 | | | | | | 8,392.80 | 1,472.75* | |
| 1948 | 8,995.99 | | | | | | 8,995.99 | 1,712.89* | |
| 1949 | 9,156.45 | | | | | | 9,156.45 | 1,839.17* | |
| 1950 | 15,031.90 | 12,000.00 | | | | | 27,031.90 | 2,324.50* | |
| 1951 | 17,398.53 | 8,124.91 | | | | | 25,523.44 | 2,769.50* | |
| 1952 | 18,968.54 | 4,660.31 | | | | | 23,628.85 | 4,811.88* | |
| 1953 | 21,703.77 | 203.21 | | | | | 21,906.98 | 7,127.43* | |
| 1954 | 23,469.77 | 9,342.45 | | | | | 32,812.22 | 6,850.40* | |
| 1955 | 26,579.60 | 1,663.74 | | | | | 28,243.34 | 7,700.00* | |
| 1956 | 30,041.40 | 4,880.09 | | | | | 34,921.49 | 8,836.00* | |
| 1957 | 30,655.19 | 709.68 | | | | | 31,364.87 | 9,975.75* | |
| 1958 | 38,253.79 | 12,323.96 | | | | | 50,577.75 | 13,184.75* | |
| 1959 | 37,745.44 | 15,220.37 | | | | | 52,965.81 | 16,103.25* | |
| 1960 | 40,052.89 | 3,249.09 | | | | | 43,301.98 | 21,716.47 | 22,044.72 |
| 1961 | 39,691.20 | | | 430.50 | | | 40,121.70 | 20,712.32 | 21,311.20 |
| 1962 | 38,727.46 | 770.67 | | 5,224.04 | | | 44,722.17 | 21,760.98 | 22,519.47 |
| 1963 | 39,377.93 | 384.71 | 1,299.00 | 1,920.00 | | | 42,981.64 | 23,287.70 | 23,963.75 |
| 1964 | 46,931.47 | 1,441.72 | 211.68 | | | 400.00 | 48,984.87 | 24,171.13 | 25,102.20 |
| 1965 | 45,319.10 | 4,838.17 | 2,420.00 | | | | 52,577.27 | 24,906.67 | 26,196.49 |
| 1966 | 48,079.07 | 4,770.38 | 3,306.59 | | | 776.08 | 56,932.12 | 27,948.35 | 29,186.85 |
| 1967 | 54,370.64 | 2,390.27 | 7,687.02 | 39,403.66 | | 428.56 | 104,280.15 | 27,325.54 | 28,550.10 |
| 1968 | 71,216.76 | 2,795.54 | (2,679.63) | 35,609.62 | | 160.87 | 107,103.16 | 29,970.39 | 31,398.59 |
| 1969 | 79,859.25 | 702.17 | 2,420.23 | 180.35 | | 622.80 | 83,784.80 | 28,058.38 | 30,269.01 |
| 1970 | 89,815.28 | 4,467.69 | 19,304.51 | 111,590.49 | | 1,447.43 | 226,625.40 | 34,099.44 | 36,353.75 |
| 1971 | 89,899.12 | 3,203.41 | | 259,255.34 | | | 352,357.87 | 31,103.07 | 33,789.95 |
| 1972 | | 734.53 | | 314,493.73 | | | 315,228.26 | 58,109.44 | 60,130.65 |
| 1973 | | | 360,701.21 | 725,000.00 | | | 1,085,701.21 | 58,073.51 | 63,072.49 |
| 1974 | | | | | | | | | |

include income from other sources

ations could have been the opposition raised from time to time by residents of Millinocket, Patten, and Aroostook County towns to continued expansion of the Park and the subsequent diminution of hunting areas.

The expenditures listed in Table IX–1 show a modest and continuing increase during the two and a half decades after 1945. Most of the larger increases, such as those coming in 1949 and 1950, and in the late fifties, reflect the necessity for hiring of additional personnel as new campgrounds were opened up. For much of this period, Helon Taylor was the only year-round employee; as use of the Park increased, more full-time staff were added. Until 1963 the Authority retained all use fees raised in the Park, and the appropriation from the General Fund was adjusted to account for this. In addition, after 1943, funds were included in the appropriations to be transferred to the Maine Forestry District to pay for forest-fire protection for the Park. As park acreage increased, this payment increased as well. In most years, salaries for personnel constituted the overwhelming proportion of the expenditures. In fiscal 1951-52, for example, they constituted 72 per cent of $14,717.18. Since capital expenditures in that year accounted for 12 per cent of the total, only 16 per cent was available for equipment, supplies, and other needs.[4] This latter situation created serious problems for those working in the Park, for it was often impossible or very difficult to obtain vehicles and other equipment needed to operate effectively. The files in the Authority office illustrate the desperate need for equipment and supplies. Yet official records show that these categories were often cut sharply in the legislature. The Authority was allowed to use income received above estimates each year and noted in its appropriation request in 1955: "The operation of a park, with a small force of seasonal rangers is very dependent upon high morale, and intensely devoted personnel. The policy of using income received above estimates for use in the park has been an incentive to the men."[5] But this alleviated only part of the problem.

Aside from General Fund appropriations for regular operations, the legislature from time to time appropriated other monies for capital expenditures. The larger totals for 1950, 1958, and 1959 were for new campgrounds. The sums appropriated for other years primarily were for alterations and additions to existing campgrounds. In 1959 the Authority noted it was trying to establish a regular rotation basis for trucks, trading them in every three years or 50,000 miles, whichever came first. "Failure to replace these units on rotation," it was noted, "means additional operational and repair costs. It is to be remembered that the ranger trucks are driven over dirt and gravel roads continuously."[6] In that year the request for new vehicles was denied, and two years later a similar appeal for restoration of a $1,500 cut in the capital budget for the purchase of a truck was approved. In justifying its request the Authority stressed that the number of visitors to the Park had increased by 15 per cent each year.[7] 199

Helon Taylor's monthly reports and communications with the Authority have a great many comments on difficulties created by lack of adequate capital equipment and the ability to maintain properly machinery already held. The problem was typified by a situation that arose in 1962. In the late spring, Taylor wrote to Forest Commissioner Wilkins as follows:

> We have a problem. The Jeep. It is a 1951 with some 39000 miles on it and the hardest possible miles at that. Rodney [Sargent] has it and the front end let go on him the other day. It is not worth fixing up. This is the second time the front end has gone. The engine has been rebuilt once, the radiator leaks and that is the second one we have put on it. It needs a new fuel pump, the transmission is shot so bad you can't tell which gear you are in when you shift, the tires are not too good and the body is all shot. My estimate is that it would cost $500.00 to put it in good mechanical shape and then what have you got? Probably the rear end would go next. We need a four wheel drive vehicle the worst kind and I respectfully suggest a Chevrolet, half ton pickup with four wheel drive when and if we can afford it. In the meantime we may as well try to do without.

Taylor added that he had a friend who would pay $100 for the Jeep and could fix it himself. Wilkins responded by saying that there was no money to purchase a new one, nor were funds available to repair the Jeep. He was unwilling to authorize the sale. Taylor replied that Sargent had another vehicle to use, but argued that the Jeep was "the only 4 wheel drive we have on the Park and is much needed. It has paid for itself ten times over in the past 11 years but is not worth fixing up. We will just have to get along without it. We will just be that much less efficient that is all." Nothing more could be done, but early in November Taylor repeated his request and said: "We need a four wheel drive vehicle bad by Thanksgiving. Is there any chance to get a war surplus one?"[8] In the end, replacement had to await funding by the legislature.

Another incident involved the first snowmobile officially used in the Park. Taylor purchased one in 1960 with his own funds to inspect the Park and do law enforcement work. He did not tell the forest commissioner, at first, since he believed it was his own responsibility to find means of winter travel about the Park. He finally asked if he could charge for and keep returns from hauling the gear of winter climbers on the snowmobile. Wilkins believed that Taylor should be reimbursed for the cost and requested Baxter's permission to use income from the trust fund to reimburse him. Baxter agreed that Taylor should not have to pay for the vehicle, but he did not want trust funds used for the purpose. He finally allowed the money to be withdrawn from trust-fund income accounts, but promptly wrote a check to restore the amount.[9]

Another type of problem arising because of small appropriations was exemplified by the hiring of assistant rangers in the late fifties and early sixties. As park use mounted rapidly, the rangers at Roaring Brook, Katahdin Stream, and South Branch Pond campgrounds found it more difficult to care for the camps and do their other work as well. The Authority decided to hire assistant rangers for those camps and appealed to the legislature for the needed funds. When the request was turned down, the Authority turned successfully to the Governor and Council in 1959 and 1960 for an allocation from the contingency funds of the state, and it was able to hire three forestry students from the University of Maine during those summers.[10] In the following year the Authority, with Baxter's reluctant permission, used income from the trust fund to pay for the student rangers and to pay the salary of ranger Scott to work full-time during the year.[11] But when Baxter received a financial report that showed these transactions, he immediately wrote to Wilkins and said he would provide the money himself to pay back the trust fund. He asked that no more money be withdrawn to pay the rangers. "Maybe they are not necessary so please do not do anything about it at the present time," he added, and said: "I want to keep the TRUST FUND intact without withdrawals so please keep this in mind for I want to be consulted." Baxter provided funds for the rangers for 1961 and to repay Helon Taylor for the snowmobile. After talking with Wilkins, Baxter again agreed to pay the cost of the summer rangers for 1962. But at the end of the summer he wrote that he was certain the legislature would now provide the needed funds for the extra rangers. "Up to now I was pleased to pay this myself," he wrote, "but it really should be taken care of by the State under the regular appropriation."[12] The Authority again turned successfully to the Executive Council for funds in 1963 and 1964; and finally, in 1965, funds for the extra rangers were included in the regular park operations appropriation.[13]

Aside from the grants of land themselves, Baxter's early donations to or for the Park were rather modest. In 1945 he asked the Governor and Executive Council to establish the Baxter State Park Trust Fund, to which would be credited all rentals received from property donated to the state, gifts accepted by the Governor and Council, receipts from flowage rights, and interest earned on invested funds. Baxter established this fund, later known as the Maintenance and Improvement Fund, with $311.82 received from rentals from private sporting camps located on lands which he had recently turned over to the state.[14] As indicated in Table IX–2, the fund grew very slowly. Managed by the state, it remained unused at Baxter's request until 1963 when nearly $1,300 was used for operating expenses in the Park. Thereafter expenditures tended to increase until in 1970, after receipt of Baxter's much larger legacy, the fund was closed out and the balance transferred to the larger trust fund. In the interim the monies

## Table IX–2
## BAXTER STATE PARK
### FINANCIAL STATEMENT OF TRUST FUND ACCOUNTS
For Fiscal Years ending June 30

| | Maintenance and Improvement | | Baxter State Park Trust Fund | |
|---|---|---|---|---|
| | Income | Principal | Income | Principal |
| 1946 | | 311.82 | | |
| 1947 | | 432.71 | | |
| 1948 | | 634.89 | | |
| 1949 | | 759.53 | | |
| 1950 | 17.62 | 759.53 | | |
| 1951 | 36.60 | 759.53 | | |
| 1952 | (55.58)* | 3,275.35 | | |
| 1953 | (45.08)* | 4,020.43 | | |
| 1954 | (107.69)* | 4,878.12 | | |
| 1955 | (122.64)* | 5,825.76 | | |
| 1956 | (139.60)* | 6,765.36 | | |
| 1957 | (209.85)* | 10,529.71** | | |
| 1958 | (307.01)* | 11,561.72 | | |
| 1959 | (334.63)* | 12,596.35 | | |
| 1960 | (389.53)* | 14,504.44 | | |
| 1961 | (460.92)* | 15,740.36 | 3,591.24*** | 489,947.90 |
| 1962 | 583.60**** | 16,665.36 | 19,738.83*** | 489,947.90 |
| 1963 | (594.31)* | 18,669.19 | 14,418.50*** | 489,947.90 |
| 1964 | 667.29 | 18,476.21 | 15,597.91*** | 492,210.41 |
| 1965 | 6,427.79 | 19,423.79 | 31,715.18*** | 1,580,247.77 |
| 1966 | 5,234.00 | 23,165.19 | 49,360.02*** | 1,575,056.13 |
| 1967 | 1,296.21 | 24,086.37 | 53,484.94*** | 1,597,977.21 |
| 1968 | 11,382.64 | 24,578.72 | 63,497.29*** | 1,597,744.90 |
| 1969 | 6,098.84 | 27,680.42 | 60,652.91*** | 1,597,744.90 |
| 1970 | 1,563.63 | -0- | 68,129.71*** | 1,623,755.86 |
| 1971 | In 1970 $2,510 was trans- | | 162,563.93*** | 1,624,784.60 |
| 1972 | ferred to the General Fund | | 343,937.40*** | 1,654,119.78 |
| | and $26,010.96 to principal | | | |
| | and Baxter State Park Trust | | | |
| | Fund. Fund closed out. | | | |

* indicates transfer to principal
** income from flowage rights
*** indicates income received and does not show cumulated income or amounts spent
**** transferred to principal in 1963
The large figures for 1965 and 1966 in income from Maintenance and Improvement Fund represent timber stumpage sales; for 1968 they indicate the insurance payments on the supervisor's headquarters, which had burned.

This table was drawn from a series of reports on the "Financial Statement of Trust Fund Accounts" for the period 1946–72, prepared by William Cross, Business Manager, Baxter State Park Authority, June 30, 1972.

were used for operating expenses; purchasing special equipment such as wood chippers; repairs, personal services, and fuel and buildings.

Much more significant for the future was the establishment by Baxter and the legislature of the Baxter State Park Trust Fund in 1961. Baxter gave to the state one thousand shares, all outstanding, of the stock of the Proprietors of Portland Pier Corporation. At the time the Corporation held municipal bonds, corporate shares, and cash with a total value of nearly $490,000.

The legislature accepted the gift on an emergency basis, so that it took effect on passage, on February 16, 1961. The money was to be held in trust and managed by a Boston trust company, for the benefit of the people of Maine with the principal to be invested and reinvested and the income to be used "for the care, protection and operation of said 193,254 acres of forest land known as BAXTER STATE PARK."[15] Four years later, Baxter more than tripled the fund when he gave, under the same conditions, all outstanding—one thousand—shares of the Congress Realty Company valued at $1,106,213.42.[16]

Another grant from Baxter for the benefit of the Park came a year before his death. He asked state officials to transfer the last $88,384.79 from the Mackworth Island Trust Fund, which he had created in 1943 when he gave the island in Portland Harbor to the state for a school for the deaf, to the Baxter State Park Fund. He asked that it be kept as a separate fund "which can be used from time to time to acquire new lands for the Baxter State Park Trust Fund. In this way we will have the regular Baxter State Park Trust Fund which will be used to enlarge my gift to the State. Mackworth Island Trust Fund will be moved into the larger fund and then my money will be all in one fund only."[17] On April 24, 1968, the Executive Council authorized the transfer of the funds from the Mackworth Island Trust Fund to the Baxter State Park Trust Account. In the records of the Department of Finance and Administration's Bureau of Accounts and Control, the funds were credited to the Baxter State Park Expendable Trust Account.[18] By June 3, 1972, the account had increased to a total of $101,917.63.[19]

Baxter expected to add to the major trust fund from time to time. By then his intention was clear: "to make another magnificent gift which ultimately will result in sufficient income to make Baxter State Park independent of any general fund money for operations."[20]

The Baxter State Park Authority, which had expected to be able to use income from the fund in the year 1961, was placed in a difficult situation. Even before Baxter clarified his position regarding the funds in July, Chairman Wilkins asked Robert N. Haskell, president of the Bangor Hydro-Electric Company and a good friend of Baxter, to discuss the situation with Baxter to get him to further explain his intentions. Wilkins stressed the increasing difficulties in administering Baxter State Park because of increased use and insufficient state appropriations. He asked Haskell to urge Baxter to release income from the trust fund to hire three part-time rangers and a forester "to prepare forest management plans and do other engineering work." He also wanted to use income for some capital improvements. He said all of the suggestions "at one time or another have been explained to Governor Baxter and were acceptable at that time." He added, "I would caution being too specific to the Governor on the items under Part II, but I am reasonably sure he would feel these improvements are needed and would in no way encroach upon his wishes for preserving this as a wilderness area." He concluded by repeating again that Baxter be urged to write a letter "which will clearly spell out that the intent of the trust fund is for the income to be used for improvements and New Activities, in addition to the regular 'Current Services' budget request."[21] Baxter and Haskell undoubtedly met, though no record is left of the meeting. Baxter did provide the funds for extra park rangers personally that year, but he seemingly remained unconvinced that trust funds should be used for capital improvements.

He waited until midsummer to clarify his intentions. Then he wrote the state treasurer and Governor John Reed and the Executive Council stating his wishes. He asked the state treasurer for regular reports, to keep the fund separate from other state trust funds, and he also directed that none of the Fund be used for any purposes "until I am consulted and approve."[22] He did not intend to preclude its use completely, but wanted to minimize expenditures so that the principal could increase substantially over the years.

As indicated in Table IX–1, modest use was made of income from the major trust fund in the early sixties, with larger expenditures later in the decade. Baxter was consulted in most cases until his death. During the fall of 1961, he was asked to approve the expenditure of $500 to enlarge the office used by Reservations Clerk Helen Gifford in the Maine Forest Service office in Millinocket. In his reply to Chairman Wilkins's request, Baxter said he wanted to discuss the matter with Wilkins and the state treasurer, who "will give me some ideas. It is well to be careful about drawing on the Trust Fund which is principally to be used in the future for personnel."[23] Eventually he approved construction of the addition. But a year later, after he had approved additional expenditures for assistant park rangers and for winter or year-round work for a ranger, he asked that such expenditures be taken care of by the state and added: "I do not want the Special Trust I established to be used during my life time. This is for future emergencies."[24]

Administrators of the Park continued to hope that more income from the trust funds would be released for use. In 1965 William Cross of the Maine Forest Service, who managed the business affairs of Baxter State Park, did a study which showed that the income from the funds granted by

Baxter in 1961 and 1965, with use fees, was sufficient to operate the Park
without state appropriations and without touching the Maintenance and
Improvement Trust Fund.[25] In noting Baxter's second large grant, Supervisor Taylor wrote, "I hope there are not so many strings on it that we can't
use the interest on it."[26] During the next year, in responding to a letter concerning the finances of the Park, Attorney General Dubord, after detailing
the budgetary situation, said he "hoped that eventually this income [from
the trust fund] will be more fully available and could, as you can see, result in sufficient funds for an expanded operation of the Park over the
present budget without the need of any legislative appropriations whatsoever."[27]

Baxter gave his approval for use of trust fund income for construction
of gatehouses to control entry to the Park and for construction of the access
road near Togue Pond. However, in 1966 he first agreed to, but then rescinded, permission for use of trust fund income for construction of a new
supervisor's headquarters in the Park. During the same year he also denied
a request to use income to pay rent in Millinocket for Ranger Sargent, who
was to become acting supervisor later in the year.[28] In 1968 he gave permission to use $52,500 from the trust fund to purchase the private equity
in the Kidney Pond camps. The funds were restored by transfer of an
equal amount from contingency funds by Executive Council action.[29]
Over the years Baxter had approved trust fund payments of $32,929.99 out
of total expenditures of $107,103.16 by the fiscal year 1968–69.[30]

As of the end of February 1970, shortly after Baxter's death but before
receipt of the very large increase in the trust fund provided by his will, the
principal of the major trust fund was $1,597,744.90, while $206,123.49 in
accrued interest was also held. Since by that time the Maintenance and
Improvement Fund was overdrawn to the extent of $19,174.67, the effective
interest income available from the trust funds was $186,948.82.[31] Legisla-
tive appropriations provided most of the costs of operating the Park until
income from the greatly enlarged trust fund became available in the following year. With receipt of this income, the management and operation of
Baxter State Park was dramatically changed.

## CARIBOU IN MAINE 1963

Captured in Newfoundland, 24 caribou were successfully delivered by helicopter to Lower Togue Pond. They were herded into a corral and put to sleep so that each could be painted with an identifying number, given a preventive antibiotic shot, blindfolded and hog tied for a helicopter trip to a Mt. Katahdin plateau. Eighteen, of which one perished en route, were taken up and released before stormy weather prevented further trips that December day. The six remaining animals were later released at Roaring Brook campground. Young caribou were seen for two or three years afterward, but none have been seen for so long that it is now believed that all have perished.

Since Baxter State Park was a state institution, its employees came under the control and regulation of the Department of Personnel. Until 1961 the power of the Personnel Board over the hiring and firing practices and the conditions of work appear to have been incomplete. In that year the legislature provided that employees of the Park "shall hold office under the rules of the Personnel Law." They would be compensated at levels to be determined by the Authority, with the approval of the Board.[1] A job classification system had been developed with gradations of park ranger I, park ranger II, park supervisor I, park supervisor II and park supervisor III. Each job was placed in a certain salary range or step system that applied to jobs at similar levels throughout the state service. Finally, within each step were different salary levels to account for length of service and experience.[2] By 1960 rangers were hired on a six-month probationary basis and, if they had little or no experience and lacked a high-school diploma, were started at the level of ranger I. Most rangers during the period were at the ranger II level. Provision was made for a system of appeals to the Personnel Board if an employee whose position was terminated felt he had been mistreated. Though this was threatened once or twice before 1969, the process was not actually used. In 1969 the Personnel Board, in consultation with the Authority, developed a new classification system with appropriate salary steps or ranges. The titles were campground ranger I, campground ranger II, assistant supervisor of Baxter Park, and supervisor of Baxter Park. Classifications were also developed for clerical personnel and laborers.[3] At the same time attempts were made to shorten what had been enormously long work weeks for the park personnel who had been on a non-standard work week for several decades. Once trust fund monies became available, wives of campground rangers or other individuals were hired as assistant rangers.

The total staff of the Park increased slowly during the period after 1950. At the end of that year Helon Taylor was the only full-time employee; the four seasonal rangers had gone off the payroll. More personnel were added as campgrounds were developed. By 1960 there were eight seasonal rangers and one seasonal clerk at Millinocket to handle reservations and correspondence. Seven of the rangers were assigned regularly to camp-

grounds, while the eighth, Owen Grant, was a carpenter for the Park and filled in for the other rangers as needs dictated. Most worked seasons from twenty-eight to thirty-two weeks and in some years in the late fifties and early sixties, some stayed on longer and in some cases for nearly the whole year to build campgrounds and do similar tasks if sufficient funds were available.[4] Part-time labor was hired from time to time for specific tasks. By 1965 there were two permanent and eleven seasonal employees, and by 1970, eight permanent and twenty-four seasonal employees.[5]

Since funds were in such short supply during all of this period, little attention could be given to hiring a broader range of personnel for the Park. Overwhelming emphasis was given by the Authority and supervisor on finding individuals who could run the campgrounds satisfactorily. Some attempts were made in the late fifties to obtain funds to hire a forester to manage some of the newer sections of the Park, but the legislature was unwilling to make them available. There is no indication in the records that the Authority or supervisor expected to hire botanists or wildlife experts or rangers who could perform educative functions as well as manage campgrounds and enforce the rules of the Park. If an applicant was an expert in wildlife and flora, a good woodsman, and good at law enforcement as well as having much experience, so much the better. Supervisor Taylor described one ranger this way after hiring him to work at Chimney Pond in 1958: "Ranger Thomas Sprague came on as a new man May 1st and has done an outstanding job at Chimney Pond this summer. He is an authority on birds and wildlife, an expert woodsman, had 12 years experience with the Fish & Game Department as a Game Warden and is extra good on law enforcement work. We were lucky to get such a man."[6] More often than not in the fifties new rangers were fairly recent high school graduates, mostly from towns in the region surrounding the Park, who had had some woods experience.

Until 1958 it appears that Taylor was almost totally in charge of hiring personnel. During the 1950s the ranger force was stable: Edward Werler remained at Roaring Brook from 1951 through mid-summer 1960. Ralph Dolley served faithfully at Russell Pond from 1950 to the end of the 1960 season and was replaced by Irvin Caverly, Jr., who served for three summers before moving on to other campgrounds. Edward Beach was the first ranger at the Nesowadnehunk campground and stayed for five summers; he was followed by Irwin Sargent of Phillips, who continued there until late in the sixties. Sargent's son, Rodney, had preceded him to the Park at Chimney Pond and then as first ranger at Abol where, except for two years of military service, he remained until the late sixties. After South Branch Pond was completed in 1951, Myrle Scott served there for four years and was followed by Dalton Kirk of Monson for three years, when Frank Darling took over until 1962, to be followed by Ellsworth Damon, who remained throughout the decade. There were more frequent changes at Chimney Pond after Roland Anderson, who served from 1951 to 1954, resigned. New men were generally given that job. In 1960 Ralph Heath, brother-in-law of Frank Darling, began working there and served very well until his tragic death at the end of the 1963 season. Ironically enough, on October 22, 1963, just a week before his death, Heath had been selected by Helon Taylor to be the next ranger to serve all winter, since he was "the best fitted for the job and deserves it most."[7]

Taylor's first appointment had been Myrle Scott, his son-in-law, whom he hired soon after he came to the Park, to fill the vacancy created by the dismissal of Ralph Robinson at Roaring Brook.[8] Taylor was reluctant about hiring Scott because of the family connection, but Scott had worked for him before and Taylor thought very highly of his abilities. Scott became a very effective ranger. He served in 1950 at Roaring Brook and then took over the new campground at South Branch Pond in the following year, and in 1955 replaced Fred Pitman at Katahdin Stream. Pitman had retired the previous year at the age of seventy, after serving at Katahdin Stream since 1941.[9] By the end of the decade, Scott was working on a full-time basis and, in effect, had become assistant supervisor, though without title. In 1962 he resigned to take a job as supervisor of Lily Bay State Park for the Maine State Park Commission.[10] The concept of assistant supervisor was continued after that time, as others were chosen to work all winter and handle part of the load. However, not until 1969 was the title officially given, to Irvin Caverly.

In 1958 Taylor met with the Authority in late spring to decide on who should be hired.[11] When Austin Wilkins became forest commissioner and chairman of the Authority, he began to play a more direct role in the hiring process than his predecessors had done. Thus, in the spring of 1959, applications for new openings were collected in Augusta and Taylor again travelled there to meet with Chairman Wilkins and work with the Personnel Board, which had requested more careful screening procedures in the selection of new rangers. It was Wilkins who actually offered the positions to individuals selected. He and Taylor had agreed on the campgrounds to which the men should be assigned, and when Taylor later changed the assignments Wilkins was irritated. Taylor had opposed the selection of one of the new rangers who had a college degree and had also attended a National Park Service ranger school. The Personnel Board, however, had pushed for the man's appointment. For various reasons, the ranger, who was very able intellectually, did not work effectively as a campground ranger. The other rangers got up a petition urging that he not be rehired, so Taylor dismissed him. When asked to write a letter defending his actions, Taylor did so. While giving his reasons he noted: "Always before I have had my choice of the men available and have never picked a dud yet. One rotten apple can spoil the whole basket."[12]

In 1960 applications for new positions again came to Wilkins. They were turned over to Taylor with the request that he arrange for interviews with them and submit the names "of the three most likely applicants you would care to recommend for a final selection." Wilkins would then make the final selection "as recommended by Helon Taylor."[13] This process continued for a time thereafter, though later in the decade it appears that the supervisor was again making most of the decisions on personnel matters.

One other employee of great importance for the Park was hired in the fifties. This was Mrs. Helen Gifford, who became reservations clerk in Millinocket. Mrs. Gifford, wife of Clayton Gifford, chief forest fire warden in Millinocket, became the first regular clerical employee of the Park and the first female employee. During the mid-fifties, the Authority began accepting reservations at the various campgrounds. As the Park received more publicity the volume of mail received increased as well. Helon Taylor spent a good deal of time each month answering correspondence; in July 1956, for example, he answered 301 letters and made many reservations.[14] His monthly reports reflect the increasing time he had to spend to keep up with the flood of correspondence. It soon became obvious that unless he got some clerical help he would not be able to perform many essential parts of his job. Funds were requested and received to pay a seasonal clerk to handle correspondence and reservations, and Mrs. Gifford was hired to begin work in early May of 1957. An office was set up in the forestry department storehouse on the main road leading into Millinocket from the east.[15] However, not until 1959 was a separate telephone listing requested for the Baxter State Park reservations office in Millinocket; until that time the phone was listed only under the Maine Forest Service.[16] For a time Mrs. Gifford worked only during the summer season. In 1963 funds were obtained to have her work for eight hours each week during the winter as well. Eventually this was increased to sixteen hours per week. She was an extremely hard worker and performed many services for the Park beyond her immediate assignment. Most important perhaps was her control of radio traffic for the Park and forest service. In 1969 Supervisor Harry Kearney argued successfully that she be placed on a full-time basis during the winter season. Kearney wrote: "It is difficult to imagine how we could run the park without her assistance. . . . She works without thought of pay many many hours more than the forty-eight required of her. When there is an emergency or disaster Mrs. Gifford can be depended on to be our link from the mountain to the town, . . ."[17]

Assignment of the rangers was the job of the supervisor. Unless the ranger currently stationed at Chimney Pond wanted to stay where he was, new men were assigned to that campground. If they did well they were then moved to other positions as openings occurred. Russell Pond, also isolated, served something of the same function after Ralph Dolley left in 1960. While Fred Pitman was at Katahdin Stream campground, he, in effect, was in charge of the western side of the Park and became what amounted to an assistant supervisor. As indicated before, the practice was continued with Myrle Scott. Frank Darling was moved from South Branch Pond to Katahdin Stream in 1962 with the same understanding; also that he would work all winter.[18]

Since the work of most of the rangers was seasonal and the pay not particularly good, while the hours were long and arduous, it is understandable that there would be a certain amount of turnover. During the period up to 1962, three rangers resigned to take positions with the Maine State Park Commission. In the case of one of them, Myrle Scott, Governor Baxter was moved to complain: "It is not fair for the State Park people to take our good men."[19] Others resigned to work for the Eastern Corporation or Great Northern, or to take other jobs such as teaching school. The fact that there was not more turnover demonstrates that the rangers were extremely dedicated men and enjoyed their work. However, by the late sixties the turnover rate was high.

Rangers were made representatives or agents of the Authority to enforce the laws of the state and rules of the Authority within the park area. This included the right to arrest those violating the rules and to bring them into court. Taylor's monthly reports show that most violations that reached the courts involved fish and game laws and regulations. In 1949 and 1950 the Authority had decided to provide proper identification cards or commissions, badges, and uniforms for the rangers. The lack of funds prevented full implementation at the time and only the commissions, badges, and shoulder patches were issued. In 1952 the question of uniforms came up again. Governor Baxter made a visit to the Park and discussed this and other matters with Taylor. He then wrote to Chairman Nutting and said he wanted his views on some of the issues he and Taylor had talked about. With regard to uniforms, Baxter provided his answer before he heard or read Nutting's views. He believed no uniforms were needed since, he said, "the season is short and an arm patch is adequate to identify the rangers. Uniforms some times keep people at a distance and we want everything in the Park to be as friendly and as simple as possible."[20] This ended discussion for some years and it was not until 1960 that uniforms were finally authorized.[21] Baxter had undoubtedly changed his mind about the need for uniforms.

Once on the job, rangers had to learn their trade unless they were already trained. The Authority had a typed terms of employment sheet and a sheet of suggestions on how to handle the public that were given to the rangers. Helon Taylor and experienced rangers briefed the men on their duties and showed them how to perform various tasks and functions, but there appears to have been no formal training sessions for some years; rangers simply learned their jobs by doing them. Occasionally representatives from the forest service or the fish and game department came to the Park to brief the rangers on special tasks or aspects of their jobs. During

most of the 1950s Taylor and, increasingly, some of the rangers attended a
late winter or early spring training program for employees conducted by
the Maine Forest Service or the fish and game department.[22]

The Authority in 1958 decided to hold a training session expressly
for the park rangers soon after they reported for work. On May 4–5,
William Whitman of the forest service met with all but one of the employees of the Park. He explained in detail various developments regarding rules and regulations and policies for collecting and accounting of
park use fees. He responded to questions from all those present regarding
Authority policy on a wide range of issues. Taylor had earlier been instructed to develop work programs for each of the rangers, and then was
asked to make regular inspections of campgrounds and report the results
in forest service inspection books. Finally, the rangers had a chance to
make suggestions for changes in park policies.[23] Similar topics were discussed at the one-day session in 1959, and at a two-day session at the
Great Northern Hotel in Millinocket in 1960.[24] The training sessions were
held for a number of years thereafter.

The rangers appear to have had very little formal training in
mountaineering and mountain rescue techniques until after Ranger Ralph
Heath lost his life in October 1963. Those rangers who conducted winter
parties to the mountains, of course, learned a good deal about winter
climbing. In March of 1964, Supervisor David Priest of the fish and game
department conducted a rescue training program in the Park. It consisted
in climbing Katahdin under winter conditions and practicing various
rescue techniques. A month later several rangers travelled to New Paltz,
New York, to attend another specialized training session in the Shawana-
gunk Mountains. These were designed to prepare rangers for bringing
out the bodies of Mrs. Ivusic and Ranger Heath when they were found
later in the year. No regular training programs were instituted during the
remainder of the decade.[25]

Governor Baxter did not take an active role in the hiring process or
in the administration of personnel, since he trusted Helon Taylor so completely. He did, however, evince a real concern for the well-being
of the rangers. During his trips through the Park he often gave them
small gifts such as knives, but more often he gave them sums of money.
In 1961, when it seemed that Myrle Scott would be hired by the State
Park Commission, Taylor wrote of the development to Baxter as an
addendum to his monthly report. Baxter replied, regretting the possible loss
of Scott and said: "We should keep Myrle if we can." He asked Taylor
what the difference in wages amounted to and upon learning this, suggested that he pay Scott $1,000 annually over and above his regular salary.
Baxter sent the check for the first quarter under this arrangement early in
January 1962. Chairman Wilkins learned of the arrangement from Baxter,
who was also providing funds to pay Scott's salary for the winter months.

Wilkins evidently questioned the propriety of the arrangement. Taylor defended it in the strongest terms. He noted there was nothing illegal about it and that the Governor "gives us all money from time to time out of the goodness of his heart and to show his appreciation for the good work we are doing here on the park. He was not too pleased with the way things were going before we came here and he realizes that Myrle has as much to do with the success of this Park as I do and he hates to see him leave. If he wants to make him a gift of cash money I should consider that was strictly his business."[26]

A year later Baxter offered to increase the salaries of the park rangers and Helen Gifford by $10 per week and apparently offered to send Wilkins a lump sum check for distribution. The Authority discussed the matter among themselves and with State Controller Henry Cranshaw. They felt the proposal would conflict with the salary system set up by the Personnel Board and suggested instead that Baxter make the payment at the end of the field season as a bonus or Christmas gift. Baxter was given the names of all those involved and the amounts each would get under the proposal.[27] It is not known whether he followed through on this suggestion.

The personnel situation at the Park began to change significantly after the mid-sixties when the gatehouses were established and the labor force in the Park nearly tripled over a period of several years. The retirement of Helon Taylor and the short tenures of Rodney Sargent as acting supervisor and Irvin Caverly as supervisor did not allow much time to develop new personnel policies. Harry Kearney became supervisor just before Baxter's death, during a period of turmoil and just as a unionization movement was developing among state employees. When Baxter's trust funds became available, the personnel situation was revolutionized once more.

Space does not allow a full discussion of the work of the rangers at the campgrounds. The general nature of the activities has been dealt with elsewhere. After 1965 there is much less information available, since the system of reporting on activities in the Park was modified. Helon Taylor's monthly and annual reports provide a rich source of information on his and the rangers' activities. In reading them, one is impressed with his ability to handle a small group of men and keep them working together. He administered with an even but firm hand and was quick and profuse in his praise of good performance. At the same time he felt he had to be blunt and honest when the work of some individual needed improvement. One gets the impression of a very close group with a really strong sense of dedication and a willingness to work hard. Through Taylor's tenure this situation generally applied. During a period of more rapid growth at the end of the sixties and at a time when many aspects of American life were undergoing close scrutiny and change, his approach probably would not have worked as well.

One is also impressed by the work and dedication of the individuals.

213

A few examples will illustrate this. Taylor's report for March 1958 included
the following entry:

> March 11th Rangers Scott and Rodney Sargent flew to South
> Branch Pond, shoveled the roofs off there the 12th, snowshoed to Rus-
> sell Pond and shoveled the roofs off there the 13th. They were none
> too soon here. One leanto, the new one Ranger Dolley built last sum-
> mer, had caved in ruining one canoe and damaging another. The
> Ranger's quarters were about to cave in too. March 14th they snow-
> shoed to Roaring Brook, shoveled all the roofs there and pushed on to
> Togue Pond that night. Lucky they did for it snowed 10 inches next
> day. They had snowshoed 15½ miles and shoveled the roofs off 11
> leantos, 2 woodsheds, 1 garage & workshop, the two porches of the
> Ranger's camp and half the bunkhouse. If that isn't a good days work
> I'd like to know what is. I gave them an extra half day off that week-
> end.[28]

Two years later, while reporting on activities in August 1960, Taylor
commented on how busy it was in the Park: "Rangers have been working
away beyond the call of duty and have averaged to work a 78½ hour week.
Some of them over a hundred hours in one week. They will all be glad
when Labor Day rolls around and the crowds thin out."[29] The next winter
he reported that besides shoveling off roofs, one ranger had "hauled three
100 pound tanks of bottled gas (they weigh over 200 pounds tanks and all)
to Basin Ponds, on the way to Chimney Pond, on a moose sled. This is
some ten and a half miles from here and with a 1848 foot rise in elevation.
Yes it takes an able man to be a Ranger."[30] Finally, in August of 1965,
while making out his report for the previous month, he had started it but
did not send it out, in this way:

> This has been a hectic month. Our facilities have been filled to
> away beyond their capacity and our skeleton crew is being worked to
> a point where they are getting short tempered and hard to get along
> with. In this day and age of the 40 hour week we are working from
> 80 to over 100 hours and for no extra pay. Some of the Rangers wives
> are working the same hours and for no pay at all. I just don't know
> how we get people to work for us at all.[31]

This working situation persisted, at least during the busy months, until
the work force was increased later in the decade.

Obviously the pressure was not the same for the whole season, for
in May and June and after Labor Day, much more time could be devoted
to other activities and the work day would be much shorter and more
relaxed. In the letters received by the Authority and the supervisor, the
large majority were in praise of the rangers, whom the visitors found to be
professionals, courteous, and with a desire to be helpful. In some cases
where visitors were critical of treatment they received, the cause was ob-
214  viously tension created by overwork.[32]

One of the anomalous situations regarding Baxter State Park was the
existence of a number of leases to individuals, groups, or sporting camps within the Park. These leases, which continued in some cases into the 1970s, created confusion and sometimes controversy regarding the rules and regulations of the Park as well as its wilderness character. The leases were continuations of those in effect when Baxter purchased various pieces of property that were later included in the Park. He could have made the work of those administering his gift much simpler and easier and in the end much less costly had he not renewed the leases once land was turned over to the state. For various reasons, it was only very late in his life that he asked the Authority to begin terminating them.

The leases were concentrated in three different areas of the Park. The oldest in terms of acquisition of land by Baxter were in T3R10, southwest of Katahdin, where the Kidney Pond camps and York's Twin Pine camps on Daicey Pond were located. Next were a number of leases to private individuals and former corporate owners in T6R8 and T6R9. Finally, there were three leases in T2R9, the last acquisition made by Baxter.

His attitude toward the leases was somewhat ambivalent. However, he continued to approve them in some areas, and he retained an active interest in them until just before his death. In 1942, 1946, and 1948, he indicated that leases should not run for more than one year, an opinion that coincided with state law for state-owned property.[1] In 1955 Baxter and the Authority worked out a statement regarding leases of park land to private persons. Unlike his statements in the same year regarding the forever wild concept, which were passed by the legislature, no legislative action was requested in this case. It is worth quoting in its entirety since, had Baxter and the Authority followed through on it, many later difficulties could have been avoided:

### LEASES OF CAMP SITES IN BAXTER STATE PARK
### TO PRIVATE PERSONS

All the land and buildings in Baxter State Park are the property of the State, for when I bought this area the buildings, under the laws of the State, went with the land.

This being so, when the Authority leased to Kennedy, York, Clark, Martin, Davignon and others, no title whatsoever to the buildings could be conveyed. These leases carry ONLY the right to use these structures. This should be kept in mind in order to avoid complications in the future.

Some of the Lessees may have the idea that they acquired title to the buildings, but such is not the case. Consequently they cannot convey these buildings to other parties or assign their leases without consent of the Park Authority.

In my opinion it will be desirable, ultimately, to terminate these particular leases, preferably at such time as the present Lessees discontinue leasing. It will also be desirable ultimately to abolish all such leases on park property. With this in mind I believe it would be well to have it definitely and unequivocally understood, in addition to and separate from the legal language of the leases, that the Lessees' rights expire when they themselves cease to occupy the premises and that the only ownership the Lessees have is in the furniture and removable fittings in the camps; these and only these have they the right to sell.[2]

Why there was no follow-through by Baxter and the Authority, and why current lessees and, more important, prospective lessees were not notified of this policy statement it is impossible to determine.

Baxter approved some lease changes after that time; Kidney Pond camps changed hands twice after he made his statement of policy. He frequently stopped at the camps during his tours of the Park and he had to know of the changes. In 1956 when Earle W. York, Jr., wanted to have his mother's lease to Twin Pine camps transferred to him, Chairman Nutting of the Authority wanted the thoughts of the other members before the change was made, since it had been agreed that leases should be discontinued when present lessees were through. "I expect that Governor Baxter would okay this change," he wrote, "but I have not consulted him yet." Commissioner Cobb replied: "I am going to hope that Governor Baxter does not insist on the camp lease being transferred to Earl York, Jr. This could keep on indefinitely, and I believe that the lease should be terminated." The former governor should be consulted, he added, "but I hope he can be guided in this direction."[3] Since the transfer was made and undoubtedly made with Baxter's knowledge and approval, he apparently wished to continue a policy which ran counter to the statement he had made the year before.

Little more concerning lease policies was stated by Baxter for over a decade. Suddenly, in 1967, when he read or heard that the Kidney Pond camps were again up for sale he acted more decisively. Apparently forgetting what he had done in 1955, he suggested that the sale be considered carefully by the Authority, "for the time has just about arrived when we want to have a distinct policy on leases. In my opinion the granting of a lease may be an infringement upon the *deed of gift.*" He asked Authority members and Helon Taylor to keep in mind the terms of the trust deeds and was "interested to know what you four men think about this matter."[4] For the Authority this was the signal to begin terminating the leasing system. The process took four years and led to additional problems.

In the southwest quarter of T3R10 are a number of small lakes on either side of Nesowadnehunk Stream. Beginning in the late 19th century, sporting camps were developed on some of the ponds, camps designed to attract fishermen, hunters, and hikers to the Katahdin area. Of these, two lasted long into the 20th century—the Kidney Pond camps and York's Twin Pine camps.

During the first four decades of the 20th century, Kidney Pond had served as the base camp for thousands of fishermen, hunters, and hikers in the Katahdin region. In 1925 or 1926, Roy Bradeen and his wife Laura purchased the original owner's interests and operated the camps together until Mr. Bradeen's death in 1937. Mrs. Bradeen continued on with the lease.[5]

When Percival Baxter bought out the interest of the Garfield Land Company in T3R10 in 1941, the situation changed somewhat. With the purchase came that company's two-year lease to the one-acre site on Kidney Pond held by Mrs. Bradeen. Baxter renewed the lease in 1942 and again two years later for two-year terms, for $350 per annum.[6] Later on in 1942 a real estate dealer connected with the Maine Publicity Bureau asked Baxter to lease the Kidney Pond site to the AMC for twenty-five years. Mrs. Bradeen then wanted to sell her interests. Baxter refused to do this, and after first indicating that renewals of leases should not run for more than two years, since he didn't want encumbrances on land when he transferred it, decided that when the "present leases expire I think it best to have them run for one year at a time only and then we shall have complete control of the property."[7] He transferred his interest in the southwest section of T3R10 to the state in 1945, though the Cassidy Estate of Bangor still held an undivided interest.

This joint ownership and the precise legal power of the Authority to make leases complicated the situation when in 1945 Mrs. Bradeen, who found the operation of the camps increasingly difficult, put them on the market. A possible sale to two members of the staff at Deering High School in Portland fell through when the Authority could not guarantee a three-year lease. Later that year, after protracted negotiations, Marshall W. and Arthur T. Doxsee of Meriden, Connecticut, bought Mrs. Bradeen's interests and had the leases assigned to them.[8] Baxter, who thought that the "young men who bought out Bradeen's are almost crazy," after first arguing that the Authority did not have the right to encumber the area with a lease, agreed to a year's extension.[9] Though Baxter and Authority members seemingly did not like the Doxsees, the lease was renewed through 1948 after which the Doxsees remained tenants at will while paying the annual lease fee.[10]

After discussing the matter at length and obtaining Baxter's opinions, the Authority again renewed, this time for a larger, twenty-four acre area, a more realistic size in view of the facilities needed and actually being used to operate the camps. At the same time the Authority refused to give the Doxsees a lease for the road connecting the main tote road with the camps.

The Authority used the common form of sportsman's lease in making legal arrangements with the Doxsees and other lessees. After setting bounds and the financial terms for the year's lease, it stated that taxes would be paid by the lessee. Next it provided for rights of the lessor, its guests and employees, in use of the property, giving them the right to cut needed trees, and the use of the shores for camping, loading logs, booming and driving, driving horses and cattle, and similar operations. The lessee agreed not to strip the land or destroy growth unless specifically allowed. Lessees agreed to make no clearings, to guard fires, to post and observe the forest commissioner's notices regarding fires, and not to interfere or meddle with lumbering activities or property. They agreed also to pay rent promptly and not to make an assignment of the lease without permission of the Authority. Regarding the property, the lessees agreed that:

> they will at the termination of this lease peaceably deliver up to the said lessor or its assigns, the said premises and the buildings and improvements thereon, and, in consideration of this lease will leave on the said premises as the property of said lessor or its assigns, without any cost or liability on the part of said lessor for betterments or improvements of any kind, any further buildings, erections or additions that may be placed upon the said premises by said lessees during the term of this lease; and it is further agreed that all said further buildings, erections and additions without the necessity of any further act by either of said parties hereto, become the property of said lessor and its assigns. Lessees may remove any personal property or removable fixtures owned by them, upon the expiration of this lease.

All later leases to the sporting camps carried this provision.

Donald D. Kennedy and Valle Ewing Kennedy of Newcastle bought the Doxsee lease in 1950. The terms of the lease and the annual rent of $350 remained the same during the decade. Baxter seemed pleased with the change and visited at the camps on some of his trips thereafter.[11] The Kennedys remained at Kidney Pond until 1960, when they sold their interest to Charles J. Lipscomb of Easton, Maryland. At this time the Authority changed its leasing policy and granted a five-year lease at an increased rate of $500 per year.[12]

After three years, problems arose regarding the lease arrangement. The Fin & Feather Club of Millinocket began attacking Authority members on a variety of matters. One of the issues involved public access to Kidney and Daicey ponds. The Club also attacked special privileges granted to camp owners. In response, the Authority began to tighten up on its rules as they pertained to the camps. For years, for instance, the sporting camp owners had been allowed to kindle fires on small ponds in the area that were used by their guests. In 1963 the Authority continued to grant them permission, but only if a registered Maine Guide who held a fire permit was present. Within a month, however, the decision was rescinded on the basis that if this privilege were given to one camp, it would have to be given to all and would create a problem in policing and enforcement. When Lipscomb's lease was renewed for another five-year term in late 1965, it was modified to include officially a point of land that the camp owners had used for years for cookouts. When the Fin & Feather Club heard of this it protested so strongly that the Authority reversed itself and decided that under the trust deeds it could make no new leases or enlarge the land in existing leases. Thus the new lease was voided and the older one reissued.[13]

The situation changed radically in 1967 after Baxter signalled an end to the leasing system. The Authority moved rapidly and on July 11 voted to terminate all leases as of January 1, 1970; later this was changed to January 1, 1971.[14] For Kidney Pond camps the Authority began talking in terms of operating them as park concessions. Under such circumstances, Charles Lipscomb decided to sell his interests even before a final decision was made. He formally offered his interest in the property in the late summer or early fall of 1967. Though no record appears, it seems that the Authority had made the decision to keep the camps open on some basis once the leaseholds were terminated and was therefore interested in purchasing the equipment and furnishings of the camps. The Authority asked a Portland firm to appraise the property. In its report the firm set a fair market value of the leased fee at $65,000.[15] At an Authority meeting in late November it was decided to continue negotiations with Lipscomb on the basis of the estimate. Since certain legal questions concerning the right of the Authority to purchase property on land leased by itself had arisen, the attorney general's office was asked to render an opinion. In mid-December an assistant attorney general wrote an opinion confirming the Authority's right to do so. As part of his opinion he stated:

> All of the tangible property, capital improvements and inventory located on the leased State land is personal property and not realty. It is assumed for purposes of this opinion that the Baxter State Park Authority is either a party to, or has actual notice of, an agreement that the buildings at the time they were erected upon the land, were to be considered personal property.

Under state law, he wrote, an agreement that a building built with the consent of the owner of the land by one who was not the owner, would be considered personal property. Without such an agreement it would be "annexed to the realty."[16] No such agreement has been found in this case,

219

and Baxter and the Authority for nearly three decades had stated that at the end of the leasehold the buildings would revert to the state. On the same day the opinion was rendered, the Authority and Lipscomb signed an agreement, made two days earlier, for the transfer of Lipscomb's interest to the Authority for a cash price of $52,500, payable by April 1, 1968.[17]

Incredibly enough, given Baxter's past interest in the use of the trust funds for various purposes, he apparently was not consulted at any time prior to the final agreement.[18] Seemingly, he first heard of it when Henry L. Cranshaw, the state controller, called him in early March when the Authority asked him to draw a check on the trust fund for the purchase price. Baxter some years earlier had made an arrangement with Cranshaw that he be contacted before approving any withdrawals, even though the Authority had the legal right to make them. After he learned of the purchase, he wrote an angry letter to Cranshaw, saying he objected "to the State purchasing any portion of the land at Kidney Pond." He said the sale would be unlawful "as the State has no power to sell any portion of this land without my consent." Though he was obviously confused as to precisely what was being done, he asked Cranshaw to block the transaction.[19]

Attorney General Erwin and Chairman Wilkins met with Baxter at his Portland office and obtained his assent to the arrangement. Once the money was withdrawn and the transaction completed, Baxter apparently had second thoughts. Chairman Wilkins again met with him on March 23. Still not totally convinced, Baxter wrote another bitter letter two days later, this time to Governor Kenneth Curtis. He charged that the trust had been violated and the money had been withdrawn without his consent and insisted that it be restored promptly. Wilkins responded to the letter and explained that the money had been used to pay for Lipscomb's personal property and that the buildings were now the property of the state. He said the Authority would work with Governor Curtis to get the funds restored.[20] The Governor and Executive Council in May transferred $52,500 from the Contingent Account to the Baxter State Park Trust Fund. Reimbursement was to be made "through annual concession fee payments and from other sources of income."[21]

Before the arrangement was finally consummated, the Authority pushed plans to keep the camps operational. It decided to lease them for a five-year term on a concession basis. Advertisements asking for bids were published in Maine, New York, and Boston. Ultimately, the Authority awarded the concession to Mr. and Mrs. Charles Norris of Dixfield, Maine. Norris had indicated an interest in taking over Lipscomb's lease during the previous summer. For each of the five years the lease was to run, Norris agreed to pay the Authority $2,510.[22] Though now totally owned by the state, the operation remained a semi-commercial one, and some of the problems with other users of the Park continued after that time.

The second major lease in T3R10 involved York's Twin Pine camps. These camps, somewhat more rustic and with fewer amenities than the Kidney Pond camps, had been built very early in the century by Maurice York, a famous canoeman, who operated them until 1920, when his cousin, Everett L. York, assumed control. In 1932 they were left to Everett's son and daughter-in-law, Earle W. and Marabelle York. Prior to 1916 they were reached by boat and then trail from the railhead at Norcross on South Twin Lake. After 1915, when the road was constructed from Greenville to Sourdnahunk Field, the camps could be approached by automobile. From Sourdnahunk Field a rough tote road led along the stream for eight and a half miles to Daicey Pond and the camps. In 1932 when Everett York and his wife Vesta turned the camps over to their son, they moved to "York's Tavern," a camp at Sourdnahunk Field that was used to house guests temporarily when they were on their way into or out from Daicey Pond.[23] The old lumbering camps at Sourdnahunk Field were included in the lease. The land on which the camps lay was owned by the Cassidy Estate and the Garfield Land Company.[24] Earle York built several more cabins on land not included in the lease, though no difficulties arose until the 1960s. In addition, Frederic Hyde, a regular visitor to the area, also had a lease from the landowners until about 1930 and, on his site adjacent to York's lease, constructed a cabin for himself called "Hyde." By the 1940s this cabin was included in the York lease.[25]

Baxter was assigned a portion of the York lease in 1941 when he purchased a partial interest in the town. As with the Kidney Pond camps, the land was owned jointly by Baxter and the Cassidy Estate until 1945, when Baxter turned his interest over to the state. In 1959 he succeeded in buying the remainder of the property and deeded it to the state. After Earle York died, his wife took over the lease for the same annual rental of $200 and retained it until 1956, when it was assigned to her son Earle.[26]

After the Fin & Feather Club of Millinocket began attacking the park administration and its policies, the Authority in 1964 checked the area of land being used by the Yorks against that listed in the lease agreement. It was discovered that, inadvertently, when the number of camps was increased in the 1940s changes were not made in the official description of the property in the leases. After discussing the situation with the Yorks, the Authority ran new exterior lines, nearly doubling the size of the leasehold, and raised the annual rental to $400.[27] As the Fin & Feather Club continued its attacks on park policy and seeming favoritism to sporting camp owners, the Authority reviewed the lease situation once again in 1966, and it decided that its earlier action in increasing the size of the leased land ran counter to the trust provisions. Thus the older lease was reinstituted and the Yorks were ordered to move three of the cabins onto their legal leasehold.[28] Before this was done, Baxter had asked for an end to the leasing system.

The Authority waited until after the Kidney Pond camps problems had been settled before making any final decisions with regard to the Twin Pine camps. In early 1969 the Yorks were informed that their lease would not be renewed, though no action would be taken prior to January 1, 1970. The Yorks were told that they would be paid "a fair price, after professional appraisal for their personal property and improvements on the premises." The Authority, saying it would be guided by all considerations present in the Lipscomb lease, offered the Yorks a "life lease" to operate the camps as a concession, including the right to sublet the concession to their son until Mr. and Mrs. York were both dead.[29] The firm of Marshall and Stevens was asked to appraise the property, which appraisal, Attorney General Erwin wrote, "should find the fair market value of all the personal property belonging to the Yorks, and further should appraise the value of the improvements which they have made to the site: I take this to be the depreciated value of the cabins and other buildings there." The appraised value would then become the starting point for negotiations on a final selling price.[30]

The appraising firm set a fair market value for the Twin Pine camps at $54,200. William E. Cross was given a copy of the appraisal and wrote a lengthy critique of it. He noted that $42,301 had been assigned as the value of construction and miscellaneous items and $11,879 for contents and equipment, which included $3,450 for books. Cross thought the high values had been assigned to "take care of the factor of good will." He compared valuations given to such items as canoes with those assigned for similar items at Kidney Pond camps and concluded again that they were unrealistically high. The buildings belonged to the state and they and the improvements should not be paid for; the Authority should pay for equipment and supplies only, which by his calculations would come to $14,889. Or, he noted, "We could take the hardhearted approach and state that the lease will not be extended and let the equipment and supplies be sold by the present owner, . . ."[31] The appraiser shot back an equally strong letter in defense of his figures, especially noting that he had been told to consider the buildings as leasehold improvements.[32]

At an Authority meeting on December 16, the size of the offer to be made to the Yorks was discussed at length. While it was recognized that only about $12,000 was legally owed, all members agreed that paying such an amount would be unfair. They agreed on an offer of $36,000. When this was apparently turned down, the Authority raised its offer to $45,000, a figure which was accepted by the Yorks.[33] Once the agreement was made, Business Manager Cross had to inventory the camps and prepare a tentative breakdown of the purchase price. Again, he compared the camps unfavorably with those at Kidney Pond, and of the total purchase price he assigned $26,529 to "goodwill." Final agreement was concluded on June

30 and the payment made shortly thereafter.[34] The Authority decided to manage the camps itself by renting the cabins on a daily basis.

The continued existence of privately owned sporting camps on leased land in the Park raised some serious questions regarding rules and regulations and the rights of the general public in such areas. The Appalachian Trail, leading southward from the Nesowadnehunk tote road, skirted Grassy Pond and then skirted the north shore of Daicey Pond, through the area leased by the Yorks. Fishermen, particularly those from Millinocket, had frequented the area for years. As use of the Park soared, they increasingly came into conflict with the leaseholders at Daicey and Kidney ponds, who felt that the approach roads leading to their leases and the leased land should not be used by the general public. They posted "No Trespassing" signs, blocked parking areas beside the roads, and until 1951, stretched chains across the roads to block access by unauthorized individuals.

While there were minor differences of opinion during the first decades of the Park's existence, the problems became more significant in the decade of the 1960s when the Fin & Feather Club emerged as a strong, active, and aggressive sportsmen's/conservation group. When Baxter acquired the land in T2R9 in 1962 and deeded it to the state, the Club fought hard to keep the area open to hunting, trapping, and fishing.[35]

Access to Kidney, Daicey, and the Foss-Knowlton ponds by fishermen became an issue in 1964. The Club contacted the Authority and asked for information concerning access to Kidney and Daicey ponds, since they didn't want to bother the camp owners and had been refused access over the leased land. They had found a route along a brook to Kidney Pond, but for Daicey Pond it was more difficult, since the Appalachian Trail had many blowdowns. They sought permission to clean up the trail or to make a new one. The Authority replied that the lessees were entitled to a private right-of-way along the road. It recognized that the public should have access to the ponds concerned, but it also did not want to "get into additional established trails which would involve maintenance work on the part of park rangers, and would also involve the cutting of trees." Since the deeds of trust specifically stated that there should be no cutting of trees the Authority was bound to honor this provision.[36] Obviously the Authority was discouraging the development of alternative routes of access. Not content with the response, the Fin & Feather Club noted it had been told by Taylor that the entry roads were open to the public. It asked that trails be spotted around the leased land and offered to help mark the boundaries of the leases. When nothing more resulted, the Club submitted a petition listing its grievances to the Authority in March, 1965, and asked for a meeting with its members.[37] Among the grievances were Helon Taylor's and Austin Wilkins's refusal to allow access to the ponds by way of the roads or the Appalachian Trail; confrontations with owners of the sporting camps who warned fishermen away; the deliberate blocking of the Appalachian Trail to prevent access, the erection of "NO TRESPASSING" signs on the approach roads; illegal searches of automobiles of fishermen by park rangers on the strength of false reports by camp owners; and lack of proper markings denoting leased land.

The Authority members met with Club officers and members in June. The issues were discussed and some agreements made.[38] After the meeting, however, Chairman Wilkins wrote Helon Taylor: "I am in accord with you and will support you always that members of this Club have no right to cross leased land." Further discussions finally brought a promise that the Appalachian Trail would be respotted around Daicey Pond.[39]

Once the Club's officers learned that the Authority was extending the bounds of the leases on the two ponds, it pushed the matter of spotting a trail around the leased areas and further requested that its lease to a small area on Abol Pond and Stream be increased by addition of a small plot at Slide Dam on Nesowadnehunk Stream, where it would develop a picnic area. The Club thought it only right that this be done if the other leases were increased in size.[40] The issue was made more public during the following summer when the *Lincoln News* carried a series of articles on the matter and many letters to the editor appeared there and in other newspapers. The seeming favoritism to sporting camp owners was particularly emphasized.[41] Bowing to the criticisms, the Authority, in July 1966, reversed itself on the question of the expanded leases, advised the owner of Kidney Pond camps that the road into his camps had to be shared with the public as far as the leased boundary, and also said it was planning to relocate the Appalachian Trail around the Kidney Pond area.[42] Despite this decision, problems continued, for in 1970 the Club once more petitioned the Authority to correct a number of grievances, among which were access to Kidney Pond, the markings of the limits of leases, and access beyond Kidney to other fishing ponds.[43]

The Club and its members were looked upon as trouble makers by the Authority. There were legitimate differences of philosophy and interpretation of what park policy should be, and the Club did raise a number of pertinent policy issues that needed clarification. As long as commercial operations continued within the Park, these solutions were difficult to achieve. Obviously, the wilderness aspect, given most emphasis by Baxter and increasingly by the Authority, came into conflict with the ideas concerning recreational uses for the area.

Another group of leases was located in the northeastern section of the Park. There former landowners such as the Eastern Corporation held some temporary leases while they were cutting in the area. Some were terminated before Baxter's death, but three remained when the termination policy was instituted. None of these caused problems.

One camp on the Park did not involve a leasing arrangement. On Hudson Pond in T6R10, north of Trout Brook, a trapper by the name of Fred Harrison built a cabin sometime in the 1920s or 1930s. There he lived a hermitlike existence in contact with very few people. When Baxter bought the land and turned it over to the state the Park "sort of inherited him along with the land . . . and it was decided to let him stay there as long as he lived." Harrison committed suicide in 1961. Lest someone else move in and claim squatter's rights, Helon Taylor suggested the camp either be offered to the Fish and Game Commission to be used by the wardens, or be burned. The Commission agreed to use it for a year or two but ultimately it was burned.[44]

Another lease issue was resolved quickly. Before Baxter bought land in the southwest area of T6R10 the Eastern Corporation had leased a lot on Trout Brook to C. Howard and Mildred Steen. They operated a hunting camp out of the site and a fishing camp on Webster Lake. When the Bangor Hydro-Electric Company hired Steen as a dam tender at Grand Lake in 1948, the company president asked Baxter to grant the Steens a lease on the Trout Brook site before he turned the land over to the state. Baxter agreed and the Authority inherited the lease. In the following year Steen abandoned the camp when he concluded his hunting camp enterprise. Baxter personally provided the $200 needed to buy Steen's interest, and after the latter removed everything he wanted, the state took ownership and park officials burned the camp.[45]

Three leases still remained in 1967 when the Authority began phasing them out. Little detail is known about them. Mrs. Priscilla L. Clark of Vanceboro held a lease to a lot on Second Grand Lake in T6R9 for which she paid $25 per year. In 1970 after being told the lease would not be renewed after January 1, 1971, she was offered a choice of having the state buy her out before the lease expired or a five-year tenancy on terms similar to the lease.[46]

Similarly Dean W. Davignon, originally of Attleboro, Massachusetts, and an employee of the Eastern Corporation, held a lease in T6R9 on Second Grand Lake for which he paid $50 per year. Baxter visited the camp several times in the course of his park tours. After the Authority refused to issue a new lease, it offered a life tenancy through a letter of intent, or a lump sum settlement of $5,500. Davignon chose the latter.[47] Since then the camp has been used to house personnel from Baxter State Park and the Fish and Game Commission.

The final lease was to Louis C. Martin, who first leased his one-acre lot on the west shore of Grand Lake from the Garfield Land Company and other owners in 1940. He was originally from Lawrence, Massachusetts, but later lived in Patten and for a number of years was a fire warden for the Maine Forest Service. After Baxter bought the land in 1947, he renewed the lease for a two-year period; then, after he gave the land to the state, he authorized a continuation of the lease, which remained in force for the next two decades for an annual fee of $150. When the Martins discussed the disposition of the camp in 1970 it was agreed an inventory would be taken. After the Authority received the appraisal of $15,000 made by the assessor for the town of Patten, the Authority, rather than buy them out, offered the Martins life tenancy. Eventually, however, the Martins preferred a lump sum settlement of $10,000 offered by the Authority for their excellent cottage.[48] It has since been used by the Authority to house park personnel.

A final set of leases was centered in T2R9, at the extreme southern end of the Park, the area last acquired by Baxter. All of these leases had been made with Great Northern prior to Baxter's acquisition of the land. Some time in the 1940s or 1950s the Boy Scout organization in Millinocket leased for one dollar per year a site for a scouting camp on the north shore of Abol Pond. The lease was continued when the land was added to the Park in 1963. After the 1967 decision on leases, the scouting organization was duly informed that the lease would not be renewed, but there was no intention of closing out the camp by the Authority. After several conferences between interested parties, continued use was assured in the spring of 1970. The Scout leaders were told that the organization could "continue to use exactly the same premises described in your former lease for the same purpose, and upon the same conditions." While the Scouts would not have a property right, as in a lease, they could continue to use the premises as a "licensee for the indefinite future." Only some form of abuse or misbehavior would lead to revocation of the license.[49]

The Great Northern Paper Company in 1955 leased a lot on the north side of Togue Stream about one-half mile below Lower Togue Pond to Ronald Budreau of Millinocket. A year later it was replaced by another which added two other Millinocket residents, Daniel A. McQuarrie and Darrell F. Morrow, to the list of lessees. For $10 paid each year the group had the right to "hold until June 1, 1956 and thereafterwards from year to year so long as this lease shall not on some rent day be cancelled in writing, and subject always to the reservations and conditions on the back hereof." The reservations and conditions were the usual ones in sportsmen's leases concerning use and abuse of property.[50] A new lease along the lines of the old lease was granted by the Authority in 1963 after Baxter turned the land over to the state. In 1969, after termination proceedings had begun, Ronald Budreau, acting for his partners, asked $2,500 for his camp. The Authority declined to purchase the improvements and also told Budreau that he could not use a snowmobile to get to his camp during the winter.[51] Budreau complained to Senator Wakine Tanous of Millinocket, and also stated that the Boy Scouts were being evicted. Tanous talked with Attorney General Erwin, who explained the situation and Baxter's actions and said the Authority was terminating the leases "not because we wanted to do it, not because we liked doing it, but because the Governor . . . has told us that this was what he wanted done."[52]

In August 1970 the Authority was ready to offer Budreau and his partners a five-year tenancy or a cash settlement of $500. An assistant attorney general who was asked to check the legal aspects of the case, however, noted that Budreau had a lifetime right to renew his lease unless he violated the conditions. Since there was no evidence of violations, and unless it could be shown that the park Authority lease violated the trust indenture, and unless it could be shown that Great Northern's lease with Budreau allowed for termination, the Authority had no legal right to terminate the lease. Late in the year Chairman Wilkins indicated that Budreau had been offered the alternatives noted above and rejected them.[53]

The Fin & Feather Club of Millinocket held a lease to a lot on Abol Pond that it had originally obtained in 1958 from Great Northern and for which it paid one dollar per year since it was a non-profit organization. In 1963 the Authority renewed the lease on terms similar to those in Budreau's lease. During the same year the Club worked closely with the Authority in reclaiming Abol Pond for fishing. It built a temporary dam and spillway at the outlet to the pond, after which the existing fish were poisoned and the pond was then restocked.[54] The Authority informed the Club late in 1969 that its lease would not be renewed, but within a year, two months after members of the Authority had met with representatives of the Fin & Feather Club in Millinocket to try to iron out differences, offered it a letter of intent for use of the premises on terms similar to those issued to the Abol Boy Scout Camp "so long as they existed as a Fin and Feather Club."[55]

The cases of the Budreau lease and that of the Fin & Feather Club were combined and they began legal proceedings against the Authority for illegal cancellation of the leases.[56] No formal legal action occurred until 1974 when the Authority brought suit against the Fin & Feather Club and others to clarify the legal status of the various parties concerned. The Maine Supreme Court found that the Authority had the right to lease lands in Baxter State Park; concluded that the Authority was on solid legal ground when it negotiated a new lease with Budreau and his partners and the Fin & Feather Club after it obtained control of the property; and, most important, had the right to terminate the leases with proper notification. The court held that the leasehold rights were terminated on December 31, 1970.[57] After duly notifying the leaseholders to remove their property during the late spring of 1974 and their failure to do so, the Authority removed their property, and in June both camps on the Budreau lease were demolished. All vestiges of both leaseholds were removed.[58]

227

THE CHIMNEY TRAIL

Another facet of park administration that caused a good deal of controversy from time to time, and particularly in the late sixties and early seventies, involved rules and regulations for the use of the Park. They evolved gradually. In setting them up the Authority had to keep in mind not only the essential wilderness character of the Park and the fact that it was also a wildlife sanctuary, but the deeds of trust. New rules often came after pressures built up to control activities that could not be foreseen when those activities first started. This is particularly true with regard to the use of snowmobiles in the Park. Except for the basic terms of the trust deeds, Baxter did not involve himself nearly so deeply in this aspect of park administration and policy making as he did in other areas.

For nearly two decades after creation of the Park there were no special rules of conduct to which visitors had to conform. General state laws and fishing and hunting rules and regulations applied to the area. Since it was a game preserve, it was in a special category in relation to game laws.* Late in 1949 the Authority developed a set of rules, but for some reason did not promulgate them. Harold Dyer in his last report to the Authority in early July 1950 suggested they be adopted. His report was written in late June. On July 1 at a meeting at Katahdin Stream at which Baxter was present, and while Dyer was elsewhere in the Park, the Authority formally adopted its first set of regulations.[1] In order to use them as the basis for further discussion, they are reproduced here in their entirety.

## BAXTER STATE PARK AUTHORITY
### RULES AND REGULATIONS

1. SEASON

   The park campground[2] shall be open to the public from May 15 to October 15. As a safeguard against accidents, no person shall climb, snowshoe or ski on any mountain in the park at any time between November 1 and May 1 until he has procured a permit to do so, and no permit shall be issued until sufficient proof has

---

* See page 161 for the law of 1949 that first spelled out the policing power of the Authority within the Park.

been presented to the Park Supervisor as to the competency of
the party.

2. TRAFFIC

All vehicles shall be left in those areas provided or designated
for parking. No person shall operate any vehicle in any recreational
area in a reckless manner, or at a speed in excess of 15 miles per
hour, or in a manner so as to endanger any person or property.

3. CLOSED AREAS

During periods of critical forest fire conditions or any other emergencies, the park, or portions thereof, shall be closed at the
descretion (sic) of the Park Authority and no person shall enter,
or remain in, the park or the closed portions thereof except a law
enforcement officer in the line of duty.

4. CAMPING

Campers in organized campgrounds must register with the Ranger
before making camp. No person shall camp in any area except at
official campsites, and then only in those places provided or
designated for such camping. Camping, or the use of fires, on the
tableland or the summits of Mount Katahdin is strictly prohibited.

5. FIRES

Any fire not confined as herein provided shall be reported to the
nearest Park Ranger *at once*. No person shall build a camp, cooking
or other fire, or use an abandoned camp, cooking or other fire
except at official campsites and then only in those places provided
or designated for such purposes, and shall, before leaving such
fire, totally extinguish the same.

No person shall throw away, or discard, any burning cigarettes,
cigars, matches, or any other burning material along any road or
trail, or in, or adjacent to any woods in this park.

6. BATHING AND WASHING

All bathing and washing shall be restricted to those areas provided or designated for such purposes, and no person shall bathe,
or wash any article, in any spring, stream, or pond used as a
source of drinking water.

7. REFUSE

All trash and waste shall be placed in the containers provided,
and no person shall throw away, or discard, any can, bottle, paper,
or any other waste or trash in any spring, stream, or pond, or along
any road or trail.

8. PETS

All dogs and other pets shall be kept under restraint while in the
park.

9. FIREARMS AND FIREWORKS

The possession, or use, of any firearms, or fireworks, within the boundaries of the park is prohibited.

10. AIRCRAFT

No person shall land an aircraft on the ground, or on the waters, of the park except a law enforcement officer in the line of duty.

11. OUTBOARD MOTORS

No person shall operate, or attach to any boat, canoe or other craft, any outboard motor while on the waters of the park.

12. PROPERTY

No person shall remove, damage, or destroy any structure, or any tree, shrub, plant, wildlife, or any other natural natural (sic) feature of the park.[3]

13. VIOLATIONS

All persons found guilty of violating the rules and regulations shall be punished as provided in the Revised Statutes of Maine, 1944, Chapter 32, as amended by Chap. 78 P. L. of 1949.

The first change came within two years. In 1951 Donald Kennedy, the lessee of the Kidney Pond camps, was arrested and summoned to court by a warden supervisor for having weapons in his personal cabin at Kidney Pond. Kennedy immediately visited Baxter and also contacted Commissioner Roland Cobb.[4] The charges were apparently quietly dropped. At about the same time, the Authority received a request from lumbering operators to permit some of their men cutting on park lands to keep weapons to protect themselves against destructive bears.[5] Since one of the new rules was an absolute prohibition against firearms within the park limits, some adjustments had to be made. Commissioner Roland Cobb wrote to Baxter regarding the rule. Baxter agreed that the owners of the sporting camps should be allowed to keep weapons for emergencies, and that hunters travelling through the Park to hunt elsewhere be allowed to transport unassembled weapons.[6] By the following spring the Authority had worked out and formally adopted a revised rule regarding weapons. The process laid down in the 1949 legislation was then followed and the change became official on July 4. It reads:

FIREARMS

The use of any firearms, except by law enforcement officers on official duty, within the boundaries of the park is prohibited. Firearms can be transported through the Park by hunters or others. However, they *should* be enclosed in the car trunk or in a case.* Firearms may be

---

* Italics mine.

kept for protection by the camps located in the Park provided a record of them is kept open at all times to inspection by the Park rangers and the Inland Fish and Game wardens. Hunters staying at sporting camps within the Park may have firearms at such camps provided they are registered with the sporting camp owner.

Of all the park rules, this caused Taylor most difficulty in the fifties and early sixties.[7]

Also appended to the revised rules, but without numbers, were three other statements that were later incorporated into them. One provided that Maine state fishing licenses were required for fishing and that the state angling laws were in effect. Hunting and trapping were prohibited. Another provided: "No intoxicating beverages may be brought into or consumed within any State Park." The third stated that it was "expected that visitors will be quiet and orderly in camps, shelters and bunkhouses."

By 1955 further changes were deemed necessary. As Baxter acquired more land in the northern section of the Park, he had to make concessions regarding hunting and other issues. Since the new acquisitions included large portions of Matagamon Lakes and Webster Lake that bordered on privately owned land, some of the regulations were unworkable. Helon Taylor made a number of suggestions regarding the wording of the rules. In the summer of 1955, therefore, some changes were voted by the Authority.[8] The rule regarding firearms was amended by adding the sentence: "Hunting and trapping are prohibited" at the end of the paragraph; this had earlier been an addendum to the rules as a whole. Another paragraph was added that read: "This regulation shall not apply in the area north of Trout Brook in Township 6 Range 9 or in Township 6 Range 10, where hunting under general laws will be allowed." The absolute bans on aircraft landing in the Park and on the use of motorboats except by authorized officials was modified to exclude the Matagamon Lakes and Webster Lake. Finally, earlier addenda on fishing and the use of liquor were formally incorporated into the revised rules as numbers 14 and 15 respectively.

Two minor modifications came in early 1957.[9] The first rule was changed to provide that between October 16 and May 14 the Park would be closed except by permit. This took care of the two two-week periods when the rules apparently did not apply. The second change modified the firearms and hunting rule to add the words: "bow and arrow, sling shot, air rifle or air pistol" to the list of banned weapons, and also substituted the word "must" for "should" in the sentence providing for keeping weapons being transported through the Park in the trunk of the vehicle or in a case.

In late 1959 the Authority made several additional changes to allow better administration and control.[10] The rule on camping was modified by changing the first sentence and adding another immediately after. As

232

amended, the first two sentences read: "Campers in organized camp-grounds must register with the ranger and pay fees in advance before making camp. Check in time—before 10:00 p.m. Check out time—by 3:30 p.m."[11]

A new rule, Number 16, on reservation refunds, was added. A policy of allowing reservations to be made at campgrounds had been adopted in the mid-fifties. Much of the Authority chairman's time and that of the supervisor and the Authority itself was taken up at meetings with refund requests. The files of the Authority contain many letters of complaint about the refusal of the Authority to refund fees paid in advance when reservations were made. Often those making reservations had to change their plans at the last minute and asked for a refund, though the cost was a minor part of the total expenditures they had to make on such a trip. The final decision rested with the chairman or the Authority itself. The new rule attempted to clarify the policy. It read:

> 16. RESERVATION REFUNDS. No refund request on a late cancellation will be honored unless a good, valid reason or unusual situation is given in writing and return of unused tickets. Special form cards are provided for this purpose. The Authority has ruled that sudden sickness, injury or death in the family are acceptable as valid reasons for refund requests. Weather conditions, dissatisfaction, business reasons, dog problems, restless children, and others will not be considered. A week's notice of a cancellation on a reservation made well in advance will be favorably considered for a refund. This will permit the possibility of filling the cancelled reservation with another party.

Complaints and dissatisfaction continued, but at least the policy was more explicit.[12]

A new rule 17 in 1959 introduced a problem that was to become more acute as time passed. As use of the Park increased, the number of accidents rose, particularly on Katahdin. When the rules were first adopted in 1950, the only limitation on hiking and climbing in the Park was in the first rule, which required that permission be obtained from the supervisor, who would determine the competency of the parties for winter climbing. Helon Taylor adhered rigorously to this and almost always followed a policy of sending a ranger, usually Myrle Scott, with the party at no cost beyond normal fees. Properly prepared parties had no trouble, but he was quick to refuse permission to those not prepared. In 1955, for example, Taylor described meeting "three young men from Rhode Island on the road and they said they were going to climb the mountain. On questioning I found that they did not have ice axes, crampons or ropes. Neither did they have snowshoes or skis. I told them they had better go back to Rhode Island and come back properly equiped (sic) if they wanted to climb our mountain."[13] In 1958 three Explorer Scouts and their leader tried to cross the Knife Edge against the advice of Ranger Tom Sprague of Chimney Pond.

They were forced to spend an uncomfortable night on the side of Pamola. Taylor hoped they had learned a lesson not in the Boy Scout manual, "And that is that a Chimney Pond Ranger probably knows more about Katahdin than a Boy Scout leader. Even one from Boston."[14] It was incidents such as these that triggered adoption of the new rule.

> 17. INSPECTION AND PERMISSION TO CLIMB MT. KATAHDIN. Permission will not be granted to climb Mt. Katahdin or any other peak in the park under hazardous conditions without adequate equipment and proper wearing apparel. Final decisions shall rest with the park ranger. This shall apply to individuals not associated with outing clubs as well as outing club members.
>
> During the summer season, May 15 to October 15, it is desirable for persons to check with the park ranger on proper footwear to climb the mountain or other peaks within the park. The provisions of this rule shall not be construed as an assumption by the Authority of any liability for use of the park and its facilities.

In the winter of 1958 the Authority had voted to impose a charge of $12 per day for the rangers who were now required to accompany parties during the off season. This was in addition to the usual summer fees.[15] The fee's existence was not fully publicized for some time and this led to some public irritation.

The last rule adopted in 1959 involved the use and enjoyment of park facilities by state officials and friends of the personnel. Questions had arisen regarding the degree to which officials should or could take advantage of their positions to obtain special privileges in the park area. This rule allowed the Authority and the administrators more clout in warding off requests for special services. It reads:

> 18. USE OF PARK FACILITIES BY STATE OFFICIALS AND SPECIAL FRIENDS. There shall be no exceptions for state personnel requesting park facilities without fee unless on official duty. Special friends of the park rangers or state personnel on vacation, whether during the week or on holiday weeks, will be required to pay the required use fee.

Though not published as part of the official rules for a time, the Authority also developed a new policy in 1959 for handling larger groups from summer camps. For some time they had been housed in overflow areas, such as Avalanche Brook or Foster Field. Taylor from time to time reported having had difficulties in controlling groups from Boy Scout and other summer camps. In 1957, he reported: "We have had more than our share of bad campers at Chimney Pond this year. All from boys camps. They use the Ranger's leanto logs for wood, hack into green trees, chase the tame rabbits, bother the other campers, generally make a nuisance of themselves and leave the place in a mess. We are thankful that only a few camps are like that. . . . As a rule the girls camps put the boys camps to shame when it comes to proper camping."[16] To correct this problem the Authority asked camp directors to cooperate by not sending more than fifteen campers to a group and providing a councillor for every five campers.[17] As time passed this was more and more rigidly enforced.

The increasing number of users created problems that forced revision of the rule regarding pets. In the late fifties, increasing numbers of visitors complained of those who brought pets into the Park since they created a nuisance and disturbed wildlife. Various control proposals were discussed, such as excluding pets at Russell Pond and Chimney Pond but allowing them elsewhere as long as they were restrained. The issue was discussed at an Authority meeting in 1960, but no changes were made. Finally the supervisor and rangers held a meeting and voted unanimously to request a rule barring all pets. This was done in time for the 1962 season. Since it took a certain amount of time for the change to become widely known, there were a number of complaints during the 1962 season, as well as in later years, from those visitors who insisted on bringing their pets with them. In many cases the rangers allowed such individuals to stay one night and then asked them to move elsewhere.[18]

In 1962, for the first time, the fee schedule was included as a new rule in the list. No charges were made for children under six. Also in 1962, the reservation refund rule was modified as follows:

16. RESERVATION REFUNDS. No refund request on a late cancellation will be honored unless a good, valid reason or unusual situation is given in writing within 30 days to the Augusta office with the return of unused receipts. A week's notice of a cancellation on a reservation will be favorably considered for a refund. This will permit the possibility of filling the cancelled reservation with another party.

The usual problems and complaints about the policy continued.

Still other changes were made in time for the 1963 summer season. The rule regarding traffic was modified to make it a bit more realistic. In place of the absolute speed limit of 15 miles per hour for the whole Park, differing limits were set according to the dangers involved. The old limit was kept for campgrounds, but a limit of 25 miles per hour was set for the rest of the Park, except for the section of the perimeter road from Abol Pond to Trout Brook Crossing. The hunting provision was modified to allow hunting on the newly acquired land in T2R9. As regards fishing, a notation was added listing points in the Park where non-resident licenses could be purchased. The fee schedule was adjusted by raising the fee for the use of the rangers' services during the off season to $15 per day. Under the violations rule the precise wording of the 1949 law setting punishments for violations was added. In the reservations refund rule, the Millinocket office of the Authority was substituted for Augusta as the place where those desiring refunds should write and return unused receipts. This seemed more logical than using the chairman's time for such tasks. Questionable cases were forwarded to Augusta for a final decision. Finally, the rule on climbing Katahdin was changed to read:

INSPECTION AND PERMISSION TO CLIMB MT. KATAHDIN. Permission will not be granted to climb Mt. Katahdin or any other peak in the park during the off season under hazardous conditions without adequate equipment and proper wearing apparel. Adequate equipment shall also be required during the regular season. Final decision shall rest with the park rangers. This shall apply to individuals not associated with outing clubs as well as outing club members.

Considerable renumbering of the various rules was done.[19]

The construction of the gatehouse system for controlling entry into the Park necessitated further changes in the rules. Before the summer season began in 1967 a new rule was added which reads as follows:

GATEHOUSES AND PASSES. All persons entering and leaving Baxter State Park will be required to stop and register or by some other identification at any of the gatehouse check points located at Togue Pond, Matagamon Lake, and Nesowadnehunk Field. Basic purpose of the gate-house pass system is for reason of safety. There will be no toll fee.[20]

In 1971 the rule was modified by deleting "by some other identification" and adding "be identified." Two years later it was again revised to read:

GATEHOUSE AND PASSES: All persons entering and leaving the Park will be required to stop and register or be identified at one of the gatehouse checkpoints. During the season all park gates shall be closed at 10 p.m. and will open at 5 a.m. Campground offices will open at 7 a.m. for registration. There will be an attendant at Togue Pond Gatehouse for emergency purposes around the clock during the season.[21]

Beginning in 1968, a great many of the rules were modified in various ways and new ones added to meet changing circumstances. The reasons for these developments were several. Most important was the continuing increase in the number of users of the Park. Basic decisions had to be made as to whether facilities should be built to handle larger numbers of users, or the gatehouse system be tied to a policy of placing realistic limits on the number of campers at each campsite. The latter policy was chosen. The increasing frequency of accidents on Katahdin and in other parts of the Park led to demands for closer control of hikers in the park area. The increased use of the Park by camp groups and the attendant problems in discipline and control created other issues. If such groups stayed at campgrounds for long periods, particularly on weekends, they took up space demanded by adults. In the late sixties, a number of visitors to the Park complained of lack of space because of this. The increased interest in

A moonlight time exposure of Mt. Katahdin, taken at about 9 P.M. (at 20 below zero!) from what is now Togue Pond Road going into the Park.

Photo Paul A. Knaut, Jr.

Taken on a beautiful early summer day, when wild purple rhodora are in their full glory, at Taylor Pond, with Mt. Katahdin in the background.

Photo Paul A. Knaut, Jr.

A bull moose taken at Sandy Stream Pond, with the Katahdin Range in the background.

Photo Paul A. Knaut, Jr.

*Diapensia lapponicum*
(4,300 feet)

*Loiseleuria procumbens*
(Alpine azalea)

*Rhododendron lapponicum*
(growing beside snow, 4,300 ft.)

The chipmunk grew bold, tempted by nuts
strewn on top the mushroom.

The botanical species are reproduced courtesy Dr. A. E. Brower, Maine
Forest Service, Retired. They were all taken in 1958, in the Saddle area of
Mt. Katahdin.

The chipmunk posed for Maurice Day and was photographed by him
as one of innumerable photos made in the Maine woods and Katahdin
region for the Disney movie on *Bambi*.

hiking in the nation generally, and the enormous expansion of the use of leisure-time recreational equipment, led to other problems. During the 1960s the use of snowmobiles mushroomed and their use in the Park was virtually uncontrolled at first. The development of trail bikes and all sorts of all-terrain vehicles presented problems there and elsewhere. Increased use of house trailers, camping trailers, cabs on trucks, and similar travel conveniences posed problems. They had been allowed in the Park during the forties and fifties and on into the early sixties, but as their use grew, problems of control grew as well. Trailers sometimes used up two or three tenting sites.

The establishment of the Allagash Wilderness Waterway also posed problems, since the most logical approach to Telos Lake was through the northern end of Baxter State Park. Policies had to be developed to handle vehicles that merely crossed the Park to the Waterway. All of these issues were compounded by the social unrest in the nation during the late sixties and early seventies. The modern ecological and environmental movement presented a wholly different philosophy about the proper uses of such an area as Baxter State Park. Environmental organizations became increasingly militant in their demands for change. They were faced by equally militant groups defending the use of snowmobiles, of pesticides, of trailers. Everything was further complicated by the death of Governor Baxter in 1969.

The Authority was caught in the middle and tried to balance the various forces and demands. It met much more frequently than in the past, and much more of its time was used in discussing administration of the Park and mediating or dealing with controversies that developed. Attorney General Erwin was much more interested in the Park and in defending Baxter's concepts for it than most of his predecessors had been, and he emerged as a major leader in developing new policies for the Park.[22] In 1970 he even suggested that the Authority close the Park completely for a year to allow time to develop new policies and refurbish the facilities.[23] The suggestion was not accepted. Erwin also suggested that to have a wider public input into the policy-making process and perhaps still some of the criticisms of park administration, an Advisory Committee be established.[24] This was accepted and such a group was set up in 1970. During the period the Authority also worked on a "Statement of Purpose" providing intermediate objectives for park policy until a more complete and permanent master plan for the Park could be worked out. This was passed by the legislature in 1971.[25]

The Authority tried to develop a set of rules and regulations that would maintain the wilderness character of the Park, conform to the trust deeds and Baxter's wishes as much as possible, and meet as many as possible of the varying demands of different public groups. The job was a difficult one. In 1970, after a number of major changes were made, the public outcry was great and diverse. Erwin sent some of the letters he had received to Chairman Wilkins for reply, since as he said: "I am not going to be the sole spokesman for the Park." He went on to ask: "Did we ban motorcycles from the perimeter roads as well as the trails? I don't remember. The attached letters simply show that, if we tried to please everybody, we wouldn't have a Park left."[26]

Particularly with regard to the snowmobile issue, the correspondence in the files of the Authority is enormous. Various groups and individuals adopted widely varying points of view on this and other rules.

Only minor changes were made in the first five rules involving the season, traffic, closed areas, camping, and fires. The maximum speed limit in the Park was lowered to 20 miles per hour. Parking was prohibited on park roads, and at the campgrounds the rule was interpreted to read that cars had to be left in parking areas and could not be left beside lean-tos or tent sites. At campgrounds the time limit for checking in was moved from 10 P.M. to 8 P.M. and for checking out from 3 P.M. to noon. The rule regarding trash and refuse reflected changing thinking in parks and environmental work around the nation. It prohibited deposit of trash or waste anywhere within the Park except in official containers or authorized dumps and noted that no official containers would be available in off-road camping areas. "Where no official containers are provided, refuse must be packed out." The regulation on bathing and washing was modified by adding two sentences: "Soap and approved detergents will be available at campgrounds. No other cleaning agents will be used." The controversial rule on pets was also modified to provide that the ban on pets "or other domestic animals" did not apply to those travelling by vehicle through the Park. The firearms regulation remained the same except for a more precise spelling out of areas not subject to the ban on hunting. The sections on aircraft and outboard motors in the Park were modified to state more precisely under what circumstances they might be used in the Park. These included emergency landings for aircraft and "official search and rescue operations, law enforcement or the administrative requirements of the park" for aircraft and motors.[27]

After discussing the question for a number of years, the Authority made a firm decision on the use of motorcycles and all-terrain vehicles within the limits of the Park at its meeting on March 23, 1970. As early as 1962 the Authority had received a complaint on the use of a "Go-Kart" at the South Branch Pond campground;[28] and the "Honda situation" was a topic of discussion at an Authority meeting in 1965. No action resulted and in the following years Baxter had asked the Authority to pass a rule specifically banning the use of motor scooters and motorcycles in the Park since they would frighten wildlife.[29] His request was not followed, but by the end of the decade the problem became more severe and something had to be done. The new rule, first used in 1970, was quite comprehensive: "No

238

person shall bring into the park or operate within the park any motorcycle, trail bike or other two-wheel motor-driven vehicle, or any all-terrain vehicle, so-called, which shall include without limitation, those motor-driven vehicles operating either on endless treads or wheels which are designed to operate over any terrain off the roads and highways." Since a later rule applied to snowmobiles, they were excepted here. There was also the usual disclaimer on use by park personnel and law enforcement officers. Within three days of the announcement of the new rule a letter of protest was received.[30]

To the earlier wording on property was added a prohibition on persons bringing paint into the Park or having it in their possession. It was accompanied by a ban on tampering, altering, or removing trail signs and other markers. Prior to this there had been a rash of vandalism that included the writing of graffiti on rocks with spray paint cans. The specific ban on liquor was modified to read: "General laws of the State of Maine pertaining to alcoholic beverages apply within the confines of the park." Advance reservations were recommended and would be accepted for specific campgrounds (but not specific camping sites) for a one-week period, but could be continued depending upon availability of space.* They had to be accompanied by funds to cover the fees and would be held until 6 P.M. of the following day. These payments would no longer be refunded if the reservation was not used. Finally, it was noted that day-use facilities would be available at each campground on a first come, first served basis. This latter provision undoubtedly reflected pressures exerted by the Fin & Feather Club.

In late 1969 and early 1970, the Authority discussed and finally developed a policy on the use of trailers in the Park. *True Magazine* in April 1969 ran an article by Michael Frome in which he discussed and criticized various famous camping areas and parks around the nation. Baxter State Park was placed in the category of "camping slums."[31] This was denied by park officials, but it also led to discussions between Supervisor Kearney and Chairman Wilkins concerning the carrying load of the Park. Kearney later noted: "If all the [camping] areas are filled to optimum we can accomidate (sic) only 587 persons, not the 1200 mentioned in the article." He went on to note problems raised by trailer reservations and continued use of trailers in camping areas where they took up too much space. He wondered "if these aluminum monsters" were in keeping with Baxter's trust deeds and wishes and asked the Authority to consider the question.[32] The problem was considered and a rule adopted for the 1970 season which was modified in the following year. It provided that, except those passing through from the Matagamon gatehouse to that at Neso-

---

* In 1972, the Authority voted to accept reservations from Maine residents only, from January 1 to March 1; in 1973 this was extended to March 31.

239

wadnehunk, motor vehicles or trailers containing sleeping accommodations were excluded from the Park. Pick-up trucks with camper bodies and small van-type vehicles not exceeding 20 feet in length or 7 feet in height could be brought to the campgrounds or parked at them, but could not be used for sleeping. Pop-up tent trailers without toilet and sink facilities were allowed. This provision led to another flurry of protest letters, as well as many in praise of the new departure.

The rules regarding hiking and climbing in the Park at various seasons was modified almost yearly before 1971. Each time the policy was made more restrictive, particularly where technical rock climbing and winter activities were involved. By 1971 it read:

> CLIMBING IN THE PARK.  Permission in writing from the park supervisor is required for the following activities: Winter Climbing, Alpine Skiing, and Technical Climbing. In order to receive permission for the above activities, parties must give evidence of having adequate experienced leadership and proper clothing and equipment for the proposed undertaking. Guidelines and detailed requirements should be obtained from the park supervisor. Applicants will be required to make definite arrangements for a back-up rescue team whenever in the judgement of the supervisor the nature of the undertaking requires this. Applications for permission for winter climbing, Alpine skiing, or technical climbing shall be submitted at least 4 weeks in advance.
>
> CLIMBING AND MOUNTAIN HIKING IN THE PARK DURING OTHER THAN WINTER CONDITIONS.  Climbing or hiking may be restricted to experienced and well equipped persons during darkness or hazardous weather conditions at the discretion of the supervisor, who may delegate this authority to certain members of the park staff.[33]

The rule was further modified in later years, but the tenor remained the same. Supervisor Harry Kearney submitted a list of criteria for winter climbing parties.[34]

The various rules on use of park facilities by state officials and friends in regard to disturbances, fees, and gatehouses and passes, remained essentially the same during the period to 1971. Minor changes of wording did not change the intent of the rules, with the big exception that the $15 per day fee for the use of rangers on winter trips was dropped.[35]

The rule on snowmobiles was undoubtedly the single most controversial issue in the history of the Park up to that point. Except for the very old steam-driven, caterpillar-tread Lombard engines, which were undoubtedly used in the park area during the early 20th century, the first discussion of more modern types of snow travelling vehicles in the Park was in 1959, when there seemed to be a possibility of obtaining the use of a 19-foot, 3,500 pound half-track vehicle. Apparently plans to bring it to the Park did not materialize. Two years later, a group from Augusta visited 240    the Park in March and used a weasel to move their goods. That year also saw the first of a series of expeditions through the Park from Millinocket to the Allagash, using Polaris Sno-Travelers; it was sponsored by a Millinocket dealer in those machines. These expeditions, by 1965 called the "Polaris Safari" by Helon Taylor, grew remarkably in size. In the latter year Ranger Rodney Sargent accompanied the group into the Park where the participants camped at Nesowadnehunk and then continued on to the Allagash with them.[36] Mention has been made in another chapter that Taylor had purchased a snowmobile with his own funds and Baxter repaid the cost. By the end of 1965, a park-owned snowmobile was being used to transport the equipment and supplies of winter campers.[37] Thereafter use of the machines in the Park increased rapidly and much of Taylor's and other rangers' time was spent in policing them.

At the same time criticism of these practices mounted in intensity. At a meeting of the Authority in June the question of motor bikes was discussed, but there is no indication that a possible snowmobile ban was debated. Under considerable pressure from both sides, the Authority in the late sixties voted to limit travel in the Park by snowmobile to the regular road system which was maintained by the State Highway Commission; the logging roads on Rum Mountain built when the blowdown of 1963 was cleared; the road eastward to Katahdin Lake from Avalanche Field, and the trail to Chimney Pond campground. Chairman Wilkins said this was reviewed with Baxter, and he stated: "I am sure that in his declining years he still understood what was meant by this snowmobile regulation."[38]

The outcry and criticism mounted while snowmobile clubs and owners defended the policy. In October of 1969 the restricted areas were increased and travel permitted only on the perimeter roads regularly maintained for summer traffic by the State Highway Commission. The road eastward from Avalanche Field to Katahdin Lake was again opened in 1971.[39] Several years later, when it was learned that Baxter had written a letter opposing the widespread use of snowmobiles in the Park, the attorney general handed down a ruling that effectively banned their non-official use in the Park.[40]

As indicated earlier, the difficulties of housing and controlling summer camp groups increased as more camps brought their clients to the Park. Most caused no problems, but by the late sixties difficulties developed.[41] Not much more was done until after July 16, 1969, when Jay Barrett, a fourteen-year-old youth from Pennsylvania who was attending a boys camp in Casco, Maine, left his party with another boy while descending Cathedral Trail. Foolishly leaving the trail to look for snowfields on the extremely steep mountainside, the boy slipped and slid down the steep, wet rock face for about 125 feet and did not survive. The tragic incident was only the worst part of a camp group hike during which discipline and supervision of the hikers broke down. The incident provoked a strong reaction, since it was the eleventh death in the Park in six years, though most were not attributable to hiking accidents.[42] The Authority very quickly instructed the supervisor that no groups of hikers under the age of twenty-one be permitted in the Park unless at least one adult over twenty-one years of age was present for every five under-age hikers.[43] Also a meeting was held between members of the Authority and representatives from summer-camp organizations to hammer out a policy regarding their use of the Park. By the following April, Supervisor Kearney had compiled a suggested list of rules for summer camp groups.[44] In 1971, a regular rule promulgated in 1970 was revised to provide that campers from boys and girls summer camps would be assigned facilities in the Park at the discretion of the Authority for periods not to exceed five days, excluding Friday and Saturday, and in groups no larger than ten campers and two leaders. Camps could submit their requests for space up to May 1 and would be notified by the end of that month. Leaders had to hold a Camp Trip Leaders permit as required by state law, and each group had to have an experienced twenty-year-old counselor or leader for each five hikers. It was a strong rule and created continued discontent, but given the increasing difficulties experienced with such groups it was probably necessary.[45]

As the amount of research, not only with regard to plants and animals, but also in geology, water studies, survival techniques, and similar topics increased, the Authority felt it necessary to set down a general policy with regard to the conduct of such research. Much of this had been done in earlier years on an *ad hoc* basis, so this represented no new departure. The rule as it existed in 1971 simply provided that requests for research studies of various types in the Park had to be submitted in writing to the Authority. Requests to collect specimens would be reviewed to make certain that they comported to the wilderness concept.

The last item on the list of rules and regulations was the reprinting of the appropriate sections of the 1949 law that provided for penalties for violation of the rules and for destroying and mutilating property in the Park. Over a period of two decades the rules and regulations had increased from thirteen in 1950 to twenty-six by 1971.

Among the major issues in administration of the Park was the development and maintenance of a road system. Comparatively few conflicts arose over this issue for the developments coincided closely with Baxter's desires. But the story of road development does illustrate some of the problems that arose in trying to reconcile the wilderness concept with the needs of the public for roads to enable them to take advantage of the recreational functions of the Park.

In 1943 the road from Millinocket to Greenville by way of Baxter State Park and Ripogenus Dam was renamed the Baxter State Park Road, and in the same year the legislature began providing $2,500 annually for its upkeep. The State Highway Commission was assigned responsibility for road maintenance. Two years later $1,000 per year was provided to maintain the Roaring Brook road. During the following decades appropriations gradually increased from a total of $30,000 per year in 1955 to $32,000 in 1969. Several special appropriations were made to replace bridges and repair storm-damaged roads in the Park.[1] All of these funds were over and above the regular appropriations for park operations.

As new lands were added to the Park in the 1940s, the lack of sufficient roads made its management increasingly difficult. Baxter stipulated in 1945 that no additional roads be built in the Park. Within a very short time he recognized that this position could not be maintained. Park personnel could check the northern region only by following a circuitous route from the southern side of the Park to Millinocket, Patten, and then westward along the Grand Lake road. Also owners of desirable sections of land Baxter wanted to buy for the Park refused to sell unless they were given permission to build roads within the Park to obtain access to lands where they held cutting rights. Baxter recognized that "without proper access roads the number of persons who would enjoy the Park would be limited." The legislature in 1949 approved a change in the trust arrangement he had initiated that authorized the state to build and maintain "such roads and ways as said State as such Trustee shall deem to be in the public interest and for the proper use and enjoyment . . ." of the citizens of Maine, with the provision that such roads "be constructed and maintained in a manner not to interfere with the natural wild state now

243

### THE RIPOGENUS DAM
"The concrete wall at the right is a sluiceway down which pulpwood logs are driven into the river below," wrote photographer Allan Rinehart on the back of this photo taken in September 1937.

### LADY SLIPPERS
Photographed by Gerald Merry, who has taken many photos of Baxter State Park flora and fauna.

existing. . . ."[2] In the latter provision Baxter intended that the roads be kept few in number, very narrow, and relatively unimproved, with only a gravel surface. During the two decades remaining in his life he was able to implant this concept firmly. Soon after acceptance by the state of the amended trust deed a worried camp director from Pennsylvania wrote to Baxter asking that trappings of modern civilization not be built in the Park. Supervisor Harold Dyer eventually answered the letter and stated that basic planning with regard to roads had not been changed. "The existing single track graveled surface roads with frequent turnouts were considered sufficient. Such roads, however, must be kept passable." Other wilderness characteristics of the Park would be preserved.[3]

Baxter and the state soon took advantage of the changed trust deeds to build a vital road link in the Park. Whether Baxter or members of the Authority first thought of the idea it is impossible to determine. In any event, during the autumn of 1950, the State Highway Commission surveyed the cost of improving old logging roads or building new roads north and then northeastward for fourteen and a half miles from Little Sourdnahunk Stream at Sourdnahunk Field to Sourdnahunk Lake, past Daisey's Camp Phoenix on that lake, then to the south branch of Trout Brook to McCarty's Camp, past Burnt Mountain to the north branch of Trout Brook and down that stream to a point near its junction with the south branch. The existing Shin Pond (Grand Lake) road terminated at that point. In an interview in 1971, former Supervisor Dyer said he had opposed extension of an improved road to McCarty Field, since it would make the remote but hauntingly beautiful Wassataquoik Lake area too readily accessible.[4] Baxter agreed to pay half the cost of construction if the state would bear the remainder. The legislature passed the needed law in late April and construction began in early summer.[5]

Baxter followed the progress of the construction very closely. He was so pleased with the work that he offered to donate more funds to trim and clean up some of the more unsightly places. After the road was punched through by late August, he made the drive through the Park early the following month in the company of Helon Taylor. Afterward he pronounced the work "eminently satisfactory" and was surprised that so much could be accomplished with such limited funds.[6] Helon Taylor was even happier, since the availability of the new route saved him one hundred and twenty miles of driving each time he travelled from his headquarters to the new South Branch Pond campground.[7] Quite obviously, administration and protection of the Park was made much easier and more efficient by the new construction.

Except for the new road to South Branch Ponds, which was built in the same period, this was to be the last major road construction for general public use in the park area for over fifteen years.

In addition to roads officially opened to the public, a number of others existed, usually built by companies such as Great Northern before the lands had been sold to Baxter or while cutting rights were being exercised after he had taken control. A problem over one such road in the western half of T4R10 arose late in the 1940s, even before Baxter changed the trust terms regarding roads. At issue was the very rough and rutted portion of the old Sourdnahunk tote road leading from Sourdnahunk Field to Sourdnahunk Lake. For years Great Northern had used it in its own operations and in addition had allowed Charles Daisey, owner of Camp Phoenix on the lake, to use the road to reach his sporting camp. A locked chain was extended across the road near the field, thus keeping out unwanted visitors. When Baxter acquired the land in 1947, Camp Phoenix was not included since Daisey had earlier obtained ownership of the land. When the existence of the locked chain was brought to his attention, Baxter asked that it be removed since the "park property should be free and open to all." He also noted that under the trust deeds there should be no road at all beyond Sourdnahunk Field, "but for the time being and in order to work no hardship I do not want to suggest any action." The Authority acceded to Baxter's wishes and Daisey agreed to remove the chain.[8] Apparently it was locked again later, for in 1949, under pressure from sportsmen in the Millinocket area, the Authority again voted to open all roads in the whole area that belonged to the state of Maine.[9]

Several roads such as the one from Black Brook Farm to Webster Lake along Wadleigh Stream led northward from the Grand Lake Road and Trout Brook.[10] Most important of these was the so-called Burma Road in T6R9 leading northwestward from Trout Brook Farm. The ten-mile road was constructed in 1950 by the Diamond Match Company to provide access for lumbering crews to the upper reaches of Second Grand Lake. For a time Telos Dam was accessible by Jeeps along these routes.[11] Hunters and fishermen from the region used it before and after it came into the hands of Baxter and the state. Near the head of Second Grand Lake, Dean Davignon, an employee of the Eastern Corporation, leased a camp which remained in his hands until 1970. After the land had been acquired by the state, Forest Commissioner Nutting and Baxter had given the Huber Company permission to use the road. In 1956 Taylor and Nutting escorted Baxter on a trip along the route. Later in the summer the Grossman Company, cutting timber for the Huber concern, asked park officials to repair the bridge crossing Trout Brook at the southern terminus. Supervisor Taylor somewhat indignantly argued that it was not the responsibility of the state to repair the bridge. Taylor was irritated because Grossman Company employees had used a camp on park property at the head of Second Grand Lake without permission.[12]

A decade later, a Patten citizen wrote the Authority that the local people wanted a bridge built across the stream to open up the road, since they wanted to hunt in the Second Grand Lake area. These lands had been

opened to hunting by Baxter "by demands of the PEOPLE of the area."
The correspondent added: "Reference to Helon Taylor will be accepted
but further action by the PEOPLE involving Mr. Taylor and Mr. Baxter
if necessary can be assured." After discussing the situation with various
officials concerned, the Authority denied the request.[13] Periodically, the
public in the Patten area asked that the road, now falling into disrepair
with bridges washed out, be opened for use. Sometime during the 1960s,
apparently, the Authority granted someone permission to rebuild the
bridge at Trout Brook at his own expense. In 1970 after being pressured
strongly by sportsmen in Millinocket and Patten and by local members of
the legislature on a number of issues involving the Park, the Authority
ordered the chain removed on the Webster Lake Road out of Black Brook
Farm, and reiterated that anyone desiring to do so and willing to pay for it
could construct a bridge across Trout Brook on the Burma Road.[14]

In T4R10 and T5R10, a road leading southeastward from McCarty
Field around Lord Mountain was built in the early fifties and was used
by campers and fishermen until it was closed by the local fire warden and
a park ranger. Though they probably exceeded their authority, their action
was upheld because of the fire danger created by slash left over from
lumbering.[15] Another constructed in the 1960s ran northward from Sourdnahunk Field through the valley to the east of Center Mountain and to the
upper reaches of the South Branch of Trout Brook. Though not open to the
public, the road is still used by park officials in managing the Park.

In the same general area, near the western base of Burnt Mountain,
a lumbering concern cutting on park land for the Eastern Corporation
opened up a new road leading westward nearly to the shore of Telos Lake
and then southward west of Morse Mountain to the new park road constructed in 1951 at a point north of Camp Phoenix. The local forest fire
warden for the Maine Forest Service suggested that this route be improved
to, in effect, replace the road constructed by Baxter and the state five years
earlier. The road had been discovered already by park users. Nothing was
done at the time though the road remained in use for a number of years
after lumbering operations ceased.[16] In the late sixties the northern section
of it was improved and extended to provide access to the Allagash Wilderness Waterway. Though these and other "unofficial" roads were used by
campers for a time, most were eventually closed off or became impassable
because of lack of maintenance.

Once the basic road system had been established and funds had been
appropriated on a regular basis for their maintenance, policies to implement these actions had to be developed. Governor Baxter, members of the
Authority, Supervisor Taylor, and officials of the State Highway Commission all played a role. Baxter developed a rather close personal relationship with Highway Commissioner Stevens and sometimes bypassed members of the Authority in discussions on maintenance policy. Generally,

officials of the Highway Commission and the Authority established the general policy, which was then implemented by those on the scene in the park area. During most summers state crews maintained the roads and made repairs where winter storms had caused damage. These crews were usually housed for varying periods of time in facilities at the regular campgrounds in the Park. Relations sometimes became a bit strained between these crews and park rangers, but for the most part they were amicable.[17] Highway Commission workers attempted to do some of the work during the off-season periods, when traffic flow through the Park was not particularly heavy.

In its maintenance work, the Commission generally did an excellent job and adhered quite well to Baxter's strictures concerning the wilderness concept. Problems, however, arose in two areas—the location of gravel pits to obtain roadbuilding materials and the clearance of brush on the sides of the roads. The first of these created no real controversy until 1969, though the problem had been present for several decades. In the course of their work, highway department and lumbering company crews had opened over a dozen and a half gravel pits along the roads. At times, these were opened after consultation with the supervisor, but more often than not no pre-planning took place. As a result, a number of pits were started immediately adjacent to and visible from the roads.[18] In the period before real environmental awareness had developed, these excited little discussion. Governor Baxter on several occasions complained that lumbering company crews had created eyesores at such places as Black Brook Farm on upper Trout Brook. Not until 1969 did the Authority turn down a request to take gravel from park land for an improvement project on the state-aid highway providing access to the northeast entrance to the Park.[19]

Further controversy arose shortly after when Supervisor Kearney for a time blocked the reopening of gravel pits by State Highway Commission crews who were rebuilding the road west from Burnt Mountain for access to the Allagash Wilderness Waterway. Kearney took the forever wild provisions of the trust deeds more seriously than some of his predecessors and objected to the open pits along park roads. After the Highway Commission threatened to stop work entirely on the road and even threatened to "get out" of the Park and thus widen the controversy, a compromise was reached at a meeting of the concerned parties. The Forestry Service agreed to plant screens across most of the objectionable pits, plant grass on some, and close out some entirely.[20] In time, natural growth would cover the raw scars; future pits would be located out of sight of the roads.

An equally vexing problem for which there was no simple solution was the control of brush along the roads. Baxter had decided that park roads should be kept as simple as possible. Over the years, as a result, some of them became overgrown and were extremely dangerous for motorists. As use of the Park increased the difficulties became more severe.

248

In the late summer of 1956, Forest Commissioner Nutting as chairman of the Authority wrote to the State Highway Commissioner suggesting a conference be held between the groups to determine maintenance policies. Nutting thought that "brush cutting, followed by basal herbicide spraying, might be the answer to this type of maintenance."[21] The meeting was held in the following October, after which Nutting and officials of the highway department toured the Park and decided where the worst brush would be removed, particularly on the road northward from Sourdnahunk Field and sections of the Roaring Brook Road. After highway crews had completed maintenance of road surfaces, they spent the remainder of their time before snows closed the Park, cutting brush in these areas.[22]

The work was resumed a year later, only to be stopped by Governor Baxter, after one of his regular fall inspections of the Park with Commissioner Nutting when he observed highway crews clearing the brush. The subject recurred from time to time during the following decade. At times highway crews were forced to cut brush discreetly to correct the most dangerous situations; without some work the brush would have blocked the roads completely and made them impassable.[23] Baxter's wish to preserve the wilderness status of the Park, set against the need to provide some basic safety measures for users of the Park, created a dilemma for the Authority and the Highway Commission that was never satisfactorily resolved during his lifetime.

As travel to the Park increased, all concerned gradually came to feel that some means had to be found to restrict or control entry to and use of the Park and its roads. The construction after 1951 by Great Northern of a bridge across the West Branch at Abol Stream, and new road connections to it from near Togue Pond on the southeast and Ripogenus Dam on the northwest in connection with the construction of a power plant at the dam, eliminated the need for the company to use the Sourdnahunk Road within the Park. This made more feasible a plan that entailed the closing of one entrance to the Park, the construction of a new road, and the development of the present gatehouse control system. Just where and when the concept first arose is not known, but the first indication came in a letter from Baxter late in 1956. He stated that the control plan used at Laurentides Park in Quebec appealed to him and that "some day we may need to do that."[24] Authority members, as usual, picked up the signal and began discussing the issue among themselves and with Baxter. By the end of the decade, Baxter had promised Helon Taylor and Austin Wilkins that if he could purchase the northern portion of T2R9 he would provide $15,000 to build a new road connecting the existing Roaring Brook Road near Helon Taylor's headquarters camp to the Baxter State Park Road west of Abol Pond.[25] Late in 1959 Taylor prepared a rough map showing the proposed road, which Baxter sent on to Chairman Wilkins in the hope that it "may help you when you appear before the Governor and

Council." The map was "not necessarily accurate but it shows what we would like to accomplish."[26]

By 1960 the plan had matured. If Baxter was able to gain ownership of land in T2R9, just south of the Park as it then existed, he would authorize the construction of a gatehouse there and at other road entries into the Park and would consent to the construction and pay half the cost of a road along the horseback near Abol Pond to connect with the old Baxter State Park Road.[27] As noted elsewhere, the gatehouses had been included in the Authority's six-year building program. On the assumption that the land would be acquired and the road built, the Authority requested an increase in its legislative appropriation to allow the hiring of attendants.[28] However, although Baxter was able to purchase the property in 1962 and gave it to the state in the year following, the control plan was dropped for the time being. Presumably a report from the State Highway Commission had to be received first; actually, Baxter had again changed his mind.

Several years later the plan was revived when Forest Commissioner Wilkins and a location engineer for the highway department walked the three-mile route of the proposed road, and the highway department provided a cost estimate of $25,000.[29] When Wilkins reported this to Baxter and further suggested that an additional $10,000 be provided to build a camp for Helon Taylor, since it was planned to use his old one for a gatehouse, Baxter balked once more. "It is well for us to be content. As you know I want to keep things as simple as possible and there really is no sound reason for heavy expenditures." The cost of a road and a "new camp for Helon is more than I want to spend. This being so we will forget it and do our best with what we now have for I do not want to branch out."[30] Commissioner Wilkins regretted the delay, though he understood the reasons for Baxter's hesitation. "We will have to rest on this," he wrote to Taylor, "until the opportunity looks a little more favorable later on."[31]

The discussions continued during the year. In November Baxter again stated his new-found opposition to the scheme he had originally proposed. The cost would be considerable, an extra ranger would have to be hired, and any increase in the budget, he felt, should go to giving the existing rangers larger salaries. "You and Helon Taylor," he wrote Chairman Wilkins, "have been in charge for a long time. Throughout all that time the mountain and its visitors have been well taken care of. It is an excellent record."[32] After receiving this letter, Wilkins again visited Baxter at his Portland office and argued the need for the gatehouses to provide for the safety of park users and better control to prevent accidents and overcrowding at campgrounds and possible forest fires caused by careless people camping at illegal places.[33] Since Baxter still withheld approval, the plan was further delayed.

250 Nothing more happened for over a year, though the Authority con-

tinued to pursue the matter. Early in 1966 its members and Baxter met in Portland and Baxter seemed finally convinced of the need to construct the control gatehouses and to use accumulated income from the trust fund to defray the costs. He authorized their construction and urged that they be built of good material and "in a substantial manner worthy of the Park they protect." He said he would be responsible for the cost "which we can take from the Trust fund or me personally."[34] Since he asked to see the plans before contracts were signed, Wilkins again journeyed to Portland in the early summer to review plans for and costs of the three prefabricated log cabins to be used as gatehouses. After Baxter's approval was given, the contracts were signed and the new gatehouses were sited and delivered late that summer.[35] The control system became operational in the spring of 1967.

While planning for the gatehouses proceeded, Authority members still had to obtain Baxter's approval for the construction of the new road necessary to make the control system effective. After another meeting with Baxter in May and after Wilkins, at Baxter's insistence, coordinated the work with Highway Commissioner Chairman Stevens, the necessary approval was given. The cost would be defrayed from accumulated interest in the trust funds. After further planning during the summer, work was commenced on the new road during the fall, but it also was not completed until 1967.[36]

Prior to Baxter's death in 1969, initial plans were made for the construction or improvement of one more short segment of road in the Park. It is not known whether Baxter was aware of the situation, but it is possible he would have approved of the decision. The problem involved the road access to Telos Lake, the southern end of the newly-created and state-operated Allagash Wilderness Waterway. The State Park and Recreation Commission, as administrator of the waterway, decided that the most feasible approach to Telos Lake was by a road leading westward for four miles from the park perimeter road near Burnt Mountain to the western border of the Park, and from that point an additional nine miles westward and northward to Telos Lake. The existing tote road would be improved to conform to the standard of other roads in the Park and would be maintained by the Highway Commission. At the same time, Great Northern was in the process of constructing a new road from Millinocket to the wild area west of Baxter State Park. The new road, to be used exclusively by the company and closed to the general public, would pass to the south and west of the Park. The paper company had decided to close its private road from Harrington Lake eastward to the western border of the Park near Nesowadnehunk campground. This meant that the newly-constructed gatehouse at that point would no longer be needed. The Authority decided that it should be rebuilt and relocated on the new road west of Burnt Mountain to control traffic into and out of the Park from Telos Lake.    251

Appropriate legislation to provide authorization and funds for the Highway Commission to rebuild and maintain the new sections was approved
by the legislature early in 1969.[37]

During the following summer the Highway Commission began rebuilding the road. After $10,000 had been expended the work was suddenly
stopped during the fall, when the deed by which Baxter granted the land
to the state was examined. That deed provided that the road west of
Burnt Mountain that was constructed by the Eastern Corporation would be
closed when that company's cutting rights ceased. Almost immediately
Baxter's removal of the ban on roads in 1949 was also noted.[38] Progress
was halted while the various agencies concerned examined the deeds once
more and looked into Baxter's desires regarding limitations on roads in
the Park. Despite pressures applied by Park and Recreation Commissioner
Lawrence Stuart, and the irritation of the highway commissioner, a resolution of the problem was postponed until the summer of 1970.[39] In August
the two agencies pressured the Authority for a final decision. At a joint
meeting late in the month, the Authority "agreed that for the indefinite
future (not less than 5 years) the existing road would be improved and
maintained as access to Telos." All concerned agreed that the search for a
feasible alternative route outside the Park would continue.[40] Thereafter, the
road was completed quickly and the new gatehouse became operational.
The old entrance to the region, used by the public since 1916, was closed
and thereafter used only for special purposes, such as hauling out downed
timber.

By 1969 the road system had reached what undoubtedly will be its
nearly final form. The completion of the perimeter road allowed contact
between all major campgrounds and campsites. The principle had been
fairly well established that the interior region of the Park would not be
penetrated by roads for use by the general public. Some of the roads
built during lumbering operations or in the clean-up after the 1963 storm
remain, but most others will gradually be obliterated. Only in the northwestern section of the Park, where Baxter specifically sanctioned forest
management, are more roads likely to be constructed.

When Helon Taylor took over as supervisor in August 1950 there were three campgrounds in the Park—Katahdin Stream (called Pitman until far into the fifties), Chimney Pond, and Russell Pond. Though the state had taken ownership of the Russell Pond camps early in the forties and had razed most of William F. Tracy's buildings, the site was not considered an official campground until 1950. As the size of the Park was increased and more people visited the area (See Table XIV–1), campgrounds had to be added, until there were eight by 1969.

During the summer of 1950, after Harold Dyer resigned as supervisor of the Park, construction begun the summer before at Roaring Brook was resumed. The new supervisor, Robert Dyer, drew up three different plans for completing the work and recommended one that would provide six shelters with fireplaces and picnic tables and also development of a parking lot and tenting area.[1] There is no record to indicate the precise action taken by the Authority, but one member felt that Dyer should be allowed to "do what he thinks is the most logical."[2] Some work was done during the summer, but with major personnel problems that resulted in the resignations of Dyer and the Roaring Brook ranger late in the summer, much remained to be done. When Helon Taylor took over as supervisor in August, he found a "nice" cottage on the site, but reported that "the whole place was dirty and in a mess." No shelters had been built nor tent sites completed. The parking lots and toilets were ready, though no trails had been cut to the latter.[3] During the fall Taylor and his crew, which consisted of rangers at the various campgrounds, completed six shelters and graded the ground for six more, plus fourteen tent sites, at a total cost of under $1200.[4] In the years following, additional shelters and a bunkhouse were built as funds became available.

Attention was given to the construction of the campground at the northern end of the Park during the same year (1950). When the campground was authorized the previous year, Harold Dyer had intended to construct it on the shores of Matagamon Lake, a location which seemed to Baxter "to involve great expenditure."[5] Some consideration was given to locations in the Trout Brook Farm area, though, when work was resumed at Roaring Brook during the following summer, plans for development in

## TABLE XIV–1

### BAXTER STATE PARK
Statistics on Park Use from 1942 to 1971

| Year (Season) | Camp-grounds | REGISTER COUNT | | | PARK USE | | |
|---|---|---|---|---|---|---|---|
| | | Resident | Non-Resident | Total | Day Use | Camper Use | Total |
| 1942 | 2 | 221 | 111 | 332 | | | |
| 1943 | 2 | 151 | 77 | 228 | | | |
| 1944 | 2 | 141 | 153 | 294 | | | |
| 1945 | 2 | 196 | 179 | 375 | | | |
| 1946 | 2 | 742 | 627 | 1,369 | | | |
| 1947 | 2 | 610 | 632 | 1,242 | | | |
| 1948 | 2 | 763 | 834 | 1,597 | | | |
| 1949 | 2 | 1,051 | 980 | 2,031 | | | |
| 1950 | 4 | 1,069 | 1,066 | 2,135 | 10,000 | 9,733 | 19,733 |
| 1951 | 5 | 1,639 | 1,670 | 3,405 | 10,000 | 9,878 | 19,878 |
| 1952 | 6 | 1,727 | 2,464 | 7,167 | 11,000 | 13,409 | 24,409 |
| 1953 | 6 | 2,220 | 2,585 | 7,875 | 11,500 | 14,354 | 25,854 |
| 1954 | 6 | 2,746 | 4,200 | 8,096 | 12,000 | 16,333 | 28,333 |
| 1955 | 6 | 2,730 | 4,071 | 8,060 | 12,000 | 18,000 | 30,000 |
| 1956 | 6 | 4,400 | 5,750 | 10,150 | 10,000 | 20,877 | 30,877 |
| 1957 | 6 | 5,641 | 6,837 | 12,478 | 18,024 | 24,882 | 42,906 |
| 1958 | 7 | 6,229 | 6,756 | 12,985 | 20,165 | 29,858 | 50,023 |
| 1959 | 7 | 6,594 | 7,914 | 14,508 | 23,580 | 34,186 | 57,766 |
| 1960 | 7 | 8,487 | 8,831 | 17,318 | 21,570 | 39,041 | 60,611 |
| 1961 | 7 | 8,910 | 9,733 | 18,643 | 19,851 | 41,606 | 61,457 |
| 1962 | 7 | 7,976 | 10,614 | 18,590 | 20,553 | 41,376 | 61,929 |
| 1963 | 7 | 8,414 | 12,054 | 20,468 | | | |
| 1964 | 7 | 10,363 | 13,832 | 24,195 | | | |
| 1965 | 7 | | | | 35,288 | 54,096 | 89,384 |
| 1966 | 7 | | | | | 56,831 | |
| 1967 | 7 | | | | 26,047 | 44,930 | 70,977 |
| 1968 | 7 | | | | 25,838 | 55,338 | 81,176 |
| 1969 | 7 | | | | 19,495 | 48,752 | 68,247 |
| 1970 | 7 | | | | 19,591 | 48,899 | 68,490 |
| 1971 | 7 | | | | 19,053 | 45,312 | 64,365 |

REGISTER COUNT—Figures based upon study by Merle Scott and biennial reports. Figures from 1942 to 1949 are for Katahdin Stream only and do not include Chimney Pond. From 1951 to 1955 some campgrounds did not distinguish between resident and non-resident.

PARK USE—Figures from 1950 to 1962 based upon reports to U.S. Dept. of Interior and biennial reports after 1962.

the north were scrapped pending its completion.[6] When Taylor found the time after he became supervisor, he travelled the Trout Brook country and talked with members of the Authority and many others about possible locations. Finally, with permission of the Authority, he selected a spot on the north shore of Lower South Branch Pond, the site of Burton Howe's old lumbering camp. Materials were ordered for the campground and arrangements made to begin construction of a road to the site immediately.[7] Much work was done on the road during the late fall before rains, and then snow made further progress impossible. In the following spring and summer the road was completed, nine lean-tos were finished, toilets built, and tent sites levelled.[8] By the end of the summer the ranger cabin was livable if not completely finished inside. During the summer of 1952 the resident ranger built three more lean-tos.[9]

The pattern followed in the construction of the campgrounds at Roaring Brook and South Branch Pond was to be typical of new construction and expansion developments in the Park. Since the appropriations for new campgrounds or extension of existing ones were small or nonexistent, the work had to be done with as little expenditure of cash as possible. After approval to proceed was obtained from the Authority, the details of plans and design were worked out by Taylor and the rangers involved. Only the heaviest jobs, such as levelling the parking lots and dumping fill into low spots at Roaring Brook, or building the road into South Branch Pond, were done by non-park labor. Increasingly, in the sixties, the Authority resorted to purchased prefabricated construction for larger buildings. Otherwise, the actual construction of lean-tos, ranger cabins, toilets, water systems, storage sheds, picnic tables, and fireplaces was done by the rangers in the course of carrying out their normal duties, or else was completed after the regular park season when the flow of visitors slowed down. While some mistakes in overall planning were made, the cost of construction could be kept to an absolute minimum. Taylor exulted at one point, after attending a state park custodians' meeting, "It costs more to build one toilet at Arcadia [sic] National Park than the State Legislature appropriates to run this vast park for an entire year. $2000.00 more. I did not dare put this is my report."[10]

The Authority decided to develop another campground at Nesowadnehunk (Sourdnahunk) Field in 1952.[11] On the east side of the stream was the location of a former lumbering camp in one of the few areas of the Park that was sparsely wooded. For the development of a more permanent campground, a site was chosen bordering and across from Nesowadnehunk Stream and the field and adjacent to the access road leading to Harrington Lake and Ripogenus Dam. Early plans apparently included the construction of housekeeping cabins at the site in addition to the usual facilities. After an inspection trip through the Park in mid-June, Baxter vetoed the idea and argued, "If we go into house-keeping it in-

255

volves the purchase and care of bedding and other furniture."[12] During
the camping season, Ranger Edward Beach completed two shelters and
did a great deal of work in preparing other sites and building water lines
and other essential services.[13] In the following year the legislature appropriated funds for a ranger's camp, garage and shop, and additional shelters. Lumber and other materials were delivered during the summer and
Ranger Beach used what time he could spare from his other duties in
building the lean-tos and the ranger camp. This system worked quite well,
since new campgrounds were not usually heavily used. With some assistance for a short time from other rangers, Beach completed the camp
by himself before heavy snows closed down operations in December.[14]

By 1953 there were six campgrounds in the Park—Katahdin Stream,
Roaring Brook, Chimney Pond, Russell Pond, South Branch Pond and
Nesowadnehunk. In the park brochure for that year it is interesting to
note that "unlimited tenting space" was listed for all campgrounds except
South Branch Pond. Katahdin Stream had fifteen open-front shelters;
Roaring Brook had six, Chimney Pond had eight, South Branch had twelve,
and Nesowadnehunk had two. Bunkhouses were available at Chimney
Pond and at Russell Pond.[15] The park circular for 1955 again noted that
unlimited tenting space was available at all places, except Roaring Brook
and Katahdin Stream.[16]

About this time the Authority worked out a policy of "gradual continuing development of the park." In this they were in agreement with
Baxter. The policy envisaged development of "simple camp sites with
facilities that can be handled by one ranger. The larger area of Baxter
Park makes it possible to develop new areas as public use increases and
thus avoid mass accumulations of people at popular sites, which would tend
to destroy the intended purpose of the park."[17] This policy was reiterated by the Authority in its statements to the budget committee into the
next decade. It was also used as the basis or rationale for new campgrounds. But at the same time, additional lean-tos were built in various
campgrounds so that management by one ranger became virtually impossible in some cases. In 1957, for instance, the Authority, in a statement
requesting additional funds from the legislature to hire more personnel,
admitted: "Pitman campground at Katahdin Stream is overcrowded and
is more than one ranger can handle satisfactorily."[18] Shortly afterward, it
began seeking funds to hire three additional part-time rangers to assist at
the busier campgrounds. Baxter provided the funds for several years.

At Katahdin Stream no new lean-tos were constructed during the remainder of the decade. However, more and more day-use picnic sites
were set aside for tenters, thus creating public relations problems with
citizens of surrounding communities. In 1955 a bunkhouse was gained
when the forest service turned one over to the Authority. As funds became
available a bypass road was built around the campground, a new ranger

**ED WERLER AND DONKEY**
Ranger Werler had two burros on which he used to pack gear for campers hiking from
Roaring Brook to Russell or Chimney Pond. Here he and his heavily laden beast are
on their way to Russell Pond.

camp was completed in 1953, and several improved toilets were constructed.
Construction of improved sanitary facilities to include septic tanks and
drainage fields at ranger stations was pushed at all campgrounds in the
Park. The poor quality of these facilities was one of the most common
complaints received by the supervisor and members of the Authority.[19]

At Roaring Brook five new lean-tos were constructed during the
decade so that, by 1959, there were eleven shelters and fourteen tenting
sites. In addition, a gravity water system, a new bunkhouse, and miscellaneous toilets and outbuildings were constructed. One ranger alone might
have been able to handle this type of campground without too much difficulty, but the fact that it was the jumping-off point for Chimney Pond
and Russell Pond campgrounds complicated the situation enormously.
Ranger Edward Werler explained the situation rather effectively in his

257

report for the 1959 camping year. He noted the increase in use during the year; noted that the "complete lack of supervision at Chimney Pond during May and June, and lack of communication and cooperation, during most of the season worked a hardship on this office." In July and August, at the peak period of use, he had to coordinate and control reservations for and traffic to Chimney and Russell ponds. The policy at Roaring Brook had been for the rangers to give freely of their time and knowledge to help campers enjoy the Park. But the increase in paper work entailed by the other responsibilities made this impossible. Werler felt that the campground "should have at least some *part time help* in mid-season, to relieve the strain of continuous sixteen hour days." He noted ten items for further discussion. They involved control of traffic, parking areas, telephone communications, need for first-aid refresher courses because of an increase in accidents, the need to limit the size of groups using the campground to no more than fifteen persons, because of difficulties in supervision; a better system for disposing of wastes; and changes in sales procedures for some items handled by rangers.

One of the items illustrated a major continuing difficulty in management of the Park. A Chamber of Commerce sign in Millinocket advertised the "Roaring Brook Picnic Grounds." With eleven shelters, fourteen tent sites, and only three picnic tables at the site, Werler stated: "We are allowing day people to overrun our campgrounds, causing a great deal of confusion and mess." Since campgrounds were for overnight campers and picnic areas for daily visitors, he argued that they should be separated, and suggested building a picnic area at Avalanche Field.[20]

At Katahdin Stream early in the following decade the demand for space became so great that the rangers began reserving picnic sites for tent campers. The tables and fireplaces thus were no longer available for day-trip users. The situation led to violent criticism of the administration of the Park by the Fin & Feather Club of Millinocket. Some of the tables were freed for day users, but often without sufficient facilities.[21] Though some picnic areas were added, the problem persisted through the decade and could be solved only by more complete separation of overnight campers from day users.

At South Branch Pond construction of new facilities also led to a situation that made it impossible for one ranger to handle the campground. After its initial construction, at least six new lean-tos were added. Late in the decade, eleven tent sites were cleared and facilities provided along the east shore of the pond. The usual outbuildings and improved water and sewer systems were also constructed. In effect, the campground was doubled in size between 1957 and 1958. This action and the way in which it was done elicited a well-reasoned and thoughtful critique from a frequent park visitor who was an expert in community organization and planning. While the writer generally praised the facilities and particularly

258

the work of Ranger Frank Darling, he expressed disappointment with the additional tent sites and shelters and the plans to add more. He noted that the new campsites were "in close proximity," but even this addition did not take care of the vast numbers of campers. He objected to the development of a picnic facility close to the dock, and he argued that more attention should have been paid to "the size and arrangement of camping areas to avoid the 'mob' feeling which has partially spoiled" the area. He felt that at South Branch Pond a number of smaller camping areas separated by woods and up to a quarter of a mile from each other, which still could have been supervised by one ranger, would have been preferable to what had been done.[22] These or similar sentiments had been voiced by some rangers and other park visitors.

By the end of the decade the Authority was asking for additional seasonal assistance at South Branch Pond campground. This was provided early in the following decade. As indicated elsewhere, Baxter and members of the Authority began talking about controlling access to the Park late in the 1950s. In this connection, Ranger Ralph Dolley of Russell Pond wrote in 1958 to the Authority chairman after the annual meeting with the rangers. He argued that an "overflow area" for South Branch Pond, which park officials were talking about and had tentatively located at Trout Brook Farm, would be better located at Grand Lake.[23] What is significant here is the admission that the pressures of numbers at South Branch Pond was becoming too great and that the addition of more rangers alone would not solve the problem. During the following decade the development of a full-fledged campground at Trout Brook and the institution of control of the number of people using campgrounds, plus additional ranger help, provided a solution to the problem. The concept of a campground managed by one ranger was gradually abandoned.[24]

The size of the campground at Chimney Pond was increased gradually despite continuing reports of the adverse affect of camping and campers on the environment of the pond area. During the remainder of the fifties at least two new lean-tos were built and some of the others rebuilt and repaired. In 1958 the Authority received funds to build a new ranger cabin at the campground. The story of its planning and construction provides another good illustration of the means by which the Park was developed. Funds for the new cabin here and at Abol Pond were requested from the legislature in 1956 and appropriated the following year.[25] Since the funds were to be available for the second year of the biennium and since is was so difficult to bring in large amounts of construction materials, the Authority checked to determine whether the existing structure could be repaired. It could not be rebuilt. At one time it was proposed that a winter road be cut to Chimney Pond with a small bulldozer, a road that could later be used as the basis for a new trail from Roaring Brook.[26] While materials were gathered and stored at Togue Pond headquarters, 259

## JUSTICE WILLIAM O. DOUGLAS
On two occasions "Jake's Rangers" were joined by Douglas, who became the only other honorary member of the group besides Lester Hall. In the top photo, taken at Katahdin Stream, he wears a Jake Ranger patch sewn on his sleeve by Jake's wife. In the lower photo, Justice Douglas and Jake Rangers are on the Chimney Trail at Basin Pond.

rangers who had finished work at their regular campgrounds labored into the late fall of 1958 to lay sills for the new camp; by the time they finished on December 14, three feet of snow lay on the ground.[27] Before the snow melted the next spring the Authority had found another means of getting the pre-cut ranger station to Chimney Pond. It was able to arrange with the United States Army at Fort Devens, Massachusetts, for the use of two large helicopters. In late June, during a period of relatively calm weather, the helicopters made thirty-four round trips to move the eleven tons of materials.[28]

It was one thing to have the materials on hand and another to have the ranger camp constructed. During May and most of June no ranger was on duty at Chimney Pond. During June a new ranger, Nicholas Barth, was hired and assigned to the campground but apparently first worked out of Roaring Brook. Soon after he assumed his duties he wrote the Chairman of the Authority a masterful letter commenting on the unfortunate situation with regard to erosion at the campground. He also found conditions "somewhat disturbing" regarding sanitation facilities and the lack of progress in assembling the new ranger station.[29] Though he was expected to assist in the construction, he was not a carpenter and also felt he should not have to perform such tasks. In early July Owen Grant, a reserve ranger who was also a skilled carpenter and did most of the major construction jobs in the Park for a number of years, and two boys hired from Millinocket worked on the camp until they were pulled off the job to work elsewhere.[30] As the summer wore on and Barth did little more, Chairman Wilkins directed Supervisor Taylor to reassign Grant to the job and gave him authority to hire a part-time assistant. Grant completed the basic construction during the late summer and fall and then remained as ranger after September 26 when Barth left.[31] The inside work on the camp was completed by Ralph Heath, still another new ranger, during the following camping season.[32]

As the use of Baxter Park increased during the 1950s and the Authority declined to impose limits on campers using the various campgrounds, some of them became terribly overcrowded, particularly during holiday weekends and during the height of the summer season in July and August. This was particularly true of Katahdin Stream campground. In 1956 the Authority decided on a policy to relieve the pressure by asking the legislature for an additional ranger to assist there and also for capital funds to develop another campground at the base of the Abol Trail.[33] Even before the funds were voted, Helon Taylor cruised the area around the proposed campground and found what he thought was an ideal location on a high horseback about 2,000 feet up the trail from the road.[34] Since this location would have necessitated the construction of a road to the area, in subsequent surveys the following year, the decision was made to locate the ranger cabin fairly close to the road with the lean-tos and tent sites situated along the stream and trail uphill from that point so that only 1,000 feet of new road had to be built. Once the legislature acted, the needed materials were purchased during the summer of 1957 and construction began during the fall. When the regular camping season closed, rangers from other campgrounds gathered to assist in construction at the new site. The crew won "a race with old man winter" in mid-December by completing work on the roof of the ranger camp just before snow depths increased to unmanageable proportions. Rangers Rodney Sargent and Myrle Scott, now retained on a year-round basis, worked during the remainder of the winter completing the inside of the cabin. Sargent took charge of the campground later that spring and began site preparation and erection of the twelve lean-tos (prefabricated by park rangers at the forest service facility in Greenbush during the late winter and early spring) originally scheduled for the campground as well as for the five tent sites. As time allowed during the summer, finishing details on roads, parking areas, and similar tasks were performed.[35] In its first season the campground was not very heavily used,[36] but in ensuing years as more people learned about it and more visited the Park, it became more popular.

After completion of construction of the campground at the Abol Trail, more than a decade elapsed before any additional campgrounds were built. Perhaps a summary listing of the campgrounds and their facilities would be of some value at this point. It is presented in Table XIV-2 below. All campgrounds had ranger camps, garages (where necessary), tool sheds, woodsheds, and toilets. Chimney Pond and Russell Pond lacked water systems.

### TABLE XIV-2
#### INVENTORY OF BAXTER STATE PARK FACILITIES REVISED 3/2/60

| | Bunk House | Lean-tos | Tent Sites | Camper Capacity Overnight | Day |
|---|---|---|---|---|---|
| Katahdin Stream | 2 | 15 | 17 | 200 | 50 |
| Roaring Brook | 1 | 11 | 14 | 150 | 50 |
| Chimney Pond | 1 | 11 | 5 | 125 | — |
| Russell Pond | 1 | 4 | 5 | 50 | — |
| South Branch Pond | 1 | 15 | 17 | 200 | 50 |
| Nesowadnehunk | 1 | 12 | 12 | 100 | 50 |
| Abol | 1 | 12 | 5 | 70 | 30 |

This was attached to a memorandum from Wilkins to Authority members, March 6, 1960. Total overnight camper capacity was listed as 1,065.

The capacities listed above were often exceeded and led to serious problems regarding sanitation facilities, littering, and the like. Since there were a limited number of rangers to handle the visitors, little real supervision existed in such places as the Fowler Ponds and other isolated camp sites.[37]

In the late fifties and early sixties those individuals who were most interested and concerned about the future and development of Baxter State Park held a long series of discussions regarding construction plans. From the extant correspondence it appears that Percival Baxter was involved in a significant number of them. At times he seemingly agreed to plans for expansion, but then changed his mind.[38] Austin Wilkins took a deep interest in the Park and pushed developmental proposals that were consistent, he thought, with Baxter's wishes. To realize the plans, accrued interest in the trust funds would have to be used, but Baxter was reluctant to authorize this.

Out of the discussions emerged a six-year plan for development of facilities in the Park.[39] It provided for the construction of a Millinocket gatehouse;* tenting sites at Trout Brook and Slide Dam (to relieve congestion at South Branch Pond and Katahdin Stream campgrounds); and the addition of four lean-tos for Roaring Brook in the fiscal year 1961–62. Gatehouses at Nesowadnehunk and the northeast entrances to the Park would be built in the following year. The Authority proposed to rebuild the bunkhouse and all lean-tos and to provide thirty-five picnic tables at Chimney Pond in 1963–64. Russell Pond would see major expansion in 1964–65, with replacement of the bunkhouse and the addition of fifteen lean-tos and twenty-five tables; while in the following year less spectacular additions at Abol, a bunkhouse, three lean-tos and fifteen picnic tables; at Nesowadnehunk, three lean-tos, six tables and fireplaces and a bunkhouse; at Togue Ponds, improvements of the supervisor's headquarters were planned. The program would be capped in 1966–67 with the construction of an entirely new campground in the Fowler Ponds area, complete with bunkhouse, ranger camp, fifteen lean-tos, and thirty tables and fireplaces. Full implementation of the plan was impossible for Baxter vetoed the use of trust funds for these purposes until later in the decade.

Little more systematic work was accomplished during the following decade beyond normal maintenance and rebuilding of shelters and other structures. From time to time the rangers constructed additional shelters or tenting sites, apparently without prior authorization or permission from the Authority or, in some cases, even from the supervisor. In 1959, for example, the ranger at Russell Pond reported: "Reading the writing on the wall, with reluctance I cleared an area for an additional leanto."[40]

In ensuing years there was some discussion among members of the Authority regarding the future of Russell Pond, since the buildings and shelters were all in need of repair. Deputy Forest Commissioner Fred Holt

---

* The Millinocket gatehouse never materialized. Instead, the south entrance to the Park was moved farther in, to the Togue Pond area, where a gatehouse was constructed in 1969; and the Baxter State Park headquarters was set up at 64 Balsam Drive, Millinocket, in 1976.

visited the campground in 1962 and suggested that before anything was done, the decision should be made whether to move or repair the buildings. If the decision was for repairs, they should be substantial enough for five or ten years more use, after which the campground could serve as an overflow campground when needed. He appeared to be leaning toward moving the campground to the southwest side of Wassataquoik Lake, near Green Falls, where a good site was available that could be easily supplied by planes landing on the lake.[41] Given Baxter's reluctance to permit additional campgrounds and the state's unwillingness to finance them, nothing more was done there until 1969. Then, when some serious problems had arisen regarding the water supply and sanitation facilities, the Authority ordered the removal of the campground to a site several miles to the southeast on the banks of Wassataquoik Stream. During the following winter and spring, materials for new lean-tos were carried to the Stream, and the shelters were completed during April and May.[42] Eventually some of the problems at Russell Pond were solved and the Authority decided to retain the campground there; the new shelters were administered from the old campground.

Other major construction came at Chimney Pond. After the tragic deaths of Ranger Ralph Heath and Mrs. Margaret Ivusic in the great storm of October 1963, the AMC, as a memorial to Heath, gave the Authority $5,000 to construct two twelve-man bunkhouses at Chimney Pond to replace the rapidly aging and deteriorating structure there.[43] Construction materials were gathered and airlifted to Chimney Pond by helicopter late in 1964 and the bunkhouses were completed during the following summer.[44] But, as noted in Chapter III, the planned official dedicatory ceremonies were cancelled abruptly and Baxter repaid the monies advanced by the Club.

Though the Trout Brook Farm was considered from time to time as a possible site for a new campground, no final decision was made until 1969. In the meantime the old farm buildings and the area were used, with official authorization, to house various groups in the Park and as an overflow campsite for South Branch Pond.[45] After troubles developed over some of these uses, Baxter in 1960 had suggested that the Authority consider removing all the buildings at the site.[46] Since it was not done, either Helon Taylor or members of the Authority convinced him that they should be left. The Authority provided for the construction of a ranger camp at the site in 1969 as the first step in the development of a new tenting campground.[47] After many delays the campground was completed in the following year. A group of ninety geologists were the first persons to use it.[48]

Also in 1969 the Authority made the often-discussed decision to close the campground at Chimney Pond and relocate it at Basin Ponds.[49] By the end of the year well-separated sites in the new location had been chosen and the needed trails completed. During the winter pre-cut materials for

several shelters were carried to the site to be erected during the summer.
By late fall the lean-tos, "well built and beautifully situated" were ready,
but the facilities had not been used, since fireplaces and toilets were lacking.[50] Though everything was supposed to be ready by the following
summer, the new campground was never actually used, since during the
following winter severe winds overturned several of the lean-tos and the
decision to build the campground was reversed. Though many persons had
suggested such a move, apparently none knew of the ferocity of the winds
in the area during the winter. Better controls over a smaller campground
at Chimney Pond were instituted instead, to preserve that area.

In addition to the regular campgrounds in the Park, a number of unofficial sites were developed over the years. Many of these locations had
been used by hunters and fishermen for decades before parcels of land
were purchased by Baxter and deeded to the state. The fact that part of
Webster Lake, all of Webster Brook, and parts of First and Second Grand
lakes (Matagamon)—all long used by lumbermen, river travellers and
others—were included in the Park in the 1950s, created additional problems. Many campsites regularly used by those frequenting these areas
before the creation of the Park continued to be used, and were even listed
as legal campsites by the Maine Forest Service after they became part of
the Park. As long as park authorities lacked sufficient funds to hire adequate personnel to patrol the various areas, these individuals, usually residents of surrounding communities, continued their practices without regard to park rules or other controls. The ranger force simply was not large
enough to police the situation adequately.

As visitors increased, a number of additional locations within the park
boundaries became campgrounds or campsites. These included Foster
Field, Slide Dam, McCarty Field, Davis Pond, Wassataquoik Lake, Little Wassataquoik Lake, Pogy Ponds, and Fowler Ponds. As early as 1950,
Boy Scout groups were given free use of Foster Field, since the Authority
did not want large organized groups in the campgrounds.[51] By the end
of the 1960s, some of these areas, such as those around Fowler Ponds, were
said to shelter more visitors than the Russell Pond area.[52]

The major problems relating to these unofficial campsites were raised
by Austin Wilkins's associate in the Maine Forest Service in 1962. After his
tour of the Park in late August or early September 1962, Fred Holt wrote
several memoranda regarding problems he encountered. In one of them
he wrote of problems resulting from the use of park facilities by guests
of private sporting camps on park property and also of the use and abuse
of unofficial camping sites. Holt did not attempt to name all such locations
being used, but he did call attention to a campsite that had been set up
on an island in Wassataquoik Lake and was not listed officially, to which
"the [rangers] refer parties . . . occasionally and more often the past two
years. . . ." he noted. "Some have used it in the past and Caverly feels    265

BOOM TENDER'S CABIN ON MATAGAMON LAKE
Edmund Ware Smith, a Jake Ranger and author of a popular book of stories about
the Rangers, peers into this deserted cabin.
*Below:* a nesting loon, one of Jake Day's photographs made as background material
for the Walt Disney production of "Bambi."

he can't refuse them . . . this year." Holt felt that the practice was safe enough, but "there appears to be too loose control of what goes on," he wrote. With a very few exceptions, such as Little Wassataquoik and the Fowler Ponds, Holt argued, "all campsites on the park which are not manned should be eliminated," or at least policed regularly, since many reports of filthy conditions at these sites had been received.[53] Since legislative appropriations limited the Authority in its ability to hire additional personnel to implement Holt's suggestions, and since no absolute limit on the number of campers allowed to enter the Park was set, these sites continued to be used during the decade. When a limit was set, late in the sixties, camper use in the Park dropped sharply.

At that time, the new park supervisor, pressured by sportsmen and campers that something be done to clean up sanitary conditions around such areas as Davis Pond, Fowler Ponds, and sites on Webster Stream, surveyed the situation. He found "semi-recognized campsites" in many areas, including: four on Webster Stream or Brook, three around the Fowler Ponds, Pogy Pond, Wassataquoik Lake, Davis Pond, Ledge Falls, Slide Dam, Foster Field, Rum Brook, and Avalanche Field. Supervisor Kearney recognized that it would be unfair to forbid use of many of these sites that had been in use for generations, but insisted that the campsites should be patrolled on a regular basis by rangers assigned specifically to such tasks. He suggested various solutions.[54]

Apparently the Authority authorized Kearney to close some of the sites along Webster Lake and Stream, which led to protests by a legislator, among others. Attorney General Erwin replied that such sites were not official ones and were in violation of park rules. "The fact that they have been used over the years simply means that there was not sufficient supervision or enforcement of the Park regulations to discover and close these sites."[55]

The fact that Baxter State Park was also a state game preserve created some minor problems at such campgrounds as Roaring Brook and Katahdin Stream, from the late 1940s on. The Department of Inland Fisheries and Game was charged with maintaining the preserve and enforcing game laws. Since the commissioner of that department was a member of the Authority, the functions involved in administering and operating the Park and in enforcing fish and game rules were generally worked out without difficulty. During the 1940s four cabins had been built in what became park land, using federal funds under the Pitman-Robinson Act. They came under the jurisdiction of the fish and game department. Once all these areas were included in the Park, differences of opinion regarding the right to use them and the manner of their use arose from time to time. The friction at such places as Katahdin Stream and Roaring Brook became severe as the park staff was enlarged. In the end it became necessary for the Authority to provide new wardens' camps at locations other than the

campgrounds to free facilities needed by park personnel. In 1957–58 the
Authority constructed a new warden's camp at the old Michard campground on Nesowadnehunk Stream to replace two old camps at Katahdin
Stream and South Branch Pond that park authorities wanted to use as
bunkhouses for their personnel.[56]

A final aspect of the development of facilities at Baxter State Park
during the 1940s is the supervisor's headquarters. In 1947 Great Northern
leased a plot of land in T2R9 on an esker just above Togue Pond to the
Authority for use as a headquarters site. Construction of the cabin was
begun by the end of the decade and when Helon Taylor became supervisor he found a cottage of four rooms, neat and clean, about half finished
on the interior. During the next decade and a half the interior was improved and modified in various ways. In addition to the existing garage and
woodsheds, a good deal of money was also invested in the construction of
a crew camp and a pole barn (storehouse).[57]

In the early morning of January 21, 1967, the headquarters building
and several adjacent sheds were totally destroyed by fire. Aside from the
property loss of $11,700 and Helen Taylor's loss of $3,700 in personal
property, all of the files of the Park, which he kept in his home, were destroyed. In ensuing months and years the Authority discussed how, where,
and when to rebuild. While Taylor and most others concerned wanted to
locate a new headquarters in Millinocket, Baxter opposed this and wanted
a simple log building that would blend with its surroundings. He insisted
on seeing plans before he committed himself. During the spring, after discussing the situation with Wilkins in Portland, Baxter consented to the expenditure of $22,000 of accumulated interest in the Baxter State Park Trust
Fund to erect a new building on the old headquarter's site. Almost immediately he rescinded the permission. A contract for the prefabricated
building that had already been awarded had to be cancelled. While he
lived Baxter refused to consent to the construction of any more new buildings in the Park.[58] Taylor's successors used campground buildings as headquarters, and later housing was provided for them in Millinocket.

In 1950, as might well be imagined, the Baxter State Park trail system centered on Katahdin itself. The network had been developed over a period of nearly a century to meet the needs of those visiting the mountain. As access routes to the mountain changed, and as former owners of the land exercised their cutting rights in various sections of the Park, many of the old trails were gradually obliterated. During the 1930s, after the CCC opened the roads from Millinocket toward Roaring Brook and improved the Sourdnahunk tote road, the old approaches from the east by way of Wassataquoik Stream and Katahdin Lake were gradually abandoned. Lumbering operations on the southern flank of Katahdin in the late thirties and early forties closed several trails: the St. John Trail, the Old Basin Trail to Pamola, the Leavitt Trail, and the Abol Trail (reopened in 1949). Except for the combination of the Russell Pond Trail and the Old Pogy Road (Draper's Packhorse Trail), which connected the Roaring Brook area and McCarty Field on the South Branch of Trout Brook, there was no north-south through trail connection in the Park. During the 1940s, park officials had worked out agreements with the AMC to maintain many trails on the mountain; in addition, the Maine Appalachian Trail Club (MATC) assumed responsibility for the Appalachian Trail within the park limits.[1]

During the nearly two decades that Helon Taylor was supervisor of the Park the trail system was extended considerably. Most of the work was done by rangers as part of their regular jobs, or by volunteer groups interested in opening up particular areas. The modest appropriations from the legislature did not allow for the development and retention of a crew to work on trails exclusively during this period. Except for the development of a through-trail between Roaring Brook and South Branch Pond, no larger systematic project was developed. Helon Taylor, as a director of the MATC and one of the major sources of data for several editions of that Club's *Katahdin Section*, worked closely with officials of the Club and measured a number of trails in the Park.

For the oldest approaches to the mountain from the west and south along the Hunt and Abol trails, there were no major relocations. The Abol Trail had been closed because of fire danger from slash after the big storm

# A MAP OF SOME OF THE BETTER KNOWN TRAILS
## IN BAXTER STATE PARK

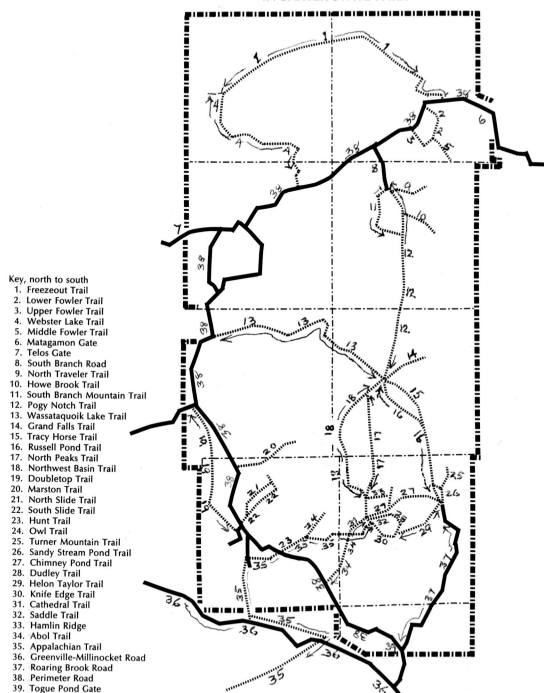

Key, north to south
 1. Freezeout Trail
 2. Lower Fowler Trail
 3. Upper Fowler Trail
 4. Webster Lake Trail
 5. Middle Fowler Trail
 6. Matagamon Gate
 7. Telos Gate
 8. South Branch Road
 9. North Traveler Trail
10. Howe Brook Trail
11. South Branch Mountain Trail
12. Pogy Notch Trail
13. Wassataquoik Lake Trail
14. Grand Falls Trail
15. Tracy Horse Trail
16. Russell Pond Trail
17. North Peaks Trail
18. Northwest Basin Trail
19. Doubletop Trail
20. Marston Trail
21. North Slide Trail
22. South Slide Trail
23. Hunt Trail
24. Owl Trail
25. Turner Mountain Trail
26. Sandy Stream Pond Trail
27. Chimney Pond Trail
28. Dudley Trail
29. Helon Taylor Trail
30. Knife Edge Trail
31. Cathedral Trail
32. Saddle Trail
33. Hamlin Ridge
34. Abol Trail
35. Appalachian Trail
36. Greenville-Millinocket Road
37. Roaring Brook Road
38. Perimeter Road
39. Togue Pond Gate

of October 1963, but it was reopened in 1965.[2] In the summers of 1965–66, members of the MATC marked and cleared a trail to the top of The Owl. The new route left the Hunt Trail about one mile from the Katahdin Stream campground. The trail crew, financed by funds donated by the AMC, completed the project in July 1966.[3]

Just before the havoc wrought in the Rum Mountain-Abol Stream area by the 1963 storm, a new trail was planned. For a number of years the Intercollegiate Outing Club Association, representing outdoor clubs from numerous colleges in the Northeast, had held a College Week in the park area during the first half of September, generally just after Labor Day. In addition to their usual hiking and climbing activities, they sometimes assisted in trail maintenance and other projects. In 1962 the Association decided to do a larger project. Gardner Perry III, its leader, visited Taylor and also talked with Ranger Rodney Sargent at Abol campground. Among the proposals mentioned and finally decided upon, was the construction of a new trail from Abol campground to South and Baxter peaks by way of Rum Mountain. Sargent, who had "had in mind to do this himself" but had not since "it is too much for one man," and Taylor both approved of the scheme. Taylor thought it would "be an added attraction, give another route onto the mountain, (many people like to make a circuit) and add to the popularity of Abol Campground." Authority Chairman Wilkins approved and asked only that the work be carefully controlled.[4] Since Supervisor Taylor did not mention any work being done by the college group in his September or year-end reports, it appears that nothing was done that year. No further mention was made of the Rum Mountain Trail until 1966 when members of the Outing Association completed it, after which a park crew measured and painted it and installed signs.[5] However, continued trouble was encountered with blowdowns and creeping rock; park authorities decided not to continue maintenance and discouraged its use. It appeared on the official list of trails for only a short period.

The trail system centering on Roaring Brook campground was modified considerably during the period after 1950. The Chimney Pond Trail, parts of which were originally located in 1887 by the AMC, was fixed as far as Basin Ponds when Great Northern in 1921 constructed a tote road to the ponds to facilitate its lumbering operations; the portion above Basin Ponds, with modifications, followed the route laid out in 1887. During the four decades that the tote road was in use as a trail, melting snows and rains gradually eroded and deepened it. The rangers at Roaring Brook and Chimney Pond never had the time to do more than give it superficial maintenance. Not until 1960 did Helon Taylor have the funds to hire the needed crew to do the job. Wherever possible, sections of the existing trail that were not eroded were used, but many new sections were cut through the woods. At the end of the season, Ranger Ralph Heath and MATC Editor Jean Stephenson blazed the relocated trail with blue paint.[6]

A new route—the Helon N. Taylor Trail—was completed in 1964. The St. John and Leavitt trails had been obliterated by lumbering operations in the late thirties, so no route to Pamola and the summit up Keep Ridge remained. The first portion of a new route was completed by Ranger Edward Werler of the Roaring Brook campground in 1952, when he located a trail from the campground to a lookout point on the side of Keep Ridge. Since then known as Ed's Lookout, this protruding rock area once offered fine views of the Sandy Stream Pond area and Turner Mountain. Little more was done until 1962–63 when a group of Millinocket Boy Scouts under the leadership of Monroe Robinson located and cleared the trail to the top of Pamola.[7] Park rangers completed the task in the late summer of 1963 and a group of high school boys were asked to "prominently mark" the trail. Clarence E. LeBell of Peabody, Massachusetts, a frequent visitor to the Park, first suggested that the trail be named in honor of the long-time supervisor. After Baxter approved and the Authority ratified the suggestion, the trail was officially dedicated, on September 28, 1963, with Baxter, Taylor, and Wilkins among those present.[8]

The trail to Russell Pond was relocated not long after Helon Taylor took over as supervisor. The valley of the South Branch of Wassataquoik Stream often had been used in the late 19th century as an approach to Katahdin from the south and east. W. F. Tracy, owner of the Russell Pond camps before Baxter bought the property, had reopened the trail in 1927 from the Roaring Brook area along the east side of Sandy Stream and Upper Whidden ponds and along the South Branch. In 1939, nearly three miles of the trail at the Roaring Brook end were relocated so that it left the Chimney Pond Trail about half a mile from Roaring Brook. To provide a more direct route to the Russell Pond campground, officially designated as such in 1950, and to avoid as many difficult crossings of the South Branch as possible, the trail was relocated so that it left directly from Roaring Brook campground along its present location. When the work was completed late in 1952, the new route was found to be 1.4 miles shorter than the older Wassataquoik South Branch Trail.[9] In 1961 when a hiking party ran into serious difficulties while crossing the dangerously high and swift South Branch and main Wassataquoik streams, Helon Taylor obtained funds to purchase materials to build a cable chair crossing over the two streams. It was completed in the winter and spring of 1962 and served effectively until the fall of 1969 when rusted cables of both spans broke under the weight of users, fortunately without injury to anyone. New log bridges were soon built to replace them.[10]

The final significant trail activity in the Roaring Brook area was the opening of a new one to the top of South Turner Mountain. Such a route had existed several decades earlier when the area was lumbered, but it gradually had become overgrown. The Sandy Stream Pond Trail, not regularly maintained by the Park, but well-worn since Sandy Stream Pond was an excellent place for visitors to see moose, provided the first portion of the route. Ranger Edward Werler laid out the extension to the top of the mountain, and in the summer of 1955 a group of geologists from Harvard who were working in the Park paid off their use fees by cutting the trail. They were assisted by the AMC trail crew.[11] Subsequently it was measured and blazed.

In addition to the trail activities on Katahdin, the outlying mountains witnessed considerable development during the period. The old trail to the top of Doubletop from the north, built to service the MFS firetower on the summit, fell into disuse when the tower was abandoned. Similarly, an old trail from the south had been abandoned. In 1955 guests at the Kidney Pond camps reopened the latter route. For the next decade or so the trail was not regularly maintained, but after the late sixties, when Baxter State Park assumed responsibility for its maintenance, its condition was improved. Late in the 1960s, park officials cut a trail southward from the Nesowadnehunk campground to the North Peak of Doubletop, thus allowing hikers to traverse the mountain.[12]

Prior to further major slides in 1932, three rock slides on O-J-I Mountain had created the letters for which it is named. The more recent slides and another which came down in late 1963 obliterated the letters. Approaches from the Nesowadnehunk tote road had been opened in the 1930s and during the following decade trails were cut to the North and South slides. The lack of maintenance virtually closed them again until Helen Taylor once more opened the trail to the South Slide. His plan to complete the route up the mountain and return by the North Slide to "give a continuous round trip that should be very interesting," was not realized due to other pressures and demands on his time.[13]

Farther to the north in the Katahdinaughuoh, Indian name for the range of mountains that begins in the south with The Owl and encircles the Klondike and ends at Pogy Mountain, another major trail was opened with volunteer labor. In late 1953 or early 1954, James L. Marston of Worcester, Massachusetts, contacted Helon Taylor and asked permission, for him and his brother Philip and a group of Explorer Scouts to open a trail from the Nesowadnehunk tote road at Slide Dam to the summit of North Brother Mountain. Taylor sought and received approval of the Authority, which gave the permission but refused to assume any responsibility for its completion or for any injuries that might be incurred. Taylor was to approve the route and the manner of construction. During the next two summers, Marston and his associates cut the spectacular trail that utilizes the long slide on South Brother to reach the plateau area and the steep summit cone of North Brother.[14] Over time, this trail made access easier to South Brother, Mt. Coe, Fort Mountain, and other parts of the range. It was officially named the Marston Trail.

Another area where major trail activity occurred was in the northeastern portion of the Park, centering on the South Branch Pond campground. Over the years the Traveler area and the smaller mountains immediately to the north had been visited on a number of occasions. Often based at the site of Burton Howe's lumber camps on the north shore of Lower South Branch Pond, hikers used game trails or opened up new routes that soon became obscured because of lack of regular use. Fishermen had for some decades developed trails into the Billfish-Littlefield-Fowler ponds area north of Traveler, but while they were more heavily travelled than some trails in other parts of the Park, they were not officially accepted as park trails. Construction at South Branch Pond quite obviously forced additional trail development to connect the new campground with the remainder of the Park and to serve the needs of hikers staying at the campground. In the summer of 1951 Ranger Ralph Dolley cut the trail linking Russell Pond campground with that at South Branch Ponds. Though the Pogy Notch Trail, as it came to be known, was rough and crude at first, its condition was gradually improved as Dolley and later rangers at both ends found time from their other work. In ensuing years an obscure side trail, not officially adopted, led from the Pogy Notch Trail eastward through Traveler Gap to Traveler Pond and subsequently to the East Branch of the Penobscot River. This route was opened from the eastern end early in the century, but the western approach became more practical after the Pogy Notch Trail was developed.[15]

Once the new campground was completed, Ranger Myrle Scott began developing a system of local trails. The most obvious location was the great star-shaped mountain, the Traveler. Apparently a complex system of routes on this mountain and on Little Peaked and Big Peaked mountains to the north was planned. The most important result of Scott's work was the fine trail leading to the top of North Traveler, which, with its long, open ridge offers spectacular views of Katahdin and many other portions of the Park and the surrounding countryside.[16] Either Scott or later rangers, or park visitors, also opened the trail along Center Ridge to the peak of the ridges on Traveler. Otherwise travel on the mountain remained a bushwhack.

The last major additions to the trail system in the Traveler region came in 1964. In that year Ranger Ellsworth Damon of the South Branch Pond campground built the half-mile trail to the falls on the outlet brook of South Branch Pond. More important, Damon opened a four-mile trail over South Branch Mountain, to the west of the ponds. At its southern end, about two miles south of the campground, it connected with the Pogy Notch Trail.[17]

Some trail changes were also made in the Russell Pond area during the period. In 1950–51 the old route between McCarty Field in the northwest corner of the Park and the Russell Pond area had been relocated by reopening and combining two older routes. Prior to this time, the Old

Pogy road was used from McCarty Field to the southeast, and a trail led from it to Little Wassataquoik Lake, Wassataquoik Lake, and on to Russell Pond by means of the Wassataquoik Lake Trail. In the relocation, Helon Taylor and his associates cleared the Old Pogy road of obstructions, but instead of continuing on to Little Wassataquoik Lake (which became a side trail), continued on the road north of the lake and over a shoulder of South Pogy Mountain. From that point, on the east side of the mountain, the route of Draper's Packhorse Trail was followed for the last two and one-half miles to Russell Pond. The Old Pogy road originally continued eastward to Old City camps near Grand Falls on the Wassataquoik at the mouth of Pogy Brook. Draper's Packhorse Trail had been built by E. B. Draper during his lumbering operations on the Wassataquoik in the period 1910–14. It connected the New City camps with the Old Pogy road by way of Russell Pond.[18] In the mid-fifties the Eastern Corporation was exercising its cutting rights in T5R10. Its operations were centered at McCarty Field and the Old Pogy road was usable by Jeeps for the first three miles.[19] Park personnel could not maintain the infrequently used trail on a regular basis during the following decades, and though it continued to be listed as an official park trail as late as 1967, it gradually deteriorated. In 1969 this trail was replaced by one leading from Nesowadnehunk campground along the tote road built by the Eastern Corporation while exercising its cutting rights in T4R10 in the valley east of Center Mountain, and on to Little Wassataquoik Lake and Russell Pond.[20]

Some trail work was also done in the immediate area of Russell Pond. The lower portion of the Wassataquoik Lake Trail, originally built in 1927 by W. F. Tracy, was relocated in 1960 to avoid the Turner Deadwater.[21] Rough trails to Lookout Ledges, north of Russell Pond, and to Inscription Rock and Grand Falls on Wassataquoik Stream, were also improved after 1950.

North of Trout Brook, the old Burma Road, a lumber tote road built in 1950 during lumbering operations in T6R8 and T6R9, was used by hunters, fishermen, and hikers to reach Second Grand Lake and Webster Stream. West of the Burma Road were other tote roads leading northward from Trout Brook toward Webster Stream and Lake that experienced decreasing use during the two decades as, after lumbering operations were completed, the roads gradually became impassable and bridges washed out. In the southwestern portion of the Park a welter of trails had been built to nearby ponds and to Sentinel Mountain from the sporting camps at Daicey and Kidney ponds. A trail also led from the Nesowadnehunk tote road to the Foss and Knowlton ponds area.[22] Though unmarked and unofficial, these trails were often better maintained and easier to follow than many of those in the regular park network.

Once the trails were in existence they had to be maintained and this created one of the major problems in the Park during the period. After campground conditions and rules, the condition of trails was probably the next most common source of complaints by park users. When Helon Taylor took over as supervisor, about fifty miles of trails could be considered official in the park area; by the end of the 1960s the total was near one hundred miles. For much of this period the number of individuals employed by the Park did not grow as rapidly as the trail system, and thus rangers were required to perform even more maintenance work.[23]

Basic responsibility for maintenance of the trails in the Park was lodged with individual campground rangers. While trail crews were hired from time to time on a short-term basis as funds became available, no regular budgetary allotments were made for hiring them until the 1970s. Most of the rangers, if they were not year-round employees, came on the job during the month of April. They cleared as many of the trails emanating from their campgrounds as possible before the larger influx of summer campers came. Typical of this process was the report of the ranger at Russell Pond in 1961: "In June after the trails were finally clear of snow I started cleaning blowdowns out of trails and repainting the blazes. I cleaned from Russell Pond to South Branch of Wassataquoik on Roaring Brook Trail. Also to Wassataquoik Lake, Grand Falls, Lookout and Deep Pond."[24] During the camping season rangers continued to maintain trails as time allowed. Campers sometimes assisted them in maintenance, but this labor could not be relied upon. When the number of visitors to the Park declined after Labor Day, larger trail or construction projects were completed, but construction work usually had precedence over trails at such times.

The rangers apparently did not receive systematic training in trail construction and maintenance. There is no evidence to indicate that any set of standards was adopted. Supervisor Taylor had the benefit of practices adopted by the Appalachian Trail Conference as a member of it. While a state game warden, he had built the Appalachian Trail along the ridge of the Bigelow Range. Those rangers coming from the Maine Forest Service also may have had some training in trail construction and maintenance; many others had none. They learned from experience or by watching older employees. Given this situation and given the differing abilities and interests in well-maintained trails among the rangers, it is understandable that their quality varied widely.

In 1966 Austin Wilkins summed up the situation in responding to a letter critical of trail and campground maintenance by stating:

> I do not wish to put myself in the position of offering excuses for some of the conditions which you have called to our attention. However, I feel I am justified in explaining that we are definitely short of park rangers who would be available to police and patrol the trails and roads of the Park outside the seven established campgrounds. We are so undermanned because of the increased impact of outdoor recreation

and the number of visitors coming into the Park that it is embarrassing.[25]

Major assistance in trail maintenance was received from the MATC and the AMC during early 1960s. The Hunt Trail had been selected as the route of the Appalachian Trail to the summit of Katahdin during the 1930s and during that decade and the one following, the MATC had provided most of the maintenance near the mountain, since it was some years before most of the route of the Appalachian Trail within the Park was actually deeded to the state. When Helon Taylor became supervisor he apparently assumed responsibility for the Appalachian Trail within the park.[26] In 1961 the MATC made a cash payment to the Authority to cover the costs of "reconditioning The Appalachian Trail on Katahdin." The gift was repeated in the following year, but no records indicating payment beyond that year have been found.[27]

More significant was the contribution of the AMC. The agreement made in 1941 between Harold Dyer, for the Authority, and the Boston-based Club has already been discussed. With extensions over the years, the Club assumed responsibility for maintaining and signing 25.25 miles of trails, which included the Dudley, Saddle, Knife Edge, Cathedral, Baxter Peak cut-off, North Peaks, North Basin, Cathedral cut-off, Hamlin Ridge, North Basin cut-off, and the Northwest Basin trails. In addition, the AMC agreed to maintain the shelter at Davis Pond on the Northwest Basin Trail. In most years after 1941, volunteer AMC work crews, usually led by Ronald Gower, visited the Park and performed needed trail work. In 1961 Taylor summed up the work performed by the crew during his tenure as supervisor: "Some years the A.M.C. crew has done an excellent job. Other years it has been more or less of a farce sending them up there. Right now their trails are in very good shape. What we need here is about a two man trail crew of hard working woodsmen. Not boys on vacation."[28]

While many of the trails were above timberline and thus relatively easy to maintain, others, such as the Northwest Basin and North Peaks trails, involved much hard work to keep them open. With the long history of AMC involvement in the Katahdin area since 1941 and earlier during the national park controversy, it was only natural that some AMC members would take a proprietary interest in the Park. This led to some friction in the 1960s.

The trail crew of the AMC found itself so deeply committed to trail work in New Hampshire and western Maine in 1959 that the Boston office of the Club asked the Authority for a modification of the 1941 agreement and suggested that the Club make an annual monetary contribution toward trail maintenance.[29] The issue was discussed by the Authority and Supervisor Taylor during the winter. Ultimately it was agreed that the AMC would make an annual contribution of $400 to the Authority, and that Helon Taylor would assume responsibility for hiring trail crews to do the needed work and report back to the AMC through Chairman Wilkins. The Club asked that the monies be used each year to maintain the trails that were formerly its responsibility and also to keep up the Davis Pond Shelter.[30] The contribution was increased to $600 in 1967, temporarily to $800 in 1969, and then back to $600, until suspended early in the 1970s.[31]

Supervisor Taylor was happy to receive the money from the two conservation and trail organizations. In 1961 two young woodsmen from Mattawamkeag were hired for a three-week period to work on the Hunt Trail and the trails on the mountain formerly maintained by the AMC. When the work was completed Taylor wrote that it was reported to him that "our mountain trails were in the best shape ever in the history of the park."[32] In 1965 it was agreed by all concerned that the entire $400 could be used to clear hazardous slash on the Abol Trail left over from the big blowdown of 1963. Due to some administrative confusion, Taylor became aware of the availability of the funds when it was too late to do anything that season. The carryover of funds allowed considerably more maintenance to be accomplished in 1966. Once the trail crew finished the AMC trails, it completed clearing the trail to The Owl and painted and signed the Rum Mountain Trail and then worked on the Togue Pond gatehouse.[33]

However, grants from the AMC were the source of some tension as well as gratification on Taylor's part. The Club was not happy with his trail crew report for 1961 and the fact that no publicity regarding the gift was prepared. When accepting the grant the following year, Chairman Wilkins promised that closer supervision would be given to the work and credit would be given to the source of the gift. C. F. Belcher, executive director of the Club, also asked that AMC members who were climbers be allowed to climb without rangers being present, even in the winter. Taylor agreed to supervise the work more closely in 1962, but felt that the AMC should provide its own publicity. He agreed to provide trail crew reports to Wilkins, who could then forward them to the AMC. On the question of members climbing on their own, he was adamant in rejecting such a policy. The summer season created no problems, but

> . . . In winter *no*. I was expecting something of this sort. They do not give $400.00 without some axe to grind. If we let them in in winter without a Ranger we might as well forget the whole thing. They are no better than anyone else. What would we say to A.T.C. members, Trail Trotters Club, Abanaki Ski Club, M.I.T. Outing Club and many others. Just as competant [sic] and some of them more so than the A.M.C. Club.[34]

While he was justified in rejecting the request and was undoubtedly fearful that outside organizations might obtain proprietary rights, he was probably overly suspicious about the motives of the AMC.

More serious was the situation with regard to the Davis Pond shelter in the Northwest Basin. The first shelter had been built by Leroy Dudley and enlarged in 1938. After it collapsed during the winter of 1939–40, it was replaced in 1942 by an AMC trail crew. During the years following, AMC members often used the shelter and included its maintenance with that of the trails on the mountain. Since the facilities at the site were limited, the Park charged no fees for its use until 1963. Maintenance of the shelter was difficult since it was far removed from other campgrounds and the limited ranger force could find little time to keep it up. The annual maintenance by AMC crews until 1960 put it in good order for a short period of time, but unless other users cleaned up before they left its condition soon became unkempt again. There were no toilet facilities and the dump for the site was often located too close to the lake or the shelter itself and was not cleaned up often enough. Users had cut much green wood in the immediate area. While the camp was located in a beautiful place with magnificent views of the headwall, it presented real problems. For entry and exit it had only one door, thus presenting real dangers to campers in case of fire. It was located in an area with a tremendous amount of combustible materials, thus posing another very serious fire threat during dry periods.[35]

The existence of the shelter presented problems for park officials. Some sort of shelter was advisable in the Northwest Basin, if even for emergency purposes, since the Basin was located so far from Russell Pond and Chimney Pond. Yet the inability to police the area properly led to abuse. Supervisor Taylor was so disgusted with the situation there in the spring of 1962 that he wrote to an AMC member: "Davis Pond Shelter is a fire trap, many violations of our rules and regulations are being committed there and it is a disgrace to our Park. I think the only solution is to burn the leanto and prohibit all camping there until such time as we can provide a Ranger to look after it." This was reported to Chairman Wilkins by Executive Director Belcher of the AMC who, after summing up the history of the shelter and noting his club's role in it, urged that before "any consideration of its demolition is taken, I think that we should do some further talking about it. In any case, I do not recommend any rash action at this time and would like to have a chance to discuss this with you and other Club officers here in Boston sometime during the next few months."[36]

The Authority discussed the situation at Davis Pond at a meeting in December. They reiterated that the shelter was the property of the state and not of the AMC. The Authority also decided to institute a use fee, which would be paid to the campground from which the using party left. Apparently the decision was also made to rebuild the shelter.[37] In 1963 the funds from the AMC were used partly to cut and prepare logs for a new lean-to at the Davis Pond location.[38] The old shelter was torn down finally in 1964 and a lean-to constructed on the site. But maintenance problems at the campsite continued through the decade.[39]

A final topic well illustrates Baxter's attitude toward the Park. In 1967 when one of the bills providing for official national recognition of the Appalachian Trail was before Congress, Baxter was asked to approve the pending legislation. The portion of the trail in Baxter Park, he noted, "must in no way be placed under the supervision of the Federal Government. . . . I disapprove of the Federal Government having control of any portion of the Trail in Maine and consequently cannot approve this pending legislation." As donor of the Park he objected to any encroachment, "no matter how slight. The erection of signs should not be permitted and the people of this State are sensitive about this matter." The Park was a state institution "and already I have had to remove signs which were erected there without the consent of the State authorities, which consent they have no right to give." He ended on an extreme note when he wrote: "Even the erection of your Trail signs is contrary to the law of Baxter State Park."[40] Nothing more on the matter was done during his lifetime.

Percival Proctor Baxter's life span was so long and his activities so varied that to do a reasonably comprehensive biography would take more space than can be allowed in this study. I will therefore give only the essential information on his life and activities. No attempt will be made to cite sources; in most cases the surviving scrapbooks and correspondence and family memorabilia in the Maine State Library in Augusta were used for reference.

He was born on November 22, 1876, the next to the youngest child of James Phinney and Mehitable Proctor Cummings Baxter. His paternal ancestors had come from England to Connecticut in the latter part of the 17th century. Percival's great-grandfather Elihu moved from Connecticut to Norwich, Vermont. There his son Elihu was born in 1781. The younger Elihu learned medicine and moved to Gorham, Maine, where he practiced for some time before moving to Portland in 1840. His son James was born in Gorham in 1831. Percival's mother's family had come to Massachusetts in the late 17th century and remained in the Salem and Peabody area. Mehitable Proctor's grandmother several times removed very nearly lost her life in the witch scare in Salem in the 1690s. Her husband, John Proctor, was hanged, but she survived—only because she was soon to have a child; by the time the child was weaned, the witch scare was over.

James Phinney Baxter was nine when his family moved to Portland. He was trained in various academies in the Portland area and at Lynn, Massachusetts. He also was tutored privately in the classics and in foreign languages. His family sent him to study law in the offices of Rufus Choate, a leader in the bar at the time. Because of failing health he gave up his legal studies and returned to Portland until he recovered. He then set up a dry goods business in partnership with William G. Davis, which expanded rapidly, and they developed wholesaling functions. Soon the two men became interested in the relatively new canning industry. They organized the Portland Packing Company, a partnership, which was profitable from the first. Davis and Baxter soon bought out their partners. The two men brought their children into the organization as its operations were extended throughout Maine and the nation. In the 1880s James retired, selling his remaining twenty per cent share in the concern to his three older sons. By 281 that time, he was one of Portland's wealthiest citizens, with holdings in real estate, banking, and ferry boats on Casco Bay, and investments in numerous corporations such as the Maine Central Railroad.

His major interests from early years were literature and history. He began publishing stories before he was twenty and continued his literary efforts for his entire life. In the 1880s he became seriously interested in the historical background of colonial Maine and New England and spent two years in England and France in the middle of that decade, copying an enormous number of manuscripts. He became a member of the Maine Historical Society, of which he was president from 1890 until 1911. The "Trelawney Papers" in the *Collections of the Maine Historical Society* and various volumes in the *Documentary History of Maine* are the most important of his widely varying publications.

A lifelong Republican, he did not take an active role in partisan politics until the last decade of the century. In 1893, when the government of the city of Portland was in the hands of the Democratic party, many questioned the honesty of the administration and asked Baxter to run for mayor. He reluctantly agreed and won by a very narrow margin. He was reelected five times, serving from 1893 to 1897 and in 1904–05. An effective mayor, he initiated construction of some major interceptor trunk sewers badly needed by the city and also projected the Back Bay boulevard (Baxter Boulevard) and a comprehensive park system. Though he was a major force in the councils of the Republican party and undoubtedly could have had a number of state or congressional positions had he desired, he preferred to work toward improving the Portland area and to pursue his intellectual activities.

Baxter loved the outdoors and was a particularly avid trout fisherman. For many years he and a close friend, Harrison Brown, made trips to the famous trout streams in Maine and other parts of the Northeast. On many of these occasions he took some of his children. Percival and a brother joined their father on one of these trips to Oquossuc in the Rangeley Lakes in 1882; and they returned two years later. This time, when they started fishing, his father promised to pay Percival $10 per pound for every fish he caught over five pounds. Within an hour the boy had hooked an eight-pound spotted trout. When asked what he was going to do with his $80, Percival said he was going to put it into a savings account. By 1957 the "Percival P. Baxter Fish Account" totalled more than $1,000.

More important, perhaps, was the trip Percival took with his father to the Katahdin area in 1903 when they stayed at the Kidney Pond camps. He was able to see Katahdin at close hand though there is no indication that he climbed it. These trips undoubtedly strongly affected young Baxter's attitude toward the wild lands and resources of Maine.

After his second wife died in 1914, James Baxter, then eighty-three years old, was cared for by his youngest son and continued to live in the

282

family mansion at 61 Deering Street in Portland. His real estate interests and other economic activities increasingly came under the direction of Percival. The two men had an extremely close relationship, and Percival, then governor of Maine, was deeply affected by his father's death on May 8, 1921. He wrote some moving reminiscences about him.

The elder Baxter's philanthropies during his lifetime were numerous. He donated public libraries to the city of Portland and the town of Gorham. He provided much of the money needed to build and beautify Baxter Boulevard. In his will he left bequests to numerous institutions. A sum of $50,000 was left to the city of Boston, with the provision that the interest be allowed to accumulate until the fund totalled one million dollars, at which time it would be used to construct a "New England Pantheon" or memorial building to the founders and early inhabitants of New England. The major part of his estate was left to his son Percival who had devoted so many years to him and his interests. The other members of his family were not particularly disappointed or disturbed, as they felt that Percy had earned such a reward.

Percival attended schools in Portland until he went to England for two years while his father collected and copied historical manuscripts. There he attended a private school. He graduated from Portland High School in 1894 and the following autumn entered Bowdoin College from which he was graduated with honors four years later, a member of Phi Beta Kappa, the scholastic honorary fraternity. At college he was a member of Delta Kappa Epsilon social fraternity, manager of the baseball team, editor of the *Bowdoin Orient,* and one of the founders and the first editor in 1897 of the *Bowdoin Quill,* a literary publication. The subject of his commencement oration was "Danton and the French Revolution."

Perhaps the most memorable experience he had at Bowdoin was the time he was arrested and put in jail for a very brief period. During the election of 1896 a Republican club was organized at Bowdoin and Baxter was elected secretary. During the course of the heated campaign, William Jennings Bryan came to Bath, the home of his Democratic running mate, Arthur Sewall. Previously, in New Haven, Bryan had been heckled and his speech disrupted by unruly students from Yale. His speech at Bath was scheduled soon after, and rumors circulated that Bowdoin students would emulate those from Yale. Bowdoin's president asked the students to behave properly, but it became obvious later that the authorities in Bath were very tense on the day of the speech. That evening, Bowdoin students, one hundred to one hundred and fifty strong, took the train to Bath and on alighting began singing college and campaign songs obviously partial to William McKinley. They were stopped by local magistrates and when Baxter tried to explain that all was going well, he was arrested and lodged in the local jail for a short period.

Baxter later sued for improper arrest, won the case, and was awarded   283

one cent in damages. (Mrs. Ethel Moyer Dyer, Baxter's grandniece, wrote
that the fine was a half-cent and that she has the coin.)* Though his father
had to pay the court costs, Baxter felt that he had been vindicated. Because of his social and economic position, the suit received extensive newspaper coverage. One unfriendly reporter noted, in language which has a
strangely modern ring, that Baxter "looked very much like a very ordinary
student of the common long haired variety. So it came to pass that his
sacred person was violated by the touch of the Marshal's hand." The
image was to change considerably in later years.

After leaving Bowdoin, Percival studied law, first at the offices of
Libby, Robinson and Turner in Portland and then at the Harvard Law
School, where he was granted the LLB in 1901. Though admitted to the
bar in both Suffolk County, Massachusetts, and Cumberland County, Maine,
in late 1901, Baxter never practiced law for a livelihood.

Instead, he began to manage his father's business affairs and to prepare himself for a political career. Most important of the business interests
were two office buildings with about 265 tenants—the Libby Building in
the Baxter Block on Congress Street, and the Trelawney Building, owned
by the Fraternity Company, on the corner of High and Congress streets.
He kept an office in the latter building for most of his life. From time to
time his management of these buildings erupted into public squabbles,
such as when he threatened to evict such prominent tenants as the Lincoln Club, a Republican organization of Portland of which he was a member (1912), or the Portland Club, of which he also was a member (1922).
His tenants accused him of maintaining the buildings inadequately. After
forty-five years, he wrote a friend that management tired him out and he
was "thinking of turning over the management to some of the younger
people in the family so they can try their wings."

Baxter also took over management of the People's Ferry Company,
which for some years had run ferries between Portland and South Portland. He was prominent in the organization of the Peaks Island Ferry
Company, which ran ferryboats to that island in competition with the
Casco Bay Steamship Company. Along the way these firms or Baxter and
others organized the Portland Pier Company to operate a pier and associated activities on the waterfront. Ultimately the assets were sold out
and the Pier Company invested its funds in securities. One of the large
contributions to the Baxter State Park Fund that Baxter made prior to
his death was the outstanding capital stock of this corporation. Very little is known about the details of the operations of these enterprises.

Baxter later was manager of the trust fund set up by his father on his
death and apparently had been given a good deal of money as well, since
it was stated publicly that he was already a millionaire when he became

---

* Half the surface of each side of the cent has been obliterated in some mysterious
284 fashion by a person unknown.

governor of Maine. He had no interest in the farflung canning businesses owned by his various brothers.

After he was graduated from the Harvard Law School Percival and his father took a long trip abroad to study municipal government operations, city planning, and other facets of public life in the places they visited. This started a long series of trips in New England, up into Quebec and around the United States; and particularly cruises to many parts of the world. In addition to their recreational value, the cruises were more important for the broad knowledge and experience Percival gained. As early as 1911 he booked passage on a cruise ship to the Caribbean with his brother James P. Baxter, Jr. Thereafter as circumstances of business, war, or politics dictated, these trips became more common. They varied from one-week cruises out of Halifax, Nova Scotia, to elaborate cruises to Africa and Latin America. His visit to the latter in 1925 encouraged him to invest heavily in nitrate, copper, and oil concerns operating there, as well as in the securities of various South American nations. He travelled to Russia in the early 1930s, to England in 1938, to Germany in 1939, and to Japan in 1940. In the course of his trips to Scandinavia and Germany, Baxter was able to see fine examples of modern forestry practices that he thought Maine citizens should emulate and which were of considerable influence in his later decisions to encourage the practice of scientific forestry in Baxter State Park. After many of these trips he wrote long descriptive and analytical articles on the nations visited, on living conditions, the economy, the political situation, and other aspects of the society that interested him. Portland papers or the *Lewiston Journal* generally printed them, and they were widely quoted and excerpted in the state's press. They gave Baxter a reputation for expertise in foreign policy and in the affairs of these nations, and led to continued suggestions that he be named to various diplomatic posts. He was particularly repulsed by what he saw in Stalin's Russia and Hitler's Germany.

In late 1903 Baxter had ably managed his father's successful campaign for reelection as mayor. This was his first real experience in politics, and he worked so effectively that newspapers of that time were predicting a bright political future for him; indeed, the *Lewiston Journal* in 1904 predicted that he would probably become governor. Shortly thereafter he announced his intention of running for the legislature from Portland and easily won in the primary and general elections. He served one term, but as a new member did not do a great deal. In 1908 he ran successfully for a seat in the Senate, and he was a leading member of the legislature in 1909. There he was most noted for his introduction into the legislature of what came to be called the Fernald Law, named for Governor Bert Fernald. This was a measure to prohibit the exportation of electric power from the state. Baxter and those supporting the measure felt that it would encourage the economic development of Maine if the seemingly plentiful

285

supplies of hydro-electric power could be developed and used within the state. The source of immense controversy in the next two decades, it remained law for nearly five decades.

In 1910 Baxter failed of reelection in the course of the Democratic sweep in Cumberland County when the Republican Party was shattered by internal feuding. As a leading member of that party, he attended the controversial Republican National Convention of 1912 where he was a staunch supporter of William Howard Taft. At this and later meetings he met Calvin Coolidge, Herbert Hoover, and other leading members of the party.

He ran successfully once more for the State House of Representatives in 1916 and was reelected in 1918. He tried for the speakership in 1916–17, but could not get sufficient support from other Republican leaders such as Guy Gannett. It was in these years that he emerged as a major and very controversial politician. Probably as a result of the fishing trips he had taken with his father, he had become increasingly concerned with the use of the resources of the state. He particularly resented the fact that Maine had sold off large blocks of land to railroads and timber companies and felt that the public lots in the wildlands of Maine should be returned to the control of the state. Detailed studies were prepared on the issues surrounding these various problems. He believed that the state should buy up and reforest burned and cut-over areas of timberland in order to ensure a sufficient supply of wood to meet future needs of the people. He introduced bills to this end in the legislature, beginning in 1917. At the same time, he began his long crusade for the development of a park in the Katahdin region.

He also had very firm ideas regarding the water-power resources of Maine. He believed that water power and water storage facilities should be used in the state and not exported. If these natural resources were developed by private corporations, the work should be done by way of leases from the state, which would assume and retain ownership and earn revenue from the franchise rights. This policy would also enable the state to take back the resources if it was felt to be in the public interest. For a time at least he believed that Maine should use the right of eminent domain where needed to obtain ownership of key storage sites. Finally, Baxter wanted the state to encourage private development of its water power by the construction of storage reservoirs. If they were built in a businesslike manner, they would return a good deal of revenue to the state and allow reduction of taxes.

The story of the long controversy in the state and within the Republican party over the Water Power Commission, which he was influential in setting up, and of the various bills he and others introduced to effect these ends is long and complicated. By 1920 he was pitted against the
286 electric companies, particularly Central Maine Power and its owners, and

PERCIVAL P. BAXTER

the large landowners, led by the Great Northern Paper Company, who were most immediately threatened by his proposals. These battles constituted a major element in his two terms as governor.

He also inherited from his father a strong anti-vivisectionist stance. He introduced a bill into the legislature to prohibit the practice of dissecting animals in the schools and colleges of Maine. In 1920 he refused to make his regular contribution as an alumnus of Bowdoin College because animals were dissected in its zoology classes and in its medical school.

Baxter ran for the Senate again in 1920. He won handily in the primary as well as the general election in September. Ever ambitious, he decided to run for the presidency of the Senate. His brother Rupert, a senator from Bath, masterminded his campaign, which he won before the legislature met in January. It was a crucial decision.

In January, soon after the new governor, Frederic H. Parkhurst, had been sworn in by Baxter, he became ill. He actually occupied his office in the State House for about four hours only. He died on the last day of the month just as Baxter was preparing to leave Portland for Augusta to keep an appointment to discuss legislative matters with him. By terms of the State Constitution, Baxter automatically became governor. At the age of forty-four he was the youngest governor in Maine's history.

What sort of individual was the man who had just become governor of the state? The author of an article in the *Woman's Home Companion* in 1923, who liked him, wrote: "The Governor is a character. Bachelor. Tall, strong and pink. Forty-six or forty-seven in the record books, but much younger with his hat on." But, he went on, "Don't misunderstand. There is nothing soft about this low-voiced, pink-cheeked, boyish man; and, for all his popularity, nothing of the hail-fellow, all-things-to-all, stein-on-the table about him. Everybody calls him Percy [to his immediate family he was Uncle Percy], but nobody calls him 'Percy, old bean!'" A number of writers at the time, including the one quoted here, commented on his large head, which, they assumed, accounted for his very considerable abilities.

Arthur Staples, the editor of the *Lewiston Journal* who accompanied Baxter to Katahdin in 1920, said: "Percy is a persistent person. He is the most patient and persistent person I ever knew. He has certain arts of retreat from difficult positions but he always takes his weapons with him when he retreats." He also kept his ammunition. Staples had followed him through the water-power controversy and noted that in his campaigns and arguments he "always had a straight course ahead and a wide open way for retreat from the position, . . ." if such retreat were necessary to prevent defeat. Staples also found him a "silent person . . . as a rule; yet not reticent. He will talk in a low soft voice on any of his favorite subjects; but never argue." He allowed others a right to an opinion, but insisted that his own right to one should be respected as well. "He is never down

cast," Staples said. "He is always able to smile, say a cheery word as well
as to be quick with ready sympathy for the unfortunate."

Baxter was one who forcefully expressed his opinions and did as much as he could to broadcast them widely. If personally attacked, he often wrote and had printed broadsides stating his position and including relevant correspondence. This occurred twice in the twenties when he had disagreements with the minister of his church in Portland. While he was governor and later on, he often used the technique of printing pamphlets and broadsides on issues. Most of his major speeches as governor were printed, and he also often had newspapers reprint for wider distribution articles on his activities that had appeared in them.

Though given his family connections and personal wealth he had entry to the highest social circles, Baxter appears not to have been active socially. One gets the impression that he was a person close to his immediate family, or at least a portion of it, and that he was a loner much of his life and, by choice, had a very restricted circle of close personal friends.

He had lived at his father's house at 61 Deering since his birth. There he took care of his father until the latter's death in 1921. Baxter had never married, though his nephew told me that his family tried to pressure him to do so. At one point, in 1921, the newspapers reported that Percival was attracted by an actress in Portland who later played on the stage in New York. It is said that his family disapproved of this romance, so nothing further developed. When asked bluntly by a journalist why he had never married, Baxter replied:

> I've always had a ready-made family. My brothers and sisters, all older than myself, married and had children while I was still too young to do so. All through my youth I was plentifully supplied with domesticity. Then, as a young man, I moved about a good deal, school here and in Europe, college at Bowdoin, law school at Cambridge. When I did settle down, it was with my father, a busy, active man, absorbed in everything that had to do with the best interests of the State of Maine. I became absorbed too. I've been in public life ever since. When my father died, my widowed sister and her two young sons came to live with me. They're with me now. You see, I have a family, and the responsibilities of family life. You might say that I have been *deflected* from matrimony.

When the journalist suggested that Baxter's statement sounded like something from Dryden, who said that somebody or other had "deviated into truth," Baxter shot back: "Say, rather, that I deviated into error!" There is no question about his concern for the children in his brothers' and sister's families; according to his nephew, he was most generous with them. He was equally kind, thoughtful, and generous to those connected with his Katahdin venture.

289

One of the consuming interests that Baxter developed as a child was a tremendous affection for animals. He was eager, while governor, to have the game preserve established at Katahdin. In 1956 he gave $50,000 to the town of Westbrook for the construction of an animal shelter, and eight years later provided a considerable sum to renovate and enlarge it. He especially loved dogs, particularly Irish setters. His father had given him one when he was about eight years old. In his Papers are copies of dog licenses for the year 1889, one for a female setter named Skip, the other for a male setter named Garry Owen. Of the fourteen setters he had over the years, several had the latter name. They were his constant companions at home in Portland and particularly when he spent the summers on Mackworth Island, where he established a cemetery for those that died.

The most memorable incident involving his dogs was the furore that arose after the death of "Garry" on June 1, 1923. This beautiful Irish setter had accompanied Baxter to the Blaine House, from which he would cross the street to the State House when Baxter was in his office. Garry had become a particular favorite of Baxter, who obtained special permission from the Maine Central Railroad to take him into the smoking cars of trains between Augusta and Portland. On Garry's death, after a long illness, Baxter ordered the flags at the Capitol to be lowered to half-mast while Garry's body was being transported to Mackworth Island for burial. Critics were enraged that the flag had been thus "desecrated"; admirers of Baxter and of animals defended his action equally vociferously. Baxter wrote and had printed a moving memorial to Garry in defense of his actions. Saying he yielded to no one in his respect and reverence for the flag, he praised dogs and Garry in particular. "My 'Garry' was a part of my life," he said, "for my dogs constitute my immediate family." After discussing the role of the flag, Garry's role in the State House, and the role of dogs in peace and war, he wrote that the reactions to his action might "arouse our people to a new realization of their responsibilities to dumb animals; if this be so one of my purposes will have been accomplished."

Baxter's tenure as governor was a controversial one, to say the least. From the outset, after getting over the shock of Parkhurst's death and his sudden elevation to the office, he argued for economy in government. Using his veto power when necessary to get the legislature to agree with him on budget cuts, he effected substantial reductions in expenditures for many state institutions. He particularly singled out the University of Maine for cutbacks and was able to make them stick. While a student at Bowdoin he had written an article for the *Orient* arguing against the creation of a law school at Orono and in favor of maintaining the University as an agricultural and mechanical college. During his term the University Law School was closed. He became involved in a number of battles while trying to enforce Prohibition laws; he tried to have the sheriff of Hancock County ousted for not working hard enough to enforce them. He demanded and obtained the resignation of the chairman of the Public Utilities Commission, who was a lobbyist in the legislature for the Associated Industries of Maine while he was on the Commission. But Baxter had a difficult time getting a successor approved. He opposed implementation of the Sheppard-Towner Act, providing for state and federal aid to dependent children in Maine, because he saw too much encroachment by the federal government on the rights of states. In refusing to declare Navy Day by proclamation in Maine, he enraged the veterans' lobbies.

Most significant were the almost continual controversies surrounding use of water and land resources, the nature of which has already been discussed. His cherished plan for creation of a state park at Katahdin fell victim to the larger controversy over control of reservoirs and dam sites and whether power should be exported from Maine. This thoroughly estranged him from the most powerful political interests in the state. Baxter was able to prevent the export of power from Maine, but he could not obtain passage of the legislation he desired. It is impossible to begin to describe it adequately in a short compass; the full story has yet to be written. For basic information, the reader should begin with Lincoln Smith's *The Power Policy of Maine* or David Smith's *Lumbering in Maine*.

Despite the controversies swirling about him, Baxter had no difficulty in being reelected in 1922. While he had alienated the most important business leaders in Maine, who accused him of being a socialist or a communist, his anti-corporate stance won him the esteem and support of a large part of the population. He had the support of much of organized labor in the state. He appointed Catholics and, for the first time, some Jewish citizens, to governmental posts. He took a strong stand against the Ku Klux Klan as it gained power during the mid-twenties. And he appointed a number of women to state positions, if admittedly minor ones. Contrary to charges made at the time that these actions were politically motivated, it appears that his lack of bigotry was genuine. His sister, Emily Poole, had become a convert of the Catholic Church at an early date, and when she died in 1921 Baxter made a number of gifts, including the family organ from his father's house, to her church. For this action he was attacked by some Protestant ministers, but he replied in strong defense of his actions coupled with pleas for tolerance.

He probably could have had a third term as governor had he desired to break the long-standing tradition against this. He chose not to and stood aside, trying to keep his party from falling apart in the bitterly contested primary battle between Owen Brewster, who had been closely tied to him in the fight for the Park, but had become too closely tied, Baxter thought, to the KKK, and Senator Frank G. Farrington, whom Baxter did not respect. Baxter urged that federal officials be called in to check the election results because of seeming fraud and corruption.

GOVERNOR BAXTER AND HELON TAYLOR, TAKEN IN THE LATE 1960s

He departed on a long tour almost as soon as he left office and then
returned to Portland and Mackworth Island. In 1926, when a vacancy occurred in Maine's United States Senate delegation, Baxter attempted to obtain the Republican nomination. The opposing faction in the party, controlled by large landowner and utility interests, put up Arthur R. Gould
of Aroostook County. Whether Baxter felt that he had enough support
for him not to have to work hard for the nomination, or whether his opposition simply put up too much money and organized more carefully in
support of the Aroostook electrical entrepreneur, it is difficult to tell. At
any rate, Baxter lost the primary election; his political career was over
as far as officeholding was concerned.

He worked hard for Hoover's election and reelection and, he indicated,
could have had an ambassadorship to a European nation had he wished.
He apparently was offered that to Canada, but did not take it. Japan
fascinated him and it was that post that he really wanted, according to
the newspapers of the day. When that went to another, his attention
turned inward toward Maine once more. He remained active in the Republican party, attending state conventions and giving speeches into the
1940s. Several times in the decades that followed, supporters started booming him for the governorship, but each time he refused to entertain the
idea. Though the New Deal helped his beloved park project, he was extremely unhappy with the economic and political forces brought into
play during the Roosevelt administration, and he probably became more
conservative politically and economically than he had been earlier.

After he withdrew from politics, he turned to his pet project of developing Baxter State Park, managing his properties and investments, and
making his tours. He spent summers on Mackworth Island until 1949, when
he turned his island house over to the state. Fortunately for Maine he
lived long enough to see a number of his favored projects consummated.

As a philanthropist Baxter is unsurpassed in Maine. In the 1940s he
gave paintings to St. Joseph's Convent and a painting and silver chalice to
the Bishop of Portland. They had been obtained by his father in Florence,
Italy, in 1885. He deeded Mackworth Island, which had been in the
hands of the family for a great many years, to the state to be used for
"STATE PUBLIC PURPOSES." He suggested that it be used as "a
home for sick and underprivileged children," but did not insist on it; he
did indicate, however, that "ITS USE FOR CHILDREN WOULD BE
ESPECIALLY PLEASING TO ME." At the same time he provided
$10,000 as a maintenance fund. A decade later, he gave the state $625,000
if it would move the state school for the deaf to the island. Of this, $125,000
was to be used to build a new bridge and causeway to replace the old
wooden bridge to the island,which was now unsafe. The remaining amount,
supplemented by state appropriations if Maine accepted his offer, was to
be used for "a new school for the Deaf or toward the construction of a new

Home and School for the wards of the State. . . ." He suggested construction of the Maine School for the Deaf first. The state accepted the offer, provided the additional funds, and began construction of what became the Governor Baxter School for the Deaf soon after. It was dedicated in 1955.

Baxter also enlarged the city's park system that his father had done so much to develop. In 1944 he gave the city of Portland six acres in the Deering section, which he promised to reforest with his own funds. Two years later, in memory of his father, he gave the city thirty acres of woods along Forest Avenue, which he wanted kept in its natural wild state without landscaping or cement sidewalks. The "Mayor Baxter Woods" were the former estate of F. O. J. Smith, the prominent and irascible 19th-century businessman and politician. James Phinney Baxter had purchased the property after Smith died.

This action was followed the next year by the installation, at Baxter's expense, of a complete and elaborate lighting system for Baxter Boulevard. He had been inspired to do this two decades earlier when, on a trip to Latin America after he left office, he had seen and enjoyed the lights around the beach at Rio de Janeiro, Brazil. When he returned from that trip he had offered to buy the lights, but city officials did not respond to his offer; this time, of course, they accepted.

Baxter followed up these gifts carefully. Several times he prevented commercial encroachment on Baxter Boulevard. If the city officials did not maintain either the Boulevard or the Woods to his liking, he would write letters to the proper officials indicating the nature of the problems and suggesting that they be attended to. His wishes were usually followed, but in a couple of cases where officials were dilatory, Baxter suggested he might go to the newspapers with his problems, and this resulted in action.

The town of Gorham benefited by Baxter's generosity again in 1956 when he gave $20,000 to establish the Percival P. Baxter Trust Fund. The income from his fund was to help defray the maintenance and repair costs of the Baxter Memorial Library and Baxter Museum established many years earlier by his father.

In addition to these major bequests made during his lifetime, there were doubtless many smaller gifts and contributions that went unrecorded. In the year before Baxter's death, a student was enabled to go to Bates College by means of funds Baxter had provided.

In his will, aside from the major endowment for Baxter State Park, he provided that $200,000 be added to the $50,000 his father had willed the city of Boston to build the memorial to the pioneers of New England. He provided $100,000 each to Portland City Hospital, Portland Public Library, Maine Medical Center, Mercy Hospital, and the Baxter School for the Deaf. To the city of Portland he gave $50,000 to be held in trust, the income to be used to maintain the Mayor Baxter Woods. The Animal

Refuge League of Portland, the town of Gorham, and the Saint Agatha School in Saint Agatha, Maine, each received $25,000. In addition, Baxter had previously made gifts to various relatives, friends, and employees.

Baxter died on June 12, 1969. During the previous decade he had been ill on a number of occasions and his ability to get around had declined gradually. He made his last trip to his beloved park in 1967. By his request, his ashes were scattered over Katahdin and Baxter State Park.

The significance and impact of Baxter's long life and contributions to the state of Maine will continue indefinitely.

GOVERNOR CURTIS AND PARTY IN 1968

When Jake was seventy-seven years old, seen here at far right, he climbed the Abol Trail, across the Knife Edge and down the Helon Taylor Trail on Katahdin with Governor Curtis and his party, photographed as they were about to set forth. Next to Day is Austin Wilkins, who was then chairman of the Baxter State Park Authority. Governor Curtis is fifth from the right.

Percival Baxter's passing marked an important milestone in the history of the Park, which was already beginning to witness significant changes. For over three decades he patiently and persistently had worked to purchase areas of land around Katahdin. While good health remained, he increased his planned purchases several times until, finally, after acquiring and deeding to the state over 200,000 acres, he felt that his goal had been achieved. As an achievement by one individual it was unparalleled in the United States.

**XVII**
Baxter's Legacy

He had lived long enough to impress upon the legislators of the state and the thinking of the population his ideas concerning the nature of his tremendous gift. Successive legislatures had accepted his grants of land on his terms, virtually without question. His continual reiteration of the wilderness nature of the Park in these laws and the clarification he provided in 1955 and 1960 make up the ruling philosophy for the Park's future. Until very nearly the end of his life, he played a major role in policy determination for the Park. While primarily interested in providing a wilderness park for the enjoyment of the people of Maine, he also had become very much interested in teaching them proper management and care of the state's forested areas. Some of his last donations, while included in the park area, were designated as areas to be managed with proper forestry techniques. The meaning and intent of some of his provisions remained unclear and subject to differing interpretations, to be settled in the courts, but their major thrust was clear and unmistakable.

To his death Baxter insisted that the Park should be administered by the forest commissioner, the commissioner of Inland Fisheries and Game and the attorney general. Usually at least one of these individuals displayed a keen interest in the well-being and future of the Park. But all of them were extremely busy individuals. There was little time for long-term planning and development of programs to meet the future needs of the Park; the Authority very often reacted to pressures as they developed rather than trying to anticipate them. Given the lack of funds to hire personnel for this purpose, this inability to plan in long-range terms is understandable. In general, the Authority, faced with many conflicting pressures and de-

297

mands, faithfully carried out Baxter's intentions and desires; but it was
a difficult and increasingly controversial task.

Throughout the period before Baxter's death, state appropriations
for maintenance of the Park, partly by his wish, remained small. This
meant that a small but extremely dedicated staff, headed for nearly two
decades by Helon N. Taylor, had to administer an increasingly large land
area. While the major job of campground operation and maintenance was
carried on adequately, many other operations could not be performed as
well as they should be. Personnel found little time to devote to educative
functions at the campgrounds. In areas set aside for scientific forestry, the
shortage of funds precluded development of an effective operating plan.
For most of the Park's history large portions remained unpoliced and uncontrolled much of the time.

When Baxter's will was probated the situation for the Park changed
dramatically. Since the 1930s, when he had so strongly opposed the
creation of a national park in the area, at first privately but then more
publicly, he had indicated that he planned to make provision for maintenance of the Park in his will. He had created an Inter Vivos Trust with
the Boston Safe Deposit and Trust Company on July 6, 1927, under which,
after his death, the state was to receive income from the trust to purchase
forest lands for the Park. This trust arrangement was amended several
times before his death. In 1967 he talked and corresponded with former
Forest Commissioner Albert Nutting regarding the establishment of a
state forest and its operation and management. At Baxter's request, Nutting drew up a proposal for a multiple-use state forest and also drafted a
statement on continuation of the Baxter State Park Authority as it was
then composed.[1] Baxter corresponded with Governor Kenneth M. Curtis
in the following year and sent him the draft of a possible trust creating a
"Maine Forests, Seashore and Lakeshore Properties Fund."[2] While final
changes were made in the trust arrangments just prior to his death, his
will remained unchanged after September 9, 1966.[3]

He named the Boston Safe Deposit and Trust Company, which "controls not only the care and custody of the bulk of my estate, but also
the distribution of the bulk of my estate," executor. After directing that
his body be cremated and his ashes be "taken to Baxter Park, the summit
of Mt. Katahdin, and there scattered to the four winds,"[4] Baxter provided
that his house and furniture and fixtures in it and in his office be sold by
the executor. Funds derived from this and other uninvested funds not yet
part of the Trust Agreement were to be turned over to the Trustee to be
added to the principal.

In the Trust Agreement he provided that the Boston Safe Deposit
and Trust Company would continue to hold the trust property and manage
298    and administer it for the following purposes:

1. To pay the net income therefrom at least as often as quarterly to the "BAXTER STATE PARK TRUST FUND" created by Chapter 21 of the Private and Special Laws of 1961 enacted by the Legislature of the State of Maine for the care, protection and operation of the forest land known as BAXTER STATE PARK, and for other forest lands hereinafter acquired by the State of Maine under the Provisions of this TRUST for recreational or reforestation purposes.

2. To pay over from the principal thereof whenever and as often as the State of Maine shall determine the desirability of the purchase or other acquisition of additional lands for said Baxter State Park or other lands for recreational or reforestation purposes, such sums as shall be requested in writing by the Treasurer of the State of Maine and shall be certified to be used for these purposes by the Governor and Executive Council of the State of Maine, and the members of the Baxter State Park Commission and the Trustee may require that any such certification contain a statement that the purchase price or acquisition cost of such lands is in their opinion fair and reasonable under all the circumstances.

3. In the State of Maine there are large areas of unproductive forest lands, burned over, cut and rocky, which are of little or no market value and which may be purchased at a low figure and allowed to reforest itself or remain as it is for scenic, recreational purposes, and for experimental scientific forestry.

All of the lands so purchased under this Trust Agreement are to be forever held by the said STATE OF MAINE in TRUST for the benefit of the People of Maine for development, improvement, use, reforestation, scientific forestry, and the production of timber and sale thereof.

I hope some of the forest land acquired by the State under this provision of my TRUST will become model forests similar to those of Germany, Scandinavia and elsewhere, producing a crop of wood to be sold by the State. The STATE OF MAINE is given full power to harvest the crop, reforest and protect these lands against damage by insects, fire or otherwise. All revenue acquired by the sale of timber shall by the State of Maine be used for the care, extension and management of said lands.

I shall be pleased if some portion of the lands purchased with my funds be made a "SANCTUARY FOR WILD LIFE," but this I must leave to the judgment of others.

The people of Maine were astounded at the size of Baxter's bequest for the Park and forest lands, since the principal totalled over $5,000,000.[5] This, added to the existing Trust Fund of nearly $1,600,000 provided a very large endowment to pay future expenses of the Park. By the late seventies, however, the rapid rate of inflation led to expenses that approached the income generated by the trust.

In the months after the will was probated, the Authority discussed the use of the funds and also made arrangements with the Trustee for orderly administration and transfer of generated income. On July 1, 1970, the Authority formally voted that no funds would be requested from the legislature for the period after July 1, 1971. Income from the endowment was sufficient to pay operating costs.[6] The legislature early in 1970 also quickly implemented Baxter's desire to improve forestry practices in Maine by establishing the Maine Forest Authority, composed of the forest commissioner, the commissioner of Inland Fisheries and Game, the director of the Maine State Park and Recreation Commission, the attorney general and one public member appointed by the governor, to receive funds from the Trustee or from other sources to purchase or otherwise obtain and manage forest lands under the terms Baxter had provided.[7] No attempt will be made here to describe its operations since that time.

In the park area, as has been indicated in earlier chapters, the new funds led to many changes. Personnel on the payroll was increased dramatically. Private leases within park boundaries were phased out and trust fund income used to pay for leaseholders' property. A number of long-delayed capital improvements were begun. However, no immediate change in direction or overall policy was made.

Baxter's death and the sudden increase in revenues which followed came at a time of turmoil in the nation at large as well as in Maine. Changing technologies in the recreation field and an increased environmental awareness led, in the late sixties, to increasing criticism of the policies and practices of the Authority. It was beset by interest groups representing widely diverse views, all of whom demanded changes in policy. Practices such as the use of pesticides to kill roadside foliage or keep down insect pests suddenly became anathema. The existence of open dumps in the Park was sharply criticized. The use of detergents in some areas by the vastly increased number of visitors led to pollution of some streams. As snowmobiles increasingly swarmed over Baxter State Park roads and trails, angry opponents of their use raised a storm of protest and eventually helped force a change in policy. The public generally became far more interested in the activities and meetings of the Authority than it had ever been before; and citizens were more willing to vent their irritation and anger over policies that they disliked.

In this situation it became obvious that the lack of a comprehensive plan for management and operation of the Park was a major weakness. The Authority began dealing with this problem in the late sixties and early seventies. An advisory committee was established in 1970 as a means of providing varied citizen input into the development of park policy. One of the first tasks of the Committee was to prepare for the Authority a "Statement of Purpose" incorporating and attempting to define Baxter's wishes and ideas. Written principally by Norman Minsky of Bangor and Dr.

Robert Ohler of Winthrop, this was introduced into the legislature early the next year by Representative Walter A. Birt of East Millinocket, a member of the Advisory Committee and one of the authors of the statement. Included in the bill, which passed without difficulty, was the provision that it shall be the object of the Authority to preserve the grandeur and beauty of the park area; "to subordinate its own wishes to the intent of Governor Baxter; [and] to recognize his wish that, in this era of change, one thing of natural beauty remain constant."[8] Late in 1972 the Authority adopted a set of interim objectives for Baxter State Park, drawn up by the Advisory Committee pending preparation of a more comprehensive master plan.[9] Early the following year, it established the position of a director to assume responsibility for overall management and planning for the Park and to prepare the master plan. After some delay, the Authority, in December, 1974, hired A. Lee Tibbs of Pennsylvania State University as director. He assumed his duties in March 1975. Soon thereafter a task force was formed, largely of members of the Advisory Committee, headed by Tibbs. It completed Section I, Policies and Concepts of a "Baxter State Park Plan" in August 1978, which was accepted by the Authority in the following month.[10]

While the long-range master plan was being developed, controversies continued on a number of fronts; some of these were resolved in the courts.[11] The Great Northern Paper Company owned cutting rights in T3R9 until December 1973. In late November of the previous year that corporation signed an agreement with the Authority by which it gave up those rights in exchange for similar rights in forest management areas in the northwestern portion of the Park. A storm of protest followed and in the end the Authority purchased all Great Northern cutting rights in the Park for $725,000, which sum came out of the principal of the trust. No attempt will be made here to deal with the intricacies of this controversy.

A greater dispute arose in the aftermath of a tremendous windstorm in November 1974, larger and more extensive than that of a decade earlier, which laid waste to 3,900 acres within the Park and additional areas of privately owned land beyond its boundaries. The Authority discussed various alternative policies with regard to the blowdowns. A consulting forestry firm, Kolman Land Consultants, Inc., of Brewer, Maine, was engaged to assess the situation and make recommendations to the Authority. Eventually it decided to restore as much of the timber as possible, using Baxter's 1955 statement to the legislature as a guide. The restoration operation began in 1975 and continued into the following year amid a good deal of controversy. Then, in August 1976, five Maine citizens were successful in obtaining a restraining order from a Superior Court justice, halting the restoration operation. The situation was complicated even more in July 1977, when a fire broke out in the blowdown area and burned 3,588 acres in the southwest corner of the Park and adjacent lands owned by Great

## THE 1977 FIRE

Out of control for 14 days, with as many as 200 people involved in fighting it at one point, the fire cost approximately $745,000. The top photo was taken from a helicopter about 6,000 feet up, flying north of the fire and looking back downriver. The beginning of Katahdin is in the background; the fire has reached Foss and Knowlton Pond. The first white streak beyond that marks the boundary between the Park and Great Northern. The West Branch of the Penobscot is to the right, and beyond that the broad light streak leads to the Ripogenus Dam. The photo of devastation in the wake of the fire was taken from Great Northern property looking toward Katahdin.

302

DIGGING A FIRELINE AHEAD OF THE FLAMES

Northern. This led to a new round of recriminations between defenders of
the policy of the Authority and staunch environmentalists.

Finally, in 1976, a group of Maine Indians—members of the Penobscot, Passamaquoddy, Micmac, and Maliseet tribes—occupied the campground at Abol to dramatize their claims to Katahdin as part of the larger
land claims issue raised by them against the state of Maine, as a "spiritual
place" that "belongs to the Indians." They discontinued their occupation,
which occurred before the Park formally opened for the summer season,
after about a week.*

While these controversies went on, the main business of the Park
continued into the late seventies. Substantial progress was being made in
correcting a number of the problems that had become so apparent by the
late sixties. While other problems remained, Baxter's basic desires were
being preserved: "Katahdin stands above the surrounding plain unique
in grandeur and glory. The works of man are short-lived. Monuments
decay, buildings crumble and wealth vanishes, but Katahdin in its massive grandeur will forever remain the mountain of the people of Maine.
Throughout the ages it will stand as an inspiration to the men and women
of this State."

## AFTERWORD

The blowdown suit to halt the BSPA's restorations operation was initiated
by a complaint filed on November 20, 1975, seeking declaratory judgment,
review of governmental action, and injunctive relief.

On January 15, 1976 a hearing was held on the plaintiff's request for
a preliminary injunction, but none was issued. Instead, hearings on both
preliminary and permanent relief were combined and held on February 26
and 27, 1976; and on August 24, 1976 the Superior Court issued its decision
recognizing the authority of the Baxter State Park Authority to clear, protect and restore the Park from the blowdown, but enjoining the Authority
from the use of heavy equipment to do so. The decision provided that:

> further clearance may continue, but without the use of heavy equip-
> ment, and in such a manner as will not unduly disturb the terrain and
> natural environment. The Baxter State Park Authority may, however,
> proceed to develop, and contract, plans for clearance of blow-down,
> which would more closely follow the terms of the trust deeds as they
> have been herein interpreted by the Court.

While the Authority elected not to proceed with the cleaning of the
blown-down trees as contemplated by the Superior Court's order, plaintiffs

---

* Settlement of the Indian Land Claims in Maine did not include any part of
Baxter Park.

filed a notice of appeal on September 21, 1976, and the Authority cross-appealed on October 6, 1976. The Maine law court upheld the Superior Court's order.

The 1977 forest fire served to strengthen the Authority's position as far as clearing up of blowdowns is concerned and it is still at cross purposes with environmentalists on this issue. But the fire itself was handled creatively.

Park Forester Vladek "Kim" Kolman evaluated potentially severe environmental impacts of some fire line construction and took prompt and effective action to remedy the situation and alleviate the danger while the fire was still going. Additional corrective measures were taken immediately following the fire. These consisted of stream bank stabilization, water bar installation, seeding and mulching of steep slopes to prevent erosion and stream and pond sedimentation. A total of 11 acres of the 1900 burned on the Park received some corrective treatment. The remaining acreage was left to be gradually restored through natural processes.

The Baxter State Park Fire Plan was updated and revised prior to the 1978 fire season, after close consultation and coordination with the Great Northern Paper Company, other abutting landowners, and the Maine Forest Service. The special and unique management objectives of Baxter Park were taken into consideration It has been concluded that under the present state of knowledge of conditions and technical capabilities the overall fire management policy for Baxter State Park must be one of control, at least for the immediate future. However, the Park's fire management plan will be reviewed annually for needed changes, and long-range studies concerning fire management are being actively considered.

The Policies and Concept Plan completed in 1978 provided for additional planning in the form of Unit Management Plans. These Unit Plans are to chart future management in detail, including appropriate aspects of environmental, economic and social consideration, management activity schedules, financial needs, and manpower requirements. They will outline action to be taken within the unit, specifying the place, method, degree, and order of priority with other activities.

Shortly after approval of the Policies and Concept Plan, multi-disciplinary task forces were formed to develop four Unit Plans: for a transportation system; fisheries and wildlife management; public use; and administration of the scientific forest management area.

The last named unit was given high priority since Governor Baxter had made this 28,594 acres a part of the Park in 1955 expressly for scientific forest management, but his desires for the area had not yet been carried out. A park forester, George M. Ruopp, was hired in September 1978 to spearhead this priority effort. The first draft of a scientific forest management plan was completed by Forester Ruopp and his task force in July 1980 and submitted to the Baxter State Park Authority and the public for review. 305

Following revisions, the Scientific Forest Management Area Unit Plan was approved by the Authority in late February 1981. Implementation of this plan is to begin immediately. Its goals are to actively and consistently improve management of the area, using the most approved practices of scientific forestry to provide for multiple use management. The primary objective is to develop the area into a showplace that will serve as both an example and an inspiration to those interested in promoting scientific forestry. The effort will be to provide for optimum levels of recreational use and enjoyment; fisheries and wildlife population, and watershed values while practicing timber management; and to provide for protection and restoration of forest resources that may be damaged or susceptible to damage by acts of nature.

Over the first five-year operational period, an average of 23,000 cord-equivalents of wood will be harvested annually. The wood removed will be primarily balsam fir because of the spruce budworm infestation that is adversely affecting this species. Also, 19 miles of primary road and 25 miles of secondary road will be completed to provide the access essential for intensive forest management.

Task forces working on the other three unit plans, coordinated by Director Tibbs, completed draft plans in December 1980. They are undergoing a public review process and are expected to be revised with final plans approved by the Authority some time in 1981.

It is probably fitting and perhaps would please Governor Baxter that the major planning documents for his beloved Park will be completed and their implementation will begin in 1981, the 50th Anniversary of Baxter State Park.

These plans collectively set the stage and establish areas within which future management actions may be taken, including a variety of more specific resource action plans that will be developed as the need arises.

BRONZE PLAQUE AT STATE HOUSE

APPENDICES

# I
## MOUNT KATAHDIN TRAGEDIES

Fortunately few explorers of the Katahdin area have suffered fatal accidents. Indeed, looking at photographs of the Knife Edge; of forbidding, steep slopes down Mt. Katahdin itself; dizzying views from it and surrounding peaks of the chasms below, one is astonished that there have not been many more serious or fatal accidents. The fact that so few have occurred is a tribute to the park rangers and their supervisors through the years.

One of the major and most publicized accidents was the death, during the week of October 28, 1963, of one of two women on a Mt. Katahdin excursion. It led to that of Baxter Park Ranger Ralph Heath, who tried to rescue her. The deaths were the first recreation connected fatalities since the creation of the Park in 1931.

Because the Authority believed that a careful review of the accident could teach many lessons toward prevention of similar occurrences, Governor John H. Reed authorized hearings on November 12, 1963, at Old Town, Maine, to be conducted jointly by the BSPA and the Maine Department of Inland Fisheries and Game.

At the meeting, Supervisor Helon Taylor was called upon to report on the weather during the week of October 28. Though it began with a warm, sunny day, Hurricane Ginny must have already been marshalling forces, for by that Monday evening a stormy wind was blowing and by Tuesday a blizzard was in progress. Sixteen inches of snow accumulated that day; increasing wind, snow, rain and sleet followed through the entire week.

Mrs. Margaret Ivusic and Mrs. Helen Mower had had uneven climbing experience: to Mrs. Ivusic mountain climbing had become a hobby which she had been pursuing ardently for two or three years, while Mrs. Mower had been climbing mountains from childhood on. However, this was her first time on Mount Katahdin. The two women, after brief conversations with rangers Rodney Sargent and Ralph Heath at the Chimney Pond campground where they had spent the previous night, started out at about 8 A.M. Monday morning and used the Cathedral Trail for a leisurely climb to Baxter Peak, where they arrived around 1:30 and stopped for lunch and picture taking and a rather long rest. The two rangers, meanwhile, were clearing the Helon Taylor Trail that day.

311

The women decided to walk out onto the Knife Edge and determine
whether to use the Dudley Trail to go back to camp or retrace their steps
and return by way of the Cathedral and Saddle trails. Mrs. Ivusic went on
ahead of her companion and in ten or fifteen minutes called out from somewhere to the left and below the Knife Edge that she had found a perfect
shortcut.

Helen Mower was afraid to leave the marked trail despite her experience as a climber (or perhaps because of it). The women were within
easy hearing distance of each other but could not see each other. They
argued which way to go for some time. In her enthusiasm Mrs. Ivusic was
determined to try her way, and since they apparently could keep in voice
contact, they decided to go their separate ways. Mrs. Mower continued
down the Knife Edge trail to the top of The Chimney (which is a technical
climbing route), where she found a sign cautioning against any but experienced climbers equipped with ropes to take that route down. She had lost
contact with Mrs. Ivusic but at that point reestablished it, only to learn that
her friend was trapped on the wall and could move neither up nor down.
Mrs. Mower shouted that she was taking the Dudley Trail down and going
for help.

When she arrived at the campground it was dark and no one was
around; but by walking to the edge of Chimney Pond in front of the camp
she could shout and still be heard by Mrs. Ivusic. She built a fire in front
of the leanto to which they had been assigned the night before and alter-
nated between keeping that up and going to the edge of the pond to talk
to Mrs. Ivusic.

Ranger Heath arrived alone about an hour later and on being told
what had happened talked with Mrs. Ivusic and established the fact that
she was uninjured. He urged her to stay exactly where she was and promised to rescue her at daybreak. He reported the matter to Supervisor Helon
Taylor and then he and Mrs. Mower had supper.

According to Mrs. Mower's report at the hearing, Ranger Heath appeared to be exhausted after his long day's work, and she urged him to get
some rest before attempting to rescue Mrs. Ivusic, who seemed to be in no
immediate danger. But around eleven a sharp weather change had taken
place and the wind was so strong that Heath decided to start out immediately. He packed Mrs. Ivusic's rucksack with extra food and clothing and
took a piton and 80 feet of rope and started out just after eleven. He came
back approximately five hours later and reported to the anxious Mrs. Mower
that he had not actually been able to reach Mrs. Ivusic for lack of sufficient
rope, but had talked with her again and believed he had convinced her to
wait where she was until he could get more help. As far as he could make
out, she was near the main waterfall west of The Chimney. He planned to
go back and attempt a rescue from below the falls.

312   Heath had breakfast, then called Supervisor Taylor for aid and left

again at 6:10 A.M. By then a message had come through that Ranger Sargent was on the way to help.

No one knows what happened: whether Ranger Heath lost his footing in the mounting snow and fell to his death before reaching the stranded woman, or both were lost in his rescue attempt. Many members of experienced mountain search teams that volunteered their help believed that neither the ranger nor Mrs. Ivusic could have survived Tuesday's hurricane winds and icy blizzard.

A team of wardens from the Maine Department of Inland Fisheries and Game, which by a Maine statute is designated as the responsible agency in the search for anyone established as missing in the woods or mountains of Maine, organized the search, which continued for a week during the most adverse of conditions. Besides students of the University of Maine, Orono, a team of instructors from Norwich College, Vermont, and Vermont State Troopers were flown in by a National Guard plane. Two Massachusetts men experienced in mountain search and rescue were called upon for assistance and were also flown to Maine. It was impossible to use an airplane at any time to help at the scene, but during what seemed a break in the violence of the storm on Thursday, a helicopter was sent out from Dow Air Force Base. It was forced back by the turbulence and high winds.

The search was finally given up on November 4th.

Review of the double tragedy did serve to point up the lack of a detailed search and rescue plan and resulted in some changes in park administration. The season for camping on and climbing any mountain in the Park above treeline was shortened; no one without a permit plus proof as to competency is now allowed to engage in any of the above activities between October 16 and May 14. Baxter Park had its own rescue team from 1969 to 1977, made up of six rangers, highly trained in rescue methods and technical climbing. Now rangers are trained in rescue and first aid techniques; and teams of highly trained volunteers coordinated by park personnel are always available in case of emergency. Medical evacuation by helicopter is also available through the National Guard. Gatehouses have been established at entrances to the Park by means of which control of the use of the Park, as well as awareness of who and where visitors are in the Park, can be maintained.

The Authority tries to keep a balance between restrictions aimed at safe usage of the Park and the freedom that Governor Baxter desired for nature lovers who visit the area and glory in its unique and blessed wilderness.

313

# II
## A DIGEST OF THE BSPA BOUNDARY
## SURVEY PROJECT REPORT
October 5, 1970–February 18, 1971

The primary objective of this survey was to traverse the entire perimeter of Baxter State Park, bushing out lines, spotting and painting line trees, re-establishing corner posts, and witnessing and chaining distances on the ground. This was done for the entire boundary except for two miles on the east line of T4R9 between the "Twin Pond Trail" and the Wassataquoik River, where thirteen inches of snow fell, bringing down the smaller tents of the side-camp and making it exceedingly difficult to move in the area which is extremely rocky and precipitous in places, with outcrops of large boulders. This section was not painted, but it was bushed out, spotted, and chained.

Eleven men selected from Fire Control personnel of the Maine Forest Service and BSP personnel to work under John S. Walker, chief of the party (who kept the daily log) and John Hinkley, his assistant, started out on October 4 for their task, which covered an estimated 107 miles in all. Four of the selected crew were released in November; the rest stayed to completion of the survey. It spanned a season that began with clear, warm autumn days, with temperatures running as high as 90 degrees, and ended in temperatures ranging from 30 to 40 degrees below zero in snow of which the average depth was 3 feet. Side-camps were established along the lines to save miles of backtracking and also valuable daylight working time.

Approximately two-thirds of the perimeter of the park area is ledgy, with huge boulders in midpath that often made it hard to chain distances accurately. Offsets had to be made, such as "breaking chain" to small increments, and "plumbing-a-line" up or down wall-type ledges. Where timber was absent along Traveler and Turner mountains, rocks were piled and painted as markers. The exterior lines of the two northern townships of the Park were bushed out, spotted, and painted a bright orange. Most of the lines were inaccessible by road and time was saved by using snow machines to reach distant areas such as the northwest corner and north line of the Park, which had to be reached by traveling up the East Branch of the Penobscot and on along the south branch of Brayley Brook.

The report, of which a number of bound copies are in existence, con-    315

sists of a general review of the project, Walker's daily log, a summary of
the hours worked, salaries earned, and other expenses incurred; and the
field notes compiled by three-man teams (head chainman, rear chainman,
and surveyor) who were each given specific lines to bush out, mark, and
chain, and were asked to provide details as to the slope and character of the
ground covered.

As Walker reports, they started out in typical fall weather, warm
enough for them to welcome the sight of a cold mountain stream at the
end of the day. On the 13th of October it was nearly 80 degrees and the
black flies and midges were swarming; yet by October 18, Walker reported:

> We woke up this morning to about a foot of snow. Our 2-man
> mountain tents collapsed in the snow. This was our roughest day yet.
> We ran 2 3/4 miles bushing, spotting, and chaining. Real rough going
> over mountainous boulders that were covered with snow and ice.
> Crevices were hidden by snow so that we would slip and down we'd
> go, lucky not to break a leg. The spruce and fir were loaded with
> heavy wet snow. Every time we limbed one or spotted a softwood
> we'd get drenched. Going over the edge of north Turner Mountain was
> almost impossible and what was even worse we had to climb back over
> tonight after finally running the line to the Wassataquoik River. . . .
> Every once in a while the wind roars down the mountain tonight like
> a wall of water almost taking our tent down. Well, back into a damp
> sleeping bag and try sleeping. There comes that wind again. My legs
> are cramped tonight from the miles walked and from being soaked.

> 22 October 1970—Thursday
> . . . I think that climbing these mountains wears a person down.
> We are either wet through from the wet brush or soaked to the skin
> with sweat. These boys are a hardy bunch and I would say about as
> tough as they come.

> 26 October 1970—Monday
> Rain again. Rain or not we have to work. . . . Today we walked
> from Traveler trail camp (from the Bench Mark) to Wassataquoik
> River where we hung up the line during the heavy snow last week. We
> ran the line from the river to the southeast corner of T5R9. Part of the
> line went over 50 chains of immense boulders, then we had to go hand
> over hand over steep ledges. We ran 2 1/2 miles of line from the river.
> We returned back to camp tonight soaked. This finished up the moun-
> tain areas on the East Line. Praise be to God!

> 28 October 1970—Wednesday
> This was the day to run the line up and over Squaw Bosom. . . .
> We walked up the Double Top Trail about two miles, a steep climb to
> an area near the base of Squaw Bosom then cut across country about
> ten chains to where we left off running the line 2 weeks ago. From
> here we started our climb bushing, spotting, painting and chaining the

line as we climbed. It's the roughest climb I have ever been over running lines. There were ledges 60 feet and over that had to be climbed hour after hour. There seemed to be no end. . . .

But despite the frightful ups and downs in weather, they made their way.

8 November 1970—Sunday
We completed the south line of 3R10 in two days. That's moving!

17 November, 1970—Tuesday
Today took us over one of our biggest and last mountain climbs. Four inches of snow hindered our running lines over Billfish Mountain. The last 500 feet to the peak was hand over hand. Upon reaching the peak, and being d____ tired, we found an old chainage station scribed 5 3/4 miles on an old dead pine stub. Even though we were tired from picking our way up over the ledges covered with snow. . . you could not help but enjoy the beauty of the surrounding mountains and valleys. . . .

7 December 1970—Monday
Returned to Soudnahunk Field today after a short weekend . . . We drove in about 7 inches of snow to reach our camp. A little more snow and we will have to use snow sleds to get here. It is becoming real cold, in fact tonight the thermometer reads about 22 degrees below zero. . . . The trees are really snapping tonight from the cold.

16 December 1970—Wednesday
A cold morning; somewhere near 30 degrees below zero. My chin is still swollen from freezing it yesterday. . . .

The group had as home base for some time the Martin's cabin on Matagamon Lake, purchased by the BSPA, in late 1970, and described when they moved into it on December 9, as beautifully constructed, with "low-beamed ceilings, pine-panelled walls, field stone fire place, varnished pine floors and the most unique kitchen wood range combined with gas"— a camp "constructed with love."

11 January 1971—Monday
. . . When I look around in and outside this camp and compare the equipment we had 22 years ago and what we have now it would make some of those old woodsmen turn over in their graves.

13 January 1971—Wednesday
This was a day of all days. I and the rest of the crew are dog tired. . . . It's hard to believe but on the way back tonight I frost-bit my eyeballs.

19 January 1971—Tuesday
It's a cold day today! 42 degrees below zero. . . .

So it went. Finally, on February 10, Walker writes: . . . "The rest of the crew finished bushing, spotting and painting the east-west line of 6R9 and 6R10. THIS FINISHES THE JOB!!"
They had come around full circle.

## BAXTER STATE PARK AUTHORITY
### Members and Chairmanship by Years

*1931*
Clement F. Robinson, Attorney General
Neil J. Violette, Com., Forestry Dept.

*1938*
Waldo N. Seavey, Com., Forestry Dept.
Franz U. Burkett, Attorney General*

*1939* Chairman:
Franz U. Burkett, Attorney General*
Waldo N. Seavey, Com., Forestry Dept.
Geo. J. Stobie, Com., Fish & Game Dept.

*1940* Chairman:
Franz U. Burkett, Attorney General*
Raymond E. Rendall, Com., Forestry Dept.
Geo. J. Stobie, Com., Fish & Game Dept.
Harold J. Dyer, Supervisor–June 1, 1940 (s)

*1941* Chairman:
Frank I. Cowan, Attorney General*
Raymond E. Rendall, Com., Forestry Dept.
Geo. J. Stobie, Com., Fish & Game Dept.
Harold J. Dyer, Supervisor

*1942* Chairman:
Frank I. Cowan, Attorney General*
Raymond E. Rendall, Com., Forestry Dept.
Geo. J. Stobie, Com., Fish & Game Dept.
Harold J. Dyer, Supervisor

*1943* Chairman:
Frank I. Cowan, Attorney General*
Geo. J. Stobie, Com., Fish & Game Dept.
Raymond E. Rendall, Com., Forestry Dept.
Harold J. Dyer, Supervisor

*1944* Chairman:
Frank I. Cowan, Attorney General*
Geo. J. Stobie, Com., Fish & Game Dept.
Raymond E. Rendall, Com., Forestry Dept.

*1945* Chairman:
Ralph W. Farris, Attorney General*
Raymond E. Rendall, Com., Forestry Dept.
Geo. J. Stobie, Com., Fish & Game Dept.

* Correspondence in these years signed by the Attorney General.
(s) Started as Supervisor of BSP.

319

1946  Chairman:  Ralph W. Farris, Attorney General*
                 Raymond E. Rendall, Com., Forestry Dept.
                 Geo. J. Stobie, Com., Fish & Game Dept.
                 Harold J. Dyer, Supervisor

1947  Chairman:  Ralph W. Farris, Attorney General*
                 Geo. J. Stobie, Com., Fish & Game Dept.
                 Raymond E. Rendall, Com., Forestry Dept.
                 Harold J. Dyer, Supervisor

1948  Chairman:  Ralph W. Farris, Attorney General*
                 Geo. J. Stobie, Com., Fish & Game Dept.
                 Albert D. Nutting, Com., Forestry Dept.
                 Harold J. Dyer, Supervisor

1949  Chairman:  Ralph W. Farris, Attorney General*
                 Geo. J. Stobie, Com., Fish & Game Dept.
                 Albert D. Nutting, Com., Forestry Dept.
                 Harold J. Dyer, Supervisor–June 10, 1950 (r)
                 Robt. H. Dyer, Supervisor–June 11, 1950 to Aug. 17, 1950
                 Fred M. Pitman, Acting Supv.–Aug. 18 to 20, 1950

1950  Chairman:  Ralph W. Farris, Attorney General*
                 Albert D. Nutting, Com., Forestry Dept.
                 Geo. J. Stobie, Com., Fish & Game Dept.
                 Helon N. Taylor, Supervisor–Aug. 21, 1950 (s)

1951  Chairman:  Albert D. Nutting, Com., Forestry Dept.
      Members:   A. A. LaFleur, Attorney General
                 R. H. Cobb, Com., Fish & Game Dept.
                 Helon N. Taylor, Supervisor

1952  Chairman:  Albert D. Nutting, Com., Forestry Dept.
      Members:   A. A. LaFleur, Attorney General
                 R. H. Cobb, Com., Fish & Game Dept.
                 Helon N. Taylor, Supervisor

1953  Chairman:  Albert D. Nutting, Com., Forestry Dept.
      Members:   A. A. LaFleur, Attorney General
                 R. H. Cobb, Com., Fish & Game Dept.
                 Helon N. Taylor, Supervisor

1954  Chairman:  Albert D. Nutting, Com., Forestry Dept.
      Members:   R. H. Cobb, Com., Fish & Game Dept.
                 A. A. LaFleur, Attorney General
                 Helon N. Taylor, Supervisor

1955  Chairman:  Albert D. Nutting, Com., Forestry Dept.
      Members:   R. H. Cobb, Com., Fish & Game Dept.
                 F. F. Harding, Attorney General
                 Helon N. Taylor, Supervisor

(r) Retired as Supervisor of BSP.

*1956* Chairman: A. D. Nutting, Com., Forestry Dept.
Members: R. H. Cobb, Com., Fish & Game Dept.
F. F. Harding, Attorney General
Helon N. Taylor, Supervisor

*1957* Chairman: A. D. Nutting, Com., Forestry Dept.
Members: R. H. Cobb, Com., Fish & Game Dept.
F. F. Harding, Attorney General
Helon N. Taylor, Supervisor

*1958* Chairman: Austin H. Wilkins, Com., Forestry Dept.
Members: R. H. Cobb, Com., Fish & Game Dept.
Frank F. Harding, Attorney General
Helon N. Taylor, Supervisor

*1959* Chairman: Austin H. Wilkins, Com., Forestry Dept.
Members: R. H. Cobb, Com., Fish & Game Dept.
F. E. Hancock, Attorney General
Helon N. Taylor, Supervisor

*1960* Chairman: Austin H. Wilkins, Com., Forestry Dept.
Members: R. H. Cobb, Com., Fish & Game Dept.
F. E. Hancock, Attorney General
Helon N. Taylor, Supervisor

*1961* Chairman: Austin H. Wilkins, Com., Forestry Dept.
Members: Roland H. Cobb., Com., Fish & Game Dept.
Frank E. Hancock, Attorney General
Helon N. Taylor, Supervisor

*1962* Chairman: Austin H. Wilkins, Com., Forestry Dept.
Members: F. E. Hancock, Attorney General
R. H. Cobb, Com., Fish & Game Dept.
Helon N. Taylor, Supervisor

*1963* Chairman: Austin H. Wilkins, Com., Forestry Dept.
Members: R. T. Speers, Com., Fish & Game Dept.
F. E. Hancock, Attorney General
Helon N. Taylor, Supervisor

*1964* Chairman: Austin H. Wilkins, Com., Forestry Dept.
Members: R. T. Speers, Com., Fish & Game Dept.
F. E. Hancock, Attorney General
Helon N. Taylor, Supervisor

*1965* Chairman: Austin H. Wilkins, Com., Forestry Dept.
Members: R. J. Dubord, Attorney General
R. T. Speers, Com., Fish & Game Dept.
Helon N. Taylor, Supervisor

1966 Chairman: Austin H. Wilkins, Com., Forestry Dept.
     Members: Ronald T. Speers, Com., Fish & Game Dept.
             R. J. Dubord, Attorney General
             Helon N. Taylor, Supervisor

1967 Chairman: Austin H. Wilkins, Com., Forestry Dept.
     Members: Ronald T. Speers, Com., Fish & Game Dept.
             Jas. S. Erwin, Attorney General
             Helon Taylor, Supervisor—Aug. 19, 1967 (r)
             Rodney H. Sargent, Acting Supervisor
                Aug. 20, 1967 to May 5, 1968

1968 Chairman: Austin H. Wilkins, Com., Forestry Dept.
     Members: James S. Erwin, Attorney General
             Ronald T. Speers, Com., Fish & Game Dept.
             I. C. Caverly, Jr., Supervisor–May 6, 1968 (s)

1969 Chairman: Austin H. Wilkins, Com., Forestry Dept.
     Members: Jas. S. Erwin, Attorney General
             Ronald T. Speers, Com., Fish & Game Dept.
             I. C. Caverly, Jr., Supervisor–March 22, 1969 (r)
             Harry Kearney, Supervisor–March 23, 1969 (s)

1970 Chairman: Austin H. Wilkins, Com., Forestry Dept.
Jan.  Members: Ronald Speers, Com., Fish & Game Dept.
to           Jas. S. Erwin, Attorney General
May         Harry Kearney, Supervisor

June  Chairman: Austin H. Wilkins, Com., Forestry Dept.
to    Members: Geo. W. Bucknam, Com., Fish & Game Dept.
Dec.         James S. Erwin, Attorney General
             Harry Kearney, Supervisor

1971 Chairman: Austin H. Wilkins, Com., Forestry Dept.
Jan.  Members: Geo. W. Bucknam, Com., Fish & Game Dept.
to           James S. Erwin, Attorney General
May         Harry Kearney, Supervisor–May 27, 1971 (r)

1971 Chairman: James S. Erwin, Attorney General
June  Members: Austin H. Wilkins, Com., Forestry Dept.
to           Geo. W. Bucknam, Com., Fish & Game Dept.
Sept.        I. C. Caverly, Jr., Supervisor–June, 1971 (s)

Oct.  Chairman: James S. Erwin, Attorney General
to    Members: Austin H. Wilkins, Com., Forestry Dept.
Dec.         Maynard F. Marsh, Com., Fish & Game Dept.
             I. C. Caverly, Jr., Supervisor

1972 Chairman: James S. Erwin, Attorney General
     Members: Austin H. Wilkins, Com., Forestry Dept.
             Maynard F. Marsh, Com., Fish & Game Dept.
             I. C. Caverly, Jr., Supervisor

1973   Chairman:   Maynard F. Marsh, Com., Fish & Game Dept.
      Members:   Fred E. Holt, Dir., Bureau of Forestry
                 Jon A. Lund, Attorney General
                 I. C. Caverly, Jr., Supervisor

1974   Chairman:   Maynard F. Marsh, Com., Fish & Game Dept.
      Members:   Fred Holt, Dir., Bureau of Forestry
                 Jon Lund, Attorney General
                 I. C. Caverly, Jr., Supervisor

1975   Chairman:   Maynard F. Marsh, Com., Fish & Game Dept.
      Members:   Fred E. Holt, Dir., Bureau of Forestry
                 Jos. E. Brennan, Attorney General
                 A. Lee Tibbs, Director–March, 1975 (s)
                 I. C. Caverly, Jr., Supervisor

1976   Chairman:   Maynard F. Marsh, Com., Fish & Wildlife Dept.
      Members:   John S. Walker, Dir., Bureau of Forestry
                 Joseph E. Brennan, Attorney General
                 A. Lee Tibbs, Director
                 I. C. Caverly, Jr., Supervisor

1977   Chairman:   Maynard F. Marsh, Com., Fish & Wildlife Dept.
      Members:   John S. Walker, Dir., Bureau of Forestry
                 Joseph E. Brennan, Attorney General
                 A. Lee Tibbs, Director
                 I. C. Caverly, Jr., Supervisor

1978   Chairman:   Maynard F. Marsh, Com., Fish & Wildlife Dept.
      Members:   John S. Walker, Dir., Bureau of Forestry
                 Joseph E. Brennan, Attorney General
                 A. Lee Tibbs, Director
                 I. C. Caverly, Jr., Supervisor

1979   Chairman:   Richard S. Cohen, Attorney General
      Members:   Glenn H. Manuel, Com., Fish & Wildlife Dept.
                 Kenneth G. Stratton, Dir., Bureau of Forestry
                 A. Lee Tibbs, Director
                 I. C. Caverly, Jr., Supervisor

1980   Chairman:   Richard S. Cohen, Attorney General
      Members:   Glenn H. Manuel, Com., Fish & Wildlife Dept.
                 Kenneth G. Stratton, Dir., Bureau of Forestry
                 A. Lee Tibbs, Director
                 I. C. Caverly, Jr., Supervisor

**IV**

STATE OF MAINE

IN THE YEAR OF OUR LORD ONE THOUSAND
NINE HUNDRED AND EIGHTY-ONE

JOINT RESOLUTION TO COMMEMORATE THE
50TH ANNIVERSARY OF THE ESTABLISHMENT OF
BAXTER STATE PARK

Whereas, on March 3, 1931, the former Governor Percival P. Baxter deeded to the State of Maine 5,960 acres of land, which included Mount Katahdin, the highest mountain in the State of Maine and "the most picturesque area of the State;" and

Whereas, in the 31 years that followed, Governor Baxter acquired an additional 195,058 acres which were given to the people of Maine as a public park and "a fitting memorial to the past century and an inspiration to the new;" and

Whereas, Governor Baxter viewed the creation of this park through his deeds as "continuing, evolving trusts," which "shall forever be retained and used for state forest, public park and recreational purposes;" and

Whereas, during his lifetime he donated over $1,500,000 to maintain this land and, on his death, he left the bulk of his estate, a trust of over $10,000,000, to forever assist in maintaining the park, and to assure it "shall forever be kept in the natural wild state;" and

Whereas, the acquisition and deeding to the State of over 200,000 acres was an achievement unparalled by any individual in the United States; now, therefore, be it

Resolved: That We, the Members of the 110th Legislature, pause in our deliberations to recognize and commemorate the deeds and actions of Governor Percival Proctor Baxter on this the 50th anniversary of this magnificent gift to the people of the State of Maine; and be it further

Resolved: That suitable copies of this Joint Resolution be sent forthwith to John L. Baxter, Sr., the living nephew of Governor Baxter, and the Baxter State Park Headquarters at Millinocket, Maine.

PUBLISHER'S NOTE
The Baxter State Park Authority and I as publisher have thought of this book in terms of the general reader, particularly the reader who had or will have at some time in his or her life experienced the unspoiled beauty of Governor Baxter's gift to the state of Maine and wondered how it came about.

Because of circumstances beyond my control there was little time for me to consult with Dr. Hakola while preparing this manuscript for publication. We did not entirely agree on treatment of his footnotes, which in my opinion were too numerous in some chapters in terms of the general reader. The best compromise that I could devise was to reduce their number, when a long paragraph or series of paragraphs dealing with one subject had a large number of superior reference figures, by linking as many of them together as possible with punctuation in the notes proper, instead of using a text-page reference for each. Thus a student could still benefit from Dr. Hakola's tremendous research.

Since this is not an orthodox approach and one that might be criticized by academicians, I feel that I should take complete responsibility for it.

Thea Wheelwright

# NOTES

## I

1. The version quoted is from John Giles, *Memoirs of Odd Adventures, Strange Deliverances, etc. in the Captivity of John Giles, esq.* Original ed. printed for William Dodge, at Boston, 1736 (Cincinnati: Spiller & Gates, printers, 1869), p. 46; Fannie Hardy Eckstorm, "The Katahdin Legends," *Appalachia*, December 1924, pp. 45–46; Stuart Trueman, *The ordeal of John Gyles; being an account of his odd adventures, strange deliverances etc. as a slave of the Maliseets* (Toronto, Montreal: McClelland and Stewart, 1966), pp. 69–80.

2. Eckstorm, *op. cit.*, pp. 39–52. See also Roger P. Ray, *The Indians of Maine: A Bibliographical Guide* (Portland, Maine: The Maine Historical Society, 1972); Eugene Vetromile, *The Abnakis and their history, or, Historical Notices on the Aborigines of Acadia* (New York: James B. Kirker, 1866), pp. 6–70; C. G. Leland, "*The Algonquian Legends of New England, Thunder Stories,*" *Century Magazine*, September 1884, pp. 225–63; Minnie Atkinson, *Hinckley Township; or, Grand Lake Stream Plantation, a sketch* (Newburyport, Massachusetts: Newburyport Press, printers [1920]), pp. 121–22; John F. Sprague, *Sebastian Rale, A Maine Tragedy of the Eighteenth Century* (Boston: Heintzmann Press, 1906), pp. 86, 93–98.

3. John Montresor, "Montresor's Journal," part of "XIII. Arnold's Letters on his Expedition to Canada in 1775," Collections of the Maine Historical Society, I (1831), 341–57. Montresor's comment is on p. 349. An undated map, probably done in 1761, accompanied the Journal. No listing is made of Panavansot Hill.

4. Eckstorm, "History of the Chadwick Survey From Fort Pownal in the District of Maine to the Province of Quebec in Canada in 1764," *Sprague's Journal of Maine History*, April-June 1926, pp. 62–89; Joseph W. Porter, "An Account of a Journey from Fort Pownal to Quebec, 1764," *Bangor Historical Society Magazine*, February 1889, p. 146. For a good description of Katahdin views from its summit, see William D. Williamson, *The History of the state of Maine from its first discovery in A.D. 1602, to the separation A.D. 1820, inclusive*, 2 v. (Hallowell: Glazier, Masters, 1832), I, 90–94.

5. Charles Turner, Jr., "A Description of Natardin or Catardin Mountain," *Massachusetts Historical Society Collections*, Second Series, 8 (1819), pp. 112–16. Reprinted in *Lewiston Journal Illustrated Magazine Section*, February 26, 1921, p. 11. See also Myron H. Avery, "Forest Fires at Mount Katahdin," *The Northern*, June 1928, p. 3; Williamson, *op. cit.*, I, 93. About 200 square miles south of

Katahdin were burned in 1795. Turner made several comments about the burned area.

6. Colin Campbell, "Extract from my Journal in Septr. and Octr. 1820 [1819]." In one line of the text on page 46 is a minute line drawing depicting the shape of Katahdin when viewed from a small lake downstream from Pemadum-cook. It is perhaps the earliest extant drawing of the mountain. (Manuscript in author's collection.)

7. Campbell, "Extract from Colin Campbell's Journals, October 19th to October 30, 1819," Barclay Papers, Maine Historical Society, Box 6. The diary for the six days between October 13 and 19 is missing. On the 1816 slide, see Williamson, *op. cit.*, I, 91.

8. L. Felix Ranlett, "Third Recorded Ascent of Katahdin, August 10, 1820," *Appalachia*, June 1968, pp. 43–52. See also C. E. Hamlin, "Reports of the Councillors for the Autumn of 1883. Natural History," *Appalachia*, December 1883, pp. 253–54. J. D. Elder of Lewiston had written to Hamlin that he had prepared a recently discovered paper on the 1820 ascent for the Maine Historical Society. (The article did not appear.) Mr. Ranlett concluded that Daniel Rose (1771–1833), an engineer in the service of the United States, a physician, surveyor, and the first warden of the Maine State Prison, may have been the author. But see Moses Greenleaf, *A Survey of the State of Maine In Reference to Its Geographical Features, Statistics and Political Economy* (Portland: Shirley and Hyde, 1829), p. 47: "Mr. Loring, United States surveyor under the treaty of Ghent, deduces the height from a series of barometrical observations in 1820, taken by himself and Mr. Odell, surveyor on the part of Great Britain. . . ."

9. For the Monument Line survey, see Avery, "The Monument Line Surveyors on Katahdin," *Appalachia*, June 1928, pp. 33–43.

10. Greenleaf, *A Survey, op. cit.*, pp. 9–37, 48; William F. Odell to Judge Chipman, Fredericton, September 18, 1819, Barclay Papers, Maine Historical Society, Box 6. Odell agreed with Greenleaf's assertions as to the height-of-land controversy.

11. Reverend Joseph Blake, "An Excursion to Mount Katahdin," *The Maine Naturalist*, June 1926, pp. 71–73, 94. *The Maine Naturalist* received this account and that of an 1856 expedition by Blake from Blake's daughter, Susan M. Blake. The accounts were probably written in the late 1860s, "for the entertainment and instruction of his children and a few intimate friends."

12. J. W. Bailey, "Account of an Excursion to Mount Katahdin, in Maine," *American Journal of Science* 32 (1837) 20–34. Reprinted in *Bangor Daily Commercial*, June 9, 1906.

13. William Clark Larrabee, "The Backwoods Expedition," in his *Rosabower: essays and miscellanies* (Cincinnati: R. P. Thompson, 1855), pp. 253–72; see Edward S. C. Smith, "Larrabee and 'The Backwoods Expedition'," *Appalachia*, February 1926, pp. 284–90. See also Charles T. Jackson, *Second Annual Report on the geology of the public lands belonging to the two states of Massachusetts and Maine* (Augusta: Luther Severance, printer, 1838), pp. 6–20. Jackson's account was used by John S. Springer in *Forest Life and Forest Trees* (New York: Harper and Brothers, 1851) and by C. A. J. Farrar in his *Guide to Moosehead Lake and the Northern Maine Wilderness*.

14. Larrabee, *op. cit.*

15. Ezekiel Holmes, *Report of an Exploration and Survey of the Territory on the Aroostook River During the Spring and Autumn of 1838* (Augusta: Smith & Robinson, Printers to the State, 1839), p. 10.

16. Avery, "The Story of the Wassataquoik, A Maine Epic," *The Maine Naturalist,* September 1929.

17. Edward Everett Hale, "An Early Ascent of Katahdin," *Appalachia,* April 1901, pp. 277–89. When the account first appeared in the *Boston Daily Advertiser,* August 15, 1845, it was signed "F. I." For the background to the trip, see Hale's *Tarry at Home Travels* (New York: The Macmillan Company, 1906), pp. 32–41. See also Atkinson, "The Molunkus House," *Sprague's Journal of Maine History* 13 (1925), 82–90.

18. Henry D. Thoreau, *The Maine Woods* (New York: Thomas Y. Crowell Company Publishers, 1909). "Ktaadn" is on pp. 3–108. Henry Seidel Canby, *Thoreau* (Boston: Houghton Mifflin Company; Cambridge: The Riverside Press, 1935); Frederick Garber, *Thoreau's Redemptive Imagination* (New York: New York University Press, 1977); William J. Wolf, *Thoreau Mystic Prophet and Ecologist* (Philadelphia: A Pilgrim Press Book from United Church Press, 1974), p. 103. Wolfe wrote: "the experience of terrifying aloneness on Katahdin" drove Thoreau down to join his friends. The experience, Wolf said, "cured him of any sentimental or romantic feelings about Nature he might have had, probably strengthened his perception that God was to be found in human communities. . . ."

On Thoreau's route, see particularly John W. Worthington, "Thoreau's Route to Katahdin," *Appalachia,* June 1946, pp. 3–14 and Robert C. Cosbey, "Thoreau on Katahdin," *Appalachia,* June 1961, pp. 409–11. Worthington believed that Thoreau got to some point near the base of the highest portion of South Peak; Cosbey asserted he got to the ridge connecting South and Baxter peaks. Most earlier writers assumed Thoreau had climbed to the tableland farther west, near to or on the Abol Slide.

19. Eckstorm, "Thoreau's 'Maine Woods'," *Atlantic Monthly* (1908), 242–50.

20. See "A Neglected Worth of Aroostook County," (Editorial) *Bangor Daily Commercial,* July 21, 1906. Also the letter signed "S.C.," probably Sidney Cook, same issue.

21. Blake, "A Second Excursion to Mount Katahdin," *The Maine Naturalist,* June 1926, p. 74.

22. Keep left no account of his 1846 trip but refers to it in later articles. For a short history of his activities on Katahdin, see Avery, "The Keep Path and Its Successors," *Appalachia,* December 1928, pp. 135–41. A picture of Keep faces p. 136. On other Keep materials available, see Smith and Avery, *An Annotated Bibliography of Katahdin,* Publication No. 6 (Washington, D.C.: Appalachian Trail Conference, reprinted 1950.)

23. For Keep's account of the 1847 trip see his letter, dated November 20, to the *Bangor Democrat,* which published it on December 7, 1847. See also "Expedition to Mt. Katahdin," *Bangor Whig and Courier,* February 15, 16, 17, 1848. This article was prepared for papers in other states but was given to the Bangor paper. Smith and Avery, *op. cit.,* ascribe it to Horace Partridge, but it is more

likely that it was written by Horace Pratt, of the Bangor Theological Seminary, who was a member of the expedition. In the Baxter Collection at the Maine State Library is a manuscript map of the "Plan of Route to Katahdin," by Lawrence J. Chamberlain of Brewer, also a member of the expedition. Chamberlain lists the other members on the reverse side; H. Partridge is not included, while H. Pratt is. The Pratt letter embodies Keep's earlier letter to the *Democrat*, with alterations.

24. Avery, "The Keep Path . . ." *op. cit.*, pp. 136, 139–40. The Keep party in 1849 gave some interesting names to the various peaks on the mountain: Pamola was named Alma; Chimney was called Etna; Cario is the present South Peak; and Mount Moriah is the current Baxter Peak. Moriah was thought to be slightly lower than Cario. The account also provided an early reference to the Northwest Basin. See also *The Bangor Whig and Courier*, August 29, 1840, for a short article on Mrs. Smith's trip; and Alice F. Lord, "Mrs. Elizabeth Oakes Smith," *Lewiston Journal Magazine Section*, November 14, 1914, for a biographical article on this fascinating individual.

25. See "News and Notes," *The Maine Naturalist*, December 1926, pp. 171–75 for the background to and personnel of the trip; also J. K. Laski, "Dr. Young's Botanical Expedition to Mount Katahdin," *The Maine Naturalist*, June 1927, pp. 38–62 (this originally appeared in the *Bangor Whig and Courier*, September 7, 8, 9, 10, 11, 1847, under the same title and signed "By one of the Party"); and George Thurber, "Notes of An Excursion to Mount Katahdin," *The Maine Naturalist*, December 1926, pp. 134–51. For Aaron Young's account, see *The Maine Farmer*, March 16, 1848 (Transmittal letter and approach); April 13, 1848 (Botanical Report); and April 20, 1848 (A brief account of Katahdin).

26. See Benjamin Browne Foster, *Down East Diary*, edited by Charles H. Foster (Orono, Maine: University of Maine at Orono Press, 1975), p. 156. The diary entry was for December 15, 1848. It reads: "*On dit* that a gold mine has been discovered in the vicinity of Ktaadn, that Doctors Young and Jackson have assayed specimens of the ore, that Veazie, Dwinel *et al* have purchased 7,000 acres of the land about, and that somebody will make a fortune without going to California." No mention of the rumor was noted in the *Bangor Daily Whig and Courier* for the immediate period.

27. John Todd, "Mount Katahdin," in *Summer Gleanings; or Sketches and Incidents of a pastor's vacation* (Northampton, Massachusetts: Hopkins, Bridgman, 1852), pp. 121–32. Collected and arranged by Todd's daughter.

28. See Charles D. Shaw, "Some Facts Relating to the Early History of Greenville and Moosehead Lake," *Historical Collections of Piscataquis County, Maine* (Dover: Observer Press, 1910) 1: 61–62.

29. William L. Jones, "Climbing Katahdin in 1853," *Lewiston Evening Journal*, November 5, 1927. This was a letter to his brother, written in Brewer on April 19, 1853.

30. See Blake, "Second Excursion," *op. cit.*, p. 78. They concluded that the East Peak was taller. See also Lucius H. Merrill, *Proceedings of the Bangor Historical Society*, 1914–1915 (Bangor, Maine: n.p., 1916), p. 21.

31. Anonymous, "Going to Mount Katahdin," *Putnam's Monthly Magazine*, September 1856, pp. 242–56. The article was reprinted in the *Bangor Daily Commercial*, July 14, 1906, and with editorial notes in *Appalachia*, June 1925, pp.

102–29. See also Allen Chamberlain "When Colonel T. W. Higginson was a Guide
to Ktaadn in 1855 and Now," *Boston Evening Transcript,* July 14, 1923.

32. Blake, "Second Excursion," *op. cit.,* pp. 74–83. Blake's herbarium is preserved at Deering Hall on the University of Maine at Orono campus. For a brief description of *Saxifraga Stellaris,* see *Mountain Flowers of New England* (Boston: Appalachian Mountain Club, 1964), p. 90.

33. Henry I. Bowditch, "A Trip to Katahdin in 1856," *Appalachia,* December 1958, pp. 145–62 and June 1959, pp. 331–48.

34. Theodore Winthrop, *Life in the Open Air, and other Papers* (Boston: Ticknor and Fields, 1863), pp. 3–119. (The account is reprinted in Farrar, *op. cit.,* pp. 230–38.)

35. Winthrop, *op. cit.,* p. 50.

36. Avery, "Artists and Katahdin," *In the Maine Woods, 1940,* pp. 12–21. This was reprinted, with omissions, as "The Artist of Katahdin American Mountain Painters III: Frederic Edwin Church, 1826–1900," *Appalachia,* December 1944, pp. 147–54. This article also deals with George Hallowell's painting "Wassataquoik River Drive," which is in the National Gallery, Washington, D.C. See also Thomas Sedgewick Steele, *Canoe and Camera, A Hundred Mile Tour Through the Maine Forests* (Boston: Estes and Lauriat, 1882), p. 133. Steele stopped at Hunt's farm on the East Branch. Another party staying there was getting ready to set out for Millinocket Lake to erect a camp on Church's 400-acre tract on the lake.

37. A. L. Holley (Arbor Ilex), "Camps and Tramps about Katahdin," *Scribner's Monthly,* May 1878, pp. 33–46.

38. Avery, "Keep Path . . ." *op. cit. Appalachia,* June 1929, p. 226. Avery interviewed Colonel Rogers. No record remains of his ascent except a comment by Marcus Keep, "The Scientific Survey No. 8 Mount Katahdin," in *The Aroostook Times,* September 20, 1861.

39. Reverend John S. Sewall, "Let Loose in the Woods," *The Maine Sportsman,* August 1904, pp. 243–48, 259.

40. *Sixth Annual Report of the Secretary of the Maine Board of Agriculture 1861* (Augusta: Stevens & Sayward, Printers to the State, 1861): See C. H. Hitchcock's "Geology of the Wild Lands," pp. 377–464. For the climb to Katahdin see pp. 393–400. Also see Kenneth A. Henderson, ed., "Penobscot East Branch in 1861 From the Diary and Letters of Alpheus Spring Packard," *Appalachia,* June 1951, pp. 414–26. Packard had just graduated from Bowdoin College when he was appointed entomologist for the trip.

41. *Sixth Annual Report . . . op. cit.,* "Report of John C. Houghton to C. H. Hitchcock, November 26, 1861," pp. 426–42, especially pp. 438–39.

42. Anonymous, "A Tramp in the Shadow of Katahdin," *The Northern Monthly,* May 1864, pp. 149–54; June 1864, pp. 224–32. The quotation starts on page 228.

43. Frederic S. Davenport, "The West Branch Route to Mt. Ktaadn," *Appalachia,* June 1919, pp. 340–52. In 1871 and 1877, Davenport relates, he made the ascent and descent in one day from the mouth of Abol Stream. See also his "Some Pioneers of Moosehead Chesuncook and Millinocket," *The Northern,* April 1922 to March 1923. The articles contain a good deal of miscellaneous his-

torical information on Greenville, Moosehead Lake, the West Branch, Katahdin and Millinocket, as well as many good photographs. For an obituary of Davenport, who was a musician in Bangor, see *The Northern*, May 1923, pp. 15–16.

44. John DeLaski, "Glacial Action on Mount Katahdin," *American Journal of Science*, Third Series, 3 (1872), 27–31. Reprinted in the *Bangor Daily Commercial*, May 19, 1906.

45. F. Lamson-Scribner, "Mt. Ktaadn and its flora," *The Botanical Gazette* 17 (February 1892), 46–54. See also Merritt C. Fernald, "Height of Mt. Ktaadn," *American Journal of Science*, Third Series, 9 (Jan.-June 1875), 238; also his "Scientific Observations on Mount Ktaadn," *Bangor Daily Whig and Courier*, November 9, 1874.

46. Alfred G. Hempstead, *The Penobscot Boom and The Development of the West Branch of the Penobscot River for Log Driving* (Orono, Maine: University Press, 1931). Most of the account in the next three paragraphs of text comes from this source.

47. For a description of life at a lumbering supply camp along this route in the early 1870s, see J. A. Thompson, "Christmas at Trout Brook Farm," *The Maine Sportsman*, December 1900, pp. 81–82. See also Steele, *Canoe and Camera, op. cit.*, pp. 133–34 for a brief description of the farm in 1881 or 1882. It had four houses, eight or ten barns and 400 acres of cleared land. See also C. A. Hall, "Three Weeks in Northern Maine," and W. N. Amory, "The Moose Country of Maine," Forest and Stream, December 16, 1899, pp. 490–91 and 487, respectively. See also Leroy T. Carleton, *Carleton's Pathfinder and Gazeteer of the Hunting and Fishing Resorts of the State of Maine*, 1899–1900 (Dover, Maine: Observer Publishing Co., 1899), pp. 113, 128; and advertisement for Patten, Maine, in *The Maine Sportsman*, October 1900, p. 28.

48. Eckstorm, *The Penobscot Man*, 2nd ed. (Boston: Houghton, Mifflin Co., 1924); Springer, *Forest Life . . . op. cit.*, revised edition with an Introduction by F. M. O'Brien (Somersworth, New Hampshire: New Hampshire Publishing Company, 1971); Richard G. Wood, *A History of Lumbering in Maine, 1820–1861*, University of Maine Studies, Second Series, No. 33 (Orono, Maine: 1935, reprinted at the University Press, 1961); and David C. Smith, *A History of Lumbering in Maine, 1861–1960*, University of Maine Studies No. 93 (Orono, Maine: University of Maine Press, 1972).

49. "Sandy Stream—An Episode of Hersey-Reed Lumber Operation of 1874," *Lewiston Journal Illustrated Magazine Section*, July 31, 1915, pp. 2–3; reprinted in *Bangor Daily Commercial*, June 23, 1917. *See also* Roland G. Gray, *Songs and Ballads of the Maine Lumberjacks* (Cambridge, Massachusetts: Harvard University Press, 1925), pp. 31–36.

50. *See* Avery, "Keep Path . . ." *op. cit.*, (1928), pp. 142–46; Charles E. Hamlin, "Routes to Ktaadn," *Appalachia*, December 1881, pp. 306–31. George H. Witherle followed the Lang and Jones Trail in 1881 and 1882.

51. See Theodore Roosevelt to Darling Bysie (Anna Roosevelt Cowles), undated, and to the same from Island Falls, September 14, 1879, in her book, *Letters from Theodore Roosevelt to Anna Roosevelt Cowles 1870–1918* (New York: Charles Scribner's Sons, 1924), pp. 7–8, 33–34. Though the undated letter is included with 1875 letters, it was clearly written about two weeks before that of

September 14, 1879. *See also* Theodore Roosevelt, *An Autobiography* (New York: The Macmillan Company, 1916), pp. 32–33, and Donald Wilhelm, *Theodore Roosevelt as an Undergraduate* (Boston: John W. Luce and Company, 1910), pp. 56–57. William Sewall was undoubtedly Roosevelt's guide on this occasion and later embellished the story considerably. As reported by Wilhelm, Sewall later wrote that it was in snowy woods, while hunting caribou, that Roosevelt lost a snowshoe while fording a rapid stream, "But with only moccasins he insisted on climbing Mt. Katahdin to where we were camped. His feet were terribly bruised but he had not uttered a whimper."

52. Avery, "Story of the Wassataquoik," *op. cit.*, pp. 86–88.

53. Avery, "Forest Fires . . . ," *op. cit.*, pp. 3–4.

54. For a description of the Tracey-Love operation in the winter of 1887 see G. M. Campbell, "Katahdin and Around There," *St. Croix Courier*, March 10, 1887. Campbell called the Tracey-Love Trail the "Eureka Trail."

55. One of the Pioneers [Mrs. Luther B. Rogers], "Katahdin," *The Lewiston Evening Journal*, July 31, 1886.

56. Avery, "Keep Path . . ." *op. cit.*, (1929), p. 225.

57. Hamlin, "Routes . . . ," *op. cit.*, p. 326. The Hunt Farm had been repaired and rebuilt but the place was not used in 1881. Perhaps it is this inn to which the commissioners of Fisheries and Game referred in their *Report* for 1880, p. 9, when they wrote of salmon fishing on the East Branch at Hunt's Farm and on the Wassataquoik, and of the increased prospects for travel to the area. They noted that "a hotel at the Hunt Farm is already projected."

58. Avery, "Story of the Wassataquoik," *op. cit.*, p. 89. Lunksoos, says Avery, is a corrupted form of Lunkasoo, spelled Lunxus by Thoreau. An English equivalent is "Indian Devil." The name refers to a wild beast—supposedly a panther—real or imaginary, which was the terror of the Indians. *See also* Hamlin, *op. cit.* p. 330.

59. Hamlin, "Observations upon the Physical Geography and Geology of Mt. Ktaadn and the Adjacent District," *Bulletin of the Museum of Comparative Zoology*, vol. 7, no. 5 (1881), pp. 206–33.

60. The question of whether or not the continental ice sheet covered all of Katahdin continued to be discussed. A geologist studying Maine's gravel deposits visited Katahdin in 1879 and concluded that the mountain had not been covered. See George H. Stone, *The Glacial Gravels of Maine and their Associated Deposits*, Monograph of the United States Geological Survey, vol. 34 (Washington: Government Printing Office, 1899), pp. 104–17, 295. Warren Upham, a geologist who had not actually visited the mountain, but who used the various articles on the topic cited earlier, also concluded that Katahdin had not been covered, in "Glaciation of Mountains in New England and New York," *Appalachia*, May 1889, pp. 291–312. Ralph S. Tarr, another geologist who studied Katahdin thoroughly in 1897 and 1899, argued convincingly that the mountain had been covered, in a fine article on "Glaciation of Mt. Ktaadn, Maine," *Bulletin of the Geological Society of America*, 2 (June 21, 1900): 433–98. His findings were questioned a decade and a half later by George C. Curtis in his "Evidence of Continental Glaciation on Mount Katahdin," *Bulletin of the Geological Society of America*, 24 (March 31, 1915): 78–79. Dabney W. Caldwell concludes that Katahdin was buried by

ice in his *The Geology of Baxter State Park and Mt. Katahdin,* Bulletin 12, Maine Geological Survey (Augusta, Maine: Department of Forestry, revised edition, 1972), p. 36.

61. Hamlin, "Routes . . . ," *op. cit.,* pp. 306–31. See also *Appalachia,* June 1879, p. 90, and December 1881, p. 368.

62. See Thompson, "A Trip to Katahdin Twenty Years Ago," *The Maine Sportsman,* March 1901, pp. 161–62, for the only other known description of the route.

63. See George H. Witherle, "Excursions North of Katahdin," *Appalachia,* December 1883, pp. 222–31, read to the Club October 12, 1883; "An Autumn Visit to the Sourdnahunk Mountains and Katahdin," *Appalachia,* December 1884, pp. 20–34, read to the Club by C. E. Hamlin on June 11, 1884; "Explorations in the Vicinity of Mount Ktaadn," *Appalachia,* June 1888, pp. 147–51, condensed from letters to C. W. Hamlin and R. B. Lawrence; *Explorations West and Northwest of Katahdin In the Late Nineteenth Century,* second ed., Myron H. Avery, editor (Augusta, Maine: Maine Appalachian Trail Club, Inc., 1950). See also C. E. Hamlin, "Notes on Ktaadn," *Appalachia,* December 1884, pp. 81–82, and Avery, "Explorations West and Northwest of Katahdin in the Nineteenth Century," *The Maine Naturalist,* September 1928, pp. 107–08.

64. "Constitution of the Appalachian Mountain Club," *Appalachia,* June 1876, p. 3.

65. Rosewell B. Lawrence, "Ktaadn Basin," *Appalachia,* December 1887, pp. 26–28. This article includes one of Hollingsworth's fine photographs of Chimney Pond and the wall of the Great Basin.

66. Avery, "Keep Path," *op. cit.,* pp. 146–47; Lawrence, "Improvements at Mount Ktaadn, Me.," *Appalachia,* June 1888, pp. 156–58.

67. Lawrence, *Ibid.,* also "Excursions for the Season of 1887 and 1888," *Appalachia,* December 1888, pp. 255–56.

68. Lore A. Rogers, "My First Trip to Katahdin," *Down East,* May 1960, pp. 36–39, 42–43, 46–48.

69. Fullerton L. Waldo, "Notes on a Recent Visit to Ktaadn," *Appalachia,* November 1896, pp. 189–94. Unable to use the Appalachian Trail, Waldo and his Harvard classmate followed the Wassataquoik to Bell's Camp, the South Branch to McLeod's Camp, and the Roger's Trail to Basin Ponds (see below). See also Augustus C. Hamlin, "Routes to Mt. Ktaadn, Paper No. 1: The Trail via Wassatacook Stream," *The Maine Sportsman,* September 1894, pp. 1, 6.

70. Avery, "Keep Path . . ." *op. cit.,* (1929), p. 228. Also see "R" [Lore A. Rogers], "Katahdin," *Forest and Stream,* February 24, 1906, pp. 298–99, for a description of this route in 1905.

71. "L" Lore A. Rogers, "Katahdin in Winter," *Forest and Stream,* April 28, 1892, p. 395; G. G. Kennedy and J. F. Collins, "Bryophytes of Mt. Katahdin," and Joseph R. Churchill, "A Botanical Excursion to Mt. Katahdin," *Rhodora,* June 1901, pp. 177 and 147–60, respectively.

72. H. H. Newcomb, "Chinobas Katahdin and An Account of Its Discovery," *Entomological News,* September 1901, p. 206, and October 1901, pp. 225–31.

73. On the 1903 fire see State of Maine, Department of Forestry, *Bulletin*

 *No. 1 of the Department of Forestry Giving Estimates of Damage, Warden Re-*

*ports, etc. of Forest Fires in April, May and June, 1903* (Augusta, Maine, 1903), NOTES
pp. 19–20. The fires burned over many areas of the present-day Park. One which
started on June 2, 1903, covered an estimated 86,000 acres of valuable timber in
T6R9, T5R9, T4R9, T5R8 and T4R8. At the same time another fire started near
Sandy Stream and burned a portion of T3R9.

74. See H. W. Rowe, "A Trip to Matagamon Lake," *The Maine Sportsman,*
August 1904, pp. 257–59, for a description of operations at Trout Brook Farm
and lumbering operations in the area by the Katahdin Pulp and Paper Company.

75. Avery, "Keep Path . . ." *op. cit.,* (1929), pp. 230–33.

76. For a brief account of caribou on Katahdin see Edward S. C. Smith, "An
Early Winter Trip to Katadin," *Appalachia,* December 1926, pp. 493–96.
Smith's party photographed caribou on the tableland; three pictures are included
with the article. Smith states that the last caribou was shot on the mountain in
October 1898, the year before the hunting of caribou was made illegal. Smith approached the mountain from the West Branch by riding sleighs to Joe Francis's
camp on Debsconeag Deadwater. They ascended the mountain by first moving
into the Klondike. For more information on caribou on Katahdin see: *Report of
Commissioners of Inland Fisheries and Game, 1895,* p. 18; *1896,* p. 11; *1898,*
pp. 16–17, 37; *1900,* p. 18; *1904,* pp. 21–24; *1906,* p. 17. In the latter year the
Commissioner reported: "There are no indications of any caribou in the state." See
also "The Caribou Returning," *The Maine Sportsman,* October 1905, pp. 9–10.
Ernest T. Seton, *Lives of Game Animals,* 4 vols. (Garden City, New York:
Doubleday, Doran & Company, Inc., 1929), vol. 3, part 1, pp. 52–94, esp. p. 59.

77. See "Up Mt. Katahdin on Horseback," *The Maine Sportsman,* May 1903,
pp. 171–72. Sandy Stream Pond could also be reached via the Sandy Stream tote
road from the south.

78. Avery, "Keep Path . . ." *op. cit.,* (1929), p. 229; Leroy H. Harvey, "An
Ecological Excursion to Mount Katahdin," *Rhodora,* February 1903, pp. 41–52;
and his *A Study of the Physiographic Ecology of Mount Ktaadn, Maine.* The
University of Maine Studies, No. 5 (Orono, Maine: n.p., 1903).

79. Avery, "Keep Path . . ." *op. cit.,* (1929), pp. 233–34. See also Annie
Lorenz, "Notes on the Hepaticae of Mt. Ktaadn," *The Bryologist,* vol. 20, no. 3
(May 1917): 41–46. For a later use of the route, see "How Two Men From
Orono Climbed Katahdin in June," *Bangor Daily Commercial,* June 16, 1920. This
party used the AMC trail guide to Katahdin.

80. Avery, "Keep Path . . ." *op. cit.,* (1929), p. 236.

81. In addition to the camps at Daicey and Kidney ponds, a number of
others were established in the late '90s or early the next century. These included:
the camp of Joe Francis, former Governor of the Penobscots, at the head of
Debsconeag Deadwater; Camp Phoenix or Sourdnahunk Lake camps, opened by
A. McLain and his son William along with two Hall brothers and taken over in
1904 by Charles Daisey; Daisey's Katahdin View camps, owned by B. C. Harris
in 1899, were located on the West Branch below Abol Stream; the Thomas camps
at Ripogenus Lake, established by Reginald C. Thomas in 1902; Camp Wellington
on Ambejejus Lake, operated by Selden T. McPheters as early as 1898; and the
camps run by C. C. Garland on First Debsconeag Lake. Other sporting camps
were located on Millinocket Lake. Those mentioned here were most commonly  335

used by visitors to Katahdin. No effort has been made to cite specific sources of information. Most came from the files of *The Maine Sportsman, In the Maine Woods,* and *Forest and Stream.* Important here are advertisements of the camp operators.

82. George K. Woodworth, "More About the Dry-Fly in Maine Woods Waters," *In the Maine Woods,* 1925, pp. 28–29. See also James Churchward, *A Big Game and Fishing Guide to North-Eastern Maine* (Bangor, Maine: Bangor & Aroostook Railroad, 1898), pp. 30–31; "Artist," "Katahdin and Big Fish Regions," *Forest and Stream,* June 11, 1898, p. 462; W. C. Squier, Jr., "In the Katahdin Region," *Forest and Stream,* June 30, 1900, pp. 503–04.

83. H. Walter Leavitt, *Katahdin Skylines,* Maine Technology Experiment Station Paper No. 40 (Orono, Maine: University of Maine Press, 1942); reprinted with revisions in 1954; reprinted 1970 as University of Maine Studies No. 90. The reference is to p. 31 of the original. See also *The Maine Sportsman,* March 1901, p. 172. In an advertisement for "Hunt's Sourdnehunk Stream Camps" and his "Kidney Pond Camps," Irving O. Hunt asked: "Do you realize that his Kidney Pond Camps are only 3 miles from Katahdin, and that a new trail permits the ascent from that side?" By 1914 Hunt had twelve cabins on Kidney Pond. See Frederic B. Hyde, "The Blind Trout of Kidney Pond," *In the Maine Woods, 1914,* p. 25.

84. For the history of the Great Northern, the best source is John E. McLeod, "The Great Northern Paper Company," typewritten manuscript, bound in six volumes, copy in Special Collections, Fogler Library, University of Maine at Orono. A seventh, index volume, was compiled by Frances C. Hartgen of the Fogler Library. See also Hempstead, *Penobscot Boom, op. cit.,* pp. 80–83; and Smith, *Lumbering in Maine, op. cit.,* ch. 10.

85. The Great Northern lumbered lands in the Sourdnahunk drainage in 1905–08 and 1909–11. See McLeod, *op. cit.,* XXI, 36. For early indications of the use of the tote road by travellers see: William H. Avis, "In the Shadow of Katahdin," *Forest and Stream,* November 3 and 17, 1900, pp. 342–43 and 383–84 respectively; and Chamberlain, *Vacation Tramps in New England Highlands* (Boston and New York; Houghton, Mifflin Co., 1919), pp. 135–55.

86. McLeod, *op. cit.,* XII, 64–68.

87. Avery, "Keep Path . . ." (1929), pp. 235–36. See issues of *Appalachia* and *In the Maine Woods* for these years for many accounts of changes occurring in the area.

88. On the history of the District, see Austin H. Wilkins, *Ten Million Acres of Timber: The Remarkable Story of Forest Protection in the Maine Forestry District (1909–1972)* (Woolwich, Maine: TBW Books, Publisher, 1978). See also the biennial *Reports of the Maine Forest Commissioner;* and The Tree Growth Tax Law, Chap. 616 P.L. 1972, Sec. 1608, Special session of Maine 104th Legislature.

89. Wilkins, *Ten Million Acres,* p. 263; Forrest H. Colby, *Forest Protection and Conservation in Maine* (Augusta, Maine: Maine Forest Service, 1919), p. 37; Chief Warden Thomas Griffin in his report recommended that the lookout be discontinued until a steel tower could be built. A new tower was never built. For a picture of this camp, see *Appalachia,* August 1921, Plate XXX, after p. 154.

# II

1. See Hitchcock, *Ibid.*, Chapter I, note 40.

2. C. E. Hamlin, "Routes . . . ," *op. cit.*, I, note 50, p. 329.

3. Prescott H. Vose, "Katahdin in '94," *Appalachia*, June 1949, pp. 334–39.

4. See Charles G. Roundy, "Changing Attitudes Toward the Maine Wilderness," (unpublished M.A. Thesis, University of Maine at Orono, 1970), pp. 68–71. Roundy notes that as the cult of the wilderness built up in the rest of the country little interest was shown in Maine. But Maine was an ideal setting for out-of-staters who wanted contact with a wilder and more natural setting. An increasing number of articles on Maine's wilderness were appearing in national magazines late in the century. A writer in a national magazine argued that northern Maine should be "permanently reserved for sport, . . ." See Alvin F. Sanborn, "The Future of Rural New England," *Atlantic Monthly*, July 1897, pp. 82–83. Roundy also noted that though Mainers themselves did not respond to the national glorification of wilderness they recognized the economic impact of tourism, which was estimated at $13,000,000 in 1901. See *Bangor Daily Commercial*, January 9, 1901. See also Smith, *A History of Lumbering . . . , op. cit.*, I, note 48, especially Chapter XIII. Most emphasis on conservation was for protection of forests and development of sustained yield programs rather than preservation for recreational purposes.

5. *The Industrial Journal*, February 15, 1895, p. 5.

6. *The Maine Sportsman*, January 24, 1896, p. 2. This was repeated eight years later (August 1904, p. 251) in an article on "What Katahdin has to Offer."

7. *Bangor Daily Commercial*, July 13, 1901. The editor noted the work of Charles E. Hamlin, Lamson-Scribner, M. L. Fernald, and George G. Kennedy, all geologists or botanists.

8. See "Under Mt. Katahdin's Shadow," *The Maine Sportsman*, February 1899, p. 13.

9. Gene Letourneau, "Sportsmen Say," *Portland Press Herald*, August 18, 1967; reprinted in his *Sportsmen Say* (Augusta: K. J. Printing, 1975), p. 217. Baxter's comment on the trip was in a statement prepared for dedication of the new gatehouse system at the Park in the summer of 1967. This is, to my knowledge, the first time he mentioned it.

10. *Legislative Record*, 1905, p. 30.

11. "Origin and Growth of the Movement to Secure the Mt. Katahdin Region as a National Reservation," *Lewiston Journal, Illustrated Magazine Section*, October 24, 1914. Mrs. Thompson said she had received considerable support for her ideas from practical foresters and academic foresters at the organizational meeting of the Maine Forestry Association on March 15, 1907, where she represented the Federation. See *Daily Kennebec Journal*, March 15, 1907.

12. Public Laws of Maine, 1909, ch. 212. *See also* "Record Book of Annual and Mid-Winter Meetings 1903–1914" for Minutes of Mid-winter meeting, January 22, 1908, and January 20, 1909, in Maine Federation of Women's Clubs Collection (Special Collections, Fogler Library, University of Maine at Orono, Box 345), pp. 170, 171, 176, 212 and 214 in minute books. See also "First Annual Report

of the State Water Storage Commission, January 1911, p. 39." *Daily Kennebec Journal,* September 23, 1908.

13. See *Daily Kennebec Journal,* September 23, 1908.

14. George Otis Smith to Baxter, June 7, 1937, BC, MSL, Folder 74.

15. 45 Cong. Rec. 2237 (1910); 48 Cong. Rec., 7588 (1912); 50 Cong. Rec., 81, 134 (1913). Guernsey's 1910 resolution was an amendment to the bill which emerged as the Weeks Act. The amendment would have added the Katahdin region to the list of areas set aside or to be acquired as national forests.

16. Weeks Act of March 1, 1911, ch. 186, 36 Stat. 961–62.

17. See newspaper clipping of the account of the annual meeting of the Association in Maine Sportsmen's Fish and Game Association Records, 1911–19, Bangor Public Library, pp. 50–51. The Association held its annual meeting in January 1913 in Augusta. As long as it remained in existence it supported the concept.

18. *Commissioners of Inland Fisheries and Game, Report,* 1912, p. 44.

19. *Maine Legislative Resolves,* 1913, ch. 1.

20. George C. Wing, Jr., "Mount Ktaadn Sometimes Mount Katahdin," *Sprague's Journal of Maine History,* July, August, September 1922, p. 134. See *Bangor Daily Commercial,* April 7, 1915, for an account of a meeting of the Bangor Historical Society at which Professor Lucius H. Merrill of the University of Maine strongly argued for the creation of a park and forest preserve. Representative Guernsey spoke at the end of the meeting and argued for a national park. See also *Commissioners of Inland Fisheries and Game, Report, 1916,* pp. 28–29 for their arguments favoring creation of forest reserves. See also 53 Cong. Rec., 6097–99 (1916) for a speech by Congressman Guernsey on April 13, 1916, supporting his national park concept.

21. *Legislative Record,* 1917, pp. 1248–55. See also pp. 171, 193, 305, 478, 585, 588, 600, 1033, 1169, 1247, 1260, 1372 and 1465 for details of action on the ill-fated bill. The forest commissioner also urged federal or state acquisition of forest lands around Katahdin. See Colby, *op. cit.,* I, note 89, xxxix-xl; see also McLeod, *op. cit.,* XII, 11. He notes that in 1917–18 Baxter "dragged in the land resources issue as ammunition in his fight against private exploitation of water power and to further his own plans for the development of a system of State parks."

22. See clippings from newspapers in Baxter Scrapbooks: *Portland Evening Express,* December 14, 1918 in BAX Scrapbook No. 5, p. 133; letter to editor *Lewiston Evening Journal,* December 14, 1918, BAX Scrapbook No. 1, p. 10. Baxter here used a technique which became more common with the passage of time; he would write a letter and have it printed in a number of papers around the state.

23. See Garret Schenck to Charles O. Small of Madison, Maine, March 25, 1918, in Great Northern Paper Company Papers, Box 842, Personnel #2 file, Special Collections, Fogler Library, UMO.

24. See letter from W. W. Ashe, Assistant Forester in Charge of Acquisition, Forest Service, Washington, D.C. to Baxter, October 25, 1918, BC, MSL. From the letter it was obvious that the national Forest Service had done a survey of the Katahdin area for possible inclusion as a national forest under the provisions of

the Weeks Act and that Baxter was doing his homework in the event that Maine might be receptive to purchase of the area. For the late January hearing, see *Lewiston Evening Journal,* January 29, 1919; *Legislative Record,* 1919, pp. 66, 102.

25. Baxter to Schenck, February 7 and 20 and March 4, 1919; Schenck to Baxter, February 12, 1919, BC, MSL. Also in the Baxter Papers is a letter from Fred A. Gilbert of Great Northern to Baxter, dated November 16, 1918, in which he acknowledged a Baxter letter and said it was being forwarded to the head office in Boston. Baxter pencilled a notation on it—"Never answered." For the February–March debates on the issue and final doom of the bill, see clippings from the Portland papers, February 19, and the *Lewiston Evening Journal,* March 5, 1919, BAX Scrapbook No. 1, pp. 16 and 14 respectively; and the *Legislative Record,* 1919, pp. 153, 188, 299, 302, 406, 492, 718.

26. See *Legislative Record, 1919,* pp. 735, 777, 782, 871; and *Public Laws of Maine, 1919,* ch. 166. It is interesting to speculate whether Baxter by this time had begun to develop his trust ideas without making them public.

27. Colby, *op. cit.,* pp. xxiv–xxvi. See also *Public Laws of Maine 1919,* ch. 43. In appropriations for general forestry purposes amounting to $5,000 for 1919 and $10,000 for 1920, the forest commissioner was granted the power to buy waste lands.

28. *Lewiston Evening Journal,* January 21, 1920.

29. Printed copy of Republican Platform adopted at Bangor Convention, March 25, 1920, BC, MSL.

30. Typical is a copy of campaign literature he used in the primary. See BAX Scrapbook No. 1, p. 30, BC, MSL.

31. Numerous accounts of the trip were written. See *Houlton Times,* March 25, 1931. In an interview after making his first grant, Baxter said "All this was born as you know, beginning on the train from Chicago . . ." Of great importance is A. G. Staples's account in the *Lewiston Journal Magazine Section,* October 2, 1920, of the planning and the first part of the trip. See also "Katahdin in Summer," *The Northern,* July 1923, p. 206; Sam E. Conner, "O'er Katahdin's Rugged Sides A Story of an Expedition up Mt. Katahdin," *In the Maine Woods,* 1921, pp. 10–20. See also copy of press release dated Portland, Maine, August 5, 1920, BAX Scrapbook, No. 15, p. 156; *Kennebec Daily Journal,* August 14, 19, and 25, 1920; clippings from *Portland Press,* August 6, 1920 and *Portland Express,* August 12, 1920, in Scrapbook No. 1, p. 31, and see other state newspapers for this period. For quote of Baxter's remark concerning Burton Howe, see Baxter to Town Clerk, Patten, Maine, August 16, 1935, BC, MSL.

32. Three years later an incident that occurred on the trip came back to haunt Baxter briefly. He was a teetotaller and a leader in the prohibition movement in Maine. During his second term as governor an unnamed member of the expedition of 1920 began circulating rumors about Baxter in an attempt to embarrass him politically. Baxter gave a straightforward account of the incident in an address to the state convention of the W.C.T.U. meeting in Pittsfield. He, along with some other members of the hiking party in 1920, was not in the best of physical condition at the beginning of the trip. As a result he was exhausted by the gruelling hike up the mountain. On his return to Chimney Pond he could not

eat or sleep, became feverish, and perspired freely. "Fearing I was developing a fever [30 miles from civilization] I took a dose of quinine and whiskey and spent a miserable night."

See *Lewiston Evening Journal*, October 4, 1923, and other newspapers. The story, generally with accompanying editorial comment, was widely published. Some seriously or jokingly suggested that instead of whiskey, it was a dose of rum, from a cache of that liquor supposedly hidden in the summit cairn by an earlier expedition. Most editors sympathized with Baxter. The identities of the individual spreading the story and that of the owner of the whiskey remain a mystery. See BAX Scrapbook No. 12, pp. 48–51, 57 for stories on the incident.

33. *Houlton Times*, March 25, 1931, clipping, BAX Scrapbook No. 3, p. 71.

34. A. G. Staples to B. W. Howe, August 12, 1920, carbon copy, BAX Scrapbook No. 5, p. 127.

35. Howe to Baxter, August 20 and 21, 1920, BP, MSL.

36. Edward P. Draper to Baxter, September 1, 1920, BP, MSL.

37. See telegrams Fred Gilbert to Schenck, December 15 and 17, and letters December 14 and 15, 1920, Gilbert (Fred Alliston) Papers, Special Collections, Fogler Library, UMO, Box 553, "Letters Garret Schenck, Sept. 1–Dec. 31, 1920" file.

38. Carbon of letter from John E. Mitchell, of Patten, to Verne Rhoades, Forest Supervisor, Pisgah National Forest and Game Preserve, September 15, 1920, BC, MSL.

39. In Baxter Papers see the following letters written in 1920: Mitchell to J. J. Fritz, September 2; Fritz to Mitchell, September 8; H. O. Staples, US Forest Service, to Mitchell, August 24; Mitchell to Staples, September 2; Rhoades to Mitchell, September 18; Mitchell to Rhoades, October 18; Mitchell to Baxter, October 12; Baxter to Mitchell, October 18; Mitchell to H. C. Brearley, New York City, October 25 and November 1; Brearley to Mitchell, October 29; George D. Pratt, Commissioner, State of New York Conservation Commission, to Mitchell, November 8. The exchange between Baxter and Mitchell shows that their efforts were not being closely coordinated.

40. See press release by Baxter for speech at Gray, September 5, 1920, BAX Scrapbook No. 15, p. 166. John A. Baxter, Sr. told this writer that Percival's older brother Rupert, Senator from Sagadahoc, was most instrumental in lining up votes needed.

41. *Daily Kennebec Journal*, January 19 and 21, 1921.

42. *Ibid.*, January 26, 1921; *Bangor Daily News*, January 27, 1921.

43. *Daily Kennebec Journal*, January 7, 1921, for Parkhurst address. See also clipping from *Portland Evening Express*, January 28, 1921, BAX Scrapbook No. 5, p. 21. But see also Schenck to Gilbert, December 15, 1920, *loc. cit.*, note 37. Schenck had visited Parkhurst in Bangor and while he was committed to the park concept he said the "state is in no condition financially to consider parks during the next 2 years."

44. See "Mount Katahdin State Park, An Address Given by Hon. Percival P. Baxter of Portland, President of the Senate, At the Annual Meeting of the Maine Sportsmen's Fish and Game Association, Hall of Representatives, State Capitol, Augusta, Maine, January 27, 1921." The Senate ordered that 2,500

copies of the speech be printed. See *Daily Kennebec Journal*, January 29, 1921.
Copies are in the Baxter Papers. The speech was widely quoted or reprinted in the press.

45. *Daily Kennebec Journal*, February 10, 1921. See also manuscript copy with corrections in BAX Scrapbook No. 16, pp. 51–63.

46. See BAX Scrapbook No. 5, p. 139 for typed copy of the lecture delivered February 9, 1921. Dawson was a guest of Baxter at the Blaine House while he was in Augusta. See also *Lewiston Evening Journal*, February 11, 1921.

47. *Daily Kennebec Journal*, February 12, 1921. See also Charles P. Barnes to Mitchell, February 8, 1921, BC, MSL. Mitchell had asked Barnes about possible appropriations for him to study park practices in other states. Barnes indicated that with economy the keynote in the session there was little chance of such appropriations and wrote, "there is no assurance that the Katahdin Park Bill will pass, . . ."

48. *Daily Kennebec Journal*, February 16, 1921.

49. For Great Northern's leadership in the fight, see Gilbert to Schenck, February 8, 9, 16, 17, 18, 1921, in "Garret Schenck Incoming Jan. 1, 1921 to Apr. 16, 1921" file; Schenck to Gilbert, January 28, February 25, March 23, 1921, in "Garret Schenck Jan. 1, 1921–June 16, 1921" file, Box 559; Schenck to Gilbert, January 10 and 25, February 3, 7, 8, and 10, 1921, in 1921 file, Box 568, Gilbert (Fred Alliston) Papers, Fogler Library, UMO. In his February 8 letter, Schenck did raise the possibility of a compromise if it seemed the bill would pass. In such a compromise the paper company would give the state 6,000 to 8,000 acres centered on the mountain, if the eminent domain provision were not included and the state agreed not to try to increase the size of the park for eight years. Gilbert strongly opposed this.

50. The preceding arguments and quotations can be found in the *Daily Kennebec Journal*, February 18, 1921; see also the strong counter-argument to Gulnac's remarks in a letter of Edward P. Ricker of Poland Spring to Editor of the *Lewiston Evening Journal*, February 23, 1921. A copy is in BAX Scrapbook No. 1, p. 77.

51. See *Daily Kennebec Journal*, February 18, 1921.

52. *Ibid.; Portland Evening Express & Advertiser*, February 17, 1921. See also Minutes of mid-winter meeting in Augusta, February 17, 1921 in Record Book of Annual and Mid-Winter Meetings, Book IV 1915–25, in Maine Federation of Women's Clubs Collection, *loc. cit.*, note 12.

53. *Daily Kennebec Journal*, March 11, 1921. See also *Bangor Commercial*, March 10, 1921 and *Lewiston Sun*, March 11, 1921 for editorials attacking Baxter's new position and defending Great Northern.

54. *Lewiston Evening Journal*, March 18 and 25, 1921; *Bangor Daily News*, March 18, 1921; *Daily Kennebec Journal*, March 24, 1921; see also clipping from *Bath Times*, March 23, 1921, BAX Scrapbook No. 1, p. 92.

55. See clipping from *Portland Evening Express*, April 13, 1921, BAX Scrapbook No. 1, p. 73. Hersey's bill never got to the floor of the House. See 61 Cong. Rec. 88 (1921) for introduction to Hersey's bill.

56. See *Annual Report of the Commissioner of Inland Fisheries and Game 1922*, pp. 14–17. This was reprinted in George C. Wing, Jr., "Mount Ktaadn

Sometimes Mount Katahdin," *Sprague's Journal of Maine History,* July, August, September 1922, pp. 115–16, 136.

57. See *Annual Report . . .* 1924, pp. 48, 49 and *Public Laws of Maine, 1923,* ch. 17. See also *Legislative Record, 1923,* pp. 65, 176, 182, 189, 226, 229; and Schenck to Gilbert, January 18, 1923 (outgoing letters 1923 file), Box 561 *loc. cit.*

58. See typed copy, "Address of Percival P. Baxter, Governor of Maine, At the Annual Meeting of the Maine Forestry Association Held at the State Capitol, Augusta, Friday, January 6th, 1922," BAX Scrapbook No. 18, p. 33. The speech was widely reported in the state's newspapers.

59. See typed copy of an Act to Establish the Mt. Katahdin State Park, BC, MSL; also *Legislative Record, 1923,* pp. 792–97 and 299, 302, 492, 718 and 725. See also Gilbert to Schenck, March 7, 23, and 29, 1923, *loc. cit.,* note 57.

60. See newspaper clippings, April and May, 1923, BAX Scrapbook No. 11, pp. 57, 82; see also Baxter to William G. Hill, Maine Sportsmen's Fish and Game Association, April 27, 1923, BAX Scrapbook No. 20, p. 25.

61. Baxter to Senator Charles L. McNary, September 27, 1923, BAX Scrapbook No. 20, p. 204.

62. See copy Baxter press release dated Augusta, March 22, 1924, BC, MSL.

63. *Portland Press Herald,* February 23, 1924; *Portland Sunday Telegram,* March 2 and 9, 1924. In the last issue it was announced that the Association was "being organized with a nation-wide membership to promote State or Federal acquisition." See also *The Maine Campus,* March 5, 1924. A Katahdin Club was organized at the University of Maine with about seventy members. Its chief object was to make Katahdin more accessible by the establishment of a line of camps in the area. Fred Gilbert reportedly offered the use of Great Northern camps and other needed materials. See also *Portland Sunday Telegram,* August 3, 1924.

64. See clippings from *Portland Press Herald,* October 17 and 18, 1924, BAX Scrapbook No. 14, p. 35.

65. Schenck to Gilbert, January 15, 1925, *loc. cit.,* note 37, Box 554.

66. *Lewiston Evening Journal,* January 7, 1925. Also see Gilbert Papers, Box 554, for numerous letters by Company officials written in late 1924 and early 1925. In mid-January Harry Ross of Bangor visited with Governor Baxter shortly before the latter left office.

67. *Legislative Journal, 1925,* pp. 153, 188, 256. A corrected copy of the bill is in BAX Scrapbook No. 5, p. 145.

68. 67 Cong. Rec. 401 (1925) and *Daily Kennebec Journal,* December 9, 1925.

69. *Daily Kennebec Journal,* September 15, 1927. In a speech to the Lions' Club in Bangor, Baxter discussed his earlier attempts.

70. Schenck to Gilbert, August 7, 1925, *loc. cit.,* note 65; see *Daily Kennebec Journal,* July 8, 9, 10, 13, 1925. See also Philip R. Shorey, "Maine Celebrities Climb to Katahdin's Peak: A Story of the Ascent made by Governor Brewster and His Party in the Summer of 1925," *In the Maine Woods, 1926,* pp. 95–99, and "Mount Katahdin," *Sun-up Magazine,* December 1925, pp. 12, 49; and Willis E. Parsons, "The State of Maine Camp at Chimney Pond," *In the Maine Woods, 1926,* p. 37.

71. Editorial, "A Corporation with a Soul," *Portland Press Herald,* December 17, 1925. For Great Northern's reaction, see Schenck to Gilbert, December 28 and 31, 1925, *loc. cit.,* note 65. In the first letter, Schenck wrote: "It doesn't seem to me to be at all in accord with what Mr. Chaplin told him, or what you have told him."

72. *Lewiston Journal Magazine Section,* October 15 and 22, 1927. The two-part article written by Emmie Bailey Whitney has a subtitle: "Katahdin No Longer Reserved for the Intrepid Climber.—The Maine Publicity Bureau, the Great Northern Company and the Appalachian Mountain Club Have Combined to Popularize the King Mountain of Maine and Make It Accessible to the Ordinary Climber."

73. "Report of the Appalachian Club," *The Northern,* April 1923, p. 13.

74. Willard Helburn, "On Ktaadn in March," *Appalachia,* April 1924, pp. 226–30; "Sandy Stream and Mt. Katahdin," *The Northern,* May 1923, pp. 5–7, 10; Edward S. C. Smith, "The First Automobile Trip over Windey Pitch Hill, Katahdin Region," *Maine Naturalist,* June 1929, pp. 74–75. For a vivid description of the terrors of this road, see Whitney article, *op. cit.,* note 72 above.

75. "The Basin Ponds Fire of August 9th," *The Northern,* December 1923, p. 14; see also the files of *Appalachia* in the period after the fire. Also Francis Harper, "The Black Bear on Mount Katahdin," *Bulletin of the Boston Society of Natural History,* October, 1928, pp. 8–12. This article contains a fine photograph of a black bear in burnt-over area near Basin Ponds. Katahdin is in the background. The burned area was two miles long and a half mile wide.

76. Rachel L. Lowe, "High Lights of My Kidney Pond Trip," *Maine Naturalist,* March 1926, p. 38.

77. Arthur C. Comey, "Exploration North of Katahdin: The Appalachian Mountain Club Makes Maps and Discoveries," *In the Maine Woods, 1926,* pp. 13–15; Corinne Danforth, "Mountain-Climbing in Maine: A Woman's Story of an Ascent of Mt. Katahdin and Some of the Experiences of Her Party," *In the Maine Woods, 1926,* pp. 13–15 and 31–35 respectively. For *Appalachia* articles not already mentioned, see: Alfred P. Wheeler, "Thanksgiving on Katahdin—1924," June 1925, pp. 182–85; Arthur Perkins, "Katahdin—August, 1926," December 1926, pp. 520–23; Arthur Comey, "Skiing at Katahdin," June 1928, pp. 24–26. More could be listed.

78. Schenck to Gilbert, November 2, 1925, *loc. cit.,* note 65.

79. See A. C., W. R. W., and H. R. B., "Field Notes: The Katahdin August Camp—1925," *Appalachia,* February 1926, pp. 371–76. The map faces pp. 372–73. It was reprinted extensively in *The Northern* and *In the Maine Woods.*

80. See *Appalachia:* "A Bibliography for Mt. Ktaadn," December 1922, pp. 334–40; "A Bibliography of Mt. Ktaadn, Revised," December 1924, pp. 59–70; and "A Bibliography of Katahdin: Supplement," June 1930, pp. 49–56. These were ultimately reworked, printed, and reprinted, *op. cit.,* I, note 22.

81. See *Public Laws of Maine, 1927,* ch. 74; Donald A. Craig, "Mapping Mt. Katahdin," *Portland Evening Express,* May 13, 1927; M. R. Stackpole, "Topographic Mapping in Maine," *Journal of the Maine Association of Engineers,* April 1928, pp. 53–55 (reprinted in *The Northern,* June 1928, p. 9).

82. See *Portland Press Herald,* October 18, 1927. In an editorial opposing

creation of a park, the Portland paper printed part of an editorial from the *Lewiston Evening Journal*, which supported it. The *Press Herald* editor noted that "the silliest proposal ever made to a Legislature was that of Governor Baxter who advocated the state's buying Mt. Katahdin and creating a state park." The paper's owners were in alliance with state water power and paper company interests.

83. See the Maine press for the period September and October, 1926. See also Schenck to Gilbert, September 15, 1926, *loc. cit.*, note 65. In this letter Schenck said, if A. R. Gould entered the race against Baxter, "Let's make it a real fight, use all points of vantage possible. You can have some money from me. Portland should not have two Senators—strong point against Baxter if *used*. Cobb I believe would use his influence. Brewster would do all he could under cover. Hale should not be in line to help Baxter, as he will have to fight the East & West question if Baxter wins. I hope Gould will make the fight." The Gilbert Papers contain numerous letters of Schenck and Gilbert which indicate their animosity and dislike for Baxter.

84. See Robert E. Dobbyn, Vice President, Boston Safe Deposit and Trust Company, to Baxter, November 15, 1966, BC, MSL.

85. *The Northern*, February 1928, pp. 1–6; McLeod, *op. cit.*, XV, 72. The Whitcomb-Gilbert fight is described in pages 12–17 of this chapter.

86. McLeod, *Ibid.*, pp. 74, 77.

87. *Ibid.*, p. 75. William A. Whitcomb and William McKay supported Baxter while William Hilton, manager of the Spruce Woods Department, was at first reluctant. Also see copy, Memorandum of Agreement, Baxter and Great Northern, November 18, 1930, Great Northern Paper Company Papers, Box 842, Special Collections, Fogler Library, UMO.

88. Memorandum of Agreement, Great Northern, William Whitcomb, President, and Baxter, January 8, 1931, BC, MSL; also in Great Northern Papers, *loc. cit.*, above.

89. Baxter to Clement F. Robinson, February 24, 1931, BSPA files; Robinson to Baxter, February 26, 1931; also two early drafts of Baxter letter to Governor Gardiner and the legislature dated February 24, 1931, BC, MSL.

90. Baxter to Robinson, undated but Saturday afternoon, BSPA files. See also clipping from *Houlton Times*, March 25, 1931, BAX Scrapbook No. 3, p. 71. Baxter said that two of the three people he had consulted in the matter suggested that he wait to make the grant until he had full ownership. He responded by saying, "Tenure of life is uncertain. I can not see how the gift can delay the negotiations, if they are to succeed."

91. Two memoranda dated Portland, February 28, 1931, from Robinson to The Governor, BSPA files.

92. *Acts and Resolves of the State of Maine, 1931*, pp. 725–26.

93. *Private and Special Laws, 1931*, ch. 23, pp. 346–47.

94. See BAX Scrapbook No. 3, pp. 56–71 for many clippings from newspapers throughout Maine.

95. Memorandum, Baxter to Robinson, March 16, 1931, BSPA.

96. McLeod, *op. cit.*, XV, 76. See also memorandum for his own use by Robinson, July 16, 1931, BSPA. Robinson was quite critical of Baxter's impa-

tience in the earlier decisions. See notes of conference in Boston office, Great Northern, June 2, 1931; Whitcomb to Baxter, June 9, 1931, and Louis C. Stearns, lawyer
from Bangor, to Baxter, September 4, 1931, BC, MSL. See also deeds, Harry Ross
to Great Northern, September 15, 1931; and Great Northern to Baxter, September
15, 1931, *loc. cit.*, note 87. Finally, see memorandum from Robinson to Governor
Gardiner, September 13, 1931, BSPA. Robinson wrote: "As you know there is
quite a question of where Baxter and the State would have 'got off' if Ross had
continued hostile but his acquiescence in putting the thing through this way is
going to result in a very real benefit for the State. Baxter's impulsiveness in going
ahead and giving the State a part interest which seemed likely at one time to
have gotten everybody into a jam will have been cured and the State will be
all right in the end. But it has undoubtedly caused both Baxter and the Great
Northern a good deal of worry and considerable money."

97. See corrected drafts of relevant documents in BSPA files, including copy
of letter from Baxter to Governor Gardiner, the Executive Council, and Forest
Commissioner Violette, October 7, 1931.

98. See *Private and Special Laws of the State of Maine, 1933*, ch. 3, and
*Resolves of the State of Maine, 1933*, ch. 103.

# III

1. Even with the care Baxter took in making certain that all claims or shares
in sections of land he purchased had been quieted, the possibility existed that at
some future date a third party such as a paper company might "claim some rights
in the land presently under the control of the Authority of which the Authority
has no knowledge for the reason that the title and all of the interest transferred
to the State of Maine have possibly not been checked." This statement was made
by Garth K. Chandler of the State Attorney General's office in the introductory
comment he provided for his survey of the deeds by which Baxter had granted
land to the state. See mimeographed, undated, untitled copies, BSPA.

2. See Baxter to Governor Edmund S. Muskie and the 97th Legislature
March 17, 1955, BC, MSL.

3. Edward M. Graham, Eastern Manufacturing Company, to Baxter,
February 6, 1932; Baxter to Graham, July 5, 1932; also see Baxter to Judge John
A. Peters, May 31, 1938, BC, MSL.

4. Charles J. Nichols to Baxter, April 20, 1937, BC, MSL. Nichols did much
of Baxter's legal work on the acquisition of land during the late thirties and early
forties.

5. Baxter to Judge Peters, May 31, June 10 and 17, 1938; see also Abstract
of Title, T5R9, W.E.L.S., Piscataquis County, Maine, November 23, 1937; Nichols
to Baxter, June 9 and November 7, 1938, BC, MSL.

6. Stephen W. Phillips, Salem, Massachusetts, to Baxter, June 15, 1938,
BC, MSL. Also see Deed from Piscataquis Land Company and others to Baxter,
June 15, 1938; Deed from St. John Smith to Baxter, December 1, 1937, BC,
MSL. Smith held 83/104 of the acreage in the township; the Piscataquis Land
Company held 21/104.

7. Baxter deeded the land on November 9, 1938. It was accepted by Forest

Commissioner Waldo N. Seavey and its acquisition approved by the Attorney General Franz U. Burkett on the same day. On November 22, 1938, Governor Lewis O. Barrows and the Executive Council formally accepted the gift for the state.

8. *Private and Special Laws, 1939*, ch. 1.

9. McLeod, *op. cit.*, XV, 77.

10. Baxter to Edward Graham, May 12, 1939; see Baxter to Judge Peters, May 21 and June 10 and June 17, 1938; Peters to Baxter June 3 and 11, 1938; and Graham to Baxter, October 24, 1938, BC, MSL.

11. Baxter to Harold H. Murchie, lawyer for Eastern Company, July 24, August 28, September 11, 1939; Murchie to Baxter, July 25 and 29, August 1, September 8, October 18, 1939; Nichols to Baxter, August 22, 1939; Murchie to Baxter, January 3, July 30, August 1, 1940, BC, MSL.

12. Baxter to Murchie, September 11, 1939, BC, MSL.

13. *Private and Special Laws of Maine, 1941*, ch. 1; *1941–42*, ch. 95. Baxter to Governor Sewall, the Senate, and House of Representatives of the 90th Legislature, January 8, 1941, in *Laws of Maine, Resolves, Communications and Proclamations*, 1941, pp. 760–61. Baxter erroneously referred to T4R9 as Traveler Town.

14. Baxter to Murchie, October 19 and 20, 1939; Murchie to Baxter, August 9 and 16, 1940, BC, MSL. The deed was signed on August 17, 1940.

15. Baxter to Governor Sewall, the Senate, and House of Representatives, April 17, 1944, in *Communications and Proclamations, Resolves of Maine, 1941*, ch. 982. Also *Private and Special Laws of Maine, 1943–1944*, ch. 91.

16. Baxter to Whitcomb, July 5, 1938, BC, MSL. See also "Index to Directors' Meetings . . . ," Great Northern Paper Company Collection, Special Collections, Fogler Library, University of Maine at Orono, Box 852. In his letter to Whitcomb, Baxter wrote: "With this section, I would be able to block the National Park plan for then I should have the entire center of the proposed National Park area with a good projection on the West."

17. See McLeod, *op. cit.*, XV, 80.

18. Whitcomb to Baxter, May 24, 1939; Baxter to Whitcomb, November 6, 1940, BC, MSL. See "Index," Great Northern, *loc. cit.* At five different meetings between September 14, 1938, and December 13, 1939, the Directors approved land sales to Baxter. Acreages for some parcels were not given, but those mentioned totalled 11,629.

19. See Abstract of "Pingree" interest in T3R10 W.E.L.S., Piscataquis County, Maine, March 24, 1941, BC, MSL. Baxter apparently traded other lands for them.

20. Murchie to Baxter, December 23, 1939 and January 16, 1940, Baxter to Murchie, December 20, 1939, BC, MSL. In his first letter to Murchie Baxter wrote that it was helpful that Great Northern had sold him the land "because otherwise I could not have traded with the Cassidy Estate."

21. Judge Peters to Baxter, November 17, 1939, BC, MSL. When the cession of land was first publicly announced two months later, Peters wrote (January 16, 1940) that he hoped Baxter would be able some day to fill in the southeast

corner (Polish Corridor) "where the big peaks come so near the line." He noted that the mountain was "a little cramped in that locality."

22. Baxter to Governor Barrows, the Senate, and House of Representatives, July 22, 1940 in *State Papers Relating to Gifts of Ex-Governor Baxter to The State of Maine* (from July 22, 1940 to May 1, 1943, except those printed in the 1941 Session Laws), in *Communications and Proclamations, Resolves of Maine, 1943,* pp. 698–99. See also *Private and Special Laws, 1939–1940* (Special Session), ch. 122. The deed was dated July 22, 1940.

23. Baxter to Governor Hildreth, the Senate, and House of Representatives, January 10, 1945, in *Resolves of Maine, 1945,* pp. 985–90. *Private and Special Laws,* 1945, ch. 1. The deed was dated January 2, 1945.

24. Baxter to Justice Edward P. Murray, July 22 and 23, 1948, BC, MSL. See also *Bangor Daily News,* August 11, 1948. The information for the paragraphs on the Cassidy suit comes from files of the attorney general that are now in the possession of the BSPA.

25. *Private and Special Laws, 1945,* ch. 1.

26. See Abstract of Title to T3R9, W.E.L.S., Piscataquis County, Maine, January 28, 1941, made by C. W. and H. M. Hayes, BC, MSL, Folder 79. See also McLeod, *op. cit.,* XV, 76, 80; and Baxter to Whitcomb, November 6, 1940, BC, MSL.

27. *Ibid.,* note 25 above.

28. See Abstract cited in note 26, and H. F. Ross to Baxter, December 19, 1938, BC, MSL.

29. Baxter to Ross, November 25 and December 16, 1939. In the latter letter Baxter repeated that he was near his goal in land acquisitions for the Park, but since he was more than sixty years old he wanted to clear it up in the event of his death. He added: "Though in my will I leave money for the Park and its development, it is better to do what one can while living, at least to get it started"; Ross to Baxter, December 19, 1939, BC, MSL.

30. Baxter to Ross, November 29, December 5 and December 6, 1940, BC, MSL. The quote is from his letter of December 5.

31. Baxter to Ross, December 14, 1940 and January 10, 1941, BC, MSL; Baxter to Governor Hildredth, the Senate, and House of Representatives, January 2, 1945, in *Communications and Resolutions, Laws of Maine, 1945,* pp. 935–39. Baxter was willing to grant cutting rights for ten years but preferred they be limited to five. On the role of Great Northern in this affair, see McLeod, *op. cit.,* XV, 81: "We have a rather obscure Memo from which we draw the conclusion that the Company took a hand in persuading Mr. Ross."

32. See *Appalachian Trailway News,* September 1940, p. 57; May 1941, pp. 25–26; May 1946, p. 22.

33. For the quotation see Ross to Baxter, March 18, 1941. See also Baxter to Ross, March 13, 14 and 19, 1941, BC, MSL.

34. Ernest H. Johnson, state tax assessor, to Baxter, March 3, 1950, BC, MSL.

35. Ralph A. Dyer, Jr., to Baxter, May 1 and November 15, 1950, BC, MSL.

36. See Baxter to Dyer, November 17, 1950; April 27 and May 28, 1951;

Dyer to Baxter, November 15, 1950; April 28, May 2 and 25, 1951. See also Baxter to Ross, April 2, 1951; Ross to Baxter, April 5, 1951, BC, MSL.

37. See Baxter to McDonald, January 7, 1954; also Baxter to Robert N. Haskell, January 6, 1954, BC, MSL. Baxter said he was transferring 8,000 acres in T3R9 to the state in 1955. See also "Index . . ." *loc. cit.* The Directors of Great Northern voted on November 18, 1953 to sell the 8,000 acres to Baxter for five dollars per acre plus cutting rights. See also unsigned memorandum dated November 9, 1953 by Vice President Hilton for the Great Northern "Index . . ." *loc. cit.* The paper company had bought the land from Ross for ten dollars per acre. Though it would lose $40,000 on the cost of the land, Hilton said the merchantable timber would more than make up for the loss. He recommended selling the land for eight dollars per acre. See also McLeod, *op. cit.*, XV, 82: ". . . the Company, actively interested in having him reach what he once more assured it was his final goal, bought from Ross . . . and sold this at once to the Governor, without it ever being on the books as land . . ."

38. Baxter to Whitcomb, November 6, 1940; also to Helon Taylor, September 28, 1951, BC, MSL. In the latter, marked "Confidential," Baxter related part of the deed to this section.

39. Baxter to Stevens, January 11, 1945, BC, MSL. Baxter reported that whenever he bought lands to be used in exchanges or to be given to the state he asked for and received tax abatements on them until they were transferred. See also Baxter to Stevens, June 7, 1946, BC, MSL, for another typical letter; also McLeod, *op. cit.*, XV, 81.

40. See communication from Baxter to Governor Hildreth, the Senate, and House of Representatives, January 2, 1945, in *Laws of Maine, 1945*, pp. 935–39. See also Baxter to Taylor, September 28, 1951, BC, MSL. The Board of Great Northern approved the sale on December 13, 1944.

In 1968, a year and a half before the cutting rights were to expire, the Authority considered the possibility of buying the rights and discussed the issue with Baxter. His "quick reaction" was to oppose any changes in the deed or the purchase of the rights since the paper company had been so good to him over the years. The matter was dropped. See Wilkins to Paul K. Patterson, Great Northern, May 10, 1968, BSPA.

41. Graham to Baxter, May 8, 1943, BC, MSL.

42. Baxter to Whitcomb, November 1, 1943, BC, MSL.

43. Baxter to Whitcomb, January 27, 1944, BC, MSL. Baxter was then trying to buy 10,000 acres in T2R9.

44. Carlisle to Baxter, April 26, May 2, July 30, 1945; Baxter to Carlisle, July 28, 1945; carbon of memorandum dated September 2, 1945 regarding purchase of lands for exchange; Baxter to Stevens, February 1, 1946, BC, MSL.

45. Baxter to Caleb Scribner, November 24, 1945, and to Whitcomb, April 12, 1946, BC, MSL.

46. Baxter to Stevens, June 12, 1946, BC, MSL. For details of Whitcomb's death, consult Maine or Massachusetts newspapers of the period. For example, see *Bangor Daily News*, June 11, 12, 13, and 14, 1946. On June 10, Whitcomb was shot three times by George E. Hardy of Westfield, New Jersey, who later that

day took his own life at his home. Though no precise reason for the murder was established, there was some evidence of a blackmailing scheme by Hardy.

47. Baxter to Governor Hildredth, October 28, 1946, BC, MSL. See also "Index . . ." *loc. cit.*: the issue was decided at a meeting on October 9, 1946. Baxter exchanged lands in T2R8, T5R7, T7R7, T8R7, T9R4, T3R2, and T3R3, a total of 11,878 acres.

48. See Baxter to Caleb Scribner, March 2, 1946, Baxter-Scribner Letters, BC, MSL. Baxter wrote: "I want to get some of 3R8 where Katahdin Lake is located. If I can get a piece of it, more may follow. That would be nice for our Park."

49. See Baxter to James Pierce of Madigan and Pierce, Timberlands Brokers, Houlton, January 11 and February 5, 1945; Pierce to Baxter, February 1, 1945, BC, MSL.

50. See Graham to Baxter, March 18, and Baxter to Graham and Haskell, March 25, 1955; Haskell to Baxter, March 28, 1955, BC, MSL. See also deed to East Branch Dam Company, October 28, 1902, Penobscot County Registry, Book 727, p. 335.

51. See Baxter to Morgan, July 3, 1947; Morgan to Baxter, July 11, 1947; Baxter to Morgan, July 14, 1947, BC, MSL. Baxter wrote: "Apparently my life span is the crux of the situation."

52. Baxter to George F. Eaton, August 19, 1947. See also Eaton to Baxter, August 7, 1947; George F. Peabody to Baxter, August 22, 1947; Baxter to Eastern Corporation, September 2, 1947, BC, MSL. Baxter in the latter letter gave a perpetual easement to the Eastern Corporation to use the so-called Headquarters camp site on the western shore of First Grand Lake. See also Eaton and Peabody to Eastern Corporation, September 3, 1947, enclosing Baxter's check for $15,000; Eaton to Baxter, September 3, 1947; Baxter to Eaton, September 5, 1947, BC, MSL.

53. *Private and Special Laws of Maine, 1949*, ch. 1.

54. Baxter to McKay, July 1, 1948, BC, MSL. Baxter said he was changing the trust deeds to allow roads to be built into the area for Great Northern operations. He offered to pay whatever price was asked.

55. See Grover C. Bradford to Baxter, February 21, 1947; Baxter to Bradford, March 11, 1947 and January 14, 1948, BC, MSL. In the latter letter, Baxter told Bradford, lawyer for the Pingree Heirs, that he was drafting an act amending the laws of 1945 and 1947 on roads in the Park and would deposit it with the Secretary of State in the event something happened to him before the legislature met in 1949. See also Stephen Wheatland, broker for the Pingree Heirs, to Baxter, October 2, 1947: Wheatland offered to sell the 1,486 acres for $7,500. See also Bradford to Baxter, October 15 and 20, 1947, and January 9, 1948; Baxter to Bradford, October 17, December 29, 1947 and January 14, 1948, BC, MSL.

56. See *Private and Special Laws of Maine, 1955*, ch. 1. Baxter deeded this 1/20 interest (76.8 acres) to the state. He had obtained the minor interests of Sada Coe Robinson of Madrone, California, on June 4, 1951 and of the Irving Pulp and Paper, Limited, on June 27, 1951.

57. Baxter to Bradford, December 17, 1951, BC, MSL.

58. See Baxter to Bradford, January 14, 1948; also to Eaton, October 12 and November 4, 1948, BC, MSL.; see also *Private and Special Laws, 1949,* ch. 1. Baxter actually transferred 19/20 or 1,486 acres of an area in T6R8; he picked up the remaining interests later in the year. Excluded in the deed was the dam lot at the outlet of First Grand Lake owned by the East Branch Improvement Company.

59. See clipping from *Houlton Pioneer Times,* January 13, 1949, attached to a letter from Baxter to Attorney General Farris, February 16, 1949, BSPA.

60. Baxter to Senator Ward, January 29, 1949: Baxter remembered the opposition, which apparently was important in his decision to allow hunting in areas he acquired later; see also Baxter to Ward, February 24, 1949, BC, MSL.

61. Farris to Baxter, April 14 and 22, 1949; Baxter to Barnes, April 14 and 20, 1949; Baxter to Farris, April 15, 1949; Ward to Baxter, April 9, 1949; Baxter to Ward, April 14 and 19, and May 9, 1949, BC, MSL. In his letter of April 14 to Ward, Baxter wrote: "Some of my cynical friends have maintained that when I no longer am here the State may lightly regard its obligations to carry out the terms of the Trust, but I always have put aside such thoughts as unworthy and still hold to my belief in the integrity of our Legislature. I do not want to be disillusioned. If I am mistaken my faith will be shattered. . . . Shall a few hunters bringing pressure on the Legislature upset my plans and thus perhaps deprive the State of benefactions that will be of material advantage to our People?" Here Baxter was referring to the trust he had set up in 1927.

See also Farris to Baxter, February 4, 1949, BSPA; *Legislative Record, 1949,* pp. 833, 1015, 1606–08; *Public Laws of Maine, 1949,* ch. 382.

Regarding the correction on boundaries, see Ward to Baxter, October 27 and November 1, 1949; Baxter to Ward, October 29, 1949, BC, MSL. Also in BSPA files see Farris to Haskell, November 13 and 17, 1950; Baxter to Deputy Attorney General John S. S. Fessenden, November 16, 1950; Haskell to Farris, June 23, November 10, and November 24, 1950; Farris to Baxter, November 17 and 20, 1950; Baxter to Farris, November 18, 1950. In his letter to Ward, Baxter at first said he wanted to do nothing about the situation. He pointed out that hunters still had 20,000 acres in T6R8 in which to hunt and that he had opened up to hunting some lands he had acquired from Harry F. Ross in T3R9. Ward noted that some legislators would not have voted for the sanctuary had they known privately owned land would be closed to hunting.

62. *Portland Press Herald,* July 12, 1949; *Bangor Daily News,* July 11, 1949. The *News* supported Baxter. For the quotation, see editorial in *Portland Sunday Telegram,* July 3, 1949, copy in BAX Scrapbook No. 4, p. 151. Letter to Editor from Earl S. Grant, *Portland Press Herald,* June 23, 1949.

63. Baxter to Haskell, January 6, 1954, BC, MSL.

64. *Kennebec Journal* and the *Bangor Daily News,* January 21 and 23, 1954; *Portland Sunday Telegram & Sunday Press Herald,* January 24, 1954.

65. Baxter to Haskell, January 18, 1954. See also carbon copy of letter of John E. Willey to Voice of the People Editor, *Portland Press Herald,* February 1, 1954, BC, MSL. Willey was Baxter's lawyer and argued his position at length.

66. *Bangor Daily News,* January 13, 21, 23, and 27, 1954.

67. Eastern Corporation to Baxter, January 4, 1954, BC, MSL. Piscataquis

County Registry of Deeds, Vol. 309, p. 78. Eastern Corporation to East Branch Improvement Company, Piscataquis County Registry of Deeds, Vol. 309, p. 81; and Piscataquis County Registry of Deeds, East Branch Improvement Company to Baxter, Vol. 315, p. 44. On preparation of the deeds, see George Peabody to Baxter, August 30, September 1 and 2, October 12, 1954; Baxter to Peabody, September 1 and October 19, 1954, BC, MSL. Baxter paid $10,000 for the property.

68. Baxter to Peabody, September 1, 1954, BC, MSL.

69. *Private and Special Laws of Maine, 1955*, ch. 4.

70. Graham to Baxter, March 18, 1955; Baxter to Graham and to Haskell, March 25, 1955, BC, MSL.; see also Haskell to Baxter, March 28, 1955; Baxter to Haskell, March 31, 1955; Baxter to Commissioner Cobb, March 31, 1955, BC, MSL. With the latter is a copy of Legislative Document No. 811, a resolve authorizing the forest commissioner to convey the flowage rights on Matagamon Lake and other rights. Baxter opposed the use of the word "convey" because he said the state lacked legal authority to "convey" lands and rights held in trust.

71. Hilton to Baxter, March 28, 1952, BC, MSL.

72. Baxter to McDonald, November 15, 1954, BC, MSL. In 1962, after acquiring his last section of land from Great Northern, Baxter told a reporter, "I used to tell the paper companies that I'd made my last purchase. Then I'd show up the next year trying to get more and we'd all get a big laugh out of it. But I won't dare go back and do that next year after saying this. I just wouldn't have the gall." See *Portland Sunday Telegram*, September 9, 1962. The interview was with Frank Sleeper.

73. See Baxter to Justice Murray, November 24, 1954; Murray to Baxter, December 3, 1954; Baxter to Haskell, December 10 and 20, 1954, and March 21, 1955; Haskell to Baxter, December 15, 1954; Harold Holden, President Eastern Corporation, to Baxter, March 11, 1955; Baxter to Holden, March 12, 1955, BC, MSL. Baxter paid $30,000 for the exchange lands.

74. *Private and Special Laws of Maine, 1955*, Ch. 61. The Bangor Hydro-Electric Company reserved a 25-acre dam lot at the foot of Webster Lake.

75. See in 1955, Baxter to Wheatland and Bradford, August 1; Wheatland to Baxter, August 8, and Baxter to Wheatland, August 9. See also Baxter to Stephen Phillips, January 16, 1956; Wheatland to Baxter, February 15, 1956; Baxter to Wheatland, February 17, 1956, BC, MSL.

76. *Private and Special Laws of Maine, 1955*, Ch. 61 and 171. See Baxter to Bradford, July 22 and 30, 1957; Bradford to Baxter, July 29, 1957; Wheatland to Baxter, October 3, 1957; Baxter to Wheatland, October 4 and 14, 1957, BC, MSL.

77. The land was purchased from the Pierce Estate of Bangor through its representative Grover C. Bradford. See Baxter to Bradford, June 17, July 11 and 12, and August 20, 1941; Bradford to Baxter, June 18, July 9, and August 22, 1941, BC, MSL.

78. Hinch & Company, Inc. and Geneva E. Hinch sold the land for $2,300. See Ballard F. Keith, attorney for Hinch, to Charles J. Nichols, Attorney for Baxter, September 8, 1944, BC, MSL.

79. Charles Shipman Payson, president, Great Northern, to Baxter, June 20, 1957; Baxter to Payson, June 22, 1957, BC, MSL.

80. Baxter to William Hilton, Woodlands Manager, Great Northern, October 14, 1959; see also A. D. Nutting to Baxter, October 7, 1959 and Baxter to Austin Wilkins, October 14, 1959. Nutting's letter made obvious Baxter's desire to hold most of the land between the Millinocket-Greenville road and the Park. This would give the state ownership of most of the Togue Ponds. Undoubtedly questions regarding private camps within this area made acquisition of the larger parcel more difficult or impossible.

81. Wilkins to Hilton, May 3, 1960, BSPA files.

82. Hilton to Baxter, June 29, 1960 (Hilton offered the right of way only); Baxter to Hilton, July 6, 1960, BC, MSL. When the land was actually purchased by Baxter, he told Taylor before informing members of the Authority. See Taylor to Baxter, August 29, 1961, BC, MSL. Taylor said he was glad to hear that there was a good chance of getting the land and went on to plan the new road, which he thought would cost $15,000.

83. Baxter to McDonald, August 30, 1961, BC, MSL.

84. See Taylor to Wilkins, October 19, 1961, and June 20, 1962, BC, MSL. See also John T. Maines, Woodlands Manager, to Controller L. G. Kewer, May 21, 1962, Great Northern Collection, "Parks" file, Box 842. Baxter paid $58,230 for the land. Also see McLeod, *op. cit.*, for quotation on Hilton's opposition. By this time Great Northern had sold Baxter about 60,000 acres.

85. *Portland Sunday Telegram*, September 9, 1962; also *Private and Special Laws of Maine, 1963*, Ch. 1.

## IV

1. "Mount Katahdin State Park," an address given by Hon. Percival P. Baxter of Portland, President of the Senate, at the Annual Meeting of the Maine Sportsmen's Fish and Game Association, Hall of Representatives, State Capitol, Augusta, Maine, January 27, 1921. The Senate ordered 2,500 copies printed. See copies in BC, MSL or in newspapers of January 28, 1921. This address was reprinted in *Mostly About People: National Magazine* in 1921. See BAX Scrapbook, No. 8, p. 32.

2. See these drafts in BC, MSL. The 1925 draft is in BAX Scrapbook No. 5, pp. 145–51.

3. Baxter to Honorable Charles L. McNary, c/o Bangor Chamber of Commerce, September 27, 1923, BAX Scrapbook No. 20, p. 204. Senator McNary of Oregon was Chairman of the United States Senate Reforestation Committee, which held a hearing in Bangor.

4. For the wording of this portion of the trust, created on July 6, 1927, see Sarah Redfield, Assistant Attorney General, to BSPA, May 20, 1976, note 1, BSPA.

5. *Private and Special Laws, 1955*, ch. 61.

6. *Ibid.*, ch. 171.

7. Baxter to Honorable Edmund S. Muskie, the Senate, and House of Representatives, May 2, 1955, in *Public Laws of Maine, 1955*, p. 1149.

8. Baxter to Governor Horace A. Hildreth, the Senate, and House of Representatives, January 2, 1945, *Private and Special Laws of Maine, 1945*, p. 985.

9. Frank Cowan to George Stobie, Raymond Rendall and Baxter, September 5, 1944, BSPA.

10. Baxter to Cowan, September 6, 1944, BSPA.

11. *Private and Special Laws, 1945*, ch. 1.

12. Baxter to Clyde B. Morgan, President, Eastern Corporation, July 3 and 14, 1947; Morgan to Baxter, July 11, 1947; George F. Eaton to Baxter, August 7, and 22, and September 3, 1947, January 7, 1948; Baxter to Eaton, August 19, 1947, January 3, 6, and 21, 1948; Baxter to Eastern Corporation, September 2, 1947; Baxter to Grover C. Bradford, December 29, 1947, January 14, 1948; Bradford to Baxter, January 9, 1948; Baxter to William O. McKay, July 1, 1948; Baxter to Edward M. Graham, January 21, 1948, all in BC, MSL. In the last letter Baxter wrote: "After much deliberation I came to the conclusion that roads really are necessary for the proper enjoyment of the state park and from now on the State is allowed to construct such roads as are necessary, the only restriction being that the natural wild state of the area shall not be unduly interfered with."

13. *Private and Special Laws, 1949*, ch. 2.

14. *Public Laws of Maine, 1949*, ch. 382.

15. Baxter to Governor Muskie, the Senate, and House of Representatives, January 11, 1955, in *Laws of Maine, Resolves and Communications, 1955*, pp. 1143–45. In this letter Baxter noted his changes regarding hunting. "This removed a controversy which is not helping any of us." Helon N. Taylor told Sarah Redfield, Assistant Attorney General, in a taped interview in the mid-seventies that Baxter changed his stance here "particularly out of consideration for the people of Patten."

16. Baxter to George Stobie, November 10, 1948, BC, MSL. See also Baxter to Caleb Scribner, January 11, 1945, Baxter-Scribner Letters, BC, MSL. Baxter noted that in transferring another sizable tract to the state he had included strong bans on roads, and "also remembering what you said, I provided that the State shall forbid air-craft to land on the ground or in the waters within the park area."

17. In 1956 Baxter authorized a flight to Russell Pond by Edmund Ware Smith and Maurice Day, who wanted to take pictures for an article for *Ford Times*. See Baxter to A. D. Nutting, April 21, 1956; Nutting to Smith and Day, April 24, 1956; Smith to A. D. Nutting, April 26, 1956, BSPA.

18. Robert Yard to Baxter, October 4 and 12, 1937; Baxter to Yard, October 6, 1937; Robert Marshall to Baxter, May 8, 1937, May 18, 1938; Baxter to Marshall, May 7 and 23, 1938, BC, MSL.

19. *Portland Sunday Telegram*, November 30, 1941, Section C, p. 1. On April 29, 1976, in commenting on an earlier draft of this chapter, John L. Baxter, Sr., Percival's nephew, made the following statement: "As to general comment, Uncle Percy often changed his mind, (some people even accused him of going back on his word)! As to the park, however, it is understandable to me that he would express certain purposes for it at one time, and different ones at others, because I know from his remarks to me from time to time that sometimes 'scientific forestry', sometimes 'forever wild', and sometimes 'enjoyment of nature etc. by

users' would be uppermost in his mind. About the only constant was that there should be no commercialization."

20. Baxter to Governor Sewall, the Senate, and House of Representatives, January 12, 1942, in *Laws of Maine, Communications, 1942,* pp. 700–701.

21. *Ibid.,* January 13, 1943, *Laws of Maine, Communications, 1943,* pp. 703–08.

22. Baxter to Governor Hildreth, the Senate, and House of Representatives of the 92nd Legislature, January 2, 1945, in *Communications and Proclamations, Resolves of Maine, 1945,* pp. 988–89.

23. Taylor to Baxter, March 16, 1952, BP, MSL. Other issues regarding removal of beaver colonies had arisen ten years earlier. See Caleb Scribner to George Stobie, October 22, 1946; Harold Dyer to Stobie, October 21, 1946; Baxter to Scribner, October 24, 1946, BC, MSL.

24. Baxter to Albert Nutting, Alexander LaFleur, and Roland Cobb, August 4, 1952, BSPA.

25. Baxter to Nutting, June 18, 1952, BSPA; Nutting to Baxter, June 23, 1952, BSPA. Taylor discussed Nutting's role in a taped interview with Sarah Redfield, Assistant Attorney General. He continually reiterated Baxter's liking for and trust in Nutting. He stressed particularly Nutting's role in developing this interpretive statement. He said that Horace Albright, former director of the National Park Service and friend of Baxter, also was consulted.

26. Baxter to Nutting, April 1, 1954, BC, MSL.

27. *Ibid.,* July 9, 1954, BC, MSL.

28. *Ibid.,* August 12, 1954; see also Charles G. Paine, vice president and general manager, Eastern Corporation, to Baxter, January 2, 1952, BC, MSL.

29. Nutting to Baxter, August 20, 1954, BC, MSL.

30. Baxter to Nutting, August 27 and November 6, 1954, BC, MSL. Baxter signed a deed to effect these changes in the event he died before the legislature met. See also Baxter to Harold Holden, December 30, 1954, BC, MSL. Baxter used this act as another lever to get more land. He noted that the document was being prepared for legislative action. "I want to provide for its future operation on a broad scale so that in the years to come, when I am no longer here, they will not say 'A dead man's hand blocks the way'."

31. *Private and Special Laws, 1955,* ch. 2.

32. Baxter to Governor John H. Reed and members of the Executive Council, May 20, 1960, BC, MSL. It was accepted and approved in Council, June 15, 1960. See also Baxter to Wilkins, April 21, 1959, BC, MSL. Baxter, after meeting personally with Wilkins, sent the latter a copy of his letter of August 27, 1954, to Nutting.

33. Baxter to Nutting, September 26 and 28, 1955; Nutting to Baxter, October 3, 1955, and November 1, 1955, BC, MSL.

34. Baxter to Nutting, June 15 and 21, 1956; Nutting to Baxter June 19, 21, and 26, 1956; and Baxter to Victor D. Davignon, June 20, 1956, BC, MSL. The clipping was from the *Portland Press Herald,* June 15, 1956.

Two years earlier Nutting had written to Alexander LaFleur on March 18, 1954, BSPA. "The other problem which I mentioned was in regard to Public Lots in Baxter Park. Governor Baxter obtained time and grass rights by purchase since the state had never sold land and mineral rights. It would seem that they still are probably in the status of lands reserved. I think this should be cleared up in the next legislature, if possible, so that someone would not try to carry on a mining business in that area." Appropriate protection was afforded by the next legislature. See *Public Laws*, 1955, ch. 80.

35. Horace Weatherbee, of Lincoln Fish and Game Club, to Roland Cobb, October 8, 1951; Baxter to Cobb, October 18, 1951, BSPA.

36. *Portland Evening Express*, June 20, 1957.

37. Baxter to Nutting, August 18, 1958, BC, MSL. See also taped interview, undated, Sarah Redfield with Helon Taylor. Nutting had asked Taylor to speak to Baxter about the possibility of cutting the magnificent spruce near Trout Brook Farm since Baxter would more readily listen to requests from Taylor. Baxter concluded the tree was more valuable where it stood than at Rockefeller Center.

38. Frank Hancock to Baxter, October 7, 1959; Baxter to Hancock, October 13, 1959, BC, MSL and BSPA; Hancock to Baxter, October 13, 1959, BC, MSL and BSPA.

39. Lucius D. Barrows, Chief Engineer, State Highway Commission, to Baxter, November 30, 1950 and also April 18, 1951, acknowledging receipt of Baxter's check for $12,500; Earl R. Bartlett to Barrows, August 10, 1951, copy to Baxter, progress report, BC, MSL.

40. Baxter to Barrows, September 11, 1951, BC, MSL. Earlier in a letter to Bartlett on August 14, 1951 Baxter offered additional funds if necessary to complete the job. He said the same thing in a letter to Barrows on the same day.

41. Baxter to David Stevens, October 24, and Stevens to Baxter, October 29, 1957, BC, MSL. In 1958, responding to a letter in praise of his roads policy, Baxter recounted this incident and concluded: "Evidently we must always be on the watch and I am doing everything I can to prevent encroachments either now or when I am no longer here." See Baxter to Freeman Tilden, August 12, 1958, BC, MSL.

Three years later a park ranger wrote to Commissioner Stevens directly praising road maintenance in the Park but asking why patrolmen were instructed not to cut brush along the roads. He stressed the dangers presented by the growth and said it had been done in the past without undesirable results. The Forest Commissioner chided the ranger for going out of proper channels with his comments and then told him of Baxter's directives. See Myrle J. Scott to David Stevens, August 15; Wilkins to Scott, August 18, 1960, BSPA.

42. William O. Douglas to Baxter, May 26; Baxter to Douglas, June 1, 1960; undated written memorandum, Fred [Holt] to Wilkins, BSPA. Baxter to Stevens, June 16, 1960, BC, MSL. In the latter letter Baxter referred to the road possibility as "just a matter of conversation which I hope will subside; . . ." In the mid-seventies, Sarah Redfield interviewed Taylor. In the course of the taped discussion he said, "I think in time I could have convinced him" of a pet scheme of Taylor's to build another road paralleling the perimeter road and making each one-way. See also Smith, "Jake's Rangers vs. the U.S. Supreme Court," in *Upriver and Down Stories from Maine Woods* (New York: Holt, Rinehart and Winston, 1955), pp. 169–87.

43. Taylor to Wilkins, May 31, 1959, BSPA.

355

44. Hilton to Baxter, June 29; Baxter to Hilton, July 6, 1960, and to McDonald, August 30, 1961, BC, MSL. See Wilkins to Hilton, May 3, 1960, BSPA.

45. Wilkins to members of BSPA and to Stevens, June 26, 1964; Vaughan M. Daggett, Chief Engineer, to Wilkins, June 25, 1964, BSPA; Wilkins to Baxter, July 6; Baxter to Wilkins, and to Taylor, July 8, 1964; BC, MSL.

46. Richard Dubord to Baxter, February 14, 1966, BSPA. Dubord stated the reasons and asked to use trust fund income. See also Baxter to Wilkins, February 14, to Dubord, February 17, and to Taylor, May 17, 1966, BC, MSL. In the letter to Dubord, Baxter authorized the use of income from the trust funds to pay costs.

47. See Forestry Department Statement to Committee on Appropriations and Financial Affairs, February 22, 1967; Wilkins to Erwin, August 24, 1967, BSPA.

48. Wilkins to Speers and Erwin, April 7, and June 1, 1967; also to Henry Cranshaw on June 1, 1967, BSPA.

49. Baxter to Wilkins, June 17, 1968, with copies and cover letters to Erwin and Speers, BSPA.

50. Wilkins to Baxter, June 26, 1968, BSPA.

51. Hancock to Wilkins, December 24, 1963, BSPA.

52. Wilkins to Fred M. Rooney, Service Forester, March 24, 1964, BSPA.

53. Wilkins to Baxter, April 2, Baxter to Wilkins, September 30, 1964, BSPA. See also Willard A. Wight to Wilkins, September 18, 1964, BSPA, for details of operations.

54. Taylor to Wilkins, October 3, 1964, BSPA.

55. Baxter to Wilkins April 8, Wilkins to Baxter, April 13, 1966; Wilkins to Cranshaw, November 30, 1965, BSPA.

56. Stevens to Baxter, January 16, 1964, BSPA.

57. Taylor to Wilkins, March 6 and 22; Wilkins to Taylor, March 22 and 26, 1962; Report of Helon Taylor for March 1962, BSPA. The latter report discusses use of the snowmobiles in the Park.

58. Donald W. McKay, of Old Town, to Editor, *Bangor Daily News,* March 25, and to Baxter, May 7, 1965, BC, MSL. The article mentioned in the text is referred to in the correspondence, but I have not been able to find it in the microfilm copy of the newspaper in the Fogler Library, UMO.

59. Taylor to Baxter, May 11, 1965, BC, MSL.

60. Baxter to Taylor, May 11, 1965, BC, MSL. During a continued investigation of this issue a decade later, the Attorney General's office contacted Helon Taylor, James Erwin, Austin Wilkins, Irvin Caverly, Rodney Sargent and Joseph Lee, Baxter's last chauffeur, to determine whether Baxter altered this position during the remainder of his life. All except Wilkins indicated that Baxter did not change his mind. See Sarah Redfield to BSPA, May 20, 1976, BSPA. On Taylor's views, see below.

61. Taylor to Wilkins, May 14, 1965, BSPA. In the taped interview with Sarah Redfield cited in note 42, Taylor stated that a Portland man had convinced Baxter that he should oppose the use of snowmobiles in the Park. Later, he said, Baxter discussed the issue at a meeting with Taylor and Authority members. "We convinced him that a snowmobile didn't do any harm," Taylor said, though Baxter did "restrict them to the roads."

62. Wilkins to Taylor, May 17, 1965, BSPA.

63. Wilkins to Richard P. Billingham of Rochester, New York, January 15, and to Senator Muskie, on the same day, 1970, BSPA. Hundreds of letters were received by the Authority protesting the new rule; some wrote first to Maine's senators and to the governor.

In November 1969, John L. Baxter, Sr. had told a reporter that the decision made the month before to allow snowmobiles in portions of the Park was "contrary to what Uncle Percy wanted." His uncle would have agreed to the use of snowmobiles "for transportation—not recreation." See Gloria Hutchinson, "Governor Baxter and the Snow Machines," *Maine Digest,* Winter, 1970, pp. 24–28.

## V

1. Archer L. Grover, "Mt. Katahdin," *Sun-up, Maine's Own Magazine,* April 1931, pp. 3, 28, 30.

2. See H. Walter Leavitt, *Katahdin Skylines,* pp. 38–45. The trail had been opened in 1923 by W. H. St. John and H. N. Walls, owners of the Togue Pond sporting camps. The upper portion of the trail traversed the route of the old Keep Path. The route fell into disuse during the 1930s as the road was extended toward Roaring Brook.

3. For an interesting article detailing the completion of the Katahdin end of the Appalachian Trail, see *Lewiston Journal Magazine Section,* October 7, 1933. Myron Avery was instrumental in completing the Katahdin end. See Avery, "Maine and the Appalachian Trail," *In the Maine Woods, 1933,* pp, 97–103. Much trail locating had been done in the mid-twenties by Arthur C. Comey, Chairman of the New England Trail Conference, but failure to follow it up with clearing forced redoing the work in the early 1930s.

4. *Twentieth Biennial Report of the Forest Commissioner of Maine, 1933–34,* p. 129.

5. See Wilkins, *Ten Million Acres of Timber, op. cit.,* pp. 264–67.

6. *Nineteenth Biennial Report of the Forest Commissioner of Maine, 1931–32,* pp. 102–03.

7. Wilfrid A. Hennessy, "Baxter Park at Mt. Katahdin," *In the Maine Woods, 1933,* p. 31.

8. See W. C. Mendenhall, acting director, U.S. Geological Survey, to Baxter, June 22, 1931; Baxter to John Cameron, U.S. Geographic Board, November 3, Cameron to Baxter, November 7, 1931, BC, MSL.

9. Baxter to Mendenhall, December 15, 1932, BC, MSL.

10. See copy of Executive Council Order 122, March 16, 1932 and a typed copy of the wording of the plaque, with changes in BAX Scrapbook No. 5, pp. 129, 131; see also in Great Northern Collection, Box 842, "Parks—National and State" file, a note, signed by Roy [Weldon?] to John McLeod on a newspaper picture of the plaque. The note reads: "Tablet installed by Baxter. We furnished Compressor & 2 men to help install it."

11. *Legislative Record, 1933,* pp. 28, 89, 100, 124, 128, 158; *Public Laws of Maine, 1933,* ch. 281; *Bangor Daily News,* December 6 and 7, 1933. In his editorial on December 6 entitled "This Bill Should Pass," the editor wrote: "The purpose of the bill is to provide competent supervision for the further de-

velopment of roads and trails on and around Mount Katahdin, the work to be done by the Civilian Conservation Corps, an opportunity that should be grasped while it offers."

12. *Twentieth Biennial Report* . . . *op. cit.*, p. 128.

13. See undated "Comments by Rep. Walter A. Birt, Member of Baxter State Park History Review Committee," on an earlier draft of this chapter, BSPA.

14. Harvey Paul McGuire, "The Civilian Conservation Corps in Maine: 1933–42" (unpublished M.A. Thesis, University of Maine, 1966), ch. I.

15. *Ibid.,* p. 20; Austin Wilkins, *The Forests of Maine,* Maine Forest Service Bulletin No. 8 (Augusta, Maine: Maine Forest Service, 1932).

16. McGuire, *op. cit.,* ch. II; *Twentieth Biennial Report* . . . *op. cit.,* pp. 112–19.

17. *Ibid.,* McGuire, pp. 150–52; *Twentieth Biennial* . . . , p. 117. To avoid having to drive long distances to work projects, the CCC in Maine made more use of side camps than was done in other New England states.

18. *Twentieth Biennial Report* . . . *op. cit.,* pp. 117–19; *Twenty-First Report, 1935–1936,* pp. 123–24; *Twenty-Second Report, 1937–1938,* pp. 128–32.

19. *Portland Press Herald,* August 25, 1933.

20. *Bangor Daily News,* September 11, 1933, and Ronald L. Gower, "Recent Changes at Katahdin," *Appalachia,* December 1934, pp. 280–81. Gower told of a meeting his group had with Baxter, James W. Sewall, Arthur C. Sylvester of the National Park Service, and a representative of the CCC.

21. *Bangor Daily News,* September 11, 1933, January 5 and 24, 1934; *Portland Press Herald,* January 19, 1934. See also BAX Scrapbook No. 3, p. 145, for a copy of a promotional pamphlet: "Proposed Extension of Route 157 from Millinocket to Greenville via Mount Katahdin and Baxter State Park," published by the Chamber of Commerce of Millinocket in 1933. See also Baxter to Governor Brann, September 7, 1933, BC, MSL. Baxter reported on his Millinocket trip, praised the work being done by the CCC, and urged the Governor to provide more state equipment for highway work.

22. Ross Abare, Memorandum Relative to Camp SP–2 Millinocket, Me. June 9, 1934, dated Greenville, Maine, June 11, 1934 in National Archives, National Park Service, Record Group 79, file 0–32, box 2940. Hereafter cited as NA, NPS, RG 79, file 0–32, box 2940. Also in NA, CCC, RG 35, box 1058.

23. For information on the work of Company 193 at Millinocket, see copies of "Baxter-News" in BC, MSL; *Bangor Daily News,* September 15, 1933; see also first two entries, note 18 above.

24. Brann to Baxter, July 7, 1933, BP, MSL; Brann to Harold W. Ickes, July 8, Ickes to Brann, July 19, 1933, and Horace M. Albright to Neil L. Violette, undated, in NA, NPS, RG 79, file 0–32, box 2940.

25. Robert Fechner to Franklin D. Roosevelt, August 24, 1933, cited in Nixon, *op. cit.,* p. 87, n. 2. At that time Fechner, noting that Brann had suggested a park in the Katahdin-Moosehead Lake area, recommended that the administration not move with undue haste since there was much cut-over land in the area.

26. See BAX Scrapbook No. 3, 138 and 147 for clippings from *Portland Press Herald* and *Portland Evening Express,* of August 30, 1933. The articles re-

iterated the trust provisions of Baxter's gift and stressed the creation of a forest preserve rather than a wilderness park. But the tenor would indicate that at this early date Brann favored federal control.

27. See James Sewall to Jacob Hoffman, National Park Service, September 2, and Donald Alexander, National Park Service, to Sewall, September 7, 1933, in NA, NPS, RG 79, file 0–32, box 2940.

28. See E. K. Burlew, Department of the Interior, to Representative John G. Utterback, March 21, 1934; Russell G. Merryman, Emergency Conservation Work, to Herbert Evison, National Parks Service, April 9, 1934; Evison to Violette, April 16, 1934; Conrad Wirth to Violette, April 26, and to Melvin B. Borgerson, of White Plains, May 1 and June 29, 1934; Telegram, Borgerson to Wirth, June 2, 1934, all in NA, NPS, RG 79, file 0–32, box 2940.

29. *Ibid.*, note 22.

30. Arthur C. Sylvester, "A Report on The Recreational Development Mount Katahdin Region, Millinocket, Maine:  General Policy for the Recreational Development of the Mount Katahdin Region," mimeographed, 1935. Copy in BSPA files. Sylvester was Project Manager, State Park Division, National Park Service. See also covering letter Sylvester to Violette, May 11, 1935. Sylvester forwarded the report and added: "Last week I had the opportunity to talk over the proposed work [for 1935] at Katahdin with ex-Governor Baxter. Mr. Baxter heartily approves of the Katahdin report and the work we propose to carry out." See also Ronald Gower, "Recent Changes at Katahdin," *op. cit.*, note 20; also Charles H. Glaster, *The West Brancher* (New York: Vantage Press, 1970), pp. 200–203.

31. See H. P. K. Agersborg, Biologist and Sr. Wildlife Technician, to Conrad Wirth, September 25, 1934. This is a cover letter for his Memorandum to Mr. Wirth of September 14–16, 1934 Re: Report on Baxter State Park, per Millinocket (SP-No. 2) Maine. In NA, NPS, RG 79, file 33, box 244. It is obvious from the memorandum that the National Park Service was thinking of national park status for Katahdin in 1934. For plans of park service geologists for advertising geological points of interest in the Katahdin area, see Wirth to Second Regional Officer, National Park Service, January 8, 1936, and H. E. Rothrock, Geologist Supervisor, to E. H. Perkins, State Geologist, July 2, 1935 in NA, NPS, RG 79, file 732, box 204.

32. Gower, "Recent Changes . . ." *op. cit.;* also "Club Arranges 120 Mile Hike from Katahdin," *Bangor Daily News,* July 2, 1934.

33. "Baxter State Park Proposed Work Program, Summer 1935, National Park Conservation Camp, Maine SP–2." This is one portion of "Recreational Development Report," *op. cit.*, note 30. No date but covering letter is May 11, 1935, BC, MSL.

34. Arthur Sylvester to Baxter, May 16, 1935, BC, MSL. See also Donald Alexander to Wayne E. Stiles, Regional Inspector, May 23, 1935 in NA, NPS, RG 79, file 601, box 243. Fred Pitman again worked on the project and was hired to look over the property during the fall and winter months.

35. See Commissioner Waldo Seavey to Gerald Hyde, Administrative Inspector, U.S. Forest Service, July 11, 1936, in NA, NPS, RG 79, file 601, box 243.

36. See note 35 above and from same source Fred T. Johnston to Regional Office, Region 1, NPS, August 21, 1936.

37. See Edouard N. Dube to Regional Director, Region One, June 10, 1938; also Melvin B. Boyson, to John S. Brown, CCC, First Corps Area, November 1, 1937; W. T. Ritenour, to The Director, CCC, July 20, 1938; Wirth to Oliver Cobb, July 5, 1938; all in NA, NPS, RG 79, file 601, box 243. This group of letters concerned the property at SP–2 and SP–3. Most of the camps at SP–3 were razed on June 27, 1938; those at SP–2 were transferred to the Maine Forest Service Office in February and July 1938. For nearly two decades Oliver R. Cobb and/or his wife disputed ownership and control of remaining structures at Avalanche Field with the Maine Forest Service or Baxter State Park. The buildings were located at the junction where the road to the Cobb's Katahdin Lake Camps led eastward from the Roaring Brook Road at Avalanche Field.

38. See H. K. Robert, to Myron Avery, July 6, 1937 in NA, NPS, RG 79, file 601, Box 243.

39. Wirth to Rendall, March 8, 1940, *Ibid.*

40. *Twenty-First Biennial Report . . . , op. cit.,* p. 24.

41. Gower, "Katahdin Circumambulated," *Appalachia,* June 1933, pp. 394–95.

42. Baxter to Gower, January 2, 1963, BC, MSL.

43. See Gower, "South From Katahdin," *Appalachia,* December 1934, p. 194; in same issue, his "Recent Changes . . . ," *op. cit.;* R.L.M.U. [Robert L. M. Underwood], "Katahdin," *Appalachia,* December 1933, p. 622; Gower, "Trail Work at Katahdin," *Appalachia,* December 1940, p. 267.

44. Esther Goodale, "Katahdin Excursion," *Appalachia,* December 1936, pp. 288–90; M. Beckett Howorth, "The Katahdin Rock-Climbing Trip," *Appalachia,* June 1936, pp. 109–12; Gower, "The Northwest Basin," *Appalachia,* December 1933, pp. 598–99; Grace E. Butcher, "The Opening Up of the Northwest Basin, Katahdin," *Appalachia,* November 1935, pp. 427–30.

45. Baxter to Cammerer, August 4, 1938, NA, NPS, RG 79, file 601, Box 243. See also Avery to Thomas J. Kennon, Secretary to Governor Barrows, August 18, 1938, and Attorney General Burkett to Baxter, September 9, 1938, BC, MSL. Barrows sent the letter to Burkett, who forwarded it to Baxter. Avery criticized the construction of the cabin at Chimney Pond because it would "increase the devastation and problems at Katahdin and is *extremely* unwise." The cabin was started in 1938.

See also Baxter to Burkett, September 19, 1939, BC, MSL. Baxter wrote that he had written Governor Barrows to get a $500 appropriation to complete the cabin. Since the Governor was out of the state, Baxter asked Burkett and the forest commissioner to arrange to move materials needed to complete the cabin at Chimney Pond and said, "I will be responsible for the bill." See also Barrows to Baxter, November 10, 1939, BC, MSL. Barrows reported that the Executive Council had approved the $500 allotment as requested by Baxter.

46. Baxter to Director, United States Geological Survey, April 21, and May 3, 1933, BC, MSL. The inscription on the bronze tablet reads: "HENRY DAVID THOREAU 1817–1862 PHILOSOPHER, NATURALIST & AUTHOR, ascended Mt. Katahdin in 1846 and wrote "THE MAINE WOODS" one of the earliest authentic descriptions of the great forest regions of Northern Maine." Also, George

C. Martin, Department of Interior, to Baxter, August 19 and December 10, 1935; Baxter to Martin, August 23 and December 10, 1935; and Martin to Governor and Executive Council, December 20, 1935, BC, MSL. Also Baxter to Governor Brann, August 1, Brann to Baxter, August 3, 1935, BC, MSL. For newspaper coverage see *Portland Press Herald*, December 22, 1935, clipping in BAX Scrapbook No. 3, p. 192.

47. See article by Myron Avery, *Portland Sunday Telegram*, August 7, 1938, in which Avery, a strong adherent of the National Park Service scheme, sharply criticized the plans to build at Chimney Pond and also criticized an offer that Baxter had made to the Millinocket Chamber of Commerce to build a hut on top of the mountain.

48. See undated "Comments by Rep. Walter A. Birt, Member of Baxter State Park History Review Committee" and undated "Comments by Former Forest Commissioner A. D. Nutting and a Former Chairman of Baxter State Park Authority" on an earlier draft of this chapter, BSPA.

49. *Public Laws of Maine, 1936*, ch. 6. This law was amended by *Public Laws of Maine, 1941*, ch. 25, to account for the changed boundaries of the Park.

# VI

1. See Robert Fechner to Roosevelt, August 24, 1933 in Nixon, *Franklin D. Roosevelt, op. cit.*, p. 87, n. 2.

2. *Bangor Daily News*, November 16, December 5, 15, 16, 18 (editorial), 19, and 20, 1933; *Public Laws of Maine, 1933*, ch. 123.

3. *Bangor Daily News*, December 28, 1933; April 13, 1934.

4. See "Parks—National and State," file, Box 842, Great Northern Collection, for dozens of letters between officers and correspondence with other paper companies. Great Northern was the leader in attempting to mobilize the paper industry of the state against the proposals.

5. See Arno Cammerer, to Roosevelt, July 6, 1937, in Nixon, *op. cit.*, Item 649, pp. 85–86.

6. A. E. Demaray, Acting Director, National Park Service to Baxter, May 5, 1937, BC, MSL.

7. Charles West, Acting Secretary of Interior, to Rene L. DeRouen, Chairman, Committee on Public Lands, May 25, 1937, BC, MSL. Alfred Mullikin to Earle A. Pritchard, National Park Service, July 21, 1936 and Pritchard to Mullikin, July 27, 1936, NA, NPS, RG 79, Box 243. In his reply Pritchard said possibilities for federal acquisition were then dubious. He noted receipt of at least four favorable reports from National Park Service employees on Katahdin.

8. Baxter to Senator Frederick Hale, April 8, 1937, BP, MSL.

9. Baxter to Pritchard, August 15, 1936, BC, MSL.

10. Pritchard to Baxter, August 29, 1936, BC, MSL.

11. See obituary, *Appalachia*, December 1952, pp. 240–41 and *Appalachian Trailway News*, September 1952, p. 35.

12. Baxter to Governor Barrows, January 15, 1937, BC, MSL, quoting three paragraphs from Avery's letter. See also Brewster to George P. Englehardt, June

3, 1937, BC, MSL. Englehardt apparently sent the letter to Baxter. Brewster re-iterated his usual arguments concerning neglect of and lack of financing for the Park.

13. Brewster to Baxter, April 14, 1937, BC, MSL. See also *Portland Press Herald*, May 13, and *Portland Sunday Telegram*, July 31, 1937.

14. See Avery, "The Katahdin National Park Bill," and Gower, "Katahdin: Its Past, Present and Future," in *Appalachia*, June 1937, pp. 447–50. Avery described the Park and its difficulties and supported the bill; Gower argued Baxter's point of view and opposed the bill. He also noted that the Council of the AMC voted on May 6, 1937, to oppose passage of the measure. See also Brewster to Baxter, April 19, 1937, BC, MSL.

15. Senator Wallace H. White to Baxter, March 10, 1937, BC, MSL.

16. Interview with John L. Baxter, Sr., February 2, 1972. In the late thirties when Brewster, a friend of his, was running for office, Mr. Baxter controlled the Republican primary vote in Brunswick. Brewster was in favor of a graduated chain-store tax to protect the small grocer; John Baxter, with the National Canners' Association, opposed the tax. Brewster came to Baxter for his support. Baxter promised it on two conditions: first, that Brewster stop plaguing Percival Baxter on the national park issue, and, second, that he lay off the chain-store tax. Brewster agreed to both. Baxter, incidentally, felt that Percival Baxter and Brewster basically were fond of each other.

17. Percival Baxter to his nephew John, April 14, 1937, BC, MSL.

18. 75th Congress, 1st Session, H. R. 5864 and H. R. 6599, dated March 23 and April 22, 1937, respectively, BC, MSL.

19. Baxter to Senator Hale (with a cc to Senator White), April 8, 1937, BC, MSL.

20. Baxter to Horace Albright, April 9, 1937 (a letter made available to me by John Baxter). Percival also wrote to Gower. His letter may account for the resolution taken by the AMC Council opposing creation of a national park.

21. Senator White to Baxter, April 13; Baxter to White, May 7; White to Baxter, May 10, 1937. See also White to William E. Wing, teacher at Deering High School, Portland, May 7, BC, MSL. White seemed to be temporizing on the federal park idea. He said he was currently opposed to it, but had "no positive commitment against the legislation, for I do not like to close my mind until I have heard the whole matter thrashed out and know all sides of it." Baxter replied at once: "I am calling on you to stand by through thick and thin because our side is the right one and there can be no compromise." White replied that his position was one of "Yankee caution"; the bill would not pass that year and he saw no need to change his mind in the future.

22. Baxter to Hale, April 17, Hale to Baxter, April 21, 1937, BC, MSL. In his letter Baxter presented a veiled political threat to Hale. He said 1938 would be a critical year for Maine and the Republicans had to work together to prevent the Democrats from gaining control. He added that he hoped Hale would continue in the Senate. See also Charles Nichols to Baxter, April 20, 1937, BC, MSL. He had talked with Senators Hale and White who urged Baxter to travel to Washington to meet with park service officials.

23. Brewster to Baxter, April 14 and 19, Baxter to Brewster, April 16, 1937, BC, MSL.

24. Baxter to Governor Barrows, April 16, Barrows to Baxter, April 19, 1937, BC, MSL.

25. *Ibid.*, note 17 above.

26. Baxter to Cammerer, April 26, 1937, BC, MSL.

27. *Public Laws of Maine, 1935*, Ch. 144.

28. Governor Barrows to Fechner, April 6; Edouard N. Dube, to Conrad Wirth, April 10; Ian Forbes and James Williams, of the park service: Memorandum to Mr. Weatherwax, April 21, 1937, in NA, NPS, RG 79, file 252, Box 242.

29. Sheldon Wardwell to Baxter, May 3; Baxter to Wardwell, May 7, 1937, BC, MSL. See also Great Northern file "Parks—national and State," *loc. cit.*, and Senator White's letters of May 7 to Baxter and to William Wing, cited in note 21 above. For one private citizen's reaction to the Brewster bill, see Daisy Brooks to White, May 6:

"What execrable taste, to say the least, for Cong. Brewster to want to take away from us such a magnificent gift as Katahdin!

The man must be crazy!

I wish your grandfather were alive to shake his fist at him; how he loved nature in its unspoiled state!

I hope you will let Mr. Brewster know how indignant Maine people are over this outragious bill. No poetry in his make up, poor man! Only the 'almighty dollar.' "

30. McLeod, *op. cit.*, XV, 77.

31. Baxter to Mr. & Mrs. David Gray, April 26, 1937. Also Cammerer to Roosevelt and Roosevelt to the Grays, in Nixon, *op. cit.*, pp. 85–87.

32. See *Portland Press Herald, Lewiston Evening Journal, Kennebec Daily Journal,* and other papers, May 3, 1937. Baxter paid for reprinting the press release for distribution to a wide range of government officials and private individuals. See his letters to Cammerer, May 3, Pritchard, May 4, and Governor Barrows, May 21, 1937, BC, MSL, for examples of letters in which copies of the releases were enclosed.

33. A. E. Demaray to Baxter, May 5, 10, and 19, 1937; Baxter to Demaray, May 15 and June 1, 1937; Baxter to Barrows, May 21, and to Secretary of Interior Ickes, May 25, 1937. Charles West, acting Secretary of the Interior, to Baxter, June 7, 1937. See also copy of Federated Garden Clubs of Maine resolution dated May 19; and Charles West to Rene Derouen, of the House of Representatives Committee on Public Lands, May 25, 1937. See BC, MSL for all of these documents.

34. Myron Avery to Herbert Evison, May 27, 1937, in NA, NPS, RG 79, file 601–03, Box 243.

35. Evison to Avery, June 16, and H. K. Roberts to E. N. Dubé, June 16, 1937; Avery to Evison, June 23, 1937, *ibid.*, reference for note 34 above.

36. Dube to Robert, June 28; Robert to Avery, July 6, 1937, *ibid.*, reference to note 34 above.

37. Yard to Baxter, July 8 and 12, 1937, BC, MSL.

38. Robert Marshall to Baxter, May 8, 1937; also Baxter to Arthur Pack, American Nature Association, October 13, 1937, BC, MSL. Pack had written supporting Baxter's views and expressing fear of the power of the National Park Service and State Park Commission. Baxter assured him that they could not get funds to buy the land.

39. Roderick Nash, *Wilderness and the American Mind* (New Haven and London: Yale University Press, 1967), pp. 206–11.

40. *Ibid.*, note 37; also Yard to Baxter, July 16, October 4 and 12, 1937; Baxter to Yard, May 27, July 14, September 20, 1937, BC, MSL.

41. No copy of the final report if it actually appeared, has been located in the National Archives or in state offices or libraries. None is in the Baxter Papers. Baxter was in the Maritime Provinces when the park service investigators were in Maine, so he knew little about their activities; see Baxter to Yard, October 6, and Yard's letter, October 12, cited above. Yard enclosed material for a forthcoming issue of *Wilderness News* (October 1937, pp. 6–9).

42. Senator Hale to Cammerer, September 20, 1937, and Demaray to Hale, in the same month, *ibid.* ref. for note 34, above. Demaray wrote: "The fine values of Baxter State Park and vicinity are fully appreciated by this Service. We have no interest in further development of Baxter State Park . . ." See also Demaray to Baxter, September 28, 1937; Baxter to White, October 28 and to Demaray, November 8, 1937; Demaray to Baxter, November 20, 1937, BC, MSL. Demaray wrote: "The particular purposes you have in mind to serve through your plans for the Mount Katahdin area will be fully respected by the National Park Service."

43. See typed copies of the press release interview dated Portland, Maine, December 2, 1937, and addressed to the Editor, BC, MSL. Most papers printed the item as Baxter had written it.

44. Baxter to Ickes, December 3, 1937, BC, MSL. Oscar Chapman, assistant secretary of the Interior, to Baxter, December 14, 1937, *ibid.*, reference for note 34 above.

45. Demarary to Baxter, December 21, 1937, Baxter to Demaray, February 28, 1938; also Yard to Baxter, March 18, 1938, BC, MSL. Yard thought the NPS would try to get passage of the law without a hearing and it would become a "request of Congress" to Maine, and would serve as a basis for "years of promotion in Maine by the Park Service and its group."

46. Avery, "Katahdin and Its Country," *Nature Magazine*, October 1937, pp. 237–41. An editorial on pp. 233–34 supported a national park. See also Yard to Baxter, December 21, 1937, BC, MSL.

47. Baxter to Demaray, June 4, 1938; Cammerer to Baxter, June 11, 1938, BC, MSL.

48. Gower, "Maine's Heritage in the Northern Wilderness, Baxter State Park," *Portland Sunday Telegram and Sunday Press Herald*, April 24, 1938. A typed copy of the same article, but titled "The Baxter State Park in Maine," is in BC, MSL. See also Baxter to Gower: "I regard you as one of the founders of the Katahdin Park and through the years have enjoyed my correspondence with you," BC, MSL.

49. Baxter to Demaray, April 25 and 28, 1938; also Cammerer to Baxter, May 4, and Baxter to Cammerer, May 8, 1938, BC, MSL. In the latter letter,

Baxter assured Cammerer that the people of Maine appreciated the great work of the park service, but, he added, this "does not prevent us from keeping our one spectacular mountain for ourselves and working in our own Down-East way."

50. Baxter to Marshall, May 7 and 23, Marshall to Baxter, May 18 and 28, 1938, BC, MSL.

51. Baxter to Demaray, April 28, and Demaray to Baxter, May 7, 1938, BC, MSL. Soon after this Demaray responded to a query on parks from Congressman Clyde H. Smith. He turned down Smith's suggestion that a national park be created at Saddleback Mountain, even when someone was apparently willing to donate needed lands. Demaray said the Katahdin area was the only national park proposed for Maine that justified consideration. See Demaray to Smith, May 29, 1938, NA, NPS, RG 79, file 0–32, Box 243.

52. *Portland Sunday Telegram and Sunday Press Herald,* July 31 and August 7, 1938. Avery sent copies of the articles to Governor Barrow's secretary. After he and the Governor read them, they were passed on to the Attorney General, who in turn sent them to Baxter. See Avery to Thomas J. Kennon, Secretary to Governor Barrows, August 18, 1938; Franz U. Burkett, Attorney General to Baxter, September 9, 1938, BSPA. Burkett and Baxter had discussed the contents earlier; see also Avery to Burkett, August 14 and September 3, 1939; Avery to Sanford Fogg, August 10, 1939; Burkett to Avery, September 20, 1939, BSPA. See also *Appalachian Trailway News,* January 1939, p. 9.

53. Baxter to Cammerer, July 6, 1938; Baxter to Yard, November 25, 1939, BC, MSL, folder 74.

54. Cammerer to Baxter, July 18, Baxter to Cammerer, August 4, 1938, NA, NPS, RG 79, file 601, Box 243. Newton B. Drury to Baxter, November 27, Baxter to Drury, December 3, 1941; also January 19, 1945; Drury to Baxter, February 19, 1945; Demaray to Baxter, August 7 and 14, Baxter to Demarary, August 12, 1941; Horace Albright to Baxter, November 12; Baxter to Dr. Jessi Nusbaum, M. R. Tillotson, and Albright, November 13, 1951; Baxter to Albright, April 10, 1952, BC, MSL.

See also George L. Collins to L. L. Bean, March 28, and to Baxter, April 14, 1944; Drury to Baxter, February 10, Baxter to Drury, February 17, 1947; Drury to Baxter, March 10, 1947, November 18 and 24, 1948, all in NA, NPS, RG 79, Box 2973.

55. Avery to Forest Commissioner Seavey, September 20, 1939, BSPA. At this time Maine was the only state not to ratify the AT Agreement. The refusal to sign was tied to a certain extent to a controversy between the Commissioner and the Patomac ATC members regarding interpretation of Maine's fire laws and the use of primus stoves on the Appalachian Trail in the state. Since 1928 the Forestry Department had considered gasoline stoves, Sterno, and similar heating devices as camp fires. See S. W. Edwards to Seavey, May 5, 1939 and to Attorney General Burkett, April 1, 1940, BSPA.

56. See Baxter to Caleb Scribner, November 24, 1950, BC, MSL. Scribner had written to Baxter about Avery's activity in the park area. "What you say about Mr. Avery is interesting," Baxter responded. "I have never seen him and recall that in the years past he was not altogether friendly. May be he has changed some of his views and I should like to meet him. Certainly I have no hostile feelings

toward him. Of course no one has any right to name places in the Park area for that is reserved for me under the Deeds of Trust."

57. Baxter to Farris, May 6, Farris to Baxter, May 19, 1952, BC, MSL.

# VII

1. *Public Laws of Maine, 1939*, ch. 6. Interestingly enough the *Maine Register* continued to list the members of the Baxter State Park Commission through 1942. Only in 1943 was the title Baxter State Park Authority used with the proper members being listed.

2. *Public Laws of Maine, 1941*, ch. 25.

3. See Baxter to George Stobie, December 18, 1942, BC, MSL. Baxter concluded this letter by saying, "With best wishes to you and the other members of the 'authority.'"

4. *Public Laws of Maine, 1949*, ch. 78.

5. Interview with Harold Dyer, July 15, 1971. During a luncheon conversation Dyer said that Baxter increasingly sought the views, and supported the arguments, of Stobie and the fish and game department.

6. Farris to Rendall, April 26, 1946, BSPA.

7. Baxter to Governor Barrows, January 3, 1939, BC, MSL.

8. Rendall and Stobie to Governor Sewall, March 19, 1941, BSPA. The budget provided for $1,500 for the park ranger; $1,000 for extra help, and $1,500 for repairs to campsites. During the 1940–41 fiscal year, $245 was collected in fees.

9. See Dyer's Report for 1941, and transmittal letter from Dyer to Cowan, January 16, 1942, BSPA. See also "Recent Developments at Katahdin," *Appalachian Trailway News*, September 1941, p. 49.

10. See "Maine Notes," *Ibid.*, September 1943, p. 1.

11. See *Resolves of Maine, 1943*, ch. 41. The legislation appropriated $1,506 to be paid to the Maine Forestry District to protect Baxter State Park. In 1945 the levy was raised to 1 1/3¢ per acre (see *Public Laws of Maine, 1945*, ch. 130); in 1949, to 3¢ (see *Public Laws of Maine, 1949*, ch. 70); in 1967, to 6¢ (see *Public Laws of Maine, 1967*, ch. 504); and in 1973, to its pro rated share of the total cost of protection for the year (see *Public Laws of Maine, 1973*, ch. 87). The cost for fiscal 1943 and 1944 was set upon the basis of 1 1/3¢ per acre on land in the Park and land which was still held by Baxter upon which he had received tax abatements. See Rendall to BSPA, June 30, 1944, BSPA.

12. See V. E. Sanborn, clerk, to members of BSPA, June 18; Rendall to Farris, October 22, 1946 (with copy of budget to support the Council request); Dyer to Farris, August 16, 1947, enclosing financial statement of BSPA for the fiscal year 1946–47, BSPA.

13. See BSPA financial statement—July 1, 1949–June 30, 1950, for Operations, Maintenance, and Baxter State Park Development, BSPA.

14. See comments of former Forest Commissioner A. D. Nutting and comments by Austin Wilkins, Chairman of Editing Committee, on an earlier draft of this chapter, BSPA.

15. Baxter to Burkett, September 19; Governor Barrows to Baxter, November

10, 1939, BC, MSL. In his letter to Burkett Baxter said that Barrows was in Idaho. He asked that Burkett and the Commissioner of Inland Fisheries and Game arrange to have Jack Grant carry the materials to Chimney Pond, "and I will be responsible for the bill."

16. See copy of "Program of The Ninth Appalachian Trail Conference, August 18–26, 1939. Held at York's Twin Pine Camps, Daicey Pond, Katahdin, Maine," BSPA. Also check *Appalachian Trailway News*, July 1939, p. 7 and January 1940, pp. 13, 18–20.

17. *Appalachian Trailway News*, January 1940, pp. 37–40.

18. See interview with Dyer, *op. cit.* A copy of the tape and a typed transcription are in the Northeast Archives of Folklore and Oral History at the University of Maine, Orono. See also *Trailway News*, January 1940, p. 39, and Avery to Dyer, August 1, 1940, BSPA, for indications that Holmes was paid by the Department of Inland Fisheries and Game.

19. *Trailway News*, p. 38. A news release of the Maine Development Commission dated August 28, 1939 was quoted.

20. No attempt has been made to document all articles on this incident. All the state's daily newspapers carried extensive coverage on the progress of the search and its aftermath. For instance, every issue of the *Daily Kennebec Journal* from July 19 through August 3 carried articles on Fendler. See Donn Fendler, *Lost on a Mountain in Maine   A Brave Boy's True Story of his Nine-Day Adventure Alone in the Mount Katahdin Wilderness, As Told to Joseph B. Egan* (Wellesley, Massachusetts: The Welles Publishing Company, Inc., 1939). See also maps on front and back covers of Fendler's book. Maine Guides E. W. York, E. W. York, Jr., Henry Soucie and Harry Kearney (then a guide at York's Twin Pine camps and later supervisor of the Park) and Forest Ranger Richard Holmes collaborated and concluded that Fendler had gone down the North Peaks Trail. See also Gower, "Fendler at Katahdin," *Appalachia*, December 1939, pp. 541–45; he thought it most likely that Fendler descended into the Northwest Basin and then followed Wassataquoik Stream, but he did not rule out the North Peaks route. Avery, "Donn Fendler Lost at Katahdin," *Appalachian Trailway News*, January 1940, pp. 21–23, argued for the North Peaks route; Vincent DeFelice, "What Ever Happened to Donn Fendler?" *Yankee*, October 1972, pp. 78–83, 174–76, 179–80, 183–84, argued persuasively that Fendler descended into the Klondike and then turned downstream in the Wassataquoik drainage. All of these individuals were extremely knowledgeable about the Katahdin region. At this distance it is difficult to determine who was correct.

21. *Portland Sunday Telegram*, July 7, 1940 and February 16, 1941, articles by Jean Stephenson of the Appalachian Trail Conference. After the ATC meeting at Daicey Pond in 1939, a metal cylinder with notebook and pencil was placed at Baxter Peak so those making the ascent could register. The ATC estimated that 10,000 people visited the Katahdin area in 1940. On installation of the cylinder see Dyer to Stobie, June 22, 1940, BSPA.

22. Minutes of BSPA meeting, December 17, 1941, BSPA. See also *Appalachian Trailway News*, September 1943, p. 1. In the interview already cited, Dyer said that the Authority had a difficult time evicting the determined and stubborn William Tracy. Finally the Authority ordered Dyer and Fred Pitman

to snowshoe to Russell Pond and burn the camps. When they left the main camp standing and placed Tracy's personal possessions in it, the attorney general was furious because they hadn't completely razed the site. Only the intercession of the other Authority members saved his job, Dyer stated.

23. Rendall to Stobie, April 4, 1941, BSPA.

24. Rendall to The Director, National Park Service, March 2; Wirth to Rendall, March 8, 1940; Rendall to Regional Director, National Park Service, June 14; E. M. Lisle, Acting Director, to Rendall, June 20 and 21, 1940; Lisle to Director, June 21; memo for the Regional Director, from Wirth, July 1; Daniel Blaney, Inspector, to Regional Director, June 17, and Fred T. Johnson, Acting Regional Director, to Rendall, July 15, 1940, NA, NPS, RG 79, file 601, box 243.

25. Rendall to Governor Barrows, Stobie, and Burkett, June 15, 1940, BSPA. This was in reference to a trip to the Park with Baxter for a meeting at which "to properly instruct Harold Dyer as to the detail of his duties, to make definite arrangements for the administration of the Katahdin Stream Camp . . ." Why Governor Barrows is listed is unknown; it was probably either done out of courtesy or the fact that Rendall forgot that the Governor was no longer a member of the governing group.

26. See Dyer interview, op. cit.; Dyer to Rendall, June 12; Dyer: suggestions for CCC work; Dyer to Stobie, June 22, 1940, BSPA.

27. Dyer to Avery, July 29, Avery to Dyer, August 1, and to Burkett, March 19, 1940, BSPA; Appalachian Trailway News, July 1939, p. 4. See Dyer interview, op. cit., for additional comments.

28. Merle Whitcomb, "Wassataquoik Lake Excursion, August 31 to September 7, 1940," and Gower, "Trail Work at Katahdin," Appalachia, December 1940, pp. 261–62 and 267. See also Dyer, "Report to Messrs. Stobie, Burkett and Rendall on the Baxter State Park," undated but September 1940, BSPA, p. 11; Appalachian Trailway News, January 1941, pp. 6–7; Avery was again critical of conditions in the park area and slighted the AMC's "temporary board signs." Also see Dyer interview, op. cit. Dyer liked and respected Gower.

29. Rendall to Burkett, September 19, 1940; Dyer, Report cited in note 28; also Dyer Interview, op. cit. (Unless other materials are used no page citations will be made in the discussion of the twenty-five page report which follows.)

30. Frank H. Speed, Secretary, Chamber of Commerce, Millinocket, to Katahdin State Park Commission, August 1; Rendall to Speed, August 8, 1940, BSPA.

31. On the program in Maine see William H. Martin, "The Pittman-Robertson Program in Maine: Where Has it Been? What Has it Done?" Maine Fish and Game, Fall 1972, pp. 6–8; "Quarterly Progress Report Wildlife Research Project 4-R-Maine, April 1, 1941, BSPA; and Report of the Commissioner of Inland Fisheries and Game, 1950, pp. 37–40.

32. Nathan Warren Fellows, Jr., Leader, Completion Report, Project 4-R, July 1, 1942, BSPA. See also Dyer, "Preliminary Plan for Wildlife Management on Baxter State Park," unpublished MS thesis, University of Maine, Orono, Maine, November, 1948.

33. See Lester Brown, Chief Warden, Department of Inland Fisheries and Game, to Dyer, June 10; Dyer to Farris, June 12, Farris to Dyer, June 23, 1948,

BSPA. Brown claimed possession of the buildings and equipment and warned Dyer away. Farris played the role of mediator.

34. See Dyer, "Preliminary Plan," *op. cit.*, pp. 58–61.

35. Jean Stephenson, editor of *Appalachian Trailway News*, to Cowan, January 10, and Cowan to Stephenson, January 14, 1942, BSPA. Stephenson asked permission to publish Cowan's letter to Avery of September 20, 1941. See also *Appalachian Trailway News*, January 1942, pp. 11–12.

36. Dyer to Cowan, February 21, 1942, an untitled, undated report in BSPA files. See also Dyer interview, *op. cit.;* Paul Wendt, Editor Colonial *Esso Road News* to Everett F. Greaton, Maine Development Commission, December 4, 1941, BSPA. Wendt wanted to know what would be done to the road before the 1942 season so he could prepare his copy properly. He noted that the keeper of Ripogenus Dam had told him "some women and timid drivers [had arrived] about out of their heads after having been over the road."

37. Charles W. Blood, "Katahdin Trails," *Appalachia*, December, 1941, pp. 555–56. Blood explained that the Appalachian Trail Conference maintained the Hunt Trail, and W. F. Tracy did those out of Russell Pond, so no one was left for the others; thus the AMC assumed the responsibility.

38. See the memorandum of this agreement, on AMC stationery, dated June 4, 1941 with Dyer's signature, in BSPA. It is reproduced in his report for that year. See also David S. Lovejoy, Trailmaster, AMC trail crew, 1941, "A Vacation with Pay," *Appalachia*, June 1942, pp. 123–25, for an interesting account of trail work done in July, 1941. See also Dyer Interview, *op. cit.* Dyer then said: "It was unfortunate that I gave them the go ahead to do it [rebuild the shelter in the fragile environment at Davis Pond]."

39. See Baxter to Cowan, September 25; Cowan to Greaton and to Stillman E. Woodman, State Highway Commission, December 23, Woodman to Cowan, December 27, 1941, BSPA. *Appalachian Trailway News*, September 1942, p. 1.

40. *Resolves of Maine, 1943*, ch. 18; *Public Laws of Maine, 1943*, ch. 71.

41. Austin Chase, "The New Davis Pond Shelter," *Appalachia*, December 1942, pp. 268–69. A picture of the shelter is opposite p. 268.

42. See Herbert Wienert, "August Camp, Katahdin, 1946," *Appalachia*, December 1946, pp. 259–60.

43. Gower to Baxter, October 20 and 26; Stobie to Cowan, November 10; Cowan to Gower, December 1 and 15; and Gower to Cowan, December 8, 1943, BSPA, in which he quoted extensively from letters Dyer to Gower, May 2, 15, and 19; Gower to Dyer, June 4, Dyer to Gower, July 30, 1941 and February 25, 1942; Rendall to Gower, August 17, 1943; Gower to Baxter, April 5, and Baxter to Gower, April 12, 1941, in which he wrote: "I have your letter of April fifth and have read it with much interest. . . . I am going to Augusta on Monday to talk with the Baxter Park Authority and will take your letter with me."

44. Cowan to Stobie, Rendall, and Baxter, September 5, 1944, BSPA.

45. *Appalachian Trailway News*, May 1942, p. 26.

46. See Dyer to Rendall, April 14, and memorandum Gowan to Rendall and Stobie, April 24, 1942, BSPA.

47. Dyer asked for a change of his 1-A draft classification, but the members of the Authority would not support his case. See Ralph E. Dyer, Clerk, Local

Board No. 4, South Portland, to Harold Dyer, May 30; Harold Dyer to Rendall, June 2; Cowan to Harold Dyer, June 5, 1942, BSPA.

After his entry into the service the Authority rejected Dyer's request for vacation pay for the time he had not taken. His use of the park vehicle for personal trips, it was argued, had used up any vacation pay accruing to him. See Rendall to Dyer, July 22, 1942, BSPA.

48. See report of Dyer dated July 3, 1942, BSPA, in which he noted that Pitman would be earning $24.42 per week or about $3.49 per day. Shortly after Dyer left, Pitman wrote the Authority and said he had been promised $4.00 per day. George Stobie, writing for the Authority, rejected Pitman's request for the increase. He had not been told of the increase by Dyer, he said, and would have to wait until another meeting had been held. See Pitman to BSPA, July 24, and Stobie to Pitman, July 28, 1942, BSPA.

49. Pitman to BSPA, July 3, 1942, BSPA. Pitman did add a suggestion for the erection of an elaborate and attractive sign at the forks of the Togue Pond-Greenville road and for the possible development of horse trails connecting Roaring Brook, South Branch Ponds, and Sourdnahunk Lake. In 1978 the cluster of signs at the junction indicated above had not been improved for 36 years.

50. Rendall to Pitman, July 8; Tracy to Rendall, July 10 and 30, and to Cowan, July 30 and August 13, 1942; BSPA to Tracy, August 25, 1942, BSPA.

51. See Rendall to Major Crowell, March 31, 1943, BSPA.

52. Rendall to Pitman, May 4, 1943; Pitman to Cowan, August 5, 1944, BSPA. See also *Appalachian Trailway News*, May 1943, p. 15; September 1945, pp. 27, 29–30. In August 1944 a MATC trail crew spent some time at Katahdin working on trails. The cylinder on top of the mountain was replaced.

53. See *Portland Sunday Telegram*, February 16, 1941; Dyer, report for 1941; Jean Stephenson, "Who builds a trail finds labor that is rest," *Appalachia*, December 1944, p. 254; Jean Stephenson "Maine Appalachian Trail Work Party," *Appalachia*, December 1946, p. 275; and *Appalachian Trailway News*, January 1947, p. 10.

54. *Appalachian Trailway News*, September 1943, p. 27.

55. George W. Outerbridge, "Trip to Traveler Mountain, Maine, September 2 to 9, 1944," *Appalachia*, December 1944, pp. 243–45; Baxter to Scribner, August 3, and to Cowan, September 6, 1944, BC, MSL. In his letter to Scribner, Baxter expressed keen anticipation about a planned trip to Lower South Branch Pond with Mr. and Mrs. Scribner: "I shall pay all the bills. You can get the eggs, bacon, flour, etc., and I shall pay for them. Also I will bring some nice canned fruit, peaches, pineapples and some canned beef and tongue. We will live well; beer if you like it. Always I have wanted to see that region. Now is the time."

For later trips, see Baxter to Scribner, August 28 and 29, 1945; October 16 and 24 and December 4, 1946; and to Laura and Caleb Scribner, September 18, 1954, BC, MSL. In the last letter listed, Baxter wrote: "You and I have been together these many years and I value your broad and generous attitudes toward our Park, yours and mine. You have been with me from the first . . . Well do I recall how we had those trips together through the woods, over the lakes. They were perfect."

56. *Ibid.* note 44 above, BSPA. See also Baxter to Cowan, September 6, 1944, BC, MSL. Baxter was noncommital concerning Cowan's suggestions.

57. *Bangor Daily News,* June 24, 25, 26, and 28, 1944; *Daily Kennebec Journal,* June 24, 26, 27, 28, and 30, 1944.

58. Stobie to Rendall, February 11, 1946; minutes of meeting of BSPA, February 19, 1946; Dyer to BSPA, March 26, with report dated April 1, 1946, enclosed, BSPA.

59. Rendall to Farris, April 17, 1946, BSPA. The letter served as the minutes of the Authority meeting held on April 10, 1946.

60. *Appalachian Trailway News,* September 1946, p. 27. Report of Harold Dyer, December 15, 1946, BSPA.

61. *Appalachian Trailway News,* September 1944, p. 27, and May 1946, p. 17. Myron Avery bemoaned the loss of wilderness because of this construction.

62. See Robley W. Nash, *Damage by the Bronze Birch Borer,* Maine Forest Service Circular No. 4, May 1942, and Bulletin No. 13, 1943.

63. *Appalachian Trailway News,* September 1944, p. 27.

64. See E. J. Jones, Great Northern, to Rendall, June 17, 1947; Farris to Stobie, June 20, 1947, BSPA. A copy of the lease is in the BSPA files.

65. See Dyer's report, June 14, 1950, BSPA. See also Baxter to Stobie, November 10, 1948, BC, MSL. Baxter alludes to the use of lumber from the old logging camp and was happy Dyer would have a comfortable camp for his family.

66. The use of packhorses was resumed later and continued on a very limited basis into the 1950s. Edward Werler, the park ranger at Chimney Pond, managed them in the first part of that decade.

67. Dyer to BSPA, April 17; Farris to Dyer, April 30, 1948, BSPA.

68. See minutes of BSPA meetings, June 23, September 2 and December 7, 1949, BSPA.

69. Dyer's report, June 14, 1950, BSPA.

70. *Ibid.,* p. 11.

71. Dyer to Farris, June 7, Farris to Dyer, June 13, 1950, BSPA.

72. Dyer to Farris, June 14, 1950, and Dyer's accompanying report.

73. See copies of State of Maine, Department of Personnel Classification Questionnaires for these employees, dated February 17, 20 and 21, 1950, BSPA. A vacancy for the Trout Brook area was included.

# VIII

1. Baxter to Scribner, July 18, 1945, Baxter-Scribner Letters, BC, MSL.

2. See comments by former Chairman, Baxter State Park Authority, A. D. Nutting, January 1979, on an earlier draft of this chapter, BSPA.

3. Maine State Park Commission (in cooperation with the National Park Service), "A Recreation Plan for Maine—1956," p. 9. For Baxter's reactions see *Portland Press Herald,* June 24, 1957.

4. Baxter to Nutting, December 22, 1956, BSPA; *Bangor Daily News,* December 26, 1956; PAS report, "The Organization and Administration of the Government of the State of Maine," dated June 12, 1956.

5. Baxter to the BSP Commission, February 16, 1967, copies in BC and BSPA. In much of his correspondence Baxter continued to use the term "Commission" rather than "Authority." See also Legislative Document No. 460, 103rd Legislature, BP, MSL; Wilkins to Ronald Speers, February 21, and to Baxter, March 3, 1967, BSPA; and Maine newspapers for the period.

6. Baxter to Wilkins, December 28, 1967 and also October 26, 1961, BSPA. In the first letter listed, Baxter wrote: "You and I will keep in touch with one another for we have much in common and I depend upon you for advice and assistance."

7. In reply to a letter from Commissioner Nutting suggesting that some arrangement be made with the Bangor Hydro-Electric Company to receive payment for wood to be cut from park property, which would be flooded if the level of Matagamon Lake were raised, Baxter replied: "My thought is to leave things just as they are until something acute develops and until they begin their construction. It will be a pity to try and solve all these problems years in advance for we do not know what the situation will be when action is taken. Let us hold fast to what we have and leave the future to be settled in the future." See Baxter to Nutting, February 17, 1956, BC, MSL.

8. Taylor to Wilkins, June 24, 1966, BSPA. Taylor discussed the old farm buildings at Trout Brook Farm, "which are only a headache to us as they are now. I have it in my six year plan to install a horseback riding stable there but that will cost money and no doubt the buildings will be gone before we ever get around to it."

9. Edward I. Heath, *Comparison of Recreational Development Plans for a Northern Maine Wilderness Tract*, Maine Agricultural Experiment Station, University of Maine, Bulletin 628, October, 1964.

10. Typical was Baxter's reaction to possible construction of a campground at Fowler Pond. Taylor, after discussing the topic with him wrote: "I could not get much out of him about the Fowler Pond project. He said no more camps. I think he meant cabins. I think he had forgotten what he said last June." Taylor to Wilkins, August 29, 1960, BSPA. An example of Baxter's role in controlling use of the roads came in 1956 when the Chairman asked him if a timber concern exercising cutting rights in land west of T6R9 could use the existing road in the latter township. Baxter had no objection to issuing a temporary, revocable permit, provided the route was not changed or any trees cut and that the concern using the road be responsible for fires. He thought that the user should sign an agreement and that it should be approved by the Attorney General. "With the above restrictions and limitations I believe it will be neighborly for us to allow this." See Baxter to Nutting, July 13, 1956, BP, MSL.

11. In 1965 the Authority issued a new brochure, which included a letter from Baxter on the origins of the Park. Permission was gained from Baxter to use the letter and use funds in a trust fund to pay for it. When the initial printing was exhausted, Austin Wilkins ordered 35,000 more, the cost to be shared by the Maine Forest Service and the Department of Economic Development. Wilkins acted "on the initial authorization of Governor Baxter," and did not think it necessary to get permission anew, "feeling that he might become confused; and I saw

no reason why his initial approval wouldn't justify the reprinting." See Wilkins to Cranshaw, State Controller, November 4, 1965, BSPA.

12. In the late fifties, after some discussion, the Authority and Baxter renewed permission for a University of Connecticut School of Forestry faculty member and students to conduct scientific work in the Park. After it was completed, Baxter wrote: "I am pleased we did not forbid him [the professor] to come into the Park with his young foresters. At first I thought we should not do so but when you and Mr. Nutting talked with me I was convinced you both were right."

13. Nutting to Baxter, September 21, 1956, BC, MSL. Baxter wrote on top of the letter "Important. Give to Secretary of State for his file." The quote appearing in the text appears on the bottom of the letter with the date September 22, 1956. The situation so frustrated some rangers in the Park that one of them, at the end of a letter in which he made suggestions for improvement of park operations, added "I am wondering if next fall we couldn't have two meetings, one with just park personnel and Commission where things could be discussed without weighing Mr. Baxter's reactions." See Ralph G. Dolley to Wilkins, September 19, 1958, BSPA.

14. However, in 1949 Baxter had given the AMC permission to erect a tablet in memory of Leroy Dudley. See Rachel Lowell Lowe, "Dedication of the Memorial Tablet to Leroy Dudley," *Appalachia*, December 1949, pp. 524–25.

15. See Baxter to Taylor, May 10, 1965, BC, MSL. Baxter mentioned a complaint from University students at Orono about the bunkhouses and added: "You are taking care of everything and should not be disturbed by suggestions from the outside"; Wilkins to Baxter, August 24, Baxter to Wilkins, August 27, 1965; BSPA. See also letters from Wilkins to various state officials, AMC officials, relatives of Ralph Heath and others regarding the ceremony dated August 18, 1965, BSPA. See *Maine Sunday Telegram*, August 22, 1965, for a picture of the plaque and its wording; Baxter to Speers and to Dubord, August 30, 1965, BSPA. See also Dubord to Baxter, September 2, 1965, BC, MSL.

16. Wilkins to Governor Curtis, December 19, 1967, BSPA. Even after his death the Authority was reluctant to allow memorials in the name of others. In 1970 when a Massachusetts man sought permission to install a plaque on top of Fort Mountain in memory of those who died in the crash of a USAAF C54 airplane in 1944, the request was denied. Chairman Wilkins explained that the request "was not consistent with the wishes of the late donor of the Park, . . . that everything be kept strictly in the name of Baxter." See Wilkins to Clarence E. Le-Bell, April 24, 1970, BSPA.

A similar situation occurred in 1965 when the Authority refused to allow the ashes of the two young Mott children who died in the Park to be scattered there. See Richard Dubord to Pelletier Funeral Home, August 12, and Wilkins to The Reverend Carl C. Allen, August 16, 1965, BSPA. See also *Kennebec Daily Journal*, August 13, 1965.

17. See Roland Cobb to Baxter, April 24, 1962, BSPA. Wilkins had relayed Baxter's request for the services of Supervisor Arthur Rogers whenever he wanted to visit the Park. Cobb indicated that he would do what he could to provide the services of Rogers, David Priest, or other employees of the Commission, but

noted that they were busy men, with large responsibilities. He asked that Baxter let him know of his needs in advance so he could make needed preparations; see also Baxter to Cobb, August 4, 1953, BC, MSL; Taylor, report for August 1953, BSPA. Taylor went to Augusta to drive Albright, Baxter, and Commissioner Nutting to the Park and surrounding areas for a period of five days.

18. In 1965 when queried by Wilkins about construction of a new camp at Togue Pond Headquarters without approval of the Authority or the Bureau of Public Improvements as required by law, Taylor replied: "About the new camp, yes, we did build a new camp. It is a replacement for an old wood shed that dates back to Harold Dyer's time and was built out of old lumber salvaged from an old lumber camp. (I understand we do not have to have a permit to build a replacement.) To be sure. It looked so good when we got it built that we insolated (sic) it, put in bunks and Rodney is now living in it. If you remember I have been asking for a crew camp for here at Togue Pond for at least five years and have always been refused. I have been talking about it for ten years. Hilda & I are tired of taking boarders the year round in this old camp where there is not room enough for our own needs. I talked this over with Governor Baxter when he was up this fall and he said to go ahead and build it. I had all the lumber, materials and labor to do so without extra cost." Taylor often knew of Baxter's thoughts and actions with regard to land purchases and like matters before members of the Authority. In 1962, for instance, when he made his last purchase Baxter discussed the matter with Taylor. Chairman Wilkins's comment on this is illuminating: "I was pleased that Governor Baxter was able to visit you and explain his success in acquiring additional land from the Great Northern. I personally had not had any direct report regarding this land transaction from either the Great Northern or Governor Baxter."

19. Baxter to Taylor, July 11, 1966, BC, MSL.

20. In 1967 when Baxter was setting up the final terms of his will and the method by which his desires to improve forestry practices in Maine might be carried out, he consulted Nutting. See Nutting to Baxter, March 27 and December 11, Baxter to Nutting, October 6 and December 28, 1967, BP, MSL. Included also is a draft copy of a proposal for "Baxter Park & Governing Board" prepared by Nutting.

21. "Baxter State Park Authority to the Committee on Appropriations and Financial Affairs of the 97th Legislature," undated, but 1955, BSPA.

22. From time to time, when the chairman of the Authority was faced with conflicting schedules, he asked one of the other members, or more often a member of his own staff, to fill in for him and speak for the Authority. This was often done at park ranger training session in the spring of each year. In 1967 when Commissioner Wilkins asked Deputy Commissioner Holt of the Forest Service to substitute for him at a meeting of the Wilderness Society at Camp Phoenix on Nesowadnehunk Lake and to answer questions regarding the Park which might arise, he was chided by Attorney General Erwin. Erwin argued: "This is exactly the blurring of the dividing line between the Baxter State Park Authority and the Maine Forest Service which we talked about." See Wilkins to Erwin and Speers, September 11; Erwin to Wilkins, September 13, 1967, BSPA. Wilkins

suggested that the others go and act officially for the Authority. He had suggested that Holt fill in for him "purely from his knowledge of some of the mechanics involved in operating and managing Baxter State Park. I thought he might be familiar with some of the detail questions which might arise." He did not ask Holt to *act* for the Authority.

23. George B. Emerson, Jr. to Erwin, March 17, 1970 (two letters), **BSPA**.

24. Erwin to Emerson, March 18, 1970, BSPA.

25. See State of Maine, Department of Personnel, Classification Questionnaire filled out by Harold Dyer on February 21, 1951, BSPA. In this questionnaire Dyer, in effect, spelled out the duties of the supervisor.

26. Taylor, report for August 1950, BSPA.

27. Ralph W. Farris to Robert H. Dyer and Ralph L. Robinson, Ranger, August 4, 1950; also Nutting to Farris, July 26, Farris to Nutting, July 27, 1950; minutes of meeting of BSPA, August 2, 1950; Robert Dyer to Farris, August 6; Robinson to Farris, August 5, Farris to Robinson and Dyer, August 15, 1950, BSPA. Dyer accepted the dismissal without argument; Robinson appealed and lost. Both were offered jobs in either the Maine Forest Service or the Department of Inland Fisheries and Game. See also Stobie to Pitman, August 15, 1950, BSPA.

28. See *Appalachia*, December 1950, p. 253; *Appalachian Trailway News*, September 1950, pp. 40–41. Also see comments by former chairman BSPA Nutting, 1979, on an earlier draft of this chapter, BSPA.

29. Harry Kearney, supervisor, to BSPA, June 26, 1969, BSPA. While praising Taylor as a man "who has done a job long and well, and who became old and tired trying to do a big job with too few personnel and too little money," he noted that Taylor had been lax in permitting highway crews to open gravel pits along the roads in the Park, allowing timber companies to leave their hovels and camps standing after work was done, and allowing violations of cutting rights.

30. See Taylor to Baxter, August 25, Baxter to Taylor, August 26, 1967, BC, MSL.

31. See minutes of BSPA meeting, April 30, 1968, BSPA.

32. Special Notice to BSP personnel from Wilkins, September 26, 1968, BSPA. Kearney had been one of the three finalists with Caverly and Sargent when the former was chosen. (Caverly returned to the rank of ranger, but was again named supervisor in the 1970s.)

## IX

1. See comments by former Chairman Nutting, of BSPA, 1979, on an early draft of this chapter, BSPA.

2. Baxter to Nutting, December 22, Nutting to Baxter, December 27, 1956, BC, MSL.

3. See Wilkins to Baxter, February 6, 1959 and BSPA statement to the Committee on Appropriations and Financial Affairs of the 99th Legislature, February 10, 1959, BSPA. In his letter to Baxter, Wilkins noted that the expansion and capital improvement request had been withdrawn and added: "You will recall we discussed this over the telephone and I am complying with your wish."

4. See appropriation requests for 1953–54 and 1954–55 in BSPA files.

5. BSPA statement to the Committee on Appropriations and Financial Affairs of the 97th Legislature, undated, BSPA.

6. *Ibid.*, 99th Legislature, February 10, 1959, BSPA.

7. *Ibid.*, 100th Legislature, January 25, 1961, BSPA.

8. Taylor to Wilkins, June 7, Wilkins to Taylor, June 20; Taylor to Wilkins, June 24 and November 8, Wilkins to Taylor, November 20, 1962, BSPA. The old Jeep was finally sold for $50.

9. Wilkins to Baxter, January 4, Baxter to Wilkins, February 15; Wilkins to Baxter, February 23 and April 11, and Baxter to Wilkins, April 24, 1962, BSPA.

10. *Ibid.*, note 7 above. See also Executive Council Orders #579 in 1959 and #617 in 1960.

11. See memoranda, Wilkins to Cobb and Hancock, June 12 and July 24, 1961, BSPA. In the first memorandum Wilkins said he had drawn the interest to hire the rangers and said: "This was a necessity and I believe we agreed this should be done if funds were available." On the same day he wrote to Baxter but did not mention his action. On July 24, he wrote: "I was able to get him [Baxter] to agree to draw $2,000 to carry Myrle Scott through the winter months and carry on the employment of the three students during the summer to serve as assistants to rangers at Roaring Brook, Katahdin Stream and South Branch Pond."

12. Baxter to Wilkins, February 15, 1962, BC, MSL. In the same place see a copy of financial information sent to Baxter by Wilkins on January 23, 1962. In 1959 when the idea of placing Myrle Scott on a year-round basis arose, Baxter agreed to pay half the salary if the Authority obtained the remainder through the Executive Council from the contingent fund. Chairman Wilkins, after discussing the matter with Governor Clauson and State Finance Commissioner Raymond Mudge, rejected the idea since he felt a bad precedent would be created. Wilkins noted that in his discussion with the Appropriations Committee of the last legislature all had agreed that there would be no increase in personnel services or extension of time of rangers. "It is most difficult to justify winter work since we have no plans or materials for the construction of improvements at any of the existing camp grounds." See Wilkins to Baxter, November 3, 1959, BSPA. See also memorandum, Wilkins to Baxter, February 23 and letter, February 26; and Mrs. Kathryn Douglas, Clerk, Department of State and Governor's Council, to Baxter, March 27, 1962, BC, MSL. Mrs. Douglas enclosed a copy of Council Order 802 approved March 21, 1962, accepting Baxter's check and transferring the funds to the Trust Fund. See Wilkins to Baxter, April 11 and to Cobb, April 24, 1962, BSPA; Baxter to Wilkins, April 24 and September 27, 1962, BC, MSL.

13. Wilkins to Executive Council member John L. Baxter, Jr., March 23, 1964, BSPA. See also Wilkins to Baxter, January 27, and to Richard Dubord, January 15, 1965, BSPA.

14. See Executive Council Order No. 281, November 7, 1945, BSPA.

15. *Private and Special Laws of Maine, 1961*, ch. 21.

16. *Ibid.*, 1965, ch. 30.

17. *Ibid.*, 1943, ch. 1. See Baxter to Cranshaw, February 8 and March 22, 1968; copies in BSPA and BC, MSL.

18. Council Order 939, April 24, 1968; Memorandum, Erwin to Cranshaw,

April 3, 1968; copy of Journal entry for account 5093, dated April 25, 1968; John Patterson, Research Assistant, to Erwin, November 11, 1969, BSPA.

19. BSP, Financial Statement of Trust Fund Accounts, June 30, 1972, BSPA.

20. Wilkins to Cobb and Hancock, July 24, 1961, BSPA.

21. Wilkins to Haskell, February 22, 1961, BSPA.

22. Baxter to Governor Reed and Executive Council, July 12, and to Frank S. Carpenter, July 19, 1961; BC, MSL.

23. Wilkins to Baxter, September 13, Baxter to Wilkins, September 18, 1961, BC, MSL.

24. Copy of letter Baxter to Wilkins, September 27, and to Hancock, October 9, 1962, BC, MSL. Baxter sent Hancock a copy of the letter to Wilkins apparently with the intention of underlining or emphasizing his desire not to have trust fund income used.

25. Memorandum, Cross to Wilkins, March 19, 1965, BSPA. Cross estimated income from the trust fund to be $45,000 annually.

26. Taylor to Wilkins, March 8, 1965, BSPA.

27. Dubord to Robert MacEachern, of the *Lincoln* (Maine) *News*, September 19, 1966, BSPA.

28. Wilkins to Erwin, Speers, and Cranshaw, July 1, 1967, BSPA. Wilkins noted that a contract with L. C. Andrews, the firm selling pre-cut log dwellings, had to be cancelled when Baxter rescinded his permission to withdraw $22,000 in trust income for the headquarters. Baxter, he said, "has other plans regarding how we are to establish some kind of headquarters for Supervisor Helon Taylor"; Wilkins to Baxter, September 6, and drafts of letter not mailed by Baxter to Wilkins, September 8, 1967, BC, MSL. Wilkins had assured Baxter by phone that the trust fund would not be disturbed. In the draft letter Baxter said trust monies were not to be used to pay Sargent and that he wanted the monies to accumulate "to build a fund for a special undisclosed purchase." He said he wanted Wilkins and his associates on the Authority to carry out his wishes. He added: "When my plans are disclosed I am sure that those of you who have charge of the park will be glad to carry out my wishes."

29. Cranshaw to Baxter, March 18; and Executive Council Contingent Allocation #1037, May 15, 1968, BC, MSL.

30. Memorandum, Cross to Wilkins, September 22, 1970, BSPA.

31. Memorandum of Status of Expendable Funds, from Cross to Wilkins, March 13, 1970, BSPA.

# X

1. See Attorney General Farris to Weldon B. Astle of Millinocket, August 25, 1950, BSPA. Astle applied for a ranger's job and was asked to obtain an application from the Personnel Board in Augusta. Also see Taylor's Report for August 1950, BSPA. He reported that several individuals had applied for the job which had been awarded to Myrle Scott.

2. *Public Laws of Maine, 1961*, ch. 1.

3. Henry Trial, Personnel Officer, Forestry Department, to Harry Kearney, March 13, 1969, BSPA.

4. See Taylor to Wilkins, October 9, 1958, BSPA: That year, funds were available to keep four men all winter. "As it stands now, Myrle Scott, Tom Sprague, Owen Grant if he is able and Ed Werler [who] has not made up his mind as yet, will be the ones to stay on this winter. None of the others want to so if Ed does not stay we may have to hire an outsider."

5. Memorandum Cross to Wilkins, September 22, 1970, BSPA.

6. Taylor's report for the year 1958, BSPA.

7. Taylor to Wilkins, October 22, Wilkins to Taylor, October 18, 1963, BSPA. The Governor and Council had approved a grant of $2,000 to allow the additional full-time person besides Taylor to serve during the winter season, as Darling had done the previous year. When Heath lost his life Rodney Sargent was selected.

8. Taylor's report for August 1950, BSPA. Apparently he made the appointment without consulting the Authority. "I hesitated about hireing (sic) them but they have both worked for me before, have had experience in the sporting business and are both good workers. If I did not feel sure that they would set a good example for the others I would not have hired them."

9. For discussion of the retirement party in Pitman's honor at Millinocket, which was attended by Baxter and many others, see *Bangor Daily News,* November 12, 1954.

10. See Scott to Wilkins, May 7, and Wilkins to Scott, May 15, 1961, BSPA. Scott was reluctant to leave Baxter State Park even though financial and living conditions would be better elsewhere. He proposed that a position such as chief ranger be created between the rangers and the supervisor. "His duties would be much like mine have been in the past few years: maintaining the busiest campground; taking charge of special work projects; assisting the supervisor with the office work, especially at the end of the campground season; and conducting winter trips in the park." The possibility of obtaining a position such as this when vacancies occurred would give rangers incentive to work hard, Scott felt. Wilkins was sympathetic but said the money to do so was not available. The topic would be discussed and money requested from future legislatures. Scott had worked all winter during 1959–60 and 1960–61 with funds supplied by the Governor and Executive Council. See Wilkins to Scott, December 15, 1961, BSPA. Scott had done extremely well on the state examination for the state park position. He remained on the Baxter Park payroll until April 1 with funds supplied by Baxter.

11. Minutes, meeting of BSPA, March 14, 1958, BSPA.

12. Taylor to Wilkins, April 3, and Wilkins to Taylor, April 7, 1959, BSPA. Taylor noted that Tom Sprague, who had been at Chimney Pond the previous summer, had first wanted to stay there when offered the vacancy at Abol created when Rodney Sargent went into the Army, but had changed his mind. Wilkins meanwhile had offered the job at Abol to Nicholas Barth, a recent college graduate, who had been hired when Taylor and Wilkins met in Augusta. Taylor assigned Barth to Chimney Pond. "I do not see how we could refuse Tom that choice when he has been here a year and has a family and the new man is single. A younger man is better for Chimney Pond anyway." Also see Taylor to Wilkins, April 9, 1959. Taylor here left the final decision to Wilkins, but stuck by his argument. "I feel that if Mr. Barth is not able to handle the Chimney Pond job he

is not what we need on this Park." See also W. E. Jackson to Taylor, September 13, Taylor to Jackson, September 17 and to Wilkins, September 26, 1959, BSPA. Taylor was pleased to get the letter since it was exactly what he needed to "prove that my decision is right. Thanks a million." See Wilkins to Taylor, October 15 and 22, 1959, BSPA. This was the first time Taylor had dismissed a ranger. Wilkins was able to convince Barth that it would be better for him to resign rather than go through the formal appeals process of the Personnel Board in an attempt to retain his job. See Wilkins to Barth, October 23, and Barth to Wilkins, October 15, 1959, BSPA. Wilkins did not object to Taylor firing Barth; he objected to the way it was done since proper Personnel Board procedures were not followed.

13. See Wilkins to Taylor, April 4, and to Hancock, April 8, 1960, BSPA.

14. Taylor's report for July 1956, BSPA.

15. *Ibid.*, May 1957, BSPA.

16. Wilkins to N.E.T. & T. Co., October 5, 1959, BSPA.

17. Wilkins to Taylor, October 22, 1963; Kearney to BSPA, September 1, and Wilkins to Mrs. Helen Gifford, October 21, 1969, BSPA.

18. Taylor to Wilkins, December 30, 1961, Wilkins to Taylor, January 4, and to Baxter, October 5, 1962, BSPA.

19. Wilkins to Taylor, April 8, 1960; Wilkins to Werler, June 20, 1962, BSPA. Wilkins had met with State Parks Director Larry Stuart to discuss the issue. See also Taylor to Wilkins, January 11, 1962, BSPA. Taylor quoted from a letter he had received from Baxter.

20. Baxter to Nutting, June 18, 1952, BP, MSL.

21. Wilkins to Taylor, January 20, 1960, BSPA. Wilkins asked Taylor not to wear his uniform until official standards were adopted. See also agenda of Annual Training School for Baxter State Park Rangers, Great Northern Hotel, Millinocket, May 2–3, 1960.

22. See typed copies, undated, of "CONDITIONS OF HIRE Baxter State Park" and "PRINCIPLES AND PRACTICES IN PUBLIC CONTACT Baxter State Park" in BSPA files. No other copies of work rules or conditions of hire exist for the period before 1969. See Taylor's report for March 1960, BSPA: "March 21st Ranger Scott and I went to Orono and attended the Maine Forestry School that day, the 22nd and the forenoon of the 23rd. It was a very interesting school and I feel that we got a lot out of it. Then March 31st I went to Orono again and attended the State Park Commission School which was also very interesting to me. That makes at least ten times I have attended a school at the University of Maine and still they have not given me a Doctor's degree."

23. Minutes, BSPA meeting, January 22, 1958; also "Baxter State Park," report of William Whitman, May 4–5, 1958, BSPA.

24. "Minutes of Meeting Spring Baxter State Park Ranger School of Instruction, Millinocket, Maine, May 4, 1959" and "Annual Training School for Baxter State Park Rangers, Great Northern Hotel—Millinocket, May 2–3, 1960, BSPA. Chairman Wilkins conducted both schools. In 1960 a cram course on first aid was presented.

25. Report of Rodney H. Sargent, ranger II, Baxter State Park, for the year 1964, to Taylor, January 6, 1965, BSPA. Curiously, none of Taylor's reports for the year list these training sessions.

26. Taylor to Wilkins, January 11, 1962, BSPA. Taylor cited a Wilkins letter of January 8, 1962, which is not available.

27. Wilkins to Baxter, May 16, 1963, BSPA. See also Taylor to Baxter, December 7, 1967, BC, MSL. Baxter had asked Taylor, after the latter's retirement, for a list of park employees for his Christmas list. Taylor, in his response, listed them according to loyalty and length of service. Taylor considered Ellsworth Damon at South Branch Pond *"the* very best Ranger on our Park."

28. Taylor's report for March 1958, BSPA.

29. *Ibid.,* August 1960, BSPA.

30. *Ibid.,* March 1961, BSPA.

31. Taylor to Wilkins, August 9, 1965, BSPA.

32. Wilkins to Mrs. Dolores Dunn, Patten, August 31, 1960, BSPA. Mrs. Dunn had complained of the rudeness of the South Branch Pond ranger. Wilkins apologized for the incident and said there were times "when the ranger gets overtired due to the increased pressure of the added use of our campgrounds." While not defending the ranger's activities, Wilkins thought it "well to explain that these men are working under pressure for long hours, with extra work, that is not expected of them but must be done because of these circumstances."

# XI

1. Baxter to Stobie, April 25, 1946, Stobie to Baxter, November 12, 1948, BSPA. See also Harold Dyer's report to BSPA, April 1, 1946, BSPA. Dyer argued for retention of the private sporting camps and the issuance of a policy statement to the "operators to dispell [sic] their fears and encourage good will."

2. Dated November 22, 1955, copy signed by Baxter in BSPA. See Attorney General Harding to Baxter, November 18, Baxter to Nutting, Cobb, and Harding, November 22, 1955. Harding prepared the document and showed it to Nutting and Cobb before sending it on to Baxter for changes and final approval.

3. Memorandum, Nutting to Harding and Cobb, July 20; Cobb to Nutting, July 24, 1956; see also comments by former Forest Commissioner Nutting on an earlier draft of this chapter, BSPA. Nutting said the Authority did notify lessees of the discontinuance of leases after the death of present owners. "This caused York and others to confer directly with Baxter. He was usually kind to them and would meet their suggestions," said Nutting.

4. Baxter to Wilkins, March 6, 1967, BSPA.

5. Issues of journals such as *Appalachia; In the Maine Woods; The Northern,* and *The Maine Sportsman* contain many articles with references to the Kidney Pond camps. Until World War II it was still possible to reach them by steamer from Norcross. See *In the Maine Woods,* 1941, p. 76.

6. See assignment of leases between Garfield Land Company and Laura P. Bradeen to Baxter, March 31, 1941; also renewal of lease, August 28, 1942, BC, MSL.

7. Baxter to Stobie, December 18, 1942, BC, MSL.

8. See Emery S. Dunfee to Rendall, March 31, Rendall to Dunfee, April 16; BSPA to Dunfee, May 1, Dunfee to Farris, May 16 and Farris to Dunfee, May

22, 1945, BSPA; see Lt. Marshall Doxsee to BSPA, October 9, Farris to Doxsee, October 24; Wilkins to Stobie, October 10; George Carlisle to Farris, October 24 and Farris to Carlisle, October 25, 1945; also assignment of lease by Laura Bradeen, November 17, 1945, BSPA.

9. Baxter to Scribner, January 25, 1946, Baxter-Scribner Letters, BC, MSL. Baxter wrote: "I don't believe I want to go there any more." See also Baxter to Stobie, April 25, 1946, BC, MSL. Baxter wrote about a small camp built by a visitor to Kidney Pond along the shore east of the main camp: "If I can have this assigned to me for such time as I may desire, it would be rather nice to feel that there is a small spot all my own in that favored location which nobody else will be permitted to use." Baxter was sure that Carlisle would approve for the Cassidy Estate. He also felt that that was the proper time to do it before any lease was made. The assignment, of course, had been done nearly six months earlier.

10. Stobie to Baxter, November 12; Doxsee to BSPA and to Farris, August 25, Farris to Doxsee, September 29, 1949; lease, BSPA with Marshall W. and Arthur T. Doxsee, of Millinocket, September 27, 1949; Dyer to Farris, September 20, 1949, BSPA.

11. Farris to Baxter, November 17 and 20, Baxter to Farris, November 18; Farris to Doxsee, November 17 and to James M. Gillen, November 20, 1950, BSPA. See BSPA files for copies of the lease during the decade.

12. Wilkins to W. A. Trafton, Jr., November 19, 1959; Wilkins to Cobb and Hancock, May 27, 1960; lease, BSPA to Charles J. Lipscomb, May 2, 1960. On one copy of the lease, Wilkins noted a discussion with Trafton, lawyer for Lipscomb. Because of the great amount of general public traffic on the approach road to the camps, Lipscomb wanted permission to post a sign reading "Private Road to Kidney Pond Camps" to discourage use by non-guests. Wilkins raised a question as to whether this legally could be done. It was decided in the affirmative. Trafton also asked permission to cut brush behind the camps and to build a fireplace on a picnic area on a sandy point near the camps. Presumably this permission was granted.

13. Wilkins to George Emerson, Jr., May 8, 1963, BSPA. The same letter went to Lipscomb and the Yorks. Emerson, of Livermore Falls, owned the Phoenix camps on Nesowadnehunk Lake. He gained access to his camps from the perimeter road within the Park and used some park lands for his activities. The ruling was probably the result of a report made the year before by Fred Holt, who had checked the Park in 1962 to find out what was going on and to make recommendations for changes. Holt found that guests at Kidney Pond camps and York's Twin Pine camps were fishing in and building fires around the small ponds in the area, and that Helon Taylor had given them permission to do so. The practice, he thought, should be stopped. See Holt to Wilkins, September 4, 1962; Wilkins to Lipscomb and E. York, Jr., August 2; to Taylor, June 14; and to Emerson and to York, June 21, 1963, BSPA. He stated that any change in rules had to be advertised. See also Wilkins to Lipscomb, January 3, and to the Fin & Feather Club, January 18, 1966; Dubord to Lipscomb, August 2; Wilkins to Lipscomb, September 1; Lipscomb to Dubord, August 30, 1966; leases, BSPA with Lipscomb, De-

cember 27, 1965 and August 24, 1966, BSPA. Both leases were for five years from May 2, 1965. See also *Bangor Daily News,* August 16 and 26, September 2 and 3, 1965, for letters to the editor and editorials on this issue.

14. Wilkins to Mr. and Mrs. York, July 24 and to Wellington F. Barto, October 31, 1967, BSPA.

15. Lipscomb to Wilkins, July 21, Fred McLeary to Wilkins, November 10, 1967. That year the assessed valuation for tax purposes was $25,000 and a tax of $460 was paid. See "Camp Lot Leases—Baxter State Park, 1967," BSPA.

16. Jerome Matus to BSPA, December 15, 1967, BSPA.

17. See payment agreement by and between the BSPA and Lipscomb, December 15, 1967, BSPA. Attached to a copy of the Matus opinion noted above was a penned comment breaking down the figures in the Authority's final offer to Lipscomb: $33,000 for all tangibles, $12,000 for capital improvement, $5,000 for all intangible values and $2,500 for inventory of supplies. The $65,000 estimate, at the Authority's request, was broken down into three components—buildings, personal property and good will. McLeary allocated $33,000 for personal property and made an arbitrary allocation of $30,000 to "Good Will." On March 26, 1968, Wilkins in a letter to Baxter explaining the Authority's decision, enclosed a copy of the face page of the inventory taken at Kidney Pond. The final round price of $52,500 was arrived at as follows: Furniture and equipment, $14,306.20; kitchen and dining equipment, $10,588.90; camp operating equipment, $13,-443.60; tools and maintenance equipment, $2,977.25; canoes and accessories, $6,100; vehicles, $2,950.00; goodwill, $1,434.05.

In 1969 a Boston lawyer writing to Erwin noted that Lipscomb's lawyer had met with Erwin and Wilkins on December 13, 1967. At the time the Authority felt there was no value to the goodwill. The round price of $52,500 was arrived at by adding the $33,000 recoverable value of Lipscomb's personal property and $18,800 of leasehold improvements. See John Simonds to Erwin, August 14, 1969, BSPA. For tax purposes Lipscomb wanted to say he had paid nothing for goodwill. Erwin to Simonds, September 18, 1969, BSPA. He sent the breakdown given in Wilkins letter above. He reported that additional personal property found at the Kidney Pond camps had a value in excess of the $1,434.05 allotted to goodwill. "Therefore the Baxter State Park Authority is willing to tell you that because the asset value is greater than expected, we do not believe that we paid anything for 'goodwill.'"

18. Wilkins to members of BSPA, November 15, 1967, BSPA. In this memorandum setting a date of November 20 for an Authority meeting to discuss the purchase from Lipscomb, Wilkins wrote that Baxter had called him that morning "as he usually does occasionally to inquire how things are going on in the Park," but apparently Wilkins did not mention the impending purchase. However, in a conversation in January 1979, Mr. Wilkins stated that Baxter was consulted on the issue before action was taken.

19. Baxter to Cranshaw, March 7, 1968, BC, MSL.

20. Wilkins and Erwin to Cranshaw, March 13, 1968, BSPA. Cranshaw was asked to draw a check for $52,500 to Lipscomb. The discussion with Baxter was noted. But see Baxter to Governor Curtis, March 25, 1968, BC, MSL. Wilkins's second visit to Baxter is mentioned in his letter to Baxter, March 26, 1968, BSPA.

21. See State of Maine, Contingent Account Allocation #1037, passed by Council and approved by Governor, May 15, 1968, BSPA.

22. Lipscomb to Wilkins, July 21, and Richard E. Whiting to Wilkins, December 20, 1967; Cross to Wilkins, February 13; Wilkins to Erwin and Speers, March 21 and to Cranshaw, April 10, 1968; minutes of BSPA meeting, April 30, 1968; Wilkins to Mr. and Mrs. Charles Norris, May 6, 1968; see License for Concession, April 30, 1968, BSPA.

23. On the camps as they existed in 1932 see Emmie B. Whitney, "Katahdin's Big Storm," *Appalachia*, June 15, 1952, pp. 21–30. Also see Frederic B. Hyde, "The Storm That Shook Katahdin: A Graphic Story of the Ravages of Rampant Waterways," *In the Maine Woods, 1953*, pp. 117–20; and *Lewiston Sunday Journal Magazine Section*, October 1, 1932, for the first photographs of the flood and slides on O-J-I and other mountains.

24. See Chapter III for details of Baxter's acquisition of the area.

25. Taylor to Wilkins, August 12, 1964, BSPA. Supervisor Harold Dyer was supposed to run new lines for the lease, but never found the time to do it.

26. See Assignment of Lease to York, dated June 7, 1940, by Garfield Land Company to Baxter, March 31, 1941; Carlisle to Baxter, August 27, 1941, and May 29, 1942, BC, MSL. See also copies of lease to Yorks for 1946 and 1953 in BSPA.

27. Taylor to Wilkins, August 12, 1964. See Wilkins to Secretary, Fin & Feather Club, January 18, 1962, BSPA. At first the Authority planned to raise the rent to $500 per year, but Taylor felt that would be prohibitive to the Yorks since "they just don't do that kind of business." He said the camps had been in the family for over 65 years but the mortgage had never been fully paid up. See also Wilkins to Taylor, July 20, 1965, BSPA. Taylor was told the exterior lines would be run by a forest service employee.

28. Attorney General Dubord to Mr. and Mrs. York, August 23, 1966, BSPA. The new lease had been dated December 27, 1965. See Wilkins to Mr. & Mrs. York, December 14, 1966; Sportsman's Lease, January 1, 1967; Erwin to Mr. and Mrs. York, March 21, and Wilkins to Mr. and Mrs. York, July 24, 1967, BSPA.

29. Horace A. Hildreth, Jr., attorney for the Yorks, to Wilkins, February 21, 1968; Erwin to Hildreth, April 9, 1969, BSPA.

30. Erwin to Wilkins, July 24, 1969. See H. N. Cates, Regional Manager, Marshall and Stevens Inc., to BSPA, November 4, 1968, BSPA.

31. Cross to Wilkins, December 9, 1969; "Camp Lot Leases—Baxter State Park, 1967," BSPA. In 1967 the camps had an assessed valuation for taxes of $10,000, and $184 in taxes were paid.

32. Cates to Wilkins, January 12, 1970, BSPA. Hildreth on January 17, 1970 also sent a copy directly to Erwin and stated: "I wanted to make sure you saw it."

33. Minutes of BSPA meetings, December 16, 1969 and May 11, 1970; Hildreth to Wilkins, April 22, 1970, BSPA.

34. Cross to Wilkins, June 29, 1970, BSPA. On the bottom of a copy of this Attorney General Erwin wrote and initialed: "This memo is offensive to me"; see Wilkins to York, July 17, 1970; Title Transfer, June 30, 1970, BSPA.

35. See voluminous correspondence between BSPA and Fin & Feather Club

from October 1962 through October 1963 in BSPA files. Helon Taylor spoke to the Chamber of Commerce in Millinocket in May 1962 to explain park rules. See his report for May 1962; Taylor to Wilkins, May 3, 1962, BSPA. Taylor thought the meeting had gone well. He wrote: "The two main agitators were conspicuous by their absence." See also Darrell Morrow, Publicity Director, to Wilkins, June 12, 1964, BSPA.

36. Wilkins to Morrow, June 16; Budreau to Wilkins, July 2, 1964, BSPA.

37. Dubord to Fin & Feather Club, March 5 and 17, Morrow to Dubord, March 16, 1965; Petition, Fin & Feather Club to BSPA, no date but March 1965, BSPA.

38. Wilkins to Budreau, June 11, 1965; Dana Brown to Dubord, February 23, 1966, BSPA.

39. Wilkins to Taylor, June 28, 1965; and to Brown, February 7, 1966, BSPA.

40. Brown to Dubord, February 23, 1966, BSPA.

41. *Lincoln News,* July 7, August 4, and November 3, 1966.

42. Dubord to Morrow, August 2, 1966, BSPA. Problems continued in early 1967. See Wilkins to Taylor, January 11, 1967, BSPA.

43. Jerome O'Kane to BSPA, May 8, 1970; presentation of the Fin and Feather Club to BSPA and Advisory Council at September 2, 1970 meeting; Wilkins to Paul Firlotte, September 14, 1970, BSPA.

44. Taylor to BSPA; Wilkins to Cobb, June 30 and July 24, Cobb to Wilkins, July 14, 1961, BSPA.

45. Haskell to Baxter, August 11 and 12; Baxter to Haskell, August 12 and 16, 1948; Haskell to Farris, September 12; Farris to Haskell, September 16, and to Dyer, October 28, 1949; Stobie to Baxter, October 27, and November 1; Baxter to Stobie, October 28, 1949; Farris to Baxter, November 3, 1949, BSPA.

46. Wilkins to Mrs. Clark, August 13, 1970, BSPA. The camp had an assessed valuation of $700 in 1967 and taxes of $12.88 were paid.

47. Wilkins to BSPA members, May 19; bill of sale for personal property as of May 20; minutes of BSPA meeting, July 1; release signed by Davignon, July 10; Wilkins to Erwin, July 16, 1970, BSPA. Davignon readily agreed that the building belonged to the state and was amenable to selling his possessions to the state. Wilkins thought the "beautifully furnished" camp could be used by park rangers or for other purposes. In 1967 it was assessed at $2,750 and $50.60 in taxes were paid on it.

48. Assignment of leases, Garfield Land Company and others to Baxter, December 12, 1947, BP, MSL. See copies of leases for 1947 and 1948 in BP and for 1950–53 in BSPA files; Martin to BSPA, July 5, Farris to Martin, July 27, 1950; minutes of meetings of BSPA, February 3 and October 8, 1970, BSPA. At the first meeting Martin's lawyer, Joseph B. Campbell, told the Authority that when his clients had built their home in the 1950s they were assured by Chairman Nutting that there would be "no problem . . . no trouble" with continuing the lease. See appraisal made by Robert L. Anderson of Patten, May 20; Campbell to Wilkins, June 2, Wilkins to Campbell, July 22, 1970; memorandum from Assistant Attorney General John Anderson to Erwin, October 7;

minutes of BSPA meeting, October 8, 1970, BSPA. Anderson had been asked for an opinion as to whether by terms of the lease the state had to pay for the buildings on its termination. In analyzing the language of the lease, which was the same as that for Kidney Pond and Twin Pine camps, Anderson concluded that the "Authority need not pay for buildings located on the leasehold." The assessed valuation in 1967 was $3,250 and taxes amounting to $52.91 were paid.

49. Wilkins to Michael Hradel, March 5, 1970, BSPA.

50. Great Northern, Lease No. 2075, February 23, 1956, BSPA.

51. See Wilkins to Erwin, December 4, Erwin to Wilkins, December 12; minutes of BSPA meeting, December 16; Wilkins to Budreau, December 18, 1969, BSPA. In his memo to Erwin, Wilkins said that it appeared that the lease did not give ownership of the camp to Budreau. He asked Erwin whether, in view of the new snowmobile rule, Budreau could bring one in on an old entry road to the Park that approached his camp. Erwin said he could not legally do so.

52. Memorandum, unsigned, for the record, December 29, 1969, BSPA. The style is that of Erwin.

53. Wilkins to Tanous, March 10, 1970; Murray to Erwin, August 5, 1970, BSPA.

54. Wilkins to Warren Metcalf, Fin and Feather Club, and to Taylor, June 20; Taylor to Wilkins, June 23; Paul Firlotte to Wilkins, November 21, 1963, BSPA. In his letter to Wilkins, Taylor commented on the fact that the Club was to assist in rebuilding the dam at Abol Pond: "Too bad we have to get mixed up with them, but I suppose that is the only way we can ever get it built."

55. Wilkins to Senator Tanous, November 10, 1970, BSPA.

56. See Club presentation cited in note 43 above; announcement of BSPA and Advisory Committee meeting, September 3; Wilkins to Tanous, December 11, 1970, BSPA.

57. See typed opinion of Justice Thomas E. Delahanty in case of State of Maine and Jon A. Lund, Maine Attorney General; Maynard F. Marsh, Commissioner of Inland Fisheries and Game; and Fred E. Holt, Maine Forest Commissioner, in their capacity as Baxter State Park Authority v. The Fin & Feather Club, et al., Law Docket No. Ken–73–8. Copy in BSPA files. See also *Bangor Daily News*, March 13, 1974.

58. Marsh to Morrow, July 6, 1976, BSPA. At a meeting with the Authority on March 12, 1974, representatives of the Fin & Feather Club asked the Authority to pay it $6,000 for the dam it had built at the outlet to Abol Pond in the reclamation effort the previous decade. The Authority, which was in the process of replacing the structure, rejected the request.

# XII

1. Minutes of BSPA meeting, July 1, 1950, BSPA.

2. This awkward phrasing was retained until 1959.

3. Because of the way this rule was written, it was completely unenforceable. If any user of the Park strayed from the trail at all, some plants and/or shrubs would be crushed.

4. Cobb to Alexander LaFleur, October 2, 1951, BSPA.

5. G. M. Austin, Eastern Corporation, to Maine State Park Commission, September 22, 1951, BSPA.

6. Baxter to Cobb, October 18, 1957, BSPA.

7. See minutes of BSP Commission [sic] meeting, April 7, 1952; BSP rules and regulations, amended 7/4/52. See Nutting to Wilkins, April 8, 1959, BSPA.

8. See Nutting to Cobb and Harding, July 7, Harding to Nutting, July 19, 1955; BSP rules and regulations, amended 9–20–54 and 6–1–55, BSPA. Harding, in response to Nutting's memorandum, pointed out a typographical error and added: "These rules and regulations appear reasonable, and I have not sufficient personal knowledge of the operation of the Park to suggest any alterations."

9. See BSP rules and regulations, amended 3/1/57, BSPA.

10. Minutes of BSPA meetings, January 22, and December 17, 1958; Wilkins to Taylor, January 6, 1959; BSP rules and regulations, undated but 1959, BSPA. In addition to the mimeographed rules to be handed out to visitors, the Authority in 1959 for the first time prepared a mimeographed sheet for each campground. On one side was a map of the campground showing trails leading from it and other pertinent information; on the reverse was information regarding the campground, fee schedules, and similar data.

11. This was tried at South Branch Pond Campground in 1968.

12. See "Minutes of Meeting, Spring BSP Ranger School of Instruction Millinocket, Maine, May 4, 1959," BSPA. At this meeting there was considerable discussion on how the rule would be handled at the park end. It was decided that Helen Gifford, Helon Taylor, or rangers could help initiate refund requests. They were directed to send a copy of the regulation with each confirmed reservation sent out. Also see minutes of BSPA meeting, January 22, and BSP report of William Whitman, May 4–5, 1958, BSPA. At the January meeting the Authority decided that reservations could be made at any time if vacancies existed, although the park brochure would still suggest that they be procured two weeks in advance. At the Ranger School it was decided that rangers could also make advance reservations for their campgrounds.

13. Taylor, report for March 1955, BSPA.

14. *Ibid.*, June 1958, BSPA.

15. Wilkins to Taylor, November 25 and 27, 1959; Robert B. Sanders to Cobb, Hancock, and Wilkins, no date but November 19, and to Taylor, dated November 19, 1959; Taylor to Sanders, November 27, 1959, BSPA. Wilkins had forgotten about the decision made by the Authority.

16. Taylor, report for July 1957; Whitman report 1958, *op. cit.*, BSPA. At the school for rangers, while discussing general park policy, the rangers asked Whitman to request that camp directors "try to limit the number to about 15 at a time at one campground."

17. Memorandum Wilkins to camp directors, March 3, 1959, BSPA.

18. See letter to Wilkins from a visitor from Cape Elizabeth, September 29, 1959 and Jean Stephenson to Wilkins, October 16, 1960, BSPA, for typical examples. The writer of the first letter complained that one ranger even had a dog. She noted that because of the numerous dogs, no wildlife was in the campground areas visited during the summer.

See also Taylor to Wilkins, July 20, Wilkins to Taylor, July 17, 1962; BSP rules and regulations revised 1962, BSPA. One park visitor complained to Wilkins about the rule and reported that two rangers had told her they did not like it. She also told Wilkins she had a dog and was allowed to remain one night. This situation disturbed Wilkins who said the new rule was put in because the rangers and Taylor had asked for it. Taylor responded and noted he had talked with the two rangers, who said they had not voted. Taylor said they had had a chance and at the meeting there were no objections. He added: "Maybe Mrs. Johnson did not tell you that she also had five cats and that we did offer her the privilege of staying two nights, one at Katahdin Stream and one at Nesowadnehunk"; Mary B. Horne and Barbara R. Carlson to BSPA, August 29, 1962, BSPA. This letter was written on a survey questionnaire form used by the Park in 1962 to obtain visitors' reactions. In his report for August 1962, Taylor noted that of the 223 people he interviewed that month, 221 liked the Park; "the other two did not like me, the Rangers, wild animals, Baxter State Park or the State of Maine. (They had a dog.) I expect their Congressman will have us all fired."

In still another case, a couple came to Roaring Brook campground with a trailer. They had a dog but were allowed to stay while the husband hiked to Russell Pond. Later the campground ranger found they also had a cat and two full-grown chickens in the trailer as well. They were escorted to a nearby private campground where Taylor hoped "the lady is very happy . . . where they do not have such unreasonable rules and regulations." See Taylor, report for July 1962, BSPA.

19. Wilkins to Taylor, December 13, 1962, BSPA. Taylor apparently did not attend the meeting where these changes were made.

20. Wilkins to members, BSPA, March 2, 1967, BSPA. It was adopted at a meeting of the Authority on April 18, 1967.

21. See papers accompanying agenda of BSPA meeting of January 19, 1971, BSPA; also BSP rules and regulations, revision 1973, BSPA.

22. Erwin in a speech made a statement regarding possible limitations on the use of the Park by non-residents which was misinterpreted and caused great consternation. See files of *Maine Times* in late sixties and into 1970 for examples. See also Erwin to Mr. and Mrs. Donald Rich of Windham, May 28, 1970, BSPA. In response to a letter critical of Supervisor Kearney's stand against use of recreational vehicles and self-contained campers, Erwin noted: "The Baxter State Park Authority is in the process of setting a new policy with respect to the protection of this unique, primitive, wilderness area. As the demands for the uses of the Park become more severe each year, it becomes necessary for the Authority to face the problems squarely." Self-contained vehicles, he thought, did not fit into the philosophy of the Authority.

23. See Erwin, "Suggested Policy for Baxter State Park," January 1970, BSPA.

24. Erwin to Wilkins, August 27 and Speers to Erwin, September 2, 1969, BSPA.

25. *Public Laws of Maine 1971*, ch. 477.

26. Erwin to Wilkins, April 28, 1970, BSPA.

27. Minutes of meetings, BSPA, December 16, 1969; January 19, and March

23, 1970, and January 19, 1971; notification of changes in rules and regulations, BSP, January 20, 1971, BSPA. Most of the changes discussed were adopted at these meetings.

With regard to the use of outboard motors in the Park after this date see Kearney to BSPA, September 15, and Wilkins to Speers, October 21, 1969, BSPA. The Inland Fish and Game Department had requested permission of the Authority to use an outboard motor to chase and tag moose in BSP as part of a research project. The Authority refused permission but the fish and game department continued the practice. At a subsequent meeting of the Authority the matter was again discussed and afterward Commissioner Speers, who was absent at the meeting, was warned again that his department should thereafter conduct "no operations other than law enforcement . . . in the Park without the authority of the Baxter State Park Authority." Wilkins added: "In view of present public sentiment we now feel that this was a proper action on our part and will look forward to your cooperation in this regard."

28. W. Robert Leach to Taylor, August 12, 1962, BSPA.

29. See agenda for BSPA meeting, June 21, 1965; Baxter to Wilkins, April 18, 1966, BSPA.

30. See Robert J. Schneider to Erwin, April 22, 1970, BSPA. Schneider was from Millinocket and wrote: "I feel suddenly cut off from some real pleasant experiences of the last three years. I've used my bike for short fishing trips or simply enjoying the beauty of the park and observing all types of game which the bike never seemed to disturb." He could not understand the ban on motorcycles when snowmobiles were allowed.

31. Michael Frome, "America's Campgrounds Are Turning Into Slums," *True Magazine*, April 1969; *Maine Sunday Telegram*, April 6, 1969; Wilkins to BSPA, April 8, 1969, BSPA. Wilkins replied to *Telegram* columnist Frank Sleeper defending the Park.

32. Kearney to BSPA, April 16, 1969, BSPA.

33. See revision in rules and regulations, BSP, August 19, 1968; also minutes of meetings BSPA, March 23, 1970 and January 19, 1971, BSPA.

34. See BSPA files for the list.

35. See discussion in and papers accompanying minutes of meeting, BSPA, January 19, 1971, BSPA.

36. Taylor to Wilkins, January 6 and 14; Wilkins to Taylor, January 6, 1959; Taylor, report for March 1961; *Ibid.*, February 1961; *Ibid.*, February 1965, BSPA. For a discussion of the 1963 expedition see George Hamilton, "The 1963 Annual Polaris Allagash Trip," *Appalachia*, XXXIV, no. 3 (June, 1963), pp. 544–48. Justice William O. Douglas had planned to take the trip but had to drop out.

37. Taylor to Larry J. Poulin, December 23, 1965, BSPA.

38. See Wilkins to Richard P. Billingham, January 13 and to Senator Muskie, January 15, 1970, BSPA.

39. See revisions 1970 and 1971 in rules and regulations BSP, BSPA.

40. See Baxter to Taylor, May 11, 1965, BC, MSL; in Sarah Redfield's statement, May 20, 1976, BSPA: "The Use of Snowmobiles Within Baxter State Park as Contemplated by the 1976 Revision of the Rules and Regulations," Baxter's letter is reproduced.

41. See Norman Minsky to Wilkins, August 15, 1966, BSPA. Minsky, a Bangor Attorney who was later involved in setting up the Advisory Committee, suggested that camp group use of the Park should be confined to weekdays as was done in the State Park system. See also Kearney to BSPA, April 16, 1969. In responding to the Authority concerning the article in *True Magazine* mentioned earlier, Kearney suggested that camp groups be assigned arbitrarily to tenting areas near the campgrounds rather than taking space in them.

42. Bradford F. Swan, "Fatality at Mt. Katahdin," *Appalachia*, XXXVII, No. 4 (December 1969), pp. 652–54 and David Webster of Camp Netop, Casco, Maine, to Wilkins, July 30, 1969 enclosing statement of Leader Richard E. Williams, July 23, 1969; see also Kearney to Wilkins, October 20, 1970, BSPA. This was in reply to a letter from Wilkins requesting information on deaths in the park area. While the data for the lumbering period were not readily available, Kearney's list appears rather complete.

43. Kearney to BSPA, September 1; Erwin to Darrah Wagner, September 11, 1969, BSPA. Kearney reported that the leaders of a boys camp from Tenant's Harbor when told they could not climb the mountain because they had one too few adults, willfully avoided the ruling by moving off from Katahdin Stream and hiding their truck in the woods nearby, then climbing the mountain. Kearney suggested they not be allowed to camp or climb another year.

44. G. B. Holmes of Camp Ettowah, Fryeburg, to BSPA, October 8, 1969 and W. D. Dilbert, State Y.M.C.A. Camp, to Wilkins, March 3, 1970, BSPA. Both sent suggestions for rules for camper groups. See Kearney to BSPA, April 4, 1970, BSPA.

45. See changes in rules and regulations, BSP, 1970 and 1971, BSPA. The 1970 ruling banned any camping by camp groups at authorized campgrounds; but no limits were placed on camper groups.

# XIII

1. *Private and Special Laws of Maine, 1943*, ch. 71. *Ibid., 1945*, ch. 92. *Ibid., 1947*, ch. 168; *1953*, ch. 93; *1955*, ch. 186; *1969*, ch. 161. *Ibid., 1949*, ch. 158; *1963*, ch. 228; *1969*, ch. 157; *Resolves*, 1951, ch. 68.

2. For the first quote see Baxter to Governor Payne, the Senate, and House of Representatives of the 94th Legislature, January 3, 1949, in *Laws of Maine, Communications, 1949*, p. 1369. For the second quotation see *Private and Special Laws, 1949*, ch. 2.

3. Harrie B. Price 3d. to Governor Payne, March 1; Payne to Dyer, March 8; Dyer to Attorney General Farris, and to Price, March 12, 1949, BSPA.

4. Dyer interview, *op. cit.* He felt that the fish and game commissioner at this time was gaining more and more control over Baxter and park policies.

5. Lucius D. Barrows, State Highway Commission, to Baxter, November 30, 1950, BC, MSL. Barrows enclosed a copy of a report of Division Engineer Earl L. Bartlett on the new route. See also Barrows to Baxter, April 18, 1951, BC, MSL, acknowledging receipt of Baxter's check for $12,000.

6. Baxter to Barrows, August 14 and September 11, and to Bartlett, August 14, 1951, BC, MSL.

7. Taylor to Baxter, August 31 and September 18, 1951, BC, MSL. After this trip Baxter sent hunting knives to Taylor and various highway commission employees who had worked on the route.

8. Copy of letter from Baxter to Stobie, June 25; Farris to Dyer, to Baxter, and to Daisey, July 16; Baxter to Farris, July 17; Daisey to Farris, July 24, 1947, BSPA. In his letter of July 17, Baxter asked the Authority to consider tearing down three unused buildings held by Daisey at Sourdnahunk Field since they were fire hazards. Dyer was directed to take proper action.

9. William Hilton of Great Northern to Farris, August 2, Farris to Hilton, August 12; Daniel Chasse of Millinocket to Farris, August 27, 1949, BSPA. Hilton recommended keeping the road closed and noted that there was a "great deal of pressure from the crowd around Millinocket" to keep it open, though he said the record of starting fires by the Millinocket group was as bad as anywhere in the state. The Chasse letter is a rejoinder to Hilton's argument.

10. See "About Katahdin," *Appalachian Trailway News*, January 1947, p. 3. The Trout Brook tote road was being improved with gravel, which had been spread on the road as far as the north branch of Trout Brook south of Black Brook Farm. The road from Black Brook Farm to Webster Lake had also been gravelled.

11. See "Katahdin Developments, Further Shrinkage of Katahdin Wilderness," *Appalachian Trailway News*, January 1951, p. 4.

12. Nutting to Taylor, July 12, Taylor to Nutting, July 14, 1956, BSPA. In the previous month, June 20, Nutting wrote to Taylor saying that the Sewall Company of Old Town had asked permission to repair and use the road and asked what Baxter's opinion might be. Taylor, June 22, agreed to the idea and said he thought Baxter "would be pleased to have this road kept open." Nutting, June 26, indicated he would check personally with Baxter before proceeding.

13. Earl Anderson, to Wilkins, August 28, Wilkins to Anderson, September 8, 1966, BSPA.

14. Memorandum Erwin to Wilkins, September 9, and to Representative Walter Birt, September 21, 1970, BSPA. Erwin was then running for governor and was receiving intense pressure regarding park policies from people and legislators in surrounding communities.

15. This was only one of the many roads constructed in this area at the time the Eastern Corporation was exercising its cutting rights in T5R10. Baxter asked them to leave a fifty-foot strip of timber on each side of such roads. The company agreed it would generally conform to his request except in areas of virgin growth "where we should for economic reasons take the growth to the roadside." See Charles Paine to Baxter, January 2, 1952, BC, MSL. Baxter's letter of December 12, 1951 has not been preserved.

16. Supervisor Pendleton to Nutting, July 7; Nutting to Roland Cobb and Frank Harding, July 13, 1956, BSPA.

17. For a typical example see Taylor to Nutting, June 22, Nutting to Taylor, June 26, 1956, BSPA. The highway crew members brought their families, so twelve individuals were involved. They lived in two lean-tos and a tent. Taylor asked if fees should be charged and noted that they were taking valuable space.

Nutting replied that a fee was not important and suggested to Taylor that he try to move them elsewhere in order to gain space for regular visitors.

18. See Myrle Scott to Wilkins, undated, but August, 1956 (first half of letter misplaced), BSPA. Scott noted that a highway department road crew would begin work within a few weeks, and asked: "What is going to be our procedure in preventing opening of more gravel pits and bulldozing along the Park roadways?"

19. Memorandum, Martin Rissell, Maine State Highway Commission, to Wilkins, June 17, Wilkins to Rissell, July 7, 1969, BSPA.

20. Kearney to BSPA, September 24, 1969; minutes of meeting, BSPA, November 19, 1969; memo Ralph Dunbar to David Stevens, June 3; memo Wilkins to Stevens, September 14, 1970, BSPA. Stevens said at the meeting with the Authority in November, 1969: "Very frankly . . . to be completely honest . . . the State Highway Commission would like to get out" of the Park. Difficulties over obtaining gravel were cited as the major cause.

Wilkins' memorandum was a report of a meeting held on May 29, 1970, at BSP. It was attended by Wilkins, Caverly, Dunbar and Lewis Hanscomb, District Maintenance Supervisor. The group checked all pits, decided which would remain open, and which were to be closed, and what screening and replanting would be done. The group agreed that the park supervisor was to approve the location of future pits and access roads to them. No pits were to be visible from the road in the future.

21. Nutting to Stevens, September 28, 1956, BSPA. In early 1979, in his comments on an earlier version of this chapter, Nutting stated that "Baxter objected largely to moving of large rocks on the road corners rather than brush removal." The written correspondence indicates otherwise.

22. Lillian Tschamler to Taylor, October 2, 1956; copy of memorandum Stuart L. Deane, Division Engineer, to John Church, Superintendent of Maintenance, October 19, 1956, BSPA.

23. Memorandum from Gordon Hunter to Ralph Dunbar. A copy, dated August 1, 1962, was sent by Hunter to Wilkins, BSPA. Hunter noted the serious driving hazards created by the brush, which threatened to engulf the roadway: desirable good growth was being hidden by these, scenic views were cut off, and the growth "in general is turning the road into a tiresome brush tunnel instead of a scenic drive designed to show the best native plant growth and natural scenery." He proposed a program of selective trimming and "judicious clearing."

24. Baxter to Nutting, December 22, 1956, BP, MSL.

25. Taylor to Wilkins, May 31, 1959, BSPA. In a letter commenting on Baxter's attempt to purchase land in T2R9 and his latest inspection trip in the Park, Taylor noted: "He has forgotten all about what he said about giving the $15,000 to build the road. When I asked him about it he said 'What road?' So I said no more about it. Off the record, he seemed a little more feeble than last fall, but he is still a grand old man and he had a fine time." See also Wilkins to Hilton, May 3, 1960, BSPA. Recounting a recent visit to Baxter's home, Wilkins said Baxter had again promised to pay for the road.

26. Baxter to Wilkins, November 27, 1959, BC, MSL.

27. Hilton to Baxter, June 29, Baxter to Hilton, July 6, 1960; Taylor to Baxter, August 29; Baxter to McDonald of Great Northern, August 30, 1961, BP, MSL.

28. Wilkins to Haskell, February 22, 1961, BSPA. Since Haskell was president of the Senate and was going to talk with Baxter about the use of income from park trust funds for operations in the Park, Wilkins sent him a copy of his budget request and asked his aid in convincing Baxter to allow trust fund income to be used to defray some of the additional costs.

29. Vaughan M. Daggett to Wilkins, June 25; Wilkins to members of BSPA, June 26, 1964; BSP "Road Location Report," by R. A. Coleman, BSPA.

30. Wilkins to Baxter, July 6, 1964, BSPA; Baxter to Wilkins and to Taylor, July 8, 1964, BP, MSL.

31. Wilkins to Taylor, July 13, 1964, BSPA.

32. Baxter to Wilkins, November 6, 1964, BSPA.

33. Wilkins to Baxter, November 15, 1964, BSPA. Wilkins said that funds for gatehouses had been included in the forthcoming budget request. He also noted that Governor Reed thought installation of the control system was of importance to the Park.

34. Baxter to Wilkins, February 14; Dubord to Baxter, February 14, Baxter to Dubord, February 17, 1966; copies in BC, MSL, and BSPA files.

35. See Baxter to Wilkins, February 15, and to Dubord, February 17, 1966, BC, MSL, on Baxter's desire to see the plans. Also Wilkins to Baxter, August 16 and 30, and September 7, 1966, BC, MSL. The receipted bills were sent to Baxter. See copies of invoices, dated August 15 and 16, 1966 from L. C. Andrews for gatehouses. The orders for the two gatehouses, which cost $2,998 each, were placed on July 18, 1966, BC. See also Edward Woodbrey of L. C. Andrews to Wilkins, June 10, 1966, BSPA, for bids on log cabins.

36. Wilkins to Baxter, May 16 and September 7, 1966; Baxter to Taylor, May 17, 1966, BC, MSL; Wilkins to Speers, June 17, and to Baxter, August 16, 1966, BC, MSL. See also Wilkins to Erwin, August 24, 1967, BSPA. The Attorney General and David Stevens had made another visit to Baxter to get his approval to pay a cost overrun for the new road from interest from the trust fund. Wilkins wanted Erwin to approve a bill from the Highway Department for the job before processing it because Baxter "might forget what he told Dave Stevens," and also because State Controller Henry Cranshaw would not approve payment without some proof of approval by Baxter. Baxter frequently called Cranshaw to check on the state of the interest account and to make certain it was not being misused.

37. See memorandum for the file on "Baxter State Park Roads" by David Stevens, November 5, 1968, BSPA. At an Authority meeting on February 3, 1970, Erwin said he felt that the late Governor "never intended this road to be a throughway." For an original copy of the act relating to BSP roads, see Wilkins to members of BSPA and Supervisor Kearney, January 8, 1969; also statement filed by Maine State Highway Commission in regard to Legislative Documents No. 285 and 286, BSPA.

38. See memorandum from Lawrence Stuart to Wilkins, October 16; and two letters Wilkins to Stevens, October 20, 1969, BSPA. The second letter was written only hours after the first. Wilkins noted: "This brings out the need more

than ever that there should be a special person from the Attorney General's Office assigned to make a careful detailed study of all deeds involving Baxter State Park."

39. Memorandum, Stuart to Wilkins, November 7, and Asa Richardson to David Stevens, December 30, 1969, BSPA.

40. Minutes of meetings, BSPA, January 15, February 3, July 1, and August 6, 1970; Stevens to Ralph Dunbar, August 19, Stuart to Wilkins, August 20, Wilkins to Stevens, August 25, and Erwin to Stuart, August 25, all 1970, BSPA. The quotation in the text is from the Erwin letter.

## XIV

1. Robert H. Dyer to Farris, July 15; Farris to Nutting and Stobie, July 18, 1950, BSPA.

2. Nutting to Farris, July 20, Farris to Nutting, July 21, 1950, BSPA.

3. Taylor, report for August 1950, BSPA.

4. *Ibid.*, October 1950, BSPA.

5. Baxter to Scribner, November 24, 1950, BC, MSL.

6. Minutes of meeting, BSPA, July 1; see also Nutting to Farris, July 20, 1950, BSPA.

7. Taylor, reports for September and October, 1950, BSPA.

8. *Ibid.*, November 1950, June, July, September, and October, 1951, BSPA.

9. *Ibid.*, May and June, 1952, BSPA. In 1953 the park brochure noted that twelve shelters were available but made no mention of tenting sites.

10. Taylor, report for October 1951, BC, MSL. In a postscript to a copy of this report that he sent to Baxter, Taylor added the comment quoted in the text.

11. The U.S. Geographic Board officially changed the name of Sourdnahunk Field, Stream and Lake to Nesowadnehunk in 1929. The former name, usually pronounced "Sowdyhunk" still remains in use. Its Indian meaning was "the mountains from Ktaadn, that stream runs among them." See MATC, *Katahdin Section*, Sixth Edition, 1965, section 1, p. 27.

12. Baxter to Nutting, June 18, 1952, BC, MSL; Nutting to Baxter, June 23, 1952, BSPA. Nutting expressed surprise at Baxter's comment on housekeeping cabins and said the Authority had not discussed their construction and he had not heard of the proposal earlier.

13. Taylor, reports for June and September, 1952, BSPA. Great Northern had been exercising its cutting rights in the area and had built a camp at Sourdnahunk. When the company employees moved out in late May, Ranger Beach moved in immediately. The camp was given to the Park by the paper company on the understanding that it could use it whenever it pleased. See Taylor, report for May 1952, BSPA.

14. Taylor, reports for August and December 1953, and the Year 1953, BSPA. In the December report, he wrote: "At Nesourdnahunk Ranger Beach has worked all alone on his camp all this month except for two days that Ranger Werler worked with him. He has his floors layed [sic], wall board up and the ceilings up in two rooms."

15. William Whitman to Attorney General Alexander LaFleur, May 7, 1953,

BSPA. Attached was a copy of the park circular for the year. LaFleur was asked to make suggestions for changes "and Mr. Nutting will be very glad to consider them."

16. Notations as to unlimited tenting were dropped from the editions after 1955.

17. BSP statement to the budget committee, October 4, 1954, BSPA. See also Wilkins, "Suggested Draft for Inclusion in the State-Wide Recreation Plan," undated but transmitted to other members of the Authority on November 15, 1966, BSPA. Wilkins, in discussing campgrounds, reiterated the one-ranger concept and said that each location "has a lay-out of four sections: area for 12 lean-tos and a bunkhouse varying from 6–12 persons per unit; area for 15 tent sites; area for day use and area for the ranger and his family. There are some variations from this standard plan."

18. BSPA statement to the Committee on Appropriations and Financial Affairs of the 98th Legislature, January 31, 1957, BSPA.

19. Most of the materials used in this paragraph come from the monthly and annual reports of Taylor.

20. Werler to Taylor and Wilkins, Roaring Brook, October 1959, BSPA. In 1960 Werler resigned his position to become Supervisor of Two Lights State Park at Cape Elizabeth, Maine.

21. See petition to correct grievances from Fin & Feather Club to BSPA, February 1965, BSPA; *Lincoln News,* July 7, August 4, 1966.

22. Mark Fortune to Taylor, whom he addressed as chairman of the Authority, August 20, 1958, BSPA.

23. Dolley to Wilkins, September 19, 1958, BSPA.

24. I have found no evidence that the Authority formally discussed abandonment or made an express decision in this regard; the policy was simply modified as time went on.

25. *Ibid.,* note 18 above. See also BSP statement to the budget committee, October 24, 1956, BSPA.

26. Report of William Whitman, BSP, May 4–5, 1958, BSPA. Whitman was an official in the Maine Forest Service who handled much of the detailed work for the administration of the Park. This was a report on a two-day meeting of park personnel with Authority members, at which Whitman asked park rangers their opinions of where future campground development should come. Basin Ponds was the first choice, though some said there was need for more camping space at the north end of the Park. In addition, the Avalanche area was suggested as a picnic area to relieve crowding at Roaring Brook.

27. Taylor, report for December 1958; see also materials accompanying agenda for BSPA meeting held December 17, 1958, BSPA. The materials for the pre-cut ranger cabin had been put out for bids. L. C. Andrews was awarded the contract for $1,904. The same firm also successfully bid $3,064 to prefabricate 5 lean-tos, 30 picnic tables, 18 supertoilets, 3 woodsheds and miscellaneous other projects for the Park.

28. Taylor, report for the year 1959. See Wilkins to Lt. Hayden, Dow Air Force Base, March 12; to Commanding General, Fort Devens, May 11; to Taylor,

394

May 29, to Cobb, June 24, and to Governor Clausen, July 20, all 1959. See Major Nash G. King, Fort Devens, to Wilkins, May 29, 1959, BSPA. On the last trip one helicopter settled to the ground after encountering an "air vacuum" and the forward rotor was damaged.

29. See Barth to Wilkins, June 12, and memorandum Wilkins to Cobb and Hancock, October 6, 1959, BSPA. In his memorandum Wilkins calls Barth's letter "a masterful piece of reporting." In his letter Barth told of the work he had done since his arrival about the first of the month. He then went on to describe in considerable detail the problem with the surface erosion at Chimney Pond campground. In comparing pictures of the campground taken in 1950 with the current situation, he noted the major problems of removal of shrubbery, the cutting of trees for wood, and the movement of the soil into the pond. He saw two possible courses of action: one, removal of the campground to the Basin Ponds area, a course of action which had been discussed from time to time for decades; and two, a three-phase plan that entailed limiting the number of campers drastically, an extensive terracing job, and a system of confining campers to certain paths within the campground. Barth had discussed the situation with Taylor, who suggested he write to Wilkins. Barth indicated he had planned to do so anyway, for, he wrote: "I have come to realize that there are many areas within Baxter State Park which Mr. Taylor doesn't seem to realize are going to be ruined for the individual who values Baxter Park for its wilderness attributes unless some sound planning is done in the very near future." Except for Harold Dyer, Barth was the first college graduate the Authority had hired. Primarily because he was unwilling to do the type of work needed to be done by rangers he was not re-hired for another season. See Taylor to Wilkins and Barth to Wilkins, October 15; Wilkins to Barth, October 23, 1959, BSPA.

In 1962 Richard D. Pardo, of the Information and Education Division of the Maine Forest Service visited Chimney Pond in the process of familarizing himself with the area in order to prepare a park brochure. He found conditions much the same. With facilities for only 60 to 70 people, he said there were often 125 there on weekends. "Ranger Heath," he went on, "hesitates to turn anyone away, one reason being the fact that they will camp in unauthorized areas and create even more of a problem than the crowding of the camp area."

30. Taylor to Wilkins, July 9, 1959, BSPA.

31. Wilkins to Taylor, August 7, 1959; Taylor, reports for August 1959, the Year 1959, and June 1960, BSPA. In his report for 1959 Taylor noted the following about Grant: "Our spare Ranger, Owen Grant, has had a busy summer too. He took charge of the prefabricating of the new Ranger's camp for Chimney Pond and did the planning and packaging of the materials to see that everything was included, helped cut the wood for Togue Pond, shingled the roof of the home camp at Togue Pond, shingled the roof of the Ranger's camp at Roaring Brook, opened camp at Russell Pond and ran it until Ranger Dolley came June 8th, built a new leanto at South Branch Pond, made four new, routed-in Park Boundary signs, built the new Ranger's camp at Chimney Pond, ran the Chimney Pond Campground from Sept. 26th until the close of the season and took charge of building the pole barn at Togue Pond."

32. Taylor, report for June 1960, BSPA. Taylor reported that the new ranger had finished the inside work on the camp and had completed five new toilet units. Of Heath, Taylor noted: "I think he is going to make a good Ranger."

33. *Ibid.* notes 18 and 25 above. $500 was requested f)r each year for this purpose.

34. Taylor to Nutting, September 1, 1956, BSPA.

35. Taylor, reports for August, October, November, December and the year 1957; and for January, February, May, June, September, and the year 1958; also Minutes of meeting of BSPA, March 14, 1958, BSPA.

36. Taylor, report for December 1958, BSPA. The 358 campers at Abol for the summer numbered about ten per cent of the totals for Katahdin Stream and Roaring Brook, and were about fifty per cent of campers at Russell Pond, the next least visited campground. Taylor said it took about five years for a campground to achieve its potential.

37. The total overnight camper capacity was listed as 1,065 in a letter from Taylor to Wilkins, February 2, 1961, BSPA. Taylor and the Authority were continually pressured by the public to open many smaller campsites in various parts of the Park. See, for instance, Jean Stephenson of the MATC to Wilkins, October 16, 1960, BSPA. Stephenson wanted the Authority to open up McCarty Field for overnight camping.

On the situation at Fowler Ponds, see Frank Hahn, to Taylor, August 30, and Taylor to Hahn, September 2, 1961, BSPA. Hahn stressed the desecration in the Middle Fowler and Lower Fowler Ponds areas. As I can attest, the situation had not changed a decade later.

38. See particularly Baxter to Nutting, August 18, 1958, BC, MSL: "As to increasing our camping facilities, I believe with you that we should hold fast to the fundamental idea of having the Park quite different from other parks." See also Baxter to Frank Hancock, October 13, 1959, BC, MSL: "I consider it best not to enlarge our facilities but to improve certain features in what we now have. This Park is really for a select group who want it left as an untouched wilderness insofar as this is possible and who are willing to put up with minor inconveniences."

Also see Taylor to Wilkins, August 29, 1960, BSPA. Baxter had just completed a trip to the Park and had continued on to Fort Kent. Taylor noted that nothing had happened about the purchase of lands in T2R9 and added: "I could not get much out of him about the Fowler Pond project. He said no more camps. I think he meant cabins. I think he has forgotin [sic] what he said last June."

39. The first mention I can find of the plan was in the minutes of the meeting, BSPA, January 22, 1958, BSPA: "The '6 Year' plan of improvements was brought up. It was decided that Mr. Nutting discuss this plan with Mr. Nilon Bates." See also "List of Capital Improvements and Construction Projects to be Included in 6 Year Program (1961–62 to 1966–67 Inc.)." Several copies of this are in the BSPA files. One is attached to a copy of the letter of Wilkins to William Hilton, August 4, 1960. See also Wilkins to Baxter, April 30, 1959, BSPA. Wilkins told Baxter that the legislature had cut the park budget for existing services but he hoped his arguments to restore cuts and fund his supplemental budget would be accepted since it included funding for an additional man as ranger at the

tenting site at Trout Brook Farm. "I am happy that you have accepted this plan since I think it will eliminate considerably the problem we now have at South Branch."

40. Report of ranger at Russell Pond for the 1959 Season, BSPA. See also Taylor, report for 1953, BSPA. Several lean-tos were built at Russell Pond in 1953.

41. Memorandum, Holt to Wilkins, August 30, 1962, BSPA.

42. Kearney to BSPA, November 2, 1969; William Warren to Wilkins, October 18, 1970, BSPA. Warren was a professional soil conservationist with the U.S. Soil Conservation Service for fifteen years and for nine years a construction engineer. He argued for retention of Russell Pond. By laying plastic pipe to outlying streams and by not increasing the total of four lean-tos and 3 tent sites there would not be too much of a load on the site. In the sixteen years he had been visiting the area no great deterioration of the vegetation had occurred, he reported. See also Kearney to BSPA, January 26 and April 22, 1970, BSPA.

43. See Wilkins to Taylor, June 10, 1964, and copy of letter from C. F. Belcher, AMC, to J. Malcolm Barter, *Down East* Magazine, October 29, 1964, BSPA. The funds came from income from the bequest made to the AMC by Evelyn H. Murphy of Philadelphia with the stipulation that it be used for the benefit of the forests of Maine. To that point most of the income had gone to the Evelyn H. Murphy-AMC Forestry Fellowship at the University of Maine. See also Taylor to Thomas Dietz, November 23, 1963, BSPA. Dietz apparently was an early advocate of construction of a bunkhouse in Heath's memory, since Taylor wrote him: "I think a bunkhouse at Chimney Pond would be fitting and proper. It is much needed and Ralph loved it up there." The Executive Council accepted the gift on June 24, 1964.

44. See unsigned Notes on Baxter Park August 4–6, 1964; Wilkins to Belcher, November 30, 1964, and June 4, 1965, BSPA.

45. In 1957 the house at Trout Brook Farm was cleaned out and fitted with furniture and appliances from state surplus in Augusta, including an old gas stove from the Blaine Mansion. During the summer a group of foresters from the University of Connecticut used the area. See Taylor, reports for June and July 1957; Edgar P. Wyman to Nutting, November 15 and 21, 1956; minutes of meeting of Baxter State Park Authority, December 17, 1958, BSPA. A Connecticut student killed a spruce partridge while at the farm, and when word reached Baxter he asked that the college thereafter be denied the right to use Trout Brook Farm for a time. In a note to the Authority on January 8, 1959, Baxter withdrew his objections.

46. Baxter to Wilkins, April 13, 1960, BC, MSL.

47. Kearney to BSPA, November 2, 1969, January 26, April 22, and November 18, 1970, BSPA.

48. Kearney to BSPA, November 18, 1970, BSPA.

49. Kearney to BSPA, November 2, 1969, BSPA. Kearney indicated the Authority had made the decision in August 1969.

50. Kearney to BSPA, April 22 and November 18, 1970, BSPA.

51. Farris to Governor Payne, June 30, 1950; minutes of BSPA meeting, July 1, 1950, BSPA. Governor Payne had forwarded a letter from a Boy Scout

executive who had complained that his scouts had been charged 25¢ for use of lean-tos at Katahdin Stream. Farris explained park policy and said if facilities such as lean-tos and toilets were used a charge had to be made. In the letter to Governor Payne and in a number of others received by the Authority over the years from Boy Scout executives, a common theme ran through them, that if park officials refused requests for free camping they were somehow being unpatriotic and un-American. Farris, who had two children who were scouts, in this case wrote: "It is not necessary for Comrade Howard to wave the flag of patriotism in behalf of the Boy Scouts to you or to the members of the Baxter State Park Authority."

52. Kearney to BSPA, May 20, 1969, BSPA. Ranger Ellsworth Damon at South Branch Pond made the comment concerning Fowler Ponds to Kearney.

53. Holt to Wilkins, September 4, 1962; Taylor, report for June 1955, BSPA. In late June Taylor went into the Foss-Knowlton Ponds area to put out a small fire left by campers. He and the forestry patrolman who accompanied him found "at least a dozen places where fires had been built in dangerous places." In his report for July 1965, Taylor reported record attendance in the Park for the month, and the use figures he gave did not include "those who camp at unsupervised campgrounds like Foster Field and Rum Brook."

54. Kearney to BSPA, May 20, 1969, BSPA. Regular visitors to the Park could add such other unofficial, but semi-recognized sites as those at the south end of Lower South Branch Pond. The Maine Forest Service had authorized some of the canoe campsites on Webster Lake and Stream. See John L. Maines, of Great Northern to Wilkins, June 24 and 25, 1963, BSPA.

55. Representative Percy G. Porter of Lincoln to James Erwin, April 2; Erwin to Porter, April 7, 1970, BSPA.

56. Cobb to Nutting, October 15; Nutting to Cobb, October 16, 1956, BSPA. In 1956 it was agreed that the wardens' camp should be moved soon. The wardens assigned to the camp felt that BSPA rangers should not use toilet facilities attached to the wardens' camp. See Taylor, reports for August, September, and the Year 1957, BSPA.

57. Taylor, report for December 1963, BSPA. Taylor's small camp could get a bit crowded. During the month reported on here, nine men from the forestry department were staying there while surveying the new acquisition. "That makes eleven men in my little old four room camp and they may be here three to four weeks. It took all the floor space for them to sleep on and there was no room to move around." Five moved to the nearby forestry camp to sleep. "It does point out the need for a bunkhouse here at Togue Pond," Taylor concluded.

58. See memo Wilkins to Speers and Erwin, January 30 and February 8, 1967. See memo of Holt, February 28; Wilkins to Speers and Erwin, April 7; Erwin to Wilkins and Speers, April 8; Wilkins to Erwin, Speers and Cranshaw, June 1, 1967; Baxter to Wilkins, June 17; Speers to Baxter, June 19, and Wilkins to Baxter, June 26, 1968, BSPA. See also Dyer interview, *op. cit.* Mr. Dyer, while he was still Director of State Parks in Maine, said he was consulted by the Authority regarding construction of additional facilities. He recommended the construction of a very large campground in the Togue Ponds area to provide

facilities for all types of campers. Facilities in existing campgrounds, he felt,

should be held at the existing level or reduced. He felt most individuals using
the new facility would not tour the Park after they had viewed the mountain.
The Authority, he stated, rejected this suggestion.

## XV

1. See "Report of Trails and Camping Facilities, by Harold J. Dyer, Supervisor of Baxter State Park (As of April 1, 1942)," in H. Walter Leavitt, *Katahdin Skylines,* Maine Technology Experiment Station, Paper No. 40, (Orono, Maine: University of Maine Press, May 1942), pp. 89–92. *Ibid.,* p. 90.

2. In the late spring of 1965 Taylor relocated the AT just south of the park boundary after the cable bridge across the West Branch of the Penobscot went out. The relocation crossed to the east bank of Nesowadnehunk Stream at the old toll dam and followed down the stream to the old West Branch tote road which led downstream to the mouth of Abol Stream and then crossed the West Branch on Great Northern's new bridge. See Taylor, report for May 1965, BSPA.

3. Taylor to William Cross, October 2, 1966, BSPA.

4. Taylor to Wilkins, August 5, 1962, BSPA: "This will be one more trail to maintain but maybe this group will take the maintenance on as a yearly project too. If we continue to get the $500.00 a year [from the MATC and AMC] we can handle it ourselves anyway." Taylor said that Perry, the leader, "is an able and experienced mountaineer. I have no doubts but they will do a good job." See also Wilkins to Taylor, August 8, 1962, BSPA.

5. Taylor to Wilkins, August 7, to Cross, October 2, 1966, BSPA. In his letter to Wilkins, Taylor noted that the Rum Mountain Trail had been completed that spring and had been blazed with bright orange paint. The latter color was being substituted for the blue previously used since it was more visible; the trail was included on the official park trail list in 1967.

6. See "Chimney Pond Trail at Katahdin," *Appalachian Trailway News,* January 1961, p. 6; Taylor to Wilkins, June 26, 1960, BSPA. Taylor noted that Edward Werler, who was soon to leave the service of the Park, had been delegated to cut out the new route. Apparently he did not really want to do the work and spent more time on the Russell Pond Trail. In 29 man-days he cut half a mile; in 8 man-days the four-man trail crew cut a mile and a half to Basin Ponds.

See also Whitman, *op. cit.,* BSPA: "The trail [to Chimney Pond]," he reported, "is becoming very hazardous, and now is more like a dried brook bed. It was suggested that the portion between Roaring Brook and Basin Pond be relocated. It would take 2 men 4 weeks to do a good job."

7. Taylor, report for June 1952, BSPA. See MATC, *Katahdin Section of the Guide to the Appalachian Trail in Maine,* Sixth Edition, 1965, Section 5, pp. 15–16.

8. Baxter to LeBell, August 1; LeBell to BSPA, August 7; Wilkins to Taylor and Baxter, August 12; Wilkins to LeBell, September 30, 1963, BSPA. At this point Baxter apparently assumed the trail had not as yet been built for in his letter to LeBell he wrote: "In building this trail great care should be taken not to cut or injure any trees and do no permanent damage to the wild forest growth." See also LeBell, "Katahdin's Keep Ridge," *Appalachia,* June 1963, pp. 420–22,

for a discussion of a bushwhacking trip made in 1962 by LeBell and his party which approximated the route of the trail.

9. *Ibid.*, note 7 above, p. 5–48; Taylor, reports for December 1951, September, and October 1952, BSPA.

10. Taylor to Wilkins, July 5 and December 28, 1961; May 3, 1962; Wilkins to Taylor, January 4, 1962; Kearney to BSPA, November 2, 1969.

11. Taylor, reports for August 1955 and for year 1955, BSPA.

12. *Ibid.* See also "New Katahdin Trails," *Appalachian Trailway News*, January 1956, p. 5. As late as 1967 the trail to Doubletop was not included on the official list of trails in the Park. See Kearney to BSPA, July 15, 1969, BSPA.

13. Taylor, report for September 1951, BSPA. Except for the discussion of Taylor's work, the information came from MATC, *Katahdin Section, op. cit.*, pp. 2–3. On the slides on O-J-I, see John W. Worthington, "Slides and Markings of O-J-I," *Appalachia*, June 1946, p. 127. For a fine illustrated description of the 1932 storm see Emmie B. Whitney, "Katahdin's Big Storm," *Appalachia*, June 1952, pp. 21–30.

14. Nutting to Taylor, January 29, 1954; Taylor, report for August 1955, BSPA. See also *Appalachia*, June 1955, p. 423.

15. See Benton L. Hatch, "September Trip to Traveler Mountain Katahdin Region, Maine," *Appalachia*, December 1938, pp. 278–81 and George W. Outerbridge, "Trip to Traveler Mountain, Maine, September 2 to 9, 1944," *Appalachia*, December 1944, pp. 243–45. See also Taylor, report for November 1951, BSPA; and MATC, *Katahdin Section, op. cit.*, p. 61.

16. Taylor, reports for September 1952 and June 1953, BSPA. In the last report, Taylor stated that Scott had "finished his new trail as far as the top of Traveler Mountain." He had gone up over Little Peaked, Big Peaked, around Howe Brook Basin, North Traveler and the Traveler.

17. Taylor, report for October 1964, BSPA.

18. MATC, *Katahdin Section, op. cit.*, pp. 53–54. See also Taylor, report for November 1951, BSPA. This is the only mention of trail relocation in the Russell Pond area during Taylor's tenure as supervisor.

19. Jean Stephenson, "Camping at Katahdin," *Appalachia*, June 1955, p. 345.

20. Kearney to BSPA, July 15, 1969, BSPA.

21. MATC, *Katahdin Section, op. cit.*, p. 52. There is nothing in the BSPA files regarding this relocation.

22. In 1965 the Fin & Feather Club accused the Authority of "deliberate destruction of a bridge on Katahdin Stream which gave access to Foss and Knowlton Ponds." See Petition, F & FC, no date but presented to BSPA at a meeting on June 21, 1965, BSPA.

23. Taylor to Anthony H. Ryan, September 8, 1960, BSPA. In responding to criticisms of campground size and maintenance of trails, Taylor noted that in the ten years he had been supervisor attendance had increased 700 per cent, while: "We still have approximately the same crew and very little more money to run on."

24. Report of Irvin Caverly, Jr., ranger, Russell Pond campground for the 1961 season, BSPA.

25. Wilkins to Carl Jordan, New York City, October 12, 1966; Jordan, NOTES
September 22, 1966, BSPA, complained of litter at Basin Ponds and around the
shelters at Wassataquoik and Little Wassataquoik lakes; of the dump at Davis
Pond, and dishwashing practices at the outlet to Davis Pond.

26. Louis Chorzempa, MATC, to Taylor, September 3, 1960, BSPA. Chorzempa noted that maintenance of the AT within Baxter State Park was under
Taylor's supervision.

27. See Jean Stephenson to Wilkins, April 21 and May 17; Wilkins to
Stephenson, April 25, and to Taylor, June 30, 1961, BSPA. In the letters of April
25 and May 17 Wilkins and Stephenson referred to a gift of $100. In the
Stephenson letter of April 21 and the Wilkins letter of June 30 they refer to a
gift of $150. On June 30 Wilkins instructed Taylor "to hire casual labor to work
under your supervision or direction through your campground rangers." In her
letter of May 17, Miss Stephenson emphasized to Wilkins that in preparing the
Council Order accepting the funds that the organization's name the *Maine* Appalachian Trail Club be written correctly so as to avoid confusion with other groups
such as the Appalachian Mountain Club; see Taylor to BSPA, report of Trail
Crew for 1962, August 27; Wilkins to Taylor, December 6, 1962. Of the MATC
gift, $43 remained unspent and permission was obtained to use it for needed
repairs on the Katahdin Stream swing cable bridge.

28. Taylor to Wilkins, January 17, 1961, BSPA. Taylor listed the trails, with
mileages, which were "supposed to be maintained" by the AMC. Wilkins had requested the list.

29. C. F. Belcher, AMC, to Wilkins, October 19, 1960, BSPA. See also a
copy of the 1941 Memorandum of Agreement between Dyer and the AMC in
BSPA files.

30. Taylor to Wilkins, January 17; Belcher to Wilkins, March 22; Wilkins
to members of BSPA and to Belcher, March 30; Wilkins to Taylor, March 31,
1961; Samuel H. Goodhue, AMC, to Wilkins, April 24; Wilkins to Belcher, April
19, 1961, BSPA. The delay in concluding a final agreement was caused by problems regarding the method of payment. Wilkins preferred to have the check go
directly to Taylor while the Club preferred the more orderly procedure of acceptance by the Governor and Council. Ultimately the Attorney General decided
that the latter process had to be followed. The AMC also volunteered to provide
any needed trail signs. Both Goodhue and Belcher hoped the BSPA would "retain
the AMC insignia on the signs." See also Belcher to Wilkins, June 23, and Goodhue to Wilkins, April 4, 1961, BSPA.

31. Wilkins to Taylor, February 2, 1967, and to Kearney, May 6, and members BSPA, July 3, 1969; Summary of Expenditures, BSP, 1960–1973, prepared
for an Authority meeting on October 8, 1970, BSPA.

32. Taylor, report for July 1961; Taylor to Wilkins, August 4, 12, and 20;
Wilkins to Taylor, August 16, 1961, BSPA. In the August 4 letter, Taylor added
a postscript: "We also got a nice log bridge at Pamola Brook out of this money.
I thought best not to put that in the regular report." The $62.80 left over from
AMC funds was used to buy trail marking paint and a new axe.

33. Belcher to Wilkins, June 19, 1962; Work Program for 1962 Trail Crew,
July 29, 1962; Taylor to BSPA, Report of Trail Crew for 1962, August 27, 1962, **401**

BSPA. Belcher requested and Taylor specifically directed the trail crew to work on club trails. See also Wilkins to Taylor July 29, 1966, BSPA. Wilkins said the AMC wanted a complete report by hours, number of men, distances of trail work done each year. Apparently Taylor had not been consistent in reporting the results of each season's work. Taylor duly provided such a report dated August 7, 1966 which Wilkins forwarded on September 27, 1966. See Wilkins to Belcher, June 8, and to Taylor, June 14 and August 17; Belcher to Taylor, August 13; Taylor to Wilkins, August 7, 1965, BSPA. See also Belcher to Wilkins, July 9, 1964, BSPA. Again Belcher wanted an accounting, particularly on the condition of trail signs, information about which had been confusing for several years; Taylor to Cross, October 7, 1966, BSPA.

34. Wilkins to Belcher, May 16, and to Taylor, June 11, 1962, BSPA. See also Taylor to Wilkins, July 20, 1962, BSPA. The men had been hired and Taylor noted: "I hope we get a better job done this year than last." See Wilkins to Taylor, May 11; Taylor to Wilkins, May 13, 1962, BSPA. Belcher's letter is not available.

35. See Taylor to BSPA, August 27, 1962, Report of Trail Crew for 1962, for a good summary of the situation at the camp.

36. Belcher to Wilkins, September 26, 1962, BSPA. In pencil on the letter is a notation by Wilkins: "Why wasn't money used to correct this fire hazard?" See also Roland Ellis to AMC, September 2, 1963; Belcher to Wilkins, September 4, 1963, BSPA. Ellis complained of the new shelter fee of 75¢ per night.

37. Minutes of meeting, BSPA, December 6, 1962, BSPA. See also Wilkins to Belcher, December 6, 1962, BSPA.

38. Taylor to Wilkins, June 23; Wilkins to Taylor, June 30, 1963, BSPA. Both letters discussed work at Davis Pond in cutting and shaping logs. Kearney to BSPA, July 15, 1969, BSPA.

39. Wilkins to Kearney, May 6, 1969, BSPA. The AMC, Wilkins related, wanted priority to be given to cleaning up the Davis Pond area, improving the toilets, and "doing a little more work in establishing rock cairns as a basis for trail marking in addition to the usual work of the party."

40. Baxter to Congressman Ray Taylor, Chairman, Subcommittee on Parks and Recreation, July 7, 1967, BC, MSL.

# XVII

1. Nutting to Baxter, March 27 and December 11; Baxter to Nutting, October 6, and December 28, 1967; "Baxter Park & Governing Board," BP, MSL. Nutting's draft of the state forest proposal was not included with the other materials.

2. Baxter to Governor Curtis, draft of "Possible Trust for your Inspection," February 1968, BP, MSL. It is not clear if this was sent to Governor Curtis.

3. See copies of Baxter's will and relevant portions of his Trust Agreement with the Boston Safe Deposit and Trust Company in BSPA files.

4. See *Portland Evening Express,* June 17, 1969. In the state plane used to carry and scatter the ashes was John L. Baxter, Jr., the governor's nephew John,

Joseph Lee, of Portland, a close friend and his last chauffeur, Chairman Austin Wilkins of the Authority, and Baxter's lawyer Daniel T. Drummond, Jr.

5. *Portland Press Herald,* and *Portland Evening Express,* June 19, 1969; *Maine Sunday Telegram,* June 29, 1969.

6. Minutes of Meeting, BSPA and Advisory Committee, July 1, 1970, BSPA.

7. *Public Laws of Maine, 1969,* Special Session, 1970, ch. 557.

8. *Ibid., 1971,* ch. 477. See also Birt to Wilkins, December 3, 1978, BSPA.

9. See "Interim Objectives for Baxter State Park," approved December 27, 1972, BSPA.

10. See BSPA files or Special Collections, Fogler Library, University of Maine at Orono, for a copy of this plan.

11. No attempt will be made here to cite the sources in this and other controversies mentioned. The press in Maine covered all of them closely and the widely varying points of view were raised. For a particularly bitter and sometimes misleading critique of park policy see Aime Gauvin, "Baxter, The Man and the Park," *Maine Sunday Telegram,* September 25, 1977. This originally appeared as "As Baxter Park burns, so burns Maine," *Audubon, The Magazine of the National Audubon Society,* September 1977, pp 146–53.

# BIBLIOGRAPHY

The bibliography of Katahdin and Baxter State Park is so extensive that no effort will be made here to list all items consulted. The footnotes reflect a majority of them. The card file at this time contains more than 750 separate entries, and this does not include a great many newspaper articles, particularly those from recent decades. Only the most important items in the areas of bibliographies, manuscripts, public documents, interviews, newspapers, journals, magazines and books are discussed below.

For the history of the Katahdin region the Maine bibliography is Smith, Edward S. C., and Avery, Myron H., compilers, *An Annotated Bibliography of Katahdin* (Washington, D.C.: Publication No. 6) The Appalachian Trail Conference, November 1936. Reprinted 1950 with Corrigenda and 1937 Supplement. First compiled in the 1920s and appearing in *Appalachia*, this is the single best listing of Katahdin materials. Most of the items published before the 1930s are listed here. It is also valuable for the listing of maps of the Katahdin region. For the history of the Park itself after 1931 it is of relatively little value.

Of the manuscript collections used, several are of great importance. For the history of the Park itself the most extensive and important are the records of the Baxter State Park Authority, housed in the office of the Authority in Millinocket. They represent records gathered from the offices of the attorney general, the fish and game commissioner and the forest commissioner as well as of the Authority itself. They contain little material for the 1930s and early 1940s. The loss of Helon N. Taylor's records when his house burned in 1967 was a great one as far as manuscripts are concerned.

At the Maine State Library is the Percival Proctor Baxter Collection. Only a portion of Governor Baxter's personal correspondence is included, though there are a good many items relating to the Park's history. The collection includes twenty-eight bound volumes of scrapbooks, mostly newspaper clippings, and four bound volumes of Baxter's speeches. The materials were used for this volume before the collection was catalogued and therefore the file numbers have not been used in referring to the correspondence. Since the collection is well indexed in a "Guide to the use of the Percival Proctor Baxter Collection," any letters cited in this work may be easily found.

The Maine State Library has also received the extensive records of Myron H. Avery, which are of considerable value. Since the Library did not receive them until 1979 and I only heard of them during the summer of that year, I did not have the opportunity to consult them prior to completion of the manuscript.

Of the many collections consulted in the Special Collections Room of the Raymond H. Fogler Library at the University of Maine at Orono, two are of special importance. The first is the Great Northern Paper Company Papers, 1896–1960; the second, the Fred Alliston Gilbert Papers. Since Gilbert was vice president of Great Northern until 1929, both are intimately concerned with company affairs. They provide materials of special importance for the controversy over creation of the Park in the 1920s, federal activities in the thirties, and the acquisition of park land by Baxter.

At the National Archives in Washington, D.C., see the papers of the National Park Service in Record Group 79. They contain materials for the history of the conflict over creation of a national park at Katahdin.

Numerous state documents were used. The *Laws of Maine* were consulted for the period from the late nineteenth century onward. The *Legislative Journal* was used for sessions in which controversies regarding particular issues involved the history of the Park. The reports of the commissioner of Inland Fisheries and Game from 1867 to 1972 and of the forestry commissioner beginning in 1891 are of great value for the information they provide on the Katahdin region. The name of the department and the title of the reports vary. The commissioner of Inland Fisheries and Game was concerned with the caribou issue late in the nineteenth century and early in the following. The reports also contain materials on the development and administration of the game preserve at Katahdin. The reports of the forest commissioner are valuable for the history of the development of a forest preserve in the Katahdin region; for the history of fires in the Katahdin area; and the work of the CCC during the 1930s. Of lesser significance were various reports and publications of the Department of Economic Development, the Department of Industry and Commerce, the Maine State Park Commission, and the Maine State Planning Board.

Oral interviews were also of considerable importance for some sections of this work. I discussed park issues on a number of occasions with William Cross, first of the Maine Forest Service and then Business Manager of Baxter State Park; with Austin H. Wilkins, forest commissioner and chairman of the Baxter State Park Authority; and with Albert D. Nutting, forest commissioner from 1948 to 1958 and chairman of the Baxter State Park Authority during that period. The comments of Wilkins and Nutting on early drafts of the work were of particular significance. I also interviewed

406 John L. Baxter, Sr., nephew of Percival P. Baxter, at Brunswick, Maine, on

February 2, 1972; Dr. Lore Rogers, of Patten, Maine, who first climbed Katahdin in the 1880s, on July 6, 1971; and Harold J. Dyer, supervisor of Baxter State Park until 1950, in Albany, New York, on July 15, 1971. The tapes are in possession of the Authority. I have also used taped interviews made by Sarah Redfield, assistant attorney general, in the mid-seventies with Mrs. Ethel Moyer Dyer, grandniece of Governor Baxter; with Helon Taylor, supervisor of Baxter State Park until 1967; and with Maurice Day, artist, frequent Katahdin area visitor, and friend of Governor Baxter. These tapes are undated and concern primarily Baxter's concept of wilderness, the use of snowmobiles, and the trust fund he created. By far the most valuable is the interview with Helon N. Taylor. Also used was Ms. Redfield's taped interview with Maynard Marsh, commissioner of Inland Fisheries and Game on July 25, 1977, the tapes of which are in the office of the attorney general.

Newspapers provided a very important source of information. The microfilm newspaper collection at the Fogler Library is the most complete in the state. Other files consulted were at the Bangor Public Library, the Maine State Library, the Maine Historical Society in Portland, and the Portland Public Library. As indicated in the footnotes, articles on Katahdin and activities in the area cropped up in a wide variety of newspapers around the state, from those in the larger cities, to religious newspapers such as *The Christian Mirror* in Portland, which ran an article by the Reverend Marcus Keep; to the *Bar Harbor Record* and the *St. Croix Courier,* and *The Maine Farmer and Journal of Useful Arts.* Most important in the course of the nineteenth century was *The Bangor Whig and Courier,* which published many articles. In the early twentieth century the *Bangor Daily Commercial* published or republished many accounts, both current news and items concerning earlier trips to the area. Most important for the period through the twenties was the *Lewiston Evening Journal,* which published many articles in its Magazine Section. At the same time, under the editorial leadership of Arthur G. Staples, it was the strongest newspaper supporter in the state of park status for the Katahdin area.

All Maine newspapers carried extensive articles on the water power and park controversy after 1917. Here the Baxter scrapbooks mentioned earlier in this essay are of particular significance, since he had hundreds of articles clipped from papers and pasted into them. The *Daily Kennebec Journal* in Augusta carried the most complete accounts, but all of the dailies, particularly those in Portland, Lewiston, and Bangor, provided extensive accounts of the controversy. Most of them opposed creation of the Park during the 1920s.

After the Park was created, all daily newspapers provided coverage of important events there and particularly of Baxter's gifts to the state. The papers did not cover routine events in the Park or meetings of the Commission or the Baxter State Park Authority with any regularity until con-   **407** servation and wilderness issues became popular and controversial in the 1960s. After 1931 the *Bangor Daily News* probably carried more articles about the Park than did other papers. In the 1970s, the *Maine Sunday Telegram* and the *Maine Times* provided more interpretive articles on controversial issues than other papers in the state.

Articles were gleaned from over fifty journals and periodicals of the scholarly and popular variety. The most important single one was *Appalachia*, published by the AMC; it is the oldest mountaineering journal in the United States. Most of the issues from the beginning carried at least one article concerning the Katahdin region. *Appalachia* files are more important for the historical background of the area than for the administrative history of the Park. The *Appalachian Trialway News*, published by the ATC, beginning in 1940, has printed many articles concerning the Park. A great many also appeared in *The Maine Sportsman* from the late 1880s to the 1920s, and in the national publication *Forest and Stream* during the same period. Both are available at the Bangor Public Library. Available there and at the Fogler Library of the University of Maine at Orono are *In the Maine Woods*, the promotional publication of the Bangor & Aroostook Railroad, which appeared from 1900 to 1952, and the Great Northern Paper Company's *The Northern*, for the period 1921 to 1928. Issues of these publications often had as many as three or four articles on the region and filled in many chinks in the history of the area.

Journals more general in their coverage and broader in their distribution were also important. Most significant here were *Scribner's Magazine*, the *Atlantic, Century Magazine, Yankee, Down East, National Geographic Magazine, Everybody's Magazine, New England Quarterly, New England Magazine*, and *American Quarterly*.

Several historical journals published in Maine were also consulted. These include *Sprague's Journal of Maine History*, the *Bangor Historical Society Magazine*, and the *Collections of the Maine Historical Society*.

During the late 19th and particularly in the first three decades of the 20th century, the journals of botanical, zoological, and other scientific organizations contained a great many references to and articles on the Katahdin area. This was during the period of scientific exploration of the region when its resources were first studied in great detail with modern scientific methods. The articles provide much material concerning the historical background and exploration of the region as well as scientific data. The most important of these was *The Maine Naturalist*, from 1921 to 1930. Very significant earlier was *Rhodora—the Journal of the New England Botanical Club*. Of lesser significance were the *Bulletin of the Boston Society of Natural History, The American Naturalist, The Auk, The Bryologist*, the *Proceedings of the Portland Society of Natural History, The Botanical Gazette*, the *Proceedings of the Washington Biological Society*,

*Bulletin of the Torrey Botanical Club,* the *Journal of Mammology* and the *Bulletin of the Museum of Comparative Zoology* at Harvard.

Other scientific journals used include the *American Journal of Science,* the *Bulletin of the Geological Society of America, Nature Magazine,* and the *Geographical Review.* Environmental journals include *The Living Wilderness, National Parks Magazine, Maine Fish and Game,* and *Audubon The Magazine of the National Audubon Society.*

More than 100 published books have references to or sections devoted to Katahdin and the park area; the most significant are cited in notes.

# INDEX
### (primarily of people and events involved in the acquisition of Baxter State Park)

Abbreviations used in this index:

| | | | |
|---|---|---|---|
| *AMC* | *Appalachian Mountain Club* | *IF&G* | *Inland Fisheries & Game* |
| *ATC* | *Appalachian Trail Conference* | *MATC* | *Maine Appalachian Trail Club* |
| *BSP* | *Baxter State Park* | *MFD* | *Maine Forestry District* |
| *BSPA* | *Baxter State Park Authority* | *MFS* | *Maine Forest Service* |
| *BSPC* | *Baxter State Park Commission* | *MSFW* | *Maine State Federation* |
| *CCC* | *Civilian Conservation Corps* | | *of Women's Clubs* |
| *F&FC* | *Fin and Feather Club* | *NPS* | *National Park Service* |
| *GNP* | *Great Northern Paper Co.* | | |